Gale Encyclopedia of
U.S. History: War

Gale Encyclopedia of U.S. History: War

VOLUME 2

GALE
CENGAGE Learning

Detroit • New York • San Francisco • New Haven, Conn • Waterville, Maine • London

Gale Encyclopedia of U.S. History: War

Project Editors: Anne Marie Hacht and Dwayne D. Hayes

Editorial: Ira Mark Milne

Rights Acquisition and Management: Leitha Etheridge-Sims, Lisa Kincade, Jacqueline Key, and Timothy Sisler

Composition: Evi Abou-El-Seoud

Manufacturing: Wendy Blurton

Imaging: Lezlie Light

Product Design: Jennifer Wahi

For product information and technology assistance, contact us at
Gale Customer Support, 1-800-877-4253.
For permission to use material from this text or product,
submit all requests online at **www.cengage.com/permissions.**
Further permissions questions can be emailed to
permissionrequest@cengage.com

Cover photographs reproduced by permission of Corbis (picture of the mushroom cloud from "Grable," the first nuclear artillery shell) and public domain (picture of Civil war image of soldiers with cannons).

While every effort has been made to ensure the reliability of the information presented in this publication, Gale, a part of Cengage Learning, does not guarantee the accuracy of the data contained herein. Gale accepts no payment for listing; and inclusion in the publication of any organization, agency, institution, publication, service, or individual does not imply endorsement of the editors or publisher. Errors brought to the attention of the publisher and verified to the satisfaction of the publisher will be corrected in future editions.

Library of Congress Cataloging-in-Publication Data

Gale encyclopedia of U.S. history : war
    p. cm. --
    Includes bibliographical references and index.
    ISBN 978-1-4144-3114-7 (set hardcover) -- ISBN 978-1-4144-3115-4 (v. 1 : hardcover) -- ISBN 978-1-4144-3116-1 (v. 2 : hardcover)
    1. United States--History, Military--Encyclopedias. I. Gale Group. II. Title: Encyclopedia of U.S. history, war. III. Title: War.

E181.G16 2008
355.00973--dc22   2007033628

Gale
27500 Drake Rd.
Farmington Hills, MI, 48331-3535

978-1-4144-3114-7 (set)   1-4144-3114-7 (set)
978-1-4144-3115-4 (vol. 1)   1-4144-3115-5 (vol. 1)
978-1-4144-3116-1 (vol. 2)   1-4144-3116-3 (vol. 2)

This title is also available as an e-book.
ISBN-13: 978-1-4144-3117-8 ISBN-10: 1-4144-3117-1
Contact your Gale sales representative for ordering information.

Printed in the United States of America
1 2 3 4 5 6 7 11 10 09 08

Contents

Contents

VOLUME 2

Introduction

How To Use This Book

The history of the Americas is fraught with conflict, from the great empires of the Aztecs and the Incas to the arrival of gun-carrying Europeans and their new way of making war, continuing on to the creation of the United States in the crucible of revolution, and on into its many wars, both foreign and domestic. Over more than five hundred years of recorded history, the scale of warfare in the Americas has grown exponentially, from skirmishes fought with flint axes and matchlock arquebuses all the way to atomic warfare—the United States being, to date, the only country to use nuclear weapons in war—and a military powerful enough to project its strength and influence around the globe.

Although virtually every corner of the Americas, from the Aleutian Islands to the Falklands, has been touched by conflict, the *Encyclopedia of U.S. History: War* focuses on the military history of the United States specifically, as it is that nation that has come to dominate both the theory and the execution of the wars of the last century. As dramatic as the last hundred years have been, this book also spends as much time focusing on the conflicts of the United States in previous centuries, as it grew from a colonial frontier populated by independent-minded sharpshooters and scouts to a power on par with Europe with armies that marched and fought in the European styles of the times.

In-depth coverage is also given to the evolving nature of conflicts and encounters between the growing United States and the native nations of North America. From the early skirmishes all the way through to the watershed events of the nineteenth century, the role and scope of the "Indian Wars" is examined over the course of several chapters.

Organization

Each chapter is arranged in such a way as to assist the student and generalist reader in gaining an in-depth appreciation of one phase of American warfare. Arranged chronologically, the chapters all follow the same structure, beginning with a short overview of the chapter and an examination of the causes that paved the path to war. The *Encyclopedia of U.S. History: War* then uses both biographies and descriptions of key battles to further illuminate the overarching nature of the phase or conflict under consideration. It is in the personal stories of the generals, leaders, soldiers, and innovators, and their role, for good or ill, on the battlefield that the true drama of America at war comes into play. Each chapter then concludes with an examination of the war's aftermath and its impact on the bigger picture of U.S. and world history.

The bigger picture is also examined in the "Homefront" and "International Context" sections. Perhaps more than any other nation, the United States' military policies have been strongly and consistently driven by events on both the domestic and international scenes. From the Great Awakening to Women's Suffrage to the Anti-War Movement of the 1960s and beyond, the Homefront articles detail the impact of non-military events at home on America's wars. Similarly, despite efforts in the past to make it so, our country has never been able to isolate itself from world politics; the United States' wars have been intrinsically linked to global events since the Seven Years War touched off the French and Indian War in colonial America.

What's Inside

The French and Indian War was but one facet of a greater conflict that is the subject of the first chapter, which focuses on conflicts with the Northeastern tribes of Native Americans. This often-overlooked period of the Indian Wars was also, demographically speaking, one of America's bloodiest conflicts.

The American Revolution, that great turning point in history, comprises the next chapter. A time of legendary leaders and battles, the epic sweep of this conflict is balanced by a focus on the simple human drama that resulted in the birth of a new kind of government and a nation quite unlike any seen before.

The focus shifts back to Native American matters with the next chapter, which examines conflicts with the tribes of the West and South as the newly-born United States began to expand westward. A crucial time in early American history, some of the country's first post-Revolutionary heroes were made in these wars, as well as some of the first enduring symbols of Native American resistance and disenfranchisement.

America once again found itself at war with Britain in 1812. A sideshow of the Napoleonic Wars then raging in Europe, the conflict was the United States' first official international war and witnessed the dramatic burning of Washington, D.C. and the equally dramatic American victory at the Battle of New Orleans, which was a tremendous morale boost for the young country even though it had no bearing on the outcome of the war, which had already concluded!

The greatest war-related territorial acquisition in U.S. history came with the subject of the next chapter, the Mexican-American War. Manifest Destiny in action, the war brought the boundaries of the United States to the Pacific Ocean (just in time for the California Gold Rush) and launched the military careers of many future Civil War generals.

The Civil War almost spelled the end of the Union a mere "four score and seven years" after its foundation. The costliest of American wars receives full coverage, from the generals and politicians who shaped the conflict on both sides to the monumental battles that determined the fate of a nation and the freedom of a people.

With the Civil War over, America turned to pacifying the last native tribes. The last phase of the Indian Wars, the conflicts with the Western tribes, is also the best known. The names and battles—Custer, Little Big Horn, Geronimo, Sitting Bull, Wounded Knee—quickly became part of the growing American mythology as the longest, and one of the most tragic, conflicts in the nation's history came to a close.

The Spanish-American War, the subject of the next chapter, marked America's true emergence onto the world stage and the country's first encounter with the complex issue of imperialism. The war was also the first great "media war", drummed up largely by competing newspaper interests. By war's end, Theodore Roosevelt had gained national notoriety and America had gained its first overseas possessions, along with the many problems that go with such acquisitions.

If the Spanish-American War constituted America's first small entry into the global scene, the two World Wars heralded its arrival in a big way. Each gets its own chapter, and each chapter examines the relevant conflict in exhaustive detail, covering not just the American soldiers and battles, but every facet of these massive wars, as well as their complex causes and the vast changes that came in their aftermath.

From the muddy fields of the Somme to the sinking of the *Lusitania* to the Russian Revolution and the Treaty of Versailles, from the rise of fascism in Europe and the Japanese invasion of China to the specter of the Holocaust and the atomic bombings of Hiroshima and Nagasaki, the tremendous scope and sweep of these two global conflicts, the costliest and deadliest in the history of the world, are captured. The immense changes brought about in America by these wars are also examined, including the rise of the first civil rights organizations, the tremendous gains made by women in political and economic arenas, and the sad legacy of Japanese internment in the Second World War.

Having become a superpower in the wake of World War II, America's subsequent wars were fought in the shadow of the Cold War, which gets its own chapter. This section covers the politicians and high-ranking generals who played out a deadly game of move and countermove for fifty years, as well as the times when the Cold War nearly became "hot", most notably during the early 1960s with such dramatic events as the Cuban Missile Crisis, the Bay of Pigs invasion, and the raising of the Berlin Wall.

The two big American wars of the Cold War era, Korea and Vietnam, are covered in two separate chapters. Both conflicts were part of much greater social and political upheavals—the de-colonialization of Asia and the burgeoning Peace Movement, for example—and these are covered in detail, as is the nuclear escalation and Cold War brinkmanship that formed the backdrop to the wars.

In the wake of the Cold War, America's military interests turned increasingly towards the Middle East starting with the Gulf War, which is covered in its own chapter. The War on Terrorism chapter is broken down into two sections: the first covers the invasion of Afghanistan which followed in the wake of the September 11 attacks; the second covers the ongoing conflict in Iraq.

The book wraps up with a five-section look at America's relations with the rest of the world, both past and present, covering covert operations, proxy wars, and U.S. political involvement in various regimes and movements.

Conclusion

The objective of this book is to take the reader on a journey through the history of the United States and the military conflicts that have shaped it and the world. Through studying America's wars and the people who have waged them, the impact history has on our lives today will hopefully become apparent to the reader.

At the very least, it is hoped that the reader will appreciate the great drama and sacrifice contained within the following chapters and will come to recognize the tremendous cost of war for those who wage it.

Chronology

c. 11,000 BCE:
Native Americans use flint-tipped spears to hunt mammoths.

c. 7,000 BCE:
Disappearance of mammoths and other "big game" in the Americas; beginning of food cultivation.

c. 1,500 BCE:
Appearance of Olmec culture in Central America.

c. 350 CE:
Rise of Old Mayan Empire.

c. 700 CE:
Rise of Mississippian culture, last of the mound building cultures of North America.

c. 1000:
Viking settlements briefly established in Newfoundland.

c. 1325:
Tenochtitlan, capital of the Aztec Empire, is constructed.

1438: Inca Empire founded in Peru.

1492: First voyage of Christopher Columbus. Funded by Spain, the Italian-born Columbus discovers "The New World."

1497: Backed by England, explorer John Cabot sails along North American coast.

1507: First reference to the New World as "America."

1513: Spaniard Ponce de Leon conducts slave raids and explores Florida and the Gulf Coast. Another Spaniard, Vasco de Balboa, crosses the Panamanian Isthmus to the Pacific Ocean.

1519: Spanish adventurer Hernán Cortés begins his conquest of Mexico. Aztec Empire falls by 1521.

1533: Spanish adventurer Francisco Pizarro conquers Peru.

1540s: Spaniard Francisco Coronado leads explorations throughout modern-U.S. Southwest.

1565: St. Augustine, oldest European settlement in the future United States, is established.

1579: Englishman Sir Francis Drake explores the California coast during his circumnavigation of the world.

1607: The English colony of Jamestown, Virginia, is founded by Captain John Smith.

1608: City of Quebec founded by Frenchman Samuel Champlain.

1609: Santa Fe, New Mexico, founded by Spanish. Henry Hudson explores Hudson River Valley.

1619: First African slaves arrive at Jamestown.

1620: Puritan settlers land at Plymouth, Massachusetts.

1626: Dutch settle on Manhattan Island, naming their colony New Amsterdam.

1630: Boston founded.

1634: Maryland established as Catholic colony.

1637: Fighting flares up between colonists and the Pequot Indians in New England.

1664: New Amsterdam seized by English, who rename it New York.

1692: Start of the Salem Witch Trials.

1699: French settlement of Louisiana begins.

1713: Queen Anne's War, a colonial conflict between France and England, ends after eleven years of hostilities.

1732: Benjamin Franklin begins publishing *Poor Richard's Almanac.*

1748: Another colonial struggle, King George's War, ends after four years.

1763: The French and Indian War, the North American portion of the Seven Years' War, concludes with French loss of all territorial possessions in Canada and the Mississippi region to the British.

1764: Stamp Act passed by the British Parliament. An effort to raise money after the costly Seven Years' War by taxing colonists on sugar and stamps, the Stamp Act proves wildly unpopular in North America and is repealed two years later.

1770: The Boston Massacre: British soldiers open fire on Bostonian mob protesting against further taxes.

1773: A group of protesting Bostonians throw English tea into the harbor in what is later dubbed the "Boston Tea Party."

1775: The battles of Lexington and Concord mark the beginning of the American Revolution.

1776: The Declaration of Independence signed on July 2 and approved on July 4, signaling the British colonies' formal break from the mother country and laying out an agenda to create a more democratically-based government. December 26: Washington's surprise victory at Trenton.

1777: Winter at Valley Forge, the low point for Washington's army.

1778: Beginning of French-American alliance.

1781: Articles of Confederation adopted. Surrender of the British General Cornwallis marks the effective end of the Revolutionary War.

1783: September 3: Treaty of Paris signed, the formally ending the American Revolution; Britain cedes all territory east of the Mississippi River. Eighty thousand Loyalists emigrate to Canada.

1786: Shays' Rebellion in Massachusetts.

1787: May 14: Constitutional Convention convened to rewrite Articles of Confederation.

1789: New U.S. Constitution ratified and put into effect. George Washington becomes the first president.

1790: U.S. population stands at 3,929,214.

1798: Alien and Sedition Acts, designed to bolster national sovereignty, are passed. Dissolution of French alliance.

1800: Federal government's capital moved to Washington, D.C. from Philadelphia. U.S. population stands at 5,308,483.

1801: American shipping encounters increasing trouble from the Barbary Pirates of North Africa.

1803: The Louisiana Purchase doubles the size of the United States.

1804: Beginning of Lewis and Clark expedition to explore the territory encompassed by the Louisiana Purchase.

1808: Slave trade outlawed by Congress.

1810: U.S. population stands at 7,239,881.

1811: Native Americans defeated in Battle of Tippecanoe in Indiana Territory.

1812: June 18: Beginning of the War of 1812 between the United States and Britain. August 19: The *Constitution* ("Old Ironsides") defeats the British *Guerriere.*

1813: September 10: Battle of Lake Erie. American forces maintain control over this body of water.

1814: August 25: British capture Washington, D.C. and put it to the torch. September 11: British defeated on Lake Champlain. December 24: Treaty of Ghent signed, ending war in stalemate.

1815: January 8: Battle of New Orleans, fought after peace declared, ends in a resounding U.S. victory.

1817: First Seminole War.

1818: U.S.-Canadian border established at 49th parallel.

1819: Florida purchased from Spain.

1820: Missouri Compromise restricts further expansion of slavery west of the Mississippi or north of the Mason-Dixon Line (except in Missouri). U.S. population stands at 9,638,453.

1821: Mexico declares its independence from Spain.

1823: President James Monroe outlines the Monroe Doctrine, creating a U.S. "sphere of influence" in Central and South America.

1825: Erie Canal opened, bringing trade to inland regions.

1828: Construction begins on first U.S. passenger railway.

1830: U.S. population stands at 12,866,020. Indian Removal Act mandates removal of Eastern Native American tribes.

1832: Black Hawk War.

1834: Indian Territory established.

1835: Second Seminole War.

1836: Battle of the Alamo and San Jacinto; Texas breaks away from Mexico, forming an independent republic.

1837: The telegraph is patented.

1838: The entire Cherokee Nation forced by American government to move from Georgia to Indian Territory, a journey known as the Trail of Tears. Thousands die along the way from disease, exposure, and privation.

1840: Opening of Oregon Trail. U.S. population stands at 17,069,453.

1844: First telegraph line established, connecting Baltimore and Washington, D.C.

1845: Republic of Texas admitted as U.S. state.

1846: 49th Parallel border with Canada extended to Oregon. Beginning of Mexican War.

1847: March 29: Capture of Veracruz by General Winfield Scott. U.S. victories in California and the taking of Mexico City follow.

1848: Treaty of Guadalupe-Hidalgo concludes U.S. war with Mexico. Mexico cedes nearly half its territory, extending U.S. border to Pacific coast.

1849: Gold discovered in California; ensuing "gold rush" brings mass movement of settlers out west.

1850: U.S. population stands at 23,191,876.

1851: Fort Laramie Treaties outline Plains Indian tribes' territories and rights. The conditions of the treaties will be systematically ignored or negated over the next forty years as white settlers stream west into Native American lands.

1853: With the Gadsden Purchase, the continental U.S. border attains its modern outline.

1857: Supreme Court issues Dred Scott decision. Tensions between pro- and anti-slavery factions escalate.

1858: Mountain Meadow Massacre in Utah.

1859: Abolitionist John Brown leads a raid on a federal armory at Harper's Ferry, Virginia.

1860: Abraham Lincoln elected president. South Carolina secedes from the United States on December 20. U.S. population stands at 31,443,321.

1861: January-June: Secession of Mississippi, Florida, Alabama, Georgia, Louisiana, Texas, Virginia, Arkansas, North Carolina, Tennessee. April 14: Firing on Fort Sumter; the American Civil War begins. July 21: First Battle of Bull Run.

1862: Ulysses S. Grant first gains notoriety with the taking of Fort Donelson in February. March 9: *Monitor vs. Virginia*, first encounter between ironclad warships. April 6–7: Battle of Shiloh. April 25: New Orleans captured by Admiral David Farragut. August 30: Second Bull Run. September 17: Battle of Antietam. December 13: Battle of Fredericksburg.

1863: January 1: Lincoln issues the Emancipation Proclamation, guaranteeing the freedom of slaves in the Confederate States. July 1–4: The Battles of Gettysburg and Vicksburg mark a turning point in the Civil War in favor of the Union. November 19: Lincoln delivers his Gettysburg Address.

1864: May 6: Battle of the Wilderness. May 11: Battle of Spottsylvania. September 2: Union General Sherman captures Atlanta and burns it; his "March to the Sea" begins in November.

1865: April 3: Richmond evacuated by Confederates. April 9: Surrender of Lee at Appomattox Courthouse, Virginia. April 14: Lincoln is assassinated. The Civil War ends; twelve-year period of Reconstruction begins in the South.

1867: "Seward's Folly" the U.S. purchases Alaska from Russia.

1868: President Andrew Johnson impeached but not convicted.

1869: Completion of Transcontinental Railroad.

1870: U.S. population stands at 38,558,371.

1876: Battle of Little Big Horn results in the death of American General Custer along with all of the men fighting with him that day.

1880: U.S. population stands at 50,189,209.

1881: July 2: President Garfield shot, mortally wounded; dies on September 19.

1886: Statue of Liberty unveiled.

1889: Oklahoma (formerly Indian Territory) opened to settlers.

1890: Wounded Knee Massacre marks an end to open warfare between the U.S. and Native American nations. U.S. population stands at 62,979,766.

1896: Supreme Court rules that "separate but equal" facilities are legal.

1898: February 15: The battleship *Maine* blows up in Havana harbor. April 25: Congress declares war on Spain. May 1: Battle of Manila. July 3: Battle of Santiago. December 10: Peace treaty signed with Spain. U.S. victory in the Spanish-American War grants America control over Cuba, Guam, Puerto Rico, and the Philippines. Beginning of fifteen-year Philippine insurgency. Hawaii annexed.

1900: American forces assist in ending Boxer Rebellion in China. U.S. population stands at 76,212,168.

1901: September 6: President McKinley assassinated; Theodore Roosevelt becomes president.

1902: Cuban Republic established.

1903: United States backs Panamanian secession from Columbia. Panama leases Canal Zone to United States.

1906: San Francisco Earthquake (and subsequent fire) destroys most of the city.

1908: Model T Ford, the first affordable, mass-produced automobile, offered for sale.

1910: U.S. population stands at 92,228,496.

1914: Opening of the Panama Canal under U.S. control.

1917: April 6: United States enters into World War I.

1918: Spanish Flu epidemic spreads worldwide, killing millions.

1919: President Woodrow Wilson promotes his Fourteen Points at Versailles. U.S. Congress fails to ratify the Treaty of Versailles and stays out of the League of Nations when it is established in 1920.

1920: Women granted the right to vote in the United States. U.S. population stands at 106,021,537.

1925: Scopes "Monkey Trial" debates the teaching of Darwinian evolution in schools.

1928: First Mickey Mouse cartoon.

1929: February 14: Mob-related St. Valentine's Day Massacre in Chicago captures nationwide attention. October 29: Crash of the New York Stock Exchange, beginning of the Great Depression.

1930: U.S. population stands at 123,202,624.

1931: Criminal kingpin Al Capone jailed for income tax evasion.

1932: Franklin D. Roosevelt elected president.

1933: Beginning of "New Deal" policy. End of Prohibition after thirteen disastrous years.

1935: Passage of Social Security Act.

1937: Golden Gate Bridge opened. May 6: *Hindenburg* disaster spells the end of lighter-than-air passenger service.

1940: U.S. population stands at 132,164,569.

1941: Mount Rushmore completed. December 7: Japanese surprise attack on Pearl Harbor, Hawaii, catalyzes U.S. entry into World War II.

1942: Japanese-Americans placed in internment camps for duration of the war. June 4–7: Battle of Midway marks turning point in Pacific War in favor of America.

1943: U.S. invasion of North Africa, Sicily, Italy. Italy surrenders and joins the Allies, but is occupied by German troops.

1944: June 6: D-Day landings in Normandy. Allies reach German border by December. German counterattack launched in last week of December, leading to "Battle of the Bulge." U.S. forces land in the Philippines beginning in October.

1945: February: Battle of Iwo Jima. April–June: Battle of Okinawa. April 12: Death of Franklin Roosevelt. May 8: "V-E Day"; end of hostilities in Europe. August 6 and 9: Dropping of atomic bombs on Hiroshima and Nagasaki. August 15: "V-J Day"; end of World War II.

1947: Marshall Plan implemented to assist in rebuilding of Europe.

1948: Berlin Airlift. Harry Truman wins the presidency in a surprise upset.

1949: NATO established.

1950: United States leads U.N. forces in Korean War. Stalemate largely reached by end of year, although the war drags on for two more years. Height of anti-Communist paranoia; McCarthy hearings begin. U.S. population stands at 151,325,798.

1953: Julius and Ethel Rosenberg convicted of spying for the Soviet Union and executed.

1954: Segregation declared illegal in Supreme Court's *Brown v. Board of Education* ruling.

1955: Disneyland opens. Rosa Parks touches off Montgomery Bus Boycott when she refuses to give up her seat on a public bus.

1959: Communist revolution in Cuba; Fidel Castro becomes dictator.

1960: U.S. population stands at 179,323,175.

1961: Soviets put first man into orbit.

1962: Cuban Missile Crisis brings world to the brink of nuclear war.

1963: November 22: Assassination of John F. Kennedy.

1965: Race riots in Los Angeles. Escalation of U.S. involvement in Vietnam. Malcolm X assassinated.

1966: Black Panther party founded. Anti-draft protests on college campuses across the country.

1968: Martin Luther King assassinated. Robert Kennedy assassinated. Tet Offensive begins turning general American opinion against the Vietnam War. Lyndon Johnson announces he will not seek re-election; Richard Nixon elected president.

1969: July 21: Neil Armstrong becomes the first man to walk on the Moon.

1970: Accusations surface of U.S. soldiers massacring Vietnamese women and children at My Lai. Kent State shootings kill four student protesters. U.S. population stands at 203,302,031.

1973: Last U.S. troops withdrawn from Vietnam. Vice President Spiro Agnew resigns amid accusations of corruption.

1974: President Richard Nixon resigns in the wake of the Watergate Scandal.

1977: Elvis Presley found dead.

1979: Iranian Revolution results in American hostages being taken in Tehran. Nuclear accident at Three Mile Island.

1980: Failed rescue attempt for Iranian hostages. May 18: Mount St. Helens erupts in Washington. Ronald Reagan elected president; his administration will drastically increase defense spending and launch the "War on Drugs." Hostages released. U.S. population stands at 226,542,199.

1981: Assassination attempt on President Reagan. AIDS first identified.

1983: Bombing of U.S. embassy in Beirut, Lebanon.

1984: Vietnam Memorial opens in Washington, D.C.

1986: 1986 Space shuttle *Challenger* explodes. Iran-Contra scandal comes to light. U.S. bombs Libya.

1988: Pan Am Flight 103 bombed over Lockerbie, Scotland.

1990: U.S. population stands at 248,709,873.

1991: The Persian Gulf War: A U.S.-led coalition defeats Iraq after that country's invasion of Kuwait.

1992: Riots in Los Angeles in wake of Rodney King verdict.

1993: World Trade Center bombed.

1995: Oklahoma City bombing; largest domestic terrorist act to date.

1999: President Bill Clinton found not guilty by the Senate after an impeachment trial.

2000: George W. Bush elected president after a controversial and divisive election. U.S. population stands at 281,421,906.

2001: September 11: Terrorists carry out the largest attack on American soil to date, hijacking planes and piloting them into the Twin Towers of the World Trade Center in New York City and the Pentagon building in Washington, D.C. America invades Afghanistan a month later.

2003: U.S. and British forces invade Iraq.

2005: Hurricane Katrina devastates New Orleans.

2006: Former Iraqi dictator Saddam Hussein executed.

2007: U.S. Coalition casualties for Iraq invasion and occupation top 4,000.

Glossary

A

AIRBORNE: Troops trained in deployment by air, either by parachute, glider, or similar assault aircraft. Can also refer to any equipment or operations related to or involving air-dropped troops.

ARMORED PERSONNEL CARRIER: Often abbreviated APC, a vehicle designed to transport troops to the battlefield in a protected environment, often alongside tanks and other armored vehicles.

ARMY: From the Latin *armata*, or "act of arming," a term that describes any land-based military force and sometimes including other branches of service as well. In modern military usage, an army is defined as a group of two or more corps. During the World Wars, the massive scale of the conflicts often saw armies being organized in turn to form Army Groups.

B

BARRAGE: A coordinated mass of artillery fire, often fired indirectly.

BATTALION: In modern military usage, a grouping of multiple companies totaling around one thousand soldiers. The smallest unit considered capable of independent, unsupported action.

BAYONET: A dagger-length blade fitted to the end of a rifle or musket. Originally developed to arm slow-firing guns with a secondary use in close combat, turning the firearm into a spear, the use of bayonet tactics was taught in European-style armies from the mid-seventeenth to the mid-twentieth century.

BEACHHEAD: A small footing gained by an army landing on enemy shores or crossing a river. Often the target of determined counterattacks.

BRIGADE: First developed by Swedish king Gustavus Adolphus during the Thirty Years War, the brigade was originally an early version of a combined arms task force consisting of several regiments of infantry, cavalry, and artillery. Modern usage places the brigade roughly on par with the regiment in terms of size.

C

CALIBER: The diameter of the bore, or inside, of a gun's barrel. Can be expressed in millimeters (i.e. 9 mm) or fractions of an inch (i.e. .50 caliber, meaning half an inch bore).

CAMPAIGN: A series of military operations, often designed towards a single objective.

CAVALRY: Soldiers who move and fight primarily from horseback. Does not generally extend to troops who use mounts to move into battle but dismount to fight, who are instead referred to as "mounted infantry."

CIVILIANS: Also called noncombatants, any non-enlisted person. As war became increasingly driven by industry in the late nineteenth and early twentieth centuries, civilians became targets of armies and the weapons of war.

COMMANDER-IN-CHIEF: A general or other leader vested with control of a nation's military forces. The United States Constitution reserves this role for the President, although only two—George Washington and James Madison—have actually led troops in the field while in office.

COMPANY: A military unit consisting of platoons, usually three or four in number, totaling anywhere from 100–200 enlisted men and officers.

CORPS: An organization of two or more divisions, grouped in turn to form armies.

D

D-DAY: A general code term for an unspecified day upon which a planned event is to take place in any given operation; the specific time is referred to as "H-hour. " Since June 6, 1944, the term has become synonymous in the popular imagination with the Normandy Invasion.

DEFILADE: A position that protects a unit from direct enemy fire.

DIVISION: A concept that first emerged during the Seven Years War of the mid-eighteenth century, the division organizes ten to twenty thousand soldiers into a single unit, forming the building block of larger armies and corps. Napoleon Bonaparte was the first general to fully adopt the divisional system; by the end of the Napoleonic Wars, all of Europe's armies would be organized by divisions, as are all modern armies.

E

ENFILADE: Also known as "flanking fire," the condition whereby a unit's flank becomes exposed to enemy fire, exposing troops beyond the front rank.

ENLISTED MAN: A term used in modern military organization to refer to the lowest ranking soldiers, often including non-commissioned officers.

F

FILE: A line of troops standing one in front of another.

FLANK: As a noun, flank is a term used to describe the side of a military unit. As a verb, the action of moving against an enemy's side or rear.

FRIENDLY FIRE: Used to describe casualties arising during battle caused by friendly forces either through mistake or accident.

FRAG: A term that became well known during the Vietnam War to describe the murder of a superior officer, usually while out in the field. "Frag" is short for "fragmentation grenade," the supposed weapon of

choice in such situations, since it would leave behind no fingerprints or other ballistic evidence and could easily be chalked up to friendly fire.

FRONT: Also called a battlefront, this is the point along which two opposing forces meet. The term can be applied to anything from local engagements up to entire theaters of war.

G

GRENADE: An explosive devise originally designed to be hurled by hand, which also sends shards of metal flying through the air.

H

HALFTRACK: A vehicle utilizing caterpillar tracks for rear propulsion and standard road wheels for front propulsion. Designed to offer the cross-country capabilities of a tank and the maneuverability of a road vehicle, military halftracks were used extensively in the Second World War as some of the first armored personnel carriers.

I

INFANTRY: The backbone of most armies throughout history, the infantry is characterized by soldiers who fight and move primarily or exclusively on foot and who are armed with relatively light weapons such as spears or rifles.

IRREGULAR: A soldier trained in non-standard military techniques, often making use of loose, open deployments.

M

MEGADEATH: A term coined in 1953 meaning one million deaths. Used to describe potential death yields from various nuclear war scenarios.

N

NO MAN'S LAND: The ground between opposing forces along a front. Can be anywhere from a few yards to a mile or more in width.

NON-COMMISSIONED OFFICER: Commonly abbreviated NCO, an enlisted man given battlefield authority by a commissioned officer. The most well-known "non-com" rank is sergeant.

O

OFFICER: Also called a commissioned officer, these are individuals vested (or "commissioned") with the ability to issue commands on the battlefield. Up until relatively recently, commissions were commonly bought and sold and did not necessarily reflect actual military skill.

P

PLATOON: Originally used to describe a small detachment of men, the platoon evolved into a modern military unit usually consisting of two to four squads totaling thirty to fifty soldiers. Usually led by a low-ranking commissioned officer such as a lieutenant.

R

RANK: A line of soldiers standing shoulder to shoulder. Most regular military units up until the First World War were trained to fight in ranks.

REGIMENT: The first post-feudal military unit, developed as armies became increasingly professional and organized during the sixteenth century. Early regiments often acted as independent military entities, conducting their own recruiting and commissioning their own officers. The modern British Army still has traces of this "regimental system" in its training and deployment of its units. Modern regiments vary widely in size depending on the army and their perceived tactical usefulness and range, anywhere from a few hundred up to three thousand soldiers.

REGULAR: Term used to distinguish trained soldiers who follow commonly accepted forms of military organization and tactical deployment.

S

SQUAD: In modern military organization, the smallest recognized unit on a battlefield, most often consisting of between eight and fourteen soldiers. Called a "section" in British and Commonwealth armies.

STRATEGY: The deployment and movement of large units, from divisions up through entire army groups, to achieve a military goal.

T

TACTICS: Military methods for defeating an enemy in individual battles.

Introduction to World War II (1939–1945)

World War II (1939–1945) was the deadliest, most costly, most widespread war in human history. The war saw the decline of the European colonial powers that had dominated global politics for the previous four centuries and the rise of the United States and the Soviet Union as superpowers. Tremendous advances in science, medicine, and military technology were made over the course of the conflict—from antibiotics to the atomic bomb—and governments spent unprecedented sums of money on research and development in the name of victory.

World War II spurred the complete mobilization of not just science but also industry, national economies, and the civilian labor force. In fact, the majority of deaths in World War II were non-military. In addition to famine and disease, civilians in war-ravaged areas found themselves deliberately targeted by hostile powers using methods ranging from strategic bombing to cold-blooded genocide in the notorious Nazi death camps. In all, more than sixty million people—soldiers and civilians—would lose their lives during World War II. Untold millions more were permanently displaced.

The roots of the conflict lay in the resolution of World War I, when Germany was placed under severe economic and military sanctions and forced to pay war reparations to the victorious powers. Meanwhile, Italy and Japan, although sharing in the victory of the Allies, felt they were not adequately rewarded for their contribution to the war effort. In World War II, these three nations and their allies, known collectively as the Axis powers, would wage war for nearly six years against an increasing number of enemies—the Allies.

The war was in many ways a clash of political and economic ideologies, pitting Western democracy, in an uneasy alliance with Soviet Communism, against imperialist and fascist aggression. The initial stages of the war were marked by stunning Axis victories in Europe and Asia—Germany found itself master of nearly all of Europe by 1941, while Japan, through a series of surprise attacks and lightning campaigns, controlled a vast Pacific realm by 1942.

That year would prove to be the turning point of the war. Germany overextended itself by invading the Soviet Union, while Japan soon found itself on the defensive after bringing the industrial and economic powerhouse of the United States into the conflict. Over the next three years, the Allies would gradually force the Axis powers to retreat over their newly acquired territories, driving them back towards their homelands.

By 1945, the Axis powers were on the verge of collapse. Italy had surrendered in 1943, and most of Germany's minor allies were similarly out of the fight or had even started fighting on the side of the Allies. Yet Germany and Japan kept fighting, spurred on by Allied calls for an unconditional surrender and the threat of retribution that policy implied.

In the end, the measures required to defeat the Axis powers would prove extreme—Germany held out until it was nearly completely overrun, crushed beneath millions of invading soldiers streaming in from the Allied nations. Japan surrendered three months later after suffering tens of thousands of civilian deaths in two devastating moments: the detonation of two atomic bombs at Hiroshima and Nagasaki.

World War II (1939–1945)

✪ Causes

German Nationalism

When Adolf Hitler (1889–1945) and the Nazi Party came to power in 1933 by popular vote, they did so largely by riding a wave of German nationalism. These nationalistic feelings were rooted in centuries of Central European conflict, were sharpened and intensified in the wake of defeat in World War I, and would reach their devastating peak in World War II (1939–1945).

The concept of a unified country called Germany is relatively new. When Kaiser Wilhelm II (1859–1941) led his nation into war in 1914, the German Empire was not yet a half-century old. Yet in that short time, Germany had quickly risen to become one of Europe's major powers. This rapid rise in power came about largely because of the population's willingness to set aside old divisions and begin working toward building a new national identity to match their much older cultural and linguistic identity, which stretched back to the Middle Ages.

The First Reich The seeds of German disunity lie in medieval power politics. At one point all of Europe was a patchwork of independent fiefdoms, loosely bound together under kings who were more often than not mere figureheads. As the Middle Ages came to a close in the fifteenth century, most of these fiefdoms were stripped of their power as the nations we know today began to take form under ever stronger kings and queens.

This process did not take place in Germany, which occupied the bulk of the Holy Roman Empire, for a variety of reasons. Chief among these were the Wars of Religion of the sixteenth and seventeenth centuries, in particular the Thirty Years War (1618–1648), which brought widespread devastation to the region and effectively transformed the more than two hundred member-states of the Holy Roman Empire into independent states, reducing the emperor to a powerless statesman.

Over the next two centuries, Central European politics was dominated by the Austrian Empire, ruled by the powerful Hapsburg dynasty. Germany, trapped between the great powers of Russia, Austria, and France, became a buffer zone and a battleground, its fractiousness encouraged as a means of maintaining the international balance of power.

Frederick the Great and the Rise of Prussia This balance would finally be upset in the eighteenth century with the rise of Prussia, an eastern German kingdom whose roots lay in the "Drive to the East," a nineteenth-century term for the migration of German-speaking peoples into the Slavic lands of Eastern Europe. Prussia itself began as the territory of the crusading Teutonic Knights, who carved the territory out of the lands of the indigenous Prussians and gradually Germanized the region.

By the mid-eighteenth century, Prussia, under the leadership of King Frederick II (1712–1786), defeated all three of its neighbors during the Seven Years War and rose to become a new power in Europe. The seeds of eventual German unification were being sown.

Romantic Nationalism The essential ingredient of unification, nationalism, did not begin in earnest until the early 1900s. French dominance in Central Europe, and resentment thereof, sparked a new recognition of the unity of German language, culture, and history. The Brothers Grimm and their collection of German folklore were a direct result of this new movement, which was soon dubbed German Romanticism. The philosophy of Romanticism represented the first expression of German nationalism, emphasizing ethnic unity in the absence of political unity.

The new philosophy espoused two central concepts of German history and culture: Pan-Germanism and *Drang Nach Osten*. Pan-Germanism sought to unite all German-speaking peoples within a single nation, where *Drang Nach Osten* ("drive to the east") explained the gradual migration of German influence from west to east

By the early 1930s, German nationalism had risen to the point that ordinary people such as these students were burning books and demonstrating "against the anti-German spirit." *AP Images*

and further implied the continuing need for German expansion to provide *Lebensraum* (living space).

This complex nationalistic philosophy, combined with the heady revolutionary atmosphere of Europe in the mid-nineteenth century, led to Germany's first attempt at unification in 1848. The Frankfurt Parliament's efforts were ultimately stymied by an inability to join the far-flung German states in a single nation. Many of the states, such as Austria-Hungary and Prussia, contained significant non-German minorities.

Blood and Iron With the failure of peaceful unification, Romanticism and Nationalism went their separate ways. The German cause was soon taken up by Prussia and its chancellor, Otto von Bismarck (1815–1898), in particular, who advocated the creation of a unified state through "blood and iron."

Bismarck was successful, although he opted to create a German state that did not encompass all German-speaking territories—missing, most notably, was Austria. Thus, the issue of pan-Germanism was left unresolved and German nationalism took on a distinctly militaristic tone.

The new militaristic brand of German nationalism, which emphasized the superiority of German culture and the need for expansion, would lead directly to two world wars. World War II in particular was a result of German nationalism expressed as national policy. Hitler's pan-Germanic dreams of expansion led to Germany's annexation of Austria and Czechoslovakia in 1938–1939.

Pan-Germanic considerations, combined with Nazi dreams of reinstituting the "drive to the East," led to the German invasion of Poland in 1939 and to the invasion of the Soviet Union in 1941. German nationalism, originally an expression of a desire for a long-fractured culture to coalesce as a sovereign nation, had turned into an instrument of militaristic imperialism. In the end, the results would prove disastrous for the very culture that German nationalism claimed to serve.

Global Economic Depression

On October 29, 1929, known as "Black Tuesday," the New York Stock Exchange crashed. The fallout of this economic crisis would set off a worldwide depression that would have profound effects on the economic, social, and political structures of virtually every industrialized country and would set the world on a path to war.

The Roaring Twenties and the Crash
The 1920s were a decade lived in the shadow of World War I. International politics focused on efforts to ensure that war on such a scale could never happen again, while Europe tried its best to rebuild after the massive destruction brought about by the conflict. The U.S. postwar economy had burgeoned, and the United States had become a global power and established strong ties with the Old World industrialized nations as well as with Japan.

Unfortunately, much of this prosperity was funneled into speculation on the stock market, which resulted in ever-increasing profits that were built on wildly overvalued stock. When the market eventually corrected itself in 1929, the resulting "crash" ruined many investors and set off a domino effect of economic failure within the United States that would eventually become a worldwide economic failure.

Domestic and International Consequences
The United States, which had already been leaning toward an isolationist foreign policy, withdrew completely from world politics as it dealt with the calamitous effects of the Great Depression, as the economic downturn was called. Hardest hit were manufacturing industries and the mining and foresting industries that supported them. To make matters worse, the American Midwest, after decades of overfarming, turned into a literal "Dust Bowl" as once-rich topsoil dried up and blew away amidst record drought. By 1932, the worst year of the Great Depression, one in four Americans was unemployed, a disastrous condition for a country with no government-sponsored support system for the poor and disadvantaged.

A strong current of isolationism accompanied the Great Depression, not only in the United States but also in Europe. England and France, still struggling to recover from the massive expenditures of World War I, were severely affected by the economic downturn—for many of the same reasons as the United States was disastrously affected. France was perhaps the hardest hit of the three, nearly crippled by riots and a general strike in the mid-1930s.

As the situation worsened, desperation led to desperate measures; fringe political parties gained considerable popularity. Democracy found itself increasingly on the defensive as the Allied victors of World War I frantically attempted to keep their governments from completely collapsing.

The Rise of Totalitarianism
Events in Spain would demonstrate how very real the possibility of government collapse was. In 1936, the country fell into civil war. The democratically elected government and a fascist insur-

gency supported by Italy and Germany clashed in a war that would cost hundreds of thousands of lives. (The terms fascist and fascism refer to a system of government marked by strong centralized economic and social authority, usually in the hands of a dictator, coupled with aggressive nationalism.) The Spanish Civil War (1936–1939) would end in a fascist victory that had in large part been assured because of the refusal of the Western democracies to intervene on behalf of the Spanish democracy.

With the major Allied powers distracted by their own internal difficulties, some nations turned to expansionist policies as their governments became increasingly radicalized in response to the global crisis.

Both Japan and Italy embarked on campaigns of territorial expansion as a means of stimulating their depressed economies—Japan attacked Manchuria and took it from China, and Italy overran the African country of Ethiopia. Both countries received international condemnation but no actual reprisals.

Japan, dependent on international trade, had been particularly hard hit by the Great Depression, which had led directly to a renewed policy of colonialism and a rejection of liberal democracy. A similar process in Germany would see the rise of Adolf Hitler and the Nazi Party.

The Great Depression and the Rise of Nazism
The German Empire was created and destroyed by war—the Franco-Prussian War and World War I, respectively. The Germany that had emerged from "the Great War" in 1919 was economically crippled and politically divided. The young nation's economic condition had never been weaker, and the worldwide economic crisis that began in 1929 only made things worse. It was this environment that allowed the National Socialist Democratic Worker's Party (or "Nazi" Party) to thrive.

The Nazis had attempted to seize power before—in a coup attempt in 1923—but the political and economic climate was not yet desperate enough to support an extremist government. The crash of 1929 changed all that. The United States, which had been propping up the German democratic government with loans, had to cut off its flow of cash. Unemployment and inflation in Germany soared and politics began to take a radical turn.

The Nazis came to power in 1933 in this environment, taking advantage of the fractiousness of their political opponents and a public increasingly desperate for solutions. One year prior to Hitler's rise to power, Franklin D. Roosevelt had been elected president of the United States. Both leaders would quickly embark on programs of renewal and rebuilding that would eventually bring their countries out of the Great Depression.

Although both programs were ultimately successful, they differed markedly in their objectives. For the Roosevelt administration, the restoration of a stable and prosperous economy was an end in itself. For Hitler, the overriding goal of Germany's economic recovery was to restore his country's military might.

The six years between the consolidation of Nazi power in 1933 and the invasion of Poland in 1939 saw Germany systematically flout or ignore nearly every provision of the Treaty of Versailles, which had put severe limits on German military, economic, and territorial expansion. With France crippled by internal strife and the United States pursuing a policy of isolation, England was left to its own response to these violations. That policy, appeasement, was largely a result of England's weakened state in the wake of the global economic depression.

As with those from Italy and Japan, the warning signs coming from Germany were ignored. The Great Depression sapped both the economic means and the political will of the Western democracies to deal with these three emerging threats until it was too late. The global economic crisis permitted the rise of Hitler and other totalitarian regimes as well as their expansion over the course of the 1930s. The seeds sown during these difficult years would be reaped in the following decade.

Anti-Semitism

Anti-Semitism, active discrimination against and hostility toward Jewish people, has a long and infamous history in Europe. From the Middle Ages onward, anti-Semitism fueled campaigns of terror against Jewish communities, often resulting in murders, mass killings, and even forced migration of entire communities. But it was not until the rise of Adolf Hitler's Nazi Party in 1933 that a nation embraced anti-Semitism as official state policy. The execution of this policy, referred to by the Nazis as the "final solution to the Jewish question," would result in the death of millions of Jews during the organized, state-run genocide known as the Holocaust.

Religious Anti-Semitism In order to understand how an event as monumentally monstrous as the Holocaust could come about, one must go back to some of the earliest Christian writings. From the beginning, many Christians felt antipathy toward the Jews, whom they viewed as stubbornly refusing to accept the coming of the Messiah. Some laid blamed on all Jews for the role played by Jewish authorities in the crucifixion of Christ. The moderate voices, such as St. Augustine of Hippo, condemned the Jews for killing Jesus the man, but exonerated them of the charge of "killing God" (for Christians, Christ was both a man and God). Other Christian thinkers were not so kind.

The common belief among medieval Christians was that the Jewish people were being punished for their deicide—they had lost their land and their temple because of God's wrath and were condemned to wander the earth. St. Thomas Aquinas (c. 1225–1274), a prominent Christian philosopher, was particularly vehement in his anti-Semitic writings, arguing at one point that the Jews should be enslaved by Christians.

In many ways, anti-Semitism arose from the Christian community's discomfort with the presence of an "alien" culture in their midst. These feelings led to the passing of laws requiring Jews to wear some sort of distinguishing clothing, most infamously a yellow star, in order to provide a visual cue for Christians.

Accusations and rumors of the most outrageous sort were spread regarding Jewish customs. It was said that Jews kidnapped Christian babies and offered them in human sacrifice to God, using their blood in Passover ceremonies. With the coming of the Black Death in the mid-fourteenth century, Jews were widely accused of causing the pestilence. Untold thousands of Jews were killed in the ensuing "reprisals."

Anti-Semitic Christian writers—both Catholic and Protestant—often went to great lengths in describing the "monstrous" appearance of Jews, as if to emphasize how alien the culture really seemed. Jews were painted as spreaders of disease, filth, death, demonic possession, and infestations. The leader of the Protestant Reformation Martin Luther (1483–1546), in what has been called the first systematic outline for the genocide of the Jewish people, claimed "we are not at fault in slaying them" and outlined a methodology for the systematic destruction of the Jews eerily reminiscent of the Holocaust.

Violence and Expulsion Organized terror campaigns directed at Jewish communities trace their lineage at least back to the First Crusade in 1096, when the first gatherings of religious zealots on their way to liberate the Holy Land, believing that killing "non-believers" in the name of God was a holy act, fell upon Jewish communities in Germany. The worst episodes occurred in the towns of Mainz and Worms, where the resident Jewish communities were completely wiped out in what has been called "the first Holocaust."

Anti-Semitic feelings were also secularly based: Christians, forbidden by the Church from lending money at a profit, turned to Jewish moneylenders to finance their ambitions. The debt-ridden nobleman or merchant might stir up a local purge of Jewish residents simply to clear his debts.

Savvy rulers usually recognized the importance of Jewish creditors to the economies of Europe, and Jews could often count on some sort of protected legal status. The primary motivation for anti-Semitic crusades remained religious, however, so this protected status could be just as quickly rescinded, as when Edward I of England (1239–1307) expelled the Jews from his country in 1290 after two hundred years of royal sanction.

Although escalating anti-Semitism in England had led to Edward's decision, it was Spain in later centuries that would earn a particular reputation for its vehement anti-Semitism. In 1492, the same year Spain completed its *reconquista* with the conquest of the last Muslim kingdom on the peninsula, the Alhambra Decree was

The label on this Berlin bench—"Nicht fur Juden," or Not for Jews—testifies to the powerful anti-Semitism practiced by Germans in the years leading up to World War II. *Fred Ramage/Getty Images*

issued, ordering Spain's significant Jewish minority to either convert or leave the country.

Hundreds of thousands of Jews chose to leave, but many converted. This would, in the end, prove unsatisfactory. The Spanish Inquisition was in large part founded to ferret out Jewish converts who might not have been totally committed to their new religion. The Jesuit Order, founded in 1540 by the Spaniard who later became St. Ignatius of Loyola (1491–1521), required its initiates to prove non-Jewish ancestry stretching back five generations.

Racial Anti-Semitism Anti-Semitism continued to flare up in Europe through the ensuing centuries, but in the nineteenth century it would take an important turn. Throughout that century, many of the laws specifically targeting Jews were repealed throughout Europe. This so-called "emancipation of the Jews" finally recognized Jewish civil rights, granting full citizenship and equality for the first time. At the same time, anti-Semitism turned from being a religious issue and began to take on racial and cultural connotations.

In fact, the term "anti-Semitism" was first coined in the nineteenth century, at a time when the newly enfranchised Jewish community was beginning to enter into European (and American) circles that had long been closed to them. This new upward mobility, combined with the emergence of nationalism, particularly in Germany, and its emphasis on native culture and the separateness of Jewish culture, led to a major surge in anti-Semitic literature and rhetoric by the end of the nineteenth century.

That anti-Semitism was turned into a racial issue fit in nicely with the emerging theories of Charles Darwin, whose theory of evolution and "survival of the fittest" was quickly misappropriated and turned to racist ends. In effect, hatred of Judaism as a religion had been replaced with hatred of Jews as a people.

✪ Major Figures

Adolf Hitler

Adolf Hitler (1889–1945) was chancellor of Germany and headed the Nazi Party during World War II. Under Hitler, the German government attempted to enact the

In October 1939, Hitler, who had himself been wounded during World War I, spoke with a wounded soldier. © *KPA/ZUMA/Corbis*

"final solution" to the "Jewish question," resulting in the mass murder of six million Jews and three million others also deemd "undesirable" by the Nazi government.

Early Life and Career Hitler was born in Braunau, Austria, on April 20, 1889, the son of an Austrian customs agent. He moved to Vienna in 1907, where he failed as a landscape artist. He became virulently anti-Semitic while in Vienna.

In 1913, he moved to Germany. He served in the Bavarian army in World War I, winning an Iron Cross for valor. The honor gave him German citizenship. In the 1920s, he entered German politics, advocating a nationalistic form of socialism. His talent for speaking took him to leadership of the National Socialist (or Nazi) party. In 1923, he attempted to take over Bavaria, a coup attempt called the Beer Hall Putsch (putsch is another word for coup). Jailed for the attempt, he wrote *Mein Kampf*, outlining his political philosophy.

After release from prison, he resumed leadership of the Nazis. He was elected chancellor of Germany in 1933 and soon took absolute power.

Opening of World War II Hitler remilitarized Germany in defiance of the Versailles Treaty that ended World War I. He rebuilt the German Navy, including a prohibited submarine fleet, created an air force, the Luftwaffe, and expanded the army well beyond the 100,000-man limit set by the Treaty of Versailles. Hitler reintroduced conscription in 1935, also in violation of the treaty.

In 1936, Germany reoccupied the Rhineland, demilitarized after World War I. Germany absorbed Austria in March 1938, annexed the German-speaking Sudetenland districts of Czechoslovakia in September 1938, and occupied Bohemia and Moravia in March 1939.

In September 1939, Hitler demanded Danzig, an ethnically German city-state and important port. He also wanted to give East Prussia land access to Germany. The Polish Corridor, which gave otherwise land-locked Poland access to the Baltic Sea, separated the two parts of Germany.

The reaction of England and France to Hitler's previous violations of the Versailles Treaty ranged from passive to supine. In 1938, British Prime Minister Neville Chamberlain (1869–1940) negotiated away part of its ally, Czechoslovakia, giving Germany the Sudetenland in exchange for a promise that Hitler would seek no more territorial gains. Chamberlain called the agreement "peace in our time." Hitler expected the Western allies to behave as passively with Poland as they had previously.

Hitler signed an alliance with the Soviet Union. It split Poland between the two nations and gave the Soviets the Baltic States and parts of Romania and Finland. In exchange, Hitler got a guarantee of neutrality from the Soviets. Britain and France, meanwhile, finally decided to try to set some limits and refused to allow Hitler to take control of the Polish Corridor.

When Germany moved into Poland in September 1939, France and Britain declared war. As Hitler conquered Poland, France and Britain sat passively on the western German border. In the spring of 1940, Germany moved north, gaining control of Denmark, Norway, the Netherlands, Belgium, Luxembourg, and, soon thereafter, France.

Hitler next tried to subdue Britain through air power, using the Luftwaffe. The Royal Air Force defended Britain from the Luftwaffe. Hitler then attempted to starve Britain out using a submarine blockade, but the British stood fast and were never subdued by the Nazis.

Invasion of Russia Stymied in the west, Hitler turned east. Hitler sent German reinforcements to help his Italian ally in North Africa. In May 1941, he invaded the Balkans, occupying Yugoslavia and Greece. The invasion of Russia, Operation Barbarossa, was launched in June 1941. The Russians counterattacked in winter 1941–1942. Hitler's generals wanted to fall back and fight a mobile defense. Hitler overruled them, demanding they stand fast. The tactic worked that winter. Afterwards, Hitler refused to allow mobile defenses, insisting that Germany hold every inch of ground it took. This led to military disasters in 1943 and 1944.

Downfall In December 1941, after Japan attacked Pearl Harbor, Hitler declared war on the United States.

EVA BRAUN

Eva Braun (1912–1945) was Hitler's mistress and, in the last day before their joint suicide, his wife. She was the daughter of a Bavarian schoolteacher, educated at a convent school and known for her wholesome, classically German good looks. She met Hitler while working as an assistant at the studio of Heinrich Hoffmann, the official photographer of the Nazis. She was only seventeen years old; Hitler was forty. Little is known of the earliest years of their association, but by 1932, she was his mistress. Evidently the relationship had its troubles, because in that same year, Braun attempted suicide. She tried again, unsuccessfully, in 1935.

Though kept out of the public eye and often ignored for long periods by her busy lover, Braun enjoyed a pampered existence. She lived in luxury at Hitler's expense. In April 1945, Braun traveled to Berlin to be with Hitler even as the Soviet army approached the capital. The two were married on April 29 in a short civil ceremony. They committed suicide together on April 30—Eva by taking poison and Hitler by both poisoning and shooting himself.

Initially, things went well for Germany in 1942, but by year's end, the momentum passed to the Allies. The Allies advanced throughout 1943 and early 1944, aided by Hitler's blunders. The Western allies captured Sicily, landed in Italy, and captured Rome on June 4, 1944. Two days later they landed in Normandy, France. The Soviets pushed across the steppes, reoccupying most of their former territory, by spring 1944. Allied air power devastated German cities.

Hitler refused to acknowledge what was happening. He insisted on impossible military offensives. He became increasingly paranoid. The paranoia increased after an assassination attempt on July 20, 1944, organized by army officers. On April 29, 1945, after the Soviets entered Berlin, he committed suicide in his Berlin command bunker.

Victor Emmanuel III

Victor Emmanuel III (1869–1947) was the last king of Italy. The Italian people abolished their monarchy in a plebiscite following World War II. This was largely due to Victor Emmanuel's involvement with the fascists in the prewar years, and his actions during World War II.

Early Life and Reign   Victor Emmanuel was born in Naples on November 11, 1869. He was the only son of Umberto I, King of Italy (1844–1900). Victor Emmanuel became king of Italy as Victor Emmanuel III on July 29, 1900, after his father was assassinated.

At the outset of World War I in 1914, Italy was allied with Germany and Austria-Hungary. It chose to remain neutral at first. By 1915 Italy had negotiated a treaty to enter World War I on the side of the Allies (France, Great Britain, and Russia). When the Italian legislature opposed entry, Victor Emmanuel overrode the legislature and declared war. Italian casualties were high, and the gains of the Italians were minimal. The war was unpopular, as it left Italy victorious but in financial ruins.

Fascist Rise and Rule   Benito Mussolini (1883–1945) was the first of the major fascist leaders in World War II to seize power in his nation. In part, this was due to Victor Emmanuel's actions. Italy suffered a severe depression in the years immediately following World War I, which led to the rise of Mussolini's Fascist Party.

When Mussolini made his march on Rome in 1922, Victor Emmanuel refused to sign a proclamation of martial law that would have allowed the existing Italian parliamentary government to use the army against Mussolini. The king ordered the army to dismantle roadblocks around Rome and admit the fascist marchers to the capital.

The government resigned. Victor Emmanuel invited Mussolini to form the new government. The king stood aside as Mussolini transformed the Italian Republic into a dictatorship. He remained silent after political leaders opposing Mussolini were assassinated.

World War II   While Italy remained neutral at the beginning of World War II, it entered the war on the side of Germany in June 1940. France was collapsing, and Italy wanted parts of southeastern France. The French army limited Italian gains to a few thousand yards. Italy found itself in a major war, allied to Germany.

A disastrous invasion of Greece in 1940 led to the loss of a quarter of the Italian colony of Albania. The Italians had to be rescued by the Germans in 1941. Italy quickly lost most of its African Empire to Britain, except for Libya. Libya was held only due to German intervention with the introduction of the *Deutches Afrika Korps*. Even Libya was lost by the end of 1942.

On July 25, 1943, after losing Sicily to Allied invasion, Victor Emmanuel called Mussolini to the palace. Victor Emmanuel demanded and received Mussolini's resignation as prime minister. He had Mussolini arrested and directed Pietro Badoglio to form a new government. The king also instructed Badoglio to negotiate an armistice.

An armistice between Italy and the Allies was signed on September 3. The Allies announced the armistice five days later, on September 8. Victor Emmanuel did not inform the Italian army of the armistice, nor did he order the army to defend its country. As a result, Germany disarmed the Italian army and occupied Italy. The king left Rome.

The combination of his long association with fascism and his flight from Rome ahead of a German invasion left the king highly unpopular. He did not abdicate, but transferred most of his royal powers to his son, the Crown Prince Umberto (1904–1983), shortly after leaving Rome.

Postwar Years In 1946, Italy held a referendum on the monarchy. While Victor Emmanuel's son was well regarded, Victor Emmanuel was still king and deeply unpopular. To sway the vote in favor of monarchy, Victor Emmanuel abdicated May 9, 1946. The act focused attention on the old king's shortcomings, reminding voters why they wanted to eliminate the monarchy. The referendum abolishing the monarchy passed with 54 percent of the vote a month later.

Victor Emmanuel died in exile in Alexandria, Egypt, on December 28, 1947.

Benito Mussolini

Early Life and Career Benito Mussolini (1883–1945), Italy's fascist wartime leader, was born on July 29, 1883. His father was a blacksmith and his mother was a teacher. Both favored socialism. Mussolini became a socialist politician as a young man. He wrote and edited socialist newspapers prior to World War I, moving between Italy, Switzerland, and Austria-Hungary.

Mussolini served in the Italian army from 1915 through 1917, fighting in World War I. After the war, he created a new political movement blending socialism, Italian nationalism, and centralized government control. The movement was called fascism.

With assistance from Italian industrialists and the king of Italy, Victor Emmanuel III, Mussolini was named head of the Italian government. Once in charge, Mussolini consolidated power and made himself the supreme leader of Italy. He was a model imitated by Hitler in Germany and Francisco Franco (1892–1975) in Spain.

As head of Italy, he centralized the economy and started Italy on a series of foreign adventures with the lofty aim of reconstituting the Roman Empire. By 1939, he had conquered Albania and Ethiopia and had assisted the Nationalists in Spain.

World War II Mussolini led Italy when World War II started. Initially, he remained neutral, but he brought Italy into the war in 1940, allied to Germany. The decision was taken against the counsel of his military advisors. Mussolini's motivations were complex. He did not think Germany would succeed. The Italian military was in poor shape. Mussolini was also a little jealous of Adolf Hitler. Mussolini entered the 1930s as Europe's leading fascist dictator. By 1939, Italy had slipped. It was the junior member of the German-Italian Axis. By remaining neutral, Mussolini asserted his independence from Hitler.

The situation changed radically when France collapsed after the German invasion in May 1940. Italy had expansionist designs on southeastern France. These could only be realized if Italy were at war with France.

Against the advice of the Italian army's general staff, Mussolini declared war on June 10, 1940. France had already begun negotiating an armistice with Hitler.

Mussolini gained little by declaring war. The Italian army advanced only a thousand or so yards into France before being stopped by the French. The subsequent peace granted Italy only such lands as it had taken prior to the cease-fire. In exchange for a few thousand square yards of mountainside along the Franco-Italian border, Mussolini involved an unprepared Italy in a war against Britain. He also put Italy's extensive Africa holdings at risk.

By spring 1941, Mussolini's military misadventures required German assistance. In December 1940, the British invaded Libya and invaded Italian East Africa in early 1940. By February 1940, the British had cleared the Italians out of the eastern half of Libya. In May 1941, Italian East Africa fell.

German intervention saved Italy. Germany sent an armored corps to Africa to reinforce the Italians. Despite initial Axis successes, the British, who were joined by the United States in December 1941, pushed the Axis powers out of Libya at the end of 1942, and out of Africa entirely in early 1943.

Fall from Power By 1943, the Italian economy was collapsing, the armed forces were demoralized, and the alliance with Germany was intensely unpopular. Since Mussolini still controlled the army and the national police, he ignored the unrest.

In July 1943, the Allies invaded Sicily. Most of Mussolini's political allies within Italy were abandoning him. Mussolini called a meeting of the Italian Grand Council on July 24. The council passed a no-confidence resolution against Mussolini, which he ignored.

King Victor Emmanuel III soon demanded and received Mussolini's resignation. When Mussolini left the palace, he was arrested. The Italian government moved Mussolini from one prison to another for the next two months. Finally, he was placed in a hotel atop Gran Sasso, a mountaintop ski resort in peacetime. On September 12, 1943, a German rescue freed Mussolini. The Germans landed gliders in front of the hotel to get troops to Mussolini.

Italy negotiated an armistice on September 3, 1943, and declared war on Germany on October 13. The Nazis organized the German-controlled portion of Italy as the Italian Social Republic, with Mussolini as the head. From September 1943 until April 1945 Mussolini "ruled" the Italian Social Republic. In actuality, he ran northern Italy for Hitler.

The Germans left northern Italy in April 1945. Mussolini attempted to flee to Switzerland but was caught by antifascist guerrillas and shot, along with his mistress. He died on April 28, 1945.

Emperor Hirohito

Hirohito (1901–1989) was Emperor of Japan from 1926 until his death in 1989. He is now known in Japan through his posthumous title, Emperor Showa.

Early Life   Hirohito was born on April 29, 1901. He was the oldest son of Crown Prince Yoshihito (later Emperor Taisho, 1879–1926). He became heir apparent in 1912 with the death of his grandfather (Emperor Meiji, 1852–1912) and the ascension of his father to the imperial throne.

When his father became ill in 1921, Hirohito was made prince regent. As prince regent, he toured Europe, the first Japanese emperor to leave Japan. Hirohito became emperor upon the death of his father on December 25, 1926.

Although until 1945 the emperor's word theoretically was law, Hirohito seldom used his absolute powers. Japan entered World War II against his desires. Once at war, Hirohito supported it until Japan's position was hopeless. He then intervened, ordering Japan's surrender.

Hirohito in the 1930s   Throughout the 1930s, Japan's government grew increasingly belligerent and militaristic. Nationalistic junior officers saw war as an opportunity for glory and fame. Any moves away from expansion were stopped by these officers, who resorted to physical intimidation and assassination to further their goals.

Many officers were willing to die for their nationalistic beliefs. A minority of senior Japanese leadership supported the militants, but they provided the militants with official cover. Moderates and those opposing Japanese expansion found themselves increasingly isolated.

As emperor, Hirohito was held to be a divine being, a direct descendant of the sun goddess Amaterasu. The emperor was theoretically an absolute ruler and commanded the Japanese military. He was, however, constrained by the Meiji Constitution (established in 1890) to be guided by parliamentary authorities, who spoke for the emperor.

Raised to defer to tradition and naturally reticent, Hirohito rarely used his absolute powers against the wishes of his cabinet. In 1928 and 1936, he acted against army officers attempting to seize power. In 1928, military plotters assassinated a Chinese leader to provoke a war with China. When the Japanese prime minister did nothing, Hirohito forced his resignation. In 1936, army officers initiated a coup, killing several civilian leaders and claiming to be acting in the emperor's name. Hirohito ordered the coup suppressed.

The Road to World War II   Hirohito did little to directly halt Japan's drift toward war. He probably supported the invasion of China in 1937. Hirohito blocked an alliance with Germany and Italy in 1939. He removed his objection to the alliance a year later, in September 1940, due to the insistence of his advisors and German successes.

America embargoed oil and steel shipments to Japan after it occupied French Indochina in July 1941. At that time, Japan was heavily dependent on American petroleum. Hirohito's military advisors insisted that if the embargo was not ended by October 1941, Japan would have to go to war to secure oil from the Dutch East Indies. Hirohito insisted that Japan seek a political solution to the crisis and saw that negotiators were sent to Washington, D.C.

When those negotiations failed, Prince Fumimaro Konoe (1891–1945), then the prime minister, resigned. In October, Hirohito named War Minister Hideki Tojo (1884–1948) as the new prime minister but charged Tojo with finding a diplomatic solution to the crisis. Hirohito directed that the negotiations begin anew.

Mistrust on both sides was too high for this effort to secure an agreement. Faced with exhaustion of their fuel reserves, the Imperial Government decided in November that Japan must go to war in December. Hirohito was reluctant but went along with the decision.

World War II   Once Japan was at war, Hirohito fully supported it. He became an active participant in Japan's war planning. Once Hirohito realized that Japan was losing, he began looking for ways to make peace. By July 1944, with the capture of Saipan by the United States, Japan's defeat appeared inevitable. Hirohito fired Tojo. Determined to share the danger faced by his people, he remained in the Imperial Palace at Tokyo after the American bombing campaign began in late 1944.

As Japanese losses continued, Hirohito's advisors advocated fighting literally to the last man. Only Prince Konoe opposed this, calling on Hirohito to make peace. Hirohito instead acquiesced to the "last man" strategy, a position that cost Japan an additional 1.5 million lives.

In August 1945, the United States dropped two atomic bombs on Japan, and the Soviet Union declared war on Japan. Hirohito insisted that Japan surrender unconditionally. He recorded a surrender message to be broadcast to the Japanese people. Hirohito's action sparked a revolt by militant junior officers. The coup attempt was put down, and the broadcast made.

Postwar Career   A month after Japan's surrender, U.S. General Douglas MacArthur took charge of the occupation of Japan. Hirohito met with MacArthur, accepted responsibility for Japan's entry into World War II, and offered to abdicate. Feeling that Hirohito was the only individual who could keep the occupation peaceful, MacArthur refused his offer. Hirohito became the only major Axis leader to keep his prewar position.

Japan's new constitution recast the emperor in a largely ceremonial role. Hirohito renounced claims of divinity after the war. He remained as Japan's emperor until his death on January 7, 1989. He watched Japan rebuild itself from ruins in 1945 to a major economic power in the 1970s.

He spent much of his time after the war researching marine biology, becoming one of the field's leaders. Following his death, he was renamed "Showa," or "period of enlightened peace." The term commemorates the last forty-four years of his reign, when Japan was at peace.

Erwin Rommel

Erwin Rommel (1891–1944) was a leading Nazi general who battled the British, French, and Americans in France, Africa, and Italy.

Early Life   Rommel was born on November 15, 1891, the son of a professor. At his father's insistence he entered the German army and was sent to Officers' Cadet School. He received a commission in January 1912.

Rommel fought in the German army in World War I seeing action in France, Romania, and Italy. In Italy he was part of the elite *Alpen Korps*. He gained a reputation for tactical brilliance, especially in his command of a battalion during the Battle of Caporetto (1917).

Between the wars, he remained in the German army. He served as an instructor at the Dresden Infantry School and the Potsdam War Academy. He also wrote books on infantry and armor tactics that became widely used textbooks.

He attracted the attention of Adolf Hitler. After Hitler gained power in 1933, Hitler made Rommel a liason from the *Wehrmacht* (the name of Nazi Germany's armed forces from 1935 to 1945) to the Hitler Youth (a Nazi organization designed to indoctrinate German boys). Rommel's performance in that role gained him command of the *Führerbegleitbataillon* (Hitler's personal protection battalion), a position he held from 1938 until after the start of World War II.

World War II   In February 1940, Rommel was given command of the Seventh Panzer Division (a division of armored fighting vehicles). He commanded the Seventh Panzer during the invasion of France in May, proving able and aggressive. He led the crossing of the Meuse River that proved critical to German success.

During the French Campaign, he had his first encounter with the British, at the Battle of Arras. A battle that pitted British armored units against the Seventh Panzer, Arras was a precursor of later battles between the British and Germans in Africa. Rommel failed to cut off the British retreat to the English Channel coast because he was ordered to hold his position. After the evacuation of British and allied troops at Dunkirk in late May and early July 1940, Rommel drove his division to Cherbourg and was heading towards Bordeaux, France, when France surrendered.

Rommel was then transferred to command of the Fifth Light Division, a motorized unit. It was sent to Libya in February 1941 to help Germany's Italian allies. The Fifth Light Division formed the core of the *Deutsches Afrika Korps*, which Rommel commanded. (The Fifth Light was later reorganized and redesignated the Twenty-first Panzer Division.)

In the spring of 1941, Rommel counterattacked British forces occupying Libya and chased the British out of the eastern coastal region of Libya. It was the beginning of a two-year struggle in Africa. Neither side had enough forces to push the war in Africa to a conclusion.

Small forces and the open desert terrain made Africa a war of maneuver, with both sides making long advances and retreats, depending upon supplies, reinforcements, and outside circumstances. The African campaign gave Rommel high visibility in both Germany and Britain. Hitler promoted Rommel to field marshal after one prominent victory, the capture of Tobruk. Rommel became the face of the German army to soldiers of the Western Allies.

The tide turned in Britain's favor after the United States entered the war. The British built up a decisive advantage against the *Afrika Korps* at El Alamein. Rommel's army was at its furthest advance. A British army under British General Bernard Montgomery overwhelmed the German lines, then chased the *Afrika Korps* out of Egypt and deep into Libya.

The Americans then invaded Western Africa in November 1942. Trapped between the two Allied armies, Rommel's *Afrika Korps* was pushed into Tunisia and ultimately crushed. While in Tunis, Rommel counterattacked the American army at Kasserine Pass. The inexperienced Americans suffered a significant check. The American Second Corps, beaten at Kasserine Pass, was given to General George Patton, who succeeded in chasing the Germans out of Africa.

Following Africa, Rommel was sent to Greece to protect against an Allied invasion that never happened. Then, after the Allied invasion of Sicily and the fall of Mussolini, Rommel was transferred to command of Northern Italy.

In Italy, Rommel became involved in a controversy with Field Marshal Albert Kesselring, his nominal superior. Rommel wanted to abandon southern Italy. Kesselring wanted to force the Allies to fight for every inch of Italian soil. Rommel was transferred to France in November 1943 to prepare to repel an Allied invasion.

In France commanding Army Group B, Rommel became involved in another dispute over strategy. Rommel believed Allied air superiority would prevent mobile warfare by the German armies. He felt that the place to stop the invasion was on the beaches, and he wanted German armor broken into small, battalion-sized units scattered immediately behind the beaches.

Field Marshal von Rundstedt, in overall command in France, opposed Rommel's strategy. Hitler settled the dispute with a compromise between the two strategies. It put German armor reserves too far forward to permit concentration but too far back to support the beach defenses.

Rommel also felt that the Allies were as likely to invade at Normandy as at the Pas-de-Calais region. The rest of the German high command viewed Calais as the Allied objective. Rommel spent the months before the June 1944 invasion strengthening defenses along the French coast, especially in Normandy.

Rommel proved correct in both his predictions. The Allies landed at Normandy, and Allied air superiority prevented swift movement of German reinforcements. On July 17, 1944, while supervising the defense in Normandy, Rommel was wounded by an Allied fighter that strafed his staff car, and he was hospitalized.

In spring 1944, Rommel had become disillusioned with Hitler and the Nazis. He became affiliated with a German officer's plot to kill Hitler. An assassination attempt on July 20, 1944, failed. Rommel's complicity was discovered. Because Rommel was closely tied with Hitler, he was allowed to commit suicide. His alternative would have been to allow himself to be tried and executed as a traitor—with his family executed along with him. Rommel died by his own hand on October 14, 1944.

Joseph Stalin

Joseph Stalin (1879–1953) led the Soviet Union during World War II and into the Cold War that followed. He was one of the most powerful and ruthless dictators in the world. The war fought between Nazi Germany and the Soviet Union was one of the most brutal conflicts of the twentieth century.

Early Life and Career Joseph Stalin was born Iosif Vissarionovich Dzhugashvili in Gori, Georgia, on December 21, 1879. As a young man, he became involved in revolutionary politics and adopted the name Joseph Stalin ("Stalin" means "steel" in Russian). By World War I, he was deeply involved in Marxist political activities.

He attracted the attention of Communist revolutionary leader Vladimir Lenin before World War I and was part of the Bolshevik faction that took control over Russia during the Russian Revolution (1917). Stalin was elected to the Central Committee of the Russian Communist Party in 1917. In 1922, he became General Secretary. He was able to use this position to gain control of the Soviet government after Lenin's death in 1924 (although it took him a few years to solidify his position).

In the years leading up to World War II, he ruled the Soviet Union with unparalleled ferocity. He created a famine in the Ukraine in order to starve out opponents and ruthlessly industrialized Russia. He crushed any opposition. In the late 1930s, he purged the Soviet army of over one-quarter of its officers because of a feared coup.

World War II In 1938 Stalin was absolute ruler of the Soviet Union. In 1939, Hitler and Stalin signed the Molotov-Ribbentrop Pact. Publicly it was a non-aggression pact between Germany and the Soviet Union. Secret clauses gave territorial rights in other nations to Germany and the Soviet Union. The Soviets ceded to Germany the western parts of Poland. Germany gave the Soviet Union eastern Poland, Latvia, Lithuania, and Estonia, parts of Finland and Bessarabia, an oil-rich eastern province of Romania.

When Hitler invaded Poland, a European war broke out. Germany was opposed by France, Britain, and Poland. The Molotov-Ribbentrop Pact allowed Hitler to take Germany into a European war without fear of fighting on two fronts. As Poland collapsed, Stalin occupied Eastern Poland in mid-August.

In November 1939, Stalin exercised the rest of the treaty. The Soviet Union got the Baltic States (Estonia, Latvia, and Lithuania) and Bessarabia without a fight. Finland chose to defend itself. Despite the unequal struggle, Finland repelled the initial Soviet invasion. Stalin purged the Soviet army officer corps in the late 1930s, executing anyone suspected of being less than completely loyal to Stalin. The Soviets lost many of their best military leaders to Stalin's paranoia. Finland negotiated peace with the Soviets in 1940, conceding land but maintaining its independence. The Soviet army's poor performance against Finland was one factor that encouraged the Germans to attack Russia in 1941.

Soviet intelligence warned Stalin that Germany was preparing to attack the Soviet Union. Stalin did not believe Hitler would attack the Soviet Union before ending the war against Britain and discounted the warnings. Stalin's generals ignored or disregarded warning signs for fear of angering Stalin. When Germany invaded in June 1941, the Soviet Union was unprepared.

Initially, Stalin disastrously micromanaged the Soviet military. He ordered the army to stand fast. Hundreds of thousands of Soviet soldiers were surrounded by German armor columns, cut off, and forced to surrender. Stalin's brutality in the 1920s and 1930s also led many so-called White Russians (anti-Communists) and Ukrainians to hail the Nazis as liberators.

When Stalin realized that the Russian people felt little loyalty to the Soviet government, he rallied them by telling them they fought for "Mother Russia." He restored the Russian Orthodox Church, which had been suppressed by the atheistic Communists. He used nationalistic symbols like Alexander Nevsky (who repelled the Teutonic Knights in the thirteenth century) and Tsar Alexander I (who fought Napoleon's invasion in the early nineteenth century), despite their non-Marxist backgrounds.

The Nazis actually helped by behaving with even more brutality than the Communists. Stalin changed the war from a fight over Communism to a crusade to save Russia. Stalin also instituted a "scorched earth" policy. When the Soviet army was forced to retreat, anything that could be of use to the Germans was to be destroyed.

The Soviets stabilized the situation by November 1941. Stalin continued micromanaging the war in early 1942. Demanding an early counteroffensive, he gave the Germans an opportunity to destroy the reserves the Soviets had accumulated during the winter of 1941–1942 and regain the initiative. After that, Stalin returned control of military operations to his generals.

Stalin issued an order in July 1942 declaring Soviet soldiers who surrendered as traitors. He also had political officers, or commissars, assigned to each military unit to ensure its political stability. With the entry of the Soviet Union into the war against Hitler, Stalin's image in the West changed. After the United States entered the war in December 1941, Stalin was seen as affable "Uncle Joe." As the war ended, Stalin proved a tough negotiator. At a series of international conferences with Churchill and Roosevelt, he gained major territorial concessions for the Soviet Union. Half of what was once East Prussia is still part of today's Russia. Stalin was also allowed to exert influence in the liberated nations of Eastern Europe.

Postwar Career After World War II, Stalin occupied Eastern Europe. Existing governments were replaced with Communist puppets. Stalin attempted to expand Communism, both in Europe and Asia. He acquired nuclear weapons and established the Soviet Union as a world power. The Cold War Stalin started lasted nearly fifty years.

Stalin ruled the Soviet Union until his death on March 5, 1953. The cause of death was reported to be a stroke, but rumored to have been a poisoning.

Charles de Gaulle

Charles de Gaulle (1890–1970), an officer in the French army in 1940, helped organize Free French forces in World War II. Fighting against Germany after France surrendered, he helped organize the French resistance movement. Eventually, he led French forces in the Allied armies after the Allied invasion at Normandy and during the liberation of France in 1944.

Early Life De Gaulle was born on November 22, 1890. His family came from minor French aristocracy. De Gaulle attended the French military academy at St. Cyr, graduating in 1912.

He served as a French infantry officer in World War I and was badly wounded at Verdun in 1916. He was captured by the Germans and remained a prisoner of war for the rest of the conflict. He unsuccessfully attempted to escape five times.

After release, he remained in the French army. He volunteered for the French mission to Poland in 1919 and participated in the Polish-Soviet war of 1919–1921. Based on his experiences, he wrote *The Army of the Future*. In that book he predicted the future belonged to mobile warfare using tanks rather than static defenses behind fortifications. While his views were respected outside of France, especially by the German and Soviet armies, he was ignored by his own army.

France 1940 De Gaulle was a colonel in the French army in 1939. He antagonized the French military establishment with his writings about tactics. He claimed static defenses such as the French Maginot Line (a system of concrete tank obstacles and other defenses along the French-German and French-Italian border) had been rendered obsolete by tanks and mobile warfare.

On May 15, 1940, five days after the Germans invaded France, de Gaulle gained command of the French Fourth Armored Division. The Germans had already broken through French lines and were driving into the French rear areas. De Gaulle had minor successes against the Germans, including forcing German infantry to retreat at Caumont, on May 28. He was promoted to brigadier general after this victory.

On June 6, he was made France's undersecretary of state for national defense and war by Paul Reynaud, who

had sponsored de Gaulle during the interwar years. De Gaulle opposed French surrender, arguing that France could continue fighting from Algeria (which was then controlled by France) and its overseas colonies.

The Free French Movement After France fell to the invading Nazis, Philippe Pétain (1856–1961) became head of the French government, called the Vichy Government. He negotiated an armistice. On June 17, de Gaulle rejected the French surrender and fled Bordeaux, where the French provisional government was seated, for London.

On June 18, with Winston Churhill's approval and assistance, de Gaulle spoke on the British Broadcasting System radio and appealed to the French to continue fighting. "The Appeal of June 18" rejected the decision of the legal French government to sue for peace. It also called on French people everywhere to rally to de Gaulle and continue the fight against Germany. The speech was not widely heard on its day of broadcast. It was rebroadcast and widely reprinted. It marked the beginning of the Free French movement.

The governments of conquered nations such as Poland or Norway established themselves in exile. By defying the legal government of France, de Gaulle and others fighting in the Free French armies could be treated as illegal combatants. The Vichy government later convicted de Gaulle of treason in absentia for continuing to fight.

Despite the dangers, more than half a million French officers and men eventually rallied to the call. De Gaulle remained in an ambiguous position for much of the early part of the war. Both the United States and Britain initially recognized the Vichy government as the legitimate government of France. In 1943 the United States finally recognized the Free French as the legitimate government. Even then, de Gaulle was not yet recognized as the head of the Free French Government. This was partly due to de Gaulle's prickly personality and his determination to treat Free French armed forces as independent of the Allies. He depended upon the United States and Great Britain for everything from weapons to the uniforms his men wore and the food they ate, so his allies found de Gaulle's attitude annoying. In the end, no alternative to de Gaulle emerged. By 1944, he was acknowledged as the head of the French government-in-exile.

Initially, only a few patriots joined de Gaulle. A few minor French African colonies declared themselves to be Free French. After the United States joined the war, more support swung to de Gaulle and the Free French. The pace accelerated after the capture of French North Africa. Those colonies all then flipped from Vichy control to Free French. De Gaulle set up a government in Algiers.

By the time of the Allied invasion of France in June 1944, Free French forces had grown to over 400,000 men. Additionally, de Gaulle was coordinating the French Resistance within occupied France. In August, de Gaulle moved the Free French government back to French soil, operating at first in Northern France. After

Winston Churchill gives the "V-sign" as he stepped down as prime minister in 1955, reminding the British of the encouragement his use of the "victory" symbol had offered them during World War II. *Keystone/Getty Images*

Free French soldiers liberated Paris, de Gaulle moved the government back to the traditional capital.

In addition to commanding the Free French Army, de Gaulle became president of the Provisional French Government in September 1944. He continued as president until January 1946. De Gaulle was part of the successful fight to secure a French occupation zone in Germany after World War II and to obtain a permanent seat on the United Nations Security Council.

Postwar Career After the formation of the French Fourth Republic in January 1946, de Gaulle stayed outside of the political sphere for many years, disapproving of the new French constitution. He returned to public power in 1958 during the Algerian Crisis that destroyed the Fourth Republic. He then organized the Fifth Republic, which he headed from 1958 until 1968.

While head of France, he steered an independent course. He made France the fourth nuclear power, with-

drew France from NATO, and opposed what he viewed as Anglo-American hegemony in the West.

He died in his home on November 9, 1970.

Winston Churchill

Winston Spencer Churchill (1874–1963) guided Great Britain to victory in World War II as prime minister of Britain. He rallied his nation from its darkest hour, after the fall of France and the evacuation of the British army at Dunkirk, and led Britain in a lonely fight against the Axis powers until America entered the war in December 1941.

Early Life Churchill was born in Blenheim Palace in Woodstock, Oxfordshire, on November 30, 1874. He was a descendant of John Churchill, the First Duke of Marlborough (1650–1722). His father was a younger son of the seventh duke and a prominent nineteenth-century politician.

Churchill attended Sandhurst, the British military academy, and was commissioned as a cavalry officer in

1895. After serving briefly in India, he became a war correspondent, both while in the British army and as a civilian. He entered politics following the Second Boer War (1899–1902).

He served as first lord of the admiralty and served briefly in the British army during World War I and became chancellor of the exchequer after that war. During that period he changed political parties twice, going from the Conservatives to Labour, and back to the Conservatives. By the 1930s, he had marginalized himself politically and held no prominent leadership roles.

Early World War II   Churchill spent much of the late 1930s as a Conservative Party back-bench member with no leadership positions. In part this was due to his taking unpopular positions, including support for the Duke of Windsor prior to then-King Edward VIII's abdication in 1936. It was also due to his opposition to the Conservative Party's policy of appeasing Adolf Hitler and advocacy of rearming Britain.

When World War II began, Churchill was invited into Neville Chamberlain's wartime government. Churchill was named first lord of the admiralty—the British equivalent of secretary of the navy.

During the first eight months of World War II, Britain primarily fought a naval war. As a result, Churchill had a very visible public role. In May 1940, Germany invaded France, going through Holland, Belgium, and Luxemburg. In a six-week campaign, the German army, spearheaded by panzer divisions and new *blitzkrieg* or lightning warfare tactics, defeated France and forced the British army in France to evacuate through ports along the French side of the English Channel. The British left most of their equipment in France.

In the wake of that disaster, the Chamberlain government fell. Because of the war crisis, no elections were held to elect a new government. Instead, Churchill was asked to organize a coalition wartime government.

Prime Minister Churchill   Churchill took over the government when Britain was at its darkest point. All of Britain's other allies had been defeated by Nazi Germany. Italy joined Germany and declared war on England, forcing Britain to defend its Mediterranean holdings as well as Britain. The British army was virtually unarmed, and only the Royal Navy and especially the Royal Air Force (RAF) prevented a German invasion.

Churchill remained resolute, rallying the British people to continue the fight by delivering a set of inspiring speeches. He described the crisis of 1940 as Britain's "finest hour." He proclaimed RAF fighter pilots as "the few," protecting England in the Battle of Britain, stating, "Never in the field of human conflict was so much owed by so many to so few."

Churchill skillfully used the political and military resources Britain still had to oppose Hitler. He fostered a "special relationship" with the United States, as the other great English-speaking republic, to gain support from the United States while it was still neutral. During that period he worked closely with U.S. President Franklin Roosevelt to get Britain critically needed munitions and credit.

When Germany attacked the Soviet Union in June 1941, Churchill sent aid to the Russians despite his lifelong antipathy towards Communism. He explained his support stating, "If Hitler were to invade Hell, I should find occasion to make a favourable reference to the Devil."

When the United States entered the war in December 1941 following the Japanese attack at Pearl Harbor, Churchill was relieved. Notwithstanding the losses suffered by the Americans and British in the Pacific, he viewed the war as won the day the United States joined Britain as a combatant.

After the United States entered the war and—as he had foreseen—began leading the Allied coalition to victory, Churchill began planning the shape of postwar Europe through a series of international conferences. At a total of nearly twenty such conferences, he helped redraw the map of Europe to the boundaries it generally still has today.

His primary focus was to remove Germany as a future threat to world peace. Churchill succeeded, but planted the seeds of the Cold War in the process.

Postwar Career   After the end of the war in Europe, elections in Britain voted Churchill's Conservatives out, replacing him with a Labour Party prime minister. Churchill remained active in British politics following World War II, warning against the new Communist menace much as he had warned against the Nazis in the 1930s. In 1948, he coined the term "iron curtain" to describe the divide between Western and Eastern Europe.

Churchill returned as prime minister in 1955 and held office for two years. He retired from public life afterwards, devoting himself to writing. He died on January 24, 1965, and was buried in a state funeral.

Isoroku Yamamoto

Admiral Isoroku Yamamoto (1884–1943) led the Imperial Japanese Navy from the beginning of World War II until his death in combat in 1943. He believed that Japan would lose a war against the United States. Regardless, he planned the attack on Pearl Harbor, Hawaii.

Early Life   Yamamoto was born as Isoroku Takano in Nagaoka, Niigata, on April 4, 1884. He belonged to a clan of minor samurai (a caste of military nobility in Japan). In 1916 he was adopted into the Yamamoto family, which lacked an heir to carry on the family name, and changed his name to Isoroku Yamamoto.

He attended the Imperial Japanese Naval Academy, graduating in 1904. He was subsequently assigned to

CHURCHILL THE COMMUNICATOR

More than any other leader of World War II, Churchill's strength lay in his ability to communicate. Roosevelt and Hitler were both skilled orators, but both were clumsy with the written word. Churchill could not only write and give a speech; he was one of the great authors of the twentieth century.

Churchill's books included not just political work, but also military commentaries, serious works of history and biography, and even a novel or two. He came to prominence in the late nineteenth century as a war correspondent, writing first-person accounts of British military campaigns in Africa and Asia. Later, he wrote major biographies of his father, Randolph Churchill (1849–1895), and his famous ancestor, John Churchill, First Duke of Marlborough.

Shortly before World War II, he wrote much of the magisterial four-volume *A History of the English-Speaking Peoples*, which was released in the 1950s and is still in print today. After the war he wrote a six-volume history of World War II. Churchill won the Nobel Prize for literature in 1953 on the strength of his collected works.

the cruiser *Nisshin* during the Russo-Japanese War (1904–1905). He fought at the Battle of Tsushima, where he was injured, losing two fingers, and later attended the Japanese Naval Staff College in 1914.

Yamamoto spent nearly five years in the United States after World War I, attending the U.S. Naval War College and Harvard. After graduating, he spent two terms as a naval attaché in Washington, D.C. Following his return to Japan at age forty, he transferred to naval aviation and became commander of the aircraft carrier *Akagi* in 1929. He served on the delegation to the London Naval Conferences in 1930 and 1934.

Yamamoto opposed the Japanese annexation of Manchuria (part of China) in 1931, the Japanese invasion of China in 1937, and Japan's signing the Tripartite Pact in 1940 (the pact allying Germany, Italy, and Japan against U.S. attack). The time he had spent living in the United States had given him an appreciation of the strengths of America that most of his colleagues lacked. He was opposed to a war with the United States; he felt Japan would lose. In November 1940, Yamamoto predicted the course of a Pacific war to Prime Minister Prince Fumimaro Konoe. "If I am told to fight ... I shall run wild for the first six months ... but I have utterly no confidence for the second or third year."

Prewar Planning Superiors transferred him from an assignment with the Ministry of the Navy to a seagoing command in 1939, and soon thereafter made him commander in chief of the Japanese fleet. Yamamoto made significant improvements to the fleet. A strong believer in air power, he reorganized the fleet around the aircraft carriers. He put the six largest carriers into one force, presaging the carrier fleets that fought during World War II. He downgraded the role of battleships, opposing the construction of super-battleships *Yamato* and *Musashi* as a waste of resources.

At the Naval Ministry in the 1930s, Yamamoto pushed development of the G3M (Nell) and G4M (Betty) twin engine bombers. Combining extremely long range with the ability to carry a torpedo, they gave Japan the ability to strike an enemy at long range. To escort them he fostered development of the A6M "Zero" fighter.

Once it became clear that Japan was going to fight, Yamamoto led efforts to develop the best plan to attack America. In January 1941, he recast the Japanese Navy's traditional war plan. The traditional plan envisioned weakening the American fleet as it fought its way across the Pacific by attacking with submarines and aircraft attacks. Once American losses were large enough, the Japanese fleet would fight a decisive surface battle with the Americans. But when the Japanese practiced the strategy in war games, the Japanese usually lost.

Pearl Harbor Yamamoto modified the war plan. He would start any war with a surprise strike at Pearl Harbor, Hawaii.

Yamamoto's plan involved a strike at the battleships that anchored there, the airfields around it, and the fuel and support facilities at the base. He intended to cripple the American fleet, destroy any aircraft present, and wreck the fuel and repair facilities.

The attack was launched on December 7, 1941. The Japanese successfully sank five American battleships and knocked out most of the military aircraft in Hawaii. However, the attack had three shortcomings.

The American aircraft carriers were not in port when the Japanese struck. The Japanese launched only two strikes, concentrating on the warships and airfields. The tank farm, submarine base, and repair facilities were all undamaged. Finally, the attack came before war was declared. This roused the American people against Japan and ensured that the United States would not seek a negotiated peace. President Roosevelt swiftly asked Congress for a declaration of war.

Midway and Afterwards In the six months that followed, Japan and Yamamoto's navy "ran wild." They captured the Philippines, Dutch East Indies, Malaya, and Burma. They also captured a wide swath of islands in the Central Pacific, giving Japan a wide belt of outposts for protection.

The Japanese offensive sputtered to a halt almost exactly six months after Pearl Harbor. The daring Doolittle Raid of 1942 (led by U.S. Lieutenant Colonel James Doolittle) against Tokyo caused American morale to soar and motivated the Japanese Navy to extend their defensive perimeter. Yamamoto planned an offensive that would capture Midway Island in the Central Pacific, as well as several islands in the Aleutians.

The plan was overly complicated. Four independent naval forces had to converge on Midway. As a diversion, two additional task forces were sent to the North Pacific, to strike Alaska. Unknown to the Japanese, the Americans had broken the Japanese codes. They knew when the Japanese were coming and with roughly what ships. On June 4, 1942, the U.S. Navy ambushed the Japanese carrier strike force. All four Japanese fleet carriers sent to Midway were sunk before Yamamoto and the Japanese main body arrived on the scene. After Midway, the Japanese lost the initiative and never regained it. The Americans counterattacked in the Solomon Islands, recapturing Guadalcanal. Yamamoto became locked in a naval war of attrition around the Solomons.

Yamamoto commanded the Japanese fleet at the Battles of the Eastern Solomons and the Santa Cruz Islands in August, September, and October of 1942. From the Japanese perspective, both battles were bloody draws. By February 1943, the Japanese lost Guadalcanal and were retreating up the Solomon Chain.

In April 1943, Yamamoto was planning a new offensive in the Solomons. To boost morale, he planned an inspection tour. The plans were broadcast in code. The Americans intercepted the message, decoded it, and had Yamamoto's itinerary.

A fighter ambush was arranged for a part of the tour where Yamamoto would be traveling by air in a G4M bomber. On April 14, 1943, American P-38 fighters successfully intercepted the Japanese and shot down the two Japanese bombers carrying Yamamoto and his entourage. There were no survivors on Yamamoto's airplane.

Bernard Montgomery

Field Marshal Bernard Law Montgomery, First Viscount of Alamein (1887–1976) was the leading British general of World War II. He led the British army to some of its greatest triumphs. At the same time, he was accused of battlefield slowness, which lost opportunities and may have prolonged the war. He irritated many counterparts, including both American and British generals.

Early Life Montgomery was born on November 17, 1887, in London, the son of a clergyman. Montgomery attended the Royal Military Academy at Sandhurst and received a lieutenant's commission in 1908.

At the outset of World War I, he fought with his battalion in the Royal Warwickshire Regiment during the opening days of August 1914. He was injured in battle. After recovering, he served in staff positions in France through the rest of World War I, rising to the temporary rank of lieutenant colonel.

Between the wars he remained in the British army, serving in the German Occupation and in the Irish Rebellion of 1920. In the 1930s he was posted to positions in Palestine, Egypt, and India. In 1938, he organized an amphibious landing exercise that succeeded well enough to gain him command of a division—the Eighth Infantry Division—in Palestine. In July 1939 he was transferred to command of the Third Infantry Division in Britain.

World War II Montgomery began World War II as a major general. His Third Infantry was sent to France as part of the British Expeditionary Force in 1939. Expecting a situation similar to that of the opening days of World War I, with a British retreat, Montgomery trained his division in retreat tactics.

In May 1940, the Germans invaded France, broke through the Allied lines at Sedan, and split the British and French Armies, surrounding both. Montgomery fell back to the English Channel with his division intact. He took command of the British Second Corps during Operation Dynamo, the evacuation from Dunkirk.

From June 1940 through August 1942, Montgomery, promoted to lieutenant general, commanded forces defending England from a possible German invasion. Initially he commanded the Fifth Corps, then the Twelfth Corps, and finally the South-East Army, in the invasion zone.

War in Africa German Field Marshal Erwin Rommel's *Afrika Korps* had chased the British to a defensive line deep in Egypt, near the town of El Alamein. Churchill relieved General Sir Claude Auchinleck, the British commander in Africa, with General William Gott. Gott was killed in an airplane crash, and Montgomery replaced Gott in August 1942.

Montgomery arrived August 13, coordinating the defense of Alam Halfa. Rommel attempted to encircle the strategic heights, but was repulsed in a battle fought starting August 31. Thereafter, Montgomery strengthened the British position and began planning for a counteroffensive.

Montgomery attacked October 23, 1942. He had spent nearly two months planning the attack while receiving massive reinforcements. Meticulously planned and deliberately executed, Alamein was characteristic of all of Montgomery's battles. In a twelve-day struggle, he cut through the German lines and sent them retreating back to Tripoli, in Libya.

While criticized for a slow pursuit, Montgomery took the British Eighth Army to victory. He started the Germans on a retreat that ended with the expulsion of Axis forces at Tunisia, in May 1943.

War in Europe Montgomery next led the British Eighth Army in Sicily, in July 1943. Prior to the invasion he changed the plans in a more conservative direction. The plan used had the American Seventh Army to shield the main thrust, provided by the British Eighth Army.

American commanders George Patton and Omar Bradley felt the U.S. Army could be doing more.

Montgomery's advance bogged down, and army boundaries were redefined, reducing the Americans to the role of spectators. Patton used this as an opportunity to capture Palermo. Patton then swept east to the campaign's objective, Syracuse, along Sicily's northern coast.

Montgomery next led the Eighth Army into Italy, invading at the toe and heel of the Italian peninsula. Soon afterwards he was transferred to Britain to take charge of the Twenty-first Army Group. This unit was to lead the invasion of France in spring 1944. Montgomery was glad to leave Italy, as he felt that Allied efforts were untidy and disorganized.

Montgomery commanded the ground forces during the Allied invasion of France in June 1944. Montgomery's offensive after the landings was meticulous and deliberate. Montgomery's caution irritated his American counterparts, but the British army was near the end of its strength. Montgomery wanted to minimize casualties.

Patton felt the best way to minimize casualties was to move quickly and end the war sooner. When the American Third Army raced across France, the British forces in the Twenty-first Army Group followed at a more deliberate pace.

Problems between Montgomery and the American generals worsened after the Allied offensive stalled at the German border in fall 1944. Montgomery conceived an airborne thrust through Holland, Operation Market Garden. It used airborne troops to grab a corridor for British armor to move into and hold. Montgomery's land forces moved too slowly. The furthest airborne division, the British Sixth Airborne, was cut off and destroyed by the Germans.

Following the German offensive in the Ardennes in December 1944, Montgomery was given command of the northern flank of the battlefield. He chose to spend time "tidying up the battlefield" before counterattacking. He then gave a press conference that implied the American commanders, including General Dwight D. Eisenhower, the supreme Allied commander, were not up to their jobs and had depended upon Montgomery to save the situation. Eisenhower almost relieved Montgomery of his command and was only dissuaded by the politics of such a move. Montgomery, who had not realized the impact of his words, later apologized to Eisenhower.

Postwar Career In April 1945, Montgomery accepted the surrender of German forces in Northern Germany, Denmark, and Norway. After the war, Montgomery was made the First Viscount of Alamein. He served, with mixed success, as chief of the imperial general staff from 1946 to 1948. He also helped organize NATO (the North Atlantic Treaty Organization, an alliance of Western nations) in 1950 and served as NATO's deputy director from 1950 until his retirement in 1958. He served in ceremonial roles in the British Parliament until

Hideki Tojo (1884–1948) served as Japan's Prime Minister and commander of the military throughout much of World War II. *AP Images*

1968 and thereafter retired to private life. He died on March 24, 1976.

Hideki Tojo

Hideki Tojo (1884–1948) served as prime minister of Japan from October 1940 to July 1944. A Japanese general, he was an ardent hawk who pushed Japan towards war with the United States. He was hanged as a war criminal after World War II.

Early Life Hideki Tojo was born in Tokyo on December 30, 1884. He came from a samurai family (samurais were a caste of military nobility) and pursued a professional military career. Tojo graduated from the Imperial Military Academy in 1905, and as a junior officer, saw service in the Russo-Japanese War (1904–1905).

In 1915, he graduated from the Imperial War College. Between 1919 and 1922, he was sent abroad to Europe to further his studies. Upon his return, he served as an instructor at the War College. In 1935, he went to Manchuko—the Japanese puppet state in Manchuria. He served as head of the Japanese secret police in Manchuko. In 1937, he was promoted to chief of staff of the Kwantung Army.

Tojo in the Pacific War Japan's invasion of China led to diplomatic difficulties with the United States. Japan's military hard-liners, including Tojo, wanted Japan to seek military solutions. The United States increased diplomatic isolation and economic sanctions in response to Japanese militancy. The Imperial Army then influenced the Japanese government to respond with increased belligerency.

Tojo also helped Japan to join a military alliance with Germany and Italy—the Tripartite Pact. One clause stated that if a nation not currently involved in the European war or Japan's war in China attacked Germany, Italy, or Japan, the other two nations would enter the war against the attacker. The major neutral powers in 1940 were the United States and the Soviet Union. Thus, the Tripartite Pact was a warning to these two nations that starting a war would create a conflict in both Europe and the Pacific.

The Tripartite Pact further increased American hostility against Japan. Japan had stationed military units in Indochina in September 1940 but left the French civil government in place. In July 1941, Japan occupied French Indochina. The United States responded with a total embargo of metal and petroleum products to Japan.

Rise to Prime Minister Japan's economy depended on American oil. The prime minister of Japan, Prince Fumimaro Konoe, wanted a diplomatic solution and entered negotiations to end the embargo. Tojo supported the army's position that it would not give up gains in China.

Peace negotiations broke down in September 1941. The army insisted that if the oil embargo was not lifted by October, Japan had to fight to secure the oil needed to run Japan. Konoe was unwilling to go to war and his government collapsed in October. Tojo became prime minister and Emperor Hirohito called upon him to make one last appeal for peace. Tojo sent a delegation to Washington, D.C., to negotiate an end to the embargo. At the same time, he set the Japanese army and navy in motion to prepare an offensive that would secure the strategic goods Japan needed.

War with the United States Six weeks later, when these negotiations failed to get terms acceptable to the Imperial Army, Tojo started the war. On December 7, 1941, he ordered the Japanese fleet to attack the American naval base at Pearl Harbor, Hawaii. Simultaneously, Japan launched strikes against other American Pacific possessions. The war initially went well for the Japanese. Within six months, they captured all of their initial objectives, secured the economic resources they had sought, and established the defensive perimeter they desired. Tojo expected that either the United States would seek a negotiated settlement or find it impossible to break through Japan's defenses.

The United States stopped the Japanese thrusts, refused to negotiate, and struck back militarily. When the Americans captured the Marianas Islands in July 1944, Japan was within striking range of American bombers.

The loss of these islands capped two years of Japanese military reversals. Tojo was forced to resign from office on July 18, 1944. He retired from the military and spent the rest of the war in seclusion.

Following the Japanese surrender in August 1945, the United States occupied Japan. In September, Tojo attempted suicide to forestall arrest for war crimes. He shot himself in the chest but survived. He was arrested and tried for waging aggressive war in violation of international law and for inhumane treatment of prisoners of war. In a trial that lasted two years, Tojo accepted responsibility for starting the war. He was found guilty in November 1948 and hanged on December 28, 1948.

Franklin Delano Roosevelt

Franklin Delano Roosevelt (1882–1945) was president of the United States through most of World War II. He led the United States for all but four months of its active involvement in the war. He was the architect of the grand strategy that led the Allied coalition to victory in World War II.

Early Life Roosevelt was born on January 30, 1882, in Hyde Park, New York. After graduating from Harvard University, he attended Columbia Law School but left in 1907 after passing the New York State bar examination.

He entered politics in 1910. Between 1913 and 1920, he served as the assistant secretary of the navy under President Woodrow Wilson. In 1920, he was the vice-presidential candidate on the Democratic ticket that lost to Warren G. Harding. He served as governor of New York from 1928 to 1932.

In 1932, he beat Herbert Hoover in the presidential election. Roosevelt ran on a platform of ending the Great Depression, which had started in 1929. He instituted radical economic legislation in his first hundred days in office, a package known as the "New Deal." He was reelected in a landslide in 1936. Thereafter, foreign affairs increasingly dominated his presidency.

Buildup to War Roosevelt was in his second term as president when the growing threat of fascism led him to rearm the United States. As early as 1937, Italian aggression against Ethiopia and Japanese intervention in China caused Roosevelt to regard a second world war as virtually inevitable.

Once war started in Europe, Roosevelt threw his support towards the nations fighting Germany and Italy. In 1939, Roosevelt helped modify the Neutrality Acts passed by Congress in the 1930s so that he could offer aid to European allies. The Neutrality Acts were a response to America's costly involvement in World War I and were designed to keep the U.S. out of foreign wars. Under the 1939 Neutrality Act, belligerent nations were permitted to purchase military equipment in the United States if they paid cash and transported the goods themselves.

Although in ill health, President Franklin Delano Roosevelt's optimism and charisma inspired Americans throughout World War II. *AP Images*

This system was called "cash and carry" and favored the Western Allies, like Britain and France.

After Germany conquered Scandinavia, then the Low Countries and France in 1940, Roosevelt expanded the U.S. Army. A conscription act was passed in September 1940, and the draft started in October. The nation's first peacetime draft, the act was renewed in 1941, passing by one vote.

Roosevelt chose to run for an unprecedented third term in 1940, in large part due to his desire to fight Germany. He won reelection by a wide margin. Roosevelt became more aggressive about providing aid. He brought important Republicans into his cabinet, creating an essentially coalition government. He made America "the Arsenal of Democracy," giving China, Britain, France, and later Russia access to American industry for their military needs.

Roosevelt gave Britain fifty World War I–era destroyers in exchange for long-term leases on British islands in the Caribbean and Western Atlantic. In March 1941, when Britain was running out of money, Roosevelt sponsored a "Lend-Lease" act that gave nations fighting the Axis powers munitions and other military equipment and supplies.

By mid-1941, Roosevelt committed the United States to provide the Allies with "all aid short of war." He met with British Prime Minister Winston Churchill in August 1941 in Newfoundland to declare the Atlantic Charter, stating Allied objectives for World War II.

Roosevelt baited the Germans, allowing American warships to escort British convoys halfway across the Atlantic, with orders to attack German submarines if they encountered them. On several occasions in the fall of 1941, U.S. Navy destroyers and Nazi U-boats exchanged fire.

After Pearl Harbor   Roosevelt had embargoed petroleum shipments to Japan several months earlier. Japan responded by attacking the United States in December 1941 and launching a general offensive in the Pacific and Far East to seize the strategic resources they needed.

The centerpiece of the Japanese plan was an attack on the United States Naval base at Pearl Harbor and on Army Air Corps bases in Hawaii. For maximum effect, the Japanese intended to surprise the Americans, attacking on a Sunday morning, December 7, 1941, immediately after issuing a declaration of war. Decoding problems delayed the Japanese embassy in Washington, D.C., from delivering the declaration until several hours after the attack had ended.

The next day, Monday, Roosevelt declared to a joint session of Congress that December 7, 1941, was "a date which will live in infamy" and asked for a declaration of war against Japan. Congress declared war that day, with only one dissenting vote. Three days later, Germany and Italy declared war on the United States.

Despite the Japanese attack, Roosevelt gave priority to beating Germany first. He committed the majority of American resources to the European theater, starting with an invasion of North Africa in November 1942. By June 1942, and despite the emphasis on Europe and a disastrous first six months, the situation in the Pacific began to favor the Allies.

In January 1943, a conference was held in Casablanca, Morocco, attended by Roosevelt, Churchill, and Free French leader Charles de Gaulle. The leaders set terms for victory in World War II—the Allies would demand unconditional surrender by the Axis powers.

By 1943, the Allies were harvesting the fruits of Roosevelt's prewar preparations. A "two-ocean" U.S. Navy existed, and U.S. Army and Marine Corps divisions were numerous enough to support simultaneous offensives in both the Atlantic and the Pacific. By the start of 1944, it was clear the Allies were going to win.

The Fourth Term In order to influence the end of the war and the peace to follow, Roosevelt decided to run for a fourth term as president, although he was very ill. He was reelected with 53 percent of the popular vote.

Roosevelt participated in or fostered a series of conferences to shape the postwar world. At Bretton Woods, with forty-four nations participating, the International Monetary Fund was created. Conferences at Dumbarton Oaks and San Francisco created the United Nations. The postwar fate of Germany was discussed at the Second Quebec Conference in September 1944. Finally, in 1945, conferences at Malta and Yalta set plans for postwar Europe and for Soviet entry into the war in the Pacific.

Roosevelt died in Hot Springs, Arkansas, on April 12, 1945. The presidency passed to Vice President Harry Truman. Although Truman proved a fast learner, he was unprepared for the office. Roosevelt—despite being gravely ill—had kept Truman out of the decision loop. Truman was not informed about Roosevelt's plans or intentions.

Douglas MacArthur

Douglas MacArthur (1880–1964) commanded Allied forces in the Philippines at the start of World War II.

Chased out of the Philippines, he went to Australia. There he was put in charge of Allied forces in the Southwest Pacific. He led the counteroffensive that resulted in the liberation of the Philippines, and the eventual defeat of the Japanese Empire.

Early Life and Career Douglas MacArthur was born on an army post near Little Rock, Arkansas, on January 26, 1880. He was the son of Captain Arthur MacArthur, who won a Medal of Honor during the Civil War.

MacArthur attended the U.S. Military Academy at West Point, graduating in 1903, and receiving a commission in the Army Corps of Engineers. Between graduation and the start of World War I, he served in a variety of jobs. He conducted a survey of the Philippines, worked as a military instructor, and served as aide to President Theodore Roosevelt.

When World War I began, MacArthur organized the Forty-Second Infantry Division. A unit made up of National Guard regiments from around the United States, the division was given the nickname "Rainbow Division" by MacArthur. He went overseas and fought with the unit in 1918, and commanded it in November 1918.

MacArthur was superintendent of West Point from 1919 to 1922. In June 1922, he was again transferred to the Philippines, where he served through the rest of the 1920s. In 1930 he returned to the United States, where he served as Army chief of staff through 1935. Following that, he went to the Philippines to organize their army.

The Philippines When World War II started, Douglas MacArthur was in the Philippines, an American colony scheduled for independence in 1946. He was there to create a Philippine army. In 1937 he had resigned his U.S. Army commission, having accepted the rank of field marshal in the Philippine army in 1936.

Because of increased tensions in the Far East, the Philippine army was merged into the U.S. Army in July 1941. MacArthur, still in the Philippines, was recalled to active duty in the U.S. Army as a lieutenant general and given command of U.S. Army forces in the Far East. This included the Philippines.

On December 8, 1941, in conjunction with the December 7 attack on Pearl Harbor, the Japanese invaded Luzon, the northern and major island of the Philippine archipelago.

The traditional defense plan for the Philippines hinged on retiring to the Bataan Peninsula and maintaining an army there until the U.S. Army and Navy fought their way across the Pacific to relieve Bataan. This plan hinged on supplies stored in Bataan. Prior to the war, MacArthur abandoned this plan in favor of an aggressive defense. He positioned most of his supplies and ammunition behind probable invasion beaches on Luzon.

MacArthur successfully forecast where the Japanese invasion would occur, but in 1941, the Philippine army was years away from being able to conduct the mobile defense that MacArthur's strategy demanded. The Imperial Japanese Army was able to establish beachheads and to advance around the defenders. MacArthur was forced to declare Philippine's capital, Manila, an open city and to retreat to Bataan.

Pre-positioned supplies were lost, and tens of thousands of American and Philippine soldiers were trapped in Bataan with little ammunition and less food. The troops were put on half-rations. Disease and hunger soon took their toll. The Japanese starved out the defenders by April 1942, and captured Corregidor Island soon after.

MacArthur intended to stay, but President Franklin Roosevelt ordered him out of the Philippines in March 1942. MacArthur arrived in Australia on March 20. After landing, he pledged to return to the Philippines.

Counteroffensive and Victory MacArthur was awarded the Medal of Honor and given command of Allied forces in the Southwest Pacific. In addition to United States military forces, MacArthur commanded a coalition that included Australian, New Zealand, and some British forces. MacArthur organized the defense of Australia but switched to the offensive after the Battle of Midway gave the Allies the initiative. He cleared the Japanese out of much of the northern side of New Guinea in 1942 and 1943.

MacArthur relied on air power and Allied naval superiority, developing an offensive technique called "island-hopping." The technique involved bypassing a strong Japanese garrison and instead having Allied forces attack a weaker one within the range of Allied fighter aircraft. An airbase was to be built on the captured island and bypassed garrisons allowed to wither away.

With the assistance from naval forces commanded by Admiral Chester Nimitz, MacArthur fulfilled his pledge to return to the Philippines by late 1944. In October, American forces landed on Leyte Island in the Philippines. On October 20, 1944, MacArthur waded ashore from a landing craft onto the beach at Leyte and proclaimed that the liberation of the Philippines had begun.

A long battle still lay ahead for the Allies before the Philippines were completely freed. Luzon was invaded in December 1944. Although Manila was quickly recaptured, Luzon was not secured until July 1945. Some Japanese forces did not surrender until the end of the war.

MacArthur was promoted to general of the army in December 1945. In April 1945, MacArthur was given command of all army forces in the Pacific. MacArthur oversaw the invasion of Okinawa, and was planning the invasion of Japan in August 1945, when Japan surrendered. MacArthur was part of the United States delegation that accepted the formal surrender of Japan on the quarterdeck of the battleship *Missouri*.

Following the Japanese surrender, MacArthur was appointed commander of Allied occupation forces in Japan. He allowed the Japanese emperor to remain as titular head of state. He also oversaw the development of a democratic republic in Japan.

Postwar Career In 1947, MacArthur was named commander of the army's Far East Command. He was in that post when North Korea attacked South Korea, an American ally. MacArthur led a United Nations force against North Korea and its Communist allies until April 1951. President Harry S. Truman relieved him of command for insubordination. Following his dismissal, he retired into private life. He died in Washington, D.C., on April 5, 1964.

George S. Patton

George S. Patton Jr. (1885–1945) was the leading American general during World War II. He is best known for his race across France in the late summer of 1944 when he led the Third Army from Normandy to the German border in a matter of weeks.

Prewar Career Patton was born on November 11, 1885, into a family of military tradition. Although he was a California native, Patton, the grandson of a Confederate Army officer, attended the Virginia Military Institute before transferring to the U.S. Military Academy at West Point. He graduated from West Point in 1909.

Following graduation he entered the cavalry. He became the Army's youngest "Master of the Sword," both writing an army manual on use of the saber and designing the last cavalry saber used by the U.S. Army, the 1913 model "Patton" saber. He was also part of the 1912 U.S. Olympic team, competing in the modern pentathlon.

In 1916, he participated in General John Pershing's expedition into Mexico in search of Pancho Villa (a Mexican Revolutionary general who had led a raid into U.S. territory). He accompanied Pershing to France in 1917 after America entered World War I. There, he organized and commanded the first American tank brigade. He fought at both Saint-Mihiel and the Meuse-Argonne offensives. He was injured during the latter.

Patton was assigned to the Second Armored Division at Fort Benning, Georgia, in July 1940. An early proponent of the aggressive use of armor, Patton was given command of the division in April 1941. He was promoted to commander of what became the U.S. Seventh Army in January 1942.

Africa Efficiency in training led Patton to a combat command. He took charge of Operation Torch, the United States force invading Casablanca in Morocco. He quickly captured his objectives, overcoming Vichy French resistance. (The Vichy government took control in France after the Germans conquered France; the U.S.

General George S. Patton riding through Paris after commanding the U.S. 3rd Army during the liberation of France in 1944.   © *Corbis*

considered the Free French government in exile the legitimate government of France.)

Following the defeat of the U.S. II Corps in the Battle of Kasserine Pass in March 1943, Patton was given command of the unit. He restored morale to the dispirited unit with an emphasis on strict discipline and hard training. Within a few weeks, the unit was battle-ready and participated in the final offensive that pushed the German *Afrika Korps* out of Tunisia.

Italy Patton then took the U.S. Seventh Army to Sicily. The Seventh Army landed on the southern shore of Sicily on July 10, 1943, to the left (west) of the British Eighth Army, which landed south of Syracuse.

The Seventh Army only had a supporting role, covering the British advance up the eastern shore of Sicily to Messina. General Sir Harold Alexander, in command of Allied ground forces, then shifted the boundary between the Seventh and Eighth armies westward, to give General Bernard Montgomery's Eighth Army more maneuvering room. The move squeezed most of Patton's command out of action.

Patton received permission to conduct a "reconnaissance" toward Palermo. Against orders, he then captured the town. (Patton later claimed the order stopping his reconnaissance was garbled in transmission.) His army then raced along the northern coast of Sicily, using three amphibious landings to leapfrog the Germans. The Seventh Army captured Messina on August 17.

Mussolini's government fell after Patton captured Palermo, but the Sicilian campaign had few other results. Axis forces were permitted to evacuate to Italy, where Allied forces fought them again.

Despite his success, the campaign almost ended Patton's career. He slapped two privates suffering from combat fatigue, a misjudgment that was widely publicized. General Dwight Eisenhower, supreme commander of Allied forces in Europe, relieved Patton from command of the Seventh Army. Only Patton's undeniable skill spared him from being sent home in disgrace.

Eisenhower used Patton as a decoy, a position the battle-hungry Patton found humiliating. The Germans believed that Patton would command the next invasion.

Eisenhower sent Patton to Corsica, and then to Egypt, giving the impression that the Allies would next invade Southern France or the Balkans.

Patton was brought to England and given the First U.S. Army Group (FUSAG), a dummy command that was part of the Operation Overlord deception plans (Operation Overlord was the planned Allied invasion at Normandy). German spies were permitted to learn that the unit's objective was to reach Pas-de-Calais—the Strait of Dover—where they concentrated their forces. The actual Operation Overlord invasion landed at Normandy.

France Patton was sent to France following the Normandy invasion and was finally allowed back in the action. On August 1, he took over the Third Army, which he led on a stunning offensive. He broke through the German lines at Saint-Lô in Normandy, then sent his army in three different directions. One column was sent to clear the Brittany Peninsula. A second went down the Loire. A third went east, helping General Courtney Hodges envelop German forces in the Argentan pocket.

Patton and the Third Army then raced across France. Since the Allies had air superiority, Patton let airpower guard his flanks, making his enemies worry about their own flanks. By August 21, the Third Army was on the Seine River. Patton's offensive charge finally died on August 31, when his army ran out of gas on the Moselle River outside Metz.

Patton resumed the offensive in early October, but the Germans had reinforced and resupplied the fortifications guarding Metz. Nevertheless, the seemingly unstoppable Third Army captured Metz on November, 23, 1944. Patton began planning an offensive into the Saar region of Germany.

On December 16, 1944, Germany attacked north of the Third Army, in the Ardennes. At a conference held on December 19, Patton pledge to counterattack the Germans within forty-eight hours. It proved to be his finest hour. Anticipating the seriousness of the German attack, Patton had his staff draw up plans for redeploying his forces prior to the meeting. On December 21, 1944, the Third Army began a thrust toward Bastogne, where an American force that included the 101st Airborne Division was besieged by the German Army.

A battalion of the Fourth Armored Division commanded by then Lieutenant-Colonel Creighton Abrams reached Bastogne on December 26. Patton's quick action probably saved the Airborne Division from capture and broke the back of the German offensive.

In January 1945, the Third Army resumed its march into Germany. Patton occupied southern Germany and was headed toward Prague, Czechoslovakia, when the war in Europe ended.

After the war Patton was made military governor of Bavaria. He was relieved of that command, as well as

command of the Third Army in October 1945 due to his vocal resistance to the Allies' denazification program.

He was given the Fifteenth Army, a force that existed largely on paper. Patton died on December 21, 1945, after being injured in a car accident in Heidelberg, Germany.

Dwight D. Eisenhower

Dwight D. Eisenhower (1890—1969), who led the Allied forces in Europe during World War II, was elected president of the United States in 1952 and was reelected in 1956. He was president during significant portions of the Cold War, which continued for three decades after he left office.

Born October 14, 1890, in Denison, Texas, Eisenhower was the son of David J. Eisenhower and his wife, Ida Stover. The family was impoverished and moved to Abilene, Kansas, within a year of his birth. From an early age, he helped support his family by selling vegetables and holding a job at a creamery, where his father also worked.

A better athlete than student despite his obvious intelligence and ambition, Eisenhower graduated from Abilene High School in 1909 and then worked for two years to help cover the costs of an older brother's college education. Eisenhower then got his chance for further schooling, entering West Point Military Academy in 1911. Again, his athletic pursuits, especially football, took precedence over studying, but he managed to graduate in 1915.

Launched Military Career Entering the army as a second lieutenant after leaving West Point, Eisenhower began in the infantry at Texas's Fort Sam Houston. During World War I, he led the tank training camps in the United States. Encouraged to learn military science, his ascent in the military began in earnest after he graduated from the Command and General Staff School and later the Army War College.

Eisenhower became aide to General Douglas MacArthur in 1933 and accompanied the general to his post in the Philippines. Eisenhower then became the chief of staff of the Third Army in 1939. After overseeing training for thousands of soldiers shortly before the United States entered World War II in 1941, Eisenhower joined the U.S. Army General Staff as chief of the War Plans Division.

World War II Hero Eisenhower became the commander of U.S. military forces in Great Britain in 1941. A respected and skilled commander, he was able to work well with Prime Minister Winston Churchill and British generals. Eisenhower was also skilled on the battlefield, leading the 1942 invasion of North Africa that led to the Allies controlling the area by May 1943.

Now a four-star general, Eisenhower led amphibious invasions of Sicily and Italy in 1943. By the end of the year, he was named supreme commander of Allied forces. He then prepared for and led troops at the 1944 invasion of Normandy, a key Allied victory over Germany. Eisenhower oversaw the liberation of France and was involved in the Battle of the Bulge (winter 1944–1945). It was Eisenhower's decision to allow the Soviets to capture Berlin, a city that featured prominently in the Cold War that commenced between the United States and the Soviet Union in the post-war years.

Postwar Popularity   After the war in Europe ended in 1945, Eisenhower returned to the United States as a popular war hero. He then returned to Europe to head the American-controlled zone in Germany for a time before serving a two-year stint as the Army's chief of staff in the United States. Eisenhower retired from the military in 1948 and became the president of Columbia University. A two-year term there ended when Eisenhower agreed to become the commander of NATO (the North Atlantic Treaty Organization), the alliance of Western European nations and the United States against possible invasion of Europe by the USSR.

Though he had previously stated that he had no interest in politics, Eisenhower decided to run for president as a Republican in 1952. With a large margin of victory, he won the presidency that year as well as reelection in 1956. Working with both Democrats and Republicans, Eisenhower carved a middle path as president, supporting business and limited government interference in economic matters. He also oversaw the beginnings of the civil rights movement in the United States, including the desegregation of public schools.

Cold War President   As soon as he took office, Eisenhower had to deal with the ongoing Korean War. He presided over the end of the Korean War in 1953, negotiating a truce with Communist North Korea that divided the Korean peninsula.

Again choosing a moderate course, Eisenhower supported the building up of NATO in the face of potential Soviet aggression. At the same time, he wanted to improve the United States' relationship with the Soviet Union, offering several plans to open up the relationship between the two countries. Relations became severely strained, however, after the Soviets shot down a U-2 spy plane flying over the Soviet Union in 1959.

Eisenhower had to deal with other conflicts involving Communists worldwide. After Vietnam was divided into Communist North Vietnam and non-Communist South Vietnam in 1954, the United States supported South Vietnam. He oversaw the creation of the Southeast Asia Treaty Organization (SEATO), which sought to contain the spread of Communism in the region. U.S. support for South Vietnam eventually escalated into the Vietnam War.

Closer to home, Eisenhower originally supported the Cuban regime of Fulgencio Batista, but withdrew his backing in 1958. After Batista's government collapsed and Communist Fidel Castro took over, Eisenhower cut off relations with the new ally of the Soviet Union before

THE "FAILURE" MESSAGE

Eisenhower's success as a general was due to his willingness to take necessary risks and to accept personal responsibility for those decisions, win or lose. One example of both was his decision to press on with the Normandy invasion, despite predictions of unsatisfactory weather.

Before every invasion Eisenhower prepared an announcement of failure, kept in his wallet against the need for it. Although he tore the others up, he showed the message he penned for D-Day to his naval aide, Harry C. Butcher. Butcher persuaded Eisenhower to save the message, which is presented below.

> Our landings in the Cherbourg-Havre area have failed to gain a satisfactory foothold and I have withdrawn the troops. My decision to attack at this time and place was based upon the best information available. The troops, the air and the Navy did all that bravery and devotion to duty could do. If any blame or fault attaches to the attempt it is mine alone.

The note is preserved at the Eisenhower Library.

he left office in 1961. Eisenhower also approved the Central Intelligence Agency's use of covert operations to limit Communist revolutions in Latin America.

Eisenhower had also allowed the CIA to execute a covert operation to prevent a possible Communist takeover of Iran in 1954. He later announced the Eisenhower Doctrine, which declared the United States would assist all Middle Eastern countries in the face of any Communist threat of expansion.

By the end of his presidency, Eisenhower was seeking peace worldwide and traveled to twenty-seven countries to that end. He even tried to meet with Soviet leader Nikita Khrushchev to discuss a nuclear test-ban treaty. Though this summit did not happen because of the spy plane incident, Eisenhower retired a popular, well-respected president. He became an advisor to the U.S. Army and enjoyed his hobbies in retirement. Eisenhower died on March 28, 1969, in Washington, D.C.

Chester Nimitz

Chester William Nimitz (1885–1966) led the U.S. Navy in the Pacific during World War II. He restored the morale of the Pacific Fleet after Pearl Harbor. His ability to assess risk, combined with a willingness to gamble when opportunity presented itself, allowed him to guide the Navy to victory over the Japanese Empire.

Early Life and Career   Chester Nimitz was born on February 24, 1885, in Fredericksburg, Texas. His father died before he was born, and Chester was initially raised by his mother and paternal grandfather, Charles H. Nimitz.

Lacking funds to go to college, Nimitz applied first to the U.S. Military Academy at West Point in New York, and then to the U.S. Naval Academy at Annapolis, Maryland. He received an appointment to the Naval Academy in 1901. He graduated seventh in a class of 114 in 1905.

Nimitz received an ensign's commission in 1907, commanding the gunboat *Panay* in the Philippines. He later commanded the destroyer *Decatur*, which he ran aground. He was court-martialed and reprimanded, but continued his career. Between 1909 and 1913, he served in submarines, experience he put to good use in both world wars. Between 1913 and 1917 he was chief engineer on the fleet oiler *Maumee*, designing and installing the diesel engines used to propel the ship.

Following World War I, during which he served as chief of staff to Admiral Samuel S. Robison, commander of the Atlantic Fleet Submarine Force, he was sent to Hawaii in 1920. There he oversaw construction of the submarine base at Pearl Harbor.

He attended the Naval War College from 1922 to 1923, where he developed a plan for a hypothetical naval war in the Pacific. After the Naval War College, he served in a series of seagoing commands of increasing responsibility. He was commanding a battleship division in 1939, when he was put in charge of the Bureau of Navigation (which was the Navy's personnel department).

World War II   Nimitz was in Washington, D.C., serving as chief of the Bureau of Navigation when the Japanese attacked the Pacific Fleet at Pearl Harbor on December 7, 1941. President Franklin Roosevelt picked Nimitz to replace Admiral Husband Kimmel as commander of the Pacific Fleet. Nimitz was promoted to the position over twenty-eight more-senior flag officers. Nimitz assumed command of the Pacific Fleet on December 25, 1941.

The Pacific Fleet was at its lowest point when Nimitz took charge. Five of the eight battleships at Pearl Harbor on December 7 were out of action. Guam had fallen. American forces in the Philippines were under siege. On December 22, a Navy task force sent to relieve the besieged American outpost at Wake Island received orders to return to Pearl Harbor, just as they were ready to attack the Japanese off Wake Island. The Wake Island garrison surrendered the next day.

Nimitz immediately worked to restore morale. He shifted the Pacific Fleet from a defensive to an offensive posture, using his aircraft carriers to launch raids against Japanese garrisons on isolated islands.

He also demonstrated a willingness to gamble when the situation warranted. In 1942, Nimitz sent half the available aircraft carriers in the Pacific on the Doolittle Raid against Japan. He realized that the morale effects of a successful attack on the Japanese homeland would balance the risk.

Nimitz also coordinated the American naval ambush of the Japanese fleet invading the Midway islands. The Japanese intended to draw the American fleet into a Japanese trap. Instead the badly outnumbered American force sank four Japanese fleet carriers while losing only one. The June 1942 battle proved the turning point in the Pacific.

Nimitz coordinated submarine warfare against the Japanese merchant fleet. The submarine campaign took time to become effective, primarily due to faulty torpedoes and timid commanders. The torpedo problems were fixed, and more aggressive skippers took charge of the fleet submarines by early 1943. The campaign then made a substantial contribution to the victory against Japan.

Nimitz took command of all land, sea, and air forces in the Pacific Ocean Areas in early 1942. This included coordinating activities with General Douglas MacArthur, the commander of the South West Pacific Area. MacArthur was responsible for the defense of Australia and the Pacific theater east of the Solomon Island chain.

Through subordinate commanders like Admirals William Halsey, Raymond Spruance, Marc Mitscher, Thomas Kinkaid, and Richmond Kelly Turner, Nimitz directed the American drives across the Pacific. Island-hopping campaigns up the Solomon Island chain and across the Central Pacific through the Gilbert, Marshall, and Marianas island chains took the United States from Hawaii to striking range of Japan and the Philippine Islands by the end of 1944.

Nimitz was promoted to five-star fleet admiral in December 1944. He then directed United States forces all the way to Japan in 1945, coordinating the recapture of the Philippines with MacArthur, and leading naval forces to the capture of Iwo Jima and the Ryukyu Islands.

In August 1945, Nimitz was preparing the naval portion of the planned Allied invasion of the Japanese home islands—Operations Olympic and Coronet. The Japanese surrender following the use of atomic bombs on Hiroshima and Nagasaki eliminated the need for those operations. Nimitz was part of the American delegation that received the Japanese surrender party aboard Nimitz's flagship, the battleship *New Jersey*.

Postwar Career   In December 1945, Nimitz became the chief of naval operations (CNO), replacing Admiral Ernest King. He continued as CNO until his retirement in December 1947. Following his retirement, he served in a number of high-profile and honorary diplomatic positions.

Uncomfortable about profiting from his wartime reputation, he turned down many opportunities to take high-salaried business jobs following his retirement. He served as a regent of the University of California for eight years, and helped raise funds to restore the Japanese warship *Mikasa* as a museum ship. He died following a stroke at his home on San Francisco Bay on February 20, 1966.

James Doolittle

James "Jimmy" Doolittle (1896–1993) is best known for leading the first bombing raid against the Japanese home islands in April 1942. He led the U.S. Eighth Air Force in the air war against Germany. He was also an aviation pioneer, air racer, and scientist who made major contributions to American aerospace technology in the twentieth century.

Early Life and Career   James Doolittle was born on December 14, 1896, in Alameda, California, but grew up in Nome, Alaska. He attended Los Angeles Junior College and the University of California. He enlisted in the Army Reserve in 1917, and was assigned to the Signal Corps.

Doolittle became a flying instructor during World War I, received a Regular Army commission in the Air Service, and became involved in military aviation. In 1922, he was given a degree by the University of California, and sent to the Massachusetts Institute of Technology (MIT) for advanced engineering study.

Assigned to aviation test facilities after graduating from MIT in 1925, he became a test pilot, aviation engineer, and air racer. He developed instrument flying techniques, allowing "blind" landings.

In 1930, he resigned his Regular Army commission to work as an executive for Shell Oil Company. He maintained a commission in the Army Reserves. While at Shell, he helped develop aviation fuels. He continued his activities as an air racer, becoming the first person to win every major aviation trophy. Throughout the 1930s, he served as a consultant to the United States government on military aviation issues. He returned to active duty in 1940.

World War II   In 1940, the United States was still neutral in the war in Europe, but feared the time would soon come when U.S. involvement would become necessary. Doolittle was assigned to Air Corps Procurement, where he coordinated the conversions of major American factories into military aircraft production facilities.

Doolittle was promoted to lieutenant colonel and was transferred to the Army Air Corps war planning division in January 1942. He developed a plan to attack Tokyo and four other major cities on the Japanese home islands. Japan was then too far away from American air bases to reach with land-based aircraft and too heavily defended to risk bringing an aircraft carrier close enough for aircraft to reach the Japanese homeland. Doolittle's concept involved flying Army medium bombers off a United States Navy aircraft carrier. This would allow the carriers to successfully withdraw. However, the Army bombers could not return and land on aircraft carriers. They were to fly to China, an American ally, and be given to the Chinese Air Force.

Doolittle led the raid, which used sixteen B-25 Mitchell bombers. The carrier group was discovered by the Japanese on April 18, 1942. The bombers were forced to launch earlier than they planned, too far from China to land safely. All sixteen bombers were lost after successfully bombing Japan, but the Chinese rescued most of the aircrews and spirited them to safety.

The Doolittle Raid boosted American morale at a critical phase of the war. It caused the Japanese to withdraw fighter squadrons to protect the home islands and motivated the execution of the successful Midway campaign. There the Japanese lost four major aircraft carriers.

Doolittle won a Medal of Honor for leading the raid and was promoted to brigadier general. Transferred to the European Theater of Operations, he remained there for the rest of the war. In England in the summer of 1942, he organized the Twelfth Air Force.

Doolittle commanded the Twelfth Air Force in Africa in the fall of 1942, during the Operation Torch invasion, and was promoted to major general. He commanded Army Air Forces in the Mediterranean for the African campaign and the subsequent invasion of Sicily and Italy. In March 1943, Doolittle led the Fifteenth Air Force in Italy.

In January 1944, he was transferred to command of the Eighth Air Force in England, and charged with achieving air superiority by the time the invasion of France, planned for June 1944, took place. He achieved this goal by changing the Eighth Air Force's tactics. Beginning in February 1944, his unit concentrated on striking the German aircraft industry, as well as hitting communications and transportation.

After bombers hit a target, escort fighters were allowed to operate independently against German fighters. This included strafing German airfields, destroying aircraft on the ground. By May the Allies controlled the sky. In March 1944, Doolittle was promoted to lieutenant general.

Following victory in Europe in April 1945, Doolittle prepared to move the Eighth Air Force to the Pacific. World War II ended before the unit could enter into combat against the Japanese. Doolittle became the highest-ranking U.S. reserve officer of World War II.

Postwar Career   In 1946, Doolittle returned to civilian life, rejoining Shell Oil Company as a vice president. He served on the National Advisory Committee on Aeronautics (NACA), a National Aeronautics and Space Administration (NASA) precursor. From 1948 to 1958, he worked for NACA. He was active early in the American missile and space development. He retired from both Shell and the Air Force in 1959, but remained active in aerospace.

Through special act of Congress in 1985, Doolittle was promoted to full general, on the retired list. He died on September 27, 1993.

100-OCTANE GASOLINE

Doolittle's most important contribution to the Allied victory in World War II took place before the war started. In 1930, Doolittle headed Shell Oil's aviation fuels section. He pioneered the development and use of 100-octane gasoline.

Gasoline with a higher octane rating burns more efficiently. During the 1930s most gasoline was rated at 87 octane. It worked well for automobiles and provided satisfactory power for the aircrafts of the 1920s.

Doolittle realized that 100-octane gasoline would allow the development of more powerful aircraft engines. Engine manufacturers were reluctant to design engines that needed 100-octane gasoline unless adequate stocks of the gasoline were available. Refineries were reluctant to build plants that could produce 100-octane gasoline unless there was a demand for it.

Doolittle put his prestige as an aviation pioneer behind the development of 100-octane fuel at Shell. He convinced Shell to produce it, and stockpile the chemicals required to make the fuel. As a result, American aircraft engine manufacturers built new engines to use the fuel. By the start of World War II the United States had both more powerful aircraft engines designed for high-performance gasoline and adequate stocks of 100-octane gasoline to fuel the engines.

Pietro Badoglio

Pietro Badoglio (1871–1956) led the first government of Italy after the fall of Benito Mussolini's fascist government (the term fascist refers to an ultranationalist government with strong central conrol). He negotiated Italy's surrender to the Allies and brought Italy back into the war on the side of the Allied powers.

Early Life and Career Pietro Badoglio was born in Piedmont, Italy, on September 28, 1871. He attended the Italian military academy at Turin and entered the Italian army as a lieutenant in 1892.

Between then and Italy's entry into World War I in 1916, Badoglio participated in several Italian colonial campaigns in Africa, where he distinguished himself. He was a lieutenant colonel when Italy entered World War I and fought in Northern Italy through most of the war, rising to general and to a position as an aide to the commander in chief of the Italian army.

Badoglio was named an Italian senator after World War I, but remained in the army. He participated in Italian military missions to the United States and Romania in 1920 and 1921. Badoglio initially opposed Mussolini, but later allied with the fascists. He served on the Italian General Staff and then as governor of Libya from 1929 to 1933.

Italy invaded Ethiopia (then called Abyssinia) in 1935. After initial Italian reverses, Badoglio was given command of the Italian army in Ethiopia and captured the country in 1936. Badoglio received the title of "Duke of Addis Ababa" and was promoted to marshal. He subsequently became chief of the general staff of the Italian army.

World War II Badoglio was opposed to Italy's entry into World War II. Badoglio opposed the "Pact of Steel," which allied Italy with Germany, creating the German-Italian Axis. He felt the Italian army was unready for war.

Badoglio's judgment was proven by the Italian army's poor performance against the French and subsequently when Italy invaded Greece from its then-colony, Albania. After initial Italian gains, a Greek counterattack pushed the Italians back into Albania. By mid-December, the Greeks held a quarter of Albania. Badoglio resigned as chief of staff in December. Germany rescued Italy by invading Greece in 1941.

For the next thirty months Badoglio was out of public service. Following the Allied invasion of Sicily in July 1943, King Victor Emmanuel III removed Mussolini as prime minister and appointed Badoglio in Mussolini's place.

Badoglio began secret negotiations with the Allies to conclude a separate peace. An armistice was signed on September 3, 1943. It was followed by Allied landings at the southwestern tip of Italy and at Taranto on September 8. The Allies announced the armistice on that date. Badoglio had not yet informed the Italian armed forces of the armistice.

Italian units were surprised by the switch. Most either went home voluntarily or were disarmed by the Germans. Additionally Italian-occupied areas in France and the Balkans were taken over by the Germans.

The Italian garrison of Rome collapsed, and Badoglio and the Italian government were forced to flee Rome. They relocated, first to Pescara, and then to Brindisi, in Allied-controlled Apulia (the southeastern tip of Italy). On October 13, Badoglio's government formally declared war on Germany and became a co-belligerent with the Allies.

Badoglio remained prime minister for less than a year. His ties to Mussolini's fascist government made him unpopular. On June 8, 1944, Badoglio was removed from the position of prime minister and from the position of foreign minister, which he had assumed in February 1944. He was replaced by Ivanoe Bonomi (1873–1951), a committed anti-fascist. Badoglio retired from public life after leaving office in 1944. He died on November 1, 1956.

Benjamin O. Davis Jr.

Benjamin Oliver Davis Jr. (1912–2002) led the all-black Ninety-ninth Fighter Squadron, the "Tuskegee Airmen," during World War II. The son of the U.S. Army's first African American general, he became the first African American to become a full general in the United States Air Force. Benjamin O. Davis Jr. was instrumental in the postwar desegregation of the U.S. Armed Forces.

Early Life Davis was born on December 18, 1912, in Washington, D.C. He was the son of Benjamin O. Davis Sr., then a lieutenant in the U.S. Army. His father went on to become the first black general in the Army.

Raised in a military tradition, Benjamin Davis Jr. decided two things as a child: that he wanted to become a pilot and that he wanted to attend the U.S. Military Academy at West Point.

Davis attended Western Reserve University in 1929 before transferring to the University of Chicago, which he attended from 1930 to 1932. In 1932, he received an appointment to West Point.

He was the fourth African American admitted to West Point. In his first year he was shunned—other cadets refused to speak to him, except for purposes of duty. He slept alone in a tent on bivouacs and ate silent meals alone. Despite the treatment, he stuck with it, and graduated thirty-fifth in a class of 216 in 1936.

African Americans were not then allowed to fly aircraft in the Army Air Corps. He was given an infantry commission as a second lieutenant. From 1938 until the start of World War II, he was assigned as an instructor of military science at Alabama's Tuskegee Institute (now Tuskegee University).

World War II In 1941, Davis was one of a first group of African Americans admitted to U.S. Army Air Corps pilot training. In late 1942, Davis was promoted to temporary lieutenant colonel and was given command of the Ninety-ninth Fighter Squadron. The first fighter squadron in the Air Corps with African American pilots, the squadron trained at Tuskegee Army Air Field. That gave the squadron the nickname "the Tuskegee Airmen."

Davis's unit was sent to Europe in 1943. Davis led the Ninety-ninth in combat in North Africa, Sicily, and Italy. The squadron proved both efficient and aggressive. The experiment was expanded, with other all–African American fighter squadrons joining the Ninety-ninth.

In 1943, Davis organized and commanded the 332nd Fighter Group, which was comprised of four African American fighter squadrons. In addition to the Ninety-ninth, the group contained the 100th, 301st, and 302nd fighter squadrons. Except for a brief period in November 1944, Davis commanded the 332nd from October 1943 until June 1945. The group fought in Italy, the Balkans, Germany, and Austria; they also supported the Allied invasion of southern France.

The 332nd Fighter Group shot down 111 planes and destroyed another 150 grounded planes during 15,000 sorties. Davis flew numerous combat sorties, winning a Distinguished Service Cross for leading a mission to Munich on March 9, 1944. In May 1944, he was promoted to colonel.

Postwar Career Davis remained with the Army Air Force after World War II, transferring to the U.S. Air Force when it was formed in 1947. Between 1945 and 1946, he commanded Godman Field in Kentucky.

AFRICAN AMERICAN UNITS IN WORLD WAR II

African American soldiers traditionally demonstrated excellent performance in the U.S. Army through the end of World War I. However, in World War II, most large African American units performed poorly.

Poor performance was not the fault of the individual soldiers. Most fought bravely. The problem was that units like the Ninety-second Infantry Division (Buffalo Soldiers) and Ninety-third Infantry Division (Blue Helmets) were committed undermanned and poorly equipped—often with World War I surplus weapons. Additionally, the white senior officers assigned to these units were rarely the most gifted or motivated officers.

African Americans in smaller units—such as the 332nd Fighter Group or the 761st Tank Battalion—turned in excellent performances during World War II. The difference was leadership and training. The officers, whether white or black, believed in their men, and set high standards in training and combat.

Additionally, late in World War II, casualties, especially during the Battle of the Bulge (winter 1944–1945), led to a shortage of infantrymen. Replacements were sought from support troops. This included African American volunteers who were put in white infantry squads as replacements. These men fought well. The dichotomy between the good individual performance of African Americans and the poor performance of segregated divisions was one factor that lef to the desegregation of the Army in the years following World War II.

Between 1946 and 1949, he commanded the 477th Fighter Bomber Group at Lockbourne Air Force Base in Ohio. He attended the Air Force War College, graduating in 1950.

During the Korean War he commanded the Fifty-first Fighter Interceptor Wing in Korea, and was promoted to brigadier general in October 1954. From 1957 through 1968, he was chief of staff in increasingly important commands: the Twelfth Air Force in Germany, the air forces in Europe (a position with NATO), and U.N. Command in Korea.

Davis was instrumental in the racial integration of the Air Force in 1949, and was a civil rights advocate for most of his life. He helped draft the Air Force desegregation plan.

Davis retired from the Air Force in 1970 to become director of public safety for Cleveland, Ohio. He left the post shortly after taking it due to disagreements with the Cleveland mayor. Shortly afterward, he was appointed director of civil aviation security. He organized the "sky marshal" program used today to combat skyjacking and terrorism.

In 1998, Davis received a promotion to full general, a special post-retirement promotion similar to one granted Jimmy Doolittle. Davis died on July 4, 2002.

Harry Truman was only vice president for a few months before assuming the presidency upon the death of President Franklin Roosevelt.
AP Images

Harry S. Truman

Harry S. Truman (1884–1972) succeeded Franklin D. Roosevelt as president of the United States in April 1945. The decisions Truman made between then and August, when World War II ended, shaped the peace and the Cold War that subsequently followed. His two most important decisions were that of dropping the atomic bomb on Japan and of allowing the Russians a postwar sphere in Eastern Europe.

Early Life Truman was born in Lamar, Missouri, on May 8, 1884, to a farm family. He attended public school in Independence, Missouri, graduating from high school in 1901. Following graduation he worked as a railroad timekeeper and a bank clerk before returning to work on the family farm in 1906.

He served in the Missouri National Guard between 1905 and 1911. When the United States entered World War I, Truman helped organize the Second Regiment of Missouri Field Artillery. It was called into federal service as the 129th Field Artillery and sent to France. Truman was promoted to captain and commanded Battery D. He saw combat at Vosges, Saint-Mihiel, and Meuse-Argonne. He remained in the reserves after the war, eventually gaining the rank of Colonel.

After World War I he returned to Independence, married Bess Wallace (1885–1982), and ran a haberdashery store. The business failed in 1922.

In 1922 he entered politics, running for county judge. Defeated in 1924, he was reelected to judge's positions between 1926 and 1932. In 1934, he ran for United States Senate and won. He would hold that seat until he became vice president in 1944.

World War II When World War II started, Harry Truman was a senator from Missouri. He had been sponsored by the Kansas City political machine run by Tom Pendergast (1873–1945) in his first Senate term. Truman barely won reelection in 1940 due to prior connections with Pendergast.

Following reelection, Truman became concerned about waste and corruption associated with American military buildup. He helped establish, and chaired, the Senate Special Committee to Investigate the National Defense Program in 1941. The committee, soon known as the Truman Committee, became the bane of war profiteers. By 1944 it was estimated to have saved the federal government as much as $15 billion. It gave Truman a reputation for integrity and honesty that transcended his earlier reputation as "the Senator from Pendergast."

Truman was picked to replace Henry Wallace (1888–1965) as Roosevelt's vice president in the 1944 presidential campaign. As vice president, Truman was outside Roosevelt's circle of advisors. Truman was not informed about Roosevelt's postwar intentions or even briefed about significant military projects. He did not learn about the existence of the Manhattan Project—the effort to develop an atomic bomb—until after he became president.

On April 12, 1945, Truman was called to the White House. Eleanor Roosevelt (1884–1962) informed him that President Roosevelt had died, and Truman was then sworn in as president. He had been vice president just eighty-two days.

Truman faced enormous challenges. Roosevelt made several critical foreign policy commitments immediately prior to his death. At Yalta in February, Roosevelt had agreed to allow the Soviet Union to control much of Eastern Europe at war's end and gave the Soviets greater influence in Asia. At Potsdam, Germany, in July 1945, Truman essentially ratified Roosevelt's concessions in exchange for a Soviet pledge to enter the war in the Pacific against the Japanese.

These decisions shaped much of the history of the rest of the century. It created the conditions for the creation of a Soviet Bloc in opposition to the Western powers, leading to both the Korean and Cold Wars.

The Potsdam Conference also resulted in the Potsdam Declaration. It called upon the Japanese government to surrender unconditionally or face "prompt and utter destruction." This was a veiled reference to the atomic bomb.

Truman had to decide whether to use the atomic bomb on Japan. One atomic bomb could destroy most of a city. The first bomb had been tested in July 1945, and by August, the United States had three more.

At the Battle of Okinawa, with 500,000 American troops engaged, the United States suffered 50,000 casualties, including over 12,000 dead. Conservative estimates set Allied casualties for an invasion of Japan in the hundreds of thousands. Fatality estimates ranged between 100,000 and 400,000 dead. (Japanese deaths would have ranged in the millions, but that was not a factor to the United States.)

Truman was a combat veteran who knew what ground combat was like. He had an alternative that offered a way to end the war without a bloody invasion. Truman took it. He ordered that the bomb be used. American B-29s dropped an atomic bomb on Hiroshima on August 6, 1945. When the Japanese refused to surrender, a second bomb was dropped on Nagasaki on August 9. On the same day, the Soviet Union declared war on Japan. Japan surrendered on August 15.

Postwar Years   Truman remained president until 1953. He ran for reelection in 1948 and won, but did not run again in 1952 after getting mired in the Korean War.

In the immediate postwar years, he was responsible for a number of important initiatives. The fascist threat to freedom was almost immediately supplanted by a Communist threat. The Soviet Union fostered a communist takeover in China, North Korea, and Eastern Europe, preventing free elections in all of those areas.

In response, Truman established the Marshall Plan to help restore Western Europe to economic health and the Truman Doctrine—which stated American willingness to support nations faced with communist incursion. This included military and economic aid to Greece from 1946 to 1948 and the creation of the North Atlantic Treaty Organization (NATO) in 1950.

In 1950 North Korea invaded South Korea. Truman sent American military assistance to Korea and enlisted the aid of the United Nations to assist the South. The war degenerated into a stalemate after China became involved.

Domestically, Truman instituted a set of economic policies known as the Fair Deal as a successor to the New Deal. Truman also desegregated the American armed forces.

After leaving the presidency, Truman retired to private life in Independence, Missouri. Truman died on December 26, 1972.

✪ Major Battles and Events

Anschluss

Anschluss is a German word that refers to the unification of Germany and Austria in 1938. It marked German leader Adolf Hitler's boldest flouting of international regulations to that point and fostered the development of the Munich Crisis later that year and the invasion of Poland in 1939.

Austria after World War I   The end of World War I brought major changes to Central Europe. Germany was saddled with punitive economic and military sanctions. The other major defeated power, the Empire of Austria-Hungary, ceased to exist entirely. From that one empire emerged several countries: Austria, Hungary, Czechoslovakia, Poland, and Yugoslavia.

The Treaty of Saint-Germain (1919), signed by the Allies and the newly created Republic of Austria shortly

These young German women, residents of Britain, boarded a ship that took them far enough away from the coast to qualify their votes on the annexation of Austria. © *Hulton-Deutsch Collection/Corbis*

after World War I came to a close, provided not only for the dissolution of the old empire but also for the awarding of Austrian territories to Italy and Romania. Most significantly, the treaty forbade Austria from unifying with Germany without the consent of the League of Nations.

The loss of its empire sent Austria into economic crisis during the 1920s; the concept of *Anschluss* soon gained considerable popularity. Support cooled, however, when Hitler and the Nazis came to power in 1933.

Hitler's Involvement Hitler, meanwhile, had long advocated unification of all German-speaking peoples and began working with the Austrian Nazi party as soon as he came to power, secretly providing funds and direction. In 1934, Austrian Nazis attempted a *putsch*, or uprising, against the Austrian government, which itself had developed strong ties with Italy and Benito Mussolini's fascists.

The *putsch* was quickly put down, although not before Austrian Chancellor Engelbert Dollfuss was assas-

sinated. Although Hitler had hoped to support the coup with military intervention, Mussolini's massing troops on the Austrian border dissuaded him.

The Nazis were banned in Austria—many fled to Germany and continued to collude with their northern brethren—and Austria experienced a brief spasm of civil war. Dollfuss's successor, Kurt von Schuschnigg, took extreme measures against the Nazis remaining in Austria, rounding up many of them into internment camps. Although Schuschnigg had successfully restored order, world events would soon conspire to doom Austrian independence.

The Anschluss By 1938, Hitler felt confident enough to begin pressing his expansionist agenda. His first target was Austria, which found its two main allies, France and Italy, drifting away—France, distracted by internal difficulties, was quickly stepping away from international politics, and Italy was just as quickly strengthening its ties with Germany, forging what would become the Rome-Berlin Axis alliance.

Mussolini and Hitler review seamen. Later, when British Prime Minister Neville Chamberlain returned from his meeting with Hitler and Mussolini in Munich, he announced he achieved "peace in our time." *AP Images*

Responding to German pressure, Schuschnigg met with Hitler in February 1938 in an attempt to reach an understanding. In the subsequent agreement, Germany pledged to respect Austrian independence. In return, Austria pledged to act in accordance with German interests on the international stage and to decriminalize the Nazi Party. In addition, Schuschnigg appointed two pro-Nazi administrators—Arthur Seyss-Inquart and Edmund Glaise-Horstenau—to his cabinet. Again bowing to German pressure, he also fired his army chief of staff, Alfred Jansa, who had been developing a plan to defend against a possible German invasion.

Schuschnigg could clearly see that his new cabinet appointees were actively pro-German and that a confrontation over *Anschluss* was fast approaching. He decided to force the issue, taking the huge gamble of calling for a national referendum on the issue. To eliminate the Austrian Nazis' strongest base of support, he set the minimum voting age at twenty-four. The referendum was set for March 13, 1938.

Hitler reacted to this development quickly, putting the Nazi propaganda machine into high gear. Announc-

ing that the elections were biased and fraudulent, he vowed to intervene militarily if requested. Schuschnigg was forced to resign on March 11, and Seyss-Inquart, the new chancellor, to send a telegram asking for aid in advance of the referendum. German troops were in Austria on March 12.

There was no resistance. In fact, thousands turned out to cheer the Germans as they marched further into Austria. Hitler, seated in an open-top staff car, crossed the border at his hometown of Braunau and proceeded on what amounted to a victory tour. The degree of enthusiasm that greeted his procession surprised even Hitler and his staff. Hitler would later comment:

I have in the course of my political struggle won much love from my people, but when I crossed the former frontier [into Austria] there met me such a stream of love as I have never experienced. Not as tyrants have we come, but as liberators.

The unification of Germany and Austria was announced by decree on March 13. The referendum was eventually held on April 10. Unification with Germany was approved by a vote of 99.73 percent.

The effects of *Anschluss* were significant. Absorption of Austria increased Germany's population and industrial resources and provided a common border with its Italian ally. More importantly, it signaled to Hitler the Western powers' reluctance to provoke a confrontation. The *Anschluss*, the first time the German army had crossed over to foreign soil since the end of World War I, marked the beginning of Hitler's expansionism. Within less than two years, his invasion of Poland would plunge Europe into World War II.

The Munich Pact

The Munich Pact of September 1938 marked the failure of appeasement (the policy under which European powers offered no resistance to Germany's expansion in hopes of avoiding a war) and the beginning of the end of peace in Europe. Although the Pact averted war for a time, the price was steep: Czechoslovakia, a young country created in the wake of World War I, would soon cease to exist because of the events set in motion at Munich. Furthermore, the Pact emboldened German leader Adolf Hitler in carrying out his expansionist policies and seriously damaged the standing of the Western powers, England in particular.

German Expansionism   In the aftermath of World War I, Germany was crippled by expensive war reparations imposed by the Treaty of Versailles (1919) and the worldwide economic depression of the 1930s. Hitler and the Nazi Party rode the wave of resentment and frustration caused by these conditions, and Hitler was in total control of the country by 1933. Hitler's goal was to undo the humiliations of Versailles and restore Germany's status as a world power.

Throughout the next five years, Hitler began slowly to test the resolve of France and England, the leading architects of Versailles. The Saar and the Rhineland, occupied regions on the French border, were reoccupied shortly after the Nazis' rise to power. Germany also set upon a course of rearmament, building up its air force, army, and navy, and developing new weapons and technology, all in defiance of the terms of the Treaty of Versailles. France and England barely reacted.

By 1938, having fully consolidated his power in Germany and rebuilt the military, Hitler began to show his territorial ambitions. Using the logic of the Versailles Treaty, which had attempted to divide countries among cultural or ethnic lines, Hitler had long agitated for a "pan-German" state that included all German-speaking peoples within a single border.

In March 1938, Hitler made his first expansionist move, boldly annexing Austria in a bloodless invasion known as the *Anschluss*. Although this was a clear violation of treaty terms, France and England allowed it to happen without challenge.

The Policy of Appeasement   The situation for those two great nations by the end of the 1930s was troubled.

The Great Depression had affected their economies as well as Germany's, and both popular and government opinion was against policing foreign countries. Furthermore, memories of the Great War (as World War I was known) and the horrendous casualties and ruin that it brought were still quite fresh in people's minds. Most people were eager to avoid the possibility of another war.

The task of directing the resulting policy, known as appeasement, fell to Britain. British Prime Minister Neville Chamberlain was convinced that Hitler did not want war any more than France or England did, and he felt that if he made minor concessions to Germany, the possibility of a greater war would be averted.

Appeasement was also motivated by a major miscalculation of relative military strengths. France and Britain both felt that their armies were thoroughly unprepared to fight the resurgent German military, which was actually only barely coalescing as an effective fighting force. If appeasement bought time for the Western democracies to get their armies back on a war footing, it also allowed the nascent Nazi army, the *Wehrmacht*, to mature into an efficient fighting force.

The September Crisis   After the *Anschluss*, Hitler set his sights on the Sudetenland, a strip of western Czechoslovakia that ran parallel to the German border and contained more than three million German-speaking residents, most of whom were strongly opposed to Czech rule. Hitler began making demands that Czechoslovakia cede the Sudetenland to Germany.

A British mediator was dispatched to Czechoslovakia to attempt to reach a peaceful resolution. Simultaneously, Germany began massing troops on the Czech border as Hitler instructed his agents at the bargaining table to continue increasing their demands. Unlike Austria, Czechoslovakia was not prepared to bow down to German demands and pledged to resist German invasion.

On September 15, Neville Chamberlain arranged a meeting with Hitler to try and find a peaceful solution. At the meeting, Chamberlain promised Hitler, without consulting the Czech government, that he would allow the Sudetens self-determination in the form of a national referendum. The English prime minister departed in high spirits.

It came as quite a shock when Hitler increased his demands the next week during a follow-up meeting with Chamberlain: Germany would occupy the Sudetenland before the referendum could proceed, the better to ensure the election was carried out "fairly." Even Chamberlain could not agree to this. For the first time since World War I, the major European powers began mobilizing their armies. War seemed inevitable.

It was Benito Mussolini, Italy's fascist dictator, who arranged a four-power conference at Munich in a last-ditch attempt at averting war. Mussolini, Hitler's ally, was motivated less by a desire for peace than by his recognition that Italy was not ready to be dragged into war.

The Munich Conference On September 29, 1938, Chamberlain, Mussolini, and Hitler were joined by France's Édouard Daladier at Munich. Czechoslovakia, the nation whose fate was to be discussed, was not invited to the talks, nor was the Soviet Union, despite its status as a Czech ally.

The conference ended with an agreement for Germany to gain the Sudetenland outright. In addition to the Sudeten population of three million, Czechoslovakia also lost major manufacturing sites and its previously protected border with Germany. Germany's concessions, if they can be called that, were in a separate agreement with Chamberlain. Germany agreed to use peaceful means in resolving all future disputes with England and guaranteed Czech sovereignty.

Political Fallout Reaction to the Munich Pact was mixed. German diplomats and generals were pleased, but Hitler felt that he had compromised his policies. The Soviet Union felt slighted and marginalized by the Western powers. This alienation would lead directly to the drafting of the Molotov-Ribbentrop Pact with Germany, the Soviet Union's ideological enemy, in 1939. The Czechoslovkian response was, as can be expected, outrage. Nevertheless, the Czech president Edvard Beneš had no choice but to accept terms and hand over the Sudetenland on October 10.

In England, Chamberlain was greeted as hero when he returned from Munich, famously promising that he had achieved "peace in our time." Not all were convinced. Future Prime Minister Winston Churchill, in a speech to Parliament, proclaimed:

> We have sustained a total and unmitigated defeat. We are in the midst of a disaster of the first magnitude.... Do not suppose that this is the end. It is only the beginning.

Churchill's predictions would prove all too accurate. Defenseless, Czechoslovakia was at the mercy of German expansion. On March 13, 1939, German units occupied Prague as Beneš signed over Bohemia and Moravia to Germany. The remainder of the dismembered country, Slovakia, was set up as a Nazi puppet state. Czechoslovakia had ceased to exist.

By this point, even someone as committed to appeasement as Chamberlain could see that the policy had failed and that war was inevitable. France and England began mobilizing their armies and resolved to stand firm on the next issue of German expansionism. They would not have long to wait: German armies crossed into Poland on September 1, 1939, almost eleven months to the day after the Munich Pact. France and England declared war two days later.

The Invasion of Poland

The origins of Germany's involvement in World War II, beginning with its invasion of Poland in 1939, lie mostly in the political fallout after the end of World War I. The Treaty of Versailles imposed stiff economic and military sanctions on Germany, wounding national pride and crippling the economy. Versailles also mandated Poland's independence—the country had been subjugated for 123 years. Poland was thus reassembled with territories carved out of Germany, Russia, and Austria-Hungary. The new country was also granted Baltic Sea access by means of the "Polish Corridor," the former German territory of West Prussia. The German city of Danzig (modern-day Gdansk, Poland), sitting at the outlet of the corridor, was declared a "free city." German leader Adolf Hitler and his Nazi party would come to power by trading on the frustrations and difficulties that these concessions had stirred up.

Two of Hitler's chief aims upon assuming power were incorporating all German-speaking peoples into a *Grossdeustchland*, or "Greater Germany," and regaining German territories lost after the Treaty of Versailles. With the annexations of Austria and Czechoslovakia, Hitler accomplished the first goal—but at the price of alerting the world to his imperial ambitions. Thus, when Hitler turned his gaze to Poland in 1939 and demanded Danzig and the Polish Corridor be ceded to Germany, the Western powers of France and England were ready to fight.

The invasion of Poland came as no surprise. England and France, seeking to end their policy of appeasement, had each guaranteed Poland's safety months before. What did come as a surprise was the Molotov-Ribbentrop Pact between Germany and the Soviet Union. Signed on August 23, 1939, it was a non-aggression treaty between the two ideologically opposed countries that freed Germany from the worry of fighting a two-front war, as it had in World War I. The announcement of the pact shocked the Western Allies, who had not thought that two countries that had openly agitated for the other's destruction could reach such an agreement. The reasons for Soviet leader Joseph Stalin's complicity would become all too clear in time.

The German Invasion Hitler, who felt that he had been talked out of war at the Munich Conference in 1938, was determined to flex his military might in Poland. With the Soviet Union out of the picture, there was now nothing to stop Germany from attacking Poland. So, in the late hours of August 31, 1939, German operatives disguised as Polish saboteurs staged an attack on a German radio station near the Polish border. Armed with this flimsy excuse to begin hostilities, Hitler ordered his armies across the Polish border at 8:00 on the morning of September 1.

The first shots of World War II had actually been fired a few hours earlier by the battleship *Schleswig-Holstein*, which opened fire on Polish positions near Danzig at 4:45 A.M. At around the same time, German planes began bombing Polish border towns.

Hitler's invasion of Poland in September 1939 aimed at, among other goals, the capture of the city of Danzig, a seaport. © *Corbis*

As the German armies crossed the Polish border, England and France issued ultimatums demanding an immediate withdrawal. As expected, these requests were ignored, and the Western Allies declared war on Germany on September 3.

By that point, Polish forces were engaged all along the country's long border, facing invasion from the north, west, and southwest. The defense plan was doomed to failure—there was just too much territory to protect. To make matters worse, the Poles were facing an entirely new kind of fight: *blitzkrieg*, or "lightning war."

Lightning War

The philosophy behind *blitzkrieg* was to use tanks, airplanes, and infantry in close cooperation. The planes, primarily the infamous "Stuka" dive-bomber, would act as highly mobile artillery, blasting holes in enemy lines that would then be exploited by tanks and mobile infantry. Regular infantry units, which would occupy the new positions and eliminate enemy strong points, would then follow up these exploitations.

The new tactics proved a major success, although for all the attention received by the mechanized elements of *blitzkrieg*, it is important to realize that the vast majority of the German army was still made up of old-fashioned foot-soldiers and that the majority of casualties sustained by the Polish forces in battle were caused by artillery.

Polish forces put up a spirited resistance on land and in the air, but by the second week of hostilities they were falling back toward the interior. Despite promises of opening a second front, France had made only small advances into German territory and was reluctant to move beyond the range of its great fortress guns on the Maginot Line, a system of fortifications in France near the German border. The British, likewise, were unable to offer much help and were reduced to dropping propaganda leaflets over German towns.

The Polish rallying point was the "Romanian Bridgehead," a mountainous area with its back to neutral Romania from which the Poles hoped to set up a defensive perimeter and wait out the winter, confident their Western allies would launch a major offensive in the spring and relieve the pressure.

The Soviet Invasion

Such dreams were quickly put to rest, however, when the Soviet Union, acting on a secret protocol in the Molotov-Ribbentrop Pact, invaded Poland from the east on September 17. Realizing the situation had become untenable, orders were sent out to units still in the field to go to neutral Romania—and then to France and England—and live to fight another day. In the end, 120,000 Polish soldiers and airmen escaped capture and would go on to fight under French and British command for the remainder of the war.

As the majority of the Polish army was retreating south and escaping the country, the Germans surrounded the capital city of Warsaw. In a brief siege that came to characterize the brutality of the new war,

Warsaw was pounded into rubble by relentless bombing raids and near-constant bombardment from artillery ranging from mortars to massive railway guns.

Warsaw capitulated on September 28, just four weeks after the first German troops had crossed the border. Although the Polish government never officially surrendered, the invasion of Poland was declared over by October 6. The speed of the victory shocked the world. Poland once again ceased to exist and was divided up between the victorious German and Soviet states.

The Battle of Flanders

In the spring of 1940, Hitler gave the warning order to his generals—an attack on the West was imminent. The first war plan for the invasion of the "Low Countries"— Belgium, the Netherlands, and Luxembourg—was compromised on January 10 when a German airplane crashed in Belgium with the documents of the plan on board. The Belgians were able to send intelligence from that plan to the French and British.

A new war plan, named "Sickle Stroke" took form. The plan called for a German flanking maneuver through the Ardennes Forest that would bypass the vaunted French Maginot Line, cross the Meuse River between Sedan and Dinant, and then drive quickly to the coast of the English Channel, dividing the British expeditionary force from the French army.

Hitler could not have asked for more ideal opponents for his conquest in the West. The Allied forces were not ready to fight modern warfare. Although the French had 101 divisions, many were not in fighting form. These second-class French divisions contained older reservists and out-of-shape soldiers with low morale. The French still used horse cavalry and light armored cars that were no match for the German Mark III Panzers. They were also a defensive army, not a maneuver army. Many French troops were tied down at the Maginot Line—eighty-seven miles of fortifications that cost the French government more than seven billion francs after World War I. However, despite the Maginot fortress, there were 250 miles of undefended border between France and Belgium. The Belgians, led by General Robert van Overstraeten, the chief military advisor to the Belgian King Leopold III, did not coordinate their defenses very well with the French and British, even though it was assumed most of the initial fight against the Germans would take place in Belgium. The Belgians had 600,000 troops in twenty-two divisions, but no joint defensive plans with the other Allies.

The French had more tanks than the Germans (3,000 versus 2,400), but the French assigned most of their tanks to their slow-moving infantry, and the Germans put seven of their Panzer divisions in General Gerd von Rundstedt's fast-moving Army Group A. There was no mass of Allied tanks to stop the Germans. The French had only five pure armored divisions—three active and

British soldiers, captured by the Germans at Dunkirk, begin the "Great March" to POW camps as far away as Poland. *AP Images*

one still forming. Rundstedt was to take the seven Panzer divisions through the Ardennes and then slice toward the coast. These divisions could cover thirty-five to forty miles a day and, unlike the infantry, did not have to travel on roads. The German tanks had air support from the Luftwaffe (German air force) at all times. The British had five infantry divisions in the fight and only one newly organized armored division in 1940.

Holland was strictly neutral in 1940. The Dutch had not fought a war since 1830; they sat out World War I. Their entire army consisted of ten divisions and only 125 aircraft. Upon attack, they planned to fall back into "Fortress Holland"—Amsterdam and Rotterdam— and hope the canals and dykes of the low country would delay the enemy. The tactics worked during the Eighty Years War against Spain three hundred years earlier, but this was 1940, and air power was at its height.

Germany's Luftwaffe flew over the canals and simply bombed and strafed all Dutch airfields, nearly eliminating the Dutch air force on the ground. On May 10, 1940, 2,500 German aircraft attacked airfields of Belgium, Holland, France, and Luxembourg and destroyed fleets of aircraft on the ground.

At dawn on that day, 16,000 German paratroopers, in a classic airborne operation, landed deep in Dutch territory and seized key bridges. The paratroopers held the bridges until German Panzers linked up with them

CHURCHILL'S SPEECH TO THE HOUSE OF COMMONS

Shortly after the bombing of Paris by the Nazis on June 3, 1940, British Prime Minister Winston Churchill delivered one of his many famous addresses, this one to the British House of Commons. In it, he vowed: "We shall go on to the end, we shall fight in France, we shall fight on the seas and oceans, we shall fight with growing confidence and growing strength in the air, we shall defend our Island, whatever the cost may be, we shall fight on the beaches, we shall fight on the landing grounds, we shall fight in the fields and in the streets, we shall fight in the hills; we shall never surrender . . . ."

for the drive westward. The main attack began. Two and a half million German troops—104 infantry divisions, nine motorized divisions, and nine armored divisions in three army groups began the invasion into Belgium, Holland, France, and Luxembourg.

First the German planes struck deep into the Netherlands. The Luftwaffe bombing of Rotterdam killed 814 civilians and forced Dutch Queen Wilhelmina to escape with the Royal Navy to Britain. As the Dutch army retreated to Fortress Holland, it left the flank open on the Belgians' left. The Belgians were also soon flanked by the Third and Fourth Panzer divisions on the right. By May 13, the rest of the German Army B entered Holland. Hitler demanded complete surrender by the Dutch, and they surrendered after the bombing of Rotterdam.

The Allies, expecting to see the Germans repeat their 1914 attack into Flanders, were surprised by the German advance through the Ardennes. Both Belgian and French infantry retreated at the sight or even the rumor of German tanks. Some even ran from friendly tanks. On May 17, German General Heinz Guderian's tanks had reached the River Oise. General Walther von Reichenau's army reached Brussels, and British General Bernard Montgomery's Third Division fell back toward the coast. The only bright spot for the Allies was Colonel Charles de Gaulle's Fourth Division, which counterattacked and was able to delay the Germans—but only briefly. De Gaulle was later promoted to brigadier general and given command of an armored division. However, the Allies had to fall back to the Dyle Line, to the east of Brussels. General Montgomery had his Third Armored Division dig in on the Dyle Line.

On May 20, Guderian's divisions reached Abbeville, and that divided the Allies in two. Since the French had no strategic reserves, panic went up and down the retreating French forces. French General Alphonse Georges wept openly in the French headquarters. The

Allies struggled to hold Somme-Aisne lines while the Germans sent three prongs of attacking armor columns to the northwest. Guderian's tanks captured Boulogne on the French coast and trapped the British at Calais on May 22–23. King Leopold surrendered to the Germans the next day at nearly the same area Belgium had taken up defensive positions against the Germans in World War I. The British Expeditionary Force and the French First Army were backed up to Dunkirk, on the north coast of France, and trapped.

Dunkirk

The evacuation of more than 300,000 British and allied troops from Dunkirk, on the north coast of France, in late May and early June of 1940 was viewed as a near miraculous feat. The troops were rescued in the nick of time, just ahead of the Germans, by British naval vessels along with all manner of private boats, yachts, and fishing vessels whose owners were eager to help.

The troops at Dunkirk had been cut off from the rest of allied forces by a successful German advance across France in late May. It seemed Germany was poised to crush the British and French forces outright. But on May 24, German leader Adolf Hitler inexplicably ordered all German tanks to stop for two whole days. He wanted to be sure he had enough tanks to take Paris. He did not want his tanks to be stuck in the mud of the canals around Dunkirk. He also may have wanted to have the Luftwaffe get the credit for destroying the Allies on the beaches. Hilter did not know that most of the remaining French and British army was stranded at Dunkirk. If he had, he might have had his tanks finish the job in May. Whatever the reason for stopping the German tank advance, it gave the Allies precious time to escape.

Two major breaks came the Allies' way. The British had an immediate plan to evacuate Allied troops from Dunkirk—Operation Dynamo. Meanwhile, the British were able to crack the Enigma code. Enigma was the code used by the Luftwaffe to communicate with the *Wehrmacht*. Essentially, the British knew German operational plans for the rest of the war. This is how Churchill kept up his confidence. He knew Hitler's eyes were on Paris and not on an immediate airborne, naval, and amphibious attack into Great Britain.

Hitler, however, immediately realized that the Allies were evacuating Dunkirk and sent his forces to finish them of. With a brave rear guard of French troops providing security and Allied pilots holding off the Luftwaffe, Operation Dynamo was able to commence on May 27. Fifty German aircraft were shot down that day while 850 British ships of all makes and sizes began the evacuation. The armada was made up of warships, private yachts, and fishing boats—basically anything that could float and haul troops. The group of ships picked up thousands of British and French soldiers from the beaches. In eight days, these vessels, later joined by

The 1940 occupation of Paris by German soldiers only weeks after the invasion of France began served as a blow to the morale of the Allied forces. *Hugo Jaeger/Timepix/Time Life Pictures/Getty Images*

iation after World War I. By the end of June, Nazis were marching into Paris.

First Moves on France Although they were on the other side of the English Channel, the British were as nervous as the Parisians about German aggression in the late spring of 1940. The British Isles would have been an easy target for the Germans at that time. Only five hundred heavy guns existed in England. The head of the Fighter Command, Sir Hugh Dowding, estimated that the British could last only forty-eight hours in the skies battling the Germans. The skeleton force of ground troops in England was armed only with rifles. Fortunately, the British High Command, due to the breaking of the Enigma code (the code the Germans used to encrypt their military messages), knew that Hitler was targeting Paris and had no immediate plans for Great Britain. However, the British populace did not know that, and they braced for the worst.

It was time for Winston Churchill to shine. He chastised, cajoled, enthused, and inspired his countrymen to fight. After all, there were still 136,000 British troops in western France. In addition to that force, 200,000 Polish soldiers carried on the fight as well. These were the Poles who escaped the invasion of their country by retreating through Romania, and they made it to France in time to defend Paris. Hitler reorganized and redirected his massive army toward the French capital. A total of 143 German divisions along a 140-mile front stared down at the Allies from the north.

On June 5, the Germans started the battle for France with a massive artillery and air attack. French General Maxime Weygand devised a plan to organize his defenses in echelons along the Somme and the Aisne Rivers while tying in to the existing Maginot Line. He had only sixty-five divisions and only a few bruised and battered armored regiments. Several of his divisions were filled with older reserve soldiers. His other troops manned the Maginot Line and could not maneuver. The Weygand Line still looked like a good plan on paper, but the French, British, and Poles were no match for the mass and tempo of the attacking Germans. The Weygand Line broke in many places, although it actually held in some areas where the Allies did damage to the Germans. But there were no reserves available in order to counterattack and take advantage of any favorable situation.

The Allies suffered too many casualties, ran out of ammunition, or simply melted away as the Germans advanced. The British and the French Ninth Corps had the left flank near the coast of Abbeville, but were quickly rolled up by Rommel's forces, and their backs were soon to the sea. The Royal Navy tried another Dunkirk-type of evacuation, but heavy fog stymied those plans. The Germans had barely even started the main attack and Allied forces were already in disarray. This was just the beginning of the rout.

French and Belgian ships, rescued 226,000 British soldiers and 112,000 French soldiers. Although the Germans sunk some of the ships from the air, more than 338,000 men were rescued in seven days. It took 222 naval vessels and 665 civilian boats to complete the evacuation. The British Army lost most of its equipment and began importing arms from the United States. Hitler figured that Britain would sue for peace and his attention turned first to Paris and later to the Soviet Union. He underestimated the resolve of Churchill and the British and the industrial and fighting capacity of the United States. At this point, the conquest of France was his next objective.

Battle of France

On June 3, 1940, German planes bombed Paris, killing 254 people. This only foreshadowed the violence that was to come. The Nazi plan for France was to decimate the land and its people so that they would never revolt under Nazi rule. German leader Adolf Hitler and the Third Reich would make France pay for German humil-

The main effort came from the center as Rundstedt's A Group started in Sedan on June 9, with German General Heinz Guderian's Panzers leading the way. The Germans broke out of the French defenses at Chalons and were able to strike east of Paris. The French government escaped to Bordeaux on June 10. On June 11, the French had completely lost thirty-five divisions. The French, seeing that the situation was dire, told the remaining British troops to evacuate, and a second "Dunkirk" was ordered for the British troops at Cherbourg and other ports in the area. More than 130,000 British troops escaped—and this time, they were able to keep their equipment. The advancing Germans were in close pursuit, only miles away, on June 18, the last day of the evacuation.

The French knew it was time to sue for peace. They instead deemed Paris a free city and told the Germans that no resistance would take place in Paris upon their arrival. Churchill tried to get the Americans to come to the aid of the French. He asked the French prime minister, Paul Reynaud, to send a telegram to President Franklin Roosevelt pleading for American intervention—to declare war if possible. Hitler publicly claimed in a radio interview that he had no plans of violence for North or South America. Roosevelt said the United States would do everything to help the French—support them with arms and materiel—but the United States would not declare war. By the time Roosevelt's return telegram was delivered to the French, German troops were entering Paris.

Two million people had already fled the city. The 700,000 who remained faced German martial law and nightly curfews. The Germans hung a huge swastika flag under the Arc de Triomphe, and a military band soon led the Fourth German Army as it marched down the Champs Elysées.

The Germans forced the French to sign the armistice in the same railcar in which the Germans were forced to sign their armistice following World War I. Most of France would become a zone of occupation for German troops, and all French troops became prisoners of war. The defeated French were allowed a consolation—a puppet government in the city of Vichy. Churchill told the British Parliament that the Battle of France was over and the Battle for Britain was next.

The Battle of Britain

The Battle of Britain was the struggle between German and British air forces from July through October 1940. Germany bombed England repeatedly in the hopes of neutralizing the Royal Air Force (RAF) in advance of a planned German invasion.

The Battle of Britain marked the first time a military campaign was to be decided in the air without armies and navies. In World War I, aircraft were used as tools for reconnaissance or bombers, but not as the main

A German bomber flies over the Thames River and the city of London during the Battle of Britain, 1940. © *Corbis*

means of attack. Later military planners identified bombing as a strategic asset during the Spanish Civil War. They found bombing from the air could scare and demoralize the civilian population—even breaking a whole country's will to fight. An early air-war proponent, Giulio Douhet (1869–1930), wrote that aircraft could bomb the enemy's supply and industrial base. He believed that air power could attack the factories and kill the people who made the guns and munitions. This theory formed the foundation of air power in World War II.

The Battle of Britain began on July 10, 1940, with German attacks on British ships in the English Channel. On August 13, when 1,485 Luftwaffe (German air force) planes crossed the English Channel, the British lost only fifteen airplanes, while Germany lost thirty-nine. The British were showing surprising skill in the air, and this was not what the Luftwaffe expected. By day three, the Germans had already lost 190 aircraft. This was the first phase of the German attack and it amounted to the classic force-on-force aerial dogfight.

Hitler's plan, Operation Sea Lion, was designed to first destroy the Royal Navy and the Royal Air Force and then invade the British Isles. The German army and navy prepared for an amphibious landing across the English Channel. Weapons President Frankin D. Roosevelt had promised Britain during the fall of France began arriving. The British army planned for the defense of their homeland. They were arrayed in depth and were ready to counterattack the Germans if they established a beachhead. British intercepts of coded German messages would later discover that the Germans had no plan for invasion until after they decisively won the battle in the air. This was good news for the British because it bought them time to prepare the ground defense.

But first the Royal Air Force would fight the Germans in the air. Hermann Göering's Luftwaffe was formidable. It consisted of at least 2,800 planes—900 fighters and 1,900 bombers in three fleets. But the British were not without their strengths. In addition to cracking the Enigma code (the German military's encryption code), the British had an early warning system called "Chain Home." Chain Home consisted of fifty radar warning systems that covered the southern shores of England. Radar was a British invention that sent out a pulsing radio beam to a target. The transmission was then reflected and received at the radar station. This beam was timed, and the delay of the pulse was measured. This sequence gave a reading of distance, bearing, height, and speed. Another advantage was the British industrial output. Aircraft were now being produced at a more rapid pace than they were in Germany—500 Spitfires and Hurricanes per month to the Germans 140 ME 109s and 90 ME 110s. However, the British had only around 1,500 trained pilots compared to Germany's 10,000. The Germans had a tremendous edge in bombers—nearly 1,300 heavy bomb-laden aircraft. These bombers were enough to defeat Britain, but Goering's Luftwaffe had devised no overall air plan. They improvised daily, and the British were able to buy time and hang on.

The Germans kept changing tactics and objectives. They switched to attacking the British airfields from late August until early September. Then the Luftwaffe began bombing London day and night, but this only worked to harden British resolve. The German bombing switched again to nightly raids on London—the "blitz"—until October 30. Some 40,000 British civilians were killed. This period of the war was made famous by the roof-top radio broadcasts of American reporter Edward R. Murrow (1908–1965). Murrow painted a picture of the aerial war over Britain each night for millions of Americans listening to their radios at home. The blitz resulted in an aerial stalemate as the Royal Air Force and some 2,000 antiaircraft guns confounded the Luftwaffe.

However, the Luftwaffe began to inflict more and more damage to Britain. The Germans appeared to be winning. Morale was sinking as more and more civilian areas were attacked. The bombing was so bad that some British air crewmen, mechanics, and refuelers refused to service the planes on some airfields.

During much of August, the Germans were shooting down RAF planes faster than Britain could make them. If the Germans had intensified bombing in the cities and on the airfields, the battle's outcome might have been different. Instead, German leader Adolf Hitler diverted much of the Luftwaffe to the Eastern Front in preparation for the attack on Russia. The Germans almost became the first air force to decisively win an air campaign in the history of war. The cracking of the

This propagandistic poster attempted to boost British morale in the face of harrowing blitzkrieg. *"Britain Shall Not Burn," 1940 (coloured litho), English School, (20th Century)/Private Collection, Peter Newark Historical Pictures/The Bridgeman Art Library*

Enigma code, the invention and implementation of radar, and heroic RAF flying saved the day for England.

The Lend-Lease Act

Though not yet an active player in the war, the United States became the "Arsenal of Democracy" with the Lend-Lease Act of March 1941. It was the first appearance of the United States as an industrial giant and superpower. The idea behind Lend-Lease was simple. The ally, either Britain or the Soviet Union, received military aid in the form of equipment, and would repay the United States after the war. The payback details were left up to the U.S. president to decide. The designers of the legislation did not want the Allies to be shackled to enormous war debt after hostilities ended.

Some in the State Department and in Congress wanted the British to have to repay the United States for the value of the equipment plus interest. But most people in Washington, D.C., saw the need to help the Allies against German leader Adolf Hitler and not take advantage of their plight. Lend-Lease was also seen as a way to win the war against Hitler without direct involvement by the United States. Some American negotiators wanted the British to compensate the United States after the war by supporting U.S. trade and economic policy. President Franklin Roosevelt wanted the British to see that a world interdependent on free trade with democracies supporting capitalism would be better than the imperial system of colonialism to which Britain had grown accustomed. Roosevelt looked strategically beyond the war and beyond Lend-Lease itself toward what the world order would be like in the coming decades.

Effects Abroad The British economy grew by sixty percent from 1939 to 1943, but expenditures on war material made up half of the gross national product. The British had an elaborate means of rationing all types of resources—from food to oil—but it relied on the United States for its war supplies. For example, all the British armored divisions in 1944 used American Sherman tanks. In 1941, the United States supplied 11.5 percent of the military equipment for Great Britain. By 1944, the percentage of equipment supplied by the United States climbed to at least 28 percent. The Americans also kept the British civilian population fed. The United States provided at least 29 percent of the food that the British ate each year during the war.

When Germany declared war on the United States after the Japanese attack on Pearl Harbor, Hawaii, in 1941, the Soviet Union also became a beneficiary of the Lend-Lease program. The United States sent military equipment to the Soviet Union through Vladivostok, Murmansk, and the Persian Gulf. The military aid came in equipment of all kinds, including tanks and airplanes.

But the major need the United States filled for the Soviet Union was basic vehicular transportation. The United States provided 427,000 two-and-a-half-ton Dodge trucks to the Soviets, whose combat maneuvering and logistics would not have been possible without the American trucks. The American arsenal of democracy provided much more to the Soviets, including thirteen million pairs of boots, five million tons of food, two thousand locomotives, eleven thousand freight cars, and 540 thousand tons of rails for railroads. The United States also sent the Soviet Union high-grade gasoline for aircraft fuel, since the Soviets had no way to refine oil to such a high grade of petroleum.

Effects at Home The "arsenal of democracy" concept had a huge effect on the U.S. economy, which had been mired in a depression during the 1930s. Although Roosevelt's New Deal policies put some people back to work, the economy did not recover until the nation switched to a war-footing after the Japanese attack on Pearl Harbor, Hawaii. Plants in the United States in 1939 were only working forty hours a week, and there were nearly nine million unemployed people. By 1944, plants were operating at an average of ninety hours a week, and there were nearly nineteen million new jobs in the country. The United States was producing 40 percent of the world's military equipment. For example, tank production went from a few hundred a year in 1940 to 17,565 tanks a year in 1944. The U.S. produced only 2,141 airplanes in 1940 compared to nearly 100,000 in 1944. By comparison, Germany produced fewer than 40,000 airplanes and about half that many tanks in 1944; Japan produced 28,180 airplanes and 401 tanks. The United States had come a long way from the 1930s when it had only one mechanized force—the Seventh Cavalry Brigade—with only 224 light tanks.

Japanese Expansion

The Japanese had been fighting in the Pacific since 1937. The Japanese called this theater of combat the "Greater East-Asian War." Japan had fought on the side of the Allies in World War I, but between the two wars it became more aggressive in an effort to gain more natural resources to feed its defense industry. Japanese cultural westernization, industrialization for the production of consumer goods, and modernization of the military happened at lightning speed during the two decades leading up to World War II.

Strategically, Japan eyed China for the purpose of using it as a buffer against Western encroachment. Japan planned on gobbling up China for its resources as well. In 1931, Japan occupied Manchuria, including Korea, to the north across the Sea of Japan. In 1937, Chiang Kai-shek (1887–1975) challenged Japanese plans of occupation in China, and war soon broke out. The Japanese struck in Peking, and they soon controlled the entire east coast of China. By 1938, Nanking fell, and Chiang Kai-shek retreated to the interior to Chungking. The economic rewards for the Japanese invasion of China were welcome, but were not enough to satisfy Japan. China would be able to supply most of the food requirements for Japan, but it could only meet 15 percent of Japan's need for natural resources for its industry.

Supplying the Empire To get more natural resources, particularly oil, iron, and rubber, the Japanese would have to look outside its borders. The Japanese army favored a land attack to the north against the Soviet Union, while the navy favored expansion to the so-called "Southern Resource Area," toward French Indochina and the Dutch East Indies. The army had clashed with the Soviets along the Manchurian border in 1938 and 1939, but the Japanese were no match for Soviet tanks, and further attacks against the Soviets were deemed too difficult. Attacking American interests (Wake Island, the Philippines), French colonies (Indochina), and British territories (Burma, Malaya) in the Southern Resource Area appeared to be less risky and have greater potential reward. The Japanese simply planned to take oil and other resources from the Allies by force. However, they never planned the next step—they had no plans to secure and protect the resources once they took them.

During the 1930s, in the early days of Japanese conquest, one Japanese officer stood out. General Hideki Tojo had served in Manchuria and was later promoted to vice minister of war. Tojo's fierce militarism and nationalism shone brightly. After an attempted coup failed in 1936, Tojo became the minister of war under the new Japanese head of state, Prince Konoe. The new foreign minister, Yosuke Matsuoka (1880–1946), helped Japan enter into the Tripartite Pact with Germany and Italy in 1940. Matsuoka also negotiated a neutrality agreement with the Soviet Union. The strategy to seize resources from the Southern Resource Area was in its final preparations, and now its leadership team was in place. After Tojo was named prime minister, the hardliners had their man at the reins. War with the Allies was imminent.

Engaging the Allies   The United States and Britain had long-term economic interests in China. The United States supported Chiang Kai-shek's Nationalists and had intervened in Chinese affairs since the Boxer Rebellion (1899–1901). For decades, American missionaries and teachers served in China to spread Christianity and western ideals and norms. American sailors and soldiers had also served in China. Other Americans got rich from China trade, so there were strong pro-China sentiments in the United States. Heavy sympathies toward China did not make U.S. diplomacy any easier with Japan, although there was a technological breakthrough that would work to the Americans' benefit.

The United States had cracked the Japanese diplomatic code, called "Magic," and messages intercepted from the Japanese would help the Americans decipher some Japanese intentions, but they did not thwart the Japanese military's early strikes into the south. The French and British were ill-prepared militarily in the Pacific to match the Japanese advance. The French in Indochina capitulated quickly. The French Vichy government let the Japanese use harbors in the north of Indochina, and the Japanese promptly used these locations as a jumping-off point to attack China and the Dutch West Indies.

Tojo's strategy was simple. He wanted to check Communist influence from Mao Zedong in China and destroy the Chinese nationalists under Chiang Kai-shek. He wished to conquer a host of nations and then include Indochina, Thailand, Malaya, Burma, and the East Indies (Sumatra, Java, and Borneo) under a new Japanese sphere of influence.

The first part of the plan, the occupation of French Indochina, took place on July 24, 1941. The Japanese negotiated with the Vichy government in France for permission to move Japanese troops from Hanoi in the North of Indochina to Saigon in the South.

U.S. Secretary of State Cordell Hull was alarmed at the Japanese aggression. On November 17, Hull met with the Japanese ambassador, Admiral Kichisaburo Nomura. Nomura refused to back down. Japan wanted more colonies in the Pacific and refused to give them up. President Franklin Roosevelt, in turn, froze Japanese assets in the United States and began a total embargo on oil and gasoline exports to Japan. The United States also wanted all Japanese forces removed from China and Indochina. Tojo saw these ultimatums as a de facto declaration of war.

The Japanese gave one more list of demands to Hull on November 26, but they were already mobilizing their army and navy. They would strike Hong Kong, Malaya, and the Philippines in December of 1941, in conjunction with the attack on Pearl Harbor. They planned to synchronize their attacks against the Southern Resource Area in the Pacific with an attack that was planned to destroy the U.S. Pacific fleet in Pearl Harbor, Hawaii, on December 7.

Pearl Harbor

On Sunday, December 7, 1941, the U.S. Pacific Fleet at Pearl Harbor, Hawaii, was hit by a surprise attack by Japanese aircraft. While the raid was successful, it was not a decisive or lasting victory. After the attack, the U.S. entered World War II immediately against both Japan and its ally, Germany.

The Pacific Fleet was usually headquartered in San Diego, but after the German invasion of France in 1940, the Department of the Navy decided to extend the fleet's stay in Pearl Harbor. A week earlier, the Japanese had sent a massive battle group to the South Pacific that included the Imperial Navy's best fighting ships: six new carriers and an armada of battleships, light cruisers, destroyers, and submarines.

At dawn on December 7, 230 miles north of the Hawaiian island of Oahu, the sky was dense with Japanese fighters and bombers. Three hundred sixty-six Japanese aircraft were streaking toward Pearl Harbor. Two U.S. Army privates at an experimental radar station reported the enemy planes. However, their superior officers thought these were part of a B-17 squadron flying in the area. The destroyer *Ward* had attacked a two-man Japanese submarine a few minutes earlier. The destroyer had fired some of the first American shots of World War II.

The Japanese had planned to surprise the Americans, and they kept the Pearl Harbor attack completely secret, even from the highest echelons of their command. Only a few operational planners knew about it. The 366 Japanese planes achieved total surprise on that Sunday. Four American battleships were destroyed and sunk in the harbor. Four other battleships were badly damaged, and eleven other American warships were sunk. The Japanese destroyed 188 U.S. planes and killed

The surprise attack on Pearl Harbor devastated the U.S. naval fleet. The destroyer U.S.S. *Shaw* exploded when one of the Japanese bombs dropped there hit its magazine. *National Archives and Records Administration*

2,330 U.S. personnel: 1,177 on the battleship *Arizona*. Fortunately, the American carriers were at sea and were spared. The Japanese lost only twenty-nine aircraft and five mini-submarines in the attack. Only sixty-four Japanese were killed, and one was taken prisoner.

The American ships were poorly defended. Few sailors were topside on Sunday mornings. Army personnel on land thought the Japanese planes were part of an exercise. Three-quarters of the 780 antiaircraft guns on the ships at Pearl Harbor were idle, with no one manning them. The army had only four of the thirty-one antiaircraft guns on shore engaging the enemy. A second wave of 168 Japanese fighters and bombers arrived at 9:00 A.M. and finished off the *West Virginia* and the badly damaged *Nevada*, *Maryland*, *Tennessee*, and *Pennsylvania*.

Strikes in Southeast Asia The Pearl Harbor attack, although it seemed isolated, was really part of a larger plan. The Japanese were simultaneously attacking the Southern Resource Area of Malaya, the Dutch East Indies, Burma, and the Philippines.

In Malaya, the Japanese destroyed most of the British Air Force on the ground. The Japanese made amphibious landings at Kota Bharu along the Malaya-Thai border. The British garrison stationed on the Malay Peninsula was not accustomed to jungle fighting, and they were soon overrun. A Japanese naval force landed near Bangkok, and Thailand surrendered. The British commander in Malaya attempted to put his remaining ships to sea, but they had no air cover and were easy targets for the Japanese. The British were pushed back to Singapore and later surrendered.

In the Philippines, the Japanese planned an aerial attack on the American air forces in Manila and an amphibious attack on Luzon. The American planes were inexplicably parked outside their hangars on December 8, 1941, even though the Department of the Navy told General Douglas MacArthur, commander of U.S. forces in the Far East, to keep his forces under high alert after the attack on Pearl Harbor. The Japanese destroyed most of the U.S. force in the Philippines with that single attack.

In Burma, British, Indian, and Burmese troops were no match for the Japanese. They were ill-equipped and undersized. The whole force amounted to only two small divisions. The Japanese army attacked across the

American and Filipino prisoners of war died in massive numbers as the Japanese marched them north from the Bataan Peninsula. This incident became known as the Bataan Death March. © *Corbis*

Burma-Thai border on January 12, 1942. The British retreated to Rangoon and lost most of their heavy equipment. Rangoon later fell, despite the efforts of the Chinese "Flying Tigers," an all-volunteer force of pilots from countries who had just declared war on Japan, such as the United States, Australia, and Canada.

Strikes in the Pacific This was the first stage of the plan—to attack and seize countries that would become supply points for Japan's defense industrial base. The second part of the plan was for the Japanese to construct an island chain for resupply and logistics that would run from the Kurile Islands off the coast of Siberia through Wake Island, the Marshall Islands, the Gilbert Islands, the Bismarck Islands, northern New Guinea, Malaya, and then to the Dutch East Indies. After Japan attacked and secured this logistical trail of islands, it would consolidate the territory and occupy it. Each group of islands would serve as a station to resupply Japan. The difficult part would be for Japan to hold this territory. Chief Admiral Isoroku Yamamoto warned against the Pearl Harbor attack. He compared the sneak attack on the United States to awakening a sleeping giant. Yamamoto also thought the island strategy was too frag-

mented and spread-out to be effective, but he resigned himself to implementing the plan.

Some Japanese officers wanted to modify the plan and steer the Japanese naval forces toward the remaining American carriers to finish off the U.S. fleet. But the Pearl Harbor attack had gone well—past anyone's expectations—that Yamamoto determined it was best to get his force out of harm's way and execute the rest of the island plan. The Japanese also attacked Guam, Wake, and Midway islands, protected by the United States. Yamamoto felt that it was time to turn his attention to the middle of the Pacific and begin the island strategy. He also felt he was on borrowed time; the American giant would soon be awake, and Japan would be forced to defend its newly won territories.

Bataan Death March

The Bataan Death March was the forced march of about 55,000 prisoners of war held by the Japanese from the southern tip of the Bataan Peninsula in the Philippines to Camp O'Donnell, which was to be used as a prisoner of war camp. Most of the prisoners were ill and starving and thousands died in the course of the march.

The Japanese Invasion In 1941, the Philippines was a U.S. protectorate. The islands had been a Spanish colony since the sixteenth century. In 1898, when the Americans were victorious in their war with Spain, the Philippines were turned over to the United States. By the 1930s, the Philippines had something close to a democratic form of government, and U.S. General Douglas MacArthur commanded its army. However, the Filipino army was really only a "Scout" division that numbered twelve thousand troops. It had ten other divisions that were loosely organized but not ready for combat. In 1934, Congress had passed a law that put the Filipino army under control of the United States, even though the rest of the Philippines had some form of independence. American troops seemed to have a significant footprint on the islands, but there were really only sixteen thousand troops, organized in just two regiments, plus a handful of surface ships and submarines, and just 150 aircraft.

In December 1941, MacArthur was told by radar operators that a large Japanese attack was coming from the air, but the American planes were left outside the hangars and parked right next to each other. The Japanese promptly destroyed the American air force on the Philippines. Admiral Thomas Hart (1877–1971) believed that the ships anchored at Subic Bay would be safer at sea since there was no air cover. However, that left the Philippines with no air support or naval gunfire to repel an invasion from the Japanese.

The Japanese had already started the invasion. The Fourteenth Army simply landed on the largest island at Luzon on December 10 and marched toward Manila. On January 23, General Masaharu Homma tried another amphibious landing behind the American lines in Bataan and had great success at first, but artillery fire from Corregidor was able to pin the Japanese down.

MacArthur was forced to retreat to the Bataan Peninsula and to the island fortress of Corregidor. Bataan had two mountains that were covered by jungle. MacArthur's troops chose to defend on the first mountain range, but they did not extend their defense down into the jungle of the valleys. The Japanese saw this mistake and were able to flank the first line of defenses. Now the Americans had to retreat to the alternate line of defense at the second mountain. There were only about ten square miles with 83,000 soldiers and 26,000 civilians who were refugees from the Japanese invasion. The Japanese had bombed Manila, despite it being a free city.

Supplies were low and the defenders began rationing food. MacArthur thought he had enough food and water for six months, but he did not count on all the refugees that would be involved. Everyone went from half-rations down to one-third rations. The Americans and Filipinos were running out of food, water, ammunition, and hope. They were then put on one-quarter rations, and disease and malnutrition were running rampant. Twenty-four thousand soldiers were wounded, sick, or otherwise unable to fight. President Franklin Roosevelt was in a difficult spot. He wanted MacArthur to remain in command, but it looked like the garrison would have to surrender. It would be a major coup for the Japanese and a huge blow to American morale if MacArthur were taken prisoner by the Japanese. Roosevelt ordered MacArthur to abdicate his command and leave by boat to Australia on March 12, 1942.

Surrender On April 3, the Japanese began their final offensive, and it was too much for the Americans and Filipinos trapped on Bataan and Corregidor. Homma had plenty of aircraft and artillery fire to support his attack. The assault was on a wide front and difficult to defend against. The Japanese were overrunning American and Filipino positions. General Edward King surrendered his command to the Japanese General Homma on April 8. The Japanese then shelled the island fortress of Corregidor into submission and final surrender—more than sixteen thousand Japanese artillery shells landed in Corregidor. The island had no real defense against bombing attacks from the air, and the Japanese made the defenders on Corregidor pay. Two thousand Americans died on Corregidor and over eleven thousand were taken prisoner. Total losses in the Philippines debacle totaled over twenty thousand for the Americans and Filipinos.

The March Thus began the Bataan Death March. The Japanese forced all prisoners—9,300 Americans and 45,000 Filipinos—to march ninety miles to a prison camp at Camp O'Donnell. Many died of sickness, starvation, and exhaustion along the way. Prisoners found to be lagging by the Japanese were often bayoneted on the spot. Some escaped and later formed an insurgent army that would resist the Japanese throughout the war. In fact, the Filipinos were the only native people who rebelled against Japanese rule during World War II.

Battle of the Coral Sea and Midway

The battles of the Coral Sea and Midway in May and June of 1942 marked the turning point in the U.S. war with Japan. After suffering multiple defeats in the first six months following the Japanese attack on Pearl Harbor in December 1941, U.S. forces saw the momentum shift in their favor.

After Pearl Harbor If there was anything positive to come out of the tragedy of Pearl Harbor, it was not readily apparent. However, the U.S. Navy got one break. Its fleet of carriers was out at sea during the attack, and the ships were able to escape, although the Japanese carrier fleet still outnumbered the American fleet by ten to three. The shock of Pearl Harbor would eventually awaken the American nascent defense industrial base. American shipbuilders would be able to exceed Japanese production and increase the Navy's ship count

Not surprisingly, the atrocities of the Bataan Death March fueled anti-Japanese propaganda in the United States. *National Archives & Records Administration*

across the board. The shipbuilding would come later. But first, the U.S. Navy needed a victory.

Victory would come in the sky—World War II in the Pacific would hinge on the maneuvering of aircraft carriers and the skill of the naval aviators. The Japanese carrier fleet, called the First Air Fleet, had five hundred aircraft with six large carriers and four light carriers. The Japanese had numerical superiority in carriers, and they had better aircraft. They considered the sailors serving on carriers as the elite of their navy. In 1941 and 1942, the Japanese Zero was the better fighter plane. Their Kate and Val torpedo and dive-bombers had longer ranges and greater payload capacities, although they were somewhat slower than the U.S. bombers. The Americans, on the other hand, had better pilots. The Americans spent the interwar period successfully training naval aviators.

Battle of the Coral Sea

The U.S. navy had three carriers in the Pacific: the *Lexington*, the *Saratoga*, and the *Enterprise*. The *Yorktown* and the *Hornet* would later transfer from the Atlantic fleet. Carrier warfare in 1942 was risky. It was difficult to land on carriers; there was no airborne or ship-borne guidance system. There was also no radar on the American ships at that time. The U.S. dive-bomber, called the Dauntless, was also used for reconnaissance. These planes were the eyes and ears of the fleet. Pilots and copilots had to find their way to the target with good vision, manual navigation, and luck. Naval aviators who were unable to link up with the carrier often ran their planes out of fuel and were forced to bail out. It was an exceedingly dangerous business. If the carrier changed course, the aircraft would have a difficult task in locating it again. And safely landing on the carrier was not an automatic exercise.

The Americans were fortunate to have cracked the Japanese diplomatic code. The Japanese were overconfident after their victory at Pearl Harbor, and they flashed and telegraphed their naval strategy, plans, and tactics with carelessness. This helped the U.S. Navy get back in the fight. The first battle happened close to Port Moresby, near Australia in the Coral Sea. The *Lexington* and *Yorktown* were sent to block the Japanese invasion force. The Japanese had three carriers in the attacking group. It was the first carrier-on-carrier battle in modern warfare. The U.S. and Japanese were separated by 175 miles of ocean, but dive-bombers and torpedo bombers from both sides found the enemy's carriers.

The fighting was fierce. The Japanese carrier *Shokaku* was badly damaged, and the Americans had already sunk the light carrier *Shoho* in a previous encounter. The *Yorktown* was slightly damaged, but the *Lexington* caught fire when its fuel line burst on the flight deck. The ship was abandoned before it sank. The Battle of the Coral Sea was important for the U.S. Navy. It stopped the Japanese navy in that part of the Pacific and gave the American sailors and aviators much valuable battle experience and confidence. The *Yorktown* sailed back to Pearl Harbor, and her damage was repaired in forty-five hours. She then steamed back to link up with the *Enterprise* and the *Hornet*.

Battle of Midway

In 1942, U.S. code-breakers had intercepted a new Japanese plan. The Imperial navy wanted to invade Midway, and the Japanese First Air Fleet was sent to do the job. The First Air Fleet had four carriers steaming to Midway with a total of 272 Japanese bombers and fighters. The Americans had three carriers with only 180 fighters and bombers. The U.S. navy also had aircraft on Midway Island itself—a group of Catalina amphibious flying boats and B-17 Flying Fortresses. The flying boats did an important job of reconnaissance, and one spotted the Japanese invasion fleet on June 3. This confirmed earlier intelligence, and the U.S. Navy would be in a good position to eventually defend Midway. However, the Americans garrisoned on Midway who were to defend against the Japanese attacking force were not as lucky. The Flying Fortresses and Catalinas tried to bomb the attacking Japanese vessels, but they were no match.

Aircraft from the American carriers attacked the Japanese four times, but they were unsuccessful. The Americans had luck on their side during the fifth attack. Japanese Admiral Chuichi Nagumo had planned to make a torpedo bomber attack of his own against the American carriers. However, the invading Midway force called for another bombing run against the Americans on Midway. Thus, Nagumo had his aircraft change from torpedoes to bombs. This took precious time. But he was still able—initially, at least—to repel the attacks from American torpedo bombers and dive-bombers.

There was one American bomber group that was able to get a clear shot at the Japanese carriers. One of the dive-bomber groups from the *Enterprise* had actually gotten lost. Thirty-seven Dauntless dive-bombers had flown 175 miles in the wrong direction. Lieutenant Commander Wade McClusky was able to make corrections in their course, and by happenstance, the Americans stumbled upon the Japanese carrier group. The Americans had fat targets. All of the Japanese planes were refueling; bombs and torpedoes were on the flight deck. The *Akagi* caught fire and was abandoned. The *Kaga* was next. It was hit by four American dive-bombers. The *Soryu* suffered three hits, and it lost propulsion—this made it an easy target for an American submarine, which hit it later. The *Hiryu* got away temporarily, but dive-bombers from the *Enterprise* caught up with her. The bombs set her on fire, and the Japanese crew scuttled the ship.

The Japanese navy was put on the defensive. Their shipbuilders would add only six more carriers during the rest of the war. The Americans would build fourteen new heavy carriers, nine light carriers, and sixty-six escort carriers. It would be a defensive war now for the Japanese in the Pacific—one that would be costly for the Americans.

Guadalcanal

The Battle of Guadalcanal lasted for more than six months between August of 1942 and February of 1943. It involved land, air, and sea forces of the United States and Japan in a heated fight for control of the island of Guadalcanal in the southern Solomon Islands. It was the first major victory of the Allied offensive in the Pacific during World War II.

Shift in Strategy The Battle of Midway had allowed U.S. military planners to change their way of thinking. No longer were they licking their wounds. The Americans took a new posture—they intended to go on the offensive and attack the Japanese. Still, geography favored the Japanese. The Imperial navy and army stretched for thousands of miles of ocean and islands in the Pacific. The Americans would have a lengthy and costly campaign on their hands. They would need to win back territory island by island, capture or rebuild an airfield, and then use the new airfield to launch a new attack on the next island. The main objective would be Tokyo and the home islands of Japan, but these targets were 2,000 miles from the American fleet.

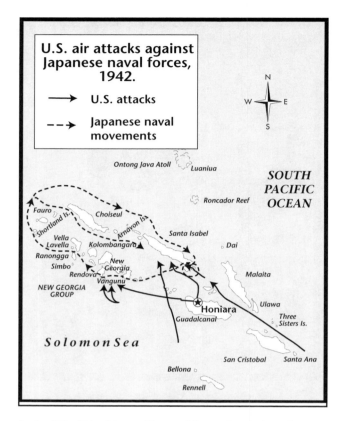

As the Allies "island-hopped" toward Japan, the number of casualties was breathtakingly high, influencing American policy makers' controversial decision to drop atomic bombs on the Japanese mainland. *Reproduced by permission of Gale, a part of Cengage Learning*

Admiral Ernest King, the chief of naval operations, and General George C. Marshall, the army chief of staff, decided to divide the responsibilities in the Pacific between two flag officers. The Pacific fleet would be led by Admiral Chester Nimitz and the army would be led by General Douglas MacArthur in the Southwest Pacific area, with his headquarters in Australia. The Navy would devise the planning and logistics for the amphibious landings that were necessary for the island hopping strategy's success.

That left the marines to fight on the ground and perform the most difficult part of the campaign. This would be particularly challenging because the marines were the smallest branch of service and had the smallest budget. To make matters more difficult, MacArthur was not popular with the navy admirals or marine generals. They saw him as a prima donna and glory-chaser. These personality conflicts made teamwork difficult in the Pacific.

Commanders of the Pacific forces finally reached a compromise. The Americans would take the southern route to attack Japan. The navy and marines would be commanded by Nimitz, although MacArthur would have some command of naval ships, naval and marine aircraft, naval logistics, and marines for certain missions in his sector. This arrangement, of course, was not popular with the navy and marines. MacArthur had inexplicably allowed his air force to be destroyed on the ground in the Philippines during the initial attacks by the Japanese in December 1941. He was warned that an attack was coming, but his planes stayed on the ground. Now he would be demanding navy and marine air support after he lost his own aircraft.

But the commanders from all the services agreed on the order of battle in the Pacific on July 2, 1942. The first task would be for Nimitz and the navy to attack and hold Guadalcanal in the Solomon Islands east of New Guinea. The second task would go to MacArthur, who would lead his army into New Guinea and its offshore island of New Britain. After holding New Guinea, MacArthur would advance on the Japanese air base at Rabaul on New Britain and link up with Nimitz. The third task would then be a combined attack.

Taking Guadalcanal The navy and marine corps drew a difficult mission with Guadalcanal. The difficulty again lay in the geography. Guadalcanal was surrounded by three other islands of the Solomons group held by the Japanese. Approach from New Zealand was the only avenue of advance to the island. This approach ("the Slot") made getting ashore very risky, and resupplying the beachhead would be difficult as well, because successfully dodging Japanese mines, submarines, and attacking aircraft while navigating the Slot would be necessary.

The amphibious landing on August 7, 1942, was not a problem. The First Marine Division established a beachhead on Guadalcanal, and it also made successful landings on the offshore islands of Tulagi, Gavutu, and Tanambogo. The Japanese had only 2,200 troops on Guadalcanal, and they were quickly swept away by the marines. The Japanese high command reacted with alarm. They saw Guadalcanal as an important part of their key defenses and decided the island needed to be retaken at once. A large Japanese force descended on the Americans. The Japanese surprised the American fleet on August 8 and 9. They sunk four U.S. cruisers and damaged one cruiser and two destroyers.

Holding Guadalcanal On August 18, the Japanese sent a marauding force back to Guadalcanal, and the reinforcements kept coming. The attackers were supported by naval gunfire and countless air attacks from Japanese fighters and bombers. The Americans had rebuilt and lengthened the original Japanese airfield and renamed it Henderson Field. The Japanese would not leave it alone, and waves of air attacks harassed the defenders on Henderson Field.

More naval battles would follow at Guadalcanal. The battle of the Eastern Solomons was a costly victory for the Americans, because the *Enterprise* was damaged.

The Americans destroyed a Japanese carrier, cruiser, and destroyer as well as about sixty aircraft, while the Americans lost twenty aircraft. The land battles on Guadalcanal were especially fierce. The Americans were learning what it was like to engage an enemy that was willing to fight to the death without surrender. American marines and soldiers suffered from the extreme conditions of relentless heat and humidity. Malaria and dysentery were common. The fight in defense of Henderson Field occurred at what was soon called "Bloody Ridge." Japanese destroyers, nicknamed the "Tokyo Express," ran the Slot to resupply their own troops and nightly navy battles took place.

One of the major battles during this time period was the Battle of Cape Esperance, in which the Americans surprised and sank a small force of Japanese carriers. The Japanese repaid the Americans with their own victory at the Battle of Santa Cruz, southeast of Guadalcanal, on October 26. They sank the carrier *Hornet* and damaged the *Enterprise*. The Americans shot down one hundred Japanese planes and lost only fifty of their own, but the loss of the *Hornet* hurt the most.

The marines fought a lonely fight at Guadalcanal. Heavy rains in October grounded U.S. planes, and this prevented air support. Japanese Zeroes were able to fly and harass the Marines with endless strafing runs. The fight switched to a significant naval battle in November called the Battle of Guadalcanal—a duel between battleships. The newer American battleships were able to take hits from the Japanese and dish out their own punishment. The Japanese lost their flagship *Hiei* on November 12, and the *Kirishima* two nights later.

By the end of 1942, both sides were sick and weary. The Americans had built up their number of ships in the region and cut off Japanese supplies, which quickly sapped the strength of the remaining soldiers on the islands. The U.S. XIV Corps took control of operations on Guadalcanal, and by February had pushed the Japanese off the island.

Battle of the Bismarck Sea

In early March 1943, U.S. and Australia air forces attacked a Japanese convoy on its way to New Guinea in the Bismarck Sea north of New Britain. They inflicted heavy troop losses and kept the Japanese on the run across the Pacific.

MacArthur Prepares In the early winter and spring of 1943, U.S. General Douglas MacArthur was readying his forces for his assigned task of taking Rabaul in New Britain, the largest island in the Bismarck Archipelago. The island-hopping strategy—taking islands and then using or improving the existing air strips to attack Japanese shipping and logistical chains—was not cost-efficient. It required large quantities of troops, ships, and airplanes. MacArthur asked for five extra divisions and 1,800 aircraft. The Pacific front already had 460,000

American troops and only 380,000 Americans were serving in Europe. A second front in the European war was to soon open in North Africa. The generals in Europe resented MacArthur's request. General George Marshall and others in Washington were exasperated by the interservice bickering going on in the various theatres.

The commanders finally agreed on a plan called Operation Cartwheel. Admiral Chester Nimitz was named commander of the entire Pacific theatre. Admiral William Halsey was given command of southern Pacific operations, while MacArthur retained his command of the Southwest Pacific area out of Australia. This soothed the egos of all three men temporarily. The plan was that MacArthur would envelop Rabaul from the south, and Halsey would come from the north. Halsey would have responsibility for the Solomons, and MacArthur would have New Guinea and the southern Bismarcks. Halsey's objective was Bougainville—located along the Solomon chain of islands. By that time, MacArthur would have the north shore of New Guinea and most of New Britain under control; he would then meet with Halsey in a two-front "pincer" movement focused on Rabaul.

The Japanese still had a say in direction of this fight. The Seventeenth Army was at Rabaul under General Hitoshi Imamura. Imperial headquarters decided on reinforcements and sent the Eighteenth Army with two new divisions under General Hatazo Adachi. In March 1943, the Japanese tried to send 7,000 troop reinforcements to Lae and Salamaua in New Guinea in the Bismarck Sea. They were discovered by American reconnaissance aircraft, and an attack force was sent to stop them.

American Success The Allies had been improving their bombing tactics. MacArthur had given a new Army air corps commander, General George Kenney, more latitude to improve bombing results. American pilots had previously almost always reported bombing successes after missions. But later research and bomb damage assessment in after-action reviews revealed less success. Kenney sought to change these results. He saw that the root of the problem lay at the air corps bombing practice of high-elevation targeting. He instead had his medium bomber aircraft pilots fly at low altitudes and use guns, cannons, and fragmentation bombs. The first attack he tried used the old high-altitude bombing technique, and only one enemy ship was sunk. The next day, 137 American bombers, using the new bombing tactics and escorted by American and Australian fighters, sunk all eight of the Japanese transport craft seeking to reinforce Rabaul. The enemy Zeroes were at high altitude and missed the Allied low-altitude bombing run. Thirty-five hundred Japanese soldiers drowned. Other craft hauling badly needed aircraft fuel and spare parts were also sunk by the American bombers. The American and Australian fighters shot down 102 out of the 150 Japanese fighters involved in the battle. The Battle of the Bismarck Sea was an important morale booster for MacArthur's forces.

THE ROAD BACK

4E1052.07   WWII: THE ROAD BACK, 1943.
Credit: The Granger Collection, New York

American cartoonist D.R. Fitzpatrick made a telling comparison between the German retreat after the Battle of Stalingrad in 1942–1943 and that of Napoleon some 130 years earlier. *The Granger Collection, New York. Reproduced by permission*

Aftermath Admiral Isoroku Yamamoto decided that the gains the Americans were making in New Guinea and the Solomons were unacceptable. He sent a large force of aircraft toward Guadalcanal and Tulagi in April 1943. The Japanese thought they had success against the U.S. navy, but Japanese aviators over-reported their success as well. Yamamoto decided to visit the front anyway and congratulate his pilots. Cryptanalysts monitoring Japanese communications intercepted the message regarding Yamamoto's visit. Admiral Nimitz saw this as an opportunity to get the Japanese leader and score a blow to Japanese morale. A squadron of P-38s intercepted Yamamoto's passenger plane on April 18 and destroyed it over Bougainville, depriving Japan of one of its key leaders.

Battle of Stalingrad

The Battle of Stalingrad (August 1942–February 1943) was, by some measures, the bloodiest battle in history. It pitted Germany against the Soviet Union in a fight for control of the Soviet city of Stalingrad. An estimated 1.5 million people died in the battle. Both sides fought ferociously, but the Soviets were finally able to claim victory.

Germany Looks East German leader Adolf Hitler's plan to occupy France and thus force Britain to sue for peace did not work out the way he envisioned. The Battle of Britain kept Hitler's forces occupied too long. He was itching to get on with the main part of his master plan, which involved an invasion of Russia. Germany and Russia had signed the Molotov-Ribbentrop non-aggression pact in 1939, but this self-serving document did little to change the fact that the Fascists in Germany and the Communists in Russia despised each other ideologically. Each side actively sought to destabilize the other, and the Fascists and Communists even used the Spanish Civil War in the late 1930s as a battleground for their conflict. However, the Molotov-Ribbentrop Pact allowed Hitler to secure his eastern front from attack while fighting to the west. For Stalin, the pact gave him security from a two-front war (against Japan in the east and Germany to the west), and there was always the possibility that Russia would get to stay out of the conflict while Western and Central Europe destroyed one another.

While he signed the treaty, Hitler never really planned to adhere to the terms of the Molotov-Ribbnetrop pact. "Lebensraum," Hitler's belief in more "living space" for the German people, focused on the Soviet Union and the Slavic people. He wished to conquer the Soviet Union and turn it into an agrarian colony for Germany. The Nazis would then control all the natural and agricultural resources of Russia. The Slav resistance would be eliminated, and the Nazis would have the living space they needed to occupy that part of Europe and Asia.

Hitler first needed to conquer the Soviet Union, and this required opening up another front of the war. In the summer of 1942, the German attack began to the north, near Kursk, with the Thirteenth, Fortieth, and Twenty-First armies attacking into Voronezh. The main avenue of approach was the so-called "Don-Donetz Corridor." This pocket was formed in the valley between the Donetz River to the west and the Don River to the east. On July 23, the Führer's Directive Number 45 (also called Operation Brunswick) instructed Army Group A to destroy the Soviets beyond Rostov on the coast of the Sea of Azov. This would deny Soviet resupply and escape lines through the Black Sea.

The Sixth Army was assigned the main effort; it would then be augmented by the Fourth Panzer Army and would speed down the Don-Donetz Corridor and seize Stalingrad. Hitler saw Stalingrad as the decisive point. If he could quickly attack and hold Stalingrad, the Germans could break the Soviet will to fight. Army Group A would then be able to rush south toward the Caucasian oil fields. The Germans enjoyed early success with this plan. The Soviet defenders seemed to melt away. The summer weather was fair, and the Germans even stopped to bathe in the Don River.

By August 1942, the Stalingrad front around the western part of the city had formed. Kletskaya and Kachalinskaya, suburbs of Stalingrad, were surrounded. Soviet defenders of Kalach, located to the west of Stalingrad, had to fall back to the city itself. Stalingrad sat in the valley of the Don and Volga Rivers. If the Germans could hold Stalingrad, they could effectively break the Soviet lines of communication from the Caspian Sea in the south to the Bryansk front in the north. The main fighting moved into the center of the city during the last weeks of August. There was a strip of wooden buildings surrounded by factories that ran for nearly twenty miles along along the west bank of the Volga River. Most of the heavy fighting was taking place there. That part of the central city was reduced to rubble during the coming weeks. The battle lines were drawn clearly around Stalingrad by the fall of 1942. Hitler looked for a quick way to end the siege of Stalingrad, but Soviet leader Joseph Stalin had other plans.

Stalin Digs In The Soviets wanted to attempt a daring counterattack. The plan was for the Soviet Sixty-second Army to destroy the Germans in the city while other Soviet troops attempted a flanking maneuver to envelop the Germans on the southern part of the Volga. However, the Soviets decided they needed every soldier to defend the city. Stalin had already rushed reinforcements and personally supervised the defense plans.

He ordered his troops to take "not a step backward." Stalin monitored his generals closely to watch for any signs of morale loss or plans of retreat. The city was getting close to falling. The Germans had torched the wooden buildings in the city's central business district. The Soviets were backing up against the Volga River—some lines were between four and ten miles away from the river. This line of defense was held by three divisions of the Sixty-second Army. The unit had sixty tanks, and its troops were skilled street fighters. However, the Germans moved three infantry divisions in one thrust—and four infantry and Panzer divisions in another—toward the street fighting from the north of the city along the Volga. It looked like the Soviets were doomed. The Germans aimed their artillery, and shells were soon falling close to the Soviet defenders.

The fight in Stalingrad was dirty and man-to-man. It was a platoon- and squad-level fight. The Germans and Soviets pounced on each other with rifle and pistol fire along with plenty of hand grenades. They used sewers as tunnels and crept along rooftops using chimneys and fire escapes to travel from building to building.

The Germans attempted one last breakthrough in mid-October. Five German infantry divisions and two tank divisions supported by some two thousand Luftwaffe sorties pushed the Soviets to the limit. They finally broke through at the Stalingrad Tractor Plant. But the advance slowed, and the front stabilized. The Soviets still held on to part of the tractor plant and part of the

Pilots from the all-African American "Tuskegee Airmen" company, in Italy, 1940. © *UPI/Bettmann/Corbis*

barricades factory. They lost the Red October Factory. The Soviets had reinforcements and hospitals to treat the wounded on the other side of the Volga, and they were able to ferry supplies, ammunition, and fresh troops to help relieve the defenders.

Perseverance Pays Italian, Romanian, and Hungarian troops—German allies—were on the outskirts of the siege. The Soviets worked to break this fragile outer shell. Marshal G. K. Zhukov's plan had two movements—one from the southwest and the city, and one from the Don River area, that consisted of three tank and eight infantry armies in total. By November 23, the pincers came together at Kalach on the Don River west of Stalingrad. The plan immediately started working. The Third and Fourth Romanian Armies were routed. The Fourth German Panzer Army was in retreat, and the Sixth Army was stuck inside Stalingrad. Stalin's counterattack had come after all.

Now the weather and the elements were on the Soviet's side. Winter was coming soon, and the Germans were not ready for it. They tried a change of

commanders and brought in new reinforcements for a winter breakthrough attack, but this failed. The German allies from Italy, Hungary, and Romania lost their will to fight during the cruel winter of 1942–1943. The German forces finally surrendered on February 2, 1943. The Soviets took control of more than 100,000 German prisoners. The Germans had lost the entire Sixth Army—twenty-two divisions. It was the first Soviet victory of the war—its story would go down in history as an epic example of Soviet solidarity and bravery.

Invasion of Sicily

The Allied invasion of Sicily was launched July 9, 1943. This amphibious and airborne attack was the beginning of the campaign to take Italy.

In the spring of 1943, German leader Adolf Hitler was occupied with several theaters of combat. The Allies had increased the rate of bombings raids over Germany. The sea battle on the Atlantic raged on, and the eastern front in the Soviet Union was dragging. Hitler was displeased with the performance of Italian troops in general, especially in North Africa. Italy simply was not

Ernest Hemingway (center) was one of many American intellectuals who supported the anti-Fascist Loyalists during the 1936–1939 Spanish Civil War.   *London Express/Getty Images*

mobilized to fight World War II. It lost 600,000 lives during World War I. Italy's economy could only provide one-tenth of what Germany's could provide to defense industries. Many of its young males had immigrated to America. Italy could also not keep up with the United States and Britain in terms of the production of tanks, ships, and airplanes. The combat equipment it did produce was often technologically generations behind the equipment of the Allies.

What was even more difficult for Italy was that many Italians did not view allied countries such as the United States and Britain as mortal enemies. The Italians who defended new conquests in North Africa often did not want to be in the fight in the first place. Thus, the number of Italians taken prisoner in East Africa in 1941, in Libya in 1941–1942, and in Tunisia was a staggering number—over 350,000. Italian cities were also receiving daily and nightly bombing raids from Allied aircraft. This weakened the country's resolve to fight. There were even plots to stage a coup against Mussolini.

Allied Offensive   The British at this time wanted to strike from southern Europe and open an offensive against Hitler's "soft underbelly" in southern France

and the Balkans. The invasion of Sicily was a surprise to Hitler, although not a surprise to Mussolini. The Allies also deceived many commanders in the region by planting fake plans on a dead body. This ruse led them to believe that the invasion would be on Corsica, Sardinia, or Greece.

The Allies planned the invasion to be in Sicily after all. In the early morning darkness on July 9–10, 1943, a huge Allied force began the attack. It was one of the first joint and combined arms invasions. The Allies again used a strategic feature that was to serve them well throughout the war—unity of command. Instead of several commands from different nationalities bickering and quarreling with one another, the Allies were led by one commander, the Supreme Allied Commander, General Dwight D. Eisenhower. Eisenhower had done an adequate job in the previous North African campaign, and diplomacy was Eisenhower's strength. He could massage the fragile egos of General George Patton and British Field Marshal Bernard Montgomery.

General Sir Harold Alexander commanded the Allied Fifteenth Army Group made up of Patton's U.S. Seventh Army and Montgomery's British Eighth Army. The attack on Sicily was the second great amphibious assault (North Africa was the first) of the war. It was a challenge for the Allies. The command staffs had to be integrated, because American, British, Canadian, and French troops took part in the invasion. And these were also joint commands with separate army, navy, and air force components and differing tactics, techniques, and procedures.

At least 160,000 troops took part in the invasion. They used 14,000 vehicles, 600 tanks, and 1,800 artillery pieces. The amphibious fleet consisted of 3,000 landing craft. The combined Allied Air Force had 3,700 aircraft commanded by British Air Marshal Arthur Tedder that used bases in Tunisia and Malta. The Axis Powers had 200,000 troops defending Sicily. The Italian Sixth Army had five ill-trained and ill-equipped coastal divisions, five infantry divisions, and two German armored divisions. The Germans and Italians had 1,600 planes.

Patton's Seventh Army landed at Licata, Gela, and Scoglitti on the western side of the island. Montgomery's Eighth Army attacked the eastern tip between Cape Passero and Syracuse. Both of the army groups used airborne troops to land behind enemy lines. However, the bad weather and wind scattered the airborne drops and also complicated the landing procedures. Despite the weather, the Allies achieved some surprise. The Germans were able to recover first and counterattacked the American landings at Gela. The American First Infantry Division suffered the brunt of these attacks. The British troops on the western side of the army defended against similar attacks. Naval gunfire and ground artillery helped both armies gain traction.

More airborne drops continued the fight on July 11 without much success. Some of these troops were killed by friendly fire. By July 12, both army groups established strong beachheads and were able to bring in reinforcements and supplies. Italian troops were melting away and the two German Panzer Divisions were conducting a fighting withdrawal.

Alexander's plan was to have Montgomery's army conduct the main effort and drive to Messina while skirting Mount Etna. This would block the German and Italian escape routes. Patton was to serve as the supporting element on the western coast, and he immediately looked at the map and saw glory. Patton commanded his forces to head north and he reached Palermo before Montgomery. On July 22, Patton was in control of Palermo and he now focused on beating Montgomery to Messina. There was difficult fighting against the retreating Germans in Troina and Fratello, but Patton was able to reach Messina before Montgomery. The Germans evacuated to the mainland of Italy and the U.S. Third Infantry Division entered Messina on August 17.

The Allies suffered 16,000 in total casualties, including 7,319 in American losses. Most of the Axis losses were Italian prisoners, but in total the casualties

were 164,000, including nearly 32,000 Germans killed, wounded, or captured.

Monte Cassino

The Allies faced the Germans in a series of battles at Monte Cassino, Italy, in the first months of 1944. They were attempting to break through German lines and head for Rome, with the aim of driving the Germans out of Italy.

Although the campaign to wrest control of Italy from the Germans had started quickly, with Field Marshal Montgomery making diversionary attacks on the southern tip of the Italian boot and General Mark Clark conducting amphibious landings at Salerno in September 1943, the Allies had bogged down in central Italy. After Mussolini's death, the Italians had negotiated for peace under Marshal Pietro Badoglio. But the Germans still remained in Italy, and they were ready to fight under General Albert Kesselring.

The Allied Invasion of Italy Kesselring first showed his mettle during the Salerno invasion, the Allied landing in Italy. On September 9, General Mark Clark's (1896–1984) Fifth Army, made up of the U.S. Sixth Corps and the British Tenth Corps, hit the beaches at Salerno. They thought they would achieve total surprise and did not even prep the landing zones with artillery fire. Kesselring had shifted a German armored division to the Sele River to meet the American and British forces. The Royal Air Force (RAF) supplied air cover, but the Germans brought down substantial machine-gun and artillery fire on the beaches. There were heavy Allied losses at first, but artillery forward observers soon called in naval gunfire, and many of the German positions were silenced. Four small beachheads were established, and troops and supplies came pouring in. However, the terrain still favored the defending Germans. The Allies were caught in the lowland of the seven-mile-wide Sele River valley.

Kesselring regrouped his forces for a counterattack on September 12 and 13. He had four armored divisions and two infantry divisions. The Germans succeeded in pushing the Americans back to the original landing zones. The Allies kept up an intense barrage of naval gunfire and air force bombing runs, but time was running out. The Eighty-second Airborne was able to join the fight and augment the Sixth Corps' area of operations. The Americans began to gain momentum. Both Allied Corps were able to finally push the Germans back. The Germans achieved what they sought—to delay the Allies at Salerno and keep Montgomery from advancing northward too quickly. The Germans could now fall back and form a tough defense along the Volturno River north of Naples that stretched east to Termoli.

Axis Defense The terrain of central Italy favored the defending Germans. The mountain ranges are as high as 10,000 feet with steep peaks and gullies all over the landscape. Kesselring put nine divisions of his best troops on the coast to protect his flanks on the Adriatic and the Mediterranean. The natural terrain of the Appenine Mountains made for a good defense. The rivers along the mountain valleys flowed quickly and were difficult to cross. The British and Americans did not communicate very well on the attack either, and the winter weather was coming on soon. If Kesselring had commanded more troops, the Italian campaign would have been even more difficult for the Allies, because they could only deploy nine divisions of their own. The Germans had fortified positions in the mountains. Rome was 120 difficult miles away.

The main Allied attack was in the west near the great fortress abbey of Monte Cassino. This location was known as the Gustav Line—the strongest position of the whole Kesselring defense. The fortifications were ten miles deep and interlocked with the Garigliano, Liri, and Rapido rivers. The Allies conducted five attacks on the Gustav Line between October 12, 1943, and January 17, 1944. The Americans pushed up toward the Volturno River but found the Germans had blown up all the bridges. The mountain fighting had gone on for a month, with heavy casualties to the Allies. They only gained about forty miles after the landings at Salerno. There were already 9,690 casualties—6,843 of these were Americans.

The Fifth Army had drawn the assignment of attacking Monte Cassino and the Gustav Line. They had to wait out winter snowstorms until January 5, when American and French units tried to attack and reach the Rapido River below the Cassino Heights. General Clark ordered the Thirty-sixth Division from the Texas National Guard to assault across the Rapido. It was an exceedingly dangerous mission. The valley was full of German mines that had to be cleared. Then the force had to use boats to cross the river while machine guns and artillery fired down from Monte Cassino.

Clark had predicted this operation would result in high casualties, and he was right. It took the Thirty-sixth Division three days to cross the river. A few of the subordinate units reached the other side, but they had no machine-gun or artillery support. Maneuvering on the other side of the river was impossible. So these units were forced to swim back to the other shore. One thousand soldiers of the six thousand–strong division died in the battle. This stopped any further attacks toward Rome up the north-south corridor of Highway 6, the most direct route. Supreme Allied Commander Dwight Eisenhower favored sending reinforcements and then making an amphibious landing at Anzio in an attack called Operation Shingle. The Allies were now attempting to bypass the Gustav Line, and it would be up to the invasion force at Anzio to break through and advance to Rome.

Anzio

The Allied difficulties on the Gustav Line and at Monte Cassino in early 1944 emphasized the need to do something different to break through the German defenses in central Italy. The planners decided to make the amphibious landing at Anzio, about fifty miles northwest of Cassino. The idea was to cut the communications of Field Marshal Albert Kesselring's Gustav Line and isolate it from resupply. If the Allies had success at Anzio, they could then move on to the Alban Hills, key terrain twenty miles south of Rome. Once the Allies were in possession of the Alban Hills, they could rain artillery fire down on German positions.

The operational art behind the planning of Anzio was superb; however, implementing the operation was going to be difficult. First, it was unusual for the main effort of an attack to have a smaller number of personnel than the support. The Allies were short on landing craft and troops. Most of the support shipping and manpower was focused on the coming Allied invasion of France (called Operation Overlord, but remembered as D-Day). The landing on Anzio was meant to be synchronous with the attacks on the Gustav Line and Monte Cassino, but those attacks were conducted too far apart to be of mutual support. Kesselring was also one of the best defensive commanders the Germans had, and some of his troops were elite forces. After some compromise at the flag-officer level, the Anzio operation called "Shingle" was finally in motion. Operation Overlord allowed some of its landing craft to be transferred to Italy, and the planners agreed to delay their attack until later in the summer. The Pacific theater contributed some ships to the Anzio landing as well. Mark Clark's Fifth Army would be assigned the job of attacking the Gustav Line and conducting the Anzio landing. British General Bernard Montgomery left the Eighth Army to assume command of parts of Operation Overlord in Britain. He was replaced by General Sir Oliver Leese. Leese would take the Eighth army on a slow advance up the Adriatic side of Italy.

Allied Landing   The Texas Thirty-sixth Infantry Division was met by the Fifteenth Panzer Grenadier Division at Monte Cassino, and the Americans lost almost two regiments (killed or captured). Kesselring sent his reserves to hold that part of the Gustav Line. This made the Anzio landing a surprise to the Germans, because they had few troops in the area. The U.S. Sixth Corps made the amphibious assault, and they were made up of about four and a half divisions of around 50,000 soldiers and 5,200 vehicles under the command of Major General John Porter Lucas. Lucas felt that he did not have enough troops for the mission. A rehearsal for the invasion resulted in a number of landing craft being sunk, and this reduced morale. The landing was successful after a heavy naval bombardment, and most of the troops were ashore by January 22, 1944, without much enemy resistance. The U.S. Rangers and British commandoes went on the beach first, and they established a beachhead for the British First Division.

Their objective was the Alban Hills, and Clark decided to wait until most of the Sixth Corps was ashore and ready to fight. Allied aircraft had the advantage in the sky, but could not immediately protect the troops. The delay in the advance gave the Germans time to go counterattack. Naval gunfire kept the Germans from overrunning the Allies. But by January 24, there were already three German divisions facing the attackers. Action on the Gustav Line simmered down, and Kesselring was able to divert troops from this stronghold to relieve Anzio. German leader Adolf Hitler ordered reinforcements from France, Germany, and the Balkans to help Anzio. General Eberhard von Mackensen moved his Fourteenth Army headquarters down from northern Italy to command the defense of Anzio. It looked like the Allies were in for a major fight.

Stalled on the Beach The early fighting favored the Germans. Three U.S. Ranger battalions were tasked to attack the Alban Hills, but they were ambushed and nearly destroyed. The U.S. Third and Forty-fifth Divisions were blocked and sputtered to a halt. The same thing happened to the British First Division and the U.S. First Armored. By early February, the Sixth Corps had not advanced beyond the same narrow beachhead. The Germans held the high terrain and continued to fire down at the Allies. There was no room for construction of a friendly airfield, and thus the Luftwaffe was able to challenge Allied air power. The German fighters constantly disrupted resupply efforts on the beachhead.

Then the Germans decided to counterattack on February 15 and push the Allies back to the sea. After two weeks of fighting, it looked like the Germans were going to get their way. Clark felt the pressure—army high command in Washington, D.C., and the media had already questioned his expertise after the failures on the Rapido River.

He had to act. He first fired Lucas and replaced him on February 23 with Major General Lucian K. Truscott Jr.,who had previously led the Third Infantry Division. Truscott was able to expand the beachhead a little, and he personally led units at the front to restore morale, but the delays were costly in manpower and planning. During the four months from the original Anzio landing and the second Allied offensive in Italy, the Americans had 23,000 casualties while the British had 9,203. The Anzio offensive still needed landing craft to haul supplies and reinforcements. That meant the landings in France would have to wait.

Onward to Rome The Americans wanted no more delay for D-Day, but Churchill thought the British could lead the attack on France from Italy through central Europe. The higher command compromised and agreed on a new all-out offensive in Italy. General Sir Harold Alexander took control of the planning in Italy and directed the Eighth Army to turn west from the Adriatic side of Italy and attack the Monte Cassino area

and then rush to the north to link up with Clark's Sixth Corps. This meant that Clark had to achieve a breakthrough at Anzio. The plan started working on May 11, but with heavy casualties.

Alexander's Fifteenth Army Group had the mission of attacking the Cassino area on the Gustav Line. The U.S. Fifth Army, the U.S. Second Corps, and a Free French Corps toiled on a front from the east coast of Italy to the Rapido River. This group moved toward the north while the Eighth Army, the British Thirteenth Corps, and a Polish Corps moved to attack the Gustav Line at Cassino. All attacks worked fairly quickly, and Clark's Sixth Corps was finally able to break out at Anzio. Truscott was ordered by Clark to take the Alban Hills before turning north to Rome. The Germans were able to escape by taking Highway 6 to the north of Rome while Clark entered Rome to parades on May 5. It would be a short celebration because attention would turn to Normandy and the D-Day landings on June 6, 1944.

Battle of Normandy

The Battle of Normandy was the massive Allied invasion of France, popularly known as D-Day. It took months of planning and preparation, as the Allies knew that the Germans occupying France were fully expecting an attempted invasion, and they would have to fight hard to land troops successfully. On June 6, 1944, Supreme Allied Commander Dwight Eisenhower gave the command for the invasion to commence.

German Preparations The Germans thought they were prepared for an Allied invasion of France. Their top two commanders, Field Marshal Gerd von Rundstedt and Field Marshal Erwin Rommel, disagreed about what to expect. Rundstedt believed that coastal defenses were only effective to slow the enemy and that it was essential for troops to remain in reserve and wait to strike the enemy at the most opportune moment. Rommel believed less in reserves and more in massing maneuver elements at critical areas. Rommel, upon arrival from a post in northern Italy, immediately ordered more mines to be laid on the avenues of approach of an amphibious invasion and on obvious landing zones to defend against raids from airborne troops.

Rommel also found that his defending force was not mobile and was mainly made up of infantry and airborne infantry tied to their positions. There were forty-six of these divisions, which would total sixty when the Panzer and Panzergrenadier divisions were added—around 500,000 German troops. Rommel did not think that he had enough tanks. If he was forced to keep his few Panzers in reserve, he knew the Allies, with their multitudes of Sherman tanks, would eventually overwhelm his defenses. Air support would also be a problem for the Germans. The vaunted Luftwaffe was down to 300 aircraft in France. The Allies would have over 12,000 aircraft on D-Day. However, the Germans were very proud

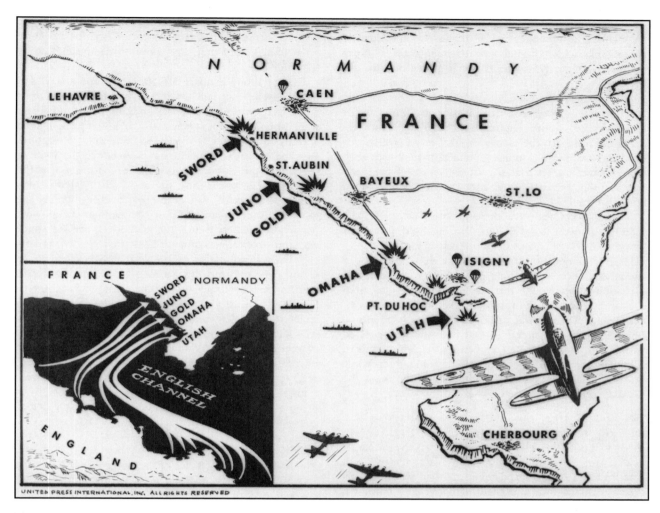

This UPI news map details the invasion launched by American, British, and Canadian trips on June 6, 1944. © *Bettmann/Corbis*

of their Atlantic Wall—the miles of entanglements and obstacles skirting the Normandy beaches. The material was taken from the old French Maginot Line (a system of fortifications along the French-German border). But this defensive fortification was not complete; Rundstedt was not much of a taskmaster, and the soldiers assigned to build the Atlantic Wall took their time.

Allied Groundwork Operation Overlord was the code name for the cross-channel invasion of Normandy. The Allies had a plan that aimed to confuse the Germans as to where the landing would take place. The Allies hoped to make the Germans think the assault would take place in the Pas-de-Calais through the Strait of Dover, the narrowest part of the English Channel. German leader Adolf Hitler, strangely enough, thought part of the Allied attack could come from Norway, and he even had eleven divisions stationed there from 1944 until the end of the war. The Allied ruse was called Operation Fortitude, and it relied on broadcasting misinformation about the plans for Pas-de-Calais. Operation Fortitude cast U.S. General

George Patton as the leader, since the Germans were more likely to believe that the fiery general would be in charge of an operation of this magnitude. Some of the German intelligence apparatus fell for the trick, but Hitler was not fooled. He knew that Normandy would be a good location for the landing, and in the spring of 1944, he told his subordinates to focus defense efforts in that area.

Rommel was still concerned about German armor. He thought it better to pick one beach and place at least one armored division there instead of keeping the whole force in reserve. If the gamble paid off, the Panzers could do a lot of damage to an amphibious landing. If the Panzers were placed badly, they could always recover and maneuver to get back into the fight. In contrast, Field Marshal von Rundstedt wanted to keep the tanks in reserve. Hitler settled the argument between the two generals and gave each three armored divisions with the instructions that Rundstedt would get Hitler's personal approval before deploying the tanks. British General

Bernard Montgomery, who had fought against Rommel frequently, thought Rommel would have total control of those tanks and would deploy them forward at Normandy. Fortunately for the Allies, Rommel did not get his way.

The Allies also had air superiority in France. This was not only important for the invasion itself, but also in the weeks and months leading up to that day. The Germans did not have the planes to do a very good reconnaissance across the English Channel. If they had, they would have known that the objective was Normandy because that was the only part of the channel deep enough for all those ships.

Operation Overlord code named the beaches of Normandy from west to east: Utah, Omaha, Gold, Juno, and Sword. The naval part of Overlord was awesome—6,483 ships, including 4,000 landing craft, were to take part in the attack. Seven battleships, twenty-three cruisers, and 104 destroyers would provide naval gunfire to prep the landing zone. One thousand Dakota transport planes would deposit three airborne divisions in France—hundreds of other aircraft would haul the gliders filled with infantry, artillery men, and engineers. Thousands of Allied bombers would be escorted by 5,000 fighters while the bombers dropped 5,000 pounds of bombs on the German defenses near the beaches.

The Fight Begins On June 6, 1944, Operation Overlord, or "D-Day" as it became known, began. More than 176,000 troops came ashore on five separate beaches on a sixty-mile stretch from Varreville to Caen. The invading troops faced mines, barbed wire, and pill boxes with machine guns and artillery. The battle on Omaha Beach was the bloodiest. There were only four paths from the beach, consisting of long and steep valleys. The Germans occupied fortified defensive positions along the entire beach. The weather was also the worst at Omaha. The troops were supposed to be supported by "floating" tanks upheld by floating canvas aprons known as "bloomers." Twenty-seven of the thirty-two tanks did not float but sank to the bottom, killing their crews. The advancing infantry troops were cut to pieces by the Germans.

The three infantry divisions were scattered by the winds of the terrible weather on D-Day. The 101st and 82nd Airborne Divisions had the most casualties, and it was difficult for them to succeed in their assigned tasks—to block the escape routes of retreating Germans.

There were difficulties throughout Normandy. The weather was terrible. The bombers and naval gunfire missed their targets. The underwater obstacles stopped or slowed the landing craft. Many soldiers were shot before they even got to the beach, and those who did make it ashore barely moved. But the leaders on the beach took over, grabbing their men and leading them up the beaches. Small groups started advancing as more troops landed on the sand. The destroyers crept close to the beaches and supplied naval gunfire to support the ground troops. The American Fifth Corps barely hung on at Omaha, but they carved out a small beachhead by that night.

The three British beaches—Gold, Juno, and Sword—were naturally protected by reefs. The British faced the same problems as the Americans and losses were heavy, but they repulsed a counterattack by the Twenty-first Panzer Division and were able to establish small beachheads. The Germans were not ready. Some of the officers, including Rommel, were not even in the area of operations during the attack. Rundstedt's plan was to slow the Allies up at the beaches and then use the tanks to finish them off. But the German tanks were needed immediately and the defenders needed quick decisions from their command—neither need was met.

The transformation of the Normandy beaches from a killing zone to a modern harbor was an amazing feat of maritime engineering. Tugboats brought in what Churchill called "floating ports." The British leader designed great concrete boxes that would be supported by a complex network of girders, beams, and plates to build a port in a matter of weeks. "Mulberry A," the American port, was destroyed by a storm, but "Mulberry B," the British port, survived. After ten days of prep work, all manner of Allied ships were transporting supplies and reinforcements to France. It was now up to the Allied ground troops to begin taking France back from the Germans.

Battle of the Bulge

The horribly bloody Battle of the Bulge pitted American and British forces against the Germans in the snow-covered Ardennes Forest starting in December 1944. The Germans "bulged" westward into Allied lines, with the aim of dividing then encircling the Allied armies. Although the Germans were ultimately unsuccessful, the battle cost the Allies dearly. The Americans suffered more than 80,000 casualties.

Progress through Europe After the breakthrough at Normandy on D-Day, the Allies gained momentum. The British were able to take Brussels on September 3, 1944, and the Allies captured Antwerp the next day. The rest of Belgium and Luxembourg was soon in Allied hands. However, there was a problem behind these triumphs: How to keep the advancing Allied armies supplied? The Allied air force had been so good at destroying the Nazi's system of logistics, especially railroads, that the fast-moving generals like Bernard Montgomery and George Patton had to depend on trucks and roads. This was a problem as winter approached. The taking of Antwerp was good news since it was the largest port in Europe. However, neither Patton nor Montgomery was pleased. They each thought the Allied advance should be on a narrower front and, of course, each general thought he alone should be getting all the food, fuel, and ammunition he requested.

Operation Autumn Mist The Germans faced many problems after their failure at Normandy. German leader Adolf Hitler thought that the Allied advance was only temporary and that it was overextended. His answer was to counterattack, a folly that had been the undoing of German armies in the Soviet Union and North Africa. Hitler first wanted reinforcements and had his generals comb through the ranks to take any person from the rear to serve in newly formed divisions. Most of these new soldiers were young and inexperienced or old, sickly, and wounded. The plan was to recreate the *blitzkrieg* successes of 1940 with a winter attack through the Ardennes Forest to retake Antwerp. This surprise attack would be called *Wacht am Rhein* or "watch on the Rhine." When the operation actually began, it was named Operation Autumn Mist. The operation included twenty-five fresh German divisions of 150,000 additional soldiers. They hoped that retaking Antwerp would allow V-2 rockets to be fired into London continually and it would allow the Germans to cut-off, encircle, and destroy the British Second and Canadian First Armies. Further attacks on the Americans would follow.

Winter in northern Europe was the worst time of year to fight; snow and ice made much of the forest impassable. The Ardennes Forest offered the Germans cover from the Allied Air Force; however, it was difficult to traverse the terrain. Most passages through the forest only allowed four tanks abreast to travel. It would be slow going. Although the Germans were able to refill old elite divisions such as the First, Second, Ninth, and Twelfth SS Panzer Divisions and the Second, Ninth, 116th, and Lehr Panzer Divisions, the new troops were far from elite. These were often rear-echelon soldiers with no combat experience; some had even been taken from Poland and Czechoslovakia. These troops did not speak German, and many actually wanted to be fighting for the Allies instead.

Autumn Mist was a good plan to achieve tactical surprise. The Americans certainly did not expect a winter attack through the Ardennes. They had only four divisions defending that area of operations—the Fourth, Twenty-eighth, and 106th Infantry Divisions plus the Ninth Armored Division. The Fourth and the Twenty-eighth were attempting to rest and refit after the Battle of the Huertgen Forest, where they had lost 9,000 troops. The 106th had never seen action, and the Ninth Armored was relatively inexperienced.

On the morning of December 16, 1944, Operation Autumn Mist began with the American Twenty-eighth Division caught on its heels. These soldiers did some damage to the attacking German Sixth and Fifth Panzer Armies, but the Americans quickly fell back. The 106th Division was surrounded.

The Germans managed to execute a plan called "Operation *Greif,*" which wreaked havoc behind Allied lines. The 150th Brigade was a German special opera-

TEHERAN CONFERENCE

The "Big Three" Allied leaders—Franklin Roosevelt, Winston Churchill, and Joseph Stalin—realized that there would be a new world order after the war, and they knew it was time to make plans for postwar reconstruction and alignment. There would have to be some balance of power among the Western democracies and the Soviet Union. Stalin saw a chance for Communism to spread into areas where developing countries could throw off the yoke of British rule and then choose Communism as their form of government. The "Big Three" met in Teheran from November 28 to December 1, 1943, to begin planning the peace now in their sights.

The immediate issue was to achieve the peace. The Allies agreed to a massive, coordinated invasion of German-occupied Europe, which would begin in the spring of 1944. The plan was codenamed "Operation Overlord," but it is more widely remembered as D-Day. They agreed that the invasion of France would need a supreme allied commander and that General Dwight Eisenhower should take that role.

The conference participants were also interested in protecting themselves, their allies, and their spheres of influence for the duration of the war and beyond. They agreed to support Turkey and Iran should they need it, but the issue of Poland's fate was more complicated. There was a Polish government in exile in London. There were also thousands of Poles now hoping for a free, independent, and democratic country after the war. But Russia had been invaded via Poland many times throughout history. Stalin was not going to let the Western democracies encroach on Poland—he demanded that about the eastern one-third of the prewar Poland be annexed to the Soviet Union. Churchill and Roosevelt reluctantly agreed. The East-West divide that characterized the Cold War had thus begun.

tions unit whose 150 members spoke flawless English and wore American uniforms. They were sent to cause confusion behind American lines through sabotage and terrorism. As a result, the Germans were able to achieve tactical and strategic surprise, push through and widen a salient toward Antwerp, and reach American fuel dumps to resupply their own tanks. It was very close to an Allied disaster. German troops commanded by First Panzer Division Lieutenant Colonel Joachim Peiper executed more than eighty American prisoners at Malmedy Road. The pocket of Germans in Allied territory created a "bulge" on the map, leading to the American name for the Ardennes operation: "Battle of the Bulge."

"Nuts!" to Surrender The American troops were able to hold their ground after the initial surprise. The Ninety-ninth and Second Divisions blocked the Sixth SS Panzer Army at the Monschau Forest and Eisenborn Ridge. The American Fourth Infantry held valiantly against the Fifth Panzer and German Seventh Army's repeated attacks. The inexperienced Ninth Armored actually did a good job at holding St. Vith. The 101st Airborne Assault Division was surrounded in Bastogne, but the "Screaming Eagles" division (as the 101st is known) held out bravely. This siege of Bastogne is remembered for the famous words from the 101st's commander in Bastogne, Brigadier General Tony McAuliffe: when handed a demand for surrender from the German commander, his reply was, "Nuts!"

Now it was the Germans who were overextended. Their wide axis of attack was divided at St. Vith and Bastogne. Montgomery brought two of his British divisions in support, but it was Patton who saved the day. Somehow, with only twenty-four hours of planning, Patton's Third Army halted its current attack going from west to east in the southern part of France near Metz. Patton then turned his army to the north and raced up to Bastogne to relieve the beleaguered 101st Airborne.

The weather finally broke on December 23 and the clear skies enabled the Allied air force to cause extensive damage to the remaining German tanks. The next day, Patton's Fourth Armored Division linked up with the 101st in Bastogne and made short work of the Germans there.

Despite its successful outcome, the Battle of the Bulge was a painful reminder to the Americans about the danger of being caught unprepared. Many of the Americans were still in their summer uniforms in December. The Germans were better prepared to fight in the cold and they were also able to hurt the Americans with the infiltrations of Operation *Greif* and its coordinated terrorist attacks behind friendly lines. The Americans were fortunate they had the personnel, spare parts, fuel, and equipment to prolong the fighting in December 1944. Without inspiring performances by many American units, the Battle of the Bulge could have been a disaster for the Allies.

Saipan

The Battle on Land   On June 15, 1944, just days after the D-Day invasion, Operation Forager began in the Pacific's Marianas Islands. The American island-hopping strategy was still in effect, as was the Japanese will to fight to the last man. The Americans established a beachhead at Saipan, but the Japanese defenders were intensely dedicated.

Admiral Marc Mitscher's Task Force 58, a battle group of aircraft carriers, softened Saipan's defenses by destroying 200 Japanese fighters and bombers while they were still on the ground. The carrier-based American planes also sank a dozen cargo ships. Admiral Richmond Turner's amphibious force of 127,000 U.S. personnel in some 530 warships came ashore. Mitscher's battleships, cruisers, and destroyers bombarded Japanese positions on Saipan. The Second and Fourth Marine Divisions came ashore and immediately engaged with

Admiral Chuichi Nagumo's Thirty-first Japanese Army. The marines barely established a beachhead, and the Twenty-seventh Infantry Division had to land as reinforcements. Mitscher's carrier battle group had to leave to join the Philippine Sea Battle, which left the Saipan invaders with no air or naval gunfire support.

The Americans advanced slowly because the Japanese had prepared a careful defense. By July 19, most of the enemy had been killed when 3,000 surviving Japanese carried out a last-ditch bayonet attack. The American losses were 3,126 killed, 13,160 wounded, and 326 missing. Japanese Admiral Nagumo and General Yoshitsugu Saito committed suicide on July 6, and three days later, 7,000 more Japanese would commit suicide rather than be captured by the Americans. Only 2,000 surrendered.

The Battle at Sea   When Saipan was attacked, Admiral Jizaburo Ozawa's fleet steamed through the southern Sulu Sea to defend it. Ozawa had a force of five battleships, five heavy and four light carriers, eleven heavy and two light cruisers, and twenty-eight destroyers. Admiral Raymond Spruance had seven heavy and eight light carriers, eight heavy and thirteen light cruisers, and sixty-nine destroyers. The Americans had 956 aircraft, and the Japanese had 473, but Ozawa could control an additional one hundred planes from the islands of Guam, Rota, and Yap in the Marianas Islands.

The sea battle started on June 19, 1944, when the Japanese spotted the Fifth Fleet's ships. These were 300 miles away from Ozawa's advance guard of four light carriers and 500 miles from his main group. Mitscher's Task Force 58 of four carrier battle groups was ninety miles northwest of Guam and 110 miles southwest of Saipan, but Spruance and his battle group were nearby. Ozawa decided to launch four successive raids, and Mitscher was ready and sent his fighters to intercept them. He also cleared his flight decks by putting his bombers in the air. American submarines in the area attacked Ozawa's ships and sank the carriers *Taiho* and *Shokaku*. *Taiho* was the newest and largest of Japan's carriers. *Shokaku*'s planes had attacked the American fleet at Pearl Harbor.

Capture of Guam and the Mariana Islands

The American capture of Guam and the Mariana Islands in the summer of 1944 marked a significant step in the American "island-hopping" campaign against Japan. By the end of the campaign, Japanese air and naval power in the Central and South Pacific would be destroyed for good, and the first regular bombing raids on the Japanese home islands would soon be staged out of airfields on the island of Guam.

Guam is the largest of the Mariana Islands at thirty miles long and nine miles wide. A U.S. possession since the Spanish-American War in 1898, the island fell to invading Japanese forces on December 11, 1941.

Although it was not fortified, its natural barriers of coral reefs and sheer sea cliffs, along with its sizeable Japanese garrison, promised a hard battle for the approaching Americans in 1944. It was, however, a target worth taking. In addition to the ability to base bombers on the island, the deep harbor at Apra was big enough for even the largest carriers and battleships and would provide an ideal naval base.

Turkey Shoot   The Marianas campaign kicked off with the invasion of the island of Saipan, and at sea, the First Battle of the Philippine Sea, which took place from June 19 through June 20, 1944. In what was later dubbed "The Great Marianas Turkey Shoot," American planes downed three hundred Japanese fighters and sank three aircraft carriers with small losses on the U.S. side. The Japanese fleet, deprived of nearly all its trained aircrew, was forced to retreat toward the home islands.

Meanwhile, because of stiff Japanese resistance, the Saipan campaign took longer than anticipated. Originally scheduled for June, the invasion of Guam was postponed until late July.

Invasion of Guam   On June 21, elements of the Third Marine and Seventy-seventh Infantry Divisions came ashore along both sides of the Orote Peninsula. The plan was to cut off the peninsula and its airfield, but the landings were slowed by Japanese artillery fire. The shelling sank twenty Marine LVTs (Landing Vehicle Tank), while the Army units, lacking amphibious assault vehicles, were forced to wade ashore from the reef line. By the end of the first day, two beachheads had been established on small strips of land on either side of the peninsula.

The first of several ferocious Japanese counterattacks were launched against the American positions that night using infiltration tactics. The attacks were repulsed amidst chaos, confusion, and high casualties on both sides.

Despite the regular counterattacks and the difficulty of supplying the units on land from beyond the coral reefs, the beachheads were finally linked on July 28. The airfield on Orote and Apra Harbor were both taken two days later. Now well supplied, the American forces began pushing inland.

The Japanese, meanwhile, had been decimated by the counterattacks. The commanding general, Takeshi Takashima, had been killed in combat on July 28 and his successor, Hideyoshi Obata, began a general withdrawal inland. In addition to the casualties sustained, the troops were running low on ammunition and provisions, and had only a few tanks and heavy guns left.

Obata intended to make a stand in the mountainous center of the island, but at the two-day battle for Mount Barrigada, the main line of Japanese resistance was broken and the withdrawal turned into a full-blown retreat with the Americans in close pursuit.

LONG-TERM HOLDOUTS

As it turned out, there were some Japanese on Guam who were not killed and did not surrender after the invasion. On December 8, 1945, four months after the end of the war, three U.S. marines were ambushed and killed by several Japanese soldiers who were still holding out in the jungle. Even more remarkably, local residents in 1972 stumbled across Shoichi Yokoi, a Japanese soldier who had been living in a jungle cave for twenty-eight years, unaware that the war was over.

The disorganized Japanese forces made their way toward the north of the island where they were eliminated piecemeal. By August 10, American forces had secured the island and declared victory. Out of the 36,000 troops who had landed on Guam, 3,000 were killed and over 7,000 were wounded. The Japanese lost more than 18,000 men. Only 450 surrendered.

In 1944, as Guam was being cleared of most of its remaining Japanese resistors, five airfields capable of handling the new B-29 Superfortress Bombers were being hastily constructed. By November of that year, regular bombing runs on the Japanese home islands were taking off from Guam as the Americans drew ever closer to their ultimate victory.

Battle of Leyte Gulf

The Battle of Leyte Gulf, fought between October 23 and October 26, 1944, marked the end of the Imperial Japanese Navy (IJN) as an effective fighting force and the beginning of U.S. naval superiority in the Pacific. A confused, running battle marked by missed opportunities on both sides, Leyte Gulf was the largest naval battle of the war. It also marked the debut of the dreaded *kamikaze* suicide attacks by Japanese fighter pilots.

Competing Strategies   By mid-1944, U.S. strategy in the Pacific was split along two possible routes of advance towards the Japanese home islands. General Douglas MacArthur, representing the army, lobbied hard for a return to the Japan-held Philippines, which he had been forced to abandon in 1942, and then an invasion of the island of Formosa (Taiwan). Ultimately, the navy plan under Admiral Chester Nimitz would win out, but in October 1944, the go-ahead was given to invade the Philippines.

The Japanese had meanwhile identified four axes along which the U.S. might advance and had prepared contingency plans for each one. Those "victory" plans called for committing nearly all available resources to a big push against the Americans in an effort to halt or reverse their advance.

When it became apparent that the Americans were targeting the Philippines, three Japanese task forces set sail. Their objective was to drive off the American navy and shell the landing beaches. A total of sixty-four warships, including the 64,000-ton super battleships *Musashi* and *Yamato*, made their way east towards the Philippine island of Leyte.

Opposing Fleets The invasion of Leyte took place under the auspices of Vice Admiral Thomas C. Kinkaid's Seventh Fleet, which boasted more than 700 vessels and 500 aircraft. Screening the landings was Admiral William Halsey's Third Fleet, a carrier-heavy task force of 100 warships and more than 1,000 planes.

The Japanese fleet, in contrast, was forced to place its hopes entirely on its battleships and heavy cruisers. The "Marianas Turkey Shoot" of the First Battle of the Philippine Sea, as well as battles around Formosa, had severely depleted the carrier-based air power of the IJN. In fact, the only role the fleet's carriers were to play in the upcoming battle was to serve as a decoy force meant to lure away Halsey's Third Fleet.

Opening Battles As the decoy carrier force steamed north, the main bulk of the Japanese fleet split into two groups for its approach to the Philippines. The objective was to circle around the island of Leyte from two directions, rendezvous, and attack the beaches, but it was not to be.

The larger of the two Japanese groups headed for the San Bernardino Strait on October 23 under the leadership of Vice Admiral Takeo Kurita. Before passing through the strait, however, the fleet was spotted by two American submarines, which quickly managed to torpedo and sink two heavy cruisers and badly damage a third. Carrier planes from Halsey's Third Fleet, alerted to the fleet's approach, also swept in, and in five assaults managed to sink the *Musashi* and cripple another heavy cruiser.

Japanese land-based aircraft in turn sank the U.S. carrier *Princeton*, but the losses at sea were too much for Kurita, who turned back, thoroughly shaken. Taking his withdrawal for a retreat, the American forces disengaged. However, after regaining his composure later in the day, Kurita once again reversed course and headed back towards the San Bernardino Strait, now behind schedule for the rendezvous with the southern fleet.

The southern task force, under Vice Admiral Shoji Nishimura, consisted of the balance of the war fleet—two battleships, a heavy cruiser, and four destroyers—and would have an even worse time of it than Kurita's fleet. Nishimura, along with a smaller following force under Vice Admiral Kiyohide Shima, headed for the Surigao Strait on the southern end of Leyte, and Kinkaid's Seventh Fleet was waiting.

Kinkaid had set up a blocking force of battleships and cruisers stretching across the narrow strait and had deployed destroyers out ahead of his blockade along the flanks of the anticipated Japanese advance.

The two sides contacted each other around midnight on October 24. In the ensuing battle, Nishimura's fleet was almost annihilated: Only a single badly damaged cruiser and a lone destroyer escaped the trap. The only American loss was a destroyer damaged by American shelling.

Shortly after Nishimura's retreat, Shima's task force also ran into the trap but managed to extricate itself with fewer losses. Nevertheless, pursuing forces sank a cruiser and destroyer. The southern strike had been stopped cold.

Final Clashes Despite learning of the destruction of Nishimura's fleet, Kurita, having reached the San Bernardino Strait, decided to press ahead on the morning of October 25. Halsey's Third Fleet should have been waiting to stop him, but instead the American force was steaming north to intercept the dummy carrier fleet—Halsey had fallen for the Japanese deception. Despite the earlier losses, a real chance now existed for Kurita to break through to the landing beaches at Leyte Gulf.

All that stood in his way was a small screening force of Seventh Fleet escort carriers and light destroyers under Admiral Clifton Sprague. Over a fearsome two-hour battle, the tiny, unarmored American destroyers fought a desperate rear-guard action against the massive Japanese warships, covering the retreat of Sprague's light escort carriers. The Japanese fleet's attack was broken up by relentless torpedo attacks and raids from the carrier planes, many of which were not equipped to fight heavy cruisers and battleships.

Despite these valiant actions, things were looking bad for the Americans: one carrier and three destroyers had fallen victim to the massive Japanese guns. But it was at this point that Kurita suddenly called off the attack. The vice admiral was increasingly worried about the return of Halsey's Third Fleet and felt that he had lost tactical control of the battle.

As Kurita retreated, Japanese airfields on Leyte launched the first-ever *kamikaze* attacks. These attacks, in which a pilot would sacrifice his own life by crashing his plane into an enemy ship, caught the Americans completely off guard, and another escort carrier was then sunk. After suffering such a mauling, pursuit of Kurita's retreating fleet was not possible. Meanwhile, far to the north, Halsey's Third Fleet had found and engaged the decoy carrier force and hurt it badly, sinking four carriers, a cruiser, and four destroyers.

The Battle of Leyte Gulf was the last major naval engagement of the war. The Imperial Japanese Navy, although not completely neutralized, had lost its effectiveness—never again would it attempt to oppose an American landing.

U.S. Recapture of the Philippines

The U.S. recapture of the Philippine Islands, which began with the landing at Leyte on October 20, 1944, fulfilled a promise made by General Douglas MacArthur when he was forced to flee the islands in March 1942. His succinct statement, "I shall return," was not an idle vow—over six months of fighting, American and Filipino forces would dislodge the Japanese from one island after another, eventually securing independence for the Philippines.

Objective: Manila By January, the Army was ready to take Luzon and the capital city of Manila. The city of Manila was home to 800,000 people and was a cosmopolitan blend of American, Spanish, and Asian influences. A colonial Spanish fort called the Intramuros dominated the city center, which was surrounded by the Pasig River. In 1942, Manila had been declared an open city to avoid damage to its historically and culturally significant architecture. Although the Japanese made no similar declaration in 1945, there was no intention to make a stand in the city.

There were no expectations of resistance in Manila from MacArthur's camp, either. After the American landings at Lingayen Gulf on January 9 and a weeklong battle for Clark Air Field, the race was on to be the first to enter the city. General William Chase formed a "flying column" from mechanized elements of his First Cavalry Division and sped toward the capital, sometimes at speeds up to fifty miles per hour. Following behind at a much slower pace was the Thirty-seventh Division.

More landings took place forty-five miles south of the city on January 15, and elements of the Eleventh Airborne Division dropped unopposed on January 31. These airborne actions and the efforts of Filipino freedom fighters made it possible for the advancing forces to move quickly across intact bridges and river fords.

Unexpected Resistance By February 3, the First Cavalry Division had reached the outskirts of the city, liberating 4,000 foreign prisoners from the makeshift internment camp at Santo Tomas University. General MacArthur reported the next day the imminent capture of the city. His staff began planning a victory parade.

Unfortunately, it was not to be. Despite the orders of their superiors, the local garrison commanders in Manila, led by Rear Admiral Iwabuchi Sanji, were determined to resist. As the Americans approached, they turned Manila into an urban fortress, strengthening its already robust concrete buildings (built to withstand earthquakes) and blockading the streets. Three army battalions (around 2,000 soldiers), plus about 16,000 naval troops, were set to defend the city to the last.

Even as MacArthur's staff were planning the victory parade, elements of the Thirty-seventh, First Cavalry and the Eleventh Airborne were reporting stiffening resistance as they approached Manila. The Thirty-seventh, in particular, was soon to encounter the toughest resistance, advancing slowly street by street and house by house in some of the most brutal urban fighting of the Pacific campaign.

Despite initial orders to avoid destruction of property whenever possible, it soon became apparent that only overwhelming firepower would dislodge the Japanese from their positions. Tanks and artillery firing at close range brought down houses that often contained civilians as well as Japanese. Meanwhile, as the Japanese retreated they would demolish their formerly occupied buildings whenever possible.

After a week of fighting, with the capture of Nichols Air Field on February 12 the encirclement of Manila was complete. The push into the city began in earnest, but the hardest fighting was yet to come.

The Intramuros, dominated by Fort Santiago, held out for five days, from February 23 to February 28. In the process of taking the fortified center, the area was nearly leveled by American artillery. With the surrender of the Financial Building on March 3, the last resistance in the city was eliminated. Out in Manila Harbor, Fort Drum held out until April and was only neutralized when 3,000 gallons of diesel fuel were pumped in and ignited. The resulting explosion destroyed the fort and the last resisters within.

A City in Ruins American casualties were around 6,000, with 1,000 of that number dead. The Japanese had lost 16,000 in their stubborn defense of the city, but it is undoubtedly the civilian population that suffered most. At least 100,000 citizens perished in the monthlong fight for the city, either caught in the crossfire or executed deliberately by the Japanese in what has come to be called the "Manila Massacre."

The Philippine Campaign Ultimately, ten U.S. divisions would take part in the capture of Luzon, a larger force than was committed to Italy or North Africa in the European theater. The effort was well worth it—the fall of Luzon gave the Allies effective control of the Philippines.

Subsequent actions throughout the Philippines gradually rooted out the last large pockets of Japanese resistance. Members of the Filipino guerilla resistance, who proved invaluable in locating hidden Japanese strongpoints in the jungles and mountains, often ably assisted these operations.

As the fighting raged in Manila in February, General MacArthur convened a meeting of leading Filipinos with the intention of declaring the restoration of the Commonwealth of the Philippines. After reminding the assemblage that his country had fulfilled its promise to return, he declared the Philippines a bastion of democracy in Asia. The United States granted Philippine independence on July 4, 1946.

Berlin Raid

The Berlin Raid of February 3, 1945, was the culminating effort of a nearly four-year strategic bombing campaign directed against the capital of Germany. The motivation of the raid—to aid advancing Soviet troops in their approach to Berlin—reflects the shifting nature of a military strategy that was never fully sure of its objectives.

Strategic Bombing At the beginning of World War II, the Allied view of strategic bombing—the use of bombers not in direct support of military operations—was decidedly negative. Bombing of civilian targets by the Luftwaffe during the Spanish Civil War seemed to only reinforce the view that such actions only strengthened civilian resistance—and that the bombers were really just war criminals.

This attitude began to shift, however, after the German terror bombing of the Dutch city of Rotterdam and especially once Great Britain came under attack during the "blitz" of 1940. Having been driven off the continent after the fall of France, the only way the British could strike back against Germany was through bombing campaigns.

At first targeting only industrial cities, the strategy was gradually expanded to include purely civilian targets as well. The commander of the Royal Air Force (RAF) bomber wing, Sir Arthur "Bomber" Harris, summarized the thinking succinctly: "[The Germans] sowed the wind, and now they are going to reap the whirlwind."

Strategic bombing even became a political tool once the Soviet Union was invaded. Joseph Stalin placed constant pressure on the Allies to open a second front, but they were in no position to do so right away. Through steady bombing of Germany, British Prime Minister Winston Churchill and U.S. President Franklin Roosevelt argued, the Allies were doing their part by disrupting German war production.

Berlin Raids By 1943, the once-reserved Allies had turned to terror-bombing of their own—the "firebombing" of Hamburg in July caused a massive firestorm that killed fifty thousand people and left one million homeless.

As bomber range improved throughout the war, Berlin increasingly became a target. Not only was it an important manufacturing center, but the attacks on the German capital were thought to have a great effect on the morale of both sides.

Although the first raid on Berlin occurred on August 25, 1940, the attacks did not begin in earnest until 1943. From November 1943 to March 1944, the RAF conducted sixteen raids that killed thousands and left hundreds of thousands homeless. In those raids, the Royal Air Force lost 500 aircraft and 2,700 crew over the city, which boasted the most extravagant air defense of the war, including the infamous "flak towers," massive concrete air-raid shelters/gun platforms.

Operation Thunderclap The United States Army Air Force (USAAF), which had concentrated on precision bombing of military and industrial targets up to this point, began formulating a plan, known as Operation Thunderclap, to carry out a mass bombing campaign in 1945 in support of the Soviet advance from the east.

The raids were launched, in part, as a sign of unity with the Soviet war effort. Although the plans for Thunderclap were scaled back somewhat, several large raids, including the infamous Dresden raid, were launched by the USAAF in the early part of the year over the objections of officers such as James Doolittle, commander of the Eighth Air Force.

The raid of February 3 was the largest ever suffered by Berlin. A total of 937 bombers and 613 fighter-escorts flew over the city that day, dropping enough bombs to kill about 3,000 people and "de-house" 120,000. Several important buildings were damaged, including the Reich Chancellery and Gestapo Headquarters.

Perhaps most notably, the February 3 raid marked the end of the career of Judge Roland Freisler, the infamous head of the People's Court who sentenced untold hundreds of political prisoners to death. Judge Freisler was crushed by a collapsing ceiling when the People's Court took a direct hit during the raid.

Legacy of Strategic Bombing Strategic bombing raids on Berlin ceased soon after the USAAF raid—the Soviet Air Force was close enough to take over the task. As for the overall effectiveness of the Berlin Raid, it seems to have had little impact. As the Allies knew going into the war (but soon forgot), indiscriminate bombing of civilian targets does not kill the will to fight and often has the opposite effect. Berlin, despite the devastation suffered during two years of prolonged bombing, continued to function as before. Civilians still went to work, even if they no longer had a house to return to. Production in the city continued to rise throughout the war, reaching a peak in December 1944.

The losses suffered in return, particularly by the RAF, were unacceptably high in the light of such small returns. Whatever gains could be realized from strategic bombing elsewhere, the raids on Berlin failed to achieve their objective of hastening the end of the war.

The Yalta Conference

The Yalta Conference, which took place during the week of February 4–11, 1945, was the last great wartime meeting of the three major Allied leaders. It was held to determine the shape of the postwar world and is seen by some as the beginning of the Cold War.

Hidden Agendas, Conflicting Personalities The resort town of Yalta, located on the Crimean Peninsula in what was then the Soviet Union, was chosen to play host to Joseph Stalin, Winston Churchill, Franklin Roosevelt, and their advisors and foreign ministers in what was only the second such meeting of the "Big Three," the first having taken place in Teheran, Iran, in 1943. The purpose of the conference was multifaceted. Roosevelt was looking for guarantees on promises Stalin had made at Teheran and to move ahead on plans for the

Winston Churchill, Franklin Roosevelt, and Joseph Stalin met in the Soviet city of Yalta in February 1945 to discuss the Soviet Union's entry into WWII and the political shape of the post-war world. *The Library of Congress*

formation of the United Nations. Stalin was looking to expand his influence in Europe and the Far East. Churchill, ever suspicious of Soviet motives, was mainly concerned with fencing in Stalin's ambitions as best he could.

The Yalta Conference was characterized by icy relations between the British and the Soviets, with Roosevelt—ailing and only two months from death—trying to act as mediator. Although Churchill did not trust Stalin, Roosevelt realized that the Western allies had no choice but to negotiate in good faith.

The Americans did manage to secure further promises from Stalin on the issue of the Far East: The Soviet Union was to declare war on Japan within three months of the end of the war in Europe. In return, the Soviet Union was promised possession of the southern Sakhalin and Kurile Islands in the Pacific as well as temporary territorial rights in Mongolia and northern China.

The other issues on the table proved more difficult to resolve. Stalin and his advisor, Vyacheslav Molotov,

were wary of the United Nations, which they regarded as a Western plot to marginalize Soviet postwar influence. Although no final agreement was reached, Stalin agreed to dispatch Molotov to the first meeting of the United Nations in San Francisco in April 1945, after Roosevelt promised him a Security Council veto and individual ambassadors for each of the Soviet Republics.

Postwar Europe The question of how to handle postwar Eastern Europe proved the most difficult to resolve. Stalin wanted to keep the lands acquired when the Soviet Union had invaded eastern Poland in 1939 as part of the Molotov-Ribbentrop Pact. He proposed shifting Poland's borders west to the Oder River, taking territory away from Germany, including the rich territory of Silesia. The former German territory of East Prussia was to be divided between Poland and the Soviet Union.

Roosevelt and Churchill agreed to this plan, somewhat reluctantly, when Stalin promised that in return

Poland would be allowed free and democratic elections "as soon as possible" after the war. This was particularly important, because there were two Polish governments in exile. The 1939 government had fled to London and had the backing of the West, while Stalin had created what amounted to a second, communist government under his sponsorship. The Poles, said Stalin, would be allowed to choose between the two.

The Yalta Conference also outlined Allied plans for the occupation of Germany. The country was to be divided in the immediate aftermath of the war into four sectors, each administered by one of the victorious allies: Great Britain, the United States, France, and the Soviet Union. Furthermore, Berlin was to be occupied by all four powers as well, regardless of what zone of control it fell under.

As for the long-term plans for Germany, the Big Three were unable to reach a consensus. Stalin favored a plan initially put forth by Henry Morgenthau Jr., U.S. secretary of the treasury. The Morgenthau Plan called for permanently dividing Germany into separate states and the complete dismantling of German industry. The apparatus of German heavy industry would then be shipped off to the victorious countries and Germany would be forced to adopt an agrarian, or farm-based, economy.

Although the Morgenthau Plan had initially met with Roosevelt's approval, public criticism and Churchill's vehement opposition had cooled his enthusiasm. As such, no final agreement was reached on how to handle German recovery after the war, and a reparations committee was formed to make further recommendations at a future time. In the end, all four Allied powers would implement the Morgenthau plan to one degree or another in the first two years after the Allied victory in Europe.

Controversial Legacy   Yalta's legacy did not become immediately clear. Stalin honored his promise to enter the war in the Pacific and attacked Japanese armies in Mongolia three months to the day after the German surrender in Berlin. However, this proved to be one of the few Yalta promises that he did honor.

Most infamously, Poland was not allowed free elections. The 1947 elections that were held were rigged in favor of the Soviet-backed party, and Poland had become a socialist state by 1949. This, along with the West's agreement to allow Stalin to keep his conquests of 1939–1940 (Eastern Poland and the Baltic states), led many in postwar America to accuse Roosevelt of "selling out" Eastern Europe to Stalinism.

It is, of course, important to consider the context of the Yalta Conference. At the time, Soviet armies had already occupied most of Poland and much of Eastern Europe. Furthermore, Roosevelt's position of bargaining in good faith was the only reasonable and productive position to adopt. There were no indications at the time

of the conference that the decisions made there would lead directly to the Cold War.

Battle of Iwo Jima

The Battle of Iwo Jima, which lasted from February 19 to March 16, 1945, was one of the bloodiest engagements of the Pacific war. Often considered the marine corps's finest hour, the order to take the island, and the payoff gained for the amount of blood spilled, remains controversial to this day.

Strategic Importance   The island of Iwo Jima is situated 1,100 miles south of Tokyo in an archipelago known as the Volcano Islands. Considered a "home island," the battle there marked the first American attack on Japanese territory.

Iwo Jima is a tiny volcanic island, eight miles square, dominated by the dormant cone of Mount Suribachi, which rises more than 500 feet above the surrounding terrain. The rest of the island is filled with volcanic crags and crevasses—some emitting foul-smelling sulfuric fumes—and covered with fine, loosely packed ash-like soil. Despite these inhospitable conditions, the order was given to take the island in early 1945.

Iwo Jima's importance lay not in the objectives of the navy or army, but in the American strategic bombing campaign. The B-29 "Superfortress," the first long-range bomber, had been flying missions against Japan since the fall of the Marianas in 1944. Possession of Iwo Jima, which hosted three airfields, would provide a base for fighter escorts. Furthermore, it would neutralize the island's role as a base for bomber interceptors and forward warning station. As preparations for the invasion of Okinawa were moving ahead, the order was given to take Iwo Jima.

Appointed to head the invasion were two masters of amphibious warfare: Marine General Holland "Howlin' Mad" Smith and Admiral Raymond Spruance. The island was expected to fall quickly. Unbeknownst to the Americans, however, Iwo Jima had slowly been turning into a giant fortress under the guidance of Lieutenant General Tadamichi Kuribayashi.

Japanese Preparations   Kuribayashi knew his appointment to head the defense of Iwo Jima in 1944 would mean his eventual death—once the Americans attacked, the island's defenders would be on their own. His strategy, then, was to sell the island dearly. It was hoped that such a fearsome defense of as tiny and insignificant an island as Iwo Jima would dissuade future invasions of Japan itself.

The strategy, developed by Kuribayashi in the months leading up to the battle, was a radical departure from previous Japanese defensive plans. Instead of trying to halt the invasion on the beaches, the Americans were to be allowed to come ashore with little harassment. The defense was to be elastic and adaptable and was to focus on killing large numbers of Americans.

Joe Rosenthal's photograph of Marines raising the American flag at Iwo Jima became iconic because of the enormous sacrifices made to take the eight-square-mile island.   *National Archives and Records Administration*

To fight against the awesome firepower that American air and naval superiority could bring to bear, Kuribayashi ordered the construction of a warren of hundreds of underground bunkers and blockhouses, many with walls up to four feet thick, connected by over eleven miles of tunnels. Manning these fortifications would be an eventual force of 22,000 men armed with hundreds of heavy guns, mortars, rockets, machine guns, and even twenty-two tank turrets mounted in static positions.

The concrete used to construct the bunkers—a mix of cement and the local volcanic ash—would prove especially strong. The tunnel defense rendered American bombs and shells almost completely ineffective.

Mount Suribachi   So it was that when—after a three-day naval bombardment that poured 6,000 tons of shells into the island—the invasion began at 9:00 A.M. on February 19, the marines coming ashore soon found themselves facing a well-prepared, entrenched enemy who was unperturbed by the preliminary shelling and determined to fight to the very end.

The initial landing wave brought 30,000 men from the Third, Fourth, and Fifth Marine Divisions ashore. As Kuribayashi had planned, the landings were unopposed, at least at first. As the beaches filled with marines, however, the Japanese opened fire from positions in front of the beaches and up on nearby Suribachi.

The volcanic soil of the beaches proved impossible to dig into and taxing to advance through, but the marines had no choice but to push ahead. Thanks to support from naval guns and tanks coming ashore, a beachhead was secured by the end of the day and Mount Suribachi was surrounded, but at great cost.

In the following days, as more of the eventual 82,000 marines came ashore, positions around Suribachi were consolidated and preparations were made to push toward the airfields on the other side of the island.

By the fourth day of battle, the marines had encountered the Japanese bunker/tunnel network and were expecting a fierce fight for Suribachi. A patrol was sent to the top of the mountain to probe resistance. The patrol, surprisingly, encountered little action on its journey to the top. Another team was sent up with an American flag to raise on the mountain's summit. Once again, there was little resistance and the flag was raised.

The ensuing story has passed into the annals of American military history. As the flag was going up, Secretary of the Navy James Forrestal was coming ashore. He reportedly saw the flag and asked for it as a souvenir. A second, larger flag was sent up to replace the first. Photographer Joe Rosenthal was on the scene as the second flag went up, but almost missed the shot, taking a quick picture "from the hip." The resulting image, "Raising the Flag on Iwo Jima," immediately became an icon of the American struggle for victory and is among the most familiar images of World War II.

Battle for the Island The fight was far from over, though. Of the six men captured in the famous photograph, only three would survive the next month of fighting. The slow advance toward the north end of the island, where Kuribayashi and most of his troops had created a strongpoint, was arduous and bloody. Bunkers thought to be "cleared" would suddenly become active again as they were reoccupied by Japanese troops moving up through the tunnel network. It came down to the work of flamethrowers, including a flamethrowing adaptation of the Sherman tank dubbed the "Zippo," and grenades to clear out and collapse the bunkers, one by one.

As the marines closed in, Japanese tactics became increasingly desperate. Toward the end several silent, nighttime wave attacks were launched and were only repelled by concentrated artillery and machine-gun fire. The last of these attacks, on one of Iwo Jima's captured airfields, lasted the length of the night of March 25. A combined force of marines, Seabees (members of naval construction batallions), and aircrew desperately defended the field against an assault of 300 Japanese that reportedly included Kuribayashi himself.

Death Toll and Legacy Despite the fact that about 1,000 Japanese remained in the tunnels below the island, Iwo Jima was declared secured the next day. Slowly, the remaining Japanese surrendered—the longest holdouts did not give themselves up until several years after the war ended—but the vast majority of the garrison had fought to the death: 20,000 Japanese died in defense of Iwo Jima.

American casualties were staggeringly high as well: nearly 7,000 killed and more than 18,000 wounded. In terms of overall casualties, the invading marines had lost more men than did the defenders. This high toll caused many to question the worth of taking the island. Using Iwo Jima as a fighter base, the original rationale for

taking the island, proved unnecessary. Other islands continued to serve as warning stations for bomber attacks until the end of the war. But the island did provide an important sanctuary for returning American bombers in desperate straits—over 2,000 B-29s would make emergency landings there over the next five months.

Perhaps most importantly, the struggle for Iwo Jima was a huge boost to the American war effort. The "Mount Suribachi" photo was immediately turned into a war bonds poster and the surviving men from the photo were brought home for publicity tours. Naval Secretary James Forrestal perhaps put it best upon seeing the first flag go up: "the raising of that flag on Suribachi means a Marine Corps for the next five hundred years."

Firebombing of Tokyo

The firebombing of Tokyo in 1945 was one of the most devastating and controversial bombing raids of World War II.

The Pacific Bombing Campaign Although the first raid on Tokyo occurred in 1942—the famous "Doolittle Raid"—regular bombing missions could not begin in earnest until 1944, when the United States Army Air Force (USAAF) was able to establish bases within bombing range of the Japanese home islands.

As the bombing raids began in earnest, American commanders in the Pacific were confronted with the same problems that had dogged strategic bombing in Europe—precision attacks on industrial and military targets were deadly, because they required bombers to fly during daylight and at a comparatively low altitude. Flying higher (at altitudes up to 40,000 feet) put the bombers safely out of range of antiaircraft fire but significantly reduced the accuracy of the bombs. Japan's high surface winds exacerbated the situation, and the early Tokyo raids were hitting their targets only 10 percent of the time.

The other option, long favored by the Royal Air Force (RAF) in Europe, was to saturate an area with bombs, dropping the explosives indiscriminately. These area raids could be undertaken at night or from high altitudes, because accuracy was not a concern. Losses could thus be greatly reduced. The downside, of course, was the fact that the bombs were bound to land mostly on civilian targets. Over time, as World War II developed into "total war," this method became part of the Allied bombing strategy—area bombing was used to try to break a civilian population's will to fight as well as to destroy the actual means of war production.

Firebombing Although the USAAF participated in only a few area bombings in Europe—the most notable example being Dresden in 1945—it soon adopted the strategy in the Pacific after the initial precision raids on Japan proved unsatisfactory. There was significant pressure from politicians and the military brass to see returns on the $4 billion investment that had been made in the B-29 bomber program, and General Haywood Hansell, an advocate of precision bombing, was replaced by General Curtis LeMay.

General LeMay immediately began to reorganize and improve the bomber fleet, replacing inefficient staff officers and raising training standards for pilots and crew. He also made the decision to switch to a strategy of area bombing, known as firebombing.

The first deliberate firebombing of the war occurred during a raid on Hamburg, Germany, in 1943. Using incendiary bombs, the aim was to create a "firestorm," essentially a self-sustaining tornado of superheated flame similar to a blast furnace. At Hamburg, the firestorm's 1,500-degree, 150-mph winds set the asphalt streets on fire, incinerated civilians inside bomb shelters, and sucked pedestrians off the streets. The effect on German morale and industry was devastating. The German armaments minister, Albert Speer, later reported that after Hamburg he feared six or seven more raids of that magnitude would drive Germany completely out of the war.

The paper and wood buildings of Japan, LeMay realized, would prove all too vulnerable to firebombing. In addition to the effect on civilian morale, LeMay reasoned that area bombing would be more effective in Japan because the country lacked large industrial centers. Most of its factories were dispersed among small businesses and cottage industries and were hard to target with precision bombing.

Target: Tokyo The first firebombing raid on Japan targeted the city of Kobe on February 3, 1945, and was judged an overwhelming success. Tokyo was first firebombed on February 23, and again on March 9.

The March 9 raid, in which Tokyo was pounded for two hours by more than 300 B-29s, was as lethal and destructive as the later atomic bomb attacks on Hiroshima and Nagasaki. Employing a mix of incendiary bombs and the first napalm bombs (napalm is a sticky, highly flammable compound), the raid destroyed sixteen square miles of the city and killed about 100,000 Japanese.

Controversy The long-term impact of the firebombings remains controversial. General LeMay remained convinced that even without the atomic attacks his bombing raids would have won the war by October, although he also later admitted, "I suppose if I had lost the war, I would have been tried as a war criminal."

His estimation of the effectiveness of the raids was borne out by Prince Fumimaro Konoe of Japan, who attributed the eventual Japanese surrender to the prolonged bombing attacks. Other Japanese officials, however, indicated the Soviet Union's entry into the war in August 1945 was the final motivating factor in Japan's surrender.

Others have pointed out that Japan's industry was already failing by the time the firebombing raids began

and that a more effective target would have been Japan's power plants. Loss of electricity would have negatively impacted civilian morale and the country's ability to wage war at a relatively low cost of life.

One thing is for certain: The firebombing of Tokyo demonstrated the effects that total war had on strategists and how much things had changed over the course of the war. In 1939, as World War II got under way, the first British bomber raids on Germany dropped propaganda leaflets, which the crew were careful to untie, lest a bound bundle fall from the sky and injure or kill any civilians. Conventional military wisdom was strongly opposed to waging war on civilians through saturation bombing. By 1945, 100,000 civilian casualties were deemed acceptable in the name of victory.

The Battle of Okinawa

Although it was not expected to be, the Battle of Okinawa was the last major engagement of World War II. The fierce fighting that took place on that island over the course of nearly three months would raise fears of the tremendous costs that would be required in the anticipated assault on Japan and would inform the subsequent decision to employ atomic weapons in an effort to break Japanese resistance without a bloody invasion.

Okinawa Island was targeted for attack due to its strategic importance. Situated in Japan's Ryukyu Island chain, an archipelago that stretches from Kyushu to Taiwan, the island, little more than 300 miles from Kyushu, was seen as an ideal staging point for an invasion of the home islands.

Opposing Forces The commander of the invading Tenth Army, Simon Bolivar Buckner Jr., was the son of a Confederate general and had distinguished himself as commander of the Alaska Defense Command earlier in the war. Bolivar's command, code-named Operation Iceberg, consisted of two marine divisions and four army divisions and would be backed up by powerful American and British naval support.

The Japanese were commanded by General Mitsuru Ushijima, who could call upon one of the best-prepared and abundantly equipped Japanese defense forces of the war. Although the Japanese navy had been effectively neutralized, Ushijima could count on air support, including the dreaded *kamikaze* suicide corps. With 100,000 troops under his command, Ushijima adopted the strategy developed during the defense of Iwo Jima and ordered his men to construct underground fortresses connected by an extensive tunnel network.

Unlike Iwo Jima, Okinawa held a large civilian population that, as in most cases, would end up suffering the greatest losses, both in life and property. To make matters worse, the Okinawans had been convinced by wartime propaganda of the brutality of the invading Americans and were prepared to sacrifice their lives rather than surrender.

Some have credited the Navajo Code Talkers, two of whom demonstrate their radio technique here, with victory at Iwo Jima.   © *Bettmann/ Corbis*

In the largest amphibious operation of the Pacific campaign, the Tenth Army came ashore on April 1, 1945. Ushijima's strategy was to not try to fight the invasion on the beaches, so the occupation of the north side of the island was relatively easy, with all resistance ceasing in that sector by April 20.

The Battle on Land   It was as the marines and soldiers pushed south that they ran up against the first determined resistance—the "Shuri line," named for the defensive lines anchored at the ancient Shuri Castle.

The fighting that ensued was slow and hellish. Every bunker became a strongpoint that could only be rooted out by using what General Buckner called "blowtorch and corkscrew" tactics. The brutal fighting quickly leveled buildings and reduced forests to fields of shattered tree stumps.

Holed up in their tunnels, the Japanese were not above sending Okinawan civilians out at gunpoint to collect water and provisions. Many of these civilians died in the "steel typhoon" that raged on the surface.

As April turned into May, and May came to a close, the seasonal monsoon rains arrived, turning the churned-up countryside into a muddy morass. In conditions reminiscent of trench warfare on the Western Front in World War I, marines and soldiers pressed grimly forward. Shuri Castle was eventually taken in an assault by elements of the First Marine Division.

The Battle at Sea   Meanwhile, out at sea, Japanese air attacks had been wreaking havoc on Allied vessels. Over the course of the battle, 4,000 sorties, many of them *kamikaze*, were launched, sinking thirty-eight U.S. ships (and damaging another 368) and killing 4,900 personnel—the worst single-battle U.S. naval losses of the war.

Elsewhere at sea, the super battleship *Yamato* put to sea on a sort of *kamikaze* mission of its own: Its objective was to shell American positions on Okinawa until destroyed, but it had barely made its way out of Japanese home waters before it was caught by torpedo-bombers and sunk. It took eight bombs and thirteen torpedoes to bring down the world's largest battleship; 3,000 of its

German General Alfred Jodl, flanked by Admiral Von Friedeburg signs the German surrender at Reims, May 7, 1945. *STP/AFP/Getty Images*

crew went down with the ship. The sinking of the *Yamato* marked the final Japanese naval action of the war.

Casualties and Aftermath After the fall of Shuri Castle, it took another month's hard fighting to take Okinawa. By June 21, the island was declared secure. Three days earlier, General Buckner, the American commander, was killed by one of the last artillery shells fired in the battle. The Japanese commander, General Ushijima, committed ritual suicide (*seppuku*) as the last Japanese resistance crumbled.

Only 7,000 Japanese voluntarily surrendered out of the initial 100,000 defenders. The vast majority, 66,000, chose death over the "dishonor" of surrender. American casualties were more than twice those suffered at Iwo Jima or Guadalcanal—7,900 dead and 72,000 total casualties, including a record number due to combat stress.

The Okinawan civilians suffered the most: A full third of the island's population, at least 140,000, were dead by the end of the battle, either caught in the crossfire or by their own hands. At least another third were wounded. It was a civilian loss rate comparable only to Stalingrad.

Surrender at Rheims

Between the beginning and the end of the Battle of Okinawa, the war's global scale had shrunk considerably.

The German surrender at Rheims on May 7, 1945, marked the cessation of hostilities between Germany and the Western Allies. The following day, known as V-E ("Victory in Europe") Day, would see the capitulation of German forces in the east and the end to war in Europe.

Unconditional Surrender The road to Rheims began two years earlier at the Casablanca Conference in Morocco, when President Franklin Roosevelt announced a new policy of accepting nothing less than unconditional surrender from the Axis powers. In other words, there could be no negotiated peace. The Axis nations had no choice but to allow the Allies to dictate terms. The rationale was that the fascist governments of Italy and Germany were in effect criminal administrations that had come to power illegally. The Allies, in refusing to deal with a "criminal" government, would delegitimize the fascist governments. This move, which demanded the complete surrender and dismantling of not only the military but also the sovereign government, was unprecedented in international law.

British Prime Minister Winston Churchill, who was meeting with Roosevelt at Casablanca to discuss war strategy, was caught off-guard with the announcement, but he quickly pledged his support despite his reservations—demanding unconditional surrender would in all likelihood stiffen Axis resistance, which is exactly what happened. Members of the German Underground, who had previously been working with the Allies to topple German leader Adolf Hitler's regime, found themselves backed against a wall. Many chose to support their country, disregarding their reservations about who was leading it.

Soviet leader Joseph Stalin was likewise upset by the call for unconditional surrender. After all, the Germans hardly needed yet another incentive to devote every last ounce of blood and sweat to the defense of their homeland against the Soviets. In typical Stalinist fashion, however, the Soviets' leader was able to turn the new policy to his own political advantage and soon threw his support behind it.

Although Italy did surrender unconditionally in 1943, the negotiations that preceded the surrender slowed the Allied advance and allowed German troops to move into the peninsula, turning Italy into a battleground.

Germany's Collapse

By May of 1945, Germany was facing a similar fate. After the Allied invasion of France in 1944, the German army had been forced back across the Rhine by a slow and steady advance along a broad front in accordance with the strategy dictated by General Dwight Eisenhower. Allied and German attempts at delivering a "knockout blow," during Operation Market Garden and the Battle of the Bulge, respectively, had failed. As unglamorous as it was, Eisenhower's strategy was winning the war.

With the crossing of the Rhine in early 1945, the Allies were able to trap 450,000 German troops in the "Ruhr Pocket." During April, the Allies tightened the noose until, as the month came to a close, more than 300,000 of the surviving German troops surrendered together.

Elsewhere, the drive into Germany had continued. Americans liberated Bavaria, which they had feared would prove a stronghold of fanatical Nazi defense. Allied units pressed further into Germany, eventually meeting advancing Soviet units at the Elbe River. Germany had been cut in half.

Meanwhile, in a bunker in Berlin, Adolf Hitler committed suicide. In one of his last official communiqués, he named Admiral Karl Dönitz as his successor, urging the architect of the U-boat campaigns to carry on the struggle. Dönitz instead wisely decided that the time had come to end the war—but not before saving as many Germans as possible from the vengeful Soviet hordes currently overrunning eastern Germany.

Dönitz's Plan

Dönitz came up with a plan to arrange for the surrender of selected units in a staggered progression, keeping up a line of resistance in the east as long as possible while units further west surrendered, thus enabling troops and civilians to flee into the unoccupied territory of Schleswig-Holstein or across Western Allied lines. This ran contrary to Allied policy, which,

under the auspices of unconditional surrender, demanded a simultaneous end to hostilities across the whole of the European theater.

Nevertheless, local units were able to arrange surrender terms with Allied commanders in Italy on May 2 and with Field Marshal Bernard Montgomery and the U.S. Sixth Army on May 5. It was only when General Eisenhower was approached by local commanders that Allied policy was put into practice and terms for total, unconditional surrender of all German forces were drawn up. Dönitz had not managed to buy as much time as he would have liked, but nonetheless about two million soldiers and civilians were able to find safety behind Western lines.

Surrender Terms

The terms signed at Rheims were straightforward. They called for a cessation of hostilities to take effect at 11:01 P.M. on May 8. They also forbade the scuttling of ships or sabotage of equipment. These provisos were put in place in response to calls from the Nazi propaganda machine encouraging Germans to resist the occupying armies and to form so-called *Werewolf* units, whose mission was to cause as much damage and mayhem as possible.

Although the surrender at Rheims only addressed military surrender, and included a provision that allowed for later peace treaties to supersede it, it is generally held to be the official end of the war, in part because what little political structure remained in Germany would soon cease to exist entirely.

Hiroshima and Nagasaki

After the German surrender in May, Japan was left with the Allies' undivided attention. The atomic bombings of Hiroshima and Nagasaki, which took place on August 6 and August 9, 1945, forced a Japanese surrender without costing the Allies a bloody invasion of the home islands. The two bombings, which remain the only nuclear attacks in history, ushered in a new age and permanently changed the nature of warfare, politics, and international diplomacy.

The roots of the atomic attacks stretched back to 1939, when a group of scientists, including the famed physicist Albert Einstein (1879–1955), concerned that Germany was developing a program to build atomic weapons, approached President Franklin Roosevelt. Such weapons, the scientists argued, were a theoretical possibility, and the United States would do well to form an exploratory committee with an eye towards developing such technology before the Nazis did.

The Manhattan Project

Roosevelt took their advice, and the exploratory committee developed into the Manhattan Project, a top-secret government effort that funneled $2 billion into building an atomic weapon. Under the guidance of a brain trust of top physicists, the theoretical possibility was on the verge of becoming an

An estimated 80,000 civilians died when the United States dropped an atomic bomb on Hiroshima, Japan on August 6, 1945. An unidentified man stands next to a tiled fireplace where a house once stood. *AP Images*

atomic reality when President Roosevelt died in April 1945.

Newly sworn-in President Harry Truman was then told of the bomb and its destructive potential. He was further informed that the bomb would be ready in four months. As it turned out, Germany did not last that long, surrendering on May 8. With the intended target of the bomb now out of the war, the question of whether to use the weapon on Japan quickly arose.

The Potsdam Declaration At the victorious Allies' German Potsdam Conference in July 1945, Truman warned Japan to surrender immediately or face "utter devastation," although he did not provide any further details. Meanwhile, in Alamogordo, New Mexico, the first atomic bomb was successfully tested on July 16.

August 1945 was the decisive month of the war in the Pacific. The Soviet Union, in accordance with agreements reached at Yalta, was gearing up to enter the war against Japan. Whether this factored into the American decision to use the atomic bomb is unknown.

What is certain is that the main reason for using the bomb was the goal of a quick surrender of Japan, which would eliminate the need for an invasion of the home islands. Such an invasion was set to begin in November. After the bloodbath on Okinawa, the prospect of fighting two million determined Japanese defending their homeland, backed by 5,000 or more *kamikaze* fighters, motivated the Americans to avoid an action that would likely result in millions of deaths and total Japanese casualties in the tens of millions.

Several options for demonstrating the bomb's capabilities in a non-lethal way—detonating it in front of a panel of international observers or dropping it into Tokyo Bay—were dismissed because a detonation failure would only strengthen Japanese resolve.

Truman authorized the use of the bomb in early August. A target committee had selected several cities that were both military and psychological targets, and from this list the city of Hiroshima, an important military-industrial center, emerged as the primary target, in part because it was the only city on the list without a POW camp.

Hiroshima and Nagasaki In the early morning hours of August 6, 1945, the B-29 *Enola Gay* took off from its base on Tinian with an escort of two other bombers carrying instrumentation and photography equipment. By 08:15 A.M., the bombers were over Hiroshima and the bomb was released. The blast, equivalent to 12,500 tons of TNT, created a fireball that reached 5,400 degrees Fahrenheit and killed around 70,000 people instantly. Outside the one-mile blast radius, fires quickly began to spread, eventually burning down four square miles of the city.

On August 8, as authorities in Tokyo began to slowly appreciate what had just happened, the Soviet Union entered the war, invading Manchuria and scything through the Japanese Kwangtung Army stationed there. The following day, ahead of a predicted weeklong period of bad weather, a second bomb was hurriedly dropped on the city of Nagasaki. The second blast was somewhat contained by the hills around the epicenter; at least 40,000 people were killed outright, including some survivors of the Hiroshima blast who had fled that city three days before.

Japanese Surrender The Japanese government, which had been making conditional peace overtures through Moscow, agreed to a near-unconditional surrender at the behest of Emperor Hirohito. The only condition the Japanese now insisted on was the preservation of the Imperial line. This was agreed to and Hirohito made a radio address on August 14—after a militarist coup attempted to stop the broadcast—announcing Japan's capitulation and asking his disbelieving subjects to "endure the unendurable."

The relative roles that the atomic bombs and the Soviet invasion played in the Japanese decision to surrender have been a source of endless debate. Even Japanese officials, in postwar interviews, seemed to give conflicting assessments. Regardless of the effectiveness of the atomic attacks, the suffering they unleashed cannot be denied.

In the confused hours after the attack on Hiroshima, Radio Tokyo supplied some of the first accounts of the aftermath of the bombing:

> With the gradual restoration of order following the disastrous ruin that struck the city of Hiroshima in the wake of the enemy's new-type bomb on Monday morning, the authorities are still unable to obtain a definite checkup on the extent of the casualties sustained by the civilian population. Medical relief agencies that were rushed from neighboring districts were unable to distinguish, much less identify, the dead from the injured. The impact of the bomb was so terrific that practically all living things, human and animal, were literally seared to death by the tremendous heat and

American physicist Robert Oppenheimer (1904–1967) was director of the Manhattan Project, which developed the atomic bomb in the early 1940s. He is pictured here with Major General Leslie Groves (1896–1970), the project's military director. *Archive Photos, Inc./Getty Images*

pressure engendered by the blast. All the dead and injured were burned beyond recognition. With houses and buildings crushed, including the emergency medical facilities, the authorities are having their hands full in giving every available relief under the circumstances. The effect of the bomb was widespread. Those outdoors burned to death while those indoors were killed by the indescribable pressure and heat.

✪ Home Front

Manhattan Project

Launched in 1942, the Manhattan Project was a secret government program charged with developing an atomic bomb. Beginning in the late 1930s, a number of leading physicists—including Enrico Fermi, Albert Einstein, and Leó Szilárd—recommended that the United States work on atomic technology because it was believed that Nazi Germany had already begun creating its own atomic weaponry. It was feared scientists working for Adolf Hitler would develop an atomic bomb first and give Germany an upper hand in World War II.

Formally called the Manhattan Engineer District, the program was overseen by the U.S. Army Corps of Engineers but relied on the efforts of many of the foremost scientists of the day as well as intelligence operatives and thousands of support staff. The Manhattan Project ultimately cost about $20 billion.

The project was managed by Brigadier General Leslie Richard Groves (1896–1970). He compartmentalized the knowledge gained throughout the Manhattan Project so that nearly everyone who worked on it only possessed a small amount of information related to his or her specific task or area. Even people who labored at one site generally had knowledge only of what they were specifically working on, and they could not talk about the project with anyone outside of work. Communication between research teams was monitored by the military, and official communications between sites was encrypted. All mail to people working on the project's sites was also censored.

Because only a select few knew how all the pieces to the Manhattan Project fit together, it was easier to maintain secrecy that way. Despite this security measure, some Soviet spies gained some knowledge of the process that made its way back to the Soviet Union before the end of World War II.

Division of Work Sites Another way secrecy was maintained was by dividing the work on the Manhattan Project between five sites scattered throughout the United States. Each location played its own significant role in the development of atomic bomb technology. In Berkeley, California, physicists at the Radiation Laboratory provided knowledge, both theoretical and practical, that was vital to the electromagnetic separation process. At the University of Chicago, the Metallurgical Laboratory was able to generate the first chain reaction and create the first small-scale production process for making plutonium. Enrico Fermi made key contributions working in Chicago, including supervising the first controlled sustained chain reaction.

There were also two massive manufacturing centers for the Manhattan Project. One industrial site was located in Oak Ridge, Tennessee, where three primary plants produced key atomic elements of the bomb in necessary quantities. There, electromagnetic separation took place on a larger scale, plutonium was produced, and uranium underwent separation. The other industrial factory was located in Hanford, Washington, where plutonium was created for use in the plutonium, or Fat Man, bomb ultimately detonated over Nagasaki, Japan.

The Los Alamos Lab The most famous site where work on the Manhattan Project took place was in Los Alamos, New Mexico. The headquarters for the science behind and the design of the atomic bomb, the laboratory was run by physicist J. Robert Oppenheimer (1904–1967), who also served as the Manhattan Project's scientific director. At Los Alamos, physicists developed the

VICTORY GARDENS

The Victory Garden movement was a government-sponsored program created to address food shortages during World War II. Even before the United States joined the conflict, the federal government encouraged Americans to plant gardens, but the initial push was not heeded by the public. By 1941, public sentiment had shifted and the U.S. Department of Agriculture promoted the concept. The agency wanted every civilian who was bodily able to plant a Victory Garden—to supplement rationed food for themselves as well as to provide produce for the hungry in other places in the world. Strongly encouraged by posters and other printed matter, adults and children planted Victory Gardens on every available piece of land. By 1943, there were 20 million Victory Gardens in the United States that produced several million tons of food in that year alone. Because of the amount of produce produced by Victory Gardens, more of the commercial harvest could be sent to soldiers and allies, another gesture that greatly helped the war effort.

theoretical data needed to construct the bomb. They also designed both of the bombs ultimately used on Japan in 1945. It was also in New Mexico, at a remote area near Alamogordo, that a test plutonium bomb, dubbed Gadget, was successfully detonated on July 16, 1945. This test blast was stronger than expected—with a one-mile radius from the blast center totally destroyed.

Manhattan Project Reaches Fruition Once it was shown that the atomic bomb technology actually worked, the Manhattan Project reached its final stages. Some scientists wanted the United States to demonstrate the new weapon's muscle before using it on Japan, or at least warn the Japanese about the bomb and its destructive power. Many who worked on the Manhattan Project were unaware the atomic bombs would be used in a military operation a short time later.

To the surprise of much of the world, President Harry Truman ordered the first atomic bomb to be dropped on Hiroshima on August 6, 1945. Truman then had another dropped on Nagasaki on August 9, 1945. Approximately 110,000 people died immediately and another 100,000 were injured in both cities because of the atomic bombs. Later, at least 200,000 more people died as a result of illness or injuries from the bombings. Many thousands faced life-long struggles with the effects of the radiation and impact-related problems.

By dropping both bombs, the United States proved to Japan that it was ready and willing to employ atomic technology to bring an end to the war. Though Japan was planning to resist the American invasion, its leader, Emperor Hirohito, decided that Japan would surrender. Japan capitulated on August 14, 1945. The Manhattan Project itself was disbanded early in 1947 when control

During World War II, Americans used government-issued ration cards to buy gasoline, butter, sugar, coffee, and other items.   © *Bettmann/Corbis*

of the United States' nuclear arsenal was transferred to the Atomic Energy Commission, a civilian entity.

The Manhattan Project and the atomic weaponry that came out of it launched the nuclear age. The way wars could be fought was changed, as was international relations, because the possession of advanced technology came to define elite power. Because of the ever-present threat of a nuclear holocaust, society and culture were also transformed. A number of the scientists who worked on the Manhattan Project later became proponents of controlling the use of nuclear weapons and promoted the use of nuclear power for peaceful purposes.

Rationing

During World War II, the United States, like many countries involved in the conflict, employed rationing policies. These policies regulated the commerce of consumer goods, especially foodstuffs, products made with metal, and rubber-based items like tires. The policies' twofold goal was to ensure military operations and American allies had the supplies they needed and to guarantee that American consumers were given fair,

but often limited, access to certain commodities in the face of war-created shortages.

Early Rationing Efforts   Rationing efforts began in the United States before the country officially entered World War II on December 8, 1941. From May 1940 to August 1941, several government entities were created in response to economic pressures created by the war then raging in Europe. These government entities ensured that prices of certain commodities, like scrap metals, remained stable, and they had limited powers until the creation of the Office of Price Administration (OPA) by several presidential executive orders in mid-1941.

While the OPA was primarily focused on controlling prices and stabilizing the cost of living as much as possible, it was also charged with overseeing American rationing efforts. The first item to be rationed was rubber tires, on December 27, 1941. By April 1942, items rationed by the OPA included cars, sugar, typewriters, and gasoline. Before the end of World War II, products being rationed included coffee, shoes, stoves, meat, cheese, butter, oils, processed foods, and bicycles. Though such products were rationed, a significant black market developed in the United States through which many of these items could be obtained by those who could afford to pay high prices.

Methods of Rationing The federal government controlled rationing through several means. Coupons, valid for a certain amount of certain products, could be used every few weeks. Other food products were rationed by the OPA through a point system combined with stamps, which allowed consumers some dietary flexibility. Every person received five blue stamps (for processed foods) and six red stamps (for meat, fat, and some dairy) every month. Each stamp was worth ten points each, and every item had a point value.

The point value of each item was determined by the OPA based on the availability of the product as well as the amount of consumer demand. Point values were not fixed for the duration of the war, but could change, especially if availability changed. For example, in 1943 there was an extraordinarily large crop of peaches in the United States, so the point value of peaches was lowered.

The use of such rationing systems was generally supported by Americans during World War II. It made ordinary citizens feel they were part of the war effort. Rationing was a patriotic, public expression of the needed sacrifice to achieve victory. Such sentiments were also expressed in communities by activities such as the planting of "Victory Gardens," as home vegetable and fruit gardens were called.

By August 1945, the rationing of certain products ended. The sale of gasoline and food products were no longer regulated after that month. All rationing ended on September 30, 1945, though price controls remained in effect to some degree through the end of 1947 to help the transition to a peacetime economy. The OPA itself ended operations on May 29, 1947.

Japanese Internment

Soon after the Japanese bombed Pearl Harbor on December 7, 1941, many Japanese Americans living on the West Coast of the United States were arrested and forced to spend years in internment camps to allay the fears of some Americans living in the same area. From December 1941 to February 1942, a number of state politicians from California, Oregon, and Washington put pressure on President Franklin D. Roosevelt to address concerns over the Japanese and Japanese Americans living in their states. At the same time, Western Defense Command head General John L. Dewitt (1880–1962) and other important army officers encouraged the president to act on the issue. Roosevelt signed Executive Order 9066 on February 19, 1942.

Under this order, anyone of Japanese ancestry serving in the armed forces was immediately removed from

Dorothea Lange was hired by the government to document the Japanese relocation program during World War II. Shown here is the Manzanar Relocation Center in California. *National Archives and Records Administration*

military service. In areas of internment, which included parts of states along the West Coast, a curfew was ordered by the army for the 110,000 Japanese and Japanese Americans living there. Over time, this curfew became increasingly restrictive.

On March 31, 1942, Executive Order 9066 was used to begin forcing internment in camps for all Japanese Americans living on the West Coast. (While there were more Japanese and Japanese Americans living in Hawaii—approximately 158,000—than on the West Coast, only 2,000 people of Japanese ancestry in Hawaii were forced to go to internment camps. It was believed that their vital importance to the Hawaiian economy was the primary reason for not forcing a mass internment there.)

Internment Starts After the order was given, Japanese Americans had to go to control stations and record the names of every member of their family. Next, they were given a time and place to show up at an assembly area. From there, they would proceed to an internment camp. Japanese Americans who were being forced to go to camps had anywhere from four to fourteen days to prepare for relocation.

Before going to the assembly area, internees had to get rid of most, if not all, of their personal property as well as their businesses. They were only allowed to bring what possessions they could physically carry to the camps. Because of this situation, other Americans sometimes paid much less than the worth of the property to internees who were desperate to get rid of their assets. Those Japanese Americans who did not sell their possessions and property sometimes lost their land to foreclosure because they were unable to make payments while living at the camps.

The federal government also benefited from this state of affairs. The Federal Reserve Bank offered to store some internees' cars, and then the army made offers to purchase these cars cheaply a short time later. By late 1942, any cars not sold to the army were seized for use in the war and their owners received nothing.

The Camps The first internment camp to open was located in southern California and was called Manzanar. Between 1942 and 1945, nine more camps opened; each held about 10,500 internees. They were located in other locations in California as well as in Arizona, Wyoming, Colorado, Utah, and Arkansas. About 120,000 Japanese Americans spent time at these camps over the three-year period.

Life inside the camps was not easy. The camps consisted of many tar paper-covered wooden barracks. Each barrack was partitioned into tiny one-room apartments that held families or groups of unrelated individuals. The small apartments were furnished only with army cots, blankets, and a light bulb. There were no private bathrooms or cooking and dining facilities, only shared spaces for those activities.

At first, there were no schools for children interned at the camps, though they were later opened up. To pass the time, internees at some camps grew their own food in gardens or started some manufacturing projects. For the most part, however, the Japanese Americans in the camps had nothing to do. Some put their unused energy into rebellion, creating more tension at some camps.

Stays in the internment camps were sometimes short. After being deemed loyal by the government, some Japanese Americans were allowed to leave. Usually not permitted to remain on the West Coast, they often moved to the East Coast or the Midwest to take jobs. Some even worked as migrant farm workers in the western states and even helped save the sugar beet crop there in the summer of 1942.

Legal Challenges Many Japanese Americans did not accept the legality of their internment and took their cases to court. College student Gordon Hirabayashi (1918–) was born in the United States and refused to accept a curfew and internment because he believed it violated his rights as an American citizen. Convicted and sentenced to jail time, his case went to the Supreme Court, which ruled against him in 1943.

Another American citizen, Fred Toyosaburo Korematsu (1919–2005) was working in the defense industry when internment began. To avoid being forced to go to a camp, he moved, changed his name, and tried to claim he had a different ethnic background. Korematsu was caught, and like Hirabayashi, convicted and sent to prison. After being paroled, he was sent to an internment camp. When Korematsu's appeal of his conviction finally reached the Supreme Court in the fall of 1944, the legality of the order was again upheld, with public safety trumping the acknowledged racism.

Leaving the Camps Though the legitimacy of internment camps was not in doubt, the end of the program was declared on December 18, 1944. All the camps were also ordered to be closed by the end of 1945, though the last camp closed on March 20, 1946. Fearing what awaited them outside of the camps, a number of internees did not want to leave as the war neared its end. To force them to go, weekly departure quotas were created in the second half of 1945. Only about half of the Japanese Americans who were sent to the camps returned to the West Coast, and those that did often found their jobs, businesses, and their property long gone.

While Japanese Americans lost hundreds of millions, if not billions, of dollars in property and wages because of internment, it took four decades for the United States to formally admit any fault. In 1988, the U.S. Congress apologized for the internment program and offered a one-time $20,000 payment for living internees as compensation. The bill was sponsored by a former internee, Congressman Norman Y. Mineta (1931–).

To soldiers returning from the war and eager to start families, the G.I. Bill offered benefits for housing and education. © *Bettmann/Corbis*

Servicemen's Readjustment Act

Passed in 1944, the Servicemen's Readjustment Act helped discharged World War II military personnel resume their civilian lives. Also known as the GI Bill of Rights or the GI Bill, this legislation originally allotted $13 million for various projects, including its best known program: a free college education for veterans. Because of the GI Bill, America was forever changed. A new group in American society was now able to obtain a college education. As a result, the American middle class expanded, and many veterans who had received higher education expected that their children would go to college as well.

Origins The GI Bill was considered important because of what had happened to returning veterans after World War I. Their postwar benefits were modest at best. They were given a train ticket to go back home and a small payment. Benefits were limited to a little vocational rehabilitation. Because of this lack of support, many discharged American soldiers had difficulty finding employment and faced financial problems. Homelessness

was also an issue. The U.S. government promised $1,000 one-time bonuses to World War I veterans in 1924, but the money was not to be paid until 1944 at the earliest. The ravages of the Great Depression compelled tens of thousands of veterans, known as the "Bonus Army," to march on Washington to demand their bonuses. In the summer of 1932, protesters had violent clashes with the police, and later, the U.S. Army.

The U.S. government hoped to better integrate the millions of World War II veterans back into American society. People also realized that the country owed returning soldiers a debt of gratitude for their defense of American interests. In addition, President Franklin D. Roosevelt, who came to office on the strength of his "New Deal" to end the Great Depression, believed generous benefits to veterans would protect the U.S. economy after the war.

Though there were some opponents of the bill—a few educators were concerned about lower admission standards for universities, for example—Congress and President Roosevelt ensured the passage of Servicemen's Readjustment Act in 1944 by enlisting the help of the

American Legion. The GI Bill was signed into law by the president on June 22, 1944. The act provided for five primary benefits for veterans who had served at least ninety days after September 1940 and were honorably discharged.

One program created by the legislation was low interest rate mortgages for veterans. Such loans allowed them to buy homes, farms, and businesses so that they could contribute to the expansion of the peacetime economy. Another program provided unemployment income of $20 per week for up to one year while veterans looked for employment. Job placement assistance, vocational training, and dishonorable discharge reviews were also provided, and more Veterans' Administration hospitals were slated to be built.

Free College Education More than fifteen million veterans had access to a free college education along with a monthly allowance as part of the GI Bill's most significant program. Specifically, each veteran received a minimum of one year of full-time schooling. Veterans were also allowed an additional educational period of time equivalent to his or her service in the military. This benefit had a limit of forty-eight months. In addition, each veteran was allotted $500 per year for tuition, books, fees, and related costs, as well as a minimum of $50 per month for living expenses.

Before this time, college was generally limited to students from higher-income families, primarily because of the high cost involved. The GI Bill led to a revolutionary change in who attended college and created a new segment of American society with access to a higher education. As a result, the new college graduates took higher-income jobs and expanded the middle class.

Because of the vast number of veterans taking advantage of the program, colleges and the college experience also changed. Universities had to deal with the large numbers of veterans who were usually older than average college students. Campuses, including classrooms and dormitories, were rapidly expanded. In 1947 alone, 49 percent of all students in American colleges were military veterans.

Existing colleges could not handle the increased demand created by the GI Bill, so new schools, primarily state universities, were established to fill the need. This demand also meant that more professors were needed to teach the students, so graduate schools and the number of people with advanced degrees also increased in number throughout the country.

The original Servicemen's Readjustment Act expired in July 1956. By that date, at least eight million veterans took advantage of its schooling and training provisions. The end cost of these programs was $14.5 billion. Similar bills were passed later in the twentieth century to provide educational and other opportunities to men and women after they complete their military service.

Television

While the technology for television existed before World War II, it was not until after that conflict ended that the broadcast medium became a widely used and society-changing phenomenon. Imagined by writers for many years, television began in the 1870s, 1880s, and 1890s when the basic components needed to create television were in place. The term itself came into being in 1900. By the 1920s, the technology had developed to the point that an image could be broadcast, though it was not yet of usable quality. John Logie Baird demonstrated an early, crude version of television at a department store in London, England, in 1925.

Experimental Broadcasts Further steps forward were made in the 1930s. By 1931, eighteen experimental television stations that developed and tested the technology were licensed by the Federal Communications Commission (FCC) and operated in the United States. However, the medium was opposed by radio broadcasters, who saw it as a threat. The Great Depression also limited the amount of available funding to improve television.

Despite such problems, several inventors continued to further develop television technology. Because of the work of people like Vladimir Zworykin and Philo Farnsworth, television had been refined to the point of being ready for commercialization by 1938. That year, RCA was prepared to manufacture televisions commercially as well as set up a national broadcasting system. But because of the opposition of RCA's competitors, the launch of commercial television was delayed by the FCC (Federal Communications Commission). However, experimental television broadcasting stations continued to work on refining the technology.

In 1940, the FCC ruled that the broadcast standards that RCA was attempting to establish would be unfair to its competitors. The FCC then revised television broadcasting standards, and announced new guidelines on May 3, 1941. Within two months, two networks, CBS and NBC, began commercial broadcasts from their New York City stations.

Commercial Broadcasts CBS and NBC offered fifteen hours of broadcasts per week, but the cost of television sets slowed the expansion of the medium. By the end of the year, as the United States prepared to enter World War II, television broadcasts were limited to a few major cities. Only about 10,000 to 20,000 television sets received these broadcasts because many Americans did not want to spend money on an expensive receiver that might soon be obsolete.

Postwar Expansion During World War II, the federal government stopped the growth of television. The FCC would not allow any new television stations to be constructed during the war because building materials were needed for the war effort. While the television industry could not expand under these restrictions, the technology did improve because of the war. New electronic devices, such as the sensitive television camera called the image orthicon, were created. Introduced by RCA in 1945, that camera proved important in television's postwar growth.

After World War II, television stations were allowed to be built again. However, it took several years for the industry to fully develop. Investors were hesitant to support the cost of constructing stations when the medium was still unproven and the profitability unknown. It cost ten times more to build a television station than a radio station, so it was established businesses—such as television set manufacturers, newspapers, radio networks, and even bigger independent radio stations—that often built stations in the early postwar years.

In the late 1940s and early 1950s, the television industry experienced rapid growth. A number of new television networks came into existence. By 1948, NBC had twenty-five national affiliates, while CBS was seen as the best news network. ABC was also in existence, but could not gain its footing until it was sold to United Paramount Theaters in 1951. Other networks, such as DuMont, also operated in television's early days, but by the early 1960s, networks other than NBC, ABC, and CBS had disappeared.

There were also technical difficulties caused by television's expansion. In 1945, the FCC developed a channel allocation plan. By 1948, the overwhelming growth of television in the Northeast United States alone meant that the plan was no longer viable. There were only thirteen VHF (very high frequency) channels available for broadcast, one of which was using the same channel as another and therefore had to be several hundred miles away in order to avoid signal interference. For cities relatively close together, such as New York City and Philadelphia, this situation created allocation difficulties for the FCC.

FCC Freeze To address these issues, the FCC froze the licensing of new television stations from 1948 until April 14, 1952. During the freeze, fewer new television stations were built, but the burgeoning industry continued to grow in other ways. Existing stations had the time to set production and broadcast standards, for example.

When the freeze ended in the spring of 1952, the FCC came up with two ways to address the channel allocation problem. While VHF channels would be cautiously allocated geographically, the FCC also allowed commercial stations on the UHF (ultrahigh frequency) band. In addition to tackling channel allocation, the FCC also dealt with a conflict between RCA and CBS over which technical standard would be used for future color television broadcasts. Each network came up with a different, incompatible system. This clash was decided in RCA's favor in 1953.

Early Programming While these situations were being dealt with and battles being fought, the growing television audience was still buying receivers and being entertained. While there were 16,000 television sets in American homes in 1947, a mere two years later, the number jumped to four million. By the beginning of 1951, there were eleven million sets in homes.

Much of television's early programming consisted of shows and stars that were popular on radio and had migrated to television. Comedies such as *Ozzie and Harriet* and *Amos and Andy*, talent shows like *Original Amateur Hour*, detective dramas such as *Dragnet*, quiz shows, and children's programs like *Superman* all were hits on radio before finding a new audience on television. News and public affairs programming and reporters also moved from radio to television. For example, reporter Edward R. Murrow found fame on the radio during World War II and became a respected news authority on television, as did the political talk show *Meet the Press.*

The most popular television format in television's early days was the variety show, which had its origins in vaudeville theater. Two well-liked programs were *Toast of the Town*, which was hosted by Ed Sullivan, and *Your Show of Shows*, which featured Sid Caesar and Imogene Coca.

The biggest early hit of television was also a variety show. Launched in 1948, *Texaco Star Theater* featured television's first superstar, Milton Berle. Berle captured nearly 95 percent of the available TV audience in the fall of 1948, but his ethnic, urban humor had limited appeal outside of the Northeast. As television expanded, Berle lost his audience and was dropped from his program in 1955. By then, television had firmly established itself as a vital entertainment and news medium in America.

✪ International Context

Sino-Japanese War

Although 1939 is commonly accepted as the first year of World War II, the initial phase of the war in Asia actually got under way in 1937 with the Second Sino-Japanese War. The conflict between Japan and China would characterize the entirety of the war in the Pacific theater until 1941 and the attack on Pearl Harbor.

The Road to War The Sino-Japanese War was the result of expansionist Japanese policies that had pursued slow and steady encroachment into China since the beginning of the twentieth century. For example, the Mukden Incident of 1931, in which the Japanese staged an attack on their own railway and then blamed it on the Chinese, had allowed Japan to take control of the northern territory of Manchuria.

Japanese influence in Asia had risen considerably after Japan's victory in the Russo-Japanese War of 1904–1905. The Japanese position in China was further strengthened by China's serious internal divisions, particularly the Nationalists under Chiang Kai-shek competing for power with Mao Zedong's Communists.

Although Mukden heightened tensions in the area, the war proper did not start until six years later, when a minor skirmish on July 7, 1937, between Japanese and Chinese troops at the Marco Polo Bridge in Peking rapidly escalated, at the encouragement of the Japanese government, into full-blown hostilities.

A Multilayered Conflict   The Japanese, worried about the possibility of war with the Soviet Union, hoped to turn the Marco Polo Bridge incident to their advantage by forcing a negotiated settlement with the Nationalists. As fighting spread in the north, Japanese forces encountered resistance at the vital port city of Shanghai, the gateway to the Nationalist capital at Nanking. Chiang Kai-shek, after allying with the Communists, had decided on a policy of total war with Japan. Shanghai was to be the proving ground of that new strategy.

For three months the two armies fought a bitter and bloody battle in the streets of Shanghai and on nearby beaches, where the Japanese conducted amphibious assaults in an attempt to flank the city. The Chinese were hopelessly outmatched militarily, and the battle failed to elicit any foreign offers of aid. By November, the city had fallen and the Japanese were moving inland. However, Chinese resistance at Shanghai had a major negative effect on the morale of the Japanese troops, who had been taught to view themselves as superior to their Chinese enemies and were shocked to encounter such fierce fighting. Furthermore, the delay of the Japanese advance bought the Nationalists valuable time to relocate vital industrial and governmental infrastructure further inland.

Rejecting Japanese calls for surrender, Chiang Kai-shek fled Nanking ahead of the invaders, relocating his capital to Chungking, in the west of China. The Japanese fell upon Nanking, taking the city on December 12, 1937. Until February 1938, the city's citizens would suffer looting, murder, rape, arson, and a host of other atrocities at the hands of the Japanese army in what would come to be known as the "Rape of Nanking."

The Rape of Nanking strengthened Chinese resolve to resist the Japanese to the bitter end. It also drew international condemnation, with President Roosevelt calling for an economic "quarantine" of Japan and the League of Nations issuing a censure of Japan. Yet no aid or intervention was offered, and the Japanese armies, 300,000 strong, continued to push into China's interior.

The Chinese, Communists and Nationalists alike, did all they could to slow the Japanese advance, even breaking dams on the Yellow River to cause floods and wash out bridges. Gradually, these efforts, combined with the sheer vastness of the country, sapped the invaders' momentum and brought about stalemate.

During this period, the Chinese Communist Party made significant gains in membership and support, especially in Japanese-occupied territories. As stalemate with Japan set in, the Nationalists began to oppose their Communist rivals, who were also subject to Japanese attacks. Nevertheless, the Communists were able to lay claim to vast areas of occupied land behind Japanese lines, waging continual guerilla attacks on railways and isolated garrisons.

Japan's "No-Win" Situation   By the time the events of December 1941 brought the United States and its allies into the war in the Pacific, which effectively merged the Sino-Japanese conflict with the greater Pacific war, the Nationalists controlled the inland territories of China. The Japanese controlled the coast, major cities, and the railways that connected them, and the Communists basically controlled the rest of the country.

Japan, seeking a quick resolution in China, had been dragged into a quagmire, a "no-win" situation from which it could not extricate itself. The war in China would continue to tie down Japanese resources and manpower all the way through to 1945, when the Soviet Union, entering the Pacific war in its final weeks, would cut like a scythe through the Japanese armies in the north.

The toll of the eight years of war in human lives was enormous. Chinese losses, civilian and military, were 20 million at least and possibly as high as 35 million. Japanese military losses were probably around one million killed, wounded, or missing. In the end, the once-mighty Japanese army was destroyed, the Chinese Communists—who went from a membership of 40,000 at the beginning of the conflict to 1.2 million in 1945—continued to rise in popularity, and the involvement of the United States and the Soviet Union in Asian politics during and after the war dramatically increased.

The Rape of Nanking

The Rape of Nanking occurred during a period of several weeks in late 1937 and early 1938 in which the Japanese army ran riot through the streets of the Nationalist Chinese capital and committed atrocities upon the people. The Rape of Nanking was the most infamous event of the Second Sino-Japanese War, a conflict that lasted from 1937–1945 and eventually became part of World War II. The incident earned Japan international condemnation, greatly increasing sympathy for the Chinese war effort abroad and providing the Chinese people with even greater motivation to resist Japanese aggression. The war crime eventually led to trade embargoes and the attack at Pearl Harbor.

The Dark Side of Bushido   The underlying factors that caused the tragedy of Nanking can be traced to the new national policies adopted by Japan as it became a player on the world stage in the late nineteenth century. After three centuries of isolation, Japan raced to catch up with European advances in technology, commerce, industry, and warfare. In order to ensure its survival in international politics, Japanese policy quickly became markedly aggressive and militaristic.

The code of *bushido*, which had long guided the actions of Japan's samurai class (samurais were military nobiligy), were adopted and modified for indoctrination in all Japanese citizens. The new *bushido* emphasized fanatical devotion to the state, aggression, lack of concern for self, disdain for Japan's enemies, and the glory inherent in fighting and dying for the Japanese emperor. Gone were *bushido* codes of chivalry and compassion. Surrender was viewed as the most shameful act possible, and those who did surrender—whether friend or enemy—were to be viewed with the utmost contempt. From 1872, with the publication of the new "Soldier's Code," Japanese soldiers were trained in this new brutal and racist ideology.

The Battle of Shanghai

When war broke out with China in 1937, the Japanese armies were prepared to win a quick and easy victory, fighting against the "inferior" Chinese. When these supposed inferiors put up a three-month resistance at Shanghai, fighting off the technologically superior Japanese in an endless series of bloody engagements, the invaders' morale was shaken to the core.

When Shanghai fell in November 1937, the Japanese pressed inland, making for the capital city of Nanking. The Chinese Nationalist leader, Chiang Kai-shek, evacuated his government ahead of the advancing army, pledging to keep fighting. The Japanese, meanwhile, were hoping the fall of Nanking would signal the end of the war.

At the head of the Japanese army was aging general Iwane Matsui (1878–1948). Even before reaching Nanking, Matsui could see that his army was quickly getting out of his control. Planes strafed refugee columns, and troops looted farmhouses and villages, burning them to the ground afterwards. These actions were too widespread and well organized to have been the actions of individuals or small groups acting on their own. General Matsui scolded his subordinate officers for their complicity in these actions but was met only with derisive laughter.

Moderate voices in Japan, meanwhile, were pushing for a cease-fire before the army reached Nanking and were offering Chiang Kai-shek the opportunity to reach a negotiated settlement. But the government, dominated by warmongers, pressed for an immediate assault on the Chinese capital. After four days of heavy bombardment, the city capitulated on December 13.

Seven Weeks of Terror

General Matsui was replaced by Prince Asaka, the emperor's uncle, who issued the secret order as his troops moved into the city to "kill all the captives." Although he was probably referring to military captives, this order set the tone for what was about to occur.

Inside Nanking were about 70,000 troops and a quarter-million civilians. Many soldiers and noncombatants had fled as the Japanese approached the city—overloaded refugee boats on the Yangtze were regularly fired upon by Japanese planes—and the city government had fled with Chiang Kai-shek. The only people with any position of authority left in Nanking were a small group of foreigners—Germans, British, Americans, and Dutch, a rag-tag group of missionaries, businesspeople, and academics who were able to establish a two-mile-square "safe zone," from which they witnessed many of the atrocities committed by the Japanese as they did their best to provide comfort and shelter to the beleaguered residents of the city.

As they moved in and occupied Nanking, the Japanese troops began to run riot through the city. Their reign of terror would last seven weeks and would encompass looting, arson, murder, and rape, all on massive scales.

The looting commenced almost immediately and bore the unmistakable signs of official complicity—troops were seen loading looted items into army transport trucks by the dozens. Whole warehouses were stripped bare, as were residential homes, businesses, and even refugees, who would be stopped on the street and relieved of what meager possessions they still carried.

Looting was often followed by arson. Japanese troops made use of the extensive selection of explosives and incendiaries available to them, setting fire to entire city blocks at once. Combined with the heavy shelling the city had sustained earlier, the mass arson laid waste to what had once been one of China's most beautiful cities.

It is the Japanese treatment of Nanking's citizens, however, that assured that the war crimes committed there would be remembered as heinous. First the Japanese made promises of safe conduct for the Chinese soldiers and then later promised all males of military age, who remained in the city, would also enjoy safe conduct. Those who believed the Japanese reported to them and were tied up in large groups and machine-gunned or bayoneted.

Others were singled out and used for bayonet or sword practice. One Japanese newspaper at the time proudly reported, in a light-hearted tone, on two officers who had made a game of running through the streets of the city and seeing how many civilians they could cut down with their katanas.

Other atrocities, which were verified by eyewitness testimony, included men, women, and children being roasted alive over open fires, doused with gasoline and set on fire, burned with caustic chemicals, beheaded, gutted, or buried up to their necks and tortured.

In April 1945, American troops liberated these prisoners at Buchenwald, near Weimar, Germany.   *AP Images*

Another instrument of terror and oppression wielded by the Japanese was rape. Women and girls ranging in age from nine to seventy-six were raped, often repeatedly, and often by many soldiers at a time. Rape became so widespread that it was not unusual to see it happening on a city street in broad daylight. These incidents were often accompanied by murder, either of the victim or of her children or family. Many of the victims were kept in makeshift prisons, enslaved by Japanese officers.

The total number of Chinese deaths suffered during the Nanking campaign and occupation is unclear, but it has been estimated to be no fewer than 150,000 and perhaps as much as 300,000. At least 20,000 women were raped between December 1937 and February 1938. The economic devastation suffered by Nanking and the surrounding countryside was immense. One estimate had the average city-dweller losing the equivalent of six years' income during the seven-week occupation.

Aftermath Nanking exposed the end result of the Japanese army's policy of racist brutality. The average Japanese soldier, himself subject to harsh discipline and bleak prospects, turned his anger outward against people he had been taught to hold as sub-human.

The only Japanese general prosecuted specifically for the events at Nanking was General Matsui, who had been the one who was appalled at the initial behavior of the Japanese army. He had retired from the army and set up a temple at Nanking to pray for the victims. He offered no defense at his trial and was sentenced to death. Many of the other generals at Nanking also received death sentences for crimes committed later in the war. Prince Asaka, due to his royal connections, escaped prosecution and punishment entirely.

The Holocaust

From 1933 to 1945, under the leadership of Adolf Hitler, Germany waged an increasingly hostile campaign of hatred, exclusion, and systematized murder against its own Jewish population and the Jewish populations of its conquered territories. This horror is known as the Holocaust.

Hitler and Anti-Semitism The roots of the Holocaust lie in centuries of European anti-Semitism, the widespread hatred of and discrimination against members of the Jewish faith. Although originally based in religious bigotry, anti-Semitism began to take on ethnic and racist overtones in the nineteenth century, when

Jews were increasingly portrayed as an outsider race that had infiltrated the "pure" European population, diluting its "greatness" in the process.

Anti-Semitism was widespread in every country in Europe at the turn of the twentieth century, and these views were soon adopted by a young Austrian serving in the German army in World War I by the name of Adolf Hitler. After Germany's capitulation in 1918 and the subsequent signing of the humiliating Treaty of Versailles in 1919, Hitler was one of a great many Germans left searching for a scapegoat to blame for the defeat. He soon found solace in like-minded political groups that singled out "international Jewry," Communists, and the new German government. By 1921, Hitler had taken control of what would eventually become known as the Nazi Party.

A central goal of the Nazi agenda was a solution to "the Jewish question," although the proposed solution was often presented as an expulsion, rather than wholesale murder, of Germany's Jews. These views were not kept secret—Hitler wrote about them extensively in his autobiography, *Mein Kampf* (*My Struggle*) in the mid-1920s. When the Nazi Party came to power in 1933, Hitler wasted no time in turning his views into national policy.

"Anti-Semitism of Reason" The Nazi approach initially downplayed widespread anti-Semitic violence, attempting instead to develop, as Hitler put it, "anti-Semitism of reason." To that end, a series of escalating discrimination laws accompanied by increasingly menacing social and economic harassment by Nazi operatives slowly accrued over the next five years. The policy did meet with "success"—half of Germany's Jewish population had emigrated by 1939—but it was not working quickly enough. Furthermore, the Nuremberg Laws of 1935 had stripped German Jews of their citizenship and property rights, making it difficult, from both an economic and bureaucratic standpoint, for them to leave the country. Worse still, Jews were finding it increasingly hard to find countries that were willing to take them in for fear of inviting a flood of refugees from Germany.

The year 1938 is often cited as the first year of the Holocaust proper. That year, Germany's *Anschluss*, or unification, with Austria, brought with it a significant Jewish population. Reinhard Heydrich, head of the secret police and one of the chief architects of the Holocaust, dispatched his deputy Adolf Eichmann to Vienna to draft a plan for the systematic expulsion of the Austrian Jewish community. The methods developed there led to the forced expulsion of all Polish and Russian Jews from Germany later in the year.

Kristallnacht The night of November 9, 1938, remembered as *Kristallnacht*, or "The Night of Broken Glass," marked the first mass *pogrom*, or anti-Semitic riot, since Hitler's rise to power. Instigated by the Jewish shooting of a German ambassador, the violence was on a nationwide scale, all of it unofficially endorsed by the government—many of the rioters were members of the Gestapo (secret police) and SA (stormtroopers) in civilian clothing.

Nearly every Jewish synagogue in Germany, 1,574 in all, was either damaged or destroyed in the course of that single night. Additionally, thousands of Jewish-owned shops were vandalized, their windows smashed out with sledgehammers. About one hundred Jews were killed. Thirty thousand Jewish men, mostly academics and professionals, were rounded up and deported to concentration camps, prisons that had initially been set up to hold the Nazis' political prisoners. The event earned international condemnation, but Kristallnacht was only the beginning of the greater horror that would soon come.

The outbreak of war in 1939 and the German conquest of Poland brought one of Europe's largest Jewish communities, two million strong, within German borders. Nazi administrators, in particular, Heinrich Himmler (1900–1945), head of the Security Services (SS), became increasingly concerned with how to deal with such unprecedented numbers of "undesirables."

Ghettos and the Final Solution It was Reinhard Heydrich (1904–1942), head of the German secret police, who first suggested moving Poland's Jews into urban ghettos as a means of concentrating their population. Beginning in 1941, this plan was put into practice. The cities chosen were situated on major railway hubs, the better to facilitate later transportation, although to where exactly was still unknown.

Once they had resettled the Jews in ghettos, which crammed huge populations—the Warsaw Ghetto alone numbered 300,000—into tiny, segregated plots of land, the Nazis set about instituting a policy of "destruction through work." Thousands would die of starvation and exhaustion as they were forced to contribute to the German war effort through what amounted to slave labor.

Meanwhile, as German forces overran vast swaths of Soviet territory in 1941, millions more Jews fell under the Nazi shadow. A deadly equation of *Lebensraum* (as Germans referred to their need for "living space") plus "the Jewish question" led Himmler and Heydrich to one conclusion—eradication of the Jews would free up living space and provide a "final solution" to the issue of what to do about the Jews of Europe.

Einsatzgruppen The mass killings that characterize the Holocaust began in the rear areas of the German advance in Russia. Heydrich's SS *Einsatzgruppen*, or Special Task Forces, followed behind the army proper, rolling into recently conquered towns and villages and rounding up the local Jewish population. Their mission was simple: to make Germany's newest acquisitions *Judenfrei*—"free of Jews."

The most infamous Einsatzgruppen action took place at Babi Yar in the Ukraine. On September 29–30,

1941, over 33,000 Jews were lined up and machine-gunned in a gorge near the town. Such actions were typical; over its two-year operational period, the Special Task Forces would execute over a half-million Soviet Jews.

Yet it became clear early on that this was not a practicable solution. The mass killings took a powerful psychological toll on the executioners—Heinrich Himmler famously vomited after witnessing the execution of one hundred Jewish captives—and the *Einsatzgruppen* themselves were deemed too imprecise and too much of a drain on resources.

The Wannsee Conference Opposing Himmler and Heydrich, Luftwaffe General Hermann Göring had long advocated using Jews as a slave labor force rather than exterminating them. In an effort to end the argument once and for all, Heydrich called a conference of the top Nazi brass in the Berlin suburb of Wannsee. The Wannsee Conference, held in January 1942, provides the clearest example of the systematic and premeditated nature of what was to follow.

The plan outlined at Wannsee called for the establishment of death camps whose sole purpose would be the industrialized slaughter of Europe's Jews. The ultimate goal was nothing less than the destruction of every Jew in Europe, including those in countries not controlled by Germany. From Ireland to Cypress, all eleven million European Jews were to be exterminated. This end would be accomplished by converting several existing concentration camps into death camps. These camps would serve one purpose: the efficient and orderly murder of millions of people. One camp in particular, Auschwitz, has become the icon of the Holocaust.

Auschwitz and the Death Camps The typical Auschwitz experience began with the evacuation of a ghetto or other Jewish community. Taking only what they could carry, the ghetto residents would be herded onto freight railway cars and told they were being relocated to a resettlement camp. The journey in the open-topped cars, exposed to the elements and without food and water, could last for days, and many would die during the trip.

Upon arrival at Auschwitz, the vast majority would be sorted into a group destined for "de-lousing showers." A few—those deemed fit for manual labor or possessing special skills, or worse, singled out for medical experimentation by the infamously sadistic Dr. Josef Mengele (1911–1979)—would be spared, but the rest would be told to strip down and line up for the showers. The charade was maintained until the end—guards issued instructions to carefully sort and mark belongings for later collection and promised hot coffee and food after the showers.

The "shower rooms" were actually giant gas chambers that held around 1,000 people. The most commonly used agent, Zyklon B, was a nerve gas that would kill everyone in the chamber in twenty minutes

or less. The bodies were at first buried in mass graves, but soon giant crematoria were constructed. These huge furnaces burned hundreds of corpses at a time.

Meticulous records were kept of deportation numbers, as well as the spoils collected from victims of the camps—Jewish dentist-prisoners were forced to extract gold teeth from the gassed bodies at Auschwitz, and the prisoners' possessions that had been brought along were collected and redistributed to the German civilian population.

Resistance As their fate became increasingly clear, many in the ghettos and the camps rose up in futile rebellion. The remaining residents of the Warsaw ghetto famously held their own for four weeks before being crushed by overwhelming force. None of the ghetto uprisings were successful. There were also uprisings at Treblinka (another concentration camp) and Auschwitz, as well as periodic escape attempts, some of which were successful.

Some of these escapees were able to find someone who would believe their incredible stories, and these accounts eventually reached the ears of the Allied leadership. Initial reports were filed away as uncorroborated and too outrageous to be true, but as the evidence began to mount, the stories began to be believed. The BBC (British Broadcasting Corporation) and *New York Times* both reported on the existence of death camps in June 1944. Yet despite these stories, no one was prepared for the scale of killing uncovered as the Allied armies marched into German territories from all sides in 1945.

With the war turning against Germany, Hitler and Himmler made sure that the death camps continued to operate at full capacity, giving camp-bound trains priority even over military transports. Few realized that for Hitler the extermination of the Jews even trumped winning the war. Himmler and many other Nazi officials were terrified of the consequences to themselves that would come when the full scale of their "final solution" was discovered by the Allies.

Pressing into Germany in 1945, the Allies found concentration camps filled with starving, sick, and half-dead prisoners. Along with the Jewish captives, there were Soviet POWs who had been living in conditions nearly as miserable—two to three million died between 1941 and 1945 in the prison camps—as well as Romani and other "undesirables" (homosexuals, Freemasons, and Jehovah's Witnesses).

Reaction The reaction of soldiers and reporters upon first seeing these camps was one of sheer disbelief, horror, and outrage. BBC reporter Richard Dimbleby, reporting from the concentration camp at Bergen-Belsen, gave a typical account:

> Here over an acre of ground lay dead and dying
> people. You could not see which was which....
> The living lay with their heads against the corpses
> and around them moved the awful, ghostly

procession of emaciated, aimless people, with nothing to do and with no hope of life, unable to move out of your way, unable to look at the terrible sights around them.... Babies had been born here, tiny wizened things that could not live ..... A mother, driven mad, screamed at a British sentry to give her milk for her child, and thrust the tiny mite into his arms.... He opened the bundle and found the baby had been dead for days. This day at Belsen was the most horrible of my life.

General Eisenhower and other high-ranking Allied leaders later toured the camps and ordered that what they saw be filmed and photographed to preserve for the historical record. Local German civilians were brought in and forced to tour the camps as well, even in some cases being assigned to burial duty. The culpability of the German people as whole during the period of the Holocaust remains a hotly debated issue, but it is certain that the Holocaust could not have functioned without the cooperation of German government and industry.

The total number of Jews killed during the Holocaust will perhaps never be known exactly. The estimates range between five and six million, fully two-thirds of the prewar population. Many of those responsible for the mass murder were tried and executed, both in the immediate aftermath of the war and at the Nuremberg Trials in 1946. The three most infamous perpetrators of the Holocaust—Hitler, Himmler, and Heydrich—all met their deaths before they could be brought to justice, Hitler and Himmler both choosing suicide and Heydrich dying in 1942 at the hands of a Czech assassin.

✪ Aftermath

Rise of Communist China

During World War II, China was not directly involved with the conflict but was at war separately with Japan. From two to fifteen million Chinese died as a result of the Japanese occupation of and hostilities toward China. Though Japan was defeated by the Allies in 1945, a war continued in China. Even before Japan started a war against China, China had been suffering from an intense internal conflict. It had begun in 1912 with the end of imperial China after the 1911 Republican Revolution. China fell into political chaos while it was an ostensible republic from 1912 to 1927.

Decades of Civil War In 1920, Communism was introduced into China and soon came into conflict with the ruling Nationalist Party, or Kuomintang. The long-running civil war in China was fought between the Nationalists and the Communists. The Nationalists had gained control of China in 1927 and moved away from revolutionary policies that had been previously implemented. The Communists left their urban base and moved to the countryside, where Mao Zedong emerged as the party's leader and led a reorganization effort.

The rival parties continued their fight for a decade, until Japan invaded China in 1937 and launched the Sino-Japanese War. Japan and its control of certain territories within China were already controversial, but the invasion took this hostility to a new level. While both Chinese parties fought against the Japanese as World War II was being fought, their conflict still raged behind the scenes. The power of the Nationalist Party eroded during the eight-year conflict with the Japanese, while the Communists gained regional power.

The civil war grew more intense after the Japanese surrender in 1945, with the Communists gaining ground on the failing Nationalists. By July 1946, the whole of China was engaged in total civil war. For the next three years, the internal conflict continued, and the Communists gained control of an increasing number of major Chinese cities. Though the Communists lacked the military power and material support of the Nationalists, they gained popular support and benefited from the collapse of the corrupt and often ineffective Nationalist government.

In October 1949, at the civil war's end, the Communists, still led by Mao, were in total control of the country. The nation was then known as the People's Republic of China. The Nationalist Party removed itself to the island of Taiwan by December of that year.

Creation of Communist Society Under Mao's leadership, a Communist government was established in China and began rebuilding the shattered country using Communist principles. Nearly all westerners were expelled from China, and the extraterritorialities were ended. (Extraterritoriality was a quasi-colonial system by which other countries essentially ruled parts of China and did not have to follow Chinese laws.) Western powers soon boycotted the country.

During the 1950s, China saw economic and social reforms implemented by Communist leaders, beginning with land reform. Collectives and agricultural cooperatives were emphasized as villages were turned into communes. Though Chinese society was changing, the economy remained primarily agricultural, with little industrialization. The Communist revolution in China was initially peasant-based. Chinese society also evolved. The practice of multiple wives was banned by the Communists, for example. Women gained legal equality through the 1950 Marriage Law.

Internationally, China and the Soviet Union were initially strong allies under the 1950 Treaty of Friendship. The Soviets agreed to provide aid, including military and technological assistance, to China. However, this alliance did not last the decade. There was a dispute between them over how they handled the Korean War early in the decade. Later on, the countries split over how they interpreted communist principles. China was also upset that the Soviets would not share their knowledge of how to make an atomic bomb. The relationship turned hostile and remained so for several decades.

Controversial Movements By 1958, Mao and the Communists tried to quickly force industrialization in China through the "Great Leap Forward." This strategy continued to emphasize the establishment of rural communes as well as small steel foundries. The strategy was an economic failure. By pushing industrialization on a country still relatively undeveloped, the Communists had caused agriculture to suffer. Bad weather compounded the problem. China then experienced widespread famine. This food crisis became one of the largest ever seen in the world: between fifteen and thirty million people died of starvation.

In 1966, Mao launched another change intended to better his country by empowering youth, students, and lower-level party members. The Cultural Revolution, also known as the Great Proletarian Revolution, forced massive social and political changes on China. The Communists tried to destroy all traditions and accepted societal elements by wiping out sites of religious and historic importance and locking up teachers and intellectuals. They also tried to obliterate the concept of social class. Even the Communist Party and the Chinese government were affected by the movement. They were both purged of important leaders while retaining their basic structure, causing two years of turmoil. As a whole, the Cultural Revolution lasted until the death of Mao in September 1976, when China again began embracing a more market-centered economy and relaxing control over citizens' private lives.

Rise of the Soviet Union

During World War II, the Soviet Union suffered heavy loss of life and property. In the postwar period—as a reluctant ally of the United States and Great Britain—it enjoyed increased political importance and prestige on the world stage. From twenty to forty million Soviet citizens died between June 1941 and May 1945. Seven million of these were soldiers—the Soviet Union lost more soldiers than any other country involved in the conflict. During the two-and-a-half year German siege of Leningrad, one million Soviet civilians died. The homes of about twenty-eight million Soviets were destroyed, and at least 70,000 communities suffered extensive damage. A key aspect of the Soviet infrastructure—the railway—also saw thousands of miles of destruction. In addition, there was the loss of an extensive number of livestock and related agriculture products, which contributed to an extensive famine in the Soviet Union in 1947.

Despite this dire situation, the Soviet Union was able to rebuild and to expand its domain, and it emerged as a significant world power. Soviet leader Joseph Stalin remained in control of the Soviet Union. He had laid the groundwork for the Soviet Union's postwar recovery during World War II. The Soviet Union had marched the Red Army into Germany and several other Eastern European countries as World War II waned. In retribution for the way the German army treated Soviet soldiers and civilians when the Nazis invaded Russia in 1941, Soviet forces killed up to one million German civilians during the invasion of that country.

Expansion of Influence Before the war's end, the Allies, including the Soviet Union, decided to divide Germany into four zones. Each zone would be occupied by a major power in the war—the United States, Great Britain, France, and the Soviet Union. While the Allies had significant disagreements during the war, their differences were intensified after the war end. The Soviet Union was already Communist, and it turned the part of Germany it controlled—the eastern section—into a Communist country. Thus was the "Cold War" born—the Soviet Union became the leading Communist nation, and the Allies sought to prevent further expansion of Soviet and Communist influence in Europe and around the world by means other than war.

The Soviet Union had extended its influence to other European countries and sometimes took over whole nations and parts of nations. For example, it absorbed the Baltic countries of Lithuania, Latvia, and Estonia in the early 1940s. These three countries remained part of the Soviet Union until its dissolution in 1991. The Soviet Union also added the eastern tip of Czechoslovakia as well as parts of eastern Poland and Germany to its territory at the end of World War II.

The Eastern Bloc Soviet-influenced Germany became the country of East Germany in 1949 and was significant member of the Eastern Bloc. The Eastern Bloc of nations consisted primarily of Central and Eastern European countries that the Soviet Union had liberated from Germany at the end of World War II. These nations included Poland, Czechoslovakia, Romania, Hungary, and Bulgaria. (Yugoslavia, China, and Albania were also initially part of the group, but a conflict with Yugoslavia resulted in its expulsion in 1949. A rift between China and the Soviet Union during the 1950s led to both China and Albania withdrawing in 1959 and 1960, respectively.)

Stalin's liberation of these countries was about controlling them—although not strictly for the purpose of expanding Communism. By dominating the Eastern Bloc nations, the Soviet Union hoped to prevent invasion through those countries by another country, which had happened a number of times in the preceding centuries.

Providing financial support to reconstruct these countries, the Soviet Union put local Communist parties in power and essentially ran them. While locals initially supported the Soviet-friendly regimes because they resisted the Nazis and supported reform and social

French prisoners of war are marched from the battlefield at Dien Bien Phu, July 1954, setting the stage for the end of French power in Indochina. © *Bettmann/Corbis*

justice, popular backing soon waned under the Communist restrictions that were backed by Soviet military might. Members of the Communist Party gained the best government jobs in these countries, and noncommunists were removed from office. The media was also controlled and censored by the Soviet-dominated Communists.

While there was vast short-term economic growth from the late 1940s to the early 1950s because of industrialization and the forced implementation of collective programs, Eastern Bloc societies were also forced to undergo rapid change. These societies faced mass terror campaigns that created upheaval and unrest. The absolute Soviet dominance of the Eastern Bloc countries ended with Stalin's death on March 5, 1953. After that, Soviet control was loosened, and more civil unrest occurred. The Eastern Bloc remained intact until the late 1980s.

French-Indochina War

In the wake of World War II, tensions in an arranged power-sharing agreement between Vietnam and France over the area known as Indochina (what is now known as Laos, Cambodia, and Vietnam) erupted into full-scale war. The French-Indochina War, also known as the First Indochina War, lasted eight years and eventually led to the Vietnam War.

Background Indochina became a colony of the French during the 1880s. France continued to control the area until World War II. During the war, Ho Chi Minh (1890–1969) and his Vietnamese Communist Party wanted to bring communalism, a form of Communism that also included the values of traditional Vietnamese society, to an independent Vietnam. To that end, they founded the Viet Nam Doc Lap Dong Minh Hoi (the Revolutionary League for the Independence of Vietnam) in 1941. Commonly known as the Viet Minh, the independence movement had the support of many different nationalist groups in Vietnam.

By that time, France's hold on Indochina had temporarily ended. After France was taken over by the Germans in 1940 and the puppet Vichy government was installed, Germany's Japanese allies seized the opportunity to use Vietnam as an operations base. Within a year, Japan controlled the whole of Indochina, though the French ostensibly maintained a colonial presence. While the Viet Minh fought the Japanese, with some support of the Americans, the Japanese brutally dominated Vietnam until World War II's end in 1945.

At the immediate conclusion of World War II, the Viet Minh took advantage of the power vacuum in Vietnam. Ho declared the creation of the Democratic Republic of Vietnam, an independent country, on

September 2, 1945. This republic only lasted a few days, because liberated France wanted to reclaim control of its colonial empire in Indochina as part of a postwar rebuilding effort.

While political decisions were being made about the area, the Allies put occupation forces in Vietnam. The disarmament of the Japanese military was overseen by the Chinese Nationalist troops in the north and the British in the south. President Franklin D. Roosevelt had not supported the French colonial rule of Indochina before his death, but his successor, Harry S. Truman, was more concerned with gaining French support against the Soviets. Thus, Indochina returned to French rule with the backing of the United States. The Vietnamese, led by Ho, and the French were to share power in Vietnam, which was to be seemingly autonomous within French-controlled Indochina.

This power arrangement was undermined by both sides in several ways. There were communication breakdowns between France and Vietnam, and the power-sharing agreement was defined in imprecise terms. French economic interests put pressure on the French government to keep a significant French presence there. And Ho still wanted to gain complete independence for his country.

The War Begins   Hostilities in the region escalated when Chinese smugglers were captured and both sides claimed jurisdiction in the situation. The French and Vietnam forces began fighting in Haiphong over the matter in November 1946. France took the conflict to a new level within a few days, using air, ground, and naval forces on the city. By December, the fighting had reached Hanoi, and Ho told his people to resist the French. The French Indochina War had begun, and within a year, the conflict enveloped the whole region.

Early in the war, France removed Viet Minh forces from the cities, so Ho and his leadership went north to an area near the border with China. With his military advisors, he developed a three-pronged strategy. It began with constant, harassing guerrilla warfare, and then moved to creating a stalemate with the French by isolating and destroying smaller French units. In the final stage, a considerable offensive against the French would bring the war to an end. While the plan was not fully executed, it contributed to France's ultimate defeat.

Viet Minh Victories   The first phase of the Viet Minh strategy worked to perfection from 1947 to the middle of 1950. While the guerrilla hits on the French were successful, the Vietnamese senior military commander, Vo Nguyen Giap (c. 1911–), also had the added benefit of time to build up and train his army. The Vietnamese also gained modern weapons from the newly Communist country of China after 1949. The French checked Ho and his independence desires by reinstalling Emperor Bao Dai (1913–1997) as a figurehead on the Vietnamese throne in 1948.

Giap moved to phase two of the plan in the fall of 1950, when his 300,000-soldier army began attacking French outposts in northern Vietnam. Beginning with the small garrison at Dong Khe, the Viet Minh forced the French troops from the post and then took several more in the border region in the fall of 1950. The French were surprised and unprepared for the strength and determination of the Viet Minh and saw 6,000 troops killed or captured.

Stalemate   Under the command of Jean de Lattre de Tassigny (1889–1952) and with American aid, French troops rallied to significant victories in 1951. While the Viet Minh also had heavy troop losses at Vinh Yen, Mao Khe, and other villages in the Hanoi-Haiphong corridor, they continued to battle the French. However, the French public questioned the cost of the war and de Lattre died of cancer in early 1952, unexpectedly bringing phase two of the Viet Minh strategy back into play.

Most of 1952 and 1953 were spent in a stalemate between the two sides. While the French began building the Vietnamese National Army to augment their own forces, Giap prepared for an attack on Laos. The assault came in April 1953, and he nearly made it to the royal capital of Luang Prabang. As monsoon season came on, Giap was compelled to withdraw his troops. As the Viet Minh made their way back to Vietnam, the French decided to make their stand at the small village of Dien Bien Phu. After an intense six-month battle, the French lost Dien Bien Phu in the spring of 1954. The French-Indochina War reached its inconclusive end.

France had suffered greatly because of the conflict. Nearly 100,000 French soldiers lost their lives. The United States had also become increasingly involved in the war, and by its end, was paying about three-quarters of its cost. But because the French still controlled significant amounts of Vietnam, at war's end, the Geneva Accord saw Vietnam being artificially divided into two countries. There was a communist north, led by Ho, and a noncommunist south, led by Ngo Dinh Diem, part of the former French puppet government. The arrangement was meant to be a temporary solution until elections could be held, but, following U.S. advice, Ngo Dinh Diem delayed elections because he thought the Communists would win. When Ho tried to take over South Vietnam a few years later, the United States became involved in an even more devastating conflict in the region: the Vietnam War.

Truman Doctrine

Announced in 1947 by President Harry S. Truman, the Truman Doctrine was the president's policy vision on how to address the increasingly aggressive actions of the Soviet Union in the post–World War II period. Though it initially addressed the tumultuous situation in Greece, Truman envisioned the principles of the Truman Doctrine being applied worldwide to contain the spread of Communism. The Truman Doctrine guided American foreign policy for decades.

Origins While the Soviet Union was an ally of the United States and Great Britain during much of World War II, the Communist country proved to have its own agenda after the end of the conflict. The Soviets began creating a sphere of influence in Eastern and Central Europe as well as parts of Germany, installing and supporting Communist regimes in countries they were in charge of rebuilding beginning in 1946. Though this development concerned Great Britain and the United States because of their uncertainty about Soviet intentions, they initially did not object to the Soviet Union's actions in Europe. This attitude soon changed, in part because of fresh memories of the expansionism of Nazi Germany. During the 1930s, country after country fell under its control without any serious challenge.

As the postwar era continued to unfold, the United States and the Soviet Union emerged as the greatest powers on the world stage and intense rivals in the nascent Cold War. This rivalry saw its first clashes in Greece and Turkey. The royalist, right-wing government in Greece was threatened by Communist revolutionaries who were backed by Eastern European Communists. Nearby Turkey was also a target of pressure from the Soviet Union for partial control of the outlet from the Black Sea to the Mediterranean. Great Britain had been the primary supporter of both countries but no longer possessed the resources to continue to do so because of its own postwar problems. Britain asked the United States to intercede.

Truman's Call for Aid Truman decided to act. He decided to end appeasement of the Soviets to ensure Communism would not spread. On March 12, 1947, he delineated what became known as the Truman Doctrine in a speech before a joint session of Congress. Initially, Truman asked Congress for $400 million in military assistance for Greece and Turkey, which was granted despite a growing isolationist attitude and aversion to giving more foreign aid.

In his speech, Truman also made clear that this call for aid was only part of a new approach in American foreign policy. Because of the United States' new importance in the world, he stated, it must now act in support of all free countries threatened by military subjugation or pressures from other countries. Both economic and military support were necessary. While there was some opposition to the principles he outlined, Truman eventually gained the backing he needed, because the growing fear of Communism in the U.S. outweighed any apprehension about increased government spending.

Doctrine's Effect After the Communists were defeated in both Greece and Turkey, Truman's goal became ensuring Communism would not spread from Eastern and Central Europe through Western Europe. To further support the principles of the Truman Doctrine, the United States supported funding the Marshall Plan, which helped pay for the rebuilding of Europe. Later, America entered into its first peacetime military alliance with many other Western European countries—the North Atlantic Treaty Organization (NATO).

The Truman Doctrine expanded its scope when the Korean War broke out in 1950. There, a struggle between democratic and Communist forces led to the principles of the Truman Doctrine being applied to Asia as well as other countries around the world. Because of the doctrine, the United States later became involved in the Vietnam War, another conflict involving Communist-backed forces. While the Truman Doctrine furthered the Cold War, it also led to the end of Communist influence in nearly every country in the world before the end of the twentieth century.

Marshall Plan

A product of the Truman Doctrine to contain Communism, the Marshall Plan (also known as the European Recovery Program) was the United States' contribution to the recovery of Europe and one of the most important government initiatives of the twentieth century. It consisted of financial aid for industry, transportation, finance, and farming so that free trade and freedom would continue to be part of European life after the devastation of World War II. By supporting the rebuilding of European countries, America ensured that Communism and the influence of the Soviet Union would remain limited.

A mason works to repair a Berlin concert hall with the help of the European Recovery Program, or "Marshall Plan," in 1950. © *Bettmann/Corbis*

Background From 1939 to 1945, the duration of World War II in Europe, every country on the continent suffered physical and economic devastation because of the conflict. Numerous bombing raids on both sides obliterated many of the industrial and transportation centers all over Europe. Because of the wide swath of destruction, European nations could not easily recover on their own, even though countries like Great Britain received billions of dollars in loans. In 1948, overall economic output was 13 percent below 1938 levels in Europe. The situation was worse in Germany, where it was 55 percent lower.

The stagnant economy made life difficult for Europeans, who had little hope for the future. Refugees numbering in the millions still lived in camps for many months after the end of the war. In Great Britain and other countries, certain foodstuffs like bread were still being rationed as they had been during World War II. While the United States gave billions of dollars in aid to eleven European countries between July 1945 and March 1948, the economies of European nations deteriorated further.

At the same time, the Soviet Union's influence was on the rise. While that country also suffered greatly, perhaps more than any other nation in Europe, Soivet leader Joseph Stalin focused on consolidating Communist influence, if not control, of many Eastern and Central European countries. After gaining dominance over these countries, Soviet efforts were focused on Greece and Turkey. The Truman Doctrine's military aid ensured the Communists did not gain control in those countries, but Italy and France seemed to be the next targets by the end of 1947. Stalin encouraged Communists in every country to challenge the capitalist status quo.

Emergence of the Plan While the United States had also suffered during World War II, there had been little damage to its infrastructure. The nation was economically strong at the end of the conflict and did not have a particularly difficult transition to a peacetime economy. By 1948, American economic output was 65 percent higher than 1938 levels. As the United States was realizing its new status as a world leader, the threat of Communism to war-ravaged Europe became clearer.

Recognizing the threat, William Clayton (1880–1966), an official with the U.S. State Department, created a solution he called the European Recovery Program (ERP). Clayton wanted the United States to give European countries billions of dollars in aid and loans. These dollars were linked to initiatives created in Europe by Europeans to rebuild key industries and infrastructures and to ensure Europe's full recovery.

Secretary of State George Marshall announced the initiative at a speech at Harvard University on June 5, 1947, while accepting an honorary degree. The Marshall Plan, as the ERP became commonly known, had support within the State Department, but it needed key allies in Congress and the federal government to become a reality. The State Department worked closely with the Republicans, who controlled Congress, though many conservative Republicans held the isolationist view echoed by public opinion.

Many Americans wanted to return political focus to the United States and see an end to the high taxes that had been prevalent throughout the war. A promotional campaign worked to change the minds of Americans, reminding them that the post-World War I policy of isolating Germany and its allies led to World War II. The ERP could prevent World War III. Supporters also advocated the Marshall Plan as a means of enhancing American national security.

The Plan in Action By February 1948, the Soviets had grabbed control of Czechoslovakia, and Americans realized that isolationist policies would be detrimental to their interests. The ERP gained widespread support. As passed by Congress and signed into law on April 3, 1948, the ERP was a four-year program with at least $13.4 billion in aid. This figure included $1.5 billion in loans. The integrated plans for recovery were to be developed by the Europeans based on how best to restore their finances, create capital investments, reestablish a market economy, and rebuild the infrastructure in their countries.

The money and support of the Marshall Plan were offered to all European nations, including the Soviet Union and the Eastern and Central European countries in its sphere of influence. Stalin refused the aid and would not allow the countries controlled by the Soviets to take any money either. To further his hold on these countries, he put the so-called Molotov Plan into place, which made them economically integrated with the Soviets.

Stalin also tried to undermine American efforts by encouraging Communists in Western Europe to whip up anti-American sentiment. This effort was in vain as most Western European countries—except, most notably, Finland and Switzerland—took part in the Marshall Plan. It was welcomed by most nations and proved essential in Western Europe's economic and psychological recovery, as well as in its return political stability in the late 1940s and for decades afterwards. The Plan's programs also helped the American economy by creating a multibillion dollar market for American materials and products.

The Marshall Plan came to an end on March 31, 1951, because of the economic demands of the new Korean War and declining support in the United States. It did, however, have its desired effect in Europe. Moreover, the groundwork laid by the ERP eventually led to the formation of the European Union four decades later.

Birth of Israel

At the end of World War II, the modern state of Israel was born, to much opposition by the Arab world. The history of the modern founding of this country had its roots in the early twentieth century. Based on the teachings of nineteenth century Zionist philosopher Moses Hess, Zionist Jews who wanted to found a Jewish state in what was then Palestine began moving to the area in 1904 and continued to do so through World War I.

Palestine as British Mandate

In the aftermath of World War I, Great Britain was given the mandate for Palestine by the League of Nations. While it was the ruling power of a predominantly Arab Middle Eastern country, Britain also recognized that both Jews and Arabs were also historically connected to the land that made up Palestine, and that Jews had a claim to a Jewish state. The Balfour Declaration of 1917 formally recognized the right for a Jewish state.

Because the British mandate acknowledged the Jewish claim and supported Zionist Jews who wanted to found a Jewish state in Palestine, large numbers of Jews immigrated to Palestine in the 1920s and much of the 1930s. This population movement led to conflicts with the Arabs already inhabiting Palestine that the British could not settle. There were armed battles as Jews protected kibbutzim (agricultural settlements) from attacks by Arabs, beginning in the 1920s and continuing through the founding of Israel.

By the late 1930s, the British tried to appease the Arab population by restricting Jewish immigration, but Jewish activists living there smuggled in Jews leaving Europe to avoid the Holocaust. This situation increased tensions between Jews, Arabs, and the British government.

Palestine Divided

Before World War II ended, the British mandate was challenged by both Jews and Arabs. Each group wanted independence and its own country, but Britain no longer supported a Jewish state and continued to try to limit Jewish immigration to Palestine. In 1947, Britain bowed out of the conflict by turning over its Palestine mandate to the newly formed United Nations (UN), though it formally retained control for another year. The UN created a proposal to divide Palestine into two separate nations, one Jewish and one Arab, a concept that was supported by the United States. The UN formally voted on partitioning Palestine on November 29, 1947, and the measure passed by a vote of thirty-three to thirteen.

The plan was supported by the Jewish inhabitants of Palestine, but not the Palestinian Arabs, who wanted to retain the whole of what had been their country. Because Arabs in Palestine could not organize any opposition or count on the support of fellow Arabs in the Arab League, Palestine was officially divided on May 14, 1948, after the British ended their control of the area the previous day. The state of Israel was then officially proclaimed by David Ben-Gurion (1886–1973), the head of the governing Jewish Agency, at the Tel Aviv Museum. He also became Israel's first prime minister and minister of defense.

As soon as Israel was founded and British troops began withdrawing, nearby Arab countries that opposed the creation of Israel—Egypt, Lebanon, Iraq, Syria, and what became Jordan—invaded Israel and launched a war against the Jews. With the support of the United States (the first country to formally recognize Israel, on May 15, 1948), Israel defeated the allied Arab countries in January 1949 and signed peace treaties with each nation over the next six months. Many Palestinian Arabs were forced to leave their homes and go to newly created refugee camps in adjacent Jordan, Syria, and Egypt. The conflict between Jews and Arabs over the land lasted for decades, occasionally broke out in armed war, and continues to this day.

Indian Independence

In 1947, India gained its long-sought independence from Great Britain. Over the course of a century, Indians had pursued their independence and received it in small steps.

The Indian subcontinent was divided into often warring states for centuries, and the idea of a united Indian country stretching over the entire region was embraced only by philosophers and poets until the nineteenth century. When the British made India a colony under the auspices of the East India Company in the eighteenth century, they also gave the country a national identity, though one that was deemed inferior in every possible way to the national identity of white nations. The British also exploited the Indians economically, taking their land and raw materials and limiting the advancement of the Indian peoples within the British colonial system.

Origins of Modern India

As the Indians embraced the concept of nationalism in the mid-1850s, an independence movement was born. The first open demonstration calling for Indian independence came with the Sepoy Rebellion of 1857, known in India as the 1857 Indian Revolt. It was caused by British economic mistreatment of Indians, increased British intrusion into the states and provinces of India, and disdain for Indian religious law.

Though the rebellion was put down, the British made changes in how India was administered. With the passing of the Government of India Act, control of India was removed from the East India Company and put directly under the British government. Also, Indians were then allowed to serve as counselors to the British colonial ruler, the viceroy.

British exploitation of India and its people continued in the late nineteenth and early twentieth centuries despite these changes. Indians were only permitted to hold positions in the lowest level of civil service, and were used as a cheap police force for the whole of the British empire well into the second decade of the new century. The Indian people saw their food supply compromised as many rice farms were turned into cotton

Millions of Muslims and Hindus became refugees after the creation of the independent nations of Pakistan and India in 1947.   © *Bettmann/ Corbis*

farms to provide raw materials for cotton mills in Britain. India's own cotton industry suffered as the products of these mills entered the Indian market without tariffs.

Independence Movement Grows   Because of this British exploitation, the Indian National Union was founded in 1885. It was soon known as the Indian National Congress, and later the Congress Party. The group initially wanted to see more local Indians in political representation. Soon, the Indian National Congress became identified with the independence movement, because the British continued to act in ways that were offensive to Indians. While India supported the British war effort during World War I, sending troops and backing the British did not result in more freedom. It only led to more authoritarian legislation such as the 1919 Rowlatt Acts.

Some Indians protested the laws, resulting in the Amritsar Massacre. A British general ordered his troops to fire on Indians who were peacefully demonstrating, resulting in the deaths of four hundred Indians and injury to one thousand more. In the wake of this event, more Indians withdrew their support from the British who seemed to have supported the massacre.

New leaders of the Indian independence movement emerged in the early 1920s, including Mohandas K. Gandhi (1869–1948), known as Mahatma Gandhi. Gandhi had been educated by the British, studying law in Great Britain. Though of upper-caste Hindu background, he lived humbly and was able to garner support among both educated Indians and the masses. Gandhi came up with a noncooperation policy that proved effective in the movement. Working with Gandhi, Jawaharlal Nehru (1889–1964) also wanted independence, and both men envisioned the new country of India as a Hindu state.

While the independence movement went forward in the decades between the world wars, there was a Muslim minority living primarily in the northwest area of the subcontinent that felt threatened by the idea. A Muslim member of the Congress Party, Mohammad Ali Jinnah (1876–1948), resigned to serve as the head of the Muslim League, which wanted to found a Muslim state. This division did not greatly affect the independence movement.

Independence Nears   The British control of India was becoming a heavy load for the mother country between World War I and World War II. In addition to having a trade deficit with India, Britain could find few young British citizens to serve in the Indian civil service. Although human rights legislation was introduced in India, Great Britain did not want to enforce the laws and often lacked the means to do so. India was allowed to languish with an ineffective Indian army and no evolution in existing institutions.

Independence took another step forward in 1935 when the British parliament gave India a new constitution. More people gained the vote, and individual provinces had more independence. As Great Britain entered World War II, the British viceroy decided, without the Indian people's consent, that India would support the war effort. The Muslim League gave limited cooperation to Great Britain in the hope of gaining British support for their own separate state, because part of Prime Minister Winston Churchill's Indian policy was support of the Muslims. The Congress Party refused to assist the British in any way.

To win India's support during World War II, the British devised the Cripps Plan. The primary provision was a promise to grant full independence to India at the end of World War II. Because of previous failed promises by the British, Gandhi and Nehru demanded the British leave the subcontinent in August 1942 so that Indians could establish self-governance. Churchill and the British government put Gandhi, Nehru, and some of their supporters in prison. The Congress Party was also banned. While order was temporarily restored in India, the end was near for British rule.

Independence Achieved In prison, Gandhi went on numerous hunger strikes. Riots were also threatened by his supporters. By 1944, Gandhi, Nehru, and their followers had been freed from prison. The following year, the British tried to appease Indian demands for independence with the 1946 proposed Cabinet Mission Plan. This idea offered to create a federal state divided into provinces with significant amounts of power. It was rejected by the Indians.

A year earlier, a new administration had taken office in Great Britain, led by Labor Party leader Clement Attlee. He supported Indian independence and publicly announced it would be given as soon as the transfer of power could be safely completed. One big task remained. Though Gandhi and the Hindus did not want a divided country, the Muslim League successfully argued for a separate Muslim state called Pakistan. This division was granted with the Indian Independence Act of 1947. The last British viceroy, Lord Louis Mountbatten (1900–1979) supervised the transfer of power and the division of the subcontinent. Independence Day came on August 15, 1947, for both India and Pakistan.

BIBLIOGRAPHY

Books

Benjamin, Thomas, ed. "China, After 1945." *Encyclopedia of Western Colonialism since 1450*, vol. 1. Detroit: Macmillan Reference, 2007.

———. "Indian National Movement." *Encyclopedia of Western Colonialism since 1450*, vol. 2. Detroit: Macmillan Reference, 2007.

Buell, Hal, ed. *World War II: A Complete Photographic History*. New York: Black Dog & Leventhal, 2002.

Carlisle, Rodney, ed. "Israel." *Encyclopedia of Politics*, vol. 1: The Left. Thousand Oaks: Sage Reference, 2005.

Dupuy, Ernest. *World War II: A Compact History*. New York: Hawthorn Books, 1969.

Gilbert, Martin. *The Second World War: A Complete History*. New York: Henry Holt and Company, 1989.

Karsten, Peter, ed. "G.I. Bill." *Encyclopedia of War and American Society*, vol. 1. Thousand Oaks: Sage Reference, 2005.

———. "Marshall Plan." *Encyclopedia of War and American Society*, vol. 2. Thousand Oaks: Sage Reference, 2005.

Katz, Solomon H., ed. "Rationing." *Encyclopedia of Food and Culture*. New York: Charles Scribner's Sons, 2003.

Keegan, John. *The Second World War*. New York.: Penguin Books, 1989.

Kimball, Warren. *The Juggler: Franklin Roosevelt as Wartime Statesman*. Princeton, NJ: Princeton University Press, 1991.

Kutler, Stanley I., ed. "Manhattan Project." *Dictionary of American History*, vol. 5, 3rd ed. New York: Charles Scribner's Sons, 2003.

———. "Office of Price Administration." *Dictionary of American History*. New York: Scribner's Sons, 2003.

———. "Television." *Dictionary of American History*. New York: Scribner's Sons, 2003.

———. "Truman Doctrine." *Dictionary of American History*. New York: Scribner's Sons, 2003.

Levinson, David, and Karen Christensen, eds. "The Partition of India." *Encyclopedia of Modern Asia*, vol. 5. New York: Charles Scribner's Sons, 2002.

McNeill, William, Jerry Bentley, and David Christian, eds. "Revolution, China." *Berkshire Encyclopedia of World History*, vol. 4. Great Barrington, MA: Berkshire, 2005.

———. "Revolutions, Communist." *Berkshire Encyclopedia of World History*, vol. 4. Great Barrington, MA: Berkshire, 2005.

Merriman, John, and Jay Winter, eds. "Eastern Bloc." *Encyclopedia of Modern Europe: Europe Since 1914: Encyclopedia of the Age of War and Reconstruction*, vol. 2. Detroit: Charles Scribner's Sons, 2006.

———. "Soviet Union." *Encyclopedia of Modern Europe: Europe Since 1914: Encyclopedia of the Age of War and Reconstruction*, vol. 4. Detroit: Charles Scribner's Sons, 2006.

Miller, Donald. *The Story of World War II*. New York.: Simon and Schuster, 1945.

Overy, Richard. *Why the Allies Won*. New York: W. W. Norton and Company, 1995.

Purdue, A.W. *The Second World War.*. New York: St. Martin's Press, 1999.

Resch, John, ed. "Manhattan Project." *Americans at War*, vol. 3: 1901–1945. Detroit: Macmillan Reference USA, 2005.

———. "Marshall Plan." *Americans at War*, vol. 4. Detroit: Macmillan Reference USA, 2005.

———. "Truman Doctrine." *Americans at War*, vol. 4. Detroit: Macmillan Reference USA, 2005.

———. "Manhattan Project." *Americans at War*, vol. 3: 1901–1945. Detroit: Macmillan Reference USA, 2005.

Rommel, Erwin. *Attacks*. Provo, UT: Athena Press, 1979. Originally published in 1935.

Introduction to the Korean War (1950–1953)

When World War II ended, Korea was one of several nations artificially divided and occupied by members of the victorious Allied coalition. The 38th parallel was set as the line of demarcation separating the northern and southern halves of the peninsula. After the war, North Korea, which Japan had controlled for many years, was occupied by Soviet and American forces. The Soviets organized a Communist regime in 1948, chose longtime Communist Kim Il-sung as its first premier, and named the region north of the 38th parallel the Democratic People's Republic of Korea. Korean nationalist Syngman Rhee won a United Nations–sponsored election that same year and became president of the Republic of Korea, also known as South Korea.

Fighting along the 38th parallel kept the divided country in a constant state of crisis. Despite the continuous violence, American forces withdrew in June 1949. The South Korean army was small, ill-trained, and poorly equipped—a sharp contrast to their Soviet-backed adversary to the north.

On June 25, 1950, North Korean forces invaded South Korea without warning. Within thirty-six hours, North Korean tanks had moved into Seoul, the South Korean capital. The United States reacted quickly and with great determination. On June 27, President Harry Truman committed United States ground forces stationed in Japan as well as air and naval forces to the fight. The American forces were inadequate to stem the powerful North Korean advance. By the end of the month, more than half the South Korean army had been destroyed. By early August, American and South Korean forces had been pushed as far as Pusan, a port city located on the southeastern tip of the peninsula. After violent fighting, a defense perimeter was established around the critical port and a stable boundary was assured.

American General Douglas MacArthur, commander of the UN forces, conceived a brilliant amphibious landing at Inchon, the west coast port located a few miles from Seoul. Within an hour and a half of the start of the assault, the critical island of Wolmi Do was captured. On September 29, after two weeks of fighting, Seoul was returned to the South Korean government. On October 1, UN forces chased the North Koreans past the 38th parallel.

The single most important decision of the war came next. Public demands for a complete victory supported MacArthur's desire to pursuing the defeated foe across the demarcation line. The first crossings into North Korea took place on October 1, and China responded by sending "volunteers" to assist North Korea. By early December, UN forces found themselves in a desperate retreat southward. Throughout the rest of the winter and early spring, the lines fluctuated from south of Seoul to north of the 38th parallel. When a stalemate was finally reached in July 1951, the war had settled into trench warfare. The stalemate was a source of mounting frustration in the United States, influencing both the rise of McCarthyism and the presidential election of Dwight D. Eisenhower. A final armistice agreement was signed on July 27, 1953.

Korean War (1950–1953)

✪ Causes

Red Menace

The Red Menace, also known as the Red Scare, refers to the fear of the spread of Communism throughout the United States and the world. This anticommunist feeling, which has roots in the 1917 Russian Revolution, bloomed after World War I and World War II, causing two distinct Red Scares. Though each had its own defining characteristics, both anticommunist crusades led to the passage of anticommunist legislation, the large-scale deportation of immigrants suspected of being Communists, and the active involvement of the attorney general's office and the Federal Bureau of Investigation (FBI) in locating subversives. Several events leading up to the Korean War (also referred to as the Korean Conflict, since the United States never formally declared war) persuaded Americans that Communism posed a genuine threat to domestic security. Speeches by Winston Churchill (1874–1965) and Joseph Stalin (1879–1953) in 1946, a 1948 Communist coup in Czechoslovakia, the Soviet explosion of an atomic bomb, and the rise of Communism in China in 1949, and the sensational trials of American Communists throughout the late 1940s and early 1950s caused America's fear of Communism to evolve into the antiradical crusade that led to McCarthyism and the Cold War.

Persuasive Speeches   Before 1945, anticommunist activists and ideologues tended to inhabit the fringes of American politics. In the immediate postwar years, anticommunist thinking gained legitimacy, which brought activists closer to the mainstream. Two powerfully galvanizing 1946 speeches helped make this change a reality. Winston Churchill gave the most famous of these speeches on March 5 to an assemblage at Westminster College in Fulton, Missouri, after receiving an honorary degree. In it, Churchill warned, "From Stettin in the Baltic to Trieste in the Adriatic, an iron curtain has descended across the Continent." The legendary statesman and orator was referring to developments leading to

the mobilization of anticommunist sentiment: Stalin's refusal to allow free elections in Poland and other Eastern European countries and the subsequent realization that he intended to use the Red Army to install Communist regimes in those countries. Churchill's landmark "Iron Curtain" speech is considered by many to be the beginning of the Cold War.

A month before Churchill delivered his speech, Joseph Stalin gave his own during the Russian elections. In it, he suggested that conflict between the East and West was inevitable and that reconciliation between the two sides was impossible. The speech revealed his own hardening attitude against Western powers and hinted at the complete collapse of Russia's fragile wartime unity with the United States. Americans took the speech as a threat.

The Truman Doctrine   The growing strength of American anticommunism deepened as a result of the Truman Doctrine. The decision, announced before a joint session of Congress on March 12, 1947, was triggered by Great Britain's inability to support Greece and Turkey in their fight against Communist insurgents during the crisis of the Greek Civil War. The nation turned to President Harry S. Truman (1884–1972) for help. Truman responded by making the containment of Communism official United States policy, saying, "The free peoples of the world look to us for support in maintaining their freedoms. If we falter in our leadership, we may endanger the peace of the world—and we shall surely endanger the welfare of our own nation."

Communism Abroad   In 1949, the United States was shocked by the "loss" of China to Mao Zedong's (1893–1976) Communist Red Army. The culmination of over twenty years of civil and international war—the establishment of the People's Republic of China on October 1, 1949,—seemed to confirm the Kremlin's threat of Communist world domination. The threat had already been advanced on August 29, 1949, the day the Soviet Union tested its first atomic bomb. Once

In the era of Joseph McCarthy and the Korean War, this young woman posed with "Red Menace" chewing gum, doing her part to fight communism. *AFP/AFP/Getty Images*

a remote hypothesis, World War III now appeared to be an imminent reality. Beyond the challenge of war, tangible proof of the success of the Soviet atomic bomb project banished any lingering sense of omnipotence from the American mind. No longer certain of its technological superiority, the United States was for the first time forced to recognize the Soviet Union as a possible military equal. This disquieting realization launched the country into a national obsession with anticommunism.

Communism at Home The fear of international Soviet expansion and the spread of its ideology inspired Americans to become fixated on a supposed Communist "fifth column" that threatened to destroy the United States from within. The term "fifth column" was first used in the Spanish Civil War and refers to a group within a state that attempts to subvert and weaken the state. The dangers of external expansion and internal subversion, though real, were highly exaggerated in 1949 and 1950. Newspaper headlines reporting the sensational confessions, revelations, and trials of accused radicals only bolstered domestic fears. The confessions of former Communists were especially influential. One Communist-turned-confessor, Elizabeth Bentley (1908–1963), admitted to playing a pivotal role in a Washington, D.C., spy ring during World War II. After claiming

responsibility for passing classified documents to the Soviets, she was labeled "the spy queen" by the press. Her 1951 autobiography, *Out of Bondage*, became a best seller and helped to shape the public's perception of the Red Menace.

Whittaker Chambers (1901–1961) was revealed to be the era's most significant apostate. Chambers accused former State Department employee Alger Hiss (1904–1996) of spying for the Soviet Union and backed up his accusation with evidence he provided to the FBI, among other agencies. A New York grand jury indicted Hiss on charges of perjury. His trial blurred the line between radical activism and espionage. It also united conservatives, split liberals, polarized public opinion, and became a defining moment in Cold War history. Americans who believed in a vast domestic Communist conspiracy felt their worst suspicions were confirmed when Hiss was found guilty in January 1950.

United States election results in 1946 and 1950 revealed the impact of the era's anticommunism climate. In 1946, the Republicans, who made Communism a major campaign issue, won control of both houses for the first time since 1933. In 1950, anticommunism rhetoric was even more explicit. This time around, Republicans accused Democrats of being soft on Communism. Public opinion polls in 1947 revealed that 61 percent of Americans supported a legal ban on the Communist Party. Just one year later, 77 percent believed that Communists should be required to register their political status with the government.

✪ Major Figures

Chiang Kai-shek

Chiang Kai-shek (1887–1975) was the head of the Chinese Nationalist Party from 1926 to 1975. He was born in Zhejiang, China, to a Qikou village salt merchant father and educated mother. Chiang showed signs of his future ambitions as a small child when he played war games with the neighborhood children. Young Chiang always appointed himself commanding general and gave orders to his friends. At the age of five, Chiang began receiving lessons from a Confucian tutor. The austere teachings left a lasting imprint on his personality. In 1901, when Chiang was fourteen, he married seventeen-year-old Mao Fumei in a union his parents arranged. In 1908, Fumei gave birth to Chiang's first child, Chiang Ching-kuo.

Chiang's teenage years dovetailed with the final, cruel years of the Manchu Dynasty. Angered by the poverty and weakness of his country, Chiang, like many other Chinese youths of the time, resolved to do something to change it. He decided to become a revolutionary and began by lopping off his *queue*, the long ponytail that symbolized loyalty to the dynasty. In 1906, Chiang began his military education at the Baoding Military Academy. From 1907 to 1913, he attended the Preparatory Academy in Tokyo,

Chiang Kai-shek, photographed here with his wife, attempted to cultivate allegiances with Americans during World War II. *AP Images*

Japan. In 1908, he met Dr. Sun Yat-sen, an American-educated agitator responsible for launching seven failed attempts at revolution. In 1913, Chiang returned to China where Yat-sen was devising a plan to overthrow the country's new leader, Yüan Shih-k'ai.

Kuomintang (KMT) The Kuomintang (KMT), or Chinese Nationalist Party, was created in 1912. It grew out of a body of political parties that emerged during the 1911 revolution to topple the Manchu Dynasty. As a division commander of Sun Yat-sen's wing of the KMT, Chiang was responsible for assisting Sun with his revolutionary activities. During this time, Chiang earned a reputation for being impulsive and temperamental. He threatened to quit on several occasions, usually when Sun did not heed his advice.

In early 1923, after failing to secure military and financial aid from the West, Sun allied the KMT with the Soviet Union. That August, Sun sent Chiang to Moscow to obtain arms and study military organization. Chiang, suspicious of the Communists, warned Sun about the Soviet's "sinister designs." Instead of heeding

Chiang's warning, Sun allowed members of the Chinese Communist Party (CCP) to join the KMT. In 1924, the KMT opened the Whampoa Military Academy, a military school designed to train officers for the next revolution. Because of his abilities as leader of the National Revolution Army (NRA), Chiang Kai-shek, was appointed its commandant. The Whampoa Military Academy boasted a staff that included future officers of both the nationalist and communist armies.

In 1925, Sun Yat-sen died. A yearlong crisis of succession followed. Chiang was not a front-runner in the contest to fill the vacant position of head of the KMT. He was considered too young. But in March 1926, he appealed to the anticommunist faction as they sought to curtail the growing communist strength of the party. Despite his age, the party chairman ruled in his favor. Chiang Kai-shek would control Chinese politics for the next twenty-three years.

The Northern Expedition Between 1926 and 1928, Chiang led his NRA on an ambitious drive north to defeat warlord armies that oppressively ruled various

On November 17, 1950, these Australian soldiers rode on a tank fifty miles north of Pyongyang, towards battle with North Korean and Chinese forces. *© Hulton-Deutsch Collection/Corbis*

sections of China as independent kingdoms. Chiang's goal in this Northern Expedition was to unite China under KMT rule. His victories were swift and decisive. The NRA began with 100,000 troops in July 1926, but by November it had 264,000. The NRA was popular with the masses, but the increased troop count had as much to do with warlords deciding to join Chiang rather than fight him. When the expedition ended in June 1928, 700,000 of Chiang's men ruled virtually all of China's larger cities. Chiang set up a new base in Nanjing, secure in the knowledge that he was the clear leader of China.

One of the most significant occurrences during the Northern Expedition was the slaughter of roughly three hundred communist leaders in Shanghai. This, in effect, destroyed the Communists' largest base and ended the period of KMT-CCP collaboration. The other significant event of this time was Chiang's marriage to Soong Mei-ling, a pretty, charming, American-educated Wellesley graduate who spoke perfect English and came from a wealthy Christian family. Chiang divorced his first wife and was baptized for his second. She would go on to play an important role in Chiang's life as confidante and promoter.

The Xi'an Incident In the mid-1930s, Chiang opted to continue his anticommunist campaign rather than fight the Japanese. This angered Zhang Xueliang, a young marshal from the city of Xi'an. Zhang ordered his men to kidnap Chiang on his next visit to the city. After Chiang had been seized, Zhang offered his leader a plan to unite the KMT and the CCP in a war against Japan. Chiang replied with a counteroffer: He challenged Zhang to kill him instead. A two-week standoff ensued while China held its breath. When Communist representative Zhou Enlai argued successfully for Chiang's release, he scored a Communist victory. He had demonstrated that his party was sincere in its desire for peaceful relations with the KMT. Chiang responded by agreeing to a united front against Japan.

China and U.S. Relations In the late 1930s, the United States began sending weapons, advisors, and money to China. Thanks in large part to Henry Luce, the powerful American media mogul and staunch Chiang supporter, Americans were infatuated with the Chiangs. After the Chiangs appeared on the cover of Luce's *Time* magazine as Man and Wife of the Year in

1937, Madame Chiang entranced Americans during a seven-month visit to the United States, raising millions along the way. The United States government, on the other hand, agonized over China. They would not support the Communists, yet they found Chiang's government to be loathsome. Its rampant corruption had frustrated the Chinese people enough to want to vote Chiang out of office. American mediations between Chiang and the Communists failed many times until, finally, Chiang's forces engaged the Communists in April 1946. The Communists defeated the nationalist forces in 1948, leaving Chiang to escape to Taiwan with more than a million followers. Because of pressure from anticommunist forces, the United States continued to recognize Chiang's government in Taiwan.

Chiang managed to establish and grow a thriving economy in Taiwan over the next twenty years. A combination of economic freedom and political order, as well as a healthy influx of American capital and military hardware, helped Chiang secure the country and produce astounding growth rates. American support and excellent relations with emerging African nations helped keep Taiwan in good stead with other countries. Chiang died on April 5, 1975. Although he remained president of the Republic of China until his death, he was never able to fulfill his dream of regaining China's mainland.

Henry Luce

Henry Robinson Luce (1898–1967) was the founder and publisher of the magazine empire that included *Time*, *Fortune*, and *Life*. In the late 1930s and early 1940s, Luce was America's single most powerful and innovative mass communicator. Fervently anticommunist, Protestant, and Republican, Luce used his magazines to promote his own views regarding U.S. foreign policy, especially regarding China. His February 1941 *Life* magazine piece titled "The American Century" outlined his vision for America in a postwar world and became famous in its own right. Luce's brilliance as an editor and publisher was matched by the influential power he wielded over U.S. political policy and public opinion.

Luce's Early Years Henry Robinson Luce was born in Shandong Province, China, to American missionary parents. Raised in China, Luce first came to the United States to attend the Hotchkiss School in Lakeview, Connecticut, when he was fifteen years old. While working on the school newspaper at Hotchkiss, Luce met Briton Hadden (1898–1929), his future publishing partner. After graduation, Luce attended Yale University where he and Hadden continued together on the Yale *Daily News*. After Yale, Luce attended Oxford University from 1920 to 1921. Around this time, he and Hadden first conceived the idea of a weekly news magazine. They believed most busy Americans could not keep up with current events on a daily basis. To remedy the problem, Luce and Hadden raised $86,000 and launched *Time* magazine. The first issue appeared on March 3, 1923.

Carl Mydans, who took this self-portrait just after the landing at Inchon, photographed the Korean Conflict for Life Magazine. *Carl Mydans/Time Life Pictures/Getty Images*

For four years, *Time* ran at a loss, but was making a profit by 1927. At the age of thirty, Luce was a self-made millionaire.

Time *Magazine* *Time* was the first newsmagazine of its kind. To serve its predominantly college-educated, middle-class readership, the magazine touched on such diverse topics as architecture, religion, and politics—all with a decidedly interpretive slant. Luce's editorial influence, first seen in the pages of *Time*, would become something of a signature as his media dynasty grew. This was no accident. In the prospectus for the magazine, Luce and Hadden included six points of "Editorial Bias." Luce was often criticized for the lack of objectivity in his publications, but he was not swayed by his detractors. Objectivity, it seemed, was never one of Luce's goals. He was more concerned with conceiving editorial innovations based on the idea that news should be entertaining as well as informative. A fundamental element of *Time* editorial policy, then, was to dramatize the news. Another innovation was the use of group journalism, a concept that used teams of researchers, correspondents, and editors to produce stories.

Creating an Empire The success of *Time* inspired Luce and Hadden to create a new magazine. Because they believed business was the common denominator of leading citizens and the mark of American genius, they decided to launch a lavish monthly magazine dedicated to the topic. When Hadden died suddenly in 1929, Luce assumed sole control of *Time* and moved forward with *Fortune*. The first issue appeared in January 1930, just weeks after the stock market crashed. Despite the crash and the ensuing Great Depression, *Fortune* was a success. Luce expanded Time Inc.'s business to include a dramatized radio news broadcast that evolved into a newsreel series called "The March of Time." First screened in February 1935, the series was viewed thirteen times a year in over ten thousand movie theaters worldwide. Then Luce introduced Americans to photojournalism. *Life* magazine, with its excellent photography and light articles, appeared for the first time on November 17, 1936, to immediate success. Luce's fourth successful magazine, *Sports Illustrated*, appeared on August 16, 1954.

Luce and Domestic and Foreign Policy Throughout the 1930s, Henry Luce's foreign policy was that of a conservative businessman defending capitalism. Adamantly anti-Soviet, *Time* went so far as to introduce the idea of an international capitalist boycott of the Soviet Union as a way of toppling Stalin. Because Luce believed the world was being clearly divided into fascist and communist camps, he stood firmly on the side of the fascists.

At the beginning of World War II, Luce began to conceive of the idea of a U.S.-led international opposition to Communism. This thinking inspired him to write "The American Century," which appeared in *Life* in February 1941. An audacious declaration of American aims in a postwar world, the piece became instantly famous. In it, Luce wrote that the twentieth century was nothing less than the American century, revealing the breathtaking scope of his vision. He explained that to become a true world power, the United States would have to adopt an aggressively internationalist foreign policy that provided economic assistance and military aid to those nations that supported what he defined as American ideals. The article was not overtly anti-Soviet, but it did divide the world into forces of "tyranny" and forces of "freedom."

Luce's China Lobby Luce's anticommunism was most evident in *Time*'s coverage of China. He continually presented in its pages a picture of a country in chaos, which led some to blame the editor and publisher for contributing to America's general hysteria over Communist China. An influential member of something called the China Lobby, a group of Americans seeking increased U.S. aid for Chiang Kai-shek's nationalists, Luce called for direct American military intervention against Chinese Communists. When Chiang was eventually defeated, Luce blamed American foreign service personnel in China and State Department leaders who criticized Chiang's government for being corrupt and out of touch. Because of Luce's press, these "China Hands," American diplomats and soldiers blamed for the "loss" of China, were chased out of office. Luce's influence over China policy continued into the early 1960s. It was so powerful that government officials, including John F. Kennedy (1917–1963), were forced to recant any support of more flexible policies fearing political retaliation wrought by the powerful publisher.

Luce's hold on U.S. policy in Asia had relaxed by the time he died on February 28, 1967. His old age and waning involvement in his magazines coupled with the larger social and political climate of the times were largely responsible. By the time President Richard M. Nixon announced his visit to China, old Republican charges about the "loss" of China had lost their intimidating power.

Syngman Rhee

Syngman Rhee (1875–1965), was a Korean nationalist and anti-Japanese activist who became the first president of the Republic of Korea (South Korea) in 1948.

Early Years Syngman Rhee was born Yi Sung-man in Pyong-san, Hwanghae Province, Korea. He adopted the name by which he is known in the West when he turned thirty in 1905. Rhee was the only son of Yi Kyong-son, a member of Pyong-san's ruling class. When Rhee was very young, his family moved to the declining capital city of Seoul, where the boy studied classic literature and Chinese before enrolling in a Methodist mission school in 1894. After graduation, Rhee became the school's English instructor. His interest in Western enlightenment ideas informed his critical view of the anachronistic Korean government, which led to his eventual arrest and imprisonment in 1897. He was a political prisoner for the next seven years. While he was in jail, Rhee converted to the Methodist faith.

In 1904, two months after he was released from prison, he traveled to the United States at the request of high-level Korean government officials. Rhee and the Reverend P. K. Yoon, a representative of the largest Korean community in Hawaii, were sent to enlist U.S. aid in the protection of Korean independence. Rhee and Yoon had to wait six months for an audience with President Theodore Roosevelt (1858–1919). They were turned down. The American-Korean Treaty of 1882 had weakened and the United States was eager to cooperate with Japan now that the country had emerged victorious from the Russo-Japanese War.

An American Education Rhee continued to pursue his goal of saving Korean independence through a series of fruitless appeals. In the meantime, he enrolled at George Washington University and became a student

This 1948 ceremony, attended by Syngman Rhee and Douglas Macarthur, marked the founding of the Korean Republic.
Carl Mydans/Time Life Pictures/Getty Images

until the Japanese national and military police became unable to contain them. Despite the arrival of Japanese army and the navy forces, protests persisted for months. By the end of the demonstrations, hundreds of Japanese were killed and thousands were injured and arrested.

One outcome of the Samil Movement was the formation of a provisional government by a group of independence leaders in Seoul in April 1919. These leaders moved the provisional government to Shanghai, China, and elected Syngman Rhee the first president of the new government-in-exile. Because he still lived in the United States, Rhee had to perform his duties long-distance, which led to his being impeached in March 1925. Rhee was replaced by Kim Ku (1876–1949) as president of the government-in-exile. Despite his impeachment, Rhee continued to assert his right to the presidency, an assertion supported by the Korean populace in Hawaii.

In early 1933, Rhee traveled to Geneva, Switzerland, to appeal on behalf of Korea to the delegates at the League of Nations. Like his appeals in Washington, this one failed. The major powers were either unable or unwilling to check expansionist Japan. But his trip was not completely wasted. In Geneva, Rhee met Franziska Donner (1900–1992), who was serving as a secretary to the Austrian delegation. Rhee and Donner were married in October of that year.

Rhee's Return to Korea Syngman Rhee returned to Korea when Allied powers finally liberated the country from Japanese colonial domination in 1945. The Korean people and the American military government that was ruling the southern half of the country gave Rhee a hero's welcome. Rhee soon became leader of conservative, right-wing forces in South Korea due to his previous engagement as president of the "exile government."

Rhee continued to rise through the ranks of post-colonial South Korean politics. On May 10, 1948, the first general elections in Korean history were held to elect members of the National Assembly. Rhee's Association for the Rapid Realization of Independence won a number of seats. When the Assembly met for the first time on May 31, 1948, Rhee was elected Assembly chairman. Under his chairmanship, the National Assembly adopted the 1948 constitution of Korea, which provided for a largely democratic, presidential system of government. One of the Assembly's first official constitutional acts was to elect Rhee as Korea's first president. He was seventy-three years old.

in the spring of 1905. In 1907, he was admitted to Harvard University and earned his master's degree a year later. In 1910, the same year that Japan formally annexed its Korean protectorate, Rhee received his doctorate in political science from Princeton University. The title of his dissertation was "Neutrality as Influenced by the United States." Rhee returned to Korea in 1910 and worked as a YMCA organizer, teacher, and evangelist. In 1912, when an international conference of Methodist delegates was held in Minneapolis, Rhee attended as a lay delegate of the Korean Methodists. He decided to stay in the United States and took a prominent position at the Korean Compound School, later the Korean Institute, in Honolulu, in 1913.

The Road to Korean Independence On March 1, 1919, Koreans participated in country-wide demonstrations inspired by U.S. President Woodrow Wilson's (1956–1924) "Fourteen Points" speech that outlined the right of national self-determination. During the demonstrations, which came to be known as the Mansei Uprising or the Samil Movement or the March First Movement, thirty-three leading Korean citizens signed a declaration of independence and read it to the crowds gathered in the streets. The Japanese response to the massive uprising was immediate and violent. On March 1, over 7,500 demonstrators were killed and roughly 16,000 were wounded. Protests erupted and spread

The Korean War The new republic was only two years old when waves of North Korean troops invaded South Korea and swiftly occupied the capital of Seoul on June 25, 1950. So began the Korean War, which in several ways was a continuation of ideological disputes that had been active since the Japanese occupation. What started as a civil war quickly exploded into a superpower conflict when U.S.-led U.N. forces came to the aid of South Korea. The war raged for three years, devastating both sides as cities were occupied, abandoned, and reoccupied. A cease-fire was signed in 1953, but a formal peace treaty was never negotiated. A Demilitarized Zone and Military Demarcation Line still divides the two countries.

As Rhee grew older, he seemed less able to compromise and work with others. He was so determined to hold onto his power that he intimidated opponents and fixed elections to do so. But in April 1960, after his fourth successful presidential election, massive protests broke out in several Korean cities. Koreans had finally had enough of government corruption, police violence, election rigging, and Rhee's emphasis on foreign affairs at the expense of domestic economic development. Rhee was forced to resign the presidency after twelve years. He fled to Hawaii where he lived out the remainder of his life. After he died on July 19, 1965, his body was returned to South Korea and buried in the National Cemetery.

Matthew Ridgway

General Matthew Bunker Ridgway (1895–1993) is widely considered the most underrated American soldier of the twentieth century. His greatest contribution to modern warfare was transforming a lackluster U.N. force into a motivated killing machine that saved South Korea from certain defeat.

Ridgway's Early Years Ridgway was born on March 3, 1895, into an upper middle-class family at Fortress Monroe, Virginia. His father, Thomas, was a full colonel in World War I. His mother, Ruth, was a concert pianist from Long Island, New York. Ridgway, a well-bred and charming boy, spent his childhood moving from military post to military post. Determined to become a general, Ridgway went to West Point as soon as he could. He graduated in 1917, just two weeks after the United States entered World War I. He was eager to join the fight in the French trenches, but was instead sent to the Mexican border for the duration of the war. At the war's end, Ridgway returned to West Point where he became a Romance language instructor. Because he was the only one of six regular army officers fluent in Spanish, Ridgway won several high-level assignments in Latin America in the 1920s. During the 1930s he studied at the best military graduate schools in the country, including the U.S. Army Infantry School, the Command and General Staff School, and the Army War College. Although he rarely commanded troops in the years leading up to World War II, he proved a master motivator when given the opportunity.

Becoming a Commander Army Chief of Staff George C. Marshall was Ridgway's greatest champion during peacetime. After serving under the influential general on four separate occasions, Ridgway was promoted to

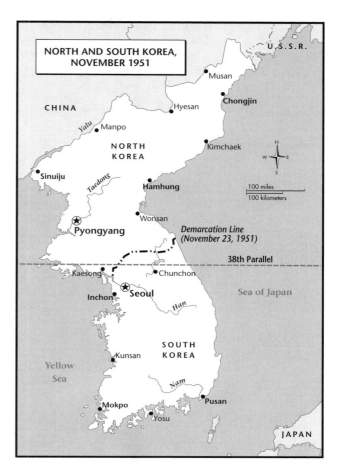

Despite high casualties, the border between North Korea and South Korea at the end of the Korean War changed little from where it stood before. *© Maryland Cartographics. Reprinted with permission*

brigadier general, assisting the command of General Omar Bradley's Eighty-Second Infantry Division after the start of World War II. When Bradley was promoted in early 1942, Ridgway was named commander. Under his tutelage, the division was transformed into one of the Army's first airborne units.

Ridgway led his forces in the invasion of Sicily in 1943, subsequent battles in Salerno, Normandy, Holland, and Germany, and the December 1944 Battle of the Bulge. His paratroopers, as they were called, fought so magnificently that their exploits became the stuff of legend. Following the Normandy invasion in 1944, Ridgway was chosen to head the Eighteenth Airborne Corps, which he commanded through Germany and across the Elbe River into advancing Soviet forces on May 3, 1945. He emerged from the war much decorated and admired. A three-star general by this time, Ridgway was regarded as one of the best Army combat corps commanders of the war. His troops found his mere presence to be awe-inspiring. His reputation was well earned. While commanding forces from the front, Ridgway often exposed himself to heavy fire and possible injury. A well-known incident involving a German grenade left Ridgway with a fragment in his shoulder after he refused medical treatment for the wound.

The Korean War In December 1950, Ridgway was appointed commander of the Eighth United States Army in Korea. Ridgway's new appointment was considered one of the most difficult of the Korean War. The Eighth Army's morale had been destroyed by Peng Dehuai's tactics. After massive Chinese forces pushed United Nations troops below the 38th parallel, mauling the First Cavalry Division, the Second Infantry Division, and the South Korean forces, the Eighth Army was exhausted. At this point, some military experts doubted the United States' ability to maintain a foothold on the Korean peninsula. But the U.S. military had faith in Ridgway, a man known for his motivational genius. To combat the superior Chinese forces, Ridgway reorganized the Eighth Army's potentially catastrophic retreat by transforming the distraught troops into a highly motivated fighting force. On February 21, 1951, he launched Operation Killer, an enormous counterattack involving eight infantry divisions of more than 100,000 troops backed by twenty-two artillery battalions, five tank battalions, and the Far East Air Force. The reinvigorated U.S. forces fought superbly. They retook Seoul and forced Chinese forces above the 38th parallel where the war stalled. The feat was regarded as one of the finest examples of military leadership of the century.

When General Douglas MacArthur was relieved of command on April 11, 1951, Ridgway was selected to serve simultaneous duties as commander in chief of the Far East command, commander in chief of the United Nations command, commander in chief of U.S. Army forces in the Far East, and supreme commander of Allied forces occupying Japan. He oversaw the war from Tokyo for the rest of the year. By now, Ridgway was celebrated as an American hero. The press, who described him in glowing terms, loved his approachability, charm, and articulate manner. Other officers, on the other hand, disliked him. They found him humorless and pretentious.

Ridgway replaced General Dwight D. Eisenhower as the supreme commander of European Allied forces and head of North Atlantic Treaty Organization (NATO) in May 1952. In 1953, he left that post to become the Army chief of staff. As chief of staff, Ridgway played a leading role in keeping the U.S. military out of the French-Indochina conflict in 1954 and steadfastly defended the Army when Republican senator Joseph McCarthy attacked it. In 1955, Ridgway retired from the Army as a four-star general and America's top soldier. He then served as director of the Mellon Industrial Research Institute in Pittsburgh until 1960.

Vietnam and Beyond During the 1960s, Ridgway became famous for his criticism of President Lyndon B. Johnson's decision to become militarily involved in the Vietnam conflict. Later, in March 1968, Johnson invited Ridgway to the White House as one of the "wise men" who advised Johnson to negotiate a withdrawal from Vietnam. Ridgway actively supported Ronald Reagan (1911–2004) during the 1980 presidential election and accompanied the president on his controversial trip to Bitburg's German army burial ground in 1985. On July 26, 1993, Matthew B. Ridgway died in Pittsburgh, Pennsylvania, at the age of ninety-eight. He was buried with full military honors in Arlington National Cemetery.

See also **World War II: Major Figures: Dwight Eisenhower**

See also **World War II: Major Figures: Douglas MacArthur**

See also **World War II: Major Figures: Harry Truman**

See also **Cold War: Major Figures: Joseph McCarthy**

See also **Cold War: Major Figures: Mao Zedong**

✪ Major Battles and Events

Seoul

Seoul's History to 1945 Seoul was the center of administration and culture during the Yi Dynasty and was chosen for its favorable and protected location. The Yi palaces and massive city wall were built on the granite base of the surrounding mountains. The well-drained floodplains of the Seoul basin and the Han River were just south of those. Although the city suffered from Manchu and Japanese invasions in the sixteenth and seventeenth centuries, the city maintained its vitality.

From 1910 to 1945, the years of the Japanese colonial regime, Seoul was forced to change. Japan built up Korea's infrastructure, especially its street and railroad systems. In Seoul, the area between the Han River and the old city became the Japanese military, residential, and commercial center. An imposing granite government building was constructed on the site of an old palace and other large banking and commercial buildings were built around the city. But Japan did not just change the Korean landscape. While Japanese leaders built up Korea's infrastructure, they simultaneously sought to eradicate the country's culture. Koreans were forced to adopt Japanese names, convert to the native Japanese religion of Shintoism, and were forbidden to speak Korean in school and at work. The March First Movement of 1919, also known as the Samil Movement or the Mansei Demonstrations, was one of the first displays of Korean nationalism. It resulted in the killing of thousands, the maiming and imprisoning of tens of thousands, and the destruction of hundreds of homes, schools, churches, and temples.

After intense fighting nearly destroyed the city of Seoul, Koreans struggled to rebuild the South Korean capital, circa 1951.   *Michael Rougier/ Time & Life Pictures/Getty Images*

When the Japanese surrendered on August 15, 1945, the Korean peninsula was divided into two distinct republics. After that date, the Soviet Union occupied Korea north of the 38th parallel, while the United States occupied the peninsula south of that line. In 1948, Seoul became the capital of the Republic of Korea, also known as South Korea. Under the auspices of the United Nations, the government of South Korea was democratic. That same year, the Communists established the Democratic People's Republic of Korea, also known as North Korea. Pyongyang became the capital of Communist North Korea. Ideological differences led to skirmishes along the 38th parallel, ultimately leading to the Korean War.

The Korean War On June 25, 1950, the North Korean Army crossed the South Korean border and started the Korean War, hoping to unify the two republics under a single Communist government. Within three days, northern forces captured Seoul, just thirty miles south of the 38th parallel. American troops were sent to assist South Korea, and Chinese Communist volunteers assisted North Korea in a war that lasted three years and claimed millions of lives on both sides.

During the course of the war, Seoul changed hands four times. North Korean forces occupied Seoul on the afternoon of June 28, 1950. After much fighting throughout September 1950, Seoul was retaken by U.N. forces at the end of that month and returned to President Rhee. In early January 1951, Seoul fell to North Korean and Chinese forces. Finally, in mid-March 1951, U.N. forces retook Seoul after expelling North Korean and Chinese troops from the city. On July 27, 1953, a cease-fire was established. The Korean War resulted in a stalemate, ending not far from where it began.

The disruption of civilian life during the back-and-forth movement of Communist and democratic forces was phenomenal. Homes and personal possessions were damaged or destroyed by shelling or bombing; crops were trampled and livestock was stolen for food; and civilians were killed or injured by stray gunfire or spontaneous violence inflicted by soldiers. Male civilians were often forcefully drafted to fight and Koreans were routinely imprisoned or summarily executed if they were suspected of supporting the "other" side. The city of Seoul was severely damaged during the conflict. The prominent buildings erected during the Japanese occupation were reduced to ravaged shells. The rest of the infrastructure became rubble after three years of intense fighting.

Invasion of Democratic People's Republic of Korea (DPRK)

When troops from the United States and the Republic of Korea (ROK), or South Korea, crossed into the Democratic People's Republic of Korea (DPRK), or North Korea, a fateful new chapter of the Korean War began. U.S. Commander Douglas MacArthur made the single most important decision of the Korean War, when he ordered the crossing despite warnings that it would provoke Chinese resistance. The bold and dangerous move resulted in the Chinese forces entering the war.

United Nations Forces Support South Korea On June 25, 1950, North Korean armed forces crossed the 38th parallel, the demarcation line that separated Communist North Korea and nationalist South Korea, thus beginning the Korean War. The South Korean army was small, ill-prepared, and poorly equipped. Their

After landing troops crossed into North Korea, paratroopers like these followed them into "Red Territory." *Howard Schurek/Time Life Pictures/Getty Images*

adversary, on the other hand, possessed a skilled army of 135,000 men equipped with a plentiful supply of Russian weapons, including 150 to 200 combat airplanes. Despite U.S. Secretary of State Dean Acheson's (1893–1971) statement on January 12, 1950, that Korea was not within the "defensive perimeter" of America's vital interests in the Far East, the United States government's reaction to the invasion was swift and determined.

Prodded by the U.S. government, the U.N. Security Council convened in a special session on the day of the attack and unanimously passed a resolution calling for the immediate withdrawal of North Korean forces to their former positions north of the 38th parallel. When the aggressors failed to comply with the resolution, the U.N. Security Council met again two days later and passed a second resolution recommending that United Nations members furnish South Korea with assistance so that they might repel their attackers. Ignoring recommendations of caution, President Harry S. Truman moved to enforce the United Nations resolution and committed U.S. military forces to South Korea. The president appointed General Douglas MacArthur as commander in chief of the Far East and supreme commander of U.N. forces.

The committed U.S. forces proved inadequate. By the end of June, more than half of the army of the Republic of Korea had been destroyed. By early August, U.N. forces had been pushed to the southeast corner of the peninsula where they dug in around the port of Pusan. After stabilizing a defense line around the important port, General MacArthur conceived of a brilliant yet risky strategy that was almost unanimously opposed. Instead of employing his forces in a frontal offensive from the Pusan Perimeter, MacArthur decided to dare an amphibious landing at Inchon, the west coast port near Seoul, behind enemy lines.

Battle of the Pusan Perimeter

The Battle of the Pusan Perimeter began shortly after U.N. forces began arriving in South Korea in mid-July 1950, and lasted until the first days of the amphibious landing at Inchon in mid-September. Inchon was a daring and controversial operation that defeated North Korean forces by driving them northward. It was conceived, in part, to give forces holding fast at Pusan a way to break past the line and help recapture Seoul for the South Koreans.

By the time U.N. forces arrived in South Korea, the mighty North Korean People's Army (KPA) had already assumed control of the majority of the peninsula. The American military landed at the far southern port city of Pusan and immediately established a defensive line, behind which they retreated and dug in. The line, which came to be called the Pusan Perimeter, marked off the southeast corner of the peninsula. Bound on the west by the Naktong River, the east by the Sea of Japan, the north by a rugged range of mountains, and the south by the Korea Strait, the perimeter enclosed the port city of Pusan,

Arms in hand, U.S. soldiers disembarked at Pohang on July 22, 1950.   *AP Images*

the arrival point of American troops and supplies, and the city of Taegu, where General Walton Walker (1889–1950) established his Eighth Army headquarters. Establishing the perimeter had been hard on Walker's troops. After numerous battle debacles and hundreds of miles of retreat, the Eighth Army was exhausted and disheartened. In a meeting in Taegu with General Walker, General Douglas MacArthur determined that the Eighth Army could retreat no farther. Soon after the meeting, on July 29, Walker issued his now-famous "Stand or Die" speech to the fatigued defenders of the Pusan Perimeter. The battle had become a holding mission, an operation that was just one part of General MacArthur's overall strategy.

The Holding Mission Begins To provide an early warning and some initial defense in case of attack, Walker positioned his forces in small manned points along the perimeter. These small groups were ordered to fade back in the case of major assaults. Although the number of troops available to Walker was growing, he could not afford to do more than hold fast at that point.

During the first two-thirds of August, that battle became a daily succession of crises that required Walker to rush men to various perimeter points to stop the North Koreans. Finally, sometime after August 21, ground fighting around the Pusan Perimeter was temporarily suspended. Because Walker and the Eighth Army had signal intelligence (SIGINT), they were able to intercept North Korean radio messages. This intelligence gave Walker information about the KPA's movements and plans, which, at that time, involved reorganizing, resupplying, and regrouping. Messages intercepted during this period revealed that the North Koreans had ordered massive quantities of ammunition and detailed maps of the Taegu area. Follow-up communications let Walker know that river-crossing equipment would be delivered to the KPA by August 23, that ammunition was being delivered around August 25, and that plans to organize a rear reconnaissance unit to annihilate the enemy using fire raids were in the works. Obviously, the KPA was planning something big.

Douglas Macarthur watching the shelling of Inchon from the USS *Mt. McKinley*, 1950.   *Reproduced by permission of Double Delta Industries, Inc.*

Deflecting North Korean Attacks By that point, General Walker's men were utterly spent. The very real prospect of being pushed off the Korean peninsula by North Korean forces did little to boost their flagging morale. Luckily, Walker's troops intercepted messages that contained very specific instructions meant for KPA units, which revealed the time and place of the planned attack. The instructions were so detailed they even disclosed the type of weapons and the battalion levels the KPA would use. One message, for example, ordered several units of North Korean soldiers and a 76-millimeter gun battalion to strike the enemy and attack its flank and rear at specific points around the perimeter. Knowing this, Walker was able to plan his strategy accordingly and organize his troops to best defend the Pusan Perimeter.

The North Koreans initiated their simultaneous coordinated assault on four fronts on August 31. Though no surprise, the attack required all of Walker's skills to keep his forces intact. The powerful North Korean effort broke through the American defenses in Masan, cut the Second Division near the Naktong in two, captured Pohang-dong, and forced Walker's headquarters from its location in Taegu to Pusan. Intercepted messages over the next two weeks alerted Walker to expect continued attacks. He called for additional personnel, weapons, and ammunition from forward locations and ordered the construction and restoration of steel bridges over the North Han, Kum, and South Han rivers. Meanwhile, Walker used information garnered from intercepted messages to continue placing his troops in the most effective positions.

Despite obvious North Korean successes, the KPA, according to various communications, appeared to be weakening in their advances. Weapons and ammunition were slow to arrive at some of the North Korean frontline divisions and officers were instructed to solve weapons problems on their own. Furious messages demanding to know why certain missions were not being carried out began to surface. Tanks were not advancing, fuel shortages were rampant, and American bombing raids were disrupting transportation. Finally, nervous messages reported the arrival of additional British and American troops in Pusan. Along with troop reinforcements, U.N. forces were also receiving antitank mines and entrenching tools. The North Koreans reported mine laying and sandbagging by U.N. forces, too.

Final Push in Pusan   The final push from U.N. forces in the Pusan Perimeter was significantly aided by the surprise amphibious attack on Inchon, a port city roughly thirty miles west of Seoul. This crowning example of General MacArthur's strategic genius was intended to trap North Korean forces between U.N. forces, outflank them, and drive them straight up the peninsula and back across the 38th parallel. Although President Truman and the Joint Chiefs of Staff thought the plan too risky, MacArthur persuaded them to let him go ahead.

Landing at Inchon

The Inchon Invasion, also known as Operation Chromite, was a controversial and daring amphibious operation on September 15, 1950, that General Douglas MacArthur conceived. Widely considered MacArthur's finest military moment, the landing at Inchon immediately changed the course of the Korean War and led to the recovery of the Korean capital city of Seoul.

The Korean War Before the Inchon Invasion   By the end of July 1950, North Korean forces had pushed U.N. forces to the southeast corner of the Korean peninsula. Unable to retreat any further, the American and South Korean troops dug in around the port of Pusan. General MacArthur, commander of U.N. troops, and Lieutenant General Walton H. Walker, commander of the U.S. Eighth Army, ordered their men to "stand or die." For the next six weeks, a bloody, desperate struggle ensued as the North Koreans battled to defeat American and South Korean forces and to gain complete control over Korea. Meanwhile, MacArthur was conceiving a strategy to move inland, retake the capital, and cut the already tenuous North Korean supply lines.

Preparing for the Strategic Landing   Operation Chromite, or the landing at Inchon, took less than three weeks to plan. Given the scope of the forces involved and the tactical challenges they faced, that time frame seems almost incomprehensible. Among the forces gathered for the operation were the First Marine Division, the Army's Seventh Infantry Division, a handful of South Korean units, virtually every available amphibious ship, and dozens of other Navy warships. The majority of Marines involved had recently arrived from the United States, while the rest were taken from the Pusan Perimeter defenses.

Inchon, located on the west coast of South Korea near Seoul, was a tactically challenging amphibious target. The primary obstacle to landing there was the area's 32-foot tidal range, which restricts landing operations to a few hours a day. The Operation Chromite planning commission determined that the tides would only be high enough to allow a big landing craft three brief hours inshore on September 15, September 27, or October 11. Beyond that, the coast would become an impassable quagmire of mud. Another challenge was the narrow channel the landing force would have to maneuver. Seawalls along the beach threatened to make the initial assault and disembarkation of vehicles and stores quite difficult.

On August 23, 1950, a contingent of high-ranking U.S. military commanders flew from Washington, D.C., to McArthur's Tokyo headquarters for a briefing on the planned mission. After the officers heard a summary of the details of the assault, including weather, landing craft, beaches, naval gunfire, and air support, Rear Admiral James H. Doyle said, "the best I can say is that Inchon is not impossible." To sell his idea to Doyle and the other doubtful officers, MacArthur relied on his well-known theatrical style. He launched into an awe-inspiring forty-five-minute speech, ending his performance with the words, "we shall land at Inchon and I shall crush them!" Three days after the briefing, MacArthur received the formal consent of the Joint Chiefs of Staff to proceed with Operation Chromite.

Lieutenant General Edward M. Almond (1892–1979), MacArthur's chief of staff, was appointed commander of the Inchon landing force, which was designated the X Corps. Two divisions, the First Marine Division and the Seventh Infantry Division, comprised the X Corps. The First Marine Division, comprised of a total of twenty thousand men, was to be the first ashore. A small fleet of cargo ships and landing ships, including six attack transport ships, eight attack cargo ships, three high-speed transports, one medium landing ship, three dock landing ships, seventeen U.S. tank landing ships, and thirty-one Japanese dock landing ships, were rounded up to move the division and their supplies from Kobe, Sasebo, and Pusan to Inchon.

The Seventh was supposed to follow the Marines in the landing, but by early August, their numbers had diminished dramatically. Nearly ten thousand of the infantry's officers and troops had already been posted in Korean divisions. To make up for the loss, over eight thousand South Koreans were sent to the Seventh Infantry Division in August. American infantry and artillery reinforcements arrived between the end of August and the beginning of September. Although the strength of the Seventh Infantry Division reached nearly 250,000 soldiers, less than half were effectively trained for battle.

A Successful Landing   Despite all odds, the amphibious landing at Inchon was a near-perfect logistical execution. Roughly 250 ships, including the flagship, two escort carriers, a bombardment force, screening and protective ships, minesweepers, supply and hospital ships, and freight and transport vessels carrying the X Corps, began their trek to Inchon as early as September 5. Air attacks began on September 10 with shore bombardment following three days later. On the morning of September 15, the Advance Attack Group, supported by naval and air forces, assaulted

On September 15, 1950, American marines made their way toward Inchon as part of a dangerous and aggressive amphibious invasion.
Hank Walker/Time & Life Pictures/Getty Images

and captured the tactically critical island of Wolmi-do in roughly an hour and a half. That afternoon, just as the tide started to come in, the order to "land the landing force" was given. That day, thirteen thousand troops and an impressive amount of assault equipment were unloaded. On September 16, the Seventh Infantry Division arrived.

General unloading was ordered, and for the next six days, unloading continued as rapidly as tidal conditions and unloading facilities would permit. During this period of time, nearly fifty thousand military personnel, five thousand vehicles, and more than twenty thousand short tons of cargo were brought ashore.

The Results of the Landing at Inchon   Over the course of the first several days of fighting, as supplies and troops poured ashore, the Marines moved relentlessly toward Seoul. On September 17, Kimpo Airfield was taken and two days later it was in use to support operations. On September 27, MacArthur received permission to pursue the retreating enemy into North Korea. On September 29, after two weeks of fighting, Seoul was returned to the South Korean government and North Korean supply lines were cut. Then, on October 1, South Korean forces chased the North Koreans past the 38th parallel. This last, fateful move marked the beginning of a new chapter in the Korean War.

The Invasion of North Korea

The decision to pursue the retreating foe across the demarcation line was fraught with peril. On the one hand, the American public was pressing for a decisive victory. On the other, Chinese Communist forces warned that an American invasion into North Korea would be met with Chinese resistance. Despite the threat, the United Nations and President Truman ordered South Korean forces north across the 38th parallel. The first crossings by United Nations and South Korean forces took place on October 1, with backup forces following eight days later. The troops sped north, nearing the Yalu River, the boundary between North Korea and Communist China. Chinese Communist troops were assembled near the Yalu, but MacArthur was unaware of their strength or position. On November 1, the leading South Korean divisions were ambushed while a U.S. regiment located at Unsan was attacked. As soon as the U.N. forces stabilized their lines after the violent setback, Chinese forces withdrew northward as quickly as they had struck.

MacArthur pressed for permission to take the fight into China, believing the only remaining course was a bold advance. His "all-out offensive" to the Yalu was met with a powerful Chinese strike on the night of November 25. Roughly 180,000 Chinese troops smashed the right flank of the Eighth Army in the west, while 120,000 others mauled the X Corps near the Chosin Reservoir. On November 28, a shaken MacArthur told the U.S. Joint Chiefs, "We face an entirely new war."

MacArthur's men fought courageously just to avoid being annihilated. They were forced to retreat southward down the peninsula past Seoul, which was recaptured on January 5, to about seventy miles south of the occupied capital. On January 15, General Matthew Ridgway, commander of the Eighth Army, began to lead U.N. troops slowly northward, inflicting heavy casualties on the Chinese and North Korean forces as they went. On March 15, his troops recaptured Seoul for the fourth and final time. MacArthur, meanwhile, stepped up efforts, pushing Washington to allow him to bomb targets in China. Being denied permission to do so enraged him. He launched a very public campaign in the press for an increase in U.S. military commitment. He sought an extension of the war into China and complained that military operations were being hamstrung by Truman's political considerations. Truman responded by relieving General MacArthur of his dual command of U.S. and U.N. forces on April 11, 1951. Ridgway took MacArthur's place and Lieutenant General James A. Van Fleet (1892–1992) replaced Ridgway as commander of the Eighth Army.

United Nations Cease-fire Resolution

Cease-fire Talks Begin   By this point in the conflict, neither side was willing to launch any new offenses and both seemed eager to begin talks leading to an armistice. On July 10, 1951, both sides sat down at Kaesong and later at Panmunjon to negotiate a cease-fire. The main objective was to restore Korean status quo. The United States refused China's demands to withdraw all foreign troops from Korea. The United States also refused to restore the 38th parallel as the border, hoping instead for the existing battle line. But the issue that caused talks to break down completely was refusal by the United States to repatriate Chinese and North Korean prisoners of war.

Talks resumed after Stalin died in March 1953 because the Soviets were eager to end the war. Dwight D. Eisenhower was now president of the United States, having won the election on a promise to "go to Korea." Although many Americans believed this to mean that he was ready to make peace, Eisenhower let it be known that he was ready to force a peace with the threat of atomic warfare. Either way, the talks showed progress despite a new obstacle. The South Korean government wanted the fighting to resume despite the clear intention between the United States and the Soviet Union to reach a permanent armistice. In the spirit of compromise, the Soviets agreed to permit the United Nations to take all prisoners of war who did not wish to go home. To retaliate, South Korea unilaterally released close to thirty thousand North Koreans it claimed had become anticommunist. This act of defiance drove the Soviets from the bargaining table for a month.

Talks resumed in late July 1953. By this time, the U.S. government had convinced the South Korean government to accept an armistice that left Korea divided. If they agreed, South Korea would receive commitment of economic aid to rebuild as well as a promise of the military support of American troops if North Korea invaded again. On July 27, 1953, the armistice was concluded. The terms of the agreement indicated that neither side had gained or lost much of anything after three years of war.

Following the Cease Fire Resolution in 1953, this U.N. landing craft brought POWs for exchange in "Operation Big Switch." *Michael Rougier/Time Life Pictures/Getty Images*

✪ The Home Front

Baby Boom

The term "baby boom" refers to the dramatic surge in childbirths in the United States between 1946 and 1964. Several historical, cultural, and economic factors led to the boom. The most obvious was the return of millions of American servicemen home from World War II. Ready to settle down, marry, and start families, many of these men fathered children within a year of their homecoming. The next factor involves the record prosperity of the United States at the time. These servicemen came home to the most prosperous and powerful nation in the world, one that provided its citizenry with unprecedented economic and physical security. Additionally, low-cost mortgages for veterans and new techniques in manufacturing housing turned millions of acres of farmland into sprawling suburbs, seemingly overnight. The third factor involves the role of women after the war. A boom in marriages preceded the boom in motherhood.

Returning veterans and their spouses were responsible for the post-war "Baby Boom" in the late 1940s and 1950s. *George Marks/Retrofile/ Getty Images*

This fact contributed to a reinforcement of the "cult of domesticity," the belief that women's proper place was in their homes. Finally, both American women and men felt a sense of urgency about living life to the fullest. After coming of age during the Great Depression and World War II, the continuing uncertainties of the atomic age prompted them to seize the American dream of having it all.

Birthrates actually began to rise as early as 1941. Between January and April of that year, twenty thousand more children were born than the same four months just one year prior. With war still on the horizon, many young couples decided to create a future by marrying and having children as quickly as they could. In 1942, 2.7 million children were born—more than any year since 1921. Those who postponed marrying and having children because of the impending war were quick to start families when it ended. There were almost

2.3 million marriages in 1946—an increase of more than 600,000 over the previous year. A year later, a record 3.8 million babies were born. In the five years between 1948 and 1953, more children were born than had been over the previous thirty years. Prompted by a low death rate, a record birthrate, and an influx of 144,000 immigrants into the country, the largest one-year population gain in American history occurred in 1954. Overall, the population of the United States jumped from 150 million in 1950 to 179 million in 1960. The birthrate stayed unusually high until 1965. The availability of a reliable oral contraceptive, together with changing attitudes about population control and family size, contributed to the mid-1960s decline in births. By the middle of the next decade, when the baby boomers started having children, birthrates were again on the rise.

The Economic Effects of the Boom   Economists in the 1950s often speculated that the growing population was a safeguard against economic stagnation. This seemed obvious, as each new birth represented new demands for food, clothing, and toys. In 1958, *Life* magazine reported on the economic consequences of the boom. The year was significant as children fifteen years old and younger in 1958 made up nearly a third of the population of the United States. *Life* found that toy sales that year reached $1.25 billion, diaper services were a $50-million business, and that a major supplier of school furniture, the American Seating Company of Grand Rapids, Michigan, had tripled its business in the thirteen years since the end of World War II.

Women's Roles During the Boom   The government and business sectors of society were eager to get America back on track after the enormous disruptions that World War II caused. A significant aspect of this normalization included moving women from the workforce back into the home. During the war, working women, symbolized by "Rosie the Riveter," were celebrated for stepping in and helping out in the defense industry, doing work their husbands, fathers, and brothers did before being called away. The culture supported working mothers during the war, but after the war everything changed. Women who were poor or single or both continued to work, but working women quickly became stigmatized. Postwar prosperity and the new American image of the family—Mom, Dad, and the children living happily in their shiny new suburban home—left no room for a working mother. It was now wholly unconventional for women to work outside the home.

Powerful men and women of the era echoed the tenets of the "cult of domesticity" in influential sociology papers, commencement speeches, women's magazines, and television shows such as *Father Knows Best*, *Ozzie and Harriet*, and *Leave it to Beaver*. From the late 1940s to the early 1960s, women were told that their fundamental status came from their roles as wife and mother. They were to be the anchor of the family, and their sphere of influence was to be the home.

The Boomers Themselves   By the sheer force of their numbers, the "baby boomers," Americans born between the mid 1940s and the mid-1960s, have shaped American society at every phase of their lives. In the 1950s, increases in school enrollment caused overcrowded classrooms. Ten and twenty years later, colleges were overfilled. In the 1960s and 1970s, twice the number of students entered higher education compared to the previous generation. In the 1970s and 1980s, the job market became glutted with floods of recent college graduates looking for work.

Several cultural elements served to inform the psychology of the baby boomers, which, in turn, affected American society at large. Although the 1950s and early 1960s were prosperous and peaceful years in American history, they followed on the heels of nuclear attacks on Hiroshima and Nagasaki in 1945. This fact made the

baby boomers the first generation to have lived with the evidence that humanity possessed the power to destroy itself. The paradox between those two states of understanding, coupled with the simmering tension of the Cold War, is widely seen as the psychological basis for later acts of revolt carried out by the baby boomers. They questioned the values handed down from the previous generation. Their contribution to the civil rights movement, the anti–Vietnam War movement, and the women's and gay liberation movements helped change the face of American society.

✪ International Context

East and West in Europe

The Cold War forced a split between Eastern and Western European countries around the time of the Korean War. This was due to the influence of the two main enemies of the Cold War—the United States and the Soviet Union. In the post–World War II atomic age, both sides were afraid of fighting each other directly. Instead of entering into a "hot" war with active fighting that could potentially destroy everything, the Soviet Union and the United States battled each other with threats and denouncements. Their most effective weapon, though, was supporting various global conflicts that reflected their respective foreign policies. This "cold" war eventually split the world into three groups: those countries with democratic political systems followed the United States, or the West; those countries with Communist political systems followed the Soviet Union, or the East; and those countries that did not want to be tied to either the West or the East remained nonaligned.

Soviet Influence Over Eastern Europe   During World War II, the Soviet Union allied itself with the Western democracies of the world in its struggle against the Axis powers of Italy, Germany, and Japan. Shortly before the war ended, though, the future of Eastern Europe became a point of conflict between the Soviet Union and its Western allies. Because the Soviet Union had been invaded by Eastern European forces in both of the world wars, and had suffered greatly for it, the nation was determined to install "friendly" regimes throughout Eastern Europe at the end of World War II. The strategy was designed to protect the Soviet Union against future invasions. By the fall of 1944, the Soviet Red Army had liberated a large part of Eastern Europe. The Soviet Union then found itself in a position to influence the type of governments that would emerge in those liberated states after the war.

The Soviet Union, believing it had an agreement with Western democracies that made Eastern Europe a Soviet sphere of influence, assumed it would have dominance over the region. At the Yalta Conference in early 1945, Soviet leader Joseph Stalin pressed the issue, categorizing Soviet control of the region as a matter of national security. Stalin also announced that he would not allow Poland, Czechoslovakia, and other Eastern European countries to elect anti-Soviet governments into power after the war. As the war neared its end, the Soviet Union quickly consolidated its control over Eastern Europe. The Red Army influenced postwar elections by intimidating voters and changing voting lists to suit its agenda. As a result, coalition governments formed after the war were predominantly Communist. The Soviet Union had succeeded in virtually annexing the Eastern European countries it conquered in World War II. Even so, Stalin was not satisfied with Communist control of Eastern Europe. He pushed Communists to influence postwar elections in Western Europe, too. By late 1946, just months after Winston Churchill declared that an "iron curtain" was descending across the European continent and the United States began favoring a policy of strong resistance against the Soviet Union, Communism was on the rise in France and Italy.

The Cold War Begins Already alarmed by Soviet expansion in Europe, the United States became increasingly concerned when, on February 21, 1947, Great Britain declared it could no longer provide the Greek government the military and financial aid it needed to fight Communist guerillas. Greece was not the only largely peasant nation in danger of being overthrown by the Communists; Turkey was also being threatened. Recognizing just how powerful the Soviet Union would be if it dominated Greece and Turkey, the United States prepared itself for a war against its former ally.

On March 12, 1947, President Truman issued a proclamation before a joint session of Congress. The proclamation, which came to be known as the Truman Doctrine, was clearly anticommunist. The president called for Communist containment and massive military and economic aid to Greece and Turkey. It was, among other things, a thinly veiled declaration of war against the Soviet Union. The essence of Truman's speech was that "it must be the policy of the United States to support free peoples who are resisting attempted subjugation by armed minorities or by outside pressure."

A few months later, on June 5, 1947, U.S. Secretary of State George C. Marshall delivered a speech at Harvard University. In it, he outlined a plan to rebuild war-torn Europe and halt the westward spread of Communism. The Marshall Plan, as it came to be known, suggested an offer of $20 million of economic aid to the desperate European nations, but only if they agreed to come together and draw up a rational plan for spending it. The stipulation ensured that they act as a single economic unit that had to work together. The plan was a success. It helped feed the hungry, shelter the homeless, and put the European economy back on its feet. Once the economies and governments of the Western European nations were stabilized, the popularity of Communist parties went into sharp decline.

Western Forces Unite The first major crisis of the Cold War came in June 1948 when Soviet forces blocked all entries into the Western-held portion of Berlin, Germany, a multinational area within the Soviet zone of the country. The blockade kept all American, British, and French road and railway transport from entering the city. President Truman responded by ordering military planes to fly food, medicine, and coal into the city. The Berlin airlift, as it came to be known, continued for almost a year. With the help of Great Britain and France, almost 2.5 million tons of supplies arrived in Berlin on roughly 280,000 flights from June 1948 to September 1949. The blockade was officially lifted in May 1949. The Berlin Blockade led to the formation of the North Atlantic Treaty Organization (NATO) in 1949, a joint military group whose purpose was to defend European countries against Soviet forces. Belgium, Britain, Canada, Denmark, France, Iceland, Italy, Luxembourg, the Netherlands, Portugal, and the United States were NATO's first member countries. Six years later, the Soviet Union and its Eastern European allies formed their own joint military group. The organization was known as the Warsaw Pact, or, more officially, The Treaty of Friendship, Cooperation, and Mutual Assistance. The Warsaw Pact survived through the Cold War, but began to crumble following the collapse of the Eastern Bloc in 1991.

Independence Movements in Asia

The most significant Asian independence movement in the twentieth century took place in India. The country's nationalist struggle for freedom from British colonial rule began with the formation of the Indian National Congress (INC) in 1885, but grew teeth when political activist and social reformer Mohandas Karamchand Gandhi became leader of the independence cause around 1918. Gandhi, a devout Hindu and proponent of nonviolent civil disobedience, was instrumental in achieving independence for India in 1947.

The Birth of the Indian National Congress One of the oldest, most unique, and most effective nationalist movements of Asia and Africa could not have happened without the Indian National Congress. Shaped by emerging Indian nationalism, the development of the colonial education system, and the rise of the new urban, Western-educated, English-speaking Indian elite, the INC was originally comprised of upper-caste Hindu lawyers, doctors, educators, and journalists. Connected through their similar educations but representing Indian diversity, the INC sought to give expression to common grievances and hopes for the country. Their first meeting in 1885 in Bombay revealed the modest demands of the founders. They praised the positive contributions of British rule, but demanded better Indian representation

After Japan's 1945 surrender, President Sukarno declared Indonesian independence from the Dutch. *The Library of Congress*

in the higher levels of civil service, a broader electoral base of the Legislative Council, and greater support and development of indigenous industries.

The second generation of the INC was more radical and drew its inspiration from Hindu revivalism. Unlike the first generation, these INC members were drawn from urban India's lower middle-class and had less exposure to English education. Because they were unable to achieve any sort of significant status or position within the new colonial order, they developed a natural sense of disdain for Britain based on religious, economic, political, and social frustrations.

But the most profound development of the INC came after World War I. The rise of Mohandas Karamchand Gandhi (1869–1948) as leader of the independence movement deeply affected the leadership, organization, appeal, methodology, and goals of the Congress. Gandhi restructured the organization of the INC into what he called a parallel government to win the loyalty of the Indian people. Among his many great gifts was his ability to attract a wide sector of Indian society. He counted among his supporters the rising indigenous industrial elite,

lawyers from small district towns, the rural peasantry, Indian traditionalists attracted to his successful political adaptation of Hindu symbology, and a large contingent of Muslims. His most powerful contribution to the INC and the system for which he is most commonly remembered, though, was his unique method of mobilizing political action through the use of nonviolent resistance, or *satyagraha*.

Inspired by the writings of nineteenth-century American transcendentalist Henry David Thoreau, Gandhi's civil disobedience relied on mass political mobilization, leadership, and organization and helped the Congress evolve from an urban, middle-class phenomenon into a highly successful movement unparalleled in the third world. One of Gandhi's first acts of mass civil disobedience involved a program of political action unlike anything the world had ever seen. To protest the Rowlatt Acts of 1919, a series of repressive laws that gave judges the power to ignore the fundamental rights of citizens in the case of political uprisings, Gandhi called for a nationwide boycott of all British institutions, including universities, shops, and governmental bodies. As a result, many Indian political leaders resigned their offices and returned honors and decorations that had been given by the British government. Students boycotted their university classes and ordinary citizens picketed shops selling British goods. For the first time in history, a nationwide action united Indians usually deeply divided by language, region, and religion.

Gandhi's civil disobedience campaigns of 1921–1922, his renowned campaign against the salt tax of 1930–1933, and the Quit India Movement of 1942 deepened the base and political appeal of the Congress and played a leading role in the success of the independence movement.

India Before and After World War II In 1935, Britain passed the Government of India Act, which outlined a framework for Indian self-rule. It allowed for elections and special seats for minority groups and was made effective in 1937. In 1939, World War II broke out. Britain responded by automatically involving India. It mobilized Indian troops and imposed economic regulations on the country. Although the INC was sympathetic to Britain's position in the conflict, it resented not being consulted and was frustrated that it had not been allowed to make decisions for India. The Muslim League opposed the INC and the divide between the two groups widened further. Initially, many Muslims followed Gandhi's lead, but the president of the Muslim League, Mohammad Ali Jinnah (1876–1948), strongly opposed *satyagraha*. Although he opposed British rule and wanted to see India free, he feared that the majority population of Hindus would not protect the rights of Muslims under Indian self-rule. Gandhi never succeeded in his many attempts to gain Jinnah's trust and cooperation.

Gandhi took advantage of Britain's preoccupation with the war and pressed for immediate independence for India. Because of violent clashes between the Hindus and the British, the Muslims became even more favored in the eyes of the colonial power. When Gandhi met with Jinnah to try to resolve the dispute, Jinnah declared that he would not support a united India. He and his fellow Muslims demanded the creation of a separate country. The country, located in the northeast region of India, would be called Pakistan, or Land of the Pure.

By the close of World War II, Britain was devastated. The nation had neither the energy nor the resources to continue fighting in India so it announced that August 15, 1947, would be India's Independence Day. It was decided that the two new nations, primarily Hindu India and Muslim Pakistan, would become self-governing dominions in the British Commonwealth of Nations. Despite the victory and the rejoicing, Hindus and Muslims continued fighting bitterly. Hindus living in Pakistan and Muslims living in India began migrating. Wherever refugees flowed over national boundary lines, fighting broke out. Gandhi, heartbroken over the division of his country, began a fast for peace. A shaky truce was reached only when Gandhi neared death. On January 30, 1948, Gandhi was assassinated by a zealot Hindu.

Western Withdrawal from Asia   Britain made India and Pakistan members of its Commonwealth of Nations when it left the subcontinent in 1947. The two countries fought several conflicts in the following decades to settle their boundaries. In less than a year, it had withdrawn from all its Asian colonies but Hong Kong. Burma (present-day Myanmar) became an independent republic in early January 1948, followed by Ceylon (present-day Sri Lanka) later in January, and Malaya (including present-day Malaysia and Singapore) in February. Other Western powers found it tougher to let go of their holdings in the East. The Netherlands, which had held the Pacific islands of modern-day Indonesia for centuries, was forced out in 1949, after four years of violent revolution. France would hold onto its colonies in Asia for a little while longer.

French Indochina—present-day Vietnam, Cambodia, and Laos—came under France's control in the late nineteenth century. After being occupied by Japan during World War II, the three countries reverted to French control, and each promptly declared its independence. The Vietnamese were lead by communist Ho Chi Minh (1890–1969) and backed by China. The resulting French-Indochina War, which lasted until 1954, became the first major struggle of Eastern and Western political philosophies after World War II. Laos and Cambodia, which fought for France in that conflict, were granted their independence in 1953, and 1954, respectively. At the end of the war, France left the peninsula, Vietnam was divided into communist North Vietnam and anti-communist South Vietnam, and the stage was set for the Vietnam Conflict in the 1960s and 1970s.

Independence Movements in Africa

In Cold War parlance, the "third world" referred to Asia, Africa, and Latin America—countries that were thought to lack the literacy, national cohesiveness, and economic power necessary to make liberal democracies work. "First world" countries, commonly referred to as the West, were capitalist, industrialized nations, while "second world" countries, commonly referred to as the East, were Communist industrialized nations. Because the world after 1945 was dominated by the first and second worlds—the liberal-democratic, capitalist world led by the United States, and the Communist-socialist world led by the Soviet Union—third world countries struggling for liberal independence had to ally themselves with one or the other.

Decolonization in Africa was one of the most significant turning developments of the postwar world. The success of the independence movement in India in 1948 gave Africans a reason to dream of a society free of European control. At that time, only Egypt, Liberia, and Ethiopia were independent nations. African decolonization began in earnest after 1945, but gained momentum between 1954 and 1970. By the mid-1970s, only scattered vestiges of colonial territories remained.

Although every occupied African country shared the common goal of decolonization, each country went about achieving that goal in very different ways. One way, the way India found to be so successful, was to find a peaceful way to shake off colonial rule, and then allow the West to assist in setting up new states based on the Western model. African countries that chose this way were assured the West's economic, military, and bureaucratic support. Another way was to decolonize by carrying out wars of national liberation. These wars were usually funded by Communists, which meant that the new state that emerged would be directed by Soviet or Chinese allies.

The Decolonization of Africa   By the end of World War II, Britain had lost the resources and the will to run an empire. At the same time, African nationalists were growing increasingly adamant in their demands for self-rule. The problem was that neither group knew how or when to dismantle the colonial machine. Beginning in West Africa, African nationalists took charge of events by putting their weight behind the independence movement. The leaders of these movements formed organizations, held elections, and negotiated new constitutions. Britain had largely relinquished its holdings on the continent between the late 1950s and late 1960s, and France withdrew from most of its holdings around 1960. By the mid-1970s, most of today's African nations were free from colonial governments, although they were hardly at peace. Cold War tensions between the United States and the Soviet Union distorted politics in Africa for much of the late twentieth century.

European settlers in South Africa, Angola, Mozambique, and Rhodesia (now Zimbabwe) wanted to cut ties

Algerians sip coffee in front of a wall urging passersby to "vote for independence" in June 1962. *STF/AFP/Getty Images*

with Britain and Portugal, but still maintain white minority rule, which excluded the African population. For their support of capitalism, a Western ideal, the white governments of South Africa and Rhodesia found their human rights violations tolerated by the international community. Angola and Mozambique, on the other hand, found financial and military support from the Soviet Union support for their campaigns for independence from European interference. At different times in the 1960s and 1970s, Guinea-Bissau, Congo, Egypt, Somalia, Ethiopia, Uganda, and Benin received some form of support from the Soviet Union, but none remained under communist influence.

✪ Aftermath

Nuclear Arms Race

The nuclear arms race, the rapid development and stockpiling of nuclear weapons by the Soviet Union and the United States, was central to the Cold War. The fear that one nation might use nuclear weapons against the other is precisely what kept the war from becoming "hot."

The United States, after nearly completely obliterating Hiroshima and Nagasaki in 1945, was the last nation to use atomic or nuclear weapons in battle, yet the fear of "the bomb" was powerful enough to keep the Cold War alive for several decades.

The Beginning of the Atomic Age The atomic age began with a $2 billion secret U.S. wartime program known as the Manhattan Project. Some of the world's most eminent scientists, including J. Robert Oppenheimer (1904–1967), collaborated in an unprecedented research effort in various sites across the country that culminated in the first successful atomic weapons test in July 1945. Less than a month later, President Truman, hoping to force Japan to surrender, ordered nuclear bombs to be dropped first on the city of Hiroshima then on the city of Nagasaki. These two events are still the only use of nuclear weapons in warfare. The cities were devastated. In Hiroshima, an estimated 45,000 people were killed on the first day. Another 19,000 died over the course of the next four months. In Nagasaki, 22,000 people were killed on the first day. Another 17,000 died

A mushroom cloud formed from A-bomb testing rises over Nevada. *© Bettmann/Corbis*

over the course of the next four months. Unrecorded deaths of military personnel and foreign workers may have added considerably to these figures.

After Japan surrendered, the United States began a rapid postwar demobilization. The American public, exhausted by the war and feeling safe in the knowledge that the United States alone possessed atomic weapons, wondered at Truman's seemingly alarmist call for economic and military aid to Greece and Turkey. Although Soviet-style totalitarianism was flourishing in European nations infiltrated by Joseph Stalin's Red Army, and Communist guerrillas threatened the takeover of both Greece and Turkey, the American public seemed beguiled by the propaganda image of a gentle "Uncle Joe" Stalin, as was his image during World War II. Anticommunism rose only after Stalin's Berlin Blockade, the 1949 Communist victory in China, and the explosion of the Soviet Union's first atomic bomb. Fearing a Soviet nuclear attack, the United States was now ready to support the passage of any U.S.

government legislation intended to arrest the spread of Communism.

The Race Is On Truman funded research to develop hydrogen bombs in January 1950. In November 1952, the United States tested a successful hydrogen bomb, just nine months before the Soviets did. Despite the development of these bombs, Truman pressed for continued moderation and a policy of Communist "containment." When Stalin suddenly died in 1953, American hopes soared, then were quickly dashed when his successors continued the relentless drive to military primacy.

Immediately following the Korean War, U.S. Navy Rear Admiral Hyman G. Rickover (1900–1986) pressed for the use of atomic energy in submarines. In 1954, the *Nautilus*, the nation's first nuclear-powered submarine, was launched. Taking a different road in the race for primacy, the Soviet Union shocked the world when it demonstrated a four-thousand-mile intercontinental ballistic missile (ICBM) in August 1957. The development realized Hitler's dream of being able to bombard the American mainland. In October of the same year, the Soviets alarmed Americans with the launch of *Sputnik I*, the first artificial satellite to successfully orbit the earth. The space race between the two superpowers had begun.

A contest was underway between the Soviet Union and the United States to perfect rockets for lofting nuclear warheads from one continent to another at supersonic speeds that compressed flight times between Moscow and Washington into mere minutes. The Soviet Union maintained an early lead by dint of the sheer size and payload of its missiles. The United States, on the other hand, used miniaturization to achieve superior sophistication and accuracy in its missiles. Fearful of falling behind in the arms race, the U.S. Congress authorized millions of dollars for new weapons, as well as programs to promote science and math education. In reality, the United States maintained a definite lead due to the accuracy of its ICBMs and the superiority of the U.S. Navy, which had the ability to deliver warheads from invulnerable submarines all over the world. When President Eisenhower left office in 1961, he was disappointed in his inability to achieve a breakthrough with the Soviets. In his farewell address, he warned of the existence of a "military industrial complex" in the United States. He explained that the inordinate influence of the defense lobby had spurred a costly arms race and the permanent militarization of the Cold War.

The Cuban Missile Crisis In 1959, Cuba had come under the revolutionary leadership of Communist Fidel Castro (1926–). Shortly thereafter, Soviet leader Nikita Khrushchev (1894–1971) made the fateful decision to place medium-range nuclear weapons in Cuba as a way of deterring ongoing American efforts to topple the Castro regime. In October 1962, the world edged toward nuclear holocaust when U.S. aerial surveillance of Cuba discovered the weapons. Estimates revealed that the missiles would be able to reach northward as far as Detroit. President John F. Kennedy (1917–1963) met with a team of advisers after confirming Soviet actions. After extensive discussions, Kennedy chose to confront the Soviets publicly by going on national television to announce the existence and location of the missiles and to demand their removal. Rather than launch a preemptive bombing, as some suggested, Kennedy announced a quarantine of Cuba. After several tense days, diplomacy prevailed and the very real possibility of nuclear war was averted. Khrushchev agreed to remove his missiles from Cuba if the United States removed its missiles from Turkey. The United States also agreed not to invade Cuba and pledged to cease efforts to overthrow Castro. In 1963, sobered by the near-catastrophe, Kennedy and Khrushchev signed the Limited Test Ban Treaty. The treaty called for the elimination of all aboveground and

undersea nuclear tests and the installation of a "hotline" for instant communication in the event of future crises.

The nuclear arms race continued. The Soviet Union pursued a steady buildup of a new navy, which prompted the United States to improve its own. In 1964, it was discovered that China also had "the bomb" and refused to agree to limitations on it. The first Strategic Arms Limitation Talks (SALT) between the Soviet Union and the United States led to the SALT I treaty of May 26, 1972. In it, the United States agreed to a five-year freeze on weapons production, which gave the Soviet Union enough of a superficial lead to deter China from attacking it. In November 1974, President Gerald R. Ford (1913–2006) and Leonid Brezhnev (1906–1982) furthered the deténte by signing an agreement at Vladivostok. The agreement raised weapons levels and, because some critics felt the terms heavily favored the Soviet Union, fear of a Soviet nuclear attack persisted through the 1980s.

Civil Rights Movement

The American civil rights movement emerged with the "separate but equal" standard set by the 1896 *Plessy v. Ferguson* Supreme Court decision. The discrete efforts of different groups were galvanized in 1954 by the *Brown v. Board of Education of Topeka, Kansas* decision ordering the integration of public schools, just as the United

Soldiers like this paratrooper stood guard with bayonets outside Little Rock's Central High School as it was integrated on September 25, 1957. © *Bettmann/Corbis*

REVEREND MARTIN LUTHER KING JR.

Martin Luther King Jr. (1929–1968) was the most famous civil rights activist of the twentieth century. The youngest man to receive a Nobel Peace Prize for his promotion of peace, nonviolence, and the equal treatment of people of all races, King followed the teachings of pacifist Indian activist Mahatma Gandhi. He became active in the civil rights movement in 1955 as the leader of the Montgomery Bus Boycott and continued to lead civil rights activists in marches and protests until his violent shooting death on April 4, 1968.

King was born on January 15, 1929, in Atlanta, Georgia. He loved books, even before he could read, and showed talent as an orator from an early age. For years he deliberated the decision to become a minister like his father, but King Sr. dissuaded him, explaining that the ministry was not a sufficiently intellectual pursuit for his bright son. In 1944, King entered Morehouse College where he majored in sociology. After graduating in 1948, he entered Crozer Theological Seminary. Despite his father's advice, King had decided to pursue a career in the ministry. As a seminary student, King attended a lecture by Howard University president, Modecai Johnson, about Indian pacifist, Mohandas "Mahatma" Gandhi. The lecture gave King his purpose and direction in life. He graduated from Crozer in 1951 and entered Boston University. He received his doctorate degree from the university in 1955. That year, King became pastor of the Dexter Avenue Baptist Church in Montgomery, Alabama.

In 1957, King and minister Ralph Abernathy founded the Southern Christian Leadership Conference (SCLC) following the success of the Montgomery Bus Boycott. The goal of the SCLC was to coordinate the action of local protest groups throughout the South. That year, King's home and church were bombed, and violence against black protestors escalated. The bombing made King conscious of the possibility of being killed, but it also reinforced his dedication to nonviolence because, as he said, "Nonviolence can touch men where the law cannot reach them." Because he was always ready to demonstrate the power of nonviolence, he made himself vulnerable to violent confrontations and run-ins with the police. He was arrested and jailed many times, was stabbed while autographing copies of his book *Stride Toward Freedom* and criticized by militant black activists, like Malcolm X (1925–1965) and Stokely Carmichael (1941–1998), who favored more extreme methods of protest.

King used visionary language and wisdom to bring people together. His now-famous "I Have a Dream" speech, delivered from the Lincoln Memorial at the March on Washington in 1963, has become one of the most eloquent and stirring speeches in American history. King's insistence on nonviolence and his gift as a powerful and persuasive orator made him the center of a whirlwind of historical events. In 1963, *Time* magazine named him Man of the Year. A year later, he was awarded the Nobel Peace Prize. He continued his work as a driven civil rights leader until he was assassinated in Memphis, Tennessee. There to assist striking garbage workers in their push for increased wages, King spoke almost prophetically about his demise. In his speech to the garbage workers, he said, "I may not get there with you, but I want you to know tonight that we as a people will get to the promised land."

States was getting involved in the Cold War. The timing of the two events was no coincidence. As Americans grew increasingly aware of the difference between their democratic right to freedom and Soviet totalitarianism, they were forced to see the hypocrisy in enforced racial segregation. The transformative effect of the Cold War was not limited to international relations. The East-West confrontation also influenced domestic life in the United States. Civil rights leaders in the late 1940s were given ammunition for their cause in light of the fact that America's self-proclaimed role as world protector of freedom and democracy flew in the face of its system of legal racial oppression. The discrepancy was not lost on President Truman. In 1947, he shocked the nation by appointing the President's Committee on Civil Rights. A year later, he issued an executive order to end segregation in the United States armed forces.

Post–1945 America The Cold War profoundly affected the politics, society, and culture of postwar America. It shaped family life, gender relations, and the trajectory of domestic policies. But it most significantly challenged the predominant social question of the era—the struggle for racial justice. Now that the Soviets were using America's "Jim Crow" segregationist policies to garner support from the rest of the world, Americans had to scrutinize more closely questions about democracy, freedom, tyranny, and oppression.

Tensions between the East and West served as the perfect vehicle for civil rights leaders to advance their domestic aims. They pointed time and again to the inconsistency between America's mission abroad and the persistence of segregation at home. Leading figures in the civil rights movement asserted relentlessly at conferences and meetings, on the radio, and in newspapers and magazines that Jim Crow was incompatible with America's international role. Martin Luther King Jr. (1929–1968), W. E. B. DuBois (1868–1963), Walter White (1893–1955) of the National Association for the Advancement of Colored People (NAACP), and other prominent activists made clear that the United States must practice at home what it preached abroad. It did not take long for their message to get through to President Truman.

Truman Supports Civil Rights In 1947, as the Cold War intensified and the United States became increasingly intolerant, President Truman shocked the nation by authorizing a fifteen-man committee on civil rights. The goal of the committee was to recommend new legislation to protect people from discrimination. That same year, Truman became the first president to address the NAACP. In his address, he announced that the federal government was working to protect African Americans against discrimination, violence, and race prejudice. In 1948, an election year, Truman continued his push for civil rights, partly out of conscience and partly out of politics. Senator Hubert Humphrey (1911–1978), a deeply committed civil rights advocate, persuaded the Democratic Party to support a strong civil rights platform in its campaign. When the platform passed at the Democratic Convention, South Carolina Governor Strom Thurmond (1902–2003) and a group of Southern delegates walked out. After the convention, Truman issued an executive order calling for the desegregation of the U.S. armed forces. His stance on civil rights won him the black vote that year—and the presidential election.

Space Race

The October 4, 1957 launch of the Soviet satellite *Sputnik I* shocked the United States into greatly accelerating its space program, thus beginning the "space race" between the world's Cold War superpowers. The Soviet launch not only made Americans feel vulnerable to attack, but it also undermined American declarations of scientific superiority.

The Space Race Begins Germany developed the world's first long-range guided missiles during World War II and used them to fire warheads into English cities. After the war, the United States recruited German rocket scientists to assist with the U.S. missile program. The Soviet Union recruited German scientists, too. When the Cold War began, the superpowers were prompted to engage in a race to develop and stockpile thermonuclear weapons and intercontinental ballistic missiles. This so-called "arms race" eventually led to the space race.

The Soviet Union tended to construct rockets capable of launching large payloads. The United States, on the other hand, concentrated on smaller, more agile rocket missiles. The success of *Sputnik I* and the launch of a dog in a second Soviet satellite a month later inspired American scientists to rethink the development of larger rockets. From 1957 to 1961, Soviet spaceships were the first to send live animals into space, orbit the sun, reach the vicinity of the moon, photograph the far side of the moon, and return live animals from space. In the meantime, the United States was focused on manned spaceflight. In 1958, Congress created the National Aeronautics and Space Administration (NASA) to oversee the civilian space program. In 1959, NASA established the Project Mercury program with a goal of

John Glenn with his spacecraft *Friendship 7* in Cape Canaveral, Florida. *© Bettmann/Corbis*

putting a man in orbit around the earth. The Soviet Union shocked the United States a second time when it was first to put a man, Yuri Gagarin (1934–1968), into orbit around the earth on April 12, 1961. Science and the Cold War arms race had converged and turned a dream into reality.

Gagarin's spaceship, the *Vostok I* weighed 10,395 pounds and orbited the globe in eighty-nine minutes at a top speed of seventeen thousand miles per hour. The flight was incredibly smooth. Gagarin reported writing a note, eating, and drinking while in orbit. His reentry into earth's atmosphere, which was faster than anticipated, damaged the capsule, but Gagarin landed unharmed four hundred miles southeast of Moscow. Soviet factories and businesses were closed during the flight so that everyone could listen to radio broadcasts about it. Because the Soviet propaganda office was prepared for the historic event, a commemorative stamp was printed the same day Gagarin reached space. Two days later, the jubilant nation celebrated its hero with a four-hour parade before the Lenin-Stalin mausoleum. That evening, Soviet President Leonid Brezhnev presented the first cosmonaut with the nation's highest award, the title of Hero of the Soviet

Union. Although America was making significant scientific space progress, the Soviet Union was clearly monopolizing the drama of space exploration.

The Race Continues Once Gagarin returned safely to earth, President John F. Kennedy congratulated the Soviet Union on a victory that, he claimed, would be beneficial to all nations. Soon after, on May 25, 1961, he announced a national goal to land an astronaut on the moon by 1970 and safely return him to earth. The pronouncement was a surprise to many, including members of the space program. Kennedy had campaigned on a promise to close the missile gap; now he was promising to close the spaceship gap. According to the president, the moon was the finish line for the space race.

On May 5, 1961, Navy Commander Alan Bartlett Shepard Jr. (1923–1998) rode *Freedom 7*, a Project Mercury capsule, 115 miles into space. Shortly thereafter, Kennedy requested a $1.8 billion appropriation for space and defense-related programs. Estimated calculations revealed that the United States would have to spend between seven and nine billion dollars between 1962 and 1967 if it wanted to take the lead in the space race. Meanwhile, in the Soviet Union, Yuri Gagarin's famous flight was followed by Major Gherman S. Titov's (1935–2000) seventeen orbits around the Earth on August 6–7, 1961. In his twenty-five hours aloft on *Vostok II*, Titov was able to record the effects of a weightless day in space on a man's capacity to work. The Soviets, it seemed, were still leading the race.

The United States Pulls Ahead For the first part of the decade, the *Vostok* launch system was veiled in secrecy. When the launch vehicle was displayed at the Paris Air Show in 1967, American space scientists were surprised by what they saw. Instead of enormous engines, the *Vostok* relied on a combination of small engines to propel and place the spaceship into orbit. This kind of technology allowed the Soviet Union to dominate the first decade of the so-called Space Age. Soviets had been the first to launch manned spacecraft, send a woman into space, create multipassenger spacecraft, send a man to walk in space, land on a planet (Venus), send a probe to the moon, send photographs from that landing, launch a functioning satellite of the moon, and carry out automated rendezvous and docking on spaceships. But by this time, the United States was scoring firsts in communications, weather satellites, and nonautomated spaceship rendezvous and docking missions. In 1962, John Glenn (1921–) became the first American to orbit the earth. Between Glenn's flight and the March 1965 two-man Gemini space flight, four manned Mercury flights were successfully launched. The heart of the U.S. lunar program, Project Apollo, was launched in 1966. The race was getting closer.

In December 1968, the first Apollo mission to orbit the moon sent amazing pictures of the planet back to earth. The public was captivated. Finally, on July 20, 1969, *Apollo 11* astronauts Edwin "Buzz" Aldrin (1930–) and Neil Armstrong (1930–) became the first human beings to walk on the moon. Roughly half a billion people around the world watched the event 240,000 miles away on live television. President Kennedy's goal had been achieved.

BIBLIOGRAPHY

Periodicals

Cavendish, Richard. "Japan's Attack on Port Arthur: February 8th and 9th, 1904". *History Today* (February, 2004).

Kennedy, Paul. "Birth Of A Superpower". *Time* (July 3, 2006).

Stoner, Lynn K. "The Santiago Campaign of 1898: A Soldier's View of the Spanish-American War". *Latin American Research Review* (Summer 1996).

Web Sites

"The American Experience, MacArthur, Korean Maps." *PBS.* <www.pbs.org/wgbh/amex/macarthur/maps/koreatxt.html> (accessed May 16, 2007).

Churchill, Winston S. "Iron Curtain Speech, March 5, 1946." *Internet Modern History Sourcebook.* <www.fordham.edu/halsall/mod/churchill-iron.html> (accessed May 11, 2007).

Frahm, Jill. "SIGINT and the Pusan Perimeter." *National Security Agency.* <www.nsa.gov/publications/publi00024.cfm#5> (accessed May 19, 2007).

"Henry R. Luce and the Rise of the American News Media." *PBS.* <www.pbs.org/wnet/americanmasters/database/luce_h.html> (accessed May 9, 2007).

Hermansen, Max. "Inchon—Operation Chromite" *United States Military Logisticsin the First Part of the Korean War.* University of Oslo. <http://vlib.iue.it/carrie/texts/carrie_books/hermansen/6.html> (accessed May 17, 2007).

"History of Korea, Part II." *Life In Korea.* <www.lifeinkorea.com/information/history2.cfm> (accessed May 15, 2007).

"Interview with Lt. Col. Charles Bussy, U.S. Army." *CNN.* <www.cnn.com/interactive/specials/0005/korea.interviews/bussey.html> (accessed May 19, 2007).

"The Korean War—The Inchon Invasion." *Naval Historical Center.* <www.history.navy.mil/photos/events/kowar/50-unof/inchon.htm> (accessed May 16, 2007).

"The Korean War Armistice." *BBC News.* <http://news.bbc.co.uk/1/hi/world/asia-pacific/2774931.stm> (accessed May 18, 2007).

"The Story of Africa: Independence." *BBC News.* <www.bbc.co.uk/worldservice/africa/features/

storyofafrica/index_section14.shtml> (accessed May 25, 2007).

Truman, Harry S. "The Truman Doctrine, President Harry S. Truman's Address Before a Joint Session of Congress, March 12, 1947." *The Avalon Project at Yale Law School.* <www.yale.edu/lawweb/ avalon/trudoc.html> (accessed May 18, 2007).

Utz, Curtis A. "MacArthur Sells Inchon." *Assault from the Sea, Amphibious Landing at Inchon.* Naval

Historical Center. <www.history.navy.mil/ download/i-16-19.pdf> (accessed May 17, 2007).

"Walton Harris Walker, General, United States Army." *ArlingtonCemetery.net.* <www.arlingtoncemetery. net/whwalker.htm> (accessed May 19, 2007).

Wormser, Richard. "Harry S. Truman Supports Civil Rights (1947–1948)." *PBS.* <www.pbs.org/wnet/ jimcrow/stories_events_truman.html> (accessed May 24, 2007).

Introduction to the Cold War (1945–1991)

The Cold War was not a war in the traditional sense. It was a political, philosophical, and economic conflict between the United States and the Soviet Union (USSR) that spanned four decades and influenced the culture of virtually every nation in the world. The Cold War did turn "hot" from time to time, as the major players applied military might to protect their interests abroad and control events in developing countries. But for the most part, the era was marked by tough rhetoric and high tension, not open combat.

Tensions between the U.S. and USSR had existed before the Cold War started. The United States, Great Britain, and France all denounced the Marxist ideas that had sparked a revolution in Russia in 1917 and led to the formation of the Communist Soviet Union. The Communists' talk of "word revolution" alarmed leaders in the United States, but the Soviets were too busy, first with a civil war and then with establishing a government, to push their political philosophy abroad in the 1920s and 1930s. As World War II came to an end, however, the United States and the Soviet Union emerged as the world's two superpowers. By the end of the 1940s, both had atomic weapons and both sought global influence.

The first Cold War "battle" was over the fate of Europe. Britain, France, the United States, and the Soviet Union had been allies during World War II. They all realized that the devastated continent, and Germany in particular, needed rebuilding. They also wanted to ensure that German aggression never again disturbed European peace. The Allies divided Germany and its capital, Berlin, into western and eastern halves. The division came to mark the spheres of influence of the Soviets and Americans. All the democratic nations of Western Europe came under the protection of the United States. All the nations of Eastern Europe, where Communist governments were soon installed, came under the influence of the Soviets. British Prime Minister Winston Churchill characterized this division as an "iron curtain"across the continent.

Tensions ran high through the 1950s and 1960s, as both the Unites States and the Soviets raced to produce as many nuclear weapons as possible. The threat of global thermonuclear war was palpable. In 1961, the two superpowers came as close as they ever did to using their devastating weapons to attack each other. Sensing weakness in newly elected President John F. Kennedy, Soviet leader Nikita Kruschev sent several dozen nuclear missiles to its ally Cuba and trained the missiles on American targets. Kennedy seriously considered military strikes against the installation, a move that would likely have led to all-out nuclear war. However, the Cuban Missile Crisis was resolved diplomatically after several nerve-jangling days.

Facing the implications of nuclear war head-on sobered U.S. and Soviet leaders. By the 1970s, the Cold War was characterized by some relaxation of tensions (known as a period of détente). The two sides began Strategic Arms Limitations Talks that led to some caps on the development of nuclear warheads. As the Vietnam War began to wind down under President Richard Nixon, the Soviets and the United States began to soften their attitudes toward one another.

In the late 1980s, a wave of democratic reform movements in the Communist Bloc nations resulted in free elections and the end of Communist rule in most of Eastern Europe. Soviet Premier Mikhail Gorbachev, who had helped foster reform in his own country, tried to maintain the vast Soviet state, but was unsuccessful. In 1991, the Soviet Union was officially dissolved. Its member states became independent nations. The Cold War had finally ended.

Cold War (1945–1991)

✪ Causes

Culture Clash on a Global Scale

A prime cause of the Cold War was the drastic difference in the ideologies of the United States and the Soviet Union. Differing views on economics, foreign policy, and domestic civil liberties set these two nations apart even before World War II and continued to drive a wedge between them during the four decades that followed World War II's end. Each nation had reasons to distrust and dislike the other, and relations between the two grew chillier as their rhetoric heated up and their nuclear arsenals grew.

U.S. Capitalism and Soviet Communism The historical, philosophical, and economic backgrounds of the U.S. and Soviet cultures are extremely complicated. In briefest outline, however, the United States can be described as a country with a capitalist economic system based on free enterprise. Philosophically, the United States believes in limited government interference in the lives of citizens, and protects what it considers to be their "rights"—things like the freedom of speech, freedom to choose their own religion (or not choose a religion), and freedom to associate with whom they please.

The Soviet Union was a nation based on a communist economic and social system that was a response to centuries of gross inequities in Russia. Russian landowners, the ruling class that made up a tiny minority of the population, controlled every aspect of the lives of the Russian peasantry, the majority of the population, and kept them in servitude and poverty. Communist leaders urged the peasants to rise up and establish a truly equal, classless society. In such a society, all land and public works would be owned and operated communally (hence the term "communism"). The idea was that there would be no rich or poor, but that all citizens would be equal and contribute to society according to their abilities. Early leaders of the Soviet Union attempted to make this idea a reality.

There are pros and cons to both the U.S. and Soviet systems, both in theory and in practice. Some of the main criticisms launched against the U.S. system are that unchecked capitalism results in a wide gap between the rich and poor, and that the poor are insufficiently cared for by the government. A criticism of the Soviet system is that by removing money as a motivating factor, workers and businesses have little incentive for operating at high efficiency, improving performance, or generating new ideas. Also, since the Soviet Union recognized only the Communist party, there was no room for political dissent. Although there were elections in the Soviet Union, and the candidates were, in theory, selected by the citizens, in reality candidates were selected by the central Communist party and most, until the late 1980s, ran unopposed. In practice, the ideals of Soviet communism did not come to fruition as planned. Because citizens had as little say in their government as ever, ruthless leaders came to power and misused their authority to violently repress the people.

The United States and the Russian Revolution U.S.-Soviet relations got off to a rocky start from the very beginning. As the Russian Revolution began in March 1917, the United States was cautiously optimistic and tried to form a workable relationship with the provisional government. The United States and Russia had enjoyed amicable but fairly distant relations during most of the century that preceded the Russian Revolution of 1917–1918. World War I had made Germany a common enemy for the United States, Russia, France, and Britain. It seemed possible this shared aim could help forge a lasting friendship between the countries.

Most U.S. citizens reacted positively to the news of the overthrow of the Russian Czar Nicholas II in March 1917. This uprising against a tyrannical regime followed President Woodrow Wilson's ideals for world democracy. By mid-March, Nicholas had abdicated and a provisional government was installed. President Wilson soon recognized the new order during the same message to

Congress in which he asked for a declaration of war against Germany. He called Russia a "fit partner for a league of honor" and began sending millions of dollars in funds to the new Russian government.

A strange twist of events over the next few months, however, caused the United States and its allies to reverse course toward Russia even while maintaining their alliance with Russia against Germany. In November 1917, revolutionary leader Vladimir Lenin mobilized workers and Bolsheviks (a faction of the Russian Communist party) to overthrow Russia's provisional government. The United States opposed the Bolsheviks for their Communist principles and because Lenin and his movement also wanted to end the war with Germany. President Wilson refused to recognize Bolshevik Russia because it had overthrown the short-lived democratic government, suppressed civil liberties, and was hostile toward private property rights. Clearly, the ideas behind the Bolshevik Revolution were contrary to several basic American principles.

With pressure from American allies Great Britain and France, the United States tried to stop the Bolsheviks from achieving a complete takeover. After much consideration, Wilson agreed to aid Russian anti-Bolsheviks. In December 1917, the United States sent funds through the British and French that ultimately reached the Russian resistance. Also in late 1917, France and Britain defined geographic areas in southern Russia in which they would assist anti-Bolshevik forces. Essentially, the Allies had entered the Russian Civil War against the Bolsheviks, even as the Bolsheviks continued to fight against Germany, their common enemy.

Meanwhile, in the hope of ending the war with Germany and its allies, the new Russian Bolshevik government signed the Treaty of Brest-Litovsk (1918), which ceded much of the western Russian empire to the Germans. The Germans, however, continued their march on Russia and took Kiev and much of the Ukraine by the spring of 1918. The new Bolshevik leaders, Lenin and Leon Trotsky, found themselves in a war against Germany again. At the same time they were still trying to secure their control of Russia itself in the face of internal opposition funded and supplied to some degree by the United States, Great Britain, and France.

President Wilson was squeamish about openly meddling in the Bolshevik conflict within Russia. The other Allies were more aggressive in their attempt to stop the Soviet government, and they pushed for the United States assistance in that effort. Wilson finally sent about 5,700 troops to Murmansk and Vladivostok in June and September 1918. He had stated publicly, however, "Whether from Vladivostok or from Murmansk and Archangel, the only legitimate object for which American or Allied troops can be employed ... is to guard military stores" for Russians to defend themselves

A 1947 photograph from Stalingrad testifies to the utter devastation sustained by Russians during World War II. *Thomas D. Mcavoy/Time Life Pictures/Getty Images*

against the aggressive enemy of Germany, not for the interference with Russian sovereignty or internal affairs.

The British and French had a different view. Winston Churchill, British war minister and later prime minister, had stated that the Allies should "strangle the Bolshevik baby in its crib." World War I ended with an armistice on November 11, 1918, but the fighting in Russia continued. The Allied still sent aid to the anti-Bolshevik movement, but only in the form of money and war materiel. Ultimately, Lenin and the Bolshevik revolutionaries cemented control of the government. They would not soon forget whose side the United States and its allies had taken during the Russian Civil War.

The First Red Scare

A fundamental part of the "American Dream" is that with hard work, ingenuity, and determination, anyone, no matter how humble his beginnings, can achieve spectacular success. Before and after the Bolshevik Revolution (this October 1917 revolution in Russia led to

IRON CURTAIN

The "Iron Curtain" was the physical, philosophical, and metaphorical divide between the countries of Western Europe and the Soviet-dominated countries of Eastern Europe. The term comes from a famous speech given in 1946 by former British Prime Minister Winston Churchill, who said: "From Stettin in the Baltic to Trieste in the Adriatic an iron curtain has descended across the Continent. Behind that line lie all the capitals of the ancient states of Central and Eastern Europe. Warsaw, Berlin, Prague, Vienna, Budapest, Belgrade, Bucharest and Sofia, all these famous cities and the populations around them lie in what I must call the Soviet sphere, and all are subject in one form or another, not only to Soviet influence but to a very high and, in some cases, increasing measure of control from Moscow."

civil war and the subsequent formation of the Soviet Union in 1922), Americans generally denounced the communist ideas on which the revolution was premised because it ran counter to their belief in the value of hard work and individual genius. Because the revolutionary rhetoric highlighted the worldwide spread of communism as a key goal, American leaders became concerned about the potential for a similar revolution in the United States. In fact, in the early part of the twentieth century, there was a variety of radical political groups, some anarchists (in favor of abolishing government altogether) and some communist, that sought to undermine the U.S. government. In 1919, in what was perhaps an overaction to the potential threat, U.S. Attorney General A. Mitchell Palmer (whose home was the target of an anarchist bomb attack) and J. Edgar Hoover, head of the General Intelligence Division of the Justice Department, raided labor union offices and private homes without warrants to find information on so-called subversives. Their agents rounded up around ten thousand individuals suspected of radicalism, tried many, and deported the foreigners they had arrested. This fear of the destructive potential of Communists and political radicals in the United States was called the "red scare." (Red was the color of the Soviet flag, and the term was used to refer to communists and other leftists.)

A Temporary Alliance During World War II, the United States and the Soviet Union placed their differences aside in order to defeat the common enemy: Germany. As the war ended and the Nazis were toppled, the Allies grew more concerned about how the Soviet Union was being operated under Joseph Stalin. At war conferences at Yalta and Potsdam, leaders from the United States, Britain, and the Soviet Union discussed postwar plans. The tensions between East and West on foreign policy began to grow. Stalin, who had risen to

power after the death of Vladimir Lenin (the Soviet Union's first head of state) in 1924, proved difficult to deal with and ruthless with his own people. The Allies believed he was planning to try to take control of Eastern Europe. The outcome of the Yalta Conference proved them at least partially right: the Soviet Union gained control of Poland, and Germany was divided into eastern and western halves, with the eastern half coming under control of the Soviet Union.

The United States and Britain were concerned because the very freedoms they fought to defend were precisely those denied to citizens of the Soviet Union. Additionally, George Kennan, a high-ranking member of the State Department working in Moscow, began to explain the motives and goals of the Soviet Union to Americans as he helped shape U.S. policy. His observations came through in his telegram to the U.S. secretary of state in 1946 and in his anonymous 1947 article in *Foreign Affairs* the following year, "The Sources of Soviet Conduct," which revealed that Soviet hostility toward American interests was largely caused by Stalin's ideology. Stalin justified his repressive tactics by arguing that they were necessary to prevent the growth of "evil" capitalism, according to Kennan. While he and the Soviet government began to exert control over East Germany, Poland, Hungary, and other Eastern European nations, Stalin claimed it was to guarantee a proletariat rule free from interference from Western imperialists.

Containment and the Truman Doctrine It was Kennan who proposed the idea of "containment" (preventing Communism from being forced on other countries) in his papers and communiqués. This idea made its way into the Truman Doctrine. In that 1947 doctrine, President Truman stated, "It must be the policy of the United States to support free peoples who are resisting attempted subjugation by armed minorities or outside pressures." Other postwar containment initiatives included the Marshall Plan in 1947 and the formation in 1949 of the North Atlantic Treaty Organization (NATO). The Marshall Plan was a mammoth package of economic assistance for war-torn Europe. NATO aligned Canada, the United States, and several Western European nations together for mutual assured protection against any attack from the Soviet Union or any other Communist Bloc country.

As the diplomatic tensions played out, both sides began the nuclear arms race. Truman had informed Stalin at Potsdam of U.S. nuclear capability after the first successful atomic bomb was exploded in New Mexico. The United States would within weeks detonate atomic bombs over Hiroshima and Nagasaki, bringing about the end of World War II. The Soviets began their work on an atomic bomb in 1945 and by 1949 had successfully conducted their first test.

Nikita S. Kruschev points his figure at Richard M. Nixon during a heated interchange that would become known as the "Kitchen Debates." *Howard Sochurek/Time Life Pictures/Getty Images*

NATO and the Warsaw Pact

The United States, Britain, and France along with other Western European nations grew further apart from the Soviet Union after World War II. The USSR, which had been their World War II ally, was increasingly seen as a potential aggressor. The United States and several Western European nations agreed that potential Soviet aggression warranted a stronger alliance among them. What resulted was the North Atlantic Treaty Organization (NATO).

The USSR had detonated its first atomic bomb in 1949, thereby raising additional concerns and solidifying the consensus in Western Europe that if the United States pulled out of Europe and went back to its former isolationist ways, Western Europe would face a Russian threat. American leaders began to believe that it would be easier to prevent another global war than to win one after it began. The United States also realized that the oceans that had protected it for years were no longer a strong defense against Russian air and missile technology.

The North Atlantic Treaty bound together the United States, Canada, and most Western European nations as a bloc promising each other assistance in case any of them were attacked. Though there was no

mention of the USSR in the treaty, it was abundantly clear that it was a Soviet attack that was feared. By 1955, the Allies formally ended their occupation of Germany and gave the new West German Republic full sovereignty. This new country was given full membership in NATO and began to rearm itself for the first time since Hitler's defeat.

The creation of NATO and the resurgence of Western Germany encouraged the USSR to create an alliance with its satellite nations—the Warsaw Pact. The USSR had essentially controlled or at least held strong influence over Poland, Albania, Bulgaria, East Germany, Romania, and Czechoslovakia. The Warsaw Pact codified the existing relationships the USSR had with those countries and both formally and publicly expressed a mutual defense arrangement on the other side of the Iron Curtain (the term used to describe the dividing line between Western and Eastern Europe). The document was signed in May 1955. It consisted of eleven articles that covered common economic interest, peaceful settlement of conflicts, and joint defense. The military component of the pact allowed for the disposition of troops under joint command for purposes of the treaty. Soviet Marshal I. S. Konev was appointed as the Warsaw Pact commander in chief, while the defense ministers of the other member nations became his deputies. Soon, key military positions in the satellite armies were given to Soviet officers. The USSR had simply expanded its military state further into Eastern Europe under the guise of a multilateral treaty.

With the dividing lines established, the West squared off with the Soviet Union for the next several decades in a Cold War of ideologies marked by considerable interference in the affairs of developing nations and, occasionaly, direct confrontations between the two superpowers.

✪ Major Figures

Nikita Khrushchev

For much of the early Cold War, the outspoken Nikita Khrushchev (1894–1971) was the leader of the Soviet Union. Vacillating between confronting the United States and backing off from hard-nosed foreign policies and threats, he also tried to institute significant domestic reforms. Khrushchev's unpredictability and uneven manner in dealing with the United States led to his removal as the Soviet premier and first secretary of the Communist party by the mid-1960s.

Born on April 17, 1894, in Kalinovka, Russia, Khrushchev was the son of Sergei Nikanorovich Khrushchev, a peasant farmer who also worked as a coal miner. When Khrushchev was able to attend school, he proved to be a gifted student. However, by the time the family moved to Yuzovka, Ukraine, so his father could be closer to the mines, his attendance was often sporadic because he worked to help support his family. By working in a factory and as a mechanic in the coal mines, he experienced the poor conditions under which the working classes labored.

Communist Party Activities After the 1917 Bolshevik Revolution forced a regime change in Russia, Khrushchev joined the ruling Communist Party in 1918. He served in the Red Army in 1919 in defense of the Communist government during the Russian Civil War. Working in the Ukrainian mines again in 1920, Khrushchev was soon put in charge of the mine's political matters. In 1922, after the death of his first wife left him a widower with young children, he went back to Yuzovka and began receiving more education through the Communist party's schools.

While attending one such institution, the Donets Industrial Institute, Khrushchev was elected to a position in the Communist Party there. Through the 1920s, he moved up through party bureaucratic ranks in the Ukraine. After the death of the first Soviet leader Vladimir Lenin in 1924, Khrushchev supported Joseph Stalin, who became the Soviet leader after party infighting.

Khrushchev's support of Stalin contributed to his rapid bureaucratic rise.

Rose Through Ranks in Moscow After moving to Moscow in 1929, Khrushchev received more education at Moscow's Academy of Heavy Industry. Soon, his political career rose to a new level. When his mentor Lazar Kaganovich became the head of the Communist Party in Moscow in 1931, Khrushchev was brought into the political administration of Moscow. Within two years, Khrushchev held the powerful position of the second secretary of the Moscow Central Committee. In 1935, Khrushchev followed Kaganovich as first secretary of the Moscow city Communist Party, after having been elected to the Soviet Central Committee in 1934.

Khrushchev was a staunch backer of Stalin even during the "purges" of the late 1930s in which many of Khrushchev's colleagues were executed or exiled. Because of Khrushchev's loyalty and his assistance conducting the purges, Stalin helped get him elected to the Supreme Soviet and the Politburo, the policy-making executive body for the Central Committee. After thousands of Ukrainian Communist Party members were purged in 1938, Khrushchev was elected the first secretary of the Ukrainian Communist Party, another influential post.

National Communist Leader Khrushchev spent several years controlling Ukrainian politics in order to improve agricultural production under the Soviet collective system, which was resisted by the locals. He also worked to bring the area under the cultural control of the Soviet Union. Nationally prominent by the beginning of the 1940s, he also became an officer in the Soviet Army when his country was invaded by Nazi Germany. Actively involved in combat for two years, he served during the Battle of Stalingrad (1942–1943) and eventually reached the rank of lieutenant general.

When the Soviets had the war under control in late 1943, Khrushchev returned to the Ukraine and reclaimed his position as the first secretary of the Communist Party. In the postwar period, he oversaw the reconstruction of the Ukraine's economy, as the chairman of the Ukrainian Council of Ministers. In 1949, Khrushchev went back to Moscow after the death of a key Soviet leader, Andrei Zhdanov, and again served as the first secretary of the Moscow Central Committee. Khrushchev consolidated his power with the aim of becoming the Soviet leader after Stalin's death.

Soviet Leader Joseph Stalin died after a stroke in March 1953. Khrushchev was selected as the first secretary of the Soviet Central Committee six months later. Stalin's chosen successor, Georgy Malenkov, became premier of the Soviet Union. A power struggle ensued in which Khrushchev gained the upper hand in 1955. He forced Malenkov out and put his ally, Nikolay Bulganin, in his place as premier. With Khrushchev in

Flanked by East Berlin soldiers, a construction worker adjusts concrete slabs on a portion of the Berlin Wall, 1961.   *Robert Lackenbach/Time Life Pictures/Getty Images*

charge of the party and Bulganin as premier, Khrushchev effectively controlled the country.

After gaining power, Khrushchev began speaking out against Stalin's policies. He alienated Communist hardliners with his de-Stalinization reforms, which began in early 1956. Khrushchev introduced more personal freedom for citizens, closed concentration and hard labor camps, freed many people who had been imprisoned by Stalin, and put certain legal processes back in place. Khrushchev also decreased the powers of the secret police and sometimes allowed more freedom of artistic expression. One reason for such reforms was to improve the Soviet Union's standing internationally.

However, such changes were not embraced by the whole of the Communist leadership in the Soviet Union. By 1957, the Politburo (the governing body of the Communist party) tried to get Khrushchev dismissed, but Khrushchev's supporters in the Central Committee blocked the move. He consolidated his hold on power by demoting or expelling party members who had led the dismissal movement. In 1958, Khrushchev took over Bulganin's place as the head of the Soviet government as well.

Cold War Leadership While Khrushchev served as the leader of the Soviet Union, the Cold War heated

up. One aspect of the rivalry between the Soviet Union and the United States was the "space race." It began when the Soviets launched the first man-made satellite to orbit the Earth, Sputnik, in October 1957. This development stunned the Western world and compelled the United States to invest heavily in its own space program. To keep up, the Soviets had to do the same.

A year later, the Cold War took on a new dimension when Khrushchev unexpectedly demanded that the West—specifically, the United States, Great Britain, and France—withdraw from their sectors in West Berlin so that the Soviet Union could control the whole of East Germany. The Soviets did not like having capitalist, Western-supported powers in Berlin. When the president of the United States, Dwight D. Eisenhower, ignored Khrushchev, the Soviet leader backed down.

The scenario repeated itself in 1961. Eisenhower's successor, John F. Kennedy, ignored Khrushchev again, and the Soviet leader yielded again. However, this time, he ordered the construction of the Berlin Wall, physically dividing the city into western and eastern halves, so people could be stopped from running from Soviet-controlled territory to the West-controlled half of the city.

SPACE RACE MILESTONES

The United States and the Soviet Union worked feverishly to establish preeminence in the area of space aeronautics. Here are some milestones of the space race:

- 1957—Russian satellite Sputnik I launched.
- 1958—Explorer I, America's first satellite, successfully launched.
- April 1961—Soviet astronaut Yuri Gagarin launched into orbit aboard the Vostok capsule.
- May 1961—Alan Shepard becomes the first American in space, leaving Earth's atmosphere for fifteen minutes; the National Aeronautics and Space Administration (NASA) launches the Apollo program with the goal of landing a man on the moon.
- 1962—John Glenn becomes the first American to orbit Earth.
- 1965—Alexei Leonov exits his Soviet spacecraft and becomes the first person to go on a "space walk."
- 1967—The first Apollo spacecraft explodes during a simulation, killing all three astronauts aboard.
- 1969—Apollo 11 lands on the moon.
- 1971—Soviet Union launches world's first space station, the Solyuz.
- 1973—America launches Skylab, a large space station.

Cold War Incidents Tensions between the United States and the Soviet Union increased in the late 1950s and early 1960s because of several significant incidents. The Soviet Union shot down an American U-2 spy plane flying over the Soviet Union in this time period, and Khrushchev skipped a planned summit meeting with Eisenhower in Paris in May 1960. The biggest incident happened in 1962: The Cuban Missile Crisis.

Because the Soviet Union did not possess nuclear missiles that could reach North America, Khrushchev placed them in Cuba, a Soviet ally located only ninety miles from the United States. After establishing a quarantine around Cuba to prevent the delivery of any more missiles, President Kennedy demanded that the Soviet missiles already in place be removed. After a tense stand-off, Khrushchev again backed down and agreed to take the missiles away if the United States promised to not invade Cuba.

Downfall After the Cuban Missile Crisis, relations between the United States and the Soviet Union improved. In addition to setting up a secure hot line between the countries, Khrushchev also signed a limited nuclear test-ban treaty in August 1963. While the Soviet leader's international position was on the rise, he still faced significant problems at home, including a lack of support for his continued reforms of the Communist

system. Khrushchev's economic reforms undermined the Soviet system, and he lost the support of military leaders by reducing the size of the Soviet Army and curtailing the powers of the secret police.

In October 1964, the Politburo succeeded in forcing the removal of Khrushchev as the first secretary of the Communist Party. He was replaced by Leonid Brezhnev. Living under guard, Khrushchev spent the rest his days in homes in Moscow and the countryside, writing a two-volume memoir and gardening. He died in Petrovo-Dalneye, on the outskirts of Moscow, on September 11, 1971, at the age of 77.

Mao Zedong

Mao Zedong (1893–1976) was the leader of the Communist Revolution in China and ruled his country for several decades until his death in the mid-1970s. Mao wanted to create stability in China and improve the lives of Chinese peasants, but many of his policies increased poverty and led to widespread oppression of his people.

He was born on December 26, 1893, in Shaoshan, Xiangtan County, in Hunan province, China. Mao was the son of Mao Jen-shen and his wife, Wen Qimei. Though his parents were peasants, they were prosperous rice farmers who eventually became landowners and had a rice trading business. When he was five years old, Mao began working in the fields. Two years later, he began his education at a local village school. Though his father wanted him to return home to work in the family business, Mao ran away at the age of thirteen to attend a better school in Changsha, the capital city of Hunan province, where he studied Chinese history and literature.

Revolutionary Ideas After graduating from a teacher's training college in Changsha in 1918, Mao went to Beijing University, where he became acquainted with the Marxist and Communist philosophies. He was one of many educated Chinese who thought the communism practiced by Vladimir Lenin in Russia might solve China's political and economic problems. Throughout Mao's young life, China had been in a state of breakdown. The power vacuum caused by the crumbling Qing dynasty caused a civil war, and a revolution in 1912 directed by Sun Yat-sen only led to more chaos.

Mao himself participated in the May Fourth Movement in which Chinese students protested the decision of the Paris Peace Conference, which ended World War I, to give German-held territories in China to Japan. Mao looked to Communism for a solution, because other parts of China were controlled by warlords and foreign countries, which created a chaotic situation.

Certain that Chinese peasants could carry out a revolution and take over China, Mao and others founded the Chinese Communist Party in 1921. Over the next six years, the party gained many supporters. By

Guerrilla leader Mao Zedong, speaking here at a meeting in November 1944, would become the president of the People's Republic of China. *Fox Photos/Getty Images*

1923, Communists began working with Nationalist Party (Kuomintang) forces led by Sun in an attempt to unite China. (Nationalist supporters wanted to keep power concentrated among those who owned land and businesses.) After Sun died in 1925, he was succeeded by Chiang Kai-shek. As the Nationalist party took control of China, Communists were forced from cities by Chiang.

Rise to Power Afraid of what the Communists would do if they had any control or influence, Chiang ordered his army to attack all Communists in April 1927. Though thousands of Communists lost their lives, many, including Mao, survived and organized a rebel government in the Kiangsi province of southern China. The number of Communist supporters grew over the next seven years as Mao built up the Communists' military force, the Red Army, and adapted guerrilla tactics to political goals.

After founding the Chinese Soviet Republic in Kiangsi and declaring himself chairman in 1931, Mao faced a new challenge. In 1934, because of continued attacks by Nationalist forces, Mao decided the Communists and their Red Army had to move their base north. The six-thousand-mile trek to Shaanxi became known as the "Long March" and was marked by hardships and battles with Nationalist forces. The journey took a year, and only eight thousand of the ninety thousand who began the march survived to reach their destination. Mao emerged as the dominant Communist leader during the march, and after they reached their destination, the Communists elected him the chairman of the party.

The Communist Revolution While the Nationalists and Communists waged a civil war for the next two years, the two sides agreed to a truce when Japan invaded China in 1937 and China was drawn into World War II. Though the two groups did not trust each other, both hated the Japanese invaders more and reluctantly worked together to rid themselves of their common enemy. When World War II ended in 1945 and the Japanese were expelled, the Nationalists and Communists began fighting for control of China. By the end of the war, the Communists were in control of parts of China with a population of nearly 100 million.

In 1949, the Communists, led by Mao, prevailed over the Nationalists, who were forced into exile on the island of Taiwan. He declared that the People's Republic of China had been founded. Mao soon signed a Sino-Soviet Treaty of Friendship, Alliance, and Mutual Assistance with the Soviets. At home, Mao remained the leader of the Communist Party and the Chinese government, though day-to-day operations were handled by Soviet-trained party bureaucrats.

Soon after taking power, Mao instructed peasants to take land and possessions from those who controlled the farmland. Because of Mao's actions, Chinese peasants were able to grow a surplus of food for the next three years. Prosperity among peasants continued in the early 1950s, after Mao ordered all farms to become cooperatives. By having peasants work tracts of land together, farm output continued to rise and continued surpluses resulted in more prosperity.

Industrial Failures By the mid-1950s, Mao wanted to change China from an agricultural to an industrial society. Because this shift required extensive capital, he took control of China's farming industry in 1956. All farms, animals, and farm equipment were now owned by the government, and cooperatives were replaced by collective farms operated under guidelines established by Chinese officials. Because peasants again received little for their work, they became impoverished, and their situation became even more dire.

In 1958, Mao started a program intended to further compel China's transformation into an industrial powerhouse. The so-called "Great Leap Forward" demanded that people work harder—and longer hours—to boost production. Citizens were encouraged to make more steel any way they could, including melting their agricultural tools. The primitive process employed only made worthless steel and took people away from food production.

The Great Leap Forward also compelled local Communist Party officials to exaggerate how much food was being produced in order to cover up the policy's failure. Because the reported amounts produced were much higher than the true figures, what the government gave back to the peasants as their share of the production was often insufficient. Nearly thirty million Chinese peasants starved to death between 1959 and 1961 as a result.

Power Shift With the failure of the Great Leap Forward and other programs, the Soviet Union no longer gave any support or aid to China. Mao stepped down as the head of the Chinese government in the early 1960s. He remained in control of the Communist Party, however, and still wielded a tremendous amount of power in China. Because the new, more moderate leaders eased

government controls and introduced a few reforms, China thrived for a few years.

By 1966, Mao was condemning the new leaders and their programs for drifting from the intent of the original revolution. He started the Cultural Revolution by telling young Chinese radicals, soon organized into battalions of Red Guards, to attack certain institutions like libraries and museums as well as people such as intellectuals, former landowners, and officials. Schools were closed and students were indoctrinated with Mao's ideas. Millions of people were publicly beaten for moving away from Mao's form of Communism, and four thousand died as a result.

Within a year, the Red Guards were in-fighting, and China fell into chaos as millions of soldiers and workers joined the battle. After Mao ordered the disbanding of the Red Guards in 1968, peace was restored, and Mao himself soon returned to power in China. A cult of Mao took hold as his ideas were published in several books and his portrait appeared everywhere in China. Mao sought to ensure that his strict version of Communism remained in control of China. Toward that end, he encouraged the development of a cult centered on his personality.

Despite ill health, Mao decided to pursue better relations with other countries in the early 1970s as a means of enhancing China's reputation on the world stage. He hosted a visit by American president Richard Nixon in 1972, which soon led to a diplomatic relationship with the Unites States. As Mao's health continued to decline, internal strife between radicals and moderates plagued the Chinese government. Mao died on September 9, 1976, in Beijing, China, and a less repressive Chinese government soon took charge.

Joseph R. McCarthy

Senator Joseph R. McCarthy (1908–1957) was America's most notorious Cold War anticommunist. For four years, from the winter of 1950 to the summer of 1954, McCarthy held the country in thrall with widely publicized charges of Communist subversion in the federal government. His reckless and unsubstantiated accusations led to the Army-McCarthy hearings, a thirty-six-day affair that was broadcast live on television to an audience of roughly twenty million viewers. After discovering a means of manipulating American anxiety over Communism, this once obscure senator became a powerful and much-feared demagogue. Though he failed to uncover a single Communist not already known to the authorities, the damage his histrionics wrought reverberated into the mid-1960s. After McCarthyism, as his reign of terror came to be known, American politicians were limited in their ability to conduct creative and realistic foreign policy with Communist countries, especially Asia. Republicans and Democrats alike saw no subtleties within the varieties of communism in the

Senator McCarthy's accusations contributed to a fear of communism both at home and abroad. *Michael Rougier/Time Life Pictures/Getty Images*

serving in the South Pacific, McCarthy took a leave of absence to campaign for the 1944 Republican nomination for the U.S. Senate. His bid for the nomination was unsuccessful. When the military denied him a second leave of absence to campaign for reelection as judge, McCarthy resigned and returned to Wisconsin. In 1946, McCarthy ran for Senate again. In the general election, he accused his Democratic opponent of ties to alleged Communist groups and won a decisive victory.

Senator McCarthy McCarthy's first years in the Senate were spent in relative obscurity. He did, however, earn a reputation for being brash, arrogant, and wildly unpredictable. He frequently violated Senate decorum by questioning the integrity of fellow senators during hearings. This extraordinary breach led to the stripping of his one major committee assignment because the chairman refused to tolerate McCarthy's presence. By 1950, the overbearing senator began to dwell on his 1952 reelection with warranted anxiety. Beyond his lackluster record, McCarthy feared being investigated for tax evasion and ethics violations. He had to figure out a way to get reelected despite these obstacles. On January 7, 1950, McCarthy was entertaining friends when someone suggested he focus on the issue of Communists in government as a way of increasing his reelection chances. McCarthy jumped at the suggestion, ignoring warnings that he do his homework and be careful with his charges.

The McCarthy Era Speaking before the Ohio County Women's Republican Club on February 9, 1950, in Wheeling, West Virginia, Senator Joseph McCarthy claimed to hold in his hands a list of 205 Communist Party members active in the State Department. He went on to say that Secretary of State Dean Acheson knew who those 205 Communist members were, but was doing nothing about it. With those two sweeping and unsubstantiated claims, McCarthy ushered in an unprecedented era of anticommunist hysteria. Domestic fears of Communism had been on the rise since the late 1940s. McCarthy simply took the existing climate of suspicion and fear and used it to his political advantage.

As public furor over McCarthy's charges began to build, his allegations changed. Two hundred and five communists became fifty-seven. When pressed by the Senate to clarify his charges, it was soon clear that McCarthy had no list, just outdated information about employees the State Department had been planning to dismiss. The whole issue would have disappeared at this point were it not for America's agitated Communist anxiety. The Democrats convened a special Senate inquiry in 1950 in an attempt to expose McCarthy. The tenacious Republican senator survived the hearings despite repeated challenges to produce evidence that did not exist. He escaped defeat by focusing his attention on accusations that incriminated various government officials for their Communist associations. The temper of the times made it possible, then, for McCarthy to

world after McCarthy. This rigid anticommunism increased the likelihood of U.S. military involvement in Vietnam as no president could tolerate having another country fall to Communism for fear of unleashing another McCarthy.

McCarthy's Early Years Joseph Raymond McCarthy was born on November 14, 1908, near Grand Chute, Wisconsin, to nearly illiterate Irish-German parents. McCarthy dropped out of school at fourteen and became a chicken farmer and then the manager of a grocery store. When he was nineteen, he returned to school and completed all four years of high school coursework in one year. In 1930, McCarthy entered Marquette University Law School in Milwaukee, Wisconsin, and graduated five years later. After law school, McCarthy opened his own law practice in Waupaca, Wisconsin, but earned so little he relied on poker winnings to make ends meet. After nine months, he moved to Shawano, Wisconsin, and took a job working with another attorney. In 1939, he ran for circuit judge in Wisconsin's tenth district and won.

McCarthy did not bother to resign his judgeship during his tenure as a marine officer in the South Pacific during World War II. He simply persuaded his fellow judges to take care of his caseload in his absence. While become the nation's leading anticommunist by making his victims guilty by association, whether they were Communist, noncommunist, or anticommunist.

McCarthy's Demise In June 1951, McCarthy accused Defense Secretary George C. Marshall (1880–1959), a national hero for his roles in ending World War II and rebuilding Western Europe in its aftermath, of aiding the Soviet Union's rise as a world power. Marshall was forced to resign in shame and disgust. When Dwight D. Eisenhower (1890–1969) was elected president and the Republicans gained control of the Senate in 1952, McCarthy's colleagues looked forward to reining him in. They never trusted him and suspected his charges were partisan politics that would cease when the Republicans ran the White House. But McCarthy outmaneuvered them by appointing himself head of the Permanent Subcommittee on Investigations, a committee that came with a generous budget and the power to issue subpoenas and hold hearings. His first investigations in 1953 were as irresponsible as the Republicans feared they would be. By the summer of 1953, McCarthy had thoroughly demoralized the Eisenhower administration and was regarded as a genuine menace by the Republicans.

When he began investigating the Army's security clearance procedures at Fort Monmouth, New Jersey, though, he actually stumbled on legitimate issues of national security. The famous Army-McCarthy hearings, held in the spring of 1954, were a tremendous spectacle and the ultimate undoing of Joseph McCarthy. The televised trial that kept the American public's rapt attention for several weeks also made millions of viewers privy to McCarthy's personal attacks, outbursts, interminable speeches, and tendency to badger and interrupt witnesses. One frustrated victim, close to tears, famously and plaintively asked his accuser, "Have you no decency, sir, at long last?" It did not take long for public opinion to turn decisively against McCarthy.

By the summer of 1954, Cold War tensions had diminished considerably, both at home and abroad. This fact and his own irresponsible and erratic behavior made McCarthy vulnerable to the many enemies he had made in the Senate. McCarthyism came to its official end on December 2, 1954, when the Republican Senate voted to censure McCarthy for violating the spirit and collegiality of the Senate. For the rest of his political life, he was largely ignored. Joseph McCarthy died on May 2, 1957, of complications related to alcoholism.

John F. Kennedy

John F. Kennedy (1917–1963) was the thirty-fifth president of the United States and took office January 20, 1961. In 1962, the United States came to the brink of nuclear war with the Soviet Union in the Cuban Missile Crisis. Also during his short time in office, Kennedy authorized the unsuccessful Bay of Pigs invasion of Cuba

and increased American involvement in the ongoing Vietnam War.

Born May 29, 1917, in Brookline, Massachusetts, Kennedy was the third child born to Joseph P. Kennedy, and his wife, Rose Fitzgerald. His father was a business executive who also served in several prestigious government posts, including a stint as the chairman of the Securities and Exchange Commission. Kennedy's maternal grandfather had a notable political career as well, serving as both the mayor of Boston and a congressman.

Despite being frequently ill throughout his childhood, Kennedy enjoyed reading and completed his education at Choate, a private preparatory school. In 1935, he entered Princeton University, but another sickness compelled him to withdraw and recover. Kennedy then went to Harvard University, majoring in government and international relations. A junior-year trip to Europe influenced his senior paper, later published in book form as *Why England Slept*. It was published in 1940, the same year Kennedy graduated with honors. He then briefly attended graduate school at Stanford University.

World War II Service In the spring of 1941, shortly before the United States entered World War II, Kennedy was refused enlistment in the U.S. Army because of a back injury. After rehabilitation, Kennedy was able to join the U.S. Navy. He began his military service as an intelligence officer in Washington, D.C. and then prepared for active duty at sea by training with the Motor Torpedo Boat Squadron.

Stationed in the South Pacific, he became commander of an armed patrol torpedo, or PT, boat in March 1943. Five months later, the boat under his command, PT-109, saw action and was cut in half by a Japanese destroyer near the Solomon Islands. Two of his men were killed, and the rest clung to life. Kennedy ensured all the men were rescued, including several wounded, by having them swim to an island three miles away. His problematic back was reinjured in the process.

The Beginnings of a Political Career After the war's end, Kennedy worked briefly as a newspaper reporter. In 1946, he ran as a Democrat for a seat representing Massachusetts in the U.S. House of Representatives. Kennedy won the seat as well as reelection in 1948 and 1950. During his terms in the House, he supported social welfare programs, including low-cost public housing, and pushed for increased regulation of business. Kennedy also spoke out against some of President Harry S. Truman's foreign policies, especially American involvement in the Korean War.

Instead of seeking reelection to the House in 1952, Kennedy decided to run for the U.S. Senate seat held by Henry Cabot Lodge, Jr. Kennedy won the election by seventy thousand votes. As a senator, he continued to back the same issues and programs he had favored as a

American intelligence photographs of missile sites in Cuba, like the one featured here, contradicted Soviet assurances that no such sites existed.   *John Fitzgerald Kennedy Library*

representative. He also attacked corruption among leaders of the nation's trade unions and supported the burgeoning civil rights movement. In addition, Kennedy helped pass bills intended to aid the economy in New England, and he sponsored bills that called for the federal government to provide financial aid to education and to ease immigration laws.

Kennedy's personal life evolved during this time period as well. He married Jacqueline Lee Bouvier in 1953, and the couple soon had children, including Caroline and John, Jr. In 1954, Kennedy's back trouble flared up again, leading to operations in 1954 and 1955. During his recovery, Kennedy wrote *Profiles in Courage*, a collection of biographies of eight U.S. senators, which won a Pulitzer Prize in 1957.

Senator to President   Kennedy was reelected to his Senate seat in 1958, and then began running for president himself in 1960. Though he secured the Democratic nomination in July 1960 and named Lyndon B. Johnson as his running mate, Kennedy had to deal with the controversy surrounding his Roman Catholic faith. All previous presidents had been Protestant. He assured voters that his religion would not play a role in how he made decisions.

After defeating his Republican opponent Richard M. Nixon in several televised debates—Kennedy and Nixon were the first presidential candidates to debate on television—Kennedy won the presidency in 1960 by only 119,450 votes. Kennedy was the first president born in the twentieth century and the youngest president ever sworn into office. While Kennedy made strides in the civil rights movement and launched the Peace Corps during his time in office, Cold War conflicts came to dominate his presidency.

President John F. Kennedy won the hearts of West Berliners encircled by the Iron Curtain when, during a 1963 visit to Berlin, he spoke of his emotion at seeing the city divided and announced, "Ich bin ein Berliner."   *AP Images*

Cold War Conflicts in Cuba, Berlin, and Asia

Four months after Kennedy became president, he authorized one Cold War battle. During the administration of his predecessor, Dwight D. Eisenhower, Cuban exiles who had escaped the Communist regime of Fidel Castro were trained for military combat by the Central Intelligence Agency. Kennedy allowed the planned invasion of Cuba by the exiles to move forward. They invaded Cuba at the Bay of Pigs on April 17, 1961. The invasion failed, partly because the United States did not provide any troops. Kennedy, however, believed that the Cuban people had to rise up and support the invasion for it to be successful. The Bay of Pigs invasion had obviously not succeeded by April 20, and the action further strained U.S. relations with the Soviet Union, Cuba's primary ally.

Two months after the Bay of Pigs fiasco, Kennedy met with his blustery Soviet counterpart, Nikita Khrushchev. The Soviet leader demanded that all three Western countries that controlled West Berlin—the United States, Great Britain, and France—leave the city by the end of 1961, or he would start a war. Kennedy believed Khrushchev was serious and in response began stockpiling weapons and shoring up the military. Instead of starting a war, Khrushchev, in August 1961, ensured Germans living under his control could not cross over to the West via Berlin. He constructed the Berlin Wall, a heavily fortified concrete wall bisecting the city. Because the wall only partially limited the flight of East Germans, Kennedy stood pat and Khrushchev did not start a war.

Cuba was also the site of another major incident in the Cold War later in Kennedy's presidency. In October 1962, Kennedy revealed that the Soviet Union was placing nuclear missiles in Cuba and that they were aimed at the United States. More missiles were being sent by ship. The United States erected a blockade around Cuba in response. The American public believed itself on the brink of nuclear war. Kennedy and Khrushchev began negotiations to resolve the matter with the help of Pope John XXIII, and the Soviets backed down after an extremely tense week. Khrushchev pledged to remove the missiles. A treaty was signed with the Soviet Union in July 1963, which included a limited ban on nuclear tests.

Kennedy had inherited another tense situation from Eisenhower: Vietnam. During Eisenhower's two terms in office, the American government had sent military aid and financial support to South Vietnam to help them combat Communist North Vietnam's attempts to take over the entire country. Kennedy continued to pour money and troops into South Vietnam, and the United States became more entangled in the civil war there. The Vietnam War would prove to be problematic for Kennedy's two successors as well.

Untimely Death On November 22, 1963, Kennedy was assassinated in Dallas, Texas. Though many conspiracy theorists believe otherwise, it is generally accepted that Lee Harvey Oswald was the only assassin of Kennedy. Oswald killed the president with a high-powered rifle from a six-story building as the president rode in a motorcade through the downtown area. After Kennedy's death, Johnson was immediately sworn in and served in the office until early 1969.

Fidel Castro

Fidel Castro (1926–), the prime minister and first secretary of the Communist Party in Cuba, helped launch the Cuban Revolution (1953–1959). He is the leader of the first Communist country in the Americas. Castro was born on August 13, 1926, on the family sugar cane plantation located near Birán, Cuba. He was the son of Angél Castro y Argiz, a native of Spain, and his second wife, Lina Ruz González.

An eager, intelligent student educated primarily at Jesuit schools, Castro did especially well in history, Spanish, and agricultural studies. He was also a strong athlete who played baseball, among other sports. Castro studied law at the University of Havana beginning in 1945, and emerged as an enthusiastic student activist. Though Castro was a strong public speaker, he did not win any student elections and remained relatively unknown. He eventually joined the Ortodoxo political party, which sought to end corruption while promoting economic independence, social justice, and political liberty in Cuba.

Revolutionary Politics While still a student, Castro showed his support of revolutionary politics by taking part in a mission to launch a coup against Rafael Trujillo, a dictator ruling the Domincan Republic, in 1947. Though the expedition was called off during the sea voyage there, Castro still swam to shore with his gun. In 1948, Castro actively participated in the Bogotazo, revolutionary riots held in the wake of the assassination of the Liberal Party leader in Colombia, Jorge E. Gaitán. On the streets of Bogotá, Castro passed out anti-American propaganda to help start the revolution. After seeking shelter in the Cuban embassy when Colombian authorities went after him and other Cuban students, Castro soon made his way back to school and graduated with his law degree in 1950.

By the early 1950s, Castro was working as a lawyer in Old Havana and decided to run for a seat in Cuba's congress, replacing the leader of the Ortodoxo Party, Eduardo Chibás. An armed takeover by Cuban military leader Fulgencio Batista tossed out the government of president Carlos Prio Socarrás and prevented elections from taking place. Castro organized his own armed resistance to Batista. He led an attack on a military barracks in the Oriente Province on July 26, 1953.

"ICH BIN EIN BERLINER"

President John F. Kennedy delivered a powerful, memorable, and policy-shaping speech in West Berlin, Germany, during the summer of 1963. The president's "Ich bin ein Berliner" speech, given from city hall near the Berlin Wall proved that America would continue to fight for the rights of those trapped in East Berlin and in other Soviet-controlled states.

Berlin had been a bone of contention between the East and West (that is, the Soviet-influenced Communist bloc and the Allied forces of the United States, Britain, and France) since the end of World War II. In dividing the German state, the Soviets occupied the eastern sector, while the other three carved up and occupied the remainder. These two sides became East and West Germany, while the capital city of Berlin, entirely surrounded by the Soviet sector, was also split in a similar fashion.

In August 1961, Premier Khrushchev and the Soviet regime responded to the mass exodus of East Berliners fleeing to freedom in the West by building the Berlin Wall. The Allies, upset by the Soviet action, unanimously agreed this act was no cause for war. But Americans called for a reaction. Kennedy had decided to travel to address the citizens of Berlin. In preparing for the speech, the White House called on a German language teacher from the State Department's Foreign Service Institute to assist Kennedy with the German pronunciations of phrases he intended to use in his speech.

Upon his arrival, Kennedy received a rock star's welcome. Kennedy eloquently pointed out what the Berliners had already expressed in their exodus. "There are people in the world today," he said, "who don't understand . . . what is the great issue between the free world and the Communist world. Let them come to Berlin. There are some that say that Communism is the wave of the future. Let them come to Berlin." He continued, saying, "Democracy is not perfect, but we have never had to put up a wall to keep our people in." Kennedy finished with his now-famous line: "Ich bin ein Berliner"—I am a Berliner. With that phrase, he underscored America's commitment to a free Germany.

Overthrowing Batista Captured and tried for his crime, Castro was convicted and sentenced to fifteen years in prison. He acted as his own lawyer and gave a speech during the trial in which he introduced his manifesto for his revolution. Two years after the incident, he was pardoned. He moved to Mexico City and, while living there, founded an anti-Batista group called the 26th of July Movement. He planned to return to Cuba and overthrow the government. The first military expedition of the small group took place in the Oriente Province. It was a disaster, with a vast majority of the eighty-one members killed or captured during encounters with Batista's army.

After this setback, Castro went into hiding in the Sierra Maestra mountains, where he came up with a plan for guerrilla warfare to remove Batista and his government. By 1958, Castro, now the leader of the primary movement to remove Batista, controlled most of rural Cuba. As Batista lost support within the military, Castro and the 26th of July Movement gained more and more control of Cuba and the Cuban government.

New Leader of Cuba   Castro and his followers took power in Cuba on January 1, 1959, and Castro took over as prime minister on February 15. Batista and his family were forced to flee the country. With his charisma and his powerful public speaking skills, Castro proved popular with the Cuban people. He promised social reforms like access to health care and education and also promised to implement democratic practices like public elections. Though Castro said he was not a Communist, he took possession of the wealth that supporters of Batista had allegedly illegally acquired. He also had a law passed that confiscated property that was inherited. In addition, Castro took measures to curtail criticism of his new regime by not allowing freedom of the press and by ensuring military leaders were his supporters.

Within a few years of gaining control of Cuba, Castro's foreign policy revealed his Communist intentions. He first stated that the United States wanted to undermine his revolution, and then he confiscated all U.S. property, including oil refineries, utilities, and sugar mills, in his country. Then he began forging diplomatic relationships with leading Communist countries, especially the Soviet Union.

Drawn into Cold War   Outgoing U.S. President Dwight D. Eisenhower ended diplomatic relations with Cuba and imposed a trade embargo on the country shortly before leaving office in 1961. The new president, John F. Kennedy, played a more active role in dealing with Castro and Cuba. Kennedy supported the failed efforts of anti-Castro Cuban exiles to invade and regain control of their native country at the Bay of Pigs in April 1961.

In October 1962, Cuba played a starring role in the worst confrontation of the Cold War. Castro had allowed his Soviet allies, led by Nikita Khrushchev, to place nuclear missiles aimed at the United States on the island. Though the confrontation nearly led to a nuclear conflict between the Soviet Union and the United States, Kennedy was able to work out a deal with Khrushchev to have the arms removed. Castro was unhappy with this outcome, feeling disgraced by his ally who left him out of the process.

Active in Latin America   The relationship between the Soviet Union and Cuba continued to be problematic in the mid-1960s, though Castro had created the Communist Party of Cuba by 1965. Castro wanted the Communist revolution to spread throughout Latin America and other parts of the world. Despite Soviet efforts to brake Castro's plans, he created several organ-

Soon after taking power in 1959, Fidel Castro traveled on what was largely a public relations mission for his regime to Washington, D.C., where he met Vice President Richard Nixon. *Keystone/Getty Images*

izations to promote his agenda. Nearly all the Cuba-supported revolutions through the late 1960s and 1970s failed, including one led by former comrade Che Guevara in Bolivia in 1967.

While promoting revolutions abroad, Castro violently suppressed any opposition to his rule in Cuba. Some critics were executed, while others were imprisoned.

Slow Decline   After the Soviet Union abandoned Communism in the early 1990s, Castro lost a key ally and supporter. The Cuban economy began to collapse, and Castro wanted to build relations with the United States to improve the situation. Efforts to get the United States to end its trade embargo were futile, because the central U.S. condition for the lifting of the embargo was the end of Communist rule in Cuba. While the relationship between the two close neighbors improved slightly in the late 1990s, with Castro even visiting the United States, the embargo was still not lifted. On its own, Cuba slowly began to make some moves toward capitalism and a free market economy.

In the early years of the twenty-first century, the aged Castro's health began to fail. He designated his younger brother Raul as the head of the Cuban military and his successor. Raul Castro's takeover seemed imminent after Castro fell ill, had several surgeries, and was not seen in public for many months in late 2006 and early 2007.

Lyndon B. Johnson

Lyndon B. Johnson (1908–1973), vice president of John F. Kennedy, took office after Kennedy's assassination in 1963. He won reelection in a landslide in 1964, and led the United States during the height of the Vietnam War. He also emphasized social programs during his time in office, including his "War on Poverty."

Lyndon Baines Johnson was born on August 27, 1908, on the family farm near Stonewall, Texas. He was the son of Sam Ealy Johnson, Jr., and his wife, Rebekah Baines. His father once served in the Texas state legislature and had been a successful businessman until he lost money on a bad cotton trading deal. Because of his father's business failures, Johnson was raised in poverty.

Living up to predictions by his paternal grandfather that he would be a politician, Johnson showed a talent for politics by the time he was in first grade. He was an unfocused student, however, and after graduating from high school, he spent three years somewhat aimlessly. Coming home after a failed trip to California, he decided to become a teacher and earned a bachelor's degree from Southwest Texas State Teachers' College in 1930.

Early Political Experience After briefly working as an educator at Houston's Sam Houston High School, Johnson moved to Washington, D.C., to join the staff of Richard Kleberg, a Texas congressman who took office in early 1931. Johnson worked as Kleberg's personal secretary and soon became a leader among the secretaries of members of Congress. He was elected to be the speaker of the secretaries' assembly.

Johnson worked on Capitol Hill and built up a network of contacts until 1935, when he returned to Texas with his new wife, Claudia Alta "Lady Bird" Taylor. Johnson then spent two years working as the state director of the National Youth Administration. Johnson was in charge of distributing money to schools and educational projects as part of this New Deal program.

In 1937, Johnson ran for and won his first political office. He became the representative for Texas's Tenth District after his predecessor died in office. Johnson won over seven other candidates in the resulting special election. Johnson retained the seat through several elections. The young congressman faced some setbacks, however. He ran for a seat in the U.S. Senate in 1941, but lost by a small margin.

As the United States entered World War II, Johnson joined the navy and went on active military duty in December 1941. He became the first member of Congress to actively serve in World War II. Johnson's war service ended later that year when President Franklin D. Roosevelt recalled all members of Congress serving in the military back to their offices.

Senator to Vice President Johnson remained a representative from Texas until 1948, when he won his long-sought seat in the U.S. Senate. He soon became a leader in the Senate and was selected to be the Democratic whip. He also had a seat on the Armed Services Committee. Johnson took on a series of leadership posts in the 1950s and was the minority leader in the Senate in 1953. He was named majority leader in 1954, when the Democrats took control of Congress.

In 1960, Johnson sought the Democratic nomination for the presidency. When Kennedy won the nomination, he selected Johnson as his running mate. Johnson's presence on the ticket and his strong campaigning skills helped Kennedy win the presidency. As vice president, Johnson continued the work he had begun while a senator on civil rights issues. He also encouraged the expansion of the U.S. space program. The Soviet Union had beat the United States to space with the 1957 launch of their Sputnik orbiting satellite, which marked the official start of the "space race."

Unexpected President Just three years after being elected president, Kennedy was assassinated in Dallas, Texas, on November 22, 1963. Johnson was sworn into the presidency the following day on Air Force One. Returning to Washington, he immediately took control of the government and worked to get some of Kennedy's pending legislation passed. One bill of particular importance was the 1964 Civil Rights Act. Johnson also launched his own initiatives, including his "Great Society" plan to address social issues and preserve natural resources.

As Johnson began his own campaign for the presidency in 1964, America's increasing involvement in the Vietnam War emerged as a primary concern for voters. Despite Republican opponent Barry Goldwater's attacks on Johnson's social programs, Johnson won an overwhelming victory, the biggest margin in the history of the United States at that time.

First Full Term in Office Johnson pressed forth with more social legislation. He increased spending on education and health care and successfully championed the 1965 Voting Rights Act. Johnson's foreign policy also had some success. He held talks with the Soviet Union on a space-related treaty. Following the protocol of the Truman Doctrine, the United States actively intervened in the affairs of Latin American countries to prevent Communist takeovers. Johnson also sent the U.S. Sixth Fleet closer to the Syrian coast during the Six-Day War between Israel and its Arab neighbors to balance any threat of Soviet military intervention in the conflict.

The Vietnam conflict was known as the first "television war." *AP Images*

Johnson's biggest challenge was the complicated conflict in Vietnam, a situation inherited from his predecessors. Johnson still believed that by supporting South Vietnam in the face of the attempted takeover by Communist North Vietnam, the United States was addressing its own security interests. Though he made campaign promises to not involve American soldiers in the conflict, Johnson approved U.S. troop increases in 1965 after two American destroyers in the Gulf of Tonkin were allegedly attacked by the North Vietnamese.

An increasing number of military men and women were sent to Vietnam over the next three years and by 1968 there were more than a half million American troops there. Johnson saw that increasing the number of troops and escalating the war did not lead to a quicker resolution to the conflict, and he faced increasing criticism at home over his handling of the matter. The relative success of North Vietnam's Tet Offensive in 1968 and Johnson's inability to get focused peace talks started compelled him to make the difficult decision not to run for another term.

Declined to Run for Full Second Term Because Johnson believed ending the war in Vietnam was his highest priority, he announced on March 31, 1968 that he would not be running for president again. Freed from running for re-election, Johnson spent the rest of his time in office working on the Vietnam situation. He was able to get peace talks started in the spring, though they accomplished little, and in November he announced that the United States would halt bombing missions over North Vietnam.

When Johnson formally left office in early 1969, he moved to his ranch near Johnson City, Texas. He focused his time and attention on caring for and selling cattle. He wrote his memoirs, executed plans for his Austin-based presidential library, and tried to improve his fragile health. Johnson died on January 22, 1973, after suffering a heart attack.

Richard M. Nixon

As a member of the House of Representatives, vice president to Dwight D. Eisenhower, and the thirty-seventh president of the United States, Richard M. Nixon (1913–1994) showed his expertise in foreign policy and played at least a minor role in many events of the Cold War. Although his presidency was marred by scandal, Nixon improved relations with China, began treaty negotiations with the Soviet Union, and oversaw America's withdrawal from Vietnam.

Difficult Childhood Richard Milhous Nixon was born on January 9, 1913, in Yorba Linda, California. He was the son of Frank Nixon, and his wife, Hannah Milhous. At the time of his birth, his father owned and operated a lemon farm. When the farm failed, Nixon's father moved his family, which included several other sons, to Whittier, California and took a job operating a grocery store and service station.

Nixon was an excellent student and emerged as a strong debater at Whittier High School before graduating with honors. Though he was offered a full-tuition scholarship to Harvard University, his family was unable to pay the rest of the costs necessary to support him. He attended Whittier College instead starting in 1930, and he continued to demonstrate his strong debating skills. He showed his growing political prowess by being elected president of his freshman class and then president of the student body as a senior. In 1934, Nixon graduated second in his class.

He attended Duke University Law School on a scholarship. Though Nixon graduated third in his class in 1937, he was unable—in the midst of the Great Depression—to find work at a law firm in New York City. He returned to Whittier to practice law.

World War II Service In the early 1940s, before the United States entered World War II, Nixon took a job in Washington, D.C. He was employed at the Office of Price Administration, part of the federal Office of Emergency Management. In August 1942, he joined the U.S. Navy as a junior officer. Nixon then spent two years in the Pacific theater, serving in the South Pacific Combat Air Transport Command as an operations officer. After his return to the United States in 1944, he returned to his practice of law in Whittier. He formally left the navy in January 1946 with the rank of lieutenant commander.

The Beginnings of a Successful Career in Politics By this time, Nixon had a new goal. Some Republicans in Whittier had asked him to run for Congress, and in November 1946 he was able to defeat a five-term incumbent in his district, Democrat Jerry Voorhis. Taking office in 1947, Nixon soon showed his expertise in foreign policy and was appointed to a special House committee that gathered supporting information for the proposed Marshall Plan for economic recovery in Europe. He was one of only two freshman members of the Select Committee on Foreign Aid, which traveled to Europe to study postwar problems. He also was appointed to the House Un-American Activities Committee and came to national prominence as a virulent anti-Communist who legally pursued Alger Hiss, for having Communist connections while working in the State Department. While Nixon charged that Hiss had been a Soviet spy in the late 1930s, Hiss denied the allegations. He was charged with and convicted of perjury in connection with his case.

THE SECOND RED SCARE

America experienced its first "red scare"—a period of widespread fear about the destructive potential of Communism in the United States—immediately after the Russian Revolution of 1917. It experienced another wave of panic, a second "red scare," during the 1950s. The person largely responsible for whipping up the frenzy of anti-Communism was Senator Joseph McCarthy of Wisconsin. McCarthy electrified the nation when he made the shocking, and unsubstantiated, claim in 1950 that he had a list of high-ranking members of the State Department who were part of a Communist spy ring. He continued making accusations and headlines for several years, ruining the careers and reputations of many inside and outside the government before he was finally censured (punished) and effectively silenced by the Senate in 1954. He died of liver disease in 1957.

McCarthy was not the only member of Congress quick to point a finger at supposed Communists. The members of the House Un-American Activities Committee, which was established as a permanent committee in 1946, began to suspect many Hollywood stars and executives of Communist sympathies in the late 1940s. Hundreds of actors, screenwriters, directors, and others associated with the motion picture industry were put before the committee. The movie studios, wary of the effect the taint of Communism might have on their profits, blacklisted (refused work to) those even accused of Communist leanings. Some managed to resume their careers in other countries; others used fake names to keep working in the United States. Most, however, were never able to rebuild their careers.

After two terms in the House, Nixon was elected to the U.S. Senate in 1950 after implying that his opponent, Democrat Helen Gahagan Douglas, had Communist inclinations. In 1952, World War II hero Dwight D. Eisenhower decided to make a run for the presidency as a Republican. He asked Nixon to join his ticket, hoping to capitalize on the support Nixon enjoyed in the western United States and to attract conservative voters through Nixon's reputation as an anti-Communist. With Nixon, Eisenhower won two terms in office, but Nixon was not fully embraced by Eisenhower's advisors.

During his time in office, Nixon changed the role of the vice president by becoming the primary political spokesman for the president and handling much of the administration's foreign travel. During his first year in office, Nixon traveled throughout Asia. In 1958, he visited Latin America and Poland, and the next year he visited the Soviet Union. Such trips deepened his knowledge of foreign affairs and created constructive relationships with these countries. Visiting Soviet leader Nikita Khrushchev in Moscow and engaging him in the so-called "kitchen debate" over the merits of capitalism versus communism, for example, later led to a meeting in the United States between Eisenhower and Khrushchev.

Lost, then Won Presidency When Eisenhower's two terms in office came to an end in 1960, Nixon ran for president himself. With running mate Henry Cabot Lodge, Nixon secured the Republican nomination. However, a series of television debates with his opponent, the handsome young Democrat, Senator John F. Kennedy, put Nixon at a disadvantage. Though Nixon debated well, on camera he looked aloof and dour next to the charming Kennedy. The election was close, with Nixon losing by about 100,000 votes. Nixon went back to California, resumed his legal career in Los Angeles, and wrote his first book, *Six Crises*. He then made an unsuccessful run for California governor in 1962. By the 1968 presidential election, Nixon had again emerged as a top Republican candidate. He secured the nomination and chose Spiro Agnew as his running mate. Nixon was able to defeat the Democratic ticket of Hubert Humphrey and Edmund Muskie.

First Term in Office Upon taking office in January 1969, Nixon said he would heal the nation, which was divided over the Vietnam War and issues of race and civil rights. Focusing on Vietnam, he tried to negotiate an end to the conflict in talks with North Vietnam held in Paris, but had no success. Though he approved the expansion of the ground war into Laos and Cambodia, Nixon was able to bring American troops home as they were replaced by the South Vietnamese soldiers. It took two years to completely remove all U.S. ground troops.

As president, Nixon also had other significant Cold War accomplishments. On a visit to Asia early in his presidency, Nixon promised material aid to free Asian countries threatened by Communism, but said he would not provide troops. When he traveled to Romania in February 1969, he became the first president to visit a Communist country. By the end of that year, Nixon had signed a treaty with the Soviet Union that called for further work on limiting the production of nuclear arms. More talks continued through the end of his first term.

In 1972, Nixon visited the Soviet Union, where he met with Soviet leader Leonid Brezhnev, and China, where he met with Chinese leader Mao Zedong. This latter event marked the first time that a sitting president had visited China. Talks were later held that resulted in the Shanghai Communiqué in which Nixon agreed to recognize the government of the People's Republic of China as the legitimate Chinese government.

Second Term Ends in Disgrace In 1972, Nixon and Agnew won reelection in a landslide over the Democratic ticket of George McGovern and Sargent Shriver. But the presidency was soon in jeopardy. During Nixon's reelection campaign, there had been a break-in at the Democratic Party national headquarters, which was located in the building complex known as the Watergate. The trial of the six men charged in the burglary revealed that many details of the burglary were covered up and that the burglars were linked to the Committee to Reelect the President.

As the investigation into the matter continued throughout 1973, many in Nixon's administration were forced to resign, including his vice president. Agnew later pleaded no contest to several significant federal charges, including receiving bribes. After the Supreme Court compelled Nixon to hand over official tapes he had made during his election campaign, it became clear that Nixon had known about the Watergate break-in—at least after the fact—and had participated in the subsequent cover-up.

Because of these revelations, which resulted in his impending impeachment, Nixon resigned on August 9, 1974. He was the first president to voluntarily leave office before his term ended. Nixon and his family went back to California and returned to private life. Nixon was succeeded by Gerald Ford, who had been named vice president after Agnew's resignation. One of Ford's first acts as president was to pardon Nixon.

Advisor to Presidents Nixon took on the role of respected statesman some years after controversy over the Watergate scandal died down. He made visits to Asia, including China, and to the Soviet Union. During the presidencies of Republican George H. W. Bush and Democrat Bill Clinton, Nixon served as an advisor, especially on international matters. Nixon also wrote his memoirs and oversaw the opening of the Richard M. Nixon presidential library in Yorba Linda. He founded the Nixon Center for Peace and Freedom, a foreign policy think tank, shortly before dying of a stroke on April 22, 1994.

Chou En-lai

An important leader in the Chinese Communist party from its earliest days, Chou En-lai (or Zhou Enlai, 1898–1976) also was the premier of the People's Republic of China under Mao Zedong. Chou was born March 5, 1898 in Huaian, Jiangsu Province, China, the son of Chou Yinen and his wife Wan Dongei. His parents were prosperous landowners, but they had fallen on hard times around the time of the birth of Chou, and both died when he was quite young. He was thereafter raised first by an aunt and then two uncles in Mukden.

After receiving his primary education at various missionary schools and Nankai Normal School, Chou traveled to Japan in 1917 to complete his education. While there, he was exposed to Marxist ideas. In 1919, Chou returned to China to participate in the May Fourth Movement, a student protest against foreign interference in China. Chou became a student at Nank'ai University. Serving as the editor of a radical newspaper and continuing related activities, Chou was arrested after a protest and spent four months in prison in 1920.

Active in the Communist Party Released later that year, Chou entered a work-study program in France.

As a member of the House Committee on Un-American Activities in 1948, Richard Nixon (l) made a name for himself as a vigilant anti-Communist. *AP Images*

There, he became influenced by both French and Chinese socialists and joined the Chinese Socialist Youth Corps. This group consisted of young Communists, and Chou soon joined the Chinese Communist Party. In 1922, Chou helped form the party's European branch and was selected to serve in the Chinese Communist Party's executive committee for the branch. He also held a similar position with the Chinese Nationalist Party, or Kuomintang, then led by Sun Yat-sen and still allied with the Communists.

Returning to China in 1924, Chou settled in Canton and was soon named the deputy director of the newly formed Whampoa Military Academy's political department. By late summer 1925, Chou was acting as the political commissar to a division in the Nationalist First Army and was then also the special commissioner of Kwangtung Province's East River District. When Chiang Kai-shek, an anti-Communist, took control of the Nationalist Party in March 1926, Chou was removed from both positions.

Increased Power Further turmoil within the Nationalist Party and the group's total break with the Communists in 1927 led Chou to take a more active role in the Communist Party. He was elected to its Central Committee and Politburo (executive body of the Communist party). Chou led thirty thousand Communist troops to take control of the town of Nanchang on August 1, 1927. Though they failed to keep control of the city, Chou remained with the Communist forces as they tried to establish a base in Kwangtung Province. Chou eventually created a secret police force, the Red Guards, to protect Communist Party leadership in Shanghai.

By 1931, Chou was working with Mao Zedong at the Communist stronghold in Kiangsi province in southwest China. There, the Communists formed the Chinese Soviet Republic. Chou served as the Communist army's political commissar and was a member of the Central Executive Committee. Forced to retreat from the area because of Nationalist attacks, the Communists decided to move their headquarters to northwest China.

Communist Leader After serving as a military officer on the so-called "Long March," Chou became the party's primary negotiator after it established a new base in Yen-an, Shensi province. This position proved important when Japan invaded the country in 1936, and Chou helped his party work with the Nationalists on key common issues related to their shared fight against the Japanese. During and after World War II, Chou also represented Chinese Communist interests in negotiations with international contingents.

Because Chou was unable to get the Communist Party into a position of power in the immediate postwar period, the civil war between Nationalist and Communist forces resumed. When the Communists defeated the Nationalists and forced their leadership into exile in 1949, Mao Zedong declared himself the founder of the People's Republic of China. Chou was named premier of the republic as well as foreign minister. He also played a role in drafting the new Chinese Constitution.

China's International Negotiator In addition to formulating the bureaucracy of the new Chinese government, Chou played a significant role in foreign relations. Early in the Korean War, he warned the United States not to cross the 38th parallel and enter what came to be known as North Korea. Because the United States disregarded this warning, American and Chinese troops came into contact with each other during the conflict. With the help of the Chinese Army, the North Koreans pushed the U.S. Army back into South Korea late in 1950 and early 1951.

Traveling to Moscow several times in the early 1950s, Chou negotiated the Chinese-Soviet alliance, a key relationship for China. Though he gave up his post as foreign minister in 1958, Chou remained active in foreign affairs. When the coalition between the Soviets and the Chinese became troubled in the early 1960s, for example, Chou led the walkout of the Chinese delegation to the Twenty-Second Congress of the Communist Party. Zhou was later able to resolve the two countries' differences and establish an uneasy peace that lasted at least until his death.

Chou also toured other countries in Asia and in Africa, often acting in support of Communist regimes and developing countries. At the end of the first French-Indochina War, he played a significant role in delineating how the French would evacuate from the area and in the partitioning of Vietnam into Communist and non-Communist halves. By 1960, Chou was successfully working on border agreements with neighbors such as Burma, Mongolia, and Afghanistan. Not all of his negotiations proved fruitful, though. He was unable to reach a border treaty agreement with India at that time, which eventually led to a brief war that ended with a Chinese victory in 1962.

Domestic Authority Although he traveled extensively, Chou remained an important leader at home as well. He

remained the head of the government's administrative system. During the brutal Cultural Revolution, which began in 1965, Chou publicly supported Mao's objectives of ensuring continued support of revolutionary Communism and purging those who did not meet these standards—but he acted behind the scenes as a moderating force. Because even high-ranking officials lost their jobs and lives as a result of the Cultural Revolution, Chou became the second-ranking member of the Chinese government by 1969.

Because of Chou's international reputation, Chinese and American relations improved in the early 1970s. President Richard Nixon and his national security advisor Henry Kissinger both traveled to the Chinese mainland. Chou convinced Nixon to drop the long-standing trade embargo and recognize Taiwan as part of the People's Republic of China, steps that led to a closer relationship between China and the United States. (Before this time, the United States had recognized exiled Nationalist Chiang Kai-shek's Republic of China—Taiwan—as the legitimate Chinese government.)

Chou remained an enthusiastic supporter of Mao in the early to mid-1970s, despite being ill with bladder cancer. He died on January 8, 1976.

Leonid Brezhnev

Succeeding Nikita Khrushchev as the leader of the Soviet Union, Leonid Brezhnev (1906–1982) oversaw the later years of the Cold War. While he forged closer ties with the United States than did his predecessors, the Soviet economy struggled under his administration and his governing style was sometimes brutal.

Brezhnev was born December 19, 1906, in Kamenskoe (now Dneprodzerzhinsk), Ukraine, the son of Ilya Yakolevich Brezhev and his wife, Nataliya Denisovna. His father was a Russian who was employed as a steelworker. When Brezhnev was seventeen years old, he joined the Communist youth organization, Komsomol. Though forced to leave full-time schooling at the age of fifteen to work in the mill with his father, he received training as a land surveyor as a part-time student. He graduated when he was twenty-one years old, and then worked for the Communist Party as an official in minor government posts.

Early Years in the Communist Party In 1931, Brezhnev became a Communist Party member and spent the next decade rising through the ranks in the Ukrainian branch of the party. He also continued his education at the Kamenskoe Metallurgical Institute, training as a metallurgical engineer. After graduating in 1935, he briefly worked as an engineer before focusing on party activities and working for the Soviet government. In the late 1930s, Brezhnev became acquainted with Nikita Khrushchev, who was by then leading the Ukrainian Communist Party. Khrushchev soon helped Brezhnev become a prominent party leader in the Ukraine.

Leonid Brezhnev (l) shakes the hand of cosmonaut Yuri Gagarin, the first man in space.   *AFP/Getty Images*

After serving as the Ukraine's military commissar and reaching the rank of major general in the Red Army during World War II, Brezhnev was tapped to become the Communist Party leader in the Moldavian Soviet Socialist Republic in 1950. This area had been annexed from Romania at the end of World War II. Having gained national prominence by taking this position, Brezhnev continued to be promoted within the party. In 1952, Brezhnev moved to Moscow and served in the Secretariat of the Central Committee of the Communist Party.

Increasing Power When Stalin died in 1953, Brezhnev was temporarily demoted from the Secretariat to lesser posts in the Ministry of Defense. When Khrushchev became the leader of the Soviet Union, Brezhnev was named the Communist Party head in Kazakhstan. There, Brezhnev found favor by successfully implementing Khrushchev's "Virgin Lands Scheme," in which

more Soviet territory was successfully converted to agricultural use. Two good harvests in 1955 and 1956 increased Brezhnev's reputation. He was soon recalled to Moscow to return to the Secretariat. Brezhnev supported Khrushchev when the Soviet leader was challenged by hard-line Communist Party members who wanted to oust him for his de-Stalinization reforms in 1957.

It became clear by the early 1960s that Brezhnev was being groomed to be Khrushchev's successor. He was elected chairman of the Party Politburo (the executive body of the Communist Party, later known as the Presidium of the Supreme Soviet), though he left three years later to return to the Secretariat because of the lack of power in the Politburo post. Brezhnev betrayed Khrushchev in 1964 when another movement to oust Khrushchev reached fruition. Brezhnev joined the faction and helped put his former mentor out of office. He

LECH WALESA AND SOLIDARITY

Lech Walesa, a carpenter by trade, spent years agitating for workers rights in Poland. He was first arrested in 1970 after participating in a strike at the Gdansk shipyard that was violently suppressed by the authorities. He spent one year in prison. After a decade of unionist political activity that cost him his job and led to several arrests, Walesa again headed a strike at the Gdansk shipyard in 1980 insisting on unionization rights for workers. This time, the whole country seemed ready to join him. The Gdansk shipyard strike led to a general worker's strike throughout Poland. Walesa's Strike Coordination Committee was soon renamed the Solidarity Trade Union after the Communist government granted strikers the right to legal organization.

Walesa, however, was arrested and imprisoned again in 1982. He won the Nobel Peace Prize in 1983, after being released from prison. In 1989, Walesa led the Solidarity organization into politics. It became the opposition party to the Communist party, and Solidarity candidates won several seats. By forming alliances with leaders of other parties that had been Communist, Walesa managed to prompt the formation of a non-Communist coalition government of Poland by the end of 1989, making Poland the first country in the Soviet bloc to abandon communism. Walesa was elected president in 1990, and served until 1995.

then took over the most important of Khrushchev's posts, first secretary (by 1966, general secretary) of the Soviet Communist Party's Central Committee. Though he held the position with the most power, Brezhnev shared control of the country with Alexei Kosygin, who had taken other posts formerly held by Khrushchev, and other party leaders.

Early Years of Soviet Leadership During the early years of Brezhnev's time in office, he rolled back many of the de-Stalinization reforms of the Khrushchev era. Literary dissent was no longer allowed, bureaucracy greatly increased, and the secret police regained their fearsome power. While the mass terrorism that was common under Stalin did not return, Soviet citizens faced more restrictions on their behavior. Economically, the Soviet Union improved under Brezhnev. The standard of living for Soviet citizens rose until the mid-1970s as more economic resources were spent on goods for consumers.

After reaching nuclear parity with the United States through a massive arms buildup, Brezhnev was able to forge closer ties to the United States by exchanging visits with President Richard M. Nixon and agreeing to arms control talks with the United States. The result was the Strategic Arms Limitation Treaty, SALT I, which stopped the production of certain nuclear weapon systems.

Slow Decline By the early 1970s, Brezhnev had essentially taken over total control of the Soviet government. He became the marshal of the Soviet Union in 1976 and then the head of state as the chairman of the Presidium of the Supreme Soviet in 1977. As his power increased, the Soviet economy began a slow decline beginning in the mid-1970s and stagnated for many years after that. While political awareness increased among those forced to be part of the Soviet Union, there was a greater attack on dissidents by the Soviets.

Wars also became more consuming. The Soviet Army invaded Afghanistan in 1979, leading to a decades-long, draining conflict. Some workers in Poland tried to lead their country to break away from the influence of the Soviet Union in 1981. Only a coup carried out by the Polish Army backed by the Soviets stopped the Polish rebellion known as Solidarity.

After years of increased understanding between the United States and the Soviet Union—including the creation of a cooperative space program in 1975, the SALT II treaty in 1979, and the Soviets purchasing an extraordinary amount of American wheat—the Cold War escalated again in the late 1970s and early 1980s. The administration of President Jimmy Carter condemned the Soviet invasion of Afghanistan. President Ronald Reagan reignited the arms race and denounced the muzzling of the Polish Solidarity movement after he took office in 1981. In poor health by the early 1980s, Brezhnev died on November 10, 1982, in Moscow.

Jimmy Carter

Elected president in 1976, Jimmy Carter (1924–) negotiated key treaties with the Soviet Union and between Israel and Egypt during his one term in office. After losing reelection in 1980, Carter continued to work for world peace and human rights as a respected elder statesman.

Carter was born on October 1, 1924, in Plains, Georgia, the oldest child of James Earl Carter, Sr., and his wife Lillian Gordy. His father was a small-time peanut and cotton farmer who also operated a peanut warehouse and store. His father later served in the Georgia legislature. His mother had worked as a nurse until her marriage. She did not accept many of the South's racist traditions and instilled in her four children a belief in racial equality and a sensitivity to the suffering of others.

Showing an outstanding work ethic from an early age, Carter was experienced in all aspects of farming by the time he graduated from Plains High School as valedictorian in 1941. He then spent a year each at Georgia Southwestern College and Georgia Institute of Technology as he sought to enter the U.S. Naval Academy.

Receiving an appointment to the academy in 1942, Carter became a cadet in 1943. As a student, he displayed skills in naval tactics and electronics. After graduating in the top ten percent of his class in 1946, Carter

The 1972 Strategic Arms Limitation Treaty, signed by U.S. President Nixon and Soviet General Secretary Leonid Brezhnev, froze the number of strategic ballistic missile launchers each nation could possess. *Dirck Halstead/Liaison/Getty Images*

volunteered for submarine duty and served aboard the USS *Pomfret*. He also worked on the first nuclear-powered submarines built by the U.S. Navy. Though he aspired to become an admiral, Carter left the service in 1953 when his father died of pancreatic cancer.

Early Political Career Returning to Georgia, Carter took over the family farm and accompanying businesses. He also was active in civic groups and activities and served on the boards of local libraries and hospitals in Plains. By the early 1960s, Carter was a very successful farmer who harbored political ambitions.

Running for office, he won a seat in the Georgia Senate in 1962 as a Democrat by one thousand votes. Carter was soon known as an effective senator. He was then reelected to his seat in 1964 and ran for governor in 1966.

Though Carter lost the Democratic gubernatorial primary that year to Lester Maddox, he did not give up on his goal to become governor. For the next four years, he traversed Georgia to learn about the concerns of the state's voters, give speeches, and essentially campaign for the post. In 1970, Carter ran again and won the governor's office.

Georgia's Governor As governor, Carter's inaugural address garnered national attention because he stated that he would seek an end to racial injustice in Georgia. As governor, he wanted to assist the needy in the state no matter what their race. He also supported education and job creation. He also increased the number of African Americans employed by the state and appointed to state boards and agencies.

During his only term in the governor's office, Carter took on positions of prominence in the national Democratic party. He served as the head of the Democratic Governors Campaign Committee in 1972 and then as the chairman of the Democratic National Campaign Committee two years later. By 1973, Carter had decided he would run for U.S. president in 1976, though he had little national name recognition. After leaving office in 1975, he began campaigning for president. It was not until January 1976 that his efforts brought him national attention as he promised to bring back ethical leadership to the office of the president.

Carter as U.S. President Carter won the Democratic nomination and named Minnesota Senator Walter Mondale as his running mate. During his campaign, he

PRAGUE SPRING

In 1968, Soviet-dominated Czechoslovakia underwent a period of rapid social and political liberalization under the administration of Alexander Dubček. Dubček launched an "Action Programme" that ushered in many Western freedoms, including freedom of the press. Dubček even made moves toward establishing a democratic, multiparty system of government. The Czech people embraced their new freedoms with fervor. Dissenting voices, silenced for so many years, found their way into the press and literature. The Western media labeled this sudden flowering of political activity the "Prague Spring." But the flower of Czech freedom was quickly crushed. In August 1968, Brezhnev sent thousands of Soviet tanks and hundreds of thousands of soldiers from five Warsaw Pact armies into Czechoslovakia to reassert Communist control. Dubček was arrested. Shortly after the invasion, tens of thousands of Czechoslovakians fled their country and sought asylum in the West.

promised to spend more federal dollars to create jobs and help businesses grow. Buoyed by the support of African Americans and the poor as well as his status as a Washington outsider, Carter defeated incumbent Gerald Ford in the 1976 general election.

After taking office, Carter was able to make the federal government more efficient by reducing redundancy in federal agencies. He also created two new federal departments: the Department of Energy and the Department of Education. While he was able to get income taxes lowered, high inflation plagued the American economy throughout his time in office and made him a relatively unpopular president by 1980.

Foreign Policy Concerns While not all of Carter's foreign policy moves were praised, he had some significant successes. In 1977, Carter signed treaties that gave control of the Panama Canal to Panama in 1999 while making sure the key waterway remained neutral. In 1979, he helped broker a peace treaty, the so-called Camp David Accords, between Israel and Egypt, which ended war between the two countries.

Carter wanted to improve the United States' relationship with the Soviet Union and bring an end to the nuclear arms race. Because of continued human rights violations by the Soviets, the United States soon adopted a more hard-line approach to Soviet-American relations. While halting grain sales to the Soviet Union, Carter worked on an arms limitation treaty with the Soviets for two-and-a-half years. At the end of negotiations in 1979, Carter signed SALT (Strategic Arms Limitation Treaty) II, which imposed limits on the number of nuclear arms possessed by each country.

The Soviet-American relationship remained tense, however. After the Soviet Union invaded Afghanistan in 1979, Carter decided that the United States would boycott the 1980 Summer Olympic Games, which were being held in Moscow. Not all dealings with Communist countries were as difficult. Carter granted China formal diplomatic recognition, opening the door for closer relations between the countries. The United States then began importing goods from China.

One major foreign policy disaster for Carter came in November 1979. A radical Iranian student group took control of the U.S. Embassy in Teheran, taking fifty-two Americans hostage. Carter's first response was to create economic pressure by cutting off Iranian imports to the United States and freezing Iranian assets in the United States. These measures did not create any change in the situation, and the hostage crisis dragged on for months. Carter authorized an armed rescue operation in April 1980. It failed, and eight Marines died during the attempt. The hostages were released in early 1981 after 444 days of captivity.

Post-Presidential Activities By the time the hostage situation ended, Carter had already lost the presidency. Because of economic problems and the situation in Iran, he was easily defeated in the 1980 presidential election by Ronald Reagan. Shortly after leaving office, Carter founded the Carter Center, which continued to promote his human rights agenda in the United States and abroad, encourage economic development, and monitor elections in emerging democracies.

Over the years, Carter has continued to personally intervene in foreign affairs as no sitting president could. In 1990, he was able to convince an opposition leader in Nicaragua, Daniel Ortega, to allow the elected president to take office in that country. Armed conflict was avoided in Somalia when Carter relayed messages from warlord Mohamed Farrah Aidid to President Bill Clinton. Later in Clinton's first term in office, Carter persuaded North Korean dictator Kim Il Sung to halt his nuclear weapons program. For his efforts, Carter was given the Presidential Medal of Freedom in 1999 and the Nobel Peace Prize in 2002.

Ronald Reagan

Ronald Reagan (1911–2004) served as president of the United States from 1981 to 1989. Because he was president during the decline and eventual disintegration of the Soviet Union, he is often credited with ending the Cold War. Staunchly anti-Communist, Reagan was a successful movie and television actor who also served as the governor of California.

Ronald Wilson Reagan was born on February 6, 1911, in Tampico, Illinois. He was the son of John Edward Reagan, and his wife, Nelle Clyde Wilson. Reagan grew up in relative poverty; his father was an alcoholic who worked as a shoe salesman but failed to retain

On June 12, 1987, President Ronald Reagan, speaking in a divided Berlin, challenged Soviet General Secretary Gorbachev to "tear down" the Berlin Wall. *© Wally McNamee/Corbis*

employment. His family moved regularly until Reagan was nine years old, when they settled in Dixon, Illinois.

A popular and talented athlete, Reagan was locally famous as a young adult for his many rescues as a lifeguard working at a park on the Rock River. During the summers from 1926 to 1933, he rescued seventy-seven people. Reagan had begun working as a lifeguard while attending Dixon High School, where he was elected student body president as a senior. After graduating in 1928, he entered Eureka College in Illinois, where he studied economics, was captain of the swim team, and was again elected student body president. Reagan completed his college education in 1932.

Radio, Television, and Film Career

Within a few years of graduating from college, Reagan began his career as a sports announcer for WOC, a radio station in Davenport, Iowa. Demonstrating promise on the radio, he soon landed a job at a bigger station, WHO, in Des Moines, Iowa. By 1937, Reagan had acting ambitions and used his position as the rebroadcaster of Chicago Cubs baseball games to get the assignment of covering the team's spring training camp in California.

Reagan soon landed a contract with Warner Brothers Studio and launched an acting career in the movies. He made his film debut starring in 1937's *Love Is on the Air*. While generally considered a "B" movie actor, he received some positive reviews and then national fame for his role as George Gipp in the 1940 classic *Knute Rockne—All American* and his role as an amputee in the 1942 film *King's Row*. By the late 1940s, Reagan's film acting career was on the decline, but his power in Hollywood was on the rise in other ways.

In 1947, Reagan was elected president of the Screen Actors Guild (SAG) in a special election. He held the post until 1952 and then served as the labor union's president again from 1959 to 1960. As the head of SAG, Reagan often expressed a deeply held anti-Communism, which he continued to espouse as he moved into television work. Though he publicly said that he would not give names of suspected Communists in Hollywood to the House Un-American Activities Committee, he appeared as a friendly witness in front of the committee, and it was later revealed that Reagan secretly provided information about suspected Communists to Congress.

Reagan found more fame as the host of the *General Electric Theater* half-hour dramatic anthology series beginning in 1954. In conjunction with his work on that show, he also made many personal appearances on behalf of General Electric (G.E.). Reagan regularly gave inspirational speeches that emphasized the importance of a free-market economy while promoting G.E.'s products. Reagan was later fired by G.E. for expressing his increasingly conservative views.

Governor of California   By the early 1960s, Reagan had political ambitions and joined the Republican Party. Supported by conservative Republicans, he ran for the governorship of California in 1966. Securing the Republican nomination with solid campaigning and extensive financial support, Reagan defeated Pat Brown in the election with fifty-eight percent of the vote. He was easily reelected in 1970. As governor, Reagan cut California's budget, raised state income taxes, and froze hiring by state agencies, all of which put California on a sound financial footing.

While serving as governor, Reagan decided to run for president. His 1968 campaign did not end in the nomination, but it did bring him to national prominence as a potential future Republican candidate. Reagan nearly won the 1976 Republican nomination, but he lost to incumbent Gerald Ford. In 1980, Reagan finally won the nomination and soundly defeated sitting Democratic president Jimmy Carter in the general election. Reagan easily won reelection in 1984 over Democratic candidate Walter Mondale.

Two-Term President   During his time in office, Reagan was generally popular with Americans and proved adept at dealing with the media. Because of this skill, he was dubbed "The Great Communicator." Rebounding from an early 1981 assassination attempt by John Hinckley, Reagan followed his promised conservative course by reducing taxes and spending on social programs while increasing defense spending. Such moves were intended to stimulate business and increase economic growth, though the American economy struggled for several years before gradually expanding.

The U.S. economy was compromised, because the federal budget had massive deficits of at least $100 billion each year. By the time Reagan left office, the national debt had reached more than $3 trillion, which bothered conservatives. Reagan also irked some conservatives by his nomination of moderate Sandra Day O'Connor to the Supreme Court.

Foreign Policy Issues   Reagan continued to express strong anti-Communist views as president and disparaged the Soviet Union as an "evil empire." Despite such tough Cold War talk, he restored the grain shipments to the Soviets that Jimmy Carter had stopped. Reagan also provided secret aid to Afghan rebels fighting Soviet occupation of their country.

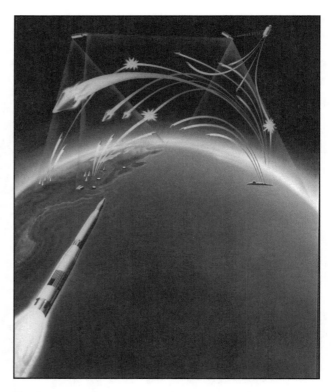

The Strategic Defense Initiative, what was commonlyu referred to as "Star Wars," rendered here by an artist, was neither the first nor last effort to develop an American defense system capable of preventing nuclear attack.   *Time Life Pictures/Department of Defense (DOD)/Time Life Pictures/Getty Images*

Reagan aggressively increased American defense spending in order to expand and modernize the military. He wanted to make it superior to the Soviet military. In 1983, he proposed the Strategic Defense Initiative, which would use satellites to shoot down missiles fired by an aggressor such as the Soviet Union. Despite proposals for such a program, Reagan continued arms control talks with Soviet leaders, especially after reformer Mikhail Gorbachev took control of the country. Reagan had face-to-face summit meetings with Gorbachev in 1985 and 1986 that eventually resulted in new arms control treaties in 1987. The INF (intermediate-range nuclear forces) Treaty led to the removal of these missiles from Western Europe.

Other foreign policy moves were meant to ensure democracy prevailed over Communism. In 1983, Reagan authorized an invasion of Grenada when it seemed Communist forces were causing problems and could potentially take over. The United States then installed a democratic, American-friendly regime, despite international criticism. Reagan received some disapproval at home for sending U.S. Marines to aid Lebanon during a civil war there early in his first term. After 240

Americans died in an attack in Lebanon, the Marines were removed.

Iran-Contra Scandal   Later in his presidency, Reagan had to deal with the fallout from the Iran-Contra scandal. In 1986 and 1987, it came to light that certain members of the Reagan administration had given a type of aid banned by Congress to Nicaragua. Arms had secretly been sold to Iran as means of gaining the release of American hostages held in Lebanon by Iranian-supported terrorists. The funds gained from the sale of these arms were sent to arm and train the Contras in Nicaragua who were trying to overthrow their country's socialist government, which was led by Daniel Ortega. The scandal led to hearings in front of a special Congressional committee known as the Tower Commission. Reagan testified he had no knowledge of the arms-for-hostages deal or the support of the Contras and claimed not to remember many conversations he allegedly had with advisors. The Tower Commission found no direct evidence that Reagan was involved in the illegal dealings, but asserted he should have been more aware of the activities of his staff. In the end, three members of Reagan's administration were indicted on various charges. These charges were later overturned on appeal or pardoned.

Post-Presidential Illness   Despite the scandal, Reagan remained publicly active and popular for several years after he left office in 1989. He left the public eye in the early 1990s when he was diagnosed with Alzheimer's disease. Reagan died on June 5, 2004, in Los Angeles.

Mikhail Gorbachev

While serving as the leader of the Soviet Union, Mikhail Gorbachev (1931–) oversaw the end of the Cold War and paved the way for political and social reforms in his country. Born Mikhail Sergeyevich Gorbachev on March 2, 1931, in Privolnoe, Stavropol, USSR, he was the son of an engine mechanic. Gorbachev was raised partially by his maternal grandparents. His grandfather, Pantelei Yefimovich Gopkalo, was a Communist party member and chairman of a local collective farm before falling victim to one of Soviet leader Joseph Stalin's purges of the late 1930s. Gorbachev began working on the farm by the age of ten and had a job as a farm machinery driver at a local machine-tractor station as a teenager. Gorbachev was also an intelligent student, though his schooling was interrupted for several years by World War II.

Joined Communist Party   After joining the Communist Party in 1952, Gorbachev entered Moscow State University and studied law. He married fellow student Raisa Titorenko in 1953 and graduated in 1955. After graduation, he went to Stavropol and became an organizer for the Young Communist League, or Komsomol.

He worked for the Communist Party and developed a reputation in the region as a successful administrator and a respected leader.

By the early 1960s, Gorbachev was taking roles of increasing responsibility in the Communist Party. In 1962, he became the Communist Party organizer for all the collective and state farms in the Stavropol region. In addition, Gorbachev soon became an important person on the Stavropol city committee. In 1966, Soviet leader Leonid Brezhnev named Gorbachev the first secretary of Stavropol. In essence, Gorbachev was the mayor of the city. He soon received more political training from the Communist Party.

Role in Regional Politics   In 1970, Gorbachev moved closer to national prominence by becoming the first secretary of the Stavropol Territorial Party Committee. Mentored by Yuri Andropov, an important national party member from the same region who was the chairman of the KGB (secret police), and others, Gorbachev went to Moscow in 1978 to become the party secretary in charge of agricultural administration. In 1980, he was made a member of the Politburo (the executive branch of the Communist party).

After the death of Brezhnev in 1982, Andropov's political star rose along with Gorbachev's. Both were interested in improving the Soviet economy by reforming obsolete and inefficient practices. Andropov became the Soviet leader, but he died two years later of kidney failure. He was briefly succeeded by Konstantin Chernenko, who died in early 1985. In March 1985, Gorbachev became the leader of the Soviet Union when he was elected the general secretary of the Soviet Communist Party.

Soviet Leader and Reformer   Regarded as a fresh young voice, Gorbachev's first order of business as Soviet leader was to improve the economic productivity of his country. He wanted to get rid of wastefulness and laziness among all workers, even in the Communist Party itself. The policy he instituted was called *perestroika*, or restructuring. Gorbachev tried to restructure the economy into one that was decentralized, not centralized, and that gave more control to local governments. He also developed a long-term plan to implement a market-style economy as the institutions needed to support it grew. Gorbachev also connected with the common Soviet citizen with frequent public appearances and promoted the concept of *glasnost*, or openness.

Gorbachev worked to improve the Soviet Union's relationship with the United States in order to end the arms race and help the Soviet economy. He wanted to figure out how to reduce Soviet defense spending so that more consumer goods could be produced. A summit meeting with President Ronald Reagan eight months after Gorbachev took office led to no real progress, though talks continued in the late 1980s.

Mikhail Gorbachev's domestic reforms bringing more openness and freedom to the lives of Soviet citizens ultimately undermined his own power as well as the stability of the USSR itself. *Getty Images*

Gorbachev continued to show his flexibility and openness in his dealings with the United States. He even visited New York City in 1987 and impressed Americans by shaking hands with them on the street. Reagan then visited Moscow a short time later. After calling for an end to the Cold War in a speech to the United Nations in 1988, in 1989 Gorbachev reduced military spending by withdrawing from Afghanistan and thus ending the Soviet military occupation of that country.

Significant internal reforms were also made in 1989. Gorbachev instituted elections that were open not just to members of the Communist Party, but to non-party candidates as well. Gorbachev also ended the special status afforded the Communist Party as guaranteed by the constitution of the Soviet Union. The government began managing the country, instead of the Communist Party managing the country. As reforms were introduced, the country's many ethnic groups and nationalities came into conflict with one another, and some demanded their independence. Gradually, the member states of the Soviet Union began establishing independent governments. After the fall of the Berlin Wall in 1989, Eastern Bloc countries also began dismantling their Communist governments and instituting democratic reforms.

Collapse of the Soviet Union Against this backdrop, the Soviet economy was failing. Industrial and agricultural production was on the decline, and the Soviet system did not address this situation any longer. Though Gorbachev received the 1990 Nobel Peace Prize, a powerful political rival emerged: former ally Boris Yeltsin. He wanted to radically reform the Soviet economy and even left the Communist Party in 1990. Yeltsin was elected the president of the Russian Republic in 1991.

Though change was imminent, staunch Communist Party conservatives—who opposed the changes that had already occurred and those anticipated for the future—detained Gorbachev in an attempted coup while he was on vacation in August 1991. The coup collapsed in a few days. The Soviet Union soon fell apart as the Ukraine and Baltic states (Estonia, Latvia, and Lithuania) declared themselves independent. Yeltsin remained in charge of the Russian Republic and banned the Communist Party. As Communism receded in Eastern Europe, Gorbachev resigned from all his public positions in December 1991, just as all non-Russian republics of the Soviet Union declared themselves independent. Although the Communist party is still active in many of these countries, the party functions as one of many legal political parties, not the sole political party of the state.

After the Fall Gorbachev published an autobiography in the United States in 1997. Continuing his support of reform, he founded several organizations such as the International Organization for Soviet Socioeconomic and Political Studies, known as the Gorbachev Foundation. Gorbachev has remained active in these pursuits for many years.

See also **World War II: Major Figures: Dwight Eisenhower**

✪ Major Battles and Events

Berlin Airlift

The Berlin Airlift was a complex mission conducted by the United States, the United Kingdom, and France in order to feed and supply the German residents of West Berlin in 1948.

The War's Aftermath Once the Allied powers defeated Nazi Germany ending World War II, Great Britain, France, the United States, and the Soviet Union began to occupy defeated Germany. Germany was divided into four sectors, and each nation was given territory to oversee. Ideological and political differences pitted the Soviet Union against the other three. The Soviet sector of Germany completely surrounded the capital city of Berlin. Berlin itself was also divided into four sections, each overseen by one of four World War II

In December 1952, the newly elected President Eisenhower fulfilled a campaign promise by visiting troops in Korea. *AP Images*

allies. The western side of the city had become aligned with the democratic and capitalist nations, but was completely surrounded by the forces of the Communist Soviet Union.

Berlin had suffered immensely over the course of the war. Round-the-clock bombing by both U.S. and British forces destroyed the city. Food was in perpetually short supply, housing was limited, and the Soviet soldiers had stripped factories of their machines and bricks and shipped these back to Russia. Only poor survivors remained, living in an economically crippled city where a black market flourished.

The United States and Britain agreed that once the Nazis were defeated, the people of Berlin should be put back on their feet. This was necessary for a healthy Europe and to prevent Communism from spreading westward. France, though less quick to befriend the nation that had occupied it during the war, typically sided with the British and Americans, while the Soviet Union did not.

Fractured Relations with the Soviet Union At a February 1948 meeting in London, representatives from the United Kingdom, France, the United States, the Netherlands, Belgium, and Luxembourg discussed the possibility of creating a new West German state. U.S. and Western European leaders believed control of West Germany was essential to stopping Communism's spread. At a later 1948 meeting that included Soviet representatives, the Soviet delegation demanded details of the prior London meeting. When American General and military governor Lucius Clay said they were not going to discuss the London meeting, Soviet leader Vasily Sokolovsky stood up and marched out with his delegation.

Eventually, the currency reform was enacted in the three sectors occupied by the United States, Britain, and France, while the Soviets refused to accept the plans or the new style of money in their eastern sector. The Soviets began to exert increased control over East Germany and East Berlin. Soon the Russians began an all-out blockade of Berlin, which meant France, the United

States, and Britain could not access their sectors of Berlin by road, rail, or canal. The Soviets offered to supply the other sectors of Berlin, but the Berliners refused the offer. French, British, and American forces remained in their parts of the city.

Operation Vittles The Berlin blockade became the first major standoff of the Cold War era. On June 21, 1948, Air Force Lieutenant General Curtis LeMay gave a mandate to supply Berlin on June 26. Battered planes from the Normandy invasion took eighty tons of food and medicine into Berlin on the first day. Initially, the combined available forces could only deliver about seven hundred tons per day into Berlin. But an estimated four thousand tons were needed to supply the Berliners with what they needed. Only an intense, detailed, and well-executed plan would save the residents of West Berlin from Soviet control.

Though the resources and logistics necessary to succeed in the early stages of the airlift did not exist at first, the combined commitment from U.S. President Harry Truman, the British, and the airmen involved resulted in a precise and successful mission. "Operation Vittles," as the Americans called it, became enhanced enough to feed and supply the beleaguered city within months. The allies called for airplanes from throughout Europe, and soon the volunteer gangs that unloaded the airplanes could do so in seven minutes. Truman had said, "The United States is going to stay, period," and he authorized additional C-54 planes to double the deliveries in July.

As the airlift continued, it became clear that even more supplies would be needed for the approaching winter. By September, five thousand tons per day reached Berlin. In February 1949, the millionth ton was delivered. The West had proved its resolve to remain in Berlin and the West German state. In May 1949, the Soviets called off their blockade. American and British flights continued to supply the city until September 1949.

The Berlin Airlift is remembered as a triumphant humanitarian effort to feed a devastated people. The West Berliners, a determined population, showed tremendous strength in fending off an attempted takeover by the Soviets.

U-2 Incident

One of the few physical encounters between the United States and the Soviet Union during the Cold War occurred in 1960 when the Soviets downed an American spy plane. United States pilot Francis Gary Powers was surveying parts of Russia to gather information on missile capability when he was shot down.

The U-2 plane was a key element in the United States's Cold War arsenal. This single-seat aircraft was designed by Lockheed. It had a range of some 2,600 miles, and flew at altitudes of 75,000 feet, well out of the

Talks between Eisenhower and Kruschev in Paris in May 1960, collapsed over the U-2 incident. Kruschev, at a press conference, rants over Eisenhower's refusal to apologize. *Carl Mydans/Time Life Pictures/Getty Images*

range of Soviet antiaircraft missiles at the time. The planes were equipped with high-tech cameras that could take detailed pictures of key military installations.

The Central Intelligence Agency (CIA), not the military, sponsored these flights that crisscrossed the Soviet Union from American bases in Pakistan and Turkey. Primarily, these U-2 planes provided snapshots for intelligence assessment and for policymaking in Washington, D.C. These flights were clearly a violation of Soviet airspace, but none had been challenged until May 1960.

Francis Gary Powers was born in a large Kentucky coal mining family but attended college and joined the Air Force after graduating. As an airman, Powers soon held the rank of first lieutenant. In 1955, the CIA recruited him and gave him the cover name Francis G. Palmer. "Palmer" was officially a pilot for Lockheed Aircraft Corporation; in reality, he was part of the agency's complex U-2 intelligence-gathering operations. Powers agreed to a three-year contract for spying over the Soviet Union. Afterward, he was to return to the Air Force.

The Ill-Fated Mission On May 1, 1960, Powers took a normal surveillance flight from Pakistan to Norway in Air Force plane 360 across the Soviet Union. The U-2

West Berliners destroy the Berlin Wall, November 10, 1989, after the German Democratic Republic (East Germany) eased travel restrictions.   *Tom Stoddart/Getty Images*

was tracked by radar early in its flight, but the Soviet MiG fighters that tried to engage it, could not reach the U-2's high altitude. As the U-2 approached the city of Sverdlovsk, a Soviet missile hit it with a surface-to-air missile. Powers tried to maintain control of his aircraft, but eventually had to bail out over Soviet territory. The townspeople of Sverdlovsk rushed to his aid, assuming he was a Russian pilot, but soon realized he was an American. His plane was severely damaged, but evidence remained that proved to the Soviet authorities that Powers was spying. Powers and what was left of the aircraft were sent to Moscow for further investigation.

The incident outraged the Soviet government and Premier Nikita Khrushchev. The United States initially took the position that it had not sponsored such a spying mission, but that this plane was merely a weather plane that had veered off course. Khrushchev produced evidence to the contrary, including the camera and a suicide needle that Powers never used. President Dwight Eisenhower finally admitted to the mission and accepted responsibility, but made no apology nor did he promise such missions would cease.

Powers was then put on public trial in Moscow and easily found guilty. He was sentenced to ten years in prison. On February 10, 1962, however, the Soviets swapped him for one of their own celebrated spies held in U.S. custody. In a simple exchange at the border of East and West Germany, intelligence officials from both sides exchanged their respective prisoners.

Powers did not exactly receive a hero's welcome back in the United States. Many felt he should have used the needle or at least remained silent about the mission. He went back to the Air Force for a while and then began teaching U-2 pilots at CIA headquarters. Afterwards, he worked for a short time at Lockheed in southern California. After the publication of his book, *Operation Overflight*, which revealed the details of his ill-fated mission over the Soviet Union, Lockheed fired him. He ended his flying career as a traffic reporter for Los Angeles radio and television stations. He died in 1977 when his helicopter crashed after running out of fuel. President Jimmy Carter granted permission for Powers to be buried in Arlington National Cemetery.

Berlin Wall

The Berlin Wall, one of the key symbols of the Cold War conflict, was constructed by the Soviet-influenced East German state in August 1961 to stop East Berlin residents from fleeing west. For nearly three decades it reminded the world of the division between East and West, between the Communist bloc and the Western allies. In 1989, the Berlin Wall came down as the Cold War ended.

A Divided Germany, A Divided Berlin The Berlin Wall was constructed during the reign of Soviet Premier Nikita Khrushchev and East German leader Walter Ulbricht. Since the end of World War II, the Potsdam and Yalta agreements made by the victorious Allies—the United States, the Soviet Union, France, and Great Britain—divided control of both Germany as a whole, and Berlin as the capital city. One of the results of this conference was that the Soviet Occupation Zone fully surrounded Berlin. The city was divided into four sectors also assigned to the respective Allied powers. Soon after the war's end, the Russian government, which had promised airspace for travel into and out of Berlin, began to block roads and trains in order to starve West Berlin into submission and in hopes of adding the entire city to its sphere of influence. The Berlin Airlift followed. For months the United States led an effort to supply the West Berliners with food and necessities so they would not have to give in to the Soviets.

Neither of the superpowers (the United States and the Soviet Union) were willing to leave Germany entirely under the other's control, prompting the creation of East and West German states, with the West aligned with the United States and the East aligned with the Soviets. However, this left the city of Berlin in the odd position of being completely surrounded by a Soviet-dominated state even while half Berlin was still under Western control.

It was clearly in Khrushchev's and Ulbricht's best interest to rid Berlin of the Western presence. A stark contrast had developed on each side of the city. West Berlin had recovered from the devastation of the war and had a booming economy. The East was drab and dreary and lacked resources or modern conveniences. While the nine-hundred-mile boundary between West and East Germany was well guarded, Berlin became the ideal place for East Germans to make their escape to the West. From the western part of the city, those fleeing Communism could fly to West Germany. Between 1949 when the German Democratic Republic was created and 1961, fully 2.8 million Germans crossed to the West. Khrushchev intended to stem this human tide.

In 1957, fleeing to the West became a crime punishable with a prison sentence. The Communist-controlled press painted a lurid picture of life in the West, with slave traders selling young vulnerable East German women into prostitution. Khrushchev began a softer line on diplomacy in terms of Berlin. After a successful tour of the United States and discussions with President Dwight Eisenhower at Camp David, Khrushchev began thinking a compromise over Berlin was possible. A Paris summit

was scheduled for this discussion. But when an American U-2 spy plane was shot down over the Soviet Union, Khrushchev lost patience and the Paris summit was canceled.

The Wall Goes Up In the early morning hours of Sunday, August 13, 1961, Berlin residents were awakened by the noise of military vehicles and unraveling coils of barbed wire in East Berlin. Trucks lined the border within the city with their headlights providing light for the East German work crews. Armed guards supervised the workers erecting barbed-wire fences and the beginnings of a brick wall. Those who had crossed the border the night before to be with friends or family were stunned to find the U-Bahn and S-Bahn, the transit systems that crisscrossed Berlin, closed. They were prevented from traveling back to their residences. As morning wore on, workers heading to one or the other side of the city were stopped from crossing the line that the East Germans had drawn. Soviet tanks took positions on the east side of the city. Though some government officials feared protests and uprisings, the streets of East Berlin remained eerily quiet.

Newly elected President John F. Kennedy sent General Lucius Clay, who had overseen West Berlin during the 1948 Airlift, and Vice President Lyndon Johnson to West Berlin to reassure the citizens of American support. He also ordered a combat unit of 1,500 to the city for reinforcement. Both the officials and the soldiers were received warmly by West Berliners. But the United States and its allies took no military action to stop construction of the wall. American support for West Berlin remained firm. Kennedy visited in 1963 and gave a famous speech expressing solidarity with the West Berliners, concluding his address with the German phrase "Ich bin ein Berliner" ("I am a Berliner").

For nearly thirty years, the Berlin Wall separated families only miles apart and served as the distinct division between the two superpowers that were hemispheres apart. But in the 1980s, the citizens of Eastern European countries began to push for reform. In Hungary and Poland, workers, students, and progressive leaders began to chip away at the Communist system that repressed them. A new Soviet leader, Mikhail Gorbachev, had taken office in 1985 and pushed dramatic reforms.

In 1987, U.S. President Ronald Reagan visited Berlin and addressed its citizens, and those listening around the world. He harked back to Kennedy's visit and reminded Berliners that the United States had not changed its views on Berlin since the wall was erected in 1961. He said that Americans admired Berliners' "courage and determination." He also called the wall a "brutal division of a continent upon the mind of the world." He then questioned Gorbachev's commitment to reform, challenging him, "Come here to this gate!

Mr. Gorbachev, open this gate! Mr. Gorbachev, tear down this wall!"

The Wall Comes Down Two years later, while East Germany was still under the oppressive regime of Erich Honecker, East Germans had been inspired by some of the revolutions against Communists in other countries. Gorbachev had recommended to Honecker to consider an East German version of the reforms underway in the Soviet Union, but Honecker refused the suggestion. When Gorbachev visited East Berlin, crowds of thousands came out into streets for torchlight marches, chanting "Gorby, Gorby, Gorby, save us." The day after Gorbachev left, a gathering of seventy thousand in Leipzig continued to challenge Honecker, who responded by ordering police to fire into the crowd. The police refused, and Honecker was ousted and replaced by a young Egon Krenz. The new prime minister fired his cabinet and looked to Gorbachev for advice. On November 4, a half a million people jammed into East Berlin's streets for a concert that became a public expression for the current generation against the old regime and the Communist oppression.

On November 9, Krenz announced that his East German government would issue visas for those wanting to visit the West. Crowds began to gather that evening at the eight crossing points in Berlin. The border guards, uncertain as to how to handle the masses lining up at these gates, called headquarters but received no clear instructions. Initially, the guards required the valid visas, but soon the trickle of East Germans heading west turned into an unstoppable flood determined to gain what they had hoped to gain for years. Soon, thousands crossed the wall for a taste of freedom. With sledgehammers, chisels, and anything else they could get their hands on, throngs of Berliners began to chip away at the wall that had divided their city for nearly three decades. Over the next two years, bit by bit, the Berlin wall was demolished. And Germany, a country divided, followed the lead of its historic capital city. The country was reunified in October 1990.

Bay of Pigs

The Bay of Pigs Invasion in 1961 was a United States-sponsored mission intended to overthrow Fidel Castro's regime in Cuba. Castro had led a successful revolution in January 1959, overthrowing the dictator Fulgencio Batista and installing his new coalition government in Havana. As Castro solidified his power, the new Cuba grew distant from the United States and began to develop close relations with the Soviet Union. The Soviet Deputy Premier Anastas Mikoyan visited Havana in February 1960 and, at the United Nations in New York in September, Castro and Russian Premier Nikita Khrushchev embraced as fellow revolutionaries.

This developing alliance disturbed American leaders. With American business interests crushed by Castro's revolution and a communist-leaning government in the United States's backyard, the CIA began a plan to overthrow Castro.

The Bay of Pigs Invasion was conceived in January 1960 and approved by President Dwight Eisenhower on March 17, 1960. The scheme entailed training Cuban exiles for a mission that would land them at the Bay of Pigs southwest of Havana. After the landing, the exiles would rally what was thought to be a strong anti-Castro movement in Cuba and overthrow the government. As late as December 1960, Eisenhower endorsed the plan for an amphibious landing of these CIA-trained paramilitary fighters. John F. Kennedy had already been elected president, but knew nothing of the mission until two days before his inauguration. Kennedy had little choice but to agree to the plan. The former general and outgoing commander in chief was solidly behind it. The Joint Chiefs of Staff supported the invasion, and presidential advisor John Foster Dulles and his brother CIA director Allen Dulles saw this as a quick way to rid America of the threat posed by Castro and weaken Soviet-Cuba connections. Kennedy agreed, but wanted the mission conducted so the United States could deny involvement.

In April, three days before the scheduled invasion, the president announced that the United States would not lead any military invasion into Cuba. On April 17, the invasion went as scheduled. In the early hours of the morning, a force of about 1,400 Cubans landed in Cuba. The mission was botched from the beginning. Both CIA planners and the Cuban exiles predicted the invasion would spark a popular anti-Castro uprising and that the United States would send military support once they achieved the beachhead at the bay. Neither of these things happened. The domestic uprising that was thought to coincide with the invasion never took place. And the United States-sponsored guerillas never received any U.S. military support because Kennedy maintained his public position that he would not intervene militarily. Castro sent his Soviet-made tanks directly at the invaders, who never made it very far inland from the beach. After a three-day standoff, about one hundred of the invading fighters were killed, fourteen were rescued by the U.S. Navy, and 1,189 were taken prisoner.

This fiasco gave Kennedy a rocky start as president and had the unintended effect of bringing Havana and Moscow closer together. The incident also damaged America's standing with Latin American countries, which began to worry that their large, powerful neighbor had aggressive imperialist intentions. Further, the failed plot led Khrushchev to view Kennedy as weak and ineffective. When Kennedy and Khrushchev met at a summit in Vienna, Austria, in June, the president told

Twenty-five years after the failed Bay of Pigs invasion, two Cubans pause before a sign claiming that one of the landing sites nearby represents "the first great defeat for imperialism in Latin America." *© Bettmann/Corbis*

his Soviet counterpart that the Bay of Pigs was a mistake. Khrushchev responded by telling Kennedy that wars of national liberation would now be won by Communists and that the United States was on the wrong side of history. The emboldened Khrushchev soon brazenly installed nuclear missiles in Cuba, aiming them at the United States.

Cuban Missile Crisis

The Cuban Missile Crisis was the closest the United States and the Soviet Union ever came to full-scale nuclear war. The conflict took place during October 1962 after the Soviet Union had shipped nuclear missiles to its ally, Cuba. After intense analysis, contemplation, and diplomacy, the crisis ended and millions of lives were saved.

The failed Bay of Pigs Invasion and a strengthening alliance between Fidel Castro and the Soviet Union encouraged Soviet Premier Nikita Khrushchev to install several dozen missiles in Cuba. Khrushchev considered this a response to the fact that the United States had already installed nuclear weapons in Turkey. It was time, Khrushchev thought, that the Americans learned what it felt like to be threatened.

On Sunday, October 14, 1962, a U-2 spy plane took aerial photographs of the missile sites under construction near San Cristobal in western Cuba. By the next morning, National Security Advisor McGeorge Bundy informed President John F. Kennedy of the discovery. On Tuesday, the president called together his chief advisors, the National Security Council, including his brother Attorney General Robert Kennedy, to discuss how they should address this volatile situation. They predicted that the missiles might become operational in two weeks, leaving only thirteen days to remove them to guarantee national security. This group agreed prompt removal was necessary, but differed greatly on the manner in which to meet this goal.

Attack or Negotiate? The first proposal was to strike the missiles before they could ever be installed. The Joint Chiefs of the armed services were the strongest advocates for this tactic. The civilian leaders—the secretaries of state and defense, and the attorney general—on the other hand, saw the political consequences of the United States attacking the small nation of Cuba, especially only a year after the debacle in the Bay of Pigs. Other concerns included the fear that the Soviet Union might retaliate by bombing Berlin.

Kennedy first approached the Soviet foreign minister Andrey Gromyko at the White House to ask about the missiles. Gromyko claimed that any assistance to Cuba was in a defensive nature only and denied that any offensive weapons had been delivered to Cuba. With no quick diplomatic solution in reach, the cabinet secretaries persuaded Kennedy that a blockade of the island would be the best course of action. A blockade would prevent additional missiles from reaching the island and show that the United States was taking this threat seriously, while it would fall short of an aggressive attack.

This solution included alerting America's B-52 bombers with nuclear weapons stationed in Europe in case the Soviets responded by attacking Berlin. Once this plan was in place, the Executive Committee of the National Security Council (ExComm) began to inform Congress and the American public of the crisis. The White House asked for airtime from the three national networks so the president could give a speech from the Oval Office. Before going public, he called a meeting of seventeen congressional leaders to explain the dilemma and how he as commander in chief planned to handle it. When Kennedy addressed the nation on live television, the military was placed on high alert, and the navy deployed 180 ships to surround Cuba in what was officially termed a "quarantine."

Khrushchev accused Kennedy of violating international law. On October 25, the Soviet ambassador to the United Nations, Valerian Zorin, challenged the United States delegate Adlai Stevenson II to prove the accusations against the Soviet Union. When Stevenson asked Zorin to answer the question of whether the Soviet Union had in fact placed these missiles in Cuba, Zorin stalled, declaring he was not in an American courtroom forced to answer in an interrogation. But Stevenson replied, "You are in the courtroom of world opinion right now and you can answer yes or no.... I am prepared to wait for my answer until hell freezes over." Stevenson presented the aerial photographs to prove what the Soviet ambassador would not confirm.

Tensions continued to mount as negotiators on both sides worked to forestall military conflict. Khrushchev sent a letter asking for a promise from the United States that it would never invade Cuba if the missiles were removed. Adlai Stevenson put forth the idea that perhaps the United States should offer to remove its missiles from Turkey. The military commanders still pushed for a full-scale invasion. A second letter from the Kremlin, which differed in tone and substance from the first, stated that in order for Russia to remove the weapons from Cuba, the United States had to remove its missiles in Turkey.

Though not everyone in the Kennedy administration agreed to this proposal, it was ultimately the compromise that saved the world from nuclear war. Robert Kennedy worked out the details of the deal with Soviet ambassador Anatoly Dobrynin. This executive agreement held that the United States would cease the quarantine and promise not to invade Cuba, and the Soviet Union would then remove the missiles. The United States also promised, though not publicly, to remove its nuclear weapons from Turkey, which it did six months later.

Crisis Averted This thirteen-day crisis had a win-win result for both sides. In the United States, it was Kennedy's finest hour. It appeared to be an American victory, especially since the U.S. missiles in Turkey were removed quietly several months later. The United States appeared once again to be master of its region. In Russia, similar relief and celebration occurred. Khrushchev called it a triumph for common sense and hailed the fact that he was able to get the United States to do what it had not done before—promise to leave Cuba alone. Those parties unhappy with the result included the U.S. Joint Chiefs, Turkey, and Fidel Castro (who was left out of the negotiations and felt betrayed by his Soviet allies). Nevertheless, Kennedy was hailed as a hero, and the Democratic victories in the midterm congressional elections gave the president's party its largest majority in the Senate in twenty years.

Strategic Arms Limitations Talks

The Strategic Arms Limitations Talks (SALT) resulted from a handful of 1960s Cold War events and issues. The confrontation between the United States and the Soviet Union during the Cuban Missile Crisis scared citizens and leaders on both sides. The brinkmanship during that October 1962 standoff luckily ended with both the United States and the Soviet Union agreeing to remove their missiles from Turkey and Cuba respectively and to limit nuclear weapons testing. The arms race had driven both nations to devote vast sums to military spending. In trying to outarm each other, the Americans and Russians endangered the economic health of their countries. And, the Soviet Union had created an antiballistic missile system that the United States would have to imitate. All of these factors led to the discussions known as SALT.

President Lyndon Johnson and Soviet Premier Aleksey Kosygin met in New Jersey in 1967. Johnson raised the issue of a ban on antiballistic missiles, to which Kosygin responded that defense is moral, while aggression is immoral. Moscow was not prepared to discuss a ban on defensive missiles, only offensive strategic missiles. The next year, the Soviet Union, United States, and Britain signed the first Nuclear Non-Proliferation Treaty, which prevented the transfer of nuclear technology from one country to another. Soon after this, the United States and the Soviet Union announced that an arms limitation, including a reduction in both offensive and defensive systems, would follow.

President Jimmy Carter and Soviet General Secretary Leonid Brezhnev shake hands at the 1979 SALT II treaty singing ceremony, in Vienna, Austria. *AP Images*

The First Talks The first arms limitation talks between the United States and the Soviet Union were set to open in Geneva in September 1968, but the United States pulled out of the meeting when the Soviets invaded Czechoslovakia in August. Once President Richard Nixon was inaugurated, the movement toward talks resumed. On November 17, 1969, the United States and the Soviet Union finally sat down at the table to negotiate in Helsinki, Finland. These discussions continued in Helsinki and later in Vienna and dragged on for years. Neither side was willing to lose its military edge. The United States had far passed the Soviets in MIRVs (multiple independently targeted reentry vehicles) and the Soviet Union had outdone the United States with its ABM (antiballistic missile) defensive system. As the negotiations inched forward, technological advances in weaponry continued and sometimes went beyond the scope of the talks.

Finally, on May 26, 1972, at a summit in Moscow, President Nixon and new Soviet Premier Leonid Brezhnev signed the agreement that became known as SALT (Strategic Arms Limitation Treaty) I. The treaty limited the number of ABMs, but SALT did not cover MIRVs, leaving the Russian advantage in missile numbers matched by America's deliverable warheads. The treaty also did not cover medium- or intermediate-range missiles, nor did it address U.S. bases in Europe. SALT I, however, ushered in a new era of détente (easing or relaxing) in relations between the Soviet Union and the United States. It also essentially froze the military balance between the two nations: each side still had the ability to destroy the other, thus causing both to refrain from taking any action. The world was safer with SALT I.

SALT II Over the next few years, under presidents Gerald Ford and Jimmy Carter, détente waxed and waned as did general Soviet-American relations. In early 1979, President Carter felt a new agreement on arms limitations should be reached. Moscow, too, was ready to negotiate. The first and only meeting between Carter and Brezhnev took place at a Vienna summit in mid-June 1979 and ended with the signing of the Strategic Arms Limitation Treaty II (SALT II). SALT II essentially made final breakthrough agreements that former president Ford and Brezhnev had reached in 1974 negotiations in Vladivostok. Both sides accepted arms production limits.

But the treaty signed by these two executives was never ratified. Carter asked the Senate to delay ratifying the treaty after the Soviet Union invaded Afghanistan in December 1979. Still, Carter promised to uphold the terms of the treaty, and President Ronald Reagan also promised his support of the agreement.

The Pueblo Incident

On January 23, 1968, the Democratic People's Republic of Korea (DPRK) captured the *U.S.S. Pueblo*, which was conducting a spy mission several miles off the Korean coast. Insisting that the ship was cruising in their territorial waters, the North Koreans took the crew hostage until they received an apology—of sorts—from the American government.

The Capture In 1968, the ongoing war in Vietnam tended to overshadow America's attention to the Korean situation. Nevertheless, the United States viewed the Communist DPRK (North Korea) as a constant threat against the democratic, American-occupied Republic of Korea (South Korea). On January 22, the DPRK attempted to assassinate South Korean leaders. Tensions on the peninsula were running high.

The American navy has always insisted that the *Pueblo* was in international waters at the time of her capture. Her captain, Commander Lloyd M. Bucher, had specific orders not to provoke an international incident. He was to conduct electronic intelligence gathering, listening for the Soviet navy, without entering South Korean territorial waters. The *Pueblo* was lightly armed, but her machine guns were under wraps and her ammunition stored below.

On January 23, a DPRK submarine chaser bore down on the *Pueblo* and demanded to know her nationality. When the ship raised American colors, the Koreans threatened to attack her if she did not heave to. The *Pueblo* tried to escape, but the much faster sub chaser was soon joined by three torpedo boats and two MiG-21 fighters. Bucher radioed the U.S. Seventh Fleet in Japan. For some reason, the Americans sent no ships or planes to help. Possibly they feared that a pitched sea battle would inevitably lead to open war.

The Koreans opened fire on the *Pueblo* with 55-mm cannon and machine guns. As still more enemy ships approached, Bucher surrendered to overwhelming odds and started to destroy all sensitive documents aboard the ship. Nevertheless, the Koreans captured a great deal of intelligence when they boarded the ship.

Eighty-three seamen, including the captain, were captured, bound, blindfolded, and beaten. One sailor was mortally wounded under the enemy fire and would die shortly thereafter.

Hostages When they were finally freed, the Americans reported that they had been regularly starved and tortured by the North Koreans. The DRPK declared that the prisoners were being treated well and released pictures of the smiling crew to the international press. However, the Koreans did not catch the cultural signifi-

cance of some of the men's hand gestures in the photographs. When asked, the sailors told their captors that an extended middle finger was a "Hawaiian Good Luck symbol."

When the photos were published, the American press crowed that the servicemen had clearly complied only under duress and with contempt. The North Koreans were furious at the loss of face, and the prisoners endured seven days of brutal reprisals, a period they would later call "Hell Week."

Bucher apparently bore the worst treatment from the beginning. In an attempt to make him confess to spying, he was dragged in front of a mock execution squad. Bucher claims that he only capitulated when the Communists threatened to murder his men in front of him, starting with the youngest.

Because of the North Koreans' poor English skills, Bucher was made to write his own confession and read it aloud. Although the DPRK diligently checked the meaning of all his words, Bucher filled his statement with puns, poor sentence structure, and mispronunciations.

"Apology" The DPRK insisted that the U.S. government admit to spying, apologize, and swear never to do it again. Americans were less than inclined to do so. Outraged hawk congressmen urged Johnson to mine the Wonsan harbor in North Korea. Even the antiwar movement was momentarily quieted in the atmosphere of general national outrage.

However, the Johnson administration hardly had time to react to the crisis. Just a week later, the Tet Offensive broke out in Vietnam. The government decided that a rescue operation in North Korea was simply not possible at the time, and that an attempt at the same would endanger the uneasy Korean armistice. In the generally overcharged political atmosphere of 1968, the issue of the *Pueblo* quickly receded from public attention.

Eleven months later, the U.S. State Department agreed to a letter of admission, apology, and assurance, though they renounced the document even before signing it. Secretary of State Dean Rusk publicly stated that the apology was a lie, with the sole purpose of reclaiming the crew. Nevertheless, the DRPK accepted the letter, blocked out the paragraph of disavowal, and released the hostages.

On returning to the United States, Bucher immediately faced a naval court of inquiry. Several high-ranking commanders were furious at the loss of the ship, which represented a major intelligence loss for the United States. In recent years, evidence has arisen that the Soviet Union may have asked North Korea to capture the *Pueblo*. The information gathered from the ship allowed the USSR to make considerable progress in their communications technology.

The court recommended that Bucher be court-martialed for surrendering his command without an attempt at resistance. Secretary of the Navy John Chafee

President Richard Nixon altered the course of the Cold War when he visited the People's Republic of China in 1972. *AP Images*

rejected the idea. "They have suffered enough," he said. The crew members were granted POW (prisoner of war) medals by the American government in 1989.

The *USS Pueblo* is still held by the DPRK in the port of Pyongyang. Guided tours are given, describing the ship as an example of American imperialist espionage.

Nixon Visits China

President Richard Nixon, a staunch anti-Communist from his early days in Congress, saw an opportunity early in his presidential administration to open relations with Communist China by exploiting the conflict between the Soviet Union and China. He did so with several changes in U.S. foreign policy toward the People's Republic of China and with a famous visit to the Communist nation.

Much had changed since Nixon's time as a congressman and vice president. In 1949, Mao Zedong and his Chinese Communist Party led a successful revolution, overthrowing the Nationalist government and its leader Chiang Kai-shek. Chiang's government fled to the island of Taiwan and formed the Republic of China,

while Mao and his followers established the People's Republic of China on the mainland. The United States strongly sided with Chiang during the World War II fight against Japan, and after Chiang established his government on Taiwan. The Soviet Union and the new Communist China enjoyed positive relations in the postwar years as they both followed Marxist principles and had a common enemy in the United States. But this relationship soured through the late 1950s and 1960s.

Rift Between Soviet Union and China The Chinese were never happy with the Soviet Union's level of support during the Korean conflict. The Soviet Union supplied no ground troops and required China to pay up front for Soviet weapons. When Soviet leader Joseph Stalin died, Mao never fully accepted Khrushchev as the head of the Communist world. In the late 1960s, with the development of the Brezhnev Doctrine—the Soviet premier's philosophy that the Soviet Union could intervene in the affairs of neighboring countries to preserve socialism—China and Mao further distanced themselves from Russia. Heavy levels of troops and warplanes on both sides guarded the long border between the two nations. In a March 1969 dispute, thirty-one Russian soldiers were killed. Mao's right-hand man, Chou Enlai, had by this time denounced the Soviet Union leaders as the "new czars."

President Nixon took office in January 1969 and saw his opportunity to capitalize on the rift between China and the Soviet Union. In early October, Nixon placed the U.S. Strategic Command on highest alert to communicate to the Soviet Union that his administration would deter a Soviet nuclear attack on China. Nixon and his closest advisors knew that many in Washington would not favor overt overtures toward China, so Nixon signaled his intentions subtly. In a *Time* magazine interview, he indicated that he would like to eventually visit China. In July 1971, Nixon secretly sent National Security Advisor Henry Kissinger to China; he was the first American official to visit China since 1949. While Kissinger was there, Chou extended an invitation to the American president, which Nixon ultimately accepted.

Nixon announced that he would travel to China within the year. Before he did, additional steps were taken to normalize relations. The United States lifted a twenty-one-year-old trade embargo it had placed on the nation. The nine thousand U.S. troops garrisoned on Taiwan were reduced. And the United States began to recognize Communist China's right to a seat in the United Nations. Meanwhile, additional troops were pulled out of Vietnam.

Nixon finally arrived in China in February 1972 for a week-long tour and talks with Mao. No actual treaty resulted from the meeting, but what became known as the Shanghai Communiqué, a simple acknowledgment of each others' positions, was signed. In the statement, the United States agreed to recognize the People's Republic of China as China's legitimate government (it had backed the exiled Nationalist government based in Taiwan since shortly after World War II).

The visit resulted in other diplomatic successes. A United States ambassador was placed in Beijing. A year later, diplomatic offices were opened in both Washington and Beijing. Nixon touted his trip as "the week that changed the world." It truly had opened some eyes to the possibilities of improved U.S.-Chinese relations.

INF Treaty

The INF (Intermediate-Range Nuclear Forces) Treaty was a landmark step in U.S-Soviet concessions that led to a thawing of the Cold War. The Treaty essentially eliminated thousands of American and Soviet missiles and proved that the easing tensions in the mid-1980s were more than symbolic. President Ronald Reagan and Soviet Premier Mikhail Gorbachev signed the treaty in December 1987, but it came as a result of a historic summit in October 1986.

Gorbachev had begun a program of openness and reform in the Soviet Union upon taking office in 1985. He wanted to bring the Soviet Union and the United States closer together. He also wanted to improve economic conditions within his country. His concern for domestic programs and his genuine desire to end hostilities between East and West encouraged him to push for peace between the two superpowers. In August 1986, Gorbachev agreed to a U.S.-Soviet meeting in Reykjavik, Iceland.

On the opening day of the conference, Gorbachev took the initiative to offer a full reduction of strategic arms, intermediate-range missiles, and space weapons. Secretary of State George Schultz accompanied President Reagan to the meeting, and they both agreed that this offer was fundamentally acceptable. The discussions moved toward the missiles that had been placed in Europe. On the second day, the pace of the discussions increased. Both Reagan and Gorbachev agreed on a complete withdrawal of intermediate-range weapons from Europe. They also agreed on cutting ballistic missiles stockpiles by fifty percent over a five-year period. Gorbachev even proposed the idea of eliminating all nuclear weapons in ten years.

Everyone—the two leaders, their representatives, and onlookers—was astonished. But before these landmark proposals could be agreed to, Gorbachev brought up Reagan's Strategic Defense Initiative that the United States had researched and partially developed. This mammoth program, mostly in the research stages, would eventually defend America from nuclear missiles with lasers from space, if Reagan had his way. The Soviets were offended by the so-called Star Wars (SDI) plan because they felt it violated the ABM Treaty, which prevented defense systems. If the United States could finalize the Star Wars Program, the deterrent of mutually assured destruction would be eliminated. The Soviets saw the program as a potential for the United States to become aggressive once they were fully defended. Gorbachev proposed that the SDI program be confined to the laboratory only.

Reagan was still pressing for his pet program and refused to accept the offer. This prevented the signing of any treaty while the leaders were in Iceland. Despite this anticlimax, great progress had been made at Reykjavik. Gorbachev stated at a post-summit press conference that in spite of all the drama, "It is a breakthrough which for the first time enabled us to look over the horizon." Reagan, as well, spoke positively of the meeting. He emphasized the significance of the conference was "not that we didn't sign the agreements in the end; the significance is that we got as close as we did."

Such attitudes by the two heads of state led to eventual ratification of the INF Treaty. Other nations had their say on the treaty before it would be finalized. West Germany, a potential Soviet target throughout

Soviet General Secretary Mikhail Gorbachev and U.S. President Ronald Reagan helped thaw the Cold War by signing a treaty eliminating intermediate-range ballistic and cruise missiles in 1987.   *AP Images*

most of the era, insisted that short-range missiles aimed at it, must be included in the treaty. The Soviets responded that similar U.S. weapons, seventy-two Pershing 1A missiles positioned in West Germany and aimed at the Soviet Union, must be removed. The United States agreed to these terms, and Gorbachev pulled back from insisting that the United States halt the SDI. Reagan and Gorbachev signed the INF Treaty in Washington, D.C., on December 8, 1987.

The treaty was of historical proportions. Both nations for the first time agreed to reduce their arsenals and to eliminate an entire category of nuclear weapons. The treaty banned all land-based missiles with a range of 1,000 to 5,500 kilometers, and short-range and inter-mediate-range weapons that could reach 500 to 1,000 kilometers. In total, the United States agreed to destroy fewer than one thousand warheads, while the Soviets would eliminate more than three thousand. The talks eventually allowed for inspections to verify enforcement of the treaties.

Reunification of Germany

After the Allied defeat of Nazi Germany in 1945, the four Allied powers either occupied or oversaw Germany until late 1990. Germany and its capital of Berlin became the epicenter of the Cold War, dividing East and West. Both the nation and the capital city were split along ideological lines. The United States, Britain, and France occupied and created West Germany, while the Soviet Union influenced and occupied East Germany. These two states formed early in the Cold War. Most Germans and Berlin citizens wanted a democracy free from Soviet influence, but the Soviet Union built a wall to stop East Berliners from escaping to the west and placed a fence with armed guards along most of the new border between the two states. By 1989, much had changed in Eastern Europe. Soviet leader Mikhail Gorbachev was instituting reforms in the Soviet Union, and Eastern Bloc nations were breaking free of Communism and the influence of the Soviet Union. In November 1989, the citizens of Berlin seized the moment and broke

On October 3, 1990, these young men donned army caps from the former East Germany to celebrate German Reunification. © *Bernard Bisson/Corbis Sygma*

through the Berlin Wall en masse and used the tools at their disposal to begin chipping away at the hated wall.

The opening of the Berlin Wall was the first step toward reunification of Germany, divided since the end of World War II. Gorbachev eyed German reunification warily as a potential security threat. A united Germany would probably join NATO (the North Atlantic Treaty Organization), an adversary of the Soviet Union and its satellites.

Gorbachev proposed discussions among the same four powers who had occupied and divided Germany in the first place. By March 18, 1990, the East Germans held an election that ousted the Communist Party and put a new democratic coalition in power. It became even clearer that reunification was going to occur.

U.S. Secretary of State James Baker, serving under President George H.W. Bush, had offered the "Four plus Two" talks. That is, the fate of Germany and whether or not it joined NATO should be decided by the four major powers that had originally divided Germany and the two German states that had existed for over a generation. The Soviet Union accepted this proposal, but it still wanted to keep a united Germany out of NATO. Talks began in May 1990. At a Washington summit, President Bush gave Gorbachev several assurances: NATO forces would not be placed in the former East Germany, Soviet forces could depart the region gradually, and the new unified Germany would have to reaffirm its commitments to neither produce nor possess nuclear weapons. The Soviets counterproposal asked for a transition period of three or four years so the four powers could set limits on Germany's armed forces and establish a structure that would prevent a resurgence of Nazi ideology. Russian foreign minister Eduard Shevardnadze had made these offers and wanted to ensure that NATO's goal was to create political, not military, alliances.

To allay Soviet fears, NATO gathered in London during a July summit and approved a declaration proclaiming the Cold War was over. The body also invited the Warsaw Pact nations to assign diplomatic liaisons with NATO and asked the organization to make a similar statement declaring that Cold War tensions had subsided. With these expressions, Germany joining NATO would make no difference. President Bush also pledged to remove nuclear weapons from Europe if the Soviet Union would reciprocate.

Both Gorbachev and Shevardnadze praised the London Declaration and Bush's offer. It became clear to the

Soviets that further delay in allowing Germany to unite and join NATO would only alienate the United States. On July 14, 1990, the Soviet leadership accepted the unification of Germany and its NATO membership. In response to this, West German chancellor Helmut Kohl promised large loans and economic aid to the Soviet Union and funds to assist the removal of Soviet troops.

With the Soviet blessing and agreements among all six nations, the East German parliament set October 3 as the date for the East to join the Federal Republic of West Germany. On September 12, the Four Allied Powers that controlled Germany's destiny since the Potsdam Conference of 1945 relinquished all power and recognized a democratic, independent Germany with the Treaty on the Final Settlement with Respect to Germany. The unification took place as scheduled, and on December 2, 1990, the Germans held their first free election since the 1920s.

✪ Homefront

The Cold War in Film and Literature

The Cold War cost Americans vast amounts of money and countless hours of worry over nuclear annihilation, but it also produced some exciting books and films. The Soviets were bad guys audiences and readers loved to hate. They were smart, crafty, dangerous, exotic—the perfect foe. From the end of World War II until the breakup of the Soviet Union, American and European novelists, screenwriters, and filmmakers created an array of suspenseful spy films, parodies, documentaries, and docudramas based on tension caused by the Cold War.

Superspies British writer Ian Fleming created the quintessential Cold War hero in his secret agent James Bond. Starting in 1953 with the publication of *Casino Royale*, readers thrilled to the adventures of the dashing British spy. Offical film versions of the books followed, starting with 1962's *Dr. No* starring Sean Connery as Bond. Bond's enemies are invariably Soviet spies or those aligned with the Soviets.

American writer Tom Clancy also got a lot of mileage out of Cold War tensions in his spy novels. His fictional hero Jack Ryan (military officer, CIA analyst, president), often faces off with Soviet enemies, notably in the highly successful 1984 novel *The Hunt for Red October*. Espionage thrillers by Robert Ludlum (author of the 1980 novel *The Bourne Identity* and many others) and John le Carré (author of such novels as the 1963 *The Spy Who Came in from the Cold*) also made successful careers spinning tales of the Cold War exploits of their superspy heroes.

Nuclear Annihilation Not all writers focused on the adventure potential of having an adversary as powerful as the Soviet Union. Many writers and filmmakers preferred to dwell on the destructive potential of Cold War ten-

4E1055.06   CARTOON: COLD WAR, 1949.
Credit: The Granger Collection, New York

This Pulitzer Prize–winning cartoon by Rube Goldberg shows the atomic bomb teetering between world peace and world destruction, the dilemma of the cold war. *The Granger Collection, New York. Reproduced by permission*

sions. Australian writer Nevil Shute's 1957 novel *On the Beach* depicts a world slowly dying after an atomic war. Dr. Helen Caldicott's 1982 Academy Award–winning short documentary *If You Love this Planet* also examines the potentially catastrophic effects of nuclear war. The year 1983 saw the release of the popular film *WarGames*, starring a young Matthew Broderick, that featured a supercomputer that almost accidentally starts World War III. The 1984 movie *Red Dawn*, a cult classic starring Patrick Swayze, tells the story of a Soviet invasion of the United States that sparks all-out war between the superpowers.

Some filmmakers managed to find humor in the threat of total nuclear destruction. One of the better-known Cold War–era films is director Stanley Kubric's *Dr. Strangelove* (1964), a black comedy about nuclear war that features British actor Peter Sellers in several different roles. In the movie's unforgettable climactic scene, Air Force Major T. J. "King" Kong (played by Slim Pickens) rides a nuclear bomb falling through the air as if it were a bucking bronco, shouting and waving his arm with gusto as he plunges toward his doom. The scene poked fun at the seemingly cowboy-like enthusiasm American military leaders had for their nuclear weapons.

A generation of schoolchildren practiced "duck and cover" skills in anticipation of a nuclear attack.   © *Bettmann/Corbis*

Television Docudramas Though they made less money than the action movies that pitted a Russian oppressor against an American hero, the docudrama productions that examined the effects of a nuclear attack brought greater attention to potential Cold War results. These movies were less about good and evil or right and wrong; they were more about the harsh realities of an atomic war. The most notable was *The Day After*, which aired on ABC in November 1983. The film was set and filmed mostly in Lawrence, Kansas. The filmmakers chose a mid-American town and followed a handful of fictional families who experienced the devastation of a nuclear attack. Other U.S. films with similar plots and themes in 1983 included *Special Bulletin* and *Testament*. *Testament* showed how a northern California community would have to handle nuclear catastrophe. In *Special Bulletin*, a radical group takes Charleston, South Carolina, hostage and threatens to detonate a nuclear bomb if nuclear weapons in the Charleston area are not immediately disarmed.

The Cold War defined how generations saw the world. Its end was a tremendous relief to both Americans and Russians. But the fading of Cold War animosities has left many fans of spy thrillers and action movies yearning for the "good old days" when our enemy and our enemy's goals were clearly defined.

✪ International Context

U.S. Military Presence Worldwide

When World War II ended, tensions increased between the Soviet Union and its former allies the United States, Great Britain, and France. The world looked on, wondering which nation and ideology would prevail, and what these nations would do to prevent another global catastrophe like World War II. The United States had emerged from the war as a true superpower, and it moved quickly to defend its interests and the interests of its allies around the world.

Atomic Power To end the war in the Asian theater, the United States had dropped atomic bombs on the Japanese cities of Hiroshima and Nagasaki. Historians debate the real motive for that decision, but few can dispute that it sent a message to potential U.S. adversaries: the United States was not to be trifled with. The United States was in exclusive control of a devastating weapon that could kill hundreds of thousands of people and wipe out a nation's infrastructure. After detonating the two weapons that caused Japan to surrender, the U.S. government continued to research and build nuclear weapons.

TIANAMEN SQUARE MASSACRE

In April 1989, several thousand Chinese students and their supporters occupied Tianamen Square in Beijing for several weeks in a peaceful protest for democratic reforms. As the occupation of the square continued through May, millions of citizens joined in the protest. The world watched as the protest took on an almost festival-like atmosphere. Hundreds of students went on a hunger strike to draw increased attention to their demands. Many wondered whether the wave of liberalization sweeping through Eastern Europe could possibly spread to China, whether the Communist regime might finally topple when faced with the people's demands for freedom.

On June 3, such hopes were dashed. Tanks rumbled into Tianamen Square and the army converged on the protestors, shooting at the unarmed protestors. Hundreds of protestors and innocent bystanders were killed. The world expressed outrage at this brutal action by the Chinese government, and Chinese efforts to improve their economic stature and political reputation internationally were severely hampered by the incident.

Protector of Europe, a Presence in Asia As American soldiers began returning home, some remained in the strategic U.S. Army stations and naval bases located throughout the world. To ensure that the defeated Axis powers honored the terms of their surrender, U.S. soldiers and military commanders occupied those nations. The United States occupied Japan until 1952, implementing policies to prevent the return of aggressive imperialism and to rebuild the country's economy. The United States took the same position in Germany, where the Allies from the West came into conflict with the Soviet Union. Ultimately, Germany was divided into two nations: West Germany, under U.S. protection, and East Germany, under Soviet protection. The U.S. military established several bases in West Germany that were key to the security of Western Europe as a whole. The United States built additional bases in other European nations throughout the Cold War era, all with the purpose of protecting its allies from Soviet aggression. In the Pacific region, the navy stayed in the islands of Guam and Midway, and maintained bases in the Philippines, South Vietnam, South Korea, and elsewhere.

The Truman Doctrine While postwar matters were still being settled in 1950, the U.S. National Security Council (NSC)—the president's primary advisory group on security issues—drafted a now famous document named NCS-68. The paper laid out the basic premise that would later form President Harry Truman's so-called Truman Doctrine: that a threat to freedom any-where was a threat to freedom everywhere, and that the advance of Communism must be contained.

The National Security Council was keeping a wary eye on the Soviet Union. They had witnessed the nation take over countries in Eastern Europe, detonate its first atomic bomb, and contribute to the takeover of China by the Chinese Communist Party. The document called for a boost of U.S. conventional forces and an enormous increase in military spending, about 350 percent per year.

Throughout the 1950s, the United States experienced a period of economic growth. Increased tax revenues were put toward Cold War aims. By 1960, defense spending amounted to nearly $50 billion—fifty-two percent of all federal spending and about ten percent of the Gross Domestic Product. By this time, the United States had nearly 1.5 million servicemen stationed around the world and another million in the civilian sector working closely with the military. Major companies like General Dynamics, Lockheed, McDonnell-Douglas, and Newport News Shipping were constructing and selling fighter jets, naval vessels, and other war materiel to the U.S. government. Defense expenditures were also the impetus for many other businesses. America's military-industrial complex, President Eisenhower warned in his farewell speech, had reached such substantial size that citizens should approach this concentration on defense cautiously over the next decades.

Military spending would continue to dominate the federal budget, and the Defense Department would be Washington's biggest employer. Not to be outdone, the Soviet Union, the world's other superpower, also devoted the majority of its resources to its military. In fact, it was the near-ruinous cost of defense spending that likely brought both countries to the conclusion that negotiations to end the arms race were necessary in the 1980s.

✪ Aftermath

China Rises Economically

China traveled down a rocky road during the Cold War, before it reached its current place in the world economy. After Mao Zedong's revolutionary takeover of mainland China in 1949, the People's Republic of China became a Communist nation. The first decades of Communist rule were marked by closed borders, a state-run centralized economy, and human rights abuses. Since the end of the Cold War, China has emerged as an economic power-house with fewer trade restrictions, the Western world as its marketplace, and membership in the World Trade Organization.

The Marxist ideals adopted by Mao in his Great Leap Forward—Communist China's second five-year plan that put rural peasant farmers to work on small industrial projects throughout the country—proved to be faulty. The public works projects that Mao ordered transferred the farmers away from their fields. This and unusually poor weather resulted in famine. It was truly a great leap backward, for it likely killed more than twenty million Chinese and was ridiculed by the Soviets, who by then began distancing themselves from their Marxist neighbor.

Deng Xiaoping and the Four Modernizations China's relations with the United States were strained, to say the least, after the 1949 revolution. No American embassy operated in Beijing, and trade between the two nations did not exist. In 1972, President Richard Nixon made a trip to China that began to mend relations. Mao welcomed him, and that trip was the first step in opening the door again to China. Mao died in the mid-1970s, and after a confusing and unstable transfer of power, Deng Xiaoping became the country's new leader. He began a program called the Four Modernizations that was aimed at enhancing agriculture, industry, science and technology, and defense. His program took China away from the failed central planning of Mao and invited foreign investment. Deng had returned many farmers from the socialist collective to the private farm, which helped increase production. A degree of capitalism had also returned to China.

Deng opened relations in other ways, too. Chinese students were sent abroad to learn advanced skills in science and technology, and foreign scholars were invited to come to China to share ideas. Tourism to China also provided additional revenue. The results over the next years were astounding. In the 1980s, real per capita incomes rose more than twenty-two percent—an unbelievable ninety percent in the countryside.

With Mao gone and Chinese citizens witnessing these improvements, Mao's influence over Chinese life also faded. The United States finished under President Jimmy Carter what Nixon had started. Carter sent his national security advisor, Zbigniew Brzezinski to China with instructions to begin a new phase in Sino-American relations. This trip was motivated not only by economic prospects for both nations, but by the desire to create an alliance against the Soviet Union. The trip was successful, and Carter announced that relations would be normalized on January 1, 1979. Deng visited the United States later that year and traveled abroad to other capitalist countries. Within five years, the United Kingdom agreed to return its colony of Hong Kong to the Chinese in 1997.

In the 1980s and 1990s, China's economy continued to grow, but distrust of Communist ways and a history of human rights abuses allowed only a very slow improvement in China's status on the world stage. By 1993, however, China had reached its pre-1939 share of world trade, and its share of world trade continued to grow after that. Many peasants among the more than one billion citizens had been lifted out of poverty. The raw materials that China needed were arriving from other nations, and Chinese manufactured goods were traveling to overseas markets. The country had even applied to become a member of the World Trade Organization (WTO). But approval of that application took some time; China had to earn the respect of the other member nations. Known for a generation of restricted trade and opposition to capitalism, China had a hard time convincing the WTO it had evolved. And Mao's legacy of inhumane treatment—millions were killed during his reign, and farmers and workers were treated harshly—was regarded as a serious impediment to membership in the WTO. But in December of 2001—after years of application, negotiation, and concessions by the Chinese—China was admitted to the WTO.

BIBLIOGRAPHY

Books

Barson, Michael and Steven Heller. *Red Scared! The Commie Menace in Propaganda and Popular Culture.* San Francisco: Chronicle Books, 2001.

Isaacs, Jeremy, and Taylor Downing. *Cold War: An Illustrated History, 1945–1991.* Boston: Little, Brown and Company, 1998.

Powaski, Ronald E. *The Cold War. The United States and Soviet Union 1917–1991.* New York: Oxford University Press, 1998.

Web Site

Internet Movie Database <http://www.imdb.com> (accessed May 29, 2007).

Introduction to the Vietnam War (1959–1975)

The Vietnam War was a struggle for control of Vietnam, a country in southeast Asia. On one side were the communist forces of North Vietnam, who sought to unite the country under a communist government. On the other side was the democratic government of South Vietnam which, with American military backing, sought to halt the spread of communism in the South. American military involvement lasted from the late 1950s until 1975. By the time it was over, more than one million Vietnamese and nearly sixty thousand Americans were dead, and the North Vietnamese were victorious. The United States—if not precisely the loser, certainly not the victor—was compelled to reexamine not only its commitment to fighting communism but the foundations of its very national identity.

The Vietnamese people had been colonized and suppressed for centuries by larger world powers, including China and France. During World War II, Japan gained control of Vietnam, which had been a French colony. Upon the Japanese surrender, France reasserted control of its colony with American support. But its control was shaky at best.

Likely the most famous Vietnamese figure in history, Ho Chi Minh was a charismatic leader who wanted to return control of Vietnam to the Vietnamese people under a communist form of government. After studying in Paris, he returned to his homeland in 1941. By 1954, Ho had achieved political prominence and sufficient military power to defeat the French at Dien Bien Phu. France relinquished its claims to the territory, and Vietnam was divided at the seventeenth parallel. To the north, Ho Chi Minh established the Democratic Republic of Vietnam, a communist regime; to the south Ngo Dinh Diem headed the anticommunist Republic of Vietnam. Diem was supported by the United States.

Soon, fighters from the North began to invade South Vietnam in an effort to unify the nation under a communist rule. Fearful of another "domino" falling to communism, President Dwight Eisenhower chose to befriend the Diem regime and sent a few hundred military personnel to support him. At first, the American military role was limited to advising and supplying equipment to the South Vietnamese government. By 1962, 11,300 American military personnel were in the region.

In 1964, U.S. and North Vietnamese ships skirmished in the Gulf of Tonkin. Shots were fired, but no one was injured. Still, the U.S. Congress voted unanimously to authorize President Lyndon Johnson to stop further aggression in Southeast Asia. The Gulf of Tonkin Resolution essentially excused the Congress from formally declaring war while it gave Johnson, the commander-in-chief, carte blanche to operate what turned into America's longest war. Within four years, there were well over half a million American troops in Vietnam.

Although initially supportive of a fight against communism, the American public became disillusioned by the bloody, seemingly endless war they saw broadcast into their homes on the news each night. By 1968, anti-war demonstrations were common throughout the country. When Richard Nixon won the presidency in that year, his first order of business was to find a way to end U.S. involvement in Vietnam. He began a military campaign he called Vietnamization—turning over the responsibility of defeating the North Vietnamese to the South Vietnamese Army and withdrawing American troops.

This process brought United States troops home, but the original goals of the Vietnam War were not achieved. Without American support, the South Vietnamese Army lost to the northern communist fighters. By 1975, the last Americans had departed Vietnam, and the entire country, now the Socialist Republic of Vietnam, was united.

Vietnam War (1959–1975)

✪ Causes

Cold War Escalation

The United States became engaged in the Vietnam conflict during the Cold War as part of its commitment to halt the spread of communism. Several presidents and Congress supported American intervention in Vietnam to halt the Communist North and Ho Chi Minh from overtaking the entire country. American support came in the form of economic aid, military supplies, and, eventually, combat troops. The process began when the United States began to assist the French in maintaining Vietnam as a colony and started to wane after American troops pulled out in early 1973. From the initial interest expressed by the United States until the midpoint of the actual war, a gradual and sometimes rapid escalation of American troop presence characterized U.S. involvement.

The United States had been waging the Cold War on several fronts, especially against Communists in Eastern Europe, South America, and now, with Vietnam, in Southeast Asia. Its main adversaries, however, were the Soviet Union and China. The Viet Minh, Ho Chi Minh's Communist force from North Vietnam, was seen as a pawn of the larger Communist forces in Asia. As the United States saw a strengthening of the Vietnamese Communists, it began to aid France in trying to quell this movement.

President Harry Truman announced on May 8, 1950, that the United States would give military and economic aid to the French in the Indochina struggle, starting with a $10 million grant. France wanted American combat troops, but Truman never gave any. At the time of Dwight Eisenhower's inauguration, the U.S. was paying for one-third of the French effort in Indochina. It supplied the French with arms and materiel, and two hundred air force technicians. The United States dramatically increased financial support and military supplies to a total of $119 million by the end of 1951; the United States supplied $815 million during 1954.

By 1954, after a defeat at Dien Bien Phu, the French lost interest in their colony. American policy toward Vietnam focused on preventing a Communist takeover. Vice President Richard Nixon was the first high-level official to pose the question: would the United States take the place of the French in Indochina to prevent the spread of communism? Within two years, 350 American military personnel were sent to Vietnam, assigned to help the Vietnamese fix the equipment the French left behind.

After the Geneva Conference of 1954, which was convened to determine the fate of Vietnam after the French defeat, Vietnam was divided at the seventeenth parallel. The United States supported Ngo Dinh Diem as the leader of South Vietnam. U.S. funds for the Diem regime grew constantly during the late 1950s—a total of $1.8 billion from the time of the Geneva Conference to mid-1959.

As American support for a democratic Vietnam grew, so did the preparation for a military campaign. A federal study group recommended in 1961 a forty-thousand man increase in the South Vietnamese Army and a major deployment of U.S. troops for training purposes. On May 11, President John F. Kennedy added four hundred Special Forces troops to the hundreds of advisors already on their way. At this time he ordered a covert campaign against North Vietnam and agreed to the National Security Council goal, "to prevent Communist domination of Vietnam." The goal had been, "to assist Vietnam to obtain its independence." In December of 1961, the first American helicopters with their crews arrived in South Vietnam. These helicopters mostly took South Vietnamese troops into battle. U.S. Secretary of Defense Robert McNamara sent President Kennedy a memorandum that declared that he and the Joint Chiefs of Staff recommended a plan to give the South Vietnamese effort more support. They felt ground troops would be necessary and this mission would not take more than 205,000 men.

Dedicated in 1982, the Vietnam Veterans Memorial offers an opportunity for Americans to reflect on the legacy of the war. *AP Images*

Diem continued to receive American support and requested the U.S. funds for a 170,000- to 270,000-man increase in his army in June 1961, and a buildup of selected elements of U.S. armed forces. In November 1961, the United States sent 948 advisors and combat support personnel to South Vietnam. By January 1962, over 2,500 were in Vietnam; by June 30, 5,576; by the end of 1962, 11,000; and by October 1963, a total of 16,732 were in country.

During this buildup of American advisors and military personnel, both President Diem and President Kennedy were murdered. Diem had proven unpopular; his coziness with the West was not appreciated by Vietnamese North or South. A coup resulted in his death. Kennedy was shot in Dallas in November 1963, which made Lyndon Johnson the new president. Johnson tackled the issue of Vietnam with force, determined not to allow Vietnam to fall to the Communists. To his ambassador to Vietnam, President Johnson declared, "I am not going to lose Vietnam. I am not going to be the one president who saw Southeast Asia go the way China went."

Johnson approved Operation Plan 34A, which was "an elaborate program of covert military operations against the state of North Vietnam, directly controlled by U.S. military commanders, using Vietnamese and Thai soldiers." By 1964, Johnson could not persuade any NATO (North Atlantic Treaty Organization) countries to join the effort against the Communists in North Vietnam. Several nations sent supplies or relief, but only five nations contributed troops—Australia, New Zealand, the Republic of Korea, Thailand, and the Philippines.

At this point, the Viet Cong (South Vietnamese Communist guerilla forces) was estimated at 170,000 soldiers. America had 23,000 troops in Vietnam, and was poised for war, but not openly committed. After a skirmish between American and North Vietnamese vessels in the Gulf of Tonkin in August of 1964, Congress issued the Gulf of Tonkin Resolution authorizing the president to commit American military troops at his discretion, without a formal declaration of war. Johnson immediately escalated American involvement in Vietnam. On March 8, 1965, the U.S. Ninth Marine Expeditionary Force came ashore at Da Nang. In February 1965, in retaliation against Viet Cong attacks against U.S. stations in the South, Operation Flaming Dart was begun with air strikes by American forces on targets in the North. Operation Rolling Thunder followed. The United States had firmly committed to defending South Vietnam.

✪ Major Figures

Ho Chi Minh

The founder of the Vietnamese Communist Party, Ho Chi Minh (1890–1969) led the movement for Vietnamese independence and served as the president of the Democratic Republic of Vietnam from 1945 to 1969. He also sought unity for the whole of Vietnam under Communist control in the face of French and American interference.

Born Nguyen Sinh Cung (some sources say Nguyen That Thanh) on May 19, 1890, in Kim Lien, Vietnam, Ho was the son of Nguyen Sinh Huy, a civil servant and local government official for the French-controlled government of his country. Ho and his two elder siblings were primarily raised by their father after the death of their mother in childbirth when Ho was ten years old. Even before his mother's death, Ho was involved in anticolonial activities because of his father.

Early Revolutionary Activities Nguyen Sinh Huy came to oppose French interference in Vietnam and ultimately resigned his position in protest. He introduced Ho to revolutionaries and anticolonial groups. By the age of nine, Ho was serving as a messenger for one such group. He continued to be an activist while attending one of the best schools in Vietnam, the National Academy in Hué. Ho was expelled from school in 1908 for participating in protests against the French.

In 1909, Ho went to southern Vietnam. He continued his education there and worked as a teacher in Saigon for a time. By 1911 or 1912, Ho was working as a cook's helper for a French-owned steamship company. He spent two years at sea, traveling the world and picking up a knowledge of languages such as Russian and English. After his tenure aboard the ship ended, Ho lived and worked first in London, then in Paris during World War I.

Emerging Communist While residing in Paris, Ho committed himself to pursuing Vietnamese independence from France. Dubbing himself Nguyen Ai Quoc, which means Nguyen "the Patriot," he tried to present a petition demanding Vietnamese independence at the Versailles Peace Conference at the end of World War I. He then spent three years as the leader of the Vietnamese community living in Paris in the early 1920s, writing pamphlets decrying French control of Indochina. Already committed to communism, Ho also had been a founding member of the French Communist Party in 1920.

Ho was invited to be educated as a revolutionary leader in the Soviet Union. In 1923, he began a two-year stint at the University of Oriental Workers, located in Moscow. Ho then spent time in China organizing a Communist movement there; he also formed a group of Vietnamese students living in Canton, China, into the Thanh Nien, or Vietnamese Revolutionary Youth League,

Ho Chi Minh. *Public Domain*

in 1925. In addition to demanding Vietnamese independence, the organization called for gender equality and land redistribution as well.

Compelled to leave China in 1927 due to a crackdown on Communists, Ho returned in 1930 to reunite the fractionalized Thanh Nien into a Communist party representing all of Indochina. Ho's revolutionary activities with the Indochinese Communist Party (ICP) continued in other cities such as Hong Kong, resulting in his arrest by the British in 1931. After two years in prison, Ho went to the Soviet Union for about seven years.

Leader of Vietnamese Independence Movement After meeting with the ICP upon his return to China in 1940, Ho served as chairman of an ICP Central Committee meeting in Vietnam in May 1941. At the time, France was occupied by the Germans, which gave Japan the opportunity to occupy most of Vietnam and establish several military bases there. The Japanese military occupation of Vietnam lasted until the end of World War II.

In conjunction with ICP, Ho formed the Viet Minh, or League for Vietnamese Independence. Ostensibly non-Communist, the group sought independence for Vietnam from both the French as well as the Japanese occupiers. Ho and his followers hoped to take advantage of the situation in France as well as greater Japanese involvement with the war to gain Vietnam's independence.

In addition to building up an ICP military force, Ho worked to gain support for Viet Minh in countries such as China and the United States. The Viet Minh aided the Americans against the Japanese during the war in hopes of gaining the support of the U.S. government for their cause.

As World War II reached its conclusion, the Viet Minh successfully pushed to take control of most of Vietnam with their August Revolution. Ho was named the president of the new Democratic Republic of Vietnam and on September 2, 1945, formally declared that Vietnam was a free and independent country. Though the French wanted to retake control of Vietnam at war's end, Ho and France agreed in March 1946 to create a free country of Vietnam within the French Union.

By the end of 1946, the French did an about face and decided to hold Vietnam as a colony, in part to enhance its reputation as a leading world power. Vietnamese forces fought French forces in the French Indochina War until the mid-1950s. The French, already drained by World War II, sought an end to the war in 1954. At a peace conference in July 1954, the agreed-upon truce saw Vietnam divided into a Communist North—the Democratic Republic of Vietnam led by Ho—and a non-Communist South—the Republic of South Vietnam. The two halves were to become one country in 1956, at which time free elections were to be held to determine who would run it.

Head of Free Vietnam   While Ho remained in control of North Vietnam, as the Democratic Republic of Vietnam was commonly known, he turned over day-to-day operations to others over the years. Remaining his country's president as well as the head of its Communist party, Ho focused primarily on putting forth Vietnamese interests on the international stage.

Domestically, Ho's actions sometimes failed, as with a mid-1950s land reform campaign that cost thousands of Vietnamese citizens their lives. Other moves had wider implications. When South Vietnam refused to hold the 1956 elections—as the Americans advised for fear the Communists would win—Ho and his fellow leaders were determined to reunite both halves of Vietnam under a Communist government.

Vietnam War   An armed conflict soon broke out between North and South Vietnam. North Vietnam supported the Viet Cong, South Vietnamese Communist rebels who engaged in guerrilla warfare in their country. They soon gained much territory in South Vietnam, and North Vietnamese soldiers soon joined the fight. From the beginning of the conflict, the United States provided money, weapons, and military advisors for South Vietnam. The Cold War compelled the United States to become involved for the sake of preventing the spread of communism and promoting democracy; Ho viewed American involvement in Vietnam as an imperialistic power grab.

As the United States became more deeply involved in the conflict in the early 1960s, Ho turned to the Soviet Union and China for important military support in his cause. However, as the Vietnam War intensified, Ho's health began to fail.

While retaining his titles, Ho gradually made fewer public appearances, had less control of his government, and was essentially a figurehead by the end of the decade. Ho died on September 3, 1969, in Hanoi, after suffering a heart attack. Several years after his death, the Democratic Republic of Vietnam defeated South Vietnam and its American supporters, taking control of the whole country. Because of his importance to Vietnamese history for his leadership in the cause of Vietnamese independence, Saigon, the former capital of South Vietnam, was renamed Ho Chi Minh City in 1975.

Robert McNamara

During the Vietnam War, Robert McNamara (1916–) was the controversial U.S. secretary of defense in the administrations of both President John F. Kennedy and President Lyndon B. Johnson. In fact, Vietnam was sometimes called "McNamara's War," because he took on primary responsibility for developing and managing America's war effort. In addition, he was a successful business executive at Ford Motor Company and later chairperson of the World Bank for thirteen years.

Robert Strange McNamara was born on June 9, 1916, in San Francisco, California. He was the son of Robert James McNamara and his wife, Clara Nell Strange. His father worked as a wholesale shoe company manager and raised his family in Piedmont, California. An outstanding student throughout his childhood, McNamara studied philosophy and economics at the University of California, Berkeley. He graduated in 1937.

Early Business Career   After graduating college, McNamara entered Harvard's business school and earned his MBA in 1939. Returning to California, he then spent a year at Price Waterhouse & Company's San Francisco office. In 1940, McNamara went back to Harvard and worked as an assistant professor of business administration.

Service during World War II   When the United States entered World War II in 1941, McNamara tried to join the navy. Because of his poor eyesight, he was not accepted for active duty, but he did serve in the U.S. Army. While remaining an educator at Harvard for a time, McNamara taught a business class for officers in the United States Army Air Forces (USAAF). He also served as a special consultant for the USAAF.

In 1943, McNamara went on leave from Harvard to focus on his consulting work for the USAAF. Stationed in England as a temporary captain, he used his background in accounting and statistics to aid the B-17 and B-29 bomber programs. McNamara also served in India, China, and the Pacific under the auspices of the USAAF.

Throughout the Vietnam War, Lyndon Johnson met with Secretary of Defense Robert McNamara. *AP Images*

Return to Business World After his war service ended in 1946, McNamara put off plans to return to Harvard in order to join a group of statistical control authorities who had served during the war and were forming a business consulting company. The "Whiz Kids," as they came to be known, wanted to use the skills they developed during the war in corporate America. The nine men who made up the Whiz Kids were hired by the financially strapped Ford Motor Company in 1946.

Because McNamara displayed the most talent of the nine, he quickly rose through Ford's corporate ranks. Moving from the manager of Ford's planning and financial offices to comptroller by 1949, he was named the Ford division's assistant general manager in 1953. McNamara gained more power in 1957 when he was named vice president in charge of all car and truck divisions of Ford. At the same time, he was elected to Ford's board of directors. In November 1960, McNamara was named president of Ford Motor Company, the first person to come from outside the Ford family to hold that position.

Named Secretary of Defense McNamara's time at the top of Ford was short-lived. He served as the company's president for only five weeks when newly elected President John F. Kennedy asked him to become the secretary of defense. With the help of the "Whiz Kids" who came with him from Ford, McNamara used his skills in finance and management to improve the Defense Department by increasing its efficiency and strength.

As defense secretary, McNamara oversaw the reorganization of the Pentagon, closed military bases that were not economical, and consolidated the assistant secretaryships from seven to five. In 1963, he introduced the first five-year projected budget plan in the history of the Pentagon. McNamara also revitalized the conventional military forces and developed many types of deterrent forces while moving away from nuclear arms as the primary deterrent defense of the country.

Oversaw Increased Involvement in Vietnam In addition to using his financial and managerial expertise to improve the operation of the Department of Defense, McNamara also became a top national security and foreign policy advisor to both Kennedy and, later, President Lyndon Johnson. During his time as defense secretary, the U.S. military became more deeply involved in Vietnam, and Vietnam became McNamara's primary focus.

While McNamara publicly supported the controversial war, he was less sure privately. He endorsed President Johnson's decisions to put American combat troops in Vietnam and begin a bombing campaign in early 1965. McNamara also consistently offered optimistic public projections about the war, which he initially believed could be won quickly.

After visiting Saigon in late 1965, however, McNamara began expressing doubts about the war in private, and these sentiments only intensified over time. Doubts tormented him, and he encouraged President Johnson to negotiate peace in 1966. McNamara commissioned a study about American involvement in the conflict in 1967, though he continued to support the war vocally in public. By this time, members of the Johnson administration could see support for McNamara declining, and Johnson planned to replace him.

Became World Bank President Because McNamara became frustrated with American policy in Vietnam, and because the stress of the job was affecting his mental and physical health, he resigned as secretary of defense in February 1968 and was named president of the World Bank. Beginning in 1968, he spent thirteen years improving the international financial body, which lends funds to poor countries for economic, educational, and social programs.

One of McNamara's primary accomplishments as president of the bank was making it the largest and most important source for international development assistance. In 1968, the World Bank was lending about $1 billion per day. In 1980, it was lending $12 billion per day, which was spent on 1,600 projects worth $100 billion in one hundred developing countries. McNamara retired from his position at the World Bank in 1981.

Writer and Lecturer in Retirement In retirement, McNamara remained active on the international stage. Becoming a public speaker and author, he commented on world poverty, development strategies, nuclear policies, and other international issues. McNamara spoke out vehemently against the proliferation of nuclear arms.

Vietnam continued to weigh heavily on McNamara's mind late in his life. He published a book, *In Retrospect: The Tragedy and Lessons of Vietnam*, in 1995. In the text, he admitted he lied to Congress and the public about why the United States became involved in the Vietnam War. McNamara also acknowledged that he did not fully understand Vietnamese and Asian politics and that these mistakes resulted in the loss of life for thousands of American soldiers. The book and McNamara's sentiments therein were regarded as highly controversial.

McNamara continues to revisit the lessons of Vietnam in his writing. He co-authored another book on Vietnam in 1999, *Argument Without End: In Search of Answers to the Vietnam Tragedy*. He was also the focus of a divisive documentary, *The Fog of War*, which was released in 2003. In the film, McNamara talks directly to the camera about the whole of his life, his place in history, and most importantly, what happened in Vietnam.

Le Duc Tho

A leader of the Democratic Republic of Vietnam (DRV) as well as a founder of the Indochinese Communist Party,

Le Duc Tho (1911–1990) played a significant role in conducting the war against South Vietnam. He also was North Vietnam's primary negotiator with the United States in peace talks. For crafting a peace treaty with American negotiator Henry Kissinger that brought an end to the war in 1973, Tho and Kissinger were jointly awarded the 1973 Nobel Peace Prize.

Born Phan Dinh Khai on October 14, 1911, in the village of Dich Le in the Nam Ha Province, Tho was the son of a civil servant in the French colonial government then ruling Vietnam. The family was most likely upper middle-class, though some sources state that they were peasants. He received his education in French schools.

Anti-French Activist As a young adult, Tho joined the burgeoning Vietnamese revolt against the French overlords and organized demonstrations against the French. In 1929, he was one of the founders of the Indochinese Communist Party, aiding its leader Ho Chi Minh. Tho was often jailed for starting antigovernment riots and other disturbances. In 1930, he was imprisoned by the French on their island prison at Poulo Condore and spent six years doing hard labor. Arrested again in 1939 on similar charges, Tho then spent time in the Son La prison camp.

Soon after his release from the camp, Tho lived primarily in the southern part of Vietnam, where he was a Communist party executive. During World War II, Vietnam was occupied by the Japanese, and Tho played a significant role in organizing resistance to the occupiers. After the war's end, France reclaimed Vietnam as its colony, though the Vietnamese wanted their independence. This struggle led to the First Indochinese War. Tho emerged as a leader of the Vietnamese Communist Party, serving as its chief commissar during the conflict.

Chief Communist Negotiator When the Americans became involved in the Second Indochinese War, commonly known as the Vietnam War, Tho was a primary player in directing the war against South Vietnam. His role for the DRV early in the conflict is unclear. Some believe that he might have played a supervisory role over the actions of the Viet Cong (South Vietnamese Communist guerilla forces) from a secret base in the jungle of South Vietnam, perhaps in the late 1950s or early 1960s.

Better known are Tho's activities in the late 1960s. Beginning in May 1968, Tho was the "special advisor" to North Vietnamese chief negotiator Xuan Thuy in the Paris-based peace talks with the Americans. It was soon clear that Tho held real power and eventually became the primary representative for the DRV. Opposite American chief negotiator Kissinger, Tho proved to be a serious opponent who would not compromise on certain points.

After a tough five years of negotiations—some held in secret because of a lack of progress and public pressure in the United States for an end to the conflict—an agreement was finally reached in January 1973 to end the American military presence in Vietnam. The treaty also called for a cease-fire and acknowledgement of General Nguyen Van Thieu as the president of South Vietnam until Vietnam-wide elections could be held to form a new government. However, some North Vietnamese troops were allowed to remain in South Vietnam while the Americans evacuated. The peace was short-lived, and fighting soon resumed between Communist and non-Communist forces in Vietnam.

Refused Nobel Prize   Though Tho and Kissinger, the chief American negotiator, were honored with the 1973 Nobel Peace Prize for their efforts to end the fighting in Vietnam, Tho refused to accept it. His refusal stemmed from the fact that the war with South Vietnam was continuing, though the Americans no longer played any role of significance. Tho supported the ongoing attacks by the North Vietnamese on South Vietnam.

After leaving Paris in 1973, Tho became the second highest ranking leader in the Communist Party and served as Le Duan's (leader of North Vietnam) senior advisor. Tho also was influential in the DRV's ongoing effort to gain control over the whole of Vietnam. Under his leadership, the final push came when the Communist forces took Saigon in 1975, after which Vietnam became one country again. Tho also might have had a part in the Vietnamese invasion of Cambodia in 1978.

After victory was achieved, Tho continued to be an active member of the Vietnamese Communist Party and its Central Committee. He also was the director of the Party Organization Department for Vietnam. Resigning from the party in 1986 after a power struggle caused by conflict over economic reforms, Tho retired to private life. He died of throat cancer on October 13, 1990, in Hanoi, Vietnam.

Robert F. Kennedy

During his 1968 presidential campaign, Democratic candidate Robert F. Kennedy (1925–1968) spoke out against President Lyndon B. Johnson's policies in Vietnam. Kennedy was a senator at the time and had previously held the position of attorney general during the presidency of his brother, John F. Kennedy. Robert Kennedy was assassinated in 1968 shortly after winning the California primary.

Born Robert Francis Kennedy on November 20, 1925, in Brookline, Massachusetts, he was the seventh of the nine children of Joseph Patrick Kennedy, Sr., and his wife Rose Fitzgerald Kennedy. Kennedy's father was a business executive who had served as the U.S. ambassador to Great Britain during the 1930s. He harbored grand political ambitions for his family that were realized by his brother John (who served as president), himself, and his younger brother Edward (longtime U.S. senator).

Educated at Harvard   Despite being overshadowed by his older brother, Kennedy developed a competitive and ambitious nature. After graduating from Milton

Academy, Kennedy entered Harvard in 1944. Kennedy's eldest brother, Joseph, served in the American military during World War II. After Joseph Kennedy was killed in combat, Kennedy left school and joined the U.S. Navy as a lieutenant. He remained in the service until the end of the war.

Kennedy went back to Harvard in 1946. He completed his bachelor's degree in 1948. Kennedy then entered the University of Virginia Law School. After earning his law degree, he went back to Massachusetts and was admitted to that state's bar in 1951.

Federal Law Career   That same year, Kennedy joined the U.S. Department of Justice's Criminal Division. He stepped down in 1952 to run his brother John's campaign for U.S. senator. His brother won the office. In 1953, Kennedy briefly worked as an assistant counsel for Senator Joseph McCarthy's permanent Senate subcommittee on investigations. While Kennedy was anti-Communist, he resigned when Democratic members of the subcommittee walked out in protest against McCarthy's bullying tactics in investigating alleged Communists.

In 1954, Kennedy rejoined the subcommittee as chief counsel for the Democratic minority. When the subcommittee was reorganized in 1955 under Senator John L. McClellan, Kennedy was named chief counsel and director of staff. Kennedy was gaining national prominence as an emerging leader.

Kennedy took on a new post in 1957. He became the chief counsel of the Senate Select Committee on Improper Activities in the Labor or Management Field, which was known as the "Rackets" Committee. The committee was chaired by Senator McClellan, and Kennedy oversaw a staff of sixty-five. Kennedy also gained media attention for his inquiries into labor and management abuses. One of his best known investigations dealt with corruption in the International Brotherhood of Teamsters, especially by the union's president, James Hoffa. Kennedy exposed the vast amount of criminal activities taking place within the union.

Kennedy as Attorney General   In 1960, Kennedy served as the campaign manager for his brother John's presidential run. When John F. Kennedy won the presidency and took office in early 1961, he appointed Robert to be the U.S. attorney general. Though many Americans believed the younger Kennedy's appointment smacked of nepotism, the president relied heavily on his brother, who was his chief advisor on all issues. Robert Kennedy came to be seen as something of an assistant president.

Kennedy supported his brother's actions during the Cuban Missile Crisis and in events related to the emerging civil rights movement. He also backed the president' decisions in the burgeoning Vietnam conflict, which included sending large amounts of financial aid, military advisors, and public officials to South Vietnam. Kennedy

Robert Kennedy grew increasingly critical of the war in Vietnam. Here he speaks on the radio-television program *Face the Nation.*   *National Archives and Records Administration*

was also an effective attorney general. In addition to using the office to protect civil rights activists, he conducted numerous investigations into organized crime groups.

U.S. Senator   In November 1963, President Kennedy was assassinated in Dallas, Texas, and Vice President Lyndon B. Johnson assumed the presidency. Kennedy remained attorney general under Johnson until September 1964. He resigned to seek a seat in the U.S. Senate representing New York and won the office with ease.

Already planning a run for president, Kennedy proved himself an outstanding liberal senator with an exceptional record. As senator, he continued to support civil rights as well as other issues related to discrimination and poverty in America. Kennedy also took on causes related to migrant farm workers and Native Americans.

In addition, Kennedy began speaking out against Johnson's policy in Vietnam in 1966. Much of his criticism was directed against the escalation of American involvement to include ground troops, bombings, and more money and weapons. Kennedy saw that such actions related to the war were creating deep divisions in American society. The senator voiced doubts about the South Vietnamese political leadership being propped up by the United States as well.

Running for President   In early 1968, Kennedy declared he was running for the Democratic presidential nomination after Johnson decided against seeking a second full term. Like fellow Democratic candidate Eugene McCarthy, Kennedy spoke out against President Johnson's policies in Vietnam and was popular among antiwar activists. He also gained the support of many African Americans because of his support of the civil rights movement. In addition, many young Americans and

Senator Eugene McCarthy's 1968 presidential campaign was not ultimately successful but it inspired, focused, and legitimized antiwar activism. *Lee Balterman/Time Life Pictures/Getty Images*

working-class Catholics backed Kennedy's campaign. Among his campaign promises was a vow to end American involvement in Vietnam.

After winning the California primary in the spring of 1968, Kennedy was shot by an assassin at a Los Angeles hotel. He died of his wounds a day later, on June 6, 1968, and was buried in Arlington National Cemetery. He was survived by his wife Ethel and their eleven children, one of whom was born after his death.

Eugene J. McCarthy

An outspoken opponent of American involvement in the Vietnam War, Eugene J. McCarthy (1916–2005) was a U.S. senator when he tried to force a public debate on Vietnam in 1967 by announcing his intention to seek the 1968 Democratic presidential nomination. McCarthy's actions helped compel President Lyndon B. Johnson to opt not to seek reelection that year. McCarthy also had a secondary career as an author.

Born Eugene Joseph McCarthy on March 29, 1916, in Watkins, Minnesota, he was the son of a farmer,

Michael J. McCarthy, and his wife, Anna Baden McCarthy. The family was devoutly Roman Catholic, and McCarthy attended the Catholic St. John's University for his undergraduate education. Completing his B.A. in 1935, he then earned his master's degree from the University of Minnesota in 1939.

While attending graduate school, McCarthy was employed as a public school educator teaching social sciences. In 1940, he went back to St. John's to work as economics and education instructor for several years before serving in military intelligence as a civilian technical assistant during World War II. In 1946, McCarthy took a position at St. Thomas College to teach economics and sociology. He remained at St. Thomas until 1949.

Political Life By this time, McCarthy had already launched a career in politics. In 1947, he served as an organizer of the newly merged Democratic-Farmer-Labor Party. McCarthy then ran for a seat in the U.S. House of Representatives representing the Fourth Congressional District. He won by 25,000 votes, despite being a liberal in a traditionally Republican district.

McCarthy spent the next ten years in the House and built a reputation as a strong liberal and internationalist. He hoped to influence the House so that liberal bills could be passed, and he often worked to limit the Central Intelligence Agency's activities. One highlight of his decade in the House was his challenge to the Communist-hunting activities of powerful U.S. Senator Joseph R. McCarthy. Representative McCarthy debated Senator McCarthy on national television in 1952, an act considered extremely brave given the senator's fearsome reputation.

Elected to U.S. Senate Realizing the limits of the House, McCarthy ran for a seat in the U.S. Senate in 1958 and won. During his first term, he emerged as a unique force in the Senate, because he was more concerned with the overall quality and focus of policy rather than drawing up bills or the extensive work of committees. However, McCarthy did chair the Special Committee on Unemployment, which sought to understand the causes of unemployment and lessen its effects.

Nearly selected as Johnson's vice-presidential running mate in 1964, McCarthy instead remained in the U.S. Senate for a second term. He came to national attention early in his second term as a critic of Johnson's foreign policies. One of his first targets was American involvement in the Dominican Republic in 1965 (the United States had invaded the politically unstable Dominican Republic to protect its interests).

Vocal Vietnam War Critic As President Johnson escalated American involvement in Vietnam in the mid-1960s, McCarthy initially accepted the administration's positions as a member of the Senate Foreign Relations Committee. McCarthy supported the 1964 Gulf of

Tonkin Resolution. He also backed Johnson's decision to authorize the sending of American ground troops to Vietnam as well as extensive bombing of the enemy in early 1965.

By 1966, the senator came to believe that the Vietnam War was unwinnable and peace would only come via a political deal with the Viet Cong (South Vietnamese Communist guerilla forces). McCarthy then spoke out against American involvement in the war at every turn, and he supported a 1966 measure that called for the repeal of the Gulf of Tonkin Resolution. Because his protests did not affect the Johnson administration's policies, McCarthy announced his intention to seek the Democratic nomination for president on November 30, 1967.

McCarthy won several primaries in early 1968 and found widespread support for his positions on the war. On March 31, Johnson announced he would not seek reelection so he could focus on solutions for Vietnam without the burden of a political campaign. McCarthy gained support but lost the nomination to Hubert Humphrey at the Democratic National Convention. McCarthy did not announce his support for the rival candidate until late in Humphrey's presidential campaign.

Post-Senate Activities   After Republican Richard M. Nixon won the White House in 1968, McCarthy announced that he would not seek reelection to Senate after his term expired in 1970. McCarthy then focused much of his time on publishing books of political commentary. He had published his first work in 1960, *Frontiers in American Democracy*. McCarthy continued to write books and articles regularly throughout the 1960s until his death. He also branched out into other genres, including children's books, such as *Mr. Raccoon and His Friends* (1977), and poetry, including *Ground Fog and Night* (1979).

Politics remained alluring to McCarthy, who sought the presidency again in 1972 and 1976. In the latter campaign, he ran as an independent candidate. By 1980, McCarthy was endorsing Republican Ronald Reagan for the presidency. In 1982, he ran again for his former seat in the U.S. Senate, but was defeated. McCarthy ran for president as a third-party candidate for the Consumers Party in 1988, but his campaign was limited.

McCarthy published his last book in January 2005, *Parting Shots From My Brittle Bow: Reflections on American Politics and Life*. The book was a collection of essays and poems. McCarthy spent the last years of his life in an assisted living facility in Washington, D.C., where he died in his sleep on December 10, 2005.

Henry Kissinger

During the administrations of presidents Richard M. Nixon and Gerald Ford, Henry Kissinger (1923–) served as the National Security Council chief, secretary of state, and chief foreign policy advisor overseeing the end of

As secretary of state, Henry Kissinger represented the United States at the 1973 Paris Peace Accords.   *AP Images*

American involvement in the Vietnam War. Because of his efforts at achieving a Vietnam solution, Kissinger was the co-winner of the 1973 Nobel Peace Prize with Le Duc Tho. Kissinger's actions as secretary of state were often controversial, and he was often criticized for his handling of American foreign policy.

Born Heinz Alfred Kissinger on May 27, 1923, in Furth, Germany, he was the son of Louis and Paula Stern Kissinger. His father was a teacher, but lost his position when the Nazis came to power, because the Kissingers were Jewish. The family, which included Kissinger's younger brother Walter, moved to England from Germany in 1938. After a few months, the Kissingers left London for the United States.

Settling in New York City, Kissinger attended high school for a year. Because of the family's financial needs, he then began working at a factory during the day and attending night school. He completed high school and then began studying accounting at the City College of New York. After the United States entered World War II, Kissinger was drafted into the U.S. Army and was stationed in Germany. There, he primarily served in Army Intelligence and worked as an interpreter for a general. Kissinger continued to work in intelligence after the war ended by spending 1946 as a civilian instructor at the Germany-based European Command Intelligence School.

Work in Academia After returning to the United States in 1947, Kissinger entered Harvard University. Earning his bachelor's degree *summa cum laude* in 1950, he went on to earn two graduate degrees at Harvard as well, a master's degree in 1952 and a Ph.D. in 1954. While completing his Ph.D., Kissinger began serving as the director for the annual summer Harvard International Seminar. He continued in this capacity until he joined the Nixon administration in 1969. Kissinger also wrote *Nuclear Weapons and Foreign Policy*, which offered his thoughts on how the United States should deal with the Soviet Union. This widely read book was published in 1957 and was created for the Council on Foreign Relations, for which he had worked for some time.

While holding other posts, Kissinger also was employed at Harvard in a teaching capacity. He became a lecturer in 1957, and by 1962 held a full professorship at his alma mater. In addition to his academic career, Kissinger also helmed an eighteen-month special studies project of the Rockefeller Brothers Fund. Kissinger also served as a consultant to several government agencies and the Rand Corporation in the 1960s, and was an informal advisor to several U.S. presidents.

By 1965, Kissinger had stepped back from working as a full-time professor at Harvard and focused much of his time on his consulting activities. That year, he became a consultant on Vietnam for the U.S. State Department and visited the country several times between 1965 and 1967. In 1968, he also aided early negotiations between the administration of President Lyndon Johnson and North Vietnam, but Kissinger's demands for both a Communist and American withdrawal from South Vietnam led to a quick end to the process. That same year, Kissinger also entered the political arena by working on Nelson Rockefeller's bid for the Republican nomination.

Nixon's Foreign Policy Advisor When Rockefeller lost the nomination to Richard M. Nixon, Rockefeller urged Nixon to consider giving a position to Kissinger. Nixon named Kissinger the head of the National Security Council during his first term in office. In this post, Kissinger acted as national security advisor and had a number of successes, primarily in dealings with the Soviet Union. He implemented the policy of détente (French for "easing") to relax relations with the Soviet Union and completed the negotiations that resulted in the signing of the Strategic Arms Limitations Treaty (SALT) with the Soviet Union in the early 1970s.

Kissinger helped the United States make progress in China as well. Though the United States had not yet recognized the Communist-controlled People's Republic of China, contact was made early in Nixon's first term. More secret communication was facilitated by the president of Pakistan, resulting in multiple visits by Kissinger to China. President Nixon himself went to China a short time later on an official state visit. The 1972 Shanghai Communiqué outlined how American-Chinese relations would be established.

End to Vietnam War The most controversial element of Kissinger's foreign policy concerned Vietnam. Though he desired a peaceful yet honorable end to the war, he also wanted to negotiate from a position of strength. To that end, Kissinger supported covert U.S. operations in Cambodia and Laos (countries neighboring Vietnam), as well as other demonstrations of military might, to compel the Viet Cong (South Vietnamese Communist guerilla forces) and North Vietnamese to stop the war. He also hoped to ensure that not all the Indochinese countries would become communist.

Kissinger began negotiating secretly with Tho in 1969, but talks made little progress over two years. In the early 1970s, however, both the Soviet Union and China cut the amount of financial aid given to the North Vietnamese. This situation contributed to more success in negotiations. While a treaty was reached between Kissinger and Tho in October 1972, Nguyen Van Thieu, the president of South Vietnam, did not support it. The United States stepped up bombings over North Vietnam to force the resumption of peace talks.

By January 1973, Kissinger was able to broker a truce with North Vietnamese leader Le Duc Tho in Paris, France. Though the South Vietnamese did not support the treaty or its contents, Kissinger and Tho were awarded the 1973 Nobel Peace Prize for their effort. Nevertheless, Kissinger was also roundly criticized for his handling of Vietnam, especially his endorsement of what some believed to be excessive use of military might. Kissinger was also criticized because the war did not end with the treaty he had crafted and North Vietnam eventually took over South Vietnam in 1975.

Named Secretary of State After Nixon won reelection in 1972, Kissinger took a new post and retained it even after Gerald Ford succeeded Nixon. As Secretary of State, Kissinger played an active role in the Middle East and tried to help restore peace to the region by facilitating negotiations between the various countries. He made eleven trips to the area in this capacity. Kissinger also remained interested in the situation in Vietnam, but could not convince Ford or Congress to send troops back there in support of the South Vietnamese.

Return to Consulting Following Ford's defeat in the 1976 presidential election by Jimmy Carter, Kissinger left office and founded his own consulting firm. Serving as the director of Kissinger Associates, he and his colleagues provided international political assessments for a variety of clients. Most of his work was done for businesses. When Republicans were in the White House,

Kissinger sometimes served as an advisor. During the presidency of Ronald Reagan, for example, Kissinger advised him on U.S. policy in the Middle East. Kissinger also served President George H.W. Bush in an informal advisory capacity.

Kissinger also wrote several books about his service in the Nixon and Ford administrations. They include *The White House Years* (1979), *Years of Upheaval* (1982), and *The Anatomy of Two Major Foreign Policy Crises* (2003). In addition, he became a professor at George-town University and was a popular lecturer.

William Westmoreland

During the Vietnam War, General William Westmoreland (1914–2005) served as the commander of all American forces from 1964 until 1968. He was removed from his post because of mounting criticism over his handling of the American effort as well as decreasing support for American involvement in the conflict. Until his death, Westmoreland believed that a strong American military buildup would have resulted in a victory in Vietnam.

William Westmoreland was born on March 26, 1914, in Spartanburg, South Carolina. His father managed a textile plant before becoming a banker. From an early age, Westmoreland embraced leadership roles and enjoyed the Boy Scouts. He served as a patrol leader of his scout troop as well as president of his senior class. Westmoreland chose the military as a career before leaving high school.

Early Military Career Westmoreland first attended the Citadel, an acclaimed military college, for a year, then gained an appointment to West Point, where he was first captain in his class. After graduating in 1936, he worked in field artillery in the United States Army. Westmoreland's first posts were in Oklahoma and Hawaii, after which he was transferred to the infantry division of Fort Bragg, North Carolina. There, he was promoted to major and put in charge of the Thirty-fourth Field Artillery Battalion.

During World War II, Westmoreland served in several positions of significance. He was an executive officer of the Ninth Division Artillery in France as well as a colonel in a Germany-based division. Promotions continued during the Korean War, where he served as the commander of the paratroopers who made up the 187th Airborne Combat Team. Serving in the Pentagon after the end of the Korean War, Westmoreland was promoted to brigadier general.

Vietnam By the mid-1950s, the United States was providing financial support and military advisors for the non-Communist half of the country. Communist North Vietnam, led by Ho Chi Minh, supported guerilla attacks against the South Vietnamese government by the Viet Cong (South Vietnamese Communist guerilla forces). The conflict soon broke out into an all-out war. Though Westmoreland became the superintendent of

West Point in 1960, he shared President John F. Kennedy's belief that the United States should expand its military presence in South Vietnam to prevent a Communist takeover, which could lead to a further expansion of communism in Southeast Asia.

By December 1963, Westmoreland was serving as the commander of the Eighteenth Airborne Corps and stationed in Vietnam. Though the United States was still providing only military advice to the South Vietnamese, Westmoreland and other generals were able to convince President Lyndon B. Johnson to increase the role of the American armed services there. Beginning in 1964, the United States joined the Vietnam conflict with combat troops, limited bombings of key targets in North Vietnam, and naval operations. While there was some controversy surrounding this shift in policy, most Americans believed in the cause.

Head of U.S. Forces in South Vietnam For the next four years, Westmoreland, by now a full general, served as the head of American forces in Vietnam as they fought the Viet Cong who engaged in both guerilla warfare as well as larger conventional attacks. By 1965, the North Vietnamese Army became more directly involved in the battle against South Vietnamese and American troops. Westmoreland did not control the bombings or the overall American strategy in the war, but directed American operations in South Vietnam. He saw his primary role as attacking the North Vietnamese Army and their bases, while secondarily helping to pacify and provide security for the South Vietnamese.

Westmoreland's actions during his four years in charge of American troops in South Vietnam were regularly criticized by the press. He believed that the conflict in Vietnam was a war of attrition (a war won by wearing one's enemy down over time) that would take years to win, and that U.S. forces never lost a battle of significance during the whole war. The American public saw the situation differently. For example, Westmoreland believed the February 1968 Tet Offensive by the Viet Cong resulted in a victory for the United States and South Vietnam. Many Americans, however, saw only that the North Vietnamese were much stronger than they had imagined and became convinced the war was unwinnable.

Removed from Post Facing intense pressure from the American public, President Johnson decided to begin removing American troops from the conflict and begin negotiations with the North Vietnamese. In July 1968, Westmoreland was removed from his post. He returned to Washington to become the U.S. Army's chief of staff, where it was his job to organize the removal of American forces from Vietnam and return the army to an all-volunteer force. Though he was roundly criticized, and often heckled, by people opposed to the war and the military, Westmoreland gave many public speeches in support of the army and the necessary transition ahead of it.

After retiring on June 30, 1972, Westmoreland returned to South Carolina, where he remained a controversial figure. He made a run for the Republican nomination for his state's governorship in 1974, but was defeated in the primary. Westmoreland remained critical of the United States' withdrawal from Vietnam as well as the government's Vietnam policy, outlining his opinions in his 1976 memoir, *A Soldier Reports.*

Libel Suit Westmoreland's actions in Vietnam haunted him for the rest of his life. On January 23, 1982, CBS aired a documentary entitled *The Uncounted Enemy: A Vietnam Deception*, which claimed that Westmoreland was involved in a cover-up that muffled or garbled American intelligence gathered about North Vietnam. Several months later, Westmoreland filed a $120 million lawsuit against the network, denying the charges and demanding an apology. Three years later, the suit was settled out of court, with CBS acknowledging some fault in the matter.

Living quietly for the rest of his life, Westmoreland died on July 18, 2005, at a retirement home in Charleston, South Carolina. He was ninety-one years old.

Nguyen Cao Ky

During the Vietnam War, Nguyen Cao Ky (1930–) was a distinguished pilot in the South Vietnamese Air Force who also played a significant role in the power politics of South Vietnam (also known as the Republic of Vietnam) during the 1960s. He helped oust Duong Van Minh (South Vietnamese leader who had seized power in a 1963 coup) in 1964, then served as prime minister and vice president himself before fading from the South Vietnamese political scene in the early 1970s.

Ky was born on September 8, 1930, in the Son Tay Province of Vietnam, the son of a teacher. After graduating from a high school in Hanoi in 1948, Ky entered a French military academy located in the northern part of Vietnam. He began his career in the military when he was drafted into the Vietnamese National Army in 1950. Ky reached the rank of lieutenant in three years.

Trained as a Pilot In 1951, Ky volunteered to be trained as a pilot with the French Air Force. He received his training in Algeria, another French colony, and France. Ky then flew practice missions in Algeria, France, and Morocco. He completed his training in 1954 and returned to Vietnam.

By the time Ky came back to Vietnam, the French Indochina War was ending. The Geneva Accords, which ended the war, divided Vietnam into two countries: a Communist-controlled North Vietnam (also known as the Democratic Republic of Vietnam) and non-Communist South Vietnam, supported by the United States and helmed by Ngo Dinh Diem. Ky chose to live in South Vietnam and joined the South Vietnamese Air Force.

Military Pilot for South Vietnam On advice from the United States, Diem refused to hold the general elections mandated by the 1954 Geneva Accords because of fears the Communists would win total control of Vietnam. Ky went to the United States that year to receive additional fighter pilot training necessary for the forthcoming war with Communist forces. He served with distinction in the South Vietnamese Air Force as the conflict between North and South Vietnam heated up, eventually reaching the rank of lieutenant general.

As part of his service, Ky began flying secret missions for the CIA (Central Intelligence Agency) in 1960. Using South Vietnamese military planes, Ky and other fighter pilots flew over North Vietnam, dropping guerrilla soldiers and experts in sabotage by parachute. These missions were intended to cut off the Communist-supported Viet Cong guerillas operating in South Vietnam from their leadership in the North.

Involved with Coups After unpopular South Vietnamese leader Diem was murdered in a coup in 1963, the political situation in South Vietnam grew more unstable with regular power shifts. In 1964, Ky himself was part of the coup which removed Duong Van Minh from power and replaced him with General Nguyen Khanh. For his assistance in the coup, Ky was named head of the South Vietnamese Air Force by Khanh.

Ky soon developed a celebrity status as a pilot and leader among younger South Vietnamese military officers. As head of the air force, he made changes to increase the effectiveness of the service. Soon after the United States began sending combat troops to South Vietnam to support their cause in 1965, Ky, with the help of Generals Nguyen Van Thieu and Nguyen Huu Co, overthrew the government in power and created a new government.

Becoming Prime Minister The three generals formed the National Leadership Committee. With the support of the Americans, Ky began his own two-year stint as the prime minister of South Vietnam. He was the youngest person to hold that post in Vietnamese history.

When Ky took over, he said he wanted to run a government that was both stable and democratic. He hoped to restore order as well as confidence in the government to further the war effort. To that end, Ky made positive changes in the South Vietnamese military and threw corrupt government officials out of office. He also began programs of land reform and built much-needed hospitals and schools.

Ky's time in office ultimately proved controversial, however. Like Diem before him, Ky ordered action against and repression of Buddhists. Ky believed they were allies of the Communists attacking South Vietnam because they disagreed with his politics. He participated in such actions himself by leading two battalions of the South Vietnamese Army against what he believed were

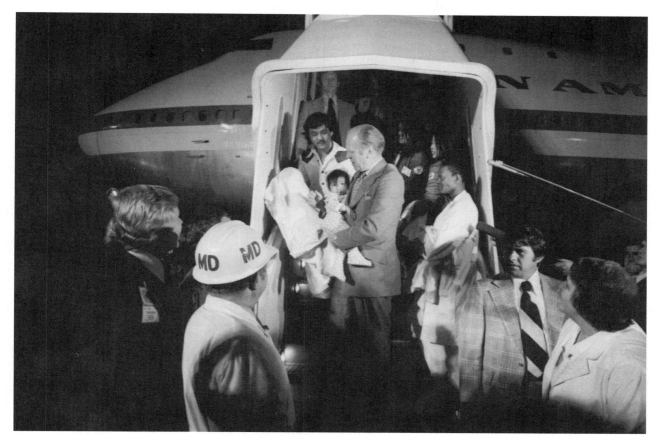

President Gerald Ford carries a baby from Clipper 1742, the plane that transported Vietnamese orphans from Saigon to the United States.   *Courtesy, Gerald R. Ford Library*

Buddhist bases of operation in Da Nang and Hué in 1966. Such moves lost Ky significant support at home and abroad, and it was believed he would not have his office without American backing.

Loss of Power   Ky held a presidential election in 1967 in an effort to legitimatize the South Vietnamese government. Ky initially ran against General Thieu for the presidency. Because of pressure from military leaders who saw his reputation as damaged, Ky ran as Thieu's vice president instead. These same military leaders rigged the elections, and Thieu and Ky won their respective offices. Their relationship was tense, however.

When elections were held again in 1971, Thieu would not permit Ky to run for the presidency. Ky left politics and again became the leader of the South Vietnamese Air Force. He continued to criticize Thieu's government through 1975, when North Vietnam won battles that gave it control over more and more of South Vietnam. Though Ky publicly stated in April 1975 he would not leave Vietnam, he left on an American military helicopter after the fall of Saigon.

At Home in America   Living in the United States with his wife and six children, Ky settled in Los Angeles,

California, where he operated a liquor store. Forced to file for bankruptcy in 1985 because of unpaid business loans and debts from gambling, he eventually wrote his autobiography, with Marvin J. Wolf, entitled *Buddha's Child: My Fight to Save Vietnam*. After its publication in 2002, Ky made a trip back to Vietnam in 2004 as part of President George W. Bush's efforts to improve relations with that country.

Gerald R. Ford

An unexpected president, Gerald R. Ford (1913–2006) took office on August 9, 1974, after the resignation of Richard M. Nixon. The only president to never be elected to the office or the vice presidency, Ford oversaw the United States' withdrawal from Vietnam and the end of American involvement in the conflict.

Ford was born Leslie King, Jr., on July 14, 1913, in Omaha, Nebraska. The son of Leslie King, Sr., and his wife Dorothy, his parents divorced when he was two years old. His mother took her son to Grand Rapids, Michigan, where she married Gerald R. Ford. Her new husband adopted her young son, and he was renamed Gerald R. Ford, Jr. Ford's adoptive father worked as a paint and varnish salesman with a successful business that withstood the Great Depression. The elder Ford instilled values of honesty and hard work in his son.

Athlete to Lawyer Throughout his childhood, Ford was an outstanding athlete. He played football at the University of Michigan while an undergraduate studying economics. In 1934, Ford, the team's center, was voted Michigan's most valuable player. After graduating from the university in 1935, he went to New Haven, Connecticut, to work as an assistant football coach for Yale. Two years later, Ford entered Yale Law School, while he continued to work as an assistant coach to support himself.

Completing his law degree in the top quarter of his class in 1941, Ford returned to Grand Rapids and opened his own legal practice. As the United States entered World War II a few months later, Ford resigned and enlisted in the U.S. Navy as an ensign. He spent forty-seven months in the service. When his tour of duty was completed, Ford again went back to Grand Rapids to resume his legal career.

Political Career In 1948, Ford began his political career by running for a seat in the House of Representatives, representing the fifth district in Michigan. Defeating the Republican incumbent in the primary, Ford won the seat and soon was known for his outstanding work ethic. Ford remained in the House for several decades and worked well with all members of his party as well as Democrats. He eventually served on the Warren Commission, which examined circumstances surrounding the assassination of President John F. Kennedy.

Because of his unblemished reputation, Ford was asked to join the Republican ticket as vice president in 1964. Ford declined, and in 1965, became the minority leader in the House. Critical of President Lyndon B. Johnson's policies in Vietnam, Ford believed that an all-out air and naval assault by the Americans would result in victory. In 1968, he served as the Republican National Convention's chairman. As a Republican candidate, Richard M. Nixon, won the White House that year; Ford worked with him during his first term, though he disagreed with some of Nixon's policies.

The Vice Presidency After Nixon and Vice President Spiro Agnew overwhelmingly won re-election in 1972, Ford was considering the end of his political career as the Democrats continued to retain control of Congress. When the Watergate scandal came to light early in Nixon-Agnew's second term (the Watergate scandal involved criminal activities within the Nixon administration), Agnew's previous improprieties also became known, and he faced prison time for racketeering and bribery. A deal was arranged that involved Agnew resigning in exchange for the dismissal of most criminal charges.

Under the Twenty-fifth Amendment to the Constitution, Nixon could appoint a replacement vice president with approval by Congress. Because Ford had the trust and respect both of Democrats and Republicans, Nixon appointed Ford to replace Agnew in 1973. As vice president, Ford kept his distance from the growing scandal surrounding President Nixon.

Became President In 1974, Watergate engulfed the president, and Nixon resigned. Ford became the first president in the history of the United States to be elected to neither the presidency nor the vice presidency. As president, Ford demonstrated his trademark modesty. Though the public initially embraced him, Ford soon lost much of their support.

On September 8, 1974, Ford pardoned Nixon for any crimes he committed while in office. Ford believed that the pardon was in the nation's best interest, but his action was viewed with disgust and suspicion by many Americans, whose confidence in their leaders had been profoundly undermined by the Watergate scandal. Ford's approval rating plummeted. Many believed rumors that there had been a secret deal between Ford and Nixon, so much so that Ford was compelled to testify before a congressional subcommittee on the matter. Ford denied that any such deal existed, but a significant number of Americans were not convinced and distrusted the president.

Short Presidency While handling the fallout from Watergate and his pardon of Nixon occupied much of Ford's 896 days as president, he also dealt with serious domestic and international issues. Increasing inflation, a stagnating economy, and high unemployment had begun during Nixon's second term, and the country endured a significant economic recession during Ford's presidency. Ford took various actions to improve the economy. Though inflation was reduced by his measures, the recession did not begin to ease until 1976.

Ford's foreign policy followed the lead set by Nixon. Ford continued trying to improve relations with the Soviet Union by following a policy of détente (French for "easing"), but relations slowly worsened during his time in office. Ford's secretary of state, Henry Kissinger, was able to lay the groundwork for SALT II (Strategic Arms Limitation Treaty II) through the Vladivostok Accords, agreed to in November 1974. Ford also pursued a similar policy with Communist China, trying to ease tensions with the country.

Vietnam Issues Vietnam remained a pressing concern as well. In January 1973, Kissinger had signed an agreement on ending the war and restoring peace in Vietnam, which saw the Communist North Vietnamese pledging to honor the sovereignty of the democratic government in South Vietnam. Two years later, North Vietnam resumed their planned conquest of South Vietnam, and Ford was unable to convince Congress to provide military aid to America's former ally. North Vietnam completed the conquest of South Vietnam in April 1975. The last Americans were evacuated by helicopter from a falling Saigon on April 30.

Post-Presidential Activities During the 1976 presidential elections, Ford won the Republican nomination over Ronald Reagan. Because of lingering distrust over his pardon of Nixon and the failing economy, however, Ford lost the election to Democrat Jimmy Carter. After leaving office in 1977, Ford remained involved in politics. Reagan even considered him for his vice president in the 1980 election.

Ford also sat on the boards of a number of corporations and gave lectures around the United States. In addition, Ford founded a charity, the Gerald R. Ford Foundation, in which he was active. Suffering from ill health in the last year of his life, Ford died on December 26, 2006, at his home in Rancho Mirage, California.

See also **Cold War: Major Figures: John F. Kennedy**

See also **Cold War: Major Figures: Lyndon B. Johnson**

See also **Cold War: Major Figures: Richard M. Nixon**

✪ Major Battles and Events

Founding of the MACV

On February 8, 1962, the Kennedy administration created the Military Assistance Command, Vietnam (MACV). Despite its tangled organizational and political structure, the MACV oversaw the deepening American presence in South Vietnam.

Containment John Kennedy's foreign policy was rooted in the prevailing theories of the Cold War. Having narrowly weathered the Cuban Missile Crisis (in which Soviet nuclear warheads were installed in Cuba and aimed at the United States), he believed that the Soviet Empire posed a real threat to America. Unwilling and unable to launch a traditional war against the Soviets, the United States opted to limit the spread of communism around the globe.

This was no small task. When European empires crumbled after World War II, nationalist movements rose up in developing countries everywhere. Many of these embraced Socialist or Communist ideals. Soviet rhetoric convinced Americans that these revolutions were, in fact, directed from Moscow. In the 1950s, President Harry Truman articulated the "domino theory"—if one country falls under Communist control, its neighbors would soon fall as well, like a row of dominos.

In response, the United States developed a policy of "universal containment," which meant squelching nascent Communist movements by any means necessary.

Like other television coverage of the war, Walter Cronkite's reports on the Tet Offensive in 1968 contributed to the growing unpopularity of the war in the United States. *Archive Photos, Inc/ Getty Images*

One of the regions of highest concern was Southeast Asia, specifically former French Indochina—Vietnam, Cambodia, and Laos.

Having thrown off French colonialism and Japanese occupation, Vietnam had separated into two warring camps. The nationalist Communist Viet Minh group, led by Ho Chi Minh, established the Democratic Republic of Vietnam (North Vietnam). They made Hanoi their capital. The pro-French and pro-American Ngo Dinh Diem declared the Republic of Vietnam (South Vietnam), with its capital in Saigon.

Around 1957, the North Vietnamese began secret attacks on the south, hoping to topple Diem's "puppet" government. With encouragement and supplies from Hanoi, southern Communists formed the National Liberation Front, also known as the Viet Cong, a force of guerilla fighters that would later prove effective against American military forces.

Buildup In 1962, trying to prevent a Communist take-over in the country, the U.S. Joint Chiefs of Staff suggested the creation of a new command dedicated to South Vietnam. Kennedy approved it, and the MACV was duly established. The new agency was to oversee

U.S. military units throughout South Vietnam. It was also to advise and support the South Vietnamese military.

That year, the number of Americans in Vietnam tripled, from 3,200 to 11,300. General Paul D. Harkins, who had served as principle staff aide under George Patton in World War II, was made Commander of the MACV (COMUSMACV). In 1964, the title passed on to General William D. Westmoreland. Two other officers would hold this title over the course of the war: Creighton Abrams and Frederick Weyand.

Hierarchy   In the beginning, the new command suffered from a tortuous and confused command structure. For one thing, a very similar agency, with overlapping responsibilities, already existed in the country. The Military Assistance Advisory Group Vietnam (MAAGV) had been created in 1955 and continued to operate independently until 1964.

In addition, the Pentagon would not grant theater-command status to MACV, limiting its authority and its ability to act. The COMUSMACV was to report to the naval commander-in-chief, Pacific (CINCPAC), who reported to the Joint Chiefs of Staff. Later, by order of the secretary of defense, MACV communications were also sent directly to the Pentagon.

These intricacies hampered the COMUSMACV's ability to conduct the war. For instance, although the war zone clearly extended into North Vietnam and Laos, those countries fell outside MACV's jurisdiction. Operations in those areas had to be cleared by Washington and CINCPAC. CINCPAC sometimes carried out such operations separately from MACV.

CINCPAC was a navy command, and yet the navy had less direct involvement with the fighting than the army or air force. Jurisdiction squabbles were particularly bitter in the air. Army helicopters, air force aviation, and navy aviation all fell under separate and often competitive commands. On top of all this, the COMUSMACV had no direct authority over the Army of the Republic of Vietnam (ARVN). The South Vietnamese were free to ignore American advice and often did.

The disunity of the American war effort often showed on the battlefield, with disastrous results. Lieutenant Colonel John Paul Vann broke with the MACV in 1963 after charging the South Vietnamese with rampant corruption and incompetence.

Consolidation   Frustrated by the organizational chaos, Westmoreland pushed for a more centralized command structure. In May 1964, the MAAGV was dissolved. The MACV took over the training and advising of the ARVN. Responsibility for this task was divided among the various field advisors instead of being centralized at headquarters. As a result, the U.S. military largely neglected the ARVN's development.

Although the navy never relinquished its overall command, other military units realigned into a more streamlined structure. As part of his efforts at consolidation, General Westmoreland became the commanding general of the U.S. Army in Vietnam (USARV). He refused to create a separate U.S. Army field headquarters. MACV headquarters therefore handled field operations, ARVN advisory efforts, and a broad range of military and political issues.

The load may have been too great for a single office to handle. Certainly the military decisions made in Vietnam have been subject to intense criticism. It is said that American soldiers sometimes painted "UUUU" on their helmets, which stood for "the unwilling, led by the unqualified, doing the unnecessary for the ungrateful." Others, especially General Westmoreland, have claimed that, militarily, the MACV was entirely successful. The war was lost, in their opinion, by politicians and journalists.

The MACV was abolished under the terms of the Paris Agreement of 1973.

The Gulf of Tonkin Incident

In the summer of 1964, the U.S. destroyer *Maddox* exchanged fire with three torpedo ships off the North Vietnamese coast. Two days later, the *Maddox*, accompanied by the destroyer *C. Turner Joy*, reported once again that they had been fired upon. Reports of the encounters were confused. It was unclear what had provoked the attacks; it was uncertain that the second attack had happened at all. Nevertheless, the administration of President Lyndon Johnson used the incident to justify a dramatic escalation of American involvement in Vietnam.

Provocation   The year 1964 was an election year. Political debate focused on the U.S.S.R and on civil rights. The United States had sent thousands of "advisors" into South Vietnam, but the war had not yet come to the forefront of the public consciousness. Incumbent President Lyndon Johnson took heavy criticism for his South Asia policy from the Republican challenger, Arizona Senator Barry Goldwater. Goldwater, a fervent anti-Communist, advocated using nuclear weapons to clear the Viet Cong's jungle cover.

The Johnson administration had in fact been more aggressive than the Republicans thought. American "advice" to South Vietnam included training, military equipment, and covert operations. In 1961, the C.I.A. launched a highly classified program known as Operation 34A, which included naval electronic intelligence cruises (called "DeSoto" missions). The South Vietnamese also launched American-supported raids on the North Vietnamese coast.

On July 31, 1964, American-trained South Vietnamese commandos attacked a radio transmitter station on Hon Nieu Island. This may have provoked the North Vietnamese to attack American ships in the area.

The navy sent the aircraft carrier USS *Constellation* to the Gulf of Tonkin in 1964, in response to reported attacks by North Vietnamese torpedo boats.   © *Bettmann/Corbis*

Incident On August 2, 1964, three North Vietnamese torpedo boats bore down fast on the *U.S.S. Maddox*, which had been on a DeSoto cruise in the Gulf of Tonkin. The *Maddox* opened fire, and the approaching boats answered with torpedoes and machine guns. Shortly afterwards, four U.S. naval airplanes from the carrier *Ticonderoga* were dispatched to strafe the enemy craft. All three North Vietnamese ships sustained damage, while the *Maddox* returned unscathed to southern waters.

Two days later, the *Maddox* returned, reinforced by the destroyer *C. Turner Joy*. The ships intercepted North Vietnamese radio messages, which they believed signaled an imminent attack. After nightfall, in the middle of a storm, radar and sonar indicated incoming torpedoes, all of which missed.

The two ships engaged in vigorous evasive maneuvering and called in air support. However, no one could make a visual sighting of the enemy. Other than an initial surprise torpedo attack, the commander noted, the whole affair might have been a product of bad weather and nervous radar operators.

Response On August 3, South Vietnamese President Nguyen Khanh told reporters that the United States

should strike back at the North Vietnamese "to save face." President Lyndon Johnson apparently agreed. In a taped conversation with Secretary of Defense Robert McNamara, he said that America "ought to always leave the impression that if you shoot at us, you're going to get hit."

Johnson publicly announced that the American ships had been on a routine patrol in international waters when they had been attacked with no provocation. He immediately sanctioned air strikes on four North Vietnamese naval bases and on an oil storage depot. In the meantime, he asked for Congressional approval of a resolution "expressing the unity and determination of the United States in supporting freedom and in protecting peace in Southeast Asia."

The Gulf of Tonkin Resolution was passed by both houses of Congress only three days after the attacks. It condemned the naval incidents as part of a "systematic campaign of aggression by North Vietnam against South Vietnam." Only two representatives voted against the bill, which gave the president full authority "to take all necessary measures to repel any armed attack against the forces of the United States."

The second part of the resolution gave the president discretion to give military aid to any member state of the

Helicopters played a crucial role in transporting American troops during the Vietnam War. *APA/Getty Images*

Southeast Asia Treaty Organization (SEATO). For practical purposes, the Gulf of Tonkin Resolution functioned as an informal declaration of war. It was to expire only at the president's discretion, unless Congress repealed it.

On August 8, Ho Chi Minh declared "the indignation and wrath of our entire people at the U.S. Government's deliberate acts of aggression against the Democratic Republic of Viet-Nam." With North Vietnam's backing, the Viet Cong increased its operations against American targets in South Vietnam.

Unlike President John Kennedy, who had sent "advisory" officials to Vietnam, Johnson deployed combat-ready American ground troops. Calling themselves "grunts," these forces were sent on aggressive "search-and-destroy" missions to find and crush Viet Cong and North Vietnamese groups. Military command theorized that the United States could win a war of attrition (a war in which one wears the enemy down over time), as long as the U.S. soldiers killed as many of the enemy as possible.

Investigation   In 1968, a congressional review made it public knowledge that the *Maddox* had actually been on a reconnaissance mission and that Americans had carried out secret attacks against North Vietnam prior to the August 2 incident. More disturbing were allegations that the reports of the August 4 incident had been mistaken or even fabricated. Antiwar activists began to charge that Johnson had already been planning to increase American involvement in Vietnam and that the affair had given him an excuse to do so.

The Gulf of Tonkin Resolution was not repealed, however, until January 13, 1971, after President Richard Nixon used it to order air raids over neutral Cambodia.

Flaming Dart

After the Gulf Of Tonkin Incident, the United States launched a series of aerial assaults on North Vietnamese targets. Flaming Dart was the first of these air war operations, which, though effective in many ways, could not guarantee victory.

Strike and Counterstrike In immediate response to the Tonkin Incident, on August 5, 1964, President Lyndon Johnson authorized Operation Pierce Arrow. Aircraft from the carriers *Ticonderoga* and *Constellation* struck a variety of North Vietnamese naval bases and petroleum storage houses. Four planes were destroyed, and one U.S. pilot died in the attack. Lieutenant Everett Alvarez was captured and was subsequently imprisoned for eight years. He became the first and longest-held American prisoner of war in Vietnam.

On February 6, 1965, the Viet Cong attacked the U.S. air base at Pleiku. They killed eight men, wounded 128, and destroyed ten airplanes. In Saigon, National Security Advisor McGeorge Bundy (1919–1996), who had come to the country on a fact-finding mission for Johnson, received the news with outrage. He sent an angry report to Washington, recommending stronger American action in Vietnam.

Beginning on February 7 and 8, 1965, the United States launched retaliatory air raids on North Vietnam, an operation code-named Flaming Dart. Planes from the sea carriers *Coral Sea* and *Hancock* hit North Vietnamese ports and army barracks. A few days later, the North Vietnamese struck U.S. billets in Qui Nhon.

In response, the United States launched Flaming Dart II. Military command carefully planned the action to take place at the exact same time as President Johnson's evening address to the nation. Whatever the political impact of the raid, militarily it did not succeed—the attack did little damage to its targets, staging and communications areas in the North.

The Ongoing Storm Johnson's aerial attacks, called Rolling Thunder, soon became a regular feature of the American campaign. American planes would target enemy locations in North and South Vietnam, as well as in the officially neutral countries Laos and Cambodia. Over the course of the Vietnam War, the United States dropped more bomb tonnage than had all of the belligerents of World War II put together.

Secretary of Defense Robert McNamara intended the air campaign to wear away resistance gradually and to force the North Vietnamese to negotiate. Aerial attacks also served as a very visible sign of American power and helped to bolster South Vietnamese morale.

The operations were an interservice effort, carried out by both air force and navy attack squadrons. Air Force F-105 and F-4 fighters flew from bases in South Vietnam and Thailand, while navy F-4, F-8, A-4, and A-6 planes took off from carriers.

Like much of the American war effort in Vietnam, Rolling Thunder suffered from muddled military and political leadership. Johnson and McNamara maintained strict control of tactical details. Much to the military's disgust, targets were chosen by the president, secretary of defense, secretary of state, and the White House press secretary. They sent airmen in attacks against barracks

POWS AND MIAS

Long after the war officially ended, the emotionally charged issue of unreturned prisoners of war (POWs) and soldiers missing in action (MIAs) continued to haunt Americans.

South Vietnam and North Vietnam had agreed to the Geneva Convention, which dictated humane treatment for captured enemy soldiers. Nevertheless, the Viet Cong, since they fought in their own country, were considered traitors and criminals and were often brutalized. In the north, the Communists declared that American aviators were guilty of "crimes against humanity." Released POWs told horrifying tales of mistreatment, torture, and murder. They also reported that the North Vietnamese still held some American prisoners.

By 1975, 1,750 soldiers were still listed as missing in action. For almost two decades, the United States refused to recognize the united Social Republic of Vietnam until a "full accountability" of the missing could be made. To this end, America insisted that Vietnam return the bodies of the fallen. In 1987, President Ronald Reagan announced that "until all our questions are fully answered, we will assume that some of our countrymen are alive."

Relations with Vietnam improved in the late 1980s. Hundreds of sets of remains were eventually flown back to the United States, and veterans groups made progress tracking down unresolved cases. In 1994, President Bill Clinton lifted the American trade embargo against Vietnam, normalizing relations between the two nations.

and military supply lines, but forbade high value targets like petroleum storage, power plants, and airfields. Because of departmental squabbles, the air campaign was hardly coordinated with the land campaign at all.

The region under attack was strictly limited by political and diplomatic considerations. At first, only southern North Vietnam came under attack, from the demilitarized zone (also called the DMZ—a narrow strip of land demarcating the divide between North and South Vietnam) to a northern "bombing line." As the war progressed, the target area expanded until it included all of North Vietnam.

Those flying these missions did so at an enormous risk. The USSR supplied North Vietnam with the latest antiaircraft artillery, including SA-2 Guideline surface-to-air missiles (SAMs). Downed aviators made up almost seventy percent of U.S. prisoners of war.

Grounding the Birds As the war dragged on, Rolling Thunder came under heavy media scrutiny and criticism. In December 1966, Harrison Salisbury reported in the *New York Times* on the collateral damage to noncombatants that he had witnessed in Hanoi. He claimed that the bombing only increased the North Vietnamese determination to fight, and he suggested that the

In a 1972 incident in which her village was mistakenly bombed by Americans with napalm, this woman's child was badly burned. *AP Images*

military was deliberately striking at civilian targets. The Pentagon furiously denied the charges.

In August 1967, Johnson reluctantly allowed attacks on high-value targets in Hanoi and Haiphong. Rolling Thunder attacks were, for a season, particularly effective. The British chargé d'affaires to Hanoi believed that the bombing came close to crippling the North Vietnamese economy in 1967. Nevertheless, following the Tet Offensive (a massive attack by the North Vietnamese and Viet Cong) in 1968, a discouraged President Johnson announced that the air campaign would be discontinued.

Battle of the Ia Drang Valley

During November 14–17, 1965, the U.S. First Airmobile Cavalry Division engaged the North Vietnamese Army (NVA) in the Ia Drang Valley in the Central Vietnamese Highlands. The pitched battle raged for four days, resulting in heavy losses for the Americans and enormous losses for the North Vietnamese.

The Battle On November 14, 1965, the U.S. Army deployed the First Battalion, Seventh Cavalry to the Ia Drang Valley, fourteen miles west of a U.S. Special Forces base at Plei Me. The 450-man force arrived on Huey helicopters, with orders to hunt down and destroy NVA troops hidden in the mountains.

As it turned out, North Vietnamese General Chu Huy Man planned to seize the base at Plei Mei and to ambush any Americans and South Vietnamese soldiers who came to the rescue. He led more than two thousand Vietnamese soldiers in the valley, waiting a few miles from where the Seventh Cavalry touched down.

The Americans had one stroke of luck—they almost immediately captured a young Vietnamese soldier. The terrified prisoner told them that three Communist battalions were hiding up the mountain and were about to start killing Americans. Sure enough, rifle fire broke out around noon. Battalion commander Lieutenant Colonel Harold Moore quickly realized that he was not only hugely outnumbered, but outflanked.

The next seventy-two hours were characterized by desperate fighting and dogged courage on both sides. The North Vietnamese took advantage of the many giant termite mounds around the field, which were as hard as cement and stood as high as fifteen feet tall. NVA soldiers would fire down from the mounds, gaining both elevation and cover against their enemies. Vietnamese snipers tied themselves to the trees on either side—when they were hit, their bodies hung gruesomely from the branches.

The Americans defended the clearing where they had landed—a flat grassy perimeter about three hundred yards across. As the NVA streamed down the mountain to the west and through the jungle, the American soldiers advanced toward the tree line on foot, bayonets fixed, to establish a perimeter around the clearing. Helicopters flew in through heavy fire to drop off ammunition and to collect the wounded.

Early in the engagement, the Second Platoon was cut off from the main division and surrounded. Led by Lieutenant Henry Herrick, the lost platoon defended a hilltop with heavy losses for the duration of the battle.

At dusk of the first day, Moore ordered a withdrawal, covered by white phosphorus smoke, to the nighttime perimeter. The fighting continued sporadically all night and all the next day.

Eventually, however, superior American firepower was brought to bear. Rocket-bearing helicopters, attack planes, B-52 bombers, and long-range howitzers did enormous damage to the North Vietnamese forces, and they withdrew on November 16.

The Army of the Republic of Vietnam (ARVN) helicopters ambushed the NVA's retreat, inflicting still more losses. But the Communists still did not give up, and reinforcements arrived from across the Laotian border every day. The next day a NVA force fell on the Second Battalion of the Seventh Cavalry, killing 155 Americans.

The Lessons The U.S. military always had difficulty determining enemy losses in Vietnam. At Ia Drang they estimated that the NVA suffered over 2,500 casualties.

The battle left 234 Americans dead and more than 300 wounded.

In some ways, the battle surprised and dismayed American leadership. It was the first time since Dien Bien Phu that the Communists had stood their ground and fought, rather than melting back into the jungle. Considering their enormous losses, the NVA had shown ferocious determination. Robert McNamara could draw only one conclusion: "It will be a long war."

Ia Drang also confirmed American fears of the level of North Vietnamese commitment to their cause. As McNamara said to President Johnson: "The rate of infiltration has increased from three battalion equivalents a month in late 1964 to a high of nine or twelve during one month this last fall." That meant that the number of enemy combatants in South Vietnam was increasing by as many as 9,600 every month.

General Westmoreland, however, still pronounced the battle a resounding victory, which demonstrated "the ability of the Americans to meet and defeat the best troops the enemy could put on the field of battle." He asked for, and received, two hundred thousand more troops to counter the increased North Vietnamese incursion.

For Westmoreland and other military leaders, Ia Drang also seemed to affirm the U.S. strategy of attrition. If America killed far more soldiers than they lost, they reasoned, eventually the Communists would give up. Over the course of the war, the United States sent more search-and-destroy missions into the Vietnamese countryside, essentially attempting to repeat the battle of Ia Drang.

In the meantime, the North Vietnamese learned to avoid conventional standing warfare, and largely returned to guerrilla tactics. American search-and-destroy missions met booby-traps, snipers, and mines more often than a direct attack. When the Communists did attack, Ia Drang had taught them to "cling to the belt"—to fight as close as possible to American troops, where U.S. long-range artillery could not be used effectively.

Military experts do not agree on the effectiveness of the attrition campaign. Some argue that, effectively, U.S. troops ran wild-goose chases in the jungle and neglected the populated coast. Others believe that the search-and-destroy missions developed a flexible and responsive fighting force in Vietnam. Certainly they inflicted heavy damage to the Communists, particularly in the Attleboro Operations of 1966, and at the Cedar Falls and Junction City Battles of 1967.

The possible military efficacy of a campaign of attrition is beside the point to some degree; American leaders fundamentally failed to grasp North Vietnamese dedication to their cause. If anything, their massive losses only seemed to goad the Communists on. In the end, it was the American public, not the American military leadership, that would give up, unwilling to support a seemingly endless war in the face of ever-mounting casualties.

The Siege of Khe Sanh

From January to April of 1968, the North Vietnamese Army (NVA) laid siege to the American base at Khe Sanh. While the United States successfully held its defenses, the battle worried and distracted American leadership. To this day, it is unclear if the NVA General Vo Nguyen Giap seriously meant to take Khe Sanh—it is possible that the battle was meant as a diversion for the Tet Offensive.

The Base In 1962, MACV (Military Assistance Command, Vietnam) set up an Army Special Forces camp at Khe Sanh, a village in the northwest region of South Vietnam. Located in hill country, about six miles from the Laotian border and fourteen miles from the demilitarized zone, the base looked down on Route 9, the major roadway between Laos and northern South Vietnam.

In 1966, General William Westmoreland ordered a marine base built close by. He did so against the vigorous opposition of Marine General Lewis W. Walt. Walt advocated a "pacification" strategy, in which U.S. troops would defend coastal populations. In his opinion, Khe Sanh was a useless outpost in the middle of nowhere.

Westmoreland, on the other hand, pushed for an "attrition" policy, in which American troops would hunt down and destroy the enemy. "Khe Sanh," he reasoned, "could serve as a patrol base blocking enemy infiltration from Laos; a base for . . . operations to harass the enemy in Laos; an airstrip for reconnaissance to survey the Ho Chi Minh Trail; a western anchor for the defenses south of the DMZ; and an eventual jumping off point for ground operations . . . ."

In the spring of 1967, the Third Marine Amphibious Force (MAF) arrived at Khe Sahn, reinforcing the undermanned base. It was not long before they saw combat. The NVA attacked the area in April and May, seeking possession of key hilltops. The Americans held on to the highlands after a series of bloody skirmishes—both sides took heavy casualties. Before long the Third Marines were relieved by the Twenty-sixth Marines, commanded by Colonel David E. Lownds.

In January, the NVA began a serious, sustained campaign against Khe Sanh, in contrast with their normal hit-and-run tactics. Westmoreland was delighted to see a relatively concentrated North Vietnamese force attack in a virtual wilderness. He reasoned that the U.S. military could bring the full weight of its artillery against the enemy without fear of massive civilian collateral.

Westmoreland sent in reinforcements. By January, Lownds commanded one marine artillery battalion, four marine infantry battalions, the South Vietnamese Thirty-seventh ARVN Ranger battalion, and various units from

American marines defend the base at Khe Sanh in the drawn-out 1968 battle.   *Dick Swanson/Time Life Pictures/Getty Images*

other services. Altogether over six thousand men defended Khe Sanh.

The Shadow of Dien Bien Phu   American interest in the base extended beyond its strategic location. Invariably, discussion of Khe Sanh brought up the specter of a similar French base at Dien Bien Phu, which had been taken by the Vietnamese in 1954. Military brass, political leaders, and wartime journalists all obsessively worried that General Giap would attempt to repeat that victory, which had ended the French presence in southeast Asia.

President Lyndon Johnson became so anxious on the subject that he repeatedly demanded reassurance from his generals. He made his Joint Chiefs of Staff sign a pledge that the base was, in fact, defensible. Westmoreland, after assessing the base's artillery and air strength, promised the president that Khe Sanh could hold out indefinitely under siege.

Having given their word, the U.S. military took trouble to back up their claims. The MACV went so far as to investigate the use of tactical nuclear weapons, but the option was never seriously proposed.

Instead Westmoreland ordered a massive wave of air strikes on North Vietnamese positions in the area, involv-

ing both tactical aircraft and B-52 bombers. Operation Niagara, as it was called, became one of the largest air assaults in American history. Altogether the assault, which lasted until the end of March, dropped almost sixty thousand tons of bombs on the Vietnamese countryside.

The Siege   The battle of Khe Sanh began on January 21, when North Vietnamese infantry launched an assault against a marine outpost on Hill 861. The NVA failed to dislodge the Americans, who had been warned of the attack the day before by a North Vietnamese defector.

Nevertheless, the fighting was brutal. Soviet-made 122-mm howitzer rockets, fired from beyond the Laotian border, pounded down on the fortifications. At one point a round hit a marine ammunition supply, setting off 1,500 tons of high explosives. Covered by the rain of artillery fire, the NVA penetrated deep into American defenses before being driven back. At the end of the day, fourteen marines were killed and another forty-three were wounded.

Many historians believe that the North Vietnamese Khe Sanh campaign was primarily a feint, designed to draw American attention away from the coastal urban centers. On January 30–31, the NVA and Viet Cong

(South Vietnamese Communist guerilla forces) initiated the massive Tet Offensive against those urban centers. The Americans quickly repelled most of the Tet attacks, but the siege of Khe Sanh continued. Feint or no, the NVA meant to take the base if they could.

The NVA had managed to block Route 9, forcing the Americans to resupply the base by air. The Communists' sophisticated antiaircraft battery made this difficult. Even covered by Operation Niagara, the air force was unable to land on the exposed airstrip. Instead they developed paradrop techniques to get food and ammunition to the troops on the ground. The Marine Corps used a combination of tactical aircraft and helicopters, called a "Super Gaggle," to supply hill outposts.

On February 7, NVA armored divisions demolished a U.S. Special Forces camp at Lang Vei, about nine miles from the Khe Sanh base. Afraid of enemy ambush, Colonel Lownds refused to send back-up. Almost 300 of the 350 defenders were killed, missing, or wounded. On February 25, a marine platoon was ambushed and took heavy losses.

On February 29, the NVA mounted an assault on a South Vietnamese Ranger battalion position. Supported by a B-52 Arc Light strike, the Rangers repelled the North Vietnamese, killing over seventy enemy soldiers. Only one of the South Vietnamese was wounded.

The Relief In April, a combined Army-Marine-RAVN force, called Operation Pegasus, managed to break through enemy lines and lift the siege. Westmoreland steadfastly refused to abandon the base, but he was recalled to Washington in June. His successor, General Creighton Abrams had the base officially closed on July 5.

The siege of Khe Sanh drew an enormous amount of press scrutiny. Marines living "in the V-ring," constantly under enemy fire, were romanticized, toasted, or pitied by the media. According to U.S. Army estimates, the NVA lost upwards of ten thousand men, while the U.S. Marines suffered around five hundred dead.

The Tet Offensive

In January 1968, the North Vietnamese Army and the Viet Cong launched a coordinated attack against hundreds of villages, towns, and cities across South Vietnam. They aimed primarily to topple the American-backed "puppet" government in Saigon. They also hoped to discredit the American government's claim that the Communists were on their last legs and that the war was almost over. While the former goal was never realized, the Tet Offensive did lend fuel to the U.S. antiwar movement and put considerable pressure on the administration of President Lyndon Johnson.

The Buildup From 1965 to 1967, the number of American troops in Vietnam increased from fewer than sixty thousand to nearly a half million. However, as casualties mounted, the American people grew increasingly weary of the war effort. In an effort to rally public

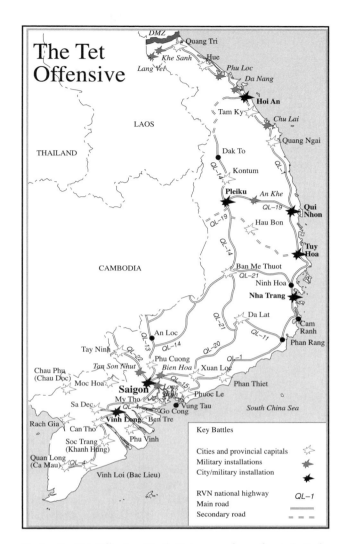

During the Tet Offensive, North Vietnamese forces focused attack efforts on American strongholds, including Saigon. *Reproduced by permission of Gale, a part of Cengage Learning*

support, the Johnson administration routinely made highly optimistic reports on America's progress. According to the U.S. military commanders, the National Liberation Front (NLF), also known as the Viet Cong, and the North Vietnamese Army (NVA) had suffered heavy losses, and they would not be able to hold out much longer. There was, the government promised, "light at the end of the tunnel."

The Vietnamese Communists, however, were still in the fight, and they had no intention of giving up. Instead, faced with a bloody stalemate, General Vo Nguyen Giap devised a massive campaign in the hopes of changing the face of the war. Called the "General Offensive-General Uprising," the action was to have two phases. First, a series of diversionary campaigns would draw American troops out of the urban centers into the countryside. Second, the Viet Cong and the

NVA would attack the major cities, prompting an uprising of the South Vietnamese people against the Saigon government.

The campaign began in October and November, as North Vietnamese forces descended on small, inland targets. Among these was the U.S. Marine base at Con Thien, across the Laotian border, as well as the towns of Loc Ninh, Song Be, and Dak To. American forces were dispersed from the coastal units to deal with these threats.

United States General Westmoreland could tell that these attacks, coupled with the massing of forces to the north, were leading up to something big. However, the army believed that the buildup was centered around the battle of Khe Sanh. They were caught off guard by the scope and coordination of the Tet Offensive.

Attack and Counterattack Hanoi's main assault was launched on January 30–31, during the Vietnamese holiday of Tet. This holiday, coinciding with the lunar New Year, was traditionally celebrated by returning to one's home village for feasting with family. In October of 1967, the North Vietnamese had agreed to a cease-fire during the festivities, a promise that they did not keep. As a result, a third of the Army of the Republic of Vietnam (ARVN) was on leave when the fighting began.

On January 30, 1968, nine NLF guerillas raided the American Embassy in Saigon, which was held by five American Marines. They managed to take control of the grounds, but could not enter the U.S. Chancery building. The next morning U.S. troops retook the compound after a bloody firefight.

At the same time, NLF and NVA strikes were launched throughout the country. Military units attacked thirty-nine provincial capitals, seventy-one district towns, and five of the six major cities.

Militarily, the offensive proved a miserable failure for the Communists. The South Vietnamese people showed no interest in a general uprising, and the ARVN fought fiercely in defense of their hometowns. With American support, most of the raids were repelled within a day. Fighting in some towns continued to the end of the week, and the former imperial city of Hué was occupied for almost a month.

The American Front From a political point of view, the Tet Offensive signaled the beginning of the end for the South Vietnamese cause, in that it ultimately cost them their most vital ally. Shocked by the ferocity and scale of the offensive, the American people began to doubt their government's glib assurance that victory was in sight. "What the hell is going on?" Walter Cronkite burst out on hearing the news, "I thought we were winning."

Cronkite, a respected news anchor, had initially supported the war. After two years of fighting, however, the Tet Offensive convinced him (and many others) that the military had made no progress. The conflict, he declared, was stalemated.

The brutality of the urban warfare also contributed to popular disillusionment, as when South Vietnam's chief of national police, Nguyen Ngoc Loan, summarily executed a Viet Cong suspect on the streets of Saigon. Having just lost several men to the NLF, he shot the man in the head before photographers and television cameras, leading to one of the most memorable—and horrifying—images of the Vietnam War. Fairly or not, Americans began to question the worthiness of their Asian allies.

More significantly, they questioned the worthiness of their own troops. American platoons had ruthlessly driven the enemy back, often with tragic cost in civilian life and property. One soldier reported after securing the village of Ben Tre, "We had to destroy the village in order to save it."

Neither side emerged from the battle as creditably as they would have liked. A month of American bombardment drove the NLF out of Hué, but left the ancient city in ruins and 116,000 townspeople homeless. On entering the city, however, they discovered an even greater atrocity. The Viet Cong had executed 2,800 Vietnamese civilians thought to be in sympathy with the South Vietnamese government and buried the bodies in shallow graves.

Johnson's Office Military commanders urged Johnson to take advantage of what they considered to be a resounding victory. Nearly forty thousand of the enemy had been killed, and the Viet Cong was in disarray. Westmoreland requested an additional two hundred thousand troops from Washington. He accurately predicted that the NLF would soon be reinforced by North Vietnam.

Johnson knew that public opinion would not permit a further escalation in Vietnam, and he worried that America would be forced away from its Southeast Asian containment policy altogether. Senator Robert Kennedy of New York and Senator Eugene McCarthy of Minnesota announced that they would be running for the Democratic presidential nomination on anti-war platforms.

On March 31, 1968, Johnson reluctantly declared that military operations in Vietnam would be scaled back. He suspended the bombing campaign on North Vietnam. He also announced that he would not run for re-election.

The My Lai Massacre

On March 16, 1968, American soldiers committed one of the worst wartime atrocities in the Vietnam War. Descending on a tiny South Vietnamese hamlet, they murdered over four hundred civilians, mostly women, children, and old men. The massacre and the subsequent

In 1968, more than 100 unarmed South Vietnamese civilians were massacred near the village of My Lai.   *Ronald S. Haeberle/Time & Life Pictures/ Getty Images*

army cover-up became an international scandal and a permanent mark on the American conscience.

The Massacre   Lieutenant William Calley commanded Charlie Company, First Battalion, Twentieth Infantry Division. On March 16, he and his men were ordered to My Lai 4, a small hamlet of the Song My village in the Quang Ngai province. Officially, they were on a search-and-destroy mission. Military intelligence had determined that the Viet Cong sheltered in the area.

The Charlie Company was on edge. Two days before, the well-beloved Sergeant George Cox had been killed by a booby trap. Wild with grief, the squad members had murdered a Vietnamese woman who had been working in a field close by. When villagers complained to Captain Ernest Medina, he told them that the woman had been holding a land mine detonator.

Calley's commanding officer, Captain Ernest "Mad Dog" Medina, had told him that all innocent Vietnamese citizens would be at the market. Everyone remaining in the village, according to intelligence, would be Viet Cong or Viet Cong sympathizers. In fact, all of the able-bodied Vietnamese men had retreated from the village the day before.

Lieutenant Colonel Frank Barker gave Calley permission to treat My Lai as an enemy stronghold. Their orders were to kill the livestock, to spoil the wells, to cut down the banana trees, and to take no prisoners. Neither Barker nor Calley explicitly included civilians in their instructions. Nevertheless, Calley believed that he had been ordered to kill everyone in the village.

At 7:40 in the morning, the soldiers marched into My Lai 4 (known to the soldiers as Pinkville.) On Calley's orders, the Americans then embarked on a ruthless, indiscriminate killing spree. They raped women and young girls; they shot mothers holding their babies. Villagers were rounded up in ditches and summarily executed. Others were clubbed, bayoneted, and even mutilated. Bodies were found with the words "C Company" carved on their chests. The U.S. Army estimates that 347 civilians were murdered. The Vietnamese put the number at 504.

A few American soldiers refused to take part in the atrocity. Pilot Hugh Thompson watched with increasing disbelief as the carnage unfolded beneath him. Finally, seeing U.S. troops chasing ten civilians, he set his helicopter down between the Vietnamese and the Americans.

Thompson had his gunners train their M60 guns on the soldiers.

Thompson jumped out and asked the officer in charge to help him get the Vietnamese out of the ditch. The officer answered that a hand grenade would do the job. "You see my guns?" Thompson replied, "If you open up, they open up."

Thompson called down two more helicopters and somehow managed to convince the ten cowering Vietnamese to board them. A little later his crew pulled a three-year-old child out of a pit full of bloody corpses. Then they flew back to base and reported what was going on to his superiors, who put a stop to the rampage.

The Uncovering   Those same superiors also immediately buried the story. If the media mentioned the incident at all, they reported that American troops had won a military victory over Viet Cong troops.

The massacre came to light in 1969 due to the efforts of a veteran, Ronald Ridenhour. He had just returned from a tour of duty, during which he had heard appalling stories from eyewitnesses of the massacre. Ridenhour's letters to the House Armed Services Committee reported that "something rather dark and bloody" had happened in My Lai; he demanded justice for the victims.

In response, General William Westmoreland initiated an army investigation, headed by Lieutenant General William Peers. The Peers Commission found that the soldiers in question had committed 224 violations of the code for military conduct. When the grisly truth of the matter became clear, the U.S. Army started trying and convicting the perpetrators in courts martial.

Twenty-five indictments were filed altogether, thirteen for war crimes and twelve for covering up the affair. Almost all of the defendants were acquitted or charges against them were dropped. The army released General Samuel Koster (Captain Medina's commanding officer) with a demotion and a letter of censure.

The army quietly published the charges, and initially the American news media did not make much of a stir. However in November 1969, freelance journalist Seymour Hersh picked up the story. He published a detailed description of the slaughter. Shortly afterwards, the Charlie Company army photographer, Ron Haeberle, published lurid photographs of the massacre in *Life* magazine. The American people were horrified. In the debacle, antiwar advocates saw proof that the United States military had lost its way, if not its soul.

The Trial of Lt. Calley   Only Lieutenant Calley, who had directly commanded Charlie Company, was convicted of any crime. He openly admitted to having shot unarmed civilians and having ordered others to do so. "I was ordered to go in there and destroy the enemy," he said. "That was the mission I was given. I did not sit down and think in terms of men, women, and children.

They were all classified the same, and that was the classification we dealt with, just as enemy soldiers." Medina denied having explicitly ordered the death of noncombatants. He also denied allegations from some troops that he had participated in the massacre. Calley was found guilty of murder by military court martial and sentenced to life imprisonment.

However, many Americans felt that Calley's conviction was deeply unfair, since his superior officers went unpunished. As the Vietnam Veterans Against the War explained, "We are all of us in this country guilty for having allowed the war to go on. We only want this country to realize that it cannot try a Calley for something which generals and presidents and our way of life encourage him to do."

Richard Nixon reduced Calley's sentence to twenty years and had him transferred from a military prison to house arrest. The U.S. Army gradually reduced his sentence to ten years. In 1974, a federal court overthrew his conviction entirely, by which time he had already been released on parole.

Secret Bombing of Cambodia

On March 18, 1969, President Richard Nixon initiated a secret B-52 bombing campaign in Cambodia, despite that country's official neutrality. When word of the attacks leaked out to the American press, the affair inspired renewed criticism of the war's legality.

Neutral Neighbors   As the Vietnam War progressed, the U.S. military became increasingly frustrated by the issue of Laos and Cambodia. Though officially neutral, these neighboring countries were essential to the North Vietnamese war effort. The North Vietnamese Army (NVA) traveled on the famed "Ho Chi Minh Trail," a system of trails and paths that snaked south from North Vietnam through neighboring Laos and Cambodia just east of the Vietnamese border. The Ho Chi Minh Trail allowed the North Vietnamese troops multiple entry points into South Vietnam.

In addition, the NVA kept arms and munitions in semipermanent bases in western Cambodia. From these locations, the Communists constantly launched lightning strikes across the border at American troops. After an attack, the Viet Cong and NVA would swiftly retreat to neutral Cambodia, where they could regroup and rearm in total safety.

The Communists had built their Cambodian bases with the permission of King Norodom Sihanouk, who had ruled Cambodia since before the country became independent from France in 1952. Unable to retain both ceremonial and political power, under the terms of the constitution, Sihanouk had abdicated in 1955. As president, the former king was still half-worshipped by the Cambodian people, despite his erratic nature and constantly shifting alliances.

An American F-100 jet drops napalm on a Cambodian target in 1970, part of Richard Nixon's effort to expand the war's territory. © *Bettmann/Corbis*

In return for their adulation, Sihanouk exerted every effort to keep his people out of the ever-deepening Vietnamese conflict. A crafty politician, he successfully negotiated the choppy diplomatic waters between the United States, the U.S.S.R, China, and the two Vietnams. "The word brinkmanship," he once remarked, "was perhaps invented for me."

In 1965, angered by America's part in the assassination of South Vietnamese President Ngo Dinh Diem and convinced that the Communists were going to win, Sihanouk broke diplomatic relations with the United States. In 1966, he gave permission to the People's Republic of China (PRC) to smuggle arms through Cambodia to Viet Cong forces. Sihanouk and his officials profited enormously from the black market in weapons that resulted.

The Menu Bombings In 1966, however, Sihanouk's government began to turn away from the left. The reinforced American army had driven an increasing number of Viet Cong across the border, where the guerrillas encouraged Cambodia's own Communist insurgents. The northwest province of Battambang witnessed a serious peasant uprising, which Defense Minister General Lon Nol brutally repressed. The surviving Cambodian

Communists escaped and regrouped in the wilderness. Sihanouk named them the Khmer Rouge. They were led by one Saloth Sar, who had taken the name Pol Pot.

Unable to fight the Khmer Rouge on his own and unwilling to count on China for help (the PRC was at the time in the midst of its "Cultural Revolution"), Sihanouk turned back to the United States. Nixon immediately responded to Cambodia's friendly overtures, sending ambassador Chester Bowles to Cambodia's capital, Phnom Penh.

In their meeting, Bowles promised that the United States would "do everything possible to avoid acts of aggression against Cambodia." However, Sihanouk gave the American military rather vague permission to cross his borders if "in hot pursuit" of the enemy.

This was more than enough license for Nixon. On March 18, 1969, Nixon and his advisors launched an air assault against Communist bases and supply points in Cambodia. Over the next fourteen months, B-52 planes flew 3,630 sorties, dropping over 100,000 tons of bombs. The individual attacks were code-named "Breakfast," "Lunch," "Snack," "Dinner," etc., and the overall campaign came to be known as "Operation Menu."

The ever-paranoid Nixon insisted that the campaign remain a profound military secret. Sihanouk later denied having giving permission for the strikes, but he did nothing to stop or expose them. The North Vietnamese government also said nothing, as it could not openly admit to the presence of its troops in neutral Cambodia.

However, the news reached the press in May 1969. The *New York Times* ran the story, which cited an unknown source in the administration. Furious, Nixon instigated a cover-up and a crackdown on suspected leaks. He began a practice of illegal surveillance that would later explode in the Watergate scandal, which in turn resulted in his resignation.

The Invasion   In 1970, General Lon Nol ousted Sihanouk while the latter was visiting France. A staunch anti-Communist, Lon Nol ordered a crack-down on ethnic Vietnamese in Cambodia. He also asked for American assistance in driving out the Viet Cong. On April 24, 1970, Nixon ordered American tactical air strikes on NVA targets in Cambodia, which were followed by a ground incursion.

The invasion had devastating consequences. The Americans and South Vietnamese troops were only permitted to penetrate nineteen miles into Cambodia, so the Viet Cong simply pushed deeper into the country. South Vietnamese soldiers slaughtered Cambodian civilians in retaliation for Lon Nol's brutality against the ethnic Vietnamese. American college campuses, the hotbed of the antiwar movement, exploded in protest, and the ground campaign was halted in May, having achieved none of its objectives.

At Lon Nol's request, however, U.S. air raids continued. American bombs continued to batter the region, destroying property and killing thousands of civilians. Rural Cambodians grew increasingly resentful of their government. They also remained devoted to Sihanouk who had, in another bizarre turnabout, aligned himself with the Khmer Rouge.

In 1971, Congress revoked the Gulf of Tonkin Resolutions. In 1973, Congress forced Nixon to stop the bombing campaign.

"Peace With Honor"   The United States people had lost patience with the war. By early 1969, 250 American soldiers were dying every week. Fearing that he might not win reelection, Nixon announced a plan for "Vietnamization," the process of gradually pulling American troops out of Southeast Asia and "transferring" the war effort to the South Vietnamese.

In August 1969, Nixon sent his national security advisor, Henry Kissinger, to conduct secret meetings with North Vietnam. These culminated in the Paris Peace Accords of 1973, which South Vietnam rejected. America signed them anyway and withdrew all U.S. troops from the region.

In April 1975, North Vietnam broke the cease-fire established by the Paris Peace Accords, invaded Saigon,

and forcibly reunited the country. Hundreds of thousands of South Vietnamese were forced into harsh "reeducation" camps. Over a million fled the country on boats, many of them dying at sea.

In the same month, the Khmer Rouge took Phnom Penh. Sihanouk was put under house arrest. The next four years of Communist rule in Cambodia were marked by mass relocations, forced labor, and genocide. The Khmer Rouge killed more than 1.5 million Cambodians before they were ousted in 1979.

Release of the Pentagon Papers

In 1967, Secretary of Defense Robert McNamara secretly commissioned a report from Pentagon officials. The document, known informally as the Pentagon Papers, described in detail American political and military decisions with regard to Vietnam. When they were leaked to the press in 1971, they sparked controversy in the United States over the government's lack of honesty about the war.

The Papers   McNamara believed that America had a moral responsibility to check the spread of communism. As secretary of defense under presidents John Kennedy and Lyndon Johnson, he fully supported both presidents' decisions to escalate the conflict in Southeast Asia. As a result, many Americans saw him as the chief architect of the Vietnam War.

By 1966, despite his public expressions of optimism, McNamara had developed private reservations about Vietnam. He worried that American political objectives could not be achieved through military means, a position that put him out of step with the Johnson administration. As his personal doubts grew, and his friction with the president intensified, McNamara sought to document and analyze U.S. policy in the war. He asked a Department of Defense analyst, Leslie Howard Gelb, to compile a detailed history of U.S. internal government decisions relating to the country's involvement in Vietnam.

Gelb assembled a team of experts—military officers, civilian analysts, and historians—who worked for the next eighteen months on a series of highly classified reports. They produced the seven thousand pages of memos, commentary, and analysis that came to be called the Pentagon Papers. While the papers did not include White House deliberations, they did provide detailed information on behind-the-scenes American policy making. The document described the government's step-by-step descent into the Vietnam War, covering such topics as the 1953 overthrow of Ngo Dinh Diem, secret peace negotiations, and game theory analysis of the ongoing combat.

The Leak   McNamara was not the only "Cold warrior" to question the Vietnam War. One of the thirty-six experts asked to work on the Pentagon Papers was Daniel Ellsberg, a consultant for the RAND Corporation

Daniel Ellsberg's leak of Defense Department papers to the *New York Times* created controversy regarding the war and the press's coverage of it. *AP Images*

California think-tank, who was then an analyst with the State Department and the Department of Defense. Ellsberg had begun his career by advocating the use of force in Southeast Asia. However, his 1965 fact-finding tour of Vietnam left him deeply troubled. He became convinced not only of the ineffectiveness and brutality of the American war effort, but of the U.S. government's duplicity.

Unable to convince any congressmen to declassify the Pentagon Papers, Ellsberg decided to take a personal stand. In February 1971, he photocopied the forty-seven volumes and gave them to Neil Sheehan, a reporter for the *New York Times*.

The *Times* published the documents in installments, causing an instant national uproar. The papers demonstrated a systematic abuse of power by three American presidents. Kennedy, Johnson, and Nixon had sidestepped Congress, the public, and even their own advisors in pursuit of their objective. They had used secrecy and misdirection to avoid public opposition to their policies.

The Nixon administration immediately went on the offensive. The publication of classified documents, they claimed, clearly endangered national security. U.S.

Attorney General John N. Mitchell charged that the newspaper had violated the Espionage Act; he threatened a lawsuit if publication was not halted. He also got a temporary court order against the *Times*, but by then the *Washington Post* and the *Boston Globe* also possessed copies of the Pentagon Papers.

In June, Alaska Senator Mike Gravel read parts of the papers aloud during a congressional hearing, thus making their contents public record. A year later, the Supreme Court heard the case *Gravel v. United States*. The Court ruled that the senator and his aide were immune from prosecution under the Speech or Debate Clause of the Constitution.

The United States government then sued the newspapers. However, on June 30, 1971, the Supreme Court upheld the right of the press to print the sensitive material.

The Plumbers Richard Nixon attributed every setback to his political opponents. He was convinced that a broad range of people plotted against him, from antiwar activists to the entire Kennedy family. Even though the Pentagon Papers primarily embarrassed Democratic predecessors John Kennedy and Lyndon Johnson, their

Within two years of the passage of the War Powers Act, North Vietnamese forces pulled a cannon past the abandoned U.S. Embassy in Saigon. *AFP/AFP/Getty Images*

release reinforced the president's essential paranoia. "We're up against an enemy conspiracy," he reportedly told his aides. "They're using any means. We're going to use any means."

In response, Nixon created a secret cadre of White House operatives called "the Plumbers." Supervised by White House Counsel John Ehrlichman, the Plumbers were told to plug the administration's "leaks." White House aides David Young and Egil "Bud" Krogh led the group, who were instructed to dig up dirt in order to discredit Ellsberg. In addition, Nixon ordered dozens of illegal phone taps on White House staff. "Anyone who opposes us, we'll destroy," said Krogh.

In September 1971, the Plumbers broke into the offices of Ellsberg's psychiatrist, Dr. Lewis Fielding, looking for incriminating material on Ellsberg. The next year, several of the same men broke into Democratic headquarters at the Watergate Complex in Washington, D.C. The burglary was shabbily managed, and the police investigation led back to the White House. The press, aided by an anonymous source in the administration calling himself "Deep Throat," traced the matter directly to the president. The resulting scandal swept Nixon out of power—he resigned in August 1974

before an imminent impeachment vote in the House could take place.

After the first release of the Pentagon Papers, Ellsberg had been charged on thirteen counts, including espionage and theft of government property. He had initially gone into hiding, but he turned himself in, asserting that he had committed no crime. His case went to court in 1973, but was dismissed because of the Plumbers's misconduct.

Passage of the War Powers Act

Throughout the Cold War, and especially in its Vietnamese theater, U.S. presidents wielded a great deal of autonomy in military matters. By 1973, many Americans believed that the Oval Office had been corrupted by a concentration of power. In response, Congress passed the War Powers Act, which was meant to limit the president's ability to personally prosecute a war.

Leader of the Free World The framers of the U.S. Constitution made every effort to check and to balance the different branches of government. In military matters, the Constitution dictates that the legislative branch is the sole branch of government that has the power to declare war. Congress also raises troops and funds the military. The executive, as commander-in-chief of the armed forces, wages war.

With the rise of communism and the nuclear age, the president of the United States took on an unprecedented amount of personal responsibility and power. President Harry Truman alone had to make the difficult decision to bomb Hiroshima, Japan, during World War II. President John Kennedy kept abreast of Russian ship movements during the Cuban Missile Crisis and personally gave the orders when those ships were to be boarded. President Lyndon Johnson ordered air strikes in retaliation for the Gulf of Tonkin incident a few hours after he received word of the attacks.

The world had changed. Correctly or not, Cold War American presidents believed themselves to be the world's chief defenders, not only against a vast Communist conspiracy, but against total global annihilation.

The Credibility Gap Presidents Woodrow Wilson and Franklin Roosevelt had delayed American entry into the World Wars because there had been little public support for intervention. In the 1950s, however, terrified of the "Red Menace" of communism, the American people largely gave their government a free hand in foreign affairs. The Gulf of Tonkin Resolution of 1964 ceded to the chief executive the right to "take all necessary measures to repel any armed attack against the forces of the United States" in Southeast Asia. As in Korea, no formal declaration of war was made in Vietnam. Yet the Vietnamese conflict became the longest sustained war in U.S. history.

As the Vietnam War dragged on, it became increasingly unpopular, and the American public began to think that presidents were abusing their power. They also became distrustful of the government's statements concerning the progress of the war, which contrasted sharply with journalists' reports from the battlefield. This "credibility gap" intensified in 1965, when the Tet Offensive cast doubt on Johnson's optimistic forecasts of victory.

In 1970 it became widely known that Nixon had ordered bombing raids over neutral Cambodia, raids that had been kept secret even from top military commanders. Antiwar activists furiously charged that the American presidency had become corrupt. The publishing of the "Pentagon Papers" in 1971 only seemed to confirm this opinion. The papers revealed that the White House had systematically withheld or misrepresented information about the war.

In 1970, two bills were introduced in Congress: the Cooper-Church and Hatfield-McGovern amendments, which attempted to cut funding for the Cambodia campaign and to force Nixon to withdraw all American troops from Vietnam. Both measures were defeated in both houses. The same year, New York Senator Jacob Javits introduced the War Powers Resolution, which was ratified only after three years of debate.

The Legislation The War Powers Act, as it came to be known, passed in November of 1973. Under the terms of the resolution, the president of the United States has to submit a written report to Congress before introducing American troops into "situations where imminent involvement in hostilities is clearly indicated by the circumstances." Once the military has been mobilized, Congress must be kept informed of all non-routine deployments. Furthermore, if Congress does not declare war or authorize the action within sixty days of the commencement of hostilities, troops must be withdrawn. If the withdrawal cannot be safely managed within that time frame, the president can extend the window to ninety days.

President Nixon vetoed the bill on the grounds that it was unconstitutional. However, because he was embroiled in the Watergate scandal at the time, he held little sway over Washington lawmakers. Congress mustered more than a two-thirds majority needed to overrule him.

Congress intended the War Powers joint resolution to limit the executive's ability to act autonomously. It was meant to ensure that the United States would not go to war without the "collective judgment of both the Congress and the president." Strangely enough, in some ways the bill actually gave the president the power to enter an undeclared conflict. As one senator put it, the president of the United States now wields an "undated ninety day declaration of war."

War Powers in Practice However, presidents have since disparaged the War Powers Act, claiming that it is unworkable and that it unconstitutionally undermines executive authority. Many have submitted the required reports, but failed to fully comply with the full terms of the resolution.

In 1975, President Gerald Ford mounted an armed rescue of the *USS Mayaguez*, which had been seized by Cambodian troops. He also ordered punitive air strikes over Cambodia. In response to congressional criticism, he argued that the War Powers Act did not apply in an emergency evacuation of American citizens. Furthermore, he said, "I did not concede that the resolution itself was legally binding on the president on constitutional grounds."

Jimmy Carter made much the same case when he unsuccessfully attempted to rescue American hostages in Teheran, Iran, in 1970. Ronald Reagan likewise shrugged aside the resolution when ordering the 1983 invasion of Grenada and the air strike against Libya in 1986.

Nevertheless, Congress still holds its War Powers prerogatives and will, on occasion, exercise them. In 1993, the House of Representatives invoked the War Powers Act to demand that U.S. troops be pulled out of Somalia.

In August 1962, President Kennedy met with volunteers for the new Peace Corps Program on the White House Lawn.   *John F. Kennedy Library.*

✪ Homefront

Peace Corps

The Peace Corps is a federal government agency that places American volunteers in developing countries to assist with medical programs, education, and economic development. The agency was created in 1961 under the control of the State Department. Since then, more than 187,000 Americans have volunteered to serve in 139 nations to pursue the Corps' goals of alleviating poverty, illiteracy, and disease.

President John F. Kennedy is largely credited with the creation of the Peace Corps, but the concept originated with his congressional colleagues, Representative Henry S. Reuss and Senator Hubert Humphrey in the late 1950s. While campaigning for the office of president, then Senator Kennedy put forth the initiative in a campaign speech at the University of Michigan. In front of thousands of students assembled to hear the candidate speak, Kennedy asked, "How many of you who are going to be doctors are willing to spend your days in Ghana? Technicians or engineers, how many of you are willing to work in the Foreign Service and spend your lives traveling around the world?" Kennedy claimed that

this type of effort would be necessary for America to compete on a global scale, and the notion went along with the famous challenge in his inaugural address on January 20, 1961: "Ask not what your country can do for you. Ask what you can do for your country." Within months, Kennedy was elected president and issued an executive order creating the Peace Corps.

He named Sargent Shriver, his brother-in-law, as its first director. In August 1961, the president hosted a ceremony in the White House Rose Garden to recognize the first class of Peace Corps volunteers who traveled to Ghana and Tanzania. When the first fifty-one American Peace Corps volunteers arrived in Ghana, they were warmly greeted with a chorus of the nation's anthem. Shriver oversaw 7,300 volunteers who assisted developing countries during his first year. He served ambitiously through the remainder of Kennedy's short life and until 1966, under Lyndon Johnson. For the agency's first year, Congress appropriated $30 million. By the time Shriver left his post, the Peace Corps had seen fourteen thousand volunteers serve in fifty-two countries and his budget expand to $110 million. Also during his tenure, the agency was given greater independence within the State Department.

Betty Friedan marches in New York City in 1970, celebrating the 50th anniversary of the passing of the 19th amendment. *© JP Laffont/Sygma/Corbis*

In the late 1960s, interest in the program decreased somewhat, due to budget cuts and a leveling off of the numbers of volunteers. Volunteers who may have opposed America's role in the Vietnam conflict also may have felt they should distance themselves from the government-sponsored program because they disagreed with United States foreign policy. Some have criticized the Peace Corps since its inception. Fiscal conservatives in Congress have questioned how much impact a relatively small group assisting localities in far away third-world countries could have on extinguishing poverty and illness. Nevertheless, the Peace Corps continues to attract many of the brightest young men and women in the United States, offering them a chance to put their skills and efforts to use in faraway lands.

Women's Movement

While America became concerned with stopping communism at the seventeenth parallel in Vietnam, it experienced a major social change at home with the Women's Movement. For more than a century, activists had pushed to expand rights—gaining the constitutional right for women to vote in 1920—and by the 1960s, the movement had gained enormous attention. Women by this time composed a large part of the U.S. workforce. In 1950, roughly 90 percent of mothers with children under the age of six did not hold jobs. Three decades later, a majority of mothers with small children did earn a living outside the home.

As more women entered the workforce and exercised their right to vote, lawmakers began to give them more attention. Many of the same progressives and reformers who sought equality for blacks also supported equality for women. In 1963, the Equal Pay Act made it illegal for employers to base wages on gender. The 1964 Civil Rights Act, mostly concerned with preventing discrimination toward African Americans, also addressed the equality of women. Title VII of the 1964 law prevented gender discrimination in hiring practices. By 1972, Congress passed Title IX of the Higher Education Act. This law requires colleges and universities to give equal attention to women's programs, particularly in the area of sports.

During this same era, the National Organization for Women (NOW) was created. Its first president was Betty Friedan. Her landmark, bestselling book, *The Feminine Mystique* (1963), argued that women need not live up to female stereotypes or assume traditional female roles. Friedan's ideas served as key goals for NOW. To forward these goals, NOW employed tactics such as holding public protests, lobbying lawmakers, filing lawsuits for equality in courts, and pressuring the federal government to enforce the gender equality laws passed by Congress. It was NOW, and other grassroots organizations and pioneering women, that caused Ivy League universities and the U.S. military to open their doors to female applicants. NOW had a membership of about three hundred when it started in 1966, and today has more than a half million members in 550 chapters throughout the country.

One of the movement's most sought-after goals was the passage of the Equal Rights Amendment (ERA), which would have amended the U.S. Constitution. The proposed amendment was first introduced in Congress in 1923. It gradually gained attention over the years until NOW made it one of its main priorities. The language of the proposed amendment was simple: "Equality of rights under the law shall not be denied on account of sex." Both the Republican and Democratic parties endorsed the amendment, and it garnered the required two-thirds vote in both the House of Representatives and the Senate. But it fell short of ratification by the necessary number of states, thirty-eight. Even supporters of equality questioned complicated matters that could have resulted from such an amendment. Labor unions wondered what might happen to the special laws for women they had worked so hard to pass. Would women be drafted into the military and have to serve in combat?

These antiwar protesters burnt draft cards on the steps of the Pentagon in 1972.   *Hulton Archive/Getty Images*

Extremists argued that unisex toilets would become the norm.

The ERA never was ratified, but the movement itself had more successes than failures. Since the 1960s, a greater number of women have been elected to public office, have served as administrators and presidents of companies, have played professional sports, and have had a profound influence on American society. In 1972, Shirley Chisholm, the first African American woman elected to Congress, became the first African American woman to run for president. In 1981, President Ronald Reagan appointed the first female Supreme Court justice: Sandra Day O'Connor; Democratic presidential nominee Walter Mondale chose Geraldine Ferraro as his running-mate in 1984. Thanks to the efforts of the women and men active in the women's movement, women enjoy freedoms and opportunities today that would have been unheard of to their grandmothers.

Antiwar Movement

For Americans, the Vietnam War proved to be one of the most unpopular wars in the nation's history. From the time that official combat began in 1964 until final U.S. with-

drawal from Saigon in 1975, dissatisfaction with the conduct of the war intensified, reaching a fever pitch in 1968.

Most Americans generally supported American involvement in Vietnam, at least initially. The American attempt to stop communism in Asia followed common Cold War policy carried out by U.S. presidents—from Harry Truman through Richard Nixon. An American presence was already in place when the 1964 Gulf of Tonkin incident occurred. Soon after, Congress handed President Lyndon Johnson virtually unchecked power to stop further aggression in Southeast Asia in the form of the Gulf of Tonkin Resolution. Public support for this measure can be gauged by the vote in Congress. Only two senators voted against the resolution, and both lost reelection bids when their terms expired.

Support Begins to Decline   As the war dragged on, however, public support for the effort began to wane. Advances in television reporting likely contributed to the growing antiwar movement. By the late 1960s, images in both print and television media gave Americans a clear and detailed view of the fighting occurring in Vietnam. Americans began to question the purposes and management of the military endeavor.

College campuses became centers for antiwar activity. Students for a Democratic Society (SDS), a group that organized on the University of Michigan campus in the early 1960s to promote civil rights, began to focus more on its antiwar agenda. Tom Hayden, one of the founding members, helped to create hundreds of chapters of the society on college campuses nationwide. One of the first notable anti-Vietnam War protests was a march in Washington, D.C., sponsored by SDS, which took place in April 1965. At that rally, an estimated twenty thousand people demonstrated against the war. A New York City protest in April 1967 saw 130,000 dissenters.

One event that decisively turned American public opinion against the war was the Tet Offensive. On January 31, 1968, during an agreed-upon truce for Tet, the Vietnamese lunar New Year festival, North Vietnamese soldiers conducted a surprise attack against more than one hundred cities, including Saigon, the capital of South Vietnam. The attack on Saigon pitted some four thousand Viet Cong against the city, especially the U.S. embassy. Headlines in American newspapers reported the attack but were no match for the moving images that were broadcast on television. The reality was that the Tet Offensive did not have the impact militarily that the North Vietnamese had hoped for, but Americans witnessed their embassy in shambles, dead American soldiers, and South Vietnamese falling dead in the street.

Leaders Oppose the War The public's confidence had been shaken. Americans began to question the practical sense of the war. Public officials, too, asked if the Vietnam War was being waged competently, or if it was a war that could be won. Senator Robert Kennedy had been in favor of stopping the spread communism since serving in his brother President John Kennedy's cabinet, but two weeks after Tet, he outlined the illusions that made the approach at that time nonproductive. He argued that the United States had misconceived the nature of warfare in Vietnam, because it was using military might to solve a conflict that required the conviction of the South Vietnamese people to win. "It is like sending a lion to halt an epidemic of jungle rot," Kennedy said. He also questioned the use of many thousands of tons of bombs, which ruined the landscape of Vietnam, both North and South. "Whatever the outcome of these battles," Kennedy continued, "it is the people we seek to defend who are the greatest losers."

Robert Kennedy's 1968 campaign for the Democratic nomination for president was gaining steam when he was assassinated in Los Angeles on June 6, just after declaring victory in the California primary election.

Democratic National Convention 1968 President Lyndon Johnson had dropped out of the presidential race, so the field was open for the Democratic nomination. When the time came for the Democratic National Convention in August, the atmosphere was fraught with

NEWS REPORTING DURING VIETNAM

Fewer than ten journalists were assigned to cover events in Vietnam in 1960 as the United States began to increase its involvement in the conflict. By 1968, about five hundred full-time reporters delivered news on a daily basis to media outlets worldwide. Most were Americans working for companies like the *New York Times*, United Press International (UPI), the Associated Press, the major television networks, and weekly news magazines. As American troop levels began to decline during President Richard Nixon's administration, so too did the number of reporters and the level of interest in the battlefield.

Reporters like David Halberstam of the *New York Times*, Peter Arnett of the Associated Press, and Neil Sheehan of UPI enjoyed less restriction and government censorship than reporters covering earlier wars. These reporters felt what they observed in the field did not square with official government reports on the progress of the war, and they openly communicated their interpretations to American readers. Leaders like General William Westmoreland and Secretary of Defense Robert McNamara frequently objected to news reports that painted a grim picture of the situation in Vietnam, arguing that many of the journalists covering the conflict were too young and too inexperienced to understand what was going on, or that they simply sought personal celebrity. What seems clear is that both the press and the military leaders had interests to protect, and the American public was often given skewed views of the truth about Vietnam.

tension. The violent deaths of Kennedy and civil rights leader Martin Luther King, Jr. (who was assassinated in April of 1968), coupled with the continued escalation of the war in Vietnam, had made many in the antiwar movement desperate. Antiwar protestors converged on the Chicago convention hoping for an opportunity to influence Vietnam policy and bring about some change. The ten thousand people who showed up were a mixture of left-wing extremists, moderate dissidents, and rabble-rousers with a variety of agendas. Most had lost confidence in the traditional political system.

Mayor Richard Daley assured citizens that he would not allow protestors to overrun the city and called out extra law enforcement. Things remained fairly peaceful until protestors marched on the International Amphitheater and were met with police rifle butts, clubs, and tear gas. The incident got the protestors publicity, but the media painted the dissidents as violent and disrespectful. What followed was the trial of the so-called Chicago Seven: seven protest leaders charged in court with the violent disturbance. Tom Hayden, one of the seven leaders, recalled his logic: "Our strategy was to show that the Democratic Party would lose all credibility if it didn't promise to end the war.... Reason had never worked; moral persuasion had never worked.... We were prepared to go to jail ... how could we protest from the sidelines?"

The events at Chicago in 1968 resulted in injuries and convictions. But another protest held at Kent State University in Ohio left four students dead. The protest came after Nixon had ordered the U.S. military into Cambodia. Protestors on several campuses burned Reserved Officers Training Corps (ROTC) buildings, and at Kent State, the National Guard had been activated. On May 4, 1970, guardsmen shot a volley into the crowd, killing four students. These killings sparked protests on more campuses across the nation. More than four hundred colleges shut down as professors and students staged strikes. Nearly 100,000 people marched on Washington, D.C. The antiwar movement had suddenly become mainstream.

Watergate

The Watergate scandal (1972–1974) involved an illegal break-in at the Democratic National Headquarters— located in an office/apartment building called the Watergate in Washington, D.C.—in 1972 that was conceived and sponsored by those tied to President Richard Nixon and the Republican Committee to Re-Elect the President (CREEP). Nixon denied any knowledge of the crime, but after an investigation ensued, he lost credibility, and it became clear that he at least knew of crucial events around the burglary. The scandal led to Nixon's eventual resignation and public disillusionment with politics in general.

Ironically, Nixon was predicted to win reelection in 1972 by a wide margin. His opponent, Democratic Sen. George McGovern, was a liberal member of his own party who stood with the antiwar movement and trailed significantly in the polls. The November election that year gave Nixon a landslide victory with 72 percent of the popular vote and 520 of the available 538 electoral votes.

The Break-In On June 17, 1972, a security guard at the Watergate Complex noticed signs of a possible burglary: there were pieces of tape over the locks of several doors. He called the police, and five burglars were caught inside the offices of the Democratic National Headquarters. Not present in the room but indicted along with them were former CIA agents G. Gordon Liddy and E. Howard Hunt, who orchestrated the break-in and monitored the burglars' activities with radio equipment from a hotel across the street. One of the accused burglars, James McCord, wrote a letter to the judge assigned to the case reporting that powerful forces in the government were attempting to cover up the burglary. The story began to evolve into the biggest American political scandal of the twentieth century.

Woodward and Bernstein As the story around this break-in unfolded, two newspaper reporters found it odd that the accused men had connections with the White House. The reporters were Bob Woodward and Carl Bernstein of the *Washington Post*. They suspected a conspiracy and probed until they turned up more information. Woodward and Bernstein had an anonymous informant, whom they nicknamed "Deep Throat," who was clearly knowledgeable and provided more information. The reporters uncovered evidence that knowledge of either the break-in or the ensuing cover-up could be traced to the highest branches of government—even the White House itself. In 2005, W. Mark Felt, a deputy director at the Federal Bureau of Investigation in the early 1970s, identified himself publicly as "Deep Throat." Woodward and Bernstein confirmed this.

Cut Tape The press was not the only entity interested in the Watergate burglary. Members of Congress, the courts, and citizens suspected the president of involvement. The common questions became, "What did the president know, and when did he know it?" Nixon began to lose credibility and conducted a full-scale cover-up, denying his involvement with or knowledge of the crime. This included withholding audio tapes of White House conversations among the conspirators and firing those in the administration who cooperated with investigators. When subpoenaed for the tapes as evidence, Nixon withheld them, claiming that executive privilege allowed him to keep conversations between him and his advisors confidential. The dispute went to the Supreme Court, which ultimately forced Nixon to hand over the evidence. Once the tapes arrived, there was an eighteen minute gap that to this day has never been explained.

In the summer of 1974, the House Judiciary Committee voted to approve articles of impeachment against Nixon. Before the vote to impeach made it to the full house, the president resigned. In a dramatic live televised speech, he announced on August 8, 1974, that he would resign the presidency effective noon the following day. That is when Vice President Gerald Ford took the oath of office and began his short tenure as president. One of his first steps was to pardon Nixon of any crimes he may have committed in the affair. Ford's purpose was to forgo a costly and distracting investigation that had already been played out in the court of public opinion. The American public, however, considered the move a miscarriage of justice. It may be what cost Ford the election in 1976.

Nixon left the White House with full retirement benefits, but with the mistrust of the American people. He was never indicted or tried. Liddy, Hunt, an aide named James McCord, and the burglars were convicted and served prison sentences. The scandal, which came after America's involvement in Vietnam had reached an

During the events Gerald Ford would refer to as a "long national nightmare," Richard Nixon resigned as president in August 1974.
© *Bettmann/Corbis*

all-time low in U.S. popularity, contributed to a distrust of government among many American citizens.

✪ International Context

Emergence of Independent African Nations

Much like Southeast Asia, the continent of Africa suffered centuries of oppression at the hands of imperialistic European powers. During the twentieth century, many African countries began to push for freedom from European control.

African Resources As early as the 1400s, Portuguese explorers made their way to Africa in search of gold, slaves, and other resources. By the late 1800s, conflicts between competing colonizing nations like Britain, France, Spain, Italy, the Netherlands, and Germany emerged as disputes over resource-rich Africa occurred. These costly battles over land brought the need for a compromise. The Berlin Conference of 1884-85 carved up the continent among the various European powers. A land mass that had housed thousands of tribes with a multitude of languages, cultures, and political systems

had been consolidated into a handful of colonies under European rule.

This system developed over the following decades with little opposition. Some tribes resisted and revolted, but the uprisings of tribesmen against the more powerful European states with modern war machines proved futile. Rarely were these attempted revolutions more than sporadic. As World War II began, only four African nations were free of European control: Liberia, created by the United States as part of a slave emancipation movement a century earlier; Ethiopia; South Africa; and Egypt. After World War II, a movement for local independence had taken place in colonies across the globe. Britain withdrew from India. The Netherlands left Indonesia. And France experienced a loss in Vietnam to the independence movement there. African veterans of World War II, commercial farmers, and scholars pushed for independence.

The Push for Independence Though the British had granted Independence to Egypt years before, there was a strong British presence in the country after WWII. Many British citizens had withdrawn, but several remained. The ascent of the aggressive Egyptian general Gamal

Abdel Nasser brought the final withdrawal of the British from the Suez Canal Zone.

In the post–World War II era, the French constitution treated Algeria as a department of the republic. During a celebration of Victory-in-Europe day in May 1945, an Algerian procession carried nationalist flags that the French police proceeded to block. A riot ensued pitting French authorities against native Algerians. Twenty-two died and forty-eight were wounded. Algerian resentment of the French only grew after this incident. By 1956, a National Council of the Algerian Revolution was formed. Over the next several years, the French tried to suppress this independence movement, but had difficulties. Neighboring Morocco and Tunisia had become independent and provided safe haven for Algerian revolutionaries. By 1962, the movement, and the armed forces that supported it, had gained control of Algeria.

In the Congo, which had been held by Belgium since the Berlin Conference, the movement toward independence intensified in the 1950s. At the time, Belgium still maintained a marked distinction between the Congolese and the Belgians, who were clearly in charge in the Congo. Only a handful of Congo's natives were permitted to attend Belgian universities and no native African held a rank higher than sergeant in Belgium's military. Such inequities inspired the creation of the Congolese national movement. By 1960, the Congo had gained its independence.

As the Congo received its independence, Mali, Chad, Niger, Cameroon, Zaire, and other Saharan nations won theirs. Those nations further south—like Angola, Mozambique, and Zimbabwe—earned independence after 1970. By 1993, the final African colony earned its sovereignty and became the independent Eritrea.

Six Day War

The Six Day War, also known as the Arab-Israeli War of 1967, was one of several conflicts between the Jewish nation of Israel and its surrounding Arab neighbors. The name "Six Day War" sums up the rapid, intense strikes that the Israeli military made on its adversaries—Egypt, Jordan, and Syria. Israel won the short war and gained additional territory. The encounter had international complications as part of the Cold War, and it proved that Israel was a force to be reckoned with.

Background The year 1967 must be seen in the context of the centuries-old struggle between Jews, Muslims, and Christians for the territory that is now Israel. All three religious groups claim the area as their "holy land," and the region has been the source of bloody disputes for thousands of years. The Christian Crusaders of Europe, for example, attempted to claim the region throughout the Middle Ages.

After World War II, the United Nations, motivated by the atrocities suffered by the Jewish population of Europe under the genocidal dictatorship of Germany's Adolf Hitler, agreed with Great Britain's plan to divide the area, which was then under British control. The UN voted to divide the region into a Jewish state and an Arab state. Israel proclaimed its independence in 1948, and the Arab-Israeli war ensued when Israel's Arab neighbors attacked. Israel gained territory in the conflict, including the area known as Palestine, a predominantly Arab region. Israel's neighbors were ill pleased to have the new Jewish state in control of an Arab territory.

During the 1960s, this dispute over Palestine was made worse when the Palestine Liberation Organization was created in 1964. One of the PLO's primary goals was to liberate Palestine from Israel, proclaiming Zionism (a political movement that supports the maintenance of a Jewish homeland) a racist movement against Islam. During the next few years, Palestinians, under no official Arab state flag, made attacks on Israeli civilians. Also during the mid-1960s, heightened anti-Israeli rhetoric and promises to annihilate and eradicate Zionism and the Israeli state compelled Israel to retaliate. Egyptian leader Gamal Abdel Nasser had gained huge popularity among Arab nations and in the third world, and felt it was his destiny to remove Israel from the map.

Nasser Makes His Move In May 1967, Nasser moved Egyptian forces into the Sinai Peninsula, which had been a demilitarized zone since the 1956 war and ousted the United Nations Emergency Forces, which had been a peacekeeping force stationed there. Afterward, he blockaded the Strait of Tiran, a common Israeli shipping path.

Israel lost little time responding. It began a mission, using its air force to attack Egyptian planes in the early hours of June 5, 1967. While Egyptian pilots ate breakfast, the Israeli Air Force destroyed three hundred of Egypt's military aircraft. With its air superiority assured, Israel then led its ground forces into Egypt and subdued them. Egypt lost six hundred of its one thousand tanks, and suffered ten thousand dead and twelve thousand prisoners. By an agreement between Nasser and Jordan's King Hussein, Jordan entered the conflict and fought hard, but suffered defeat at the hands of the determined Israelis. Syria, too, faced off with Israel only to lose the strategic point of the Golan Heights.

The war was over by June 11 and had marked consequences for the ongoing Cold War between the United States and the USSR. Moscow denounced the Israeli actions as preemptive and aggressive. They pushed for a resolution at the United Nations to condemn Israel, but it was vetoed. The United States took a cautious approach, but sided more so with Israel.

The Six Day War resulted in a stronger Israel. The new nation had proved its military prowess and reluctance to put up with Arab threats. Israel also gained considerable territory, expanding from 80,000 to 260,000 square miles with the acquisition of the Gaza Strip, the West Bank, Golan Heights, much of the Sinai

An Israeli soldier rides atop a U.S.-made Super-Sherman tank on the 1973 counteroffensive against Syrians in the Golan Heights.   *Gabriel Duval/AFP/Getty Images*

Peninsula, and Jerusalem. With these acquisitions came a population of over one million Arabs. Their victory was decisive, but the conflict would continue with another deadly encounter in the Yom Kippur War of 1973.

Yom Kippur War

The Yom Kippur War of 1973 was one of several military conflicts between Israel and its Arab neighbors. The war cast the two sides—the Israelis and the neighboring Arab states—as pawns in the Cold War clash between the Soviet Union and the United States.

Background   Israel had proven a formidable foe in the 1967 Six Day War, through which it had gained thousands of square miles of territory, including the Gaza Strip, the West Bank, and the Golan Heights. Along with these land gains came nearly a million Arabs.

Between the Israeli victory in 1967 and the commencement of the Yom Kippur War in 1973, several events took place. Anwar Sadat had become the new Egyptian president and pledged to seek revenge on Israel. The two sides had grown closer to their respective allies—the Israelis to the United States, and the Arab states, Egypt in particular, to the USSR. The Soviets, in fact, had supplied Sadat with new weaponry. The portable Sagger missile allowed a single foot soldier to take

out a tank, and SAMs (surface-to-air missiles) diminished the importance of the Israeli Air Force, which had played a decisive role in the Six Day War.

Surprise Attack   October 6, 1973, was Yom Kippur, the holiest of Jewish holy days. In Israel, no one travels, except on foot, on this celebrated day. On the Bar-Lev line (the point of Israeli defenses on the east bank of the Suez Canal) reservists waited out their tour. In the Golan Heights, to the north bordering Syria, under-manned units observed Yom Kippur. No one was ready for what was about to take place. At 2:00 PM, the Egyptians and Syrians carried out a coordinated attack on two fronts. The Egyptian forces crossed the Suez Canal and established a stronghold in the Sinai Peninsula. The Syrians attacked Israelis in the Golan Heights with both infantry and armored vehicles, as well as air support. A mere 180 Israeli tanks faced an onslaught of 1,400 Syrian tanks. In the Suez, 436 Israeli defenders were attacked by 80,000 Egyptians. When the Israeli Air Force tried to respond, the new Soviet weapons proved useful. The Israelis were quickly crippled militarily.

Though Egypt and Syria were the major players against the Jewish state on Yom Kippur, several other Arab nations had contributed to the effort. Iraq had transferred a squadron of Hunter jets to Egypt and provided a division of some eighteen thousand men and several tanks to the Golan Heights. Saudi Arabia and Kuwait committed men to battle. Libya and Algeria also provided men and materiel. The Arab states assisted in a diplomatic embargo as well. When the United States and Western Europeans showed signs of assisting Israel, Arab OPEC nations (those organized in the oil cartel) promised an oil embargo. Once the help that Israel requested from the United States, the Netherlands, and others arrived, oil shipments from the major oil providers to the West slowed, and in some cases stopped entirely.

While the fighting intensified and became public, the United Nations tried to intervene to stop the war in this volatile region. A showdown took place between the Soviet Union and the United States. Each country wielded veto power in the UN Security Council, which made it impossible to bring a decisive truce. Egypt had demanded Israel give up the territory it had won in the Six Day War and return to its pre-1967 borders. As the superpowers debated the issue at the UN, they also began supplying their friends in the Middle East.

Israel Fights Back Israel was able to recover after the initial shock. By the third day of the war, Israeli jets had struck into Syria, hitting Damascus and causing serious civilian casualties. Israel was able to drive back the Syrian army to within twenty miles of the Syrian capital. Its artillery units shelled the suburbs of the city. The fighting lasted a little more than two weeks. Israel lost 800 tanks, 115 aircraft, and 2,500 soldiers. About 9,000 were wounded. Arab losses were still greater. More than 450 planes went down and 2,000 tanks were destroyed. An estimated 8,500 Arabs died, while about 20,000 were wounded.

On October 22, the UN Security Council finally drafted a cease-fire resolution that both Egypt and Israel accepted. Syria accepted a slightly different resolution the following day. Some fighting continued along the Suez until a UN peacekeeping force arrived and an official cease fire was signed on November 11. Israel agreed to withdraw to a line that was twenty miles beyond its 1967 line at the Suez. A UN buffer zone was created between Syria and Israel. The war highlighted Isreal's weakened military position in the Middle East. No longer could it count on an easy six day victory. Tensions in the region mounted.

✪ Aftermath

OPEC Power

OPEC, the Organization of Petroleum Exporting Countries, was created in 1960 as a cartel of mostly Arab nations to protect their interests against major Western oil companies. The organization has seen a variance in its economic, and thus diplomatic, power since its creation, but in the early 1970s, as the United States was preoccupied with the Vietnam War, OPEC proved a strong inter-

This July 9, 1979, *Time* magazine cover drew attention to the country's ongoing vulnerabilities due to the dependence on foreign oil supply. © *Roberto Brosan/Time & Life Pictures/Getty Images*

national player. OPEC proved its strength against the United States during the Arab-Israeli conflict of 1973 known as the Yom Kippur War when it began an oil embargo against Israel's allies. For the next decade, if not the next generation, OPEC proved a powerful force.

Creation of OPEC After the industrial revolution a century ago, the United States was the world's leader in crude oil production. Oil found largely in Ohio, Pennsylvania, and then Texas was first used for lighting and then lubrication for heavy machinery in urban centers. After the introduction of the automobile, refining oil into gasoline expanded the need for the product even more. After World War I, the United States was responsible for about 70 percent of the world's oil production. But then, British companies discovered oil in the Middle East. By the post-World War II era, it became obvious to international oil companies that most of the world's supply of oil would come form this area. The major companies—Standard Oil, Royal Dutch Shell, British Petroleum, Chevron, Exxon, Gulf, and others—took full advantage of their discovery. They began developing Saudi Arabia, Iraq, Iran, and other Arab states, providing the machinery and know-how to extract oil from the region to sell on the global marketplace. In the eyes of many Arab leaders, these Western companies began to exploit their Arab partners.

The Arab response was the creation of OPEC. An Arab Petroleum Congress convened in Cairo, Egypt, in 1959 to discuss the situation, and another meeting took place in Baghdad in 1960, resulting in the creation of the OPEC organization. The charter countries included Saudi Arabia, Iran, Iraq, Kuwait, and Venezuela. Seven more—Qatar, Indonesia, Libya, Abu Dhabi, Algeria, Nigeria, and Ecuador—joined by 1973. OPEC's charter notes that it shall promote member interests and shall "demand that Oil Companies maintain their prices steady and free from unnecessary fluctuations and that Members shall study and formulate a system to ensure the stabilization of prices." By the early 1970s, the major Western oil companies controlled only a modest one-fifth of the world oil production. The increased dependency on oil worldwide also made OPEC an even more powerful player. From 1950 until 1972, oil consumption in the United States grew from 5.8 million barrels per day to 16.4 million. Western Europe and Japan experienced even greater increases in oil use.

The power that came with control over such a precious commodity became obvious. In September of 1973 at a meeting in Vienna, Austria, members of OPEC had already called for a new system of determining the division of revenues between the Western companies and the oil-producing states. A solution was tabled and planned to be determined in an October meeting. In the meantime, a conflict broke out between a handful of member Arab states and Israel. For more than two decades, the United States had generally sided with Israel in prior conflicts. Arab states had warned that a cozy American-Israeli relationship would likely result in an oil embargo. President Richard Nixon basically ignored these warnings. Egypt, Jordan, and Syria had all lost territory to Israel in the 1967 Six Day War and wanted to reclaim it. Saudi Arabia, too, had interest in Arab states retaking Jerusalem. The Egyptians and Syrians launched a surprise coordinated attack on the Jewish holiday, Yom Kippur, October 6, 1973.

Initially, the attack resulted in heavy Israeli losses. Israel was forced to request war materiel from the United States. The United States agreed. As the October OPEC conference approached, American air force carriers could be spotted landing in Israel with supplies. When delegates from the Persian Gulf states and one from Iran met in Kuwait to discuss the situation, OPEC asserted its power. On October 17, they imposed a five percent cut in oil shipments to states that were friendly to Israel. An additional five percent per month cut would follow until these states officially endorsed United Nations Resolution 242 that called on Israel to give back the lands they gained from the 1967 Six Day War. When President Nixon announced a $22 billion package to be sent to Israel to assist with the aggression by her neighbors, Saudi Arabia announced that all oil headed for the United States and other pro-Israeli states would stop.

The United States, its allies, and the Western oil companies all felt the impact of the embargo. American consumers drove into gas stations to find prices had gone up 40 percent. Soon signs informed them "Sorry, no gas today." The effects of the embargo were partially eased by the fact that non-Arab OPEC members did not join the embargo. Major oil companies tried to solve the crisis by rerouting shipments. The embargo ended in March 1974. OPEC had asserted the power it had been developing since its creation in 1960. It made the production and control of oil a matter for diplomacy and forced American allies to break with the United States on this issue for fear of being blacklisted by OPEC. The oil companies lost power, becoming contractors of these oil-producing states instead of controlling operations within them. And, perhaps most importantly, the oil embargo drove the price of crude oil up to four times its pre-embargo price, which made the OPEC nations even more powerful and wealthy.

BIBLIOGRAPHY

Books

Boettcher, Thomas D. *Vietnam: The Valor and the Sorrow*. Boston: Little, Brown and Company, 1985.

Dorland, Gil. *Legacy of Discord: Voices of the Vietnam War Era*. Washington: Brassey's, 2001.

Isserman, Maurice. *The Vietnam War: America At War*. New York: Facts on File, 1992.

Karnow, Stanley. *Vietnam: A History*. New York: Viking Press, 1983.

Summers, Harry G., Jr. *Historical Atlas of the Vietnam War*. Boston: Houghton Mifflin, 1995.

Video

Vietnam: A Television History. Boston: WGBH Video, 1983.

Web Site

Peace Corps. <www.peacecorps.gov> (accessed June 1, 2007).

Introduction to the Gulf War (1990–1991)

On August 3, 1990, one day after Iraqi President Saddam Hussein invaded and occupied the nation of Kuwait, U.S. President George H. W. Bush rallied international support for a unified military intervention intended to liberate the small country. The six-week war that ensued was televised from start to finish, allowing the American public to view the technologically advanced weaponry used in the action. Both air and ground offenses resulted in minimal U.S. casualties and a swift and decided victory, which established President Bush as a powerful force in world affairs. Americans, burdened for so long by the specter of the inconclusive Vietnam War, celebrated the defeat of Iraq and the might of their military.

Iraq had emerged from the Iran-Iraq War of 1980–1988 $80 billion in debt. Because Iraq historically had considered Kuwait a part of Iraq, Hussein demanded that Kuwait raise the price of oil, forgive billions of dollars in debt, pay billions more in aid, and pay $2.4 billion for Iraqi oil that it allegedly pumped illegally from the Rumaila oil field, which straddles the border between the two countries. When Kuwait did not concede to these and other demands, Hussein invaded Kuwait without warning on the morning of August 2, 1990. Within a few hours, Hussein's army occupied the entire country. Meeting little resistance, they killed hundreds of Kuwaitis and jailed and tortured hundreds more.

As soon as President Bush learned of the invasion, he and his staff began planning the military intervention dubbed "Operation Desert Storm" and organizing a mighty force of 500,000 American troops and U.N.-coalition forces from dozens of countries. By late November 1990, a massive military presence was established in nearby Saudi Arabia and in the Persian Gulf itself. Diplomats from the United Nations and the United States attempted to negotiate a peaceful end to the invasion, but Hussein would not budge. January 15, 1991, was set as the deadline for withdrawal. When Hussein ignored the ultimatum, U.S. and coalition forces unleashed an air attack on Baghdad and other military installations inside Iraq. In a matter of days, the United States' cutting-edge military technology had obliterated many of Iraq's command and control centers, munitions factories, and other military installations. After 72,000 sorties dropped 141,921 tons of bombs over five weeks of air attacks, President Bush ordered the commencement of a ground offensive.

On February 24, 1991, over 100,000 U.S. and coalition troops led by General Norman Schwarzkopf mounted a swift and well-planned ground attack. Because of the success of the previous air attack, ground troops were able to defeat the enemy within 100 hours. The Gulf War ended just six weeks after it began. There were 147 Americans killed in battle, while Iraq lost between 80,000 and 100,000 soldiers and civilians. Despite the apparent total victory, Hussein was not ousted from power. He showed no contrition for his aggression, even after his elite troops were destroyed and his military might severely reduced. President Bush, enjoying the highest approval rating of any American president, ruled against further military action in Iraq but urged the world community to maintain economic sanctions against the country.

The Gulf War (1990–1991)

✪ Causes

Invasion of Kuwait

On August 2, 1990, Iraqi armed forces invaded Kuwait, a very small, oil-rich country bordering southern Iraq, sparking the Gulf War. The conflict split the Arab community into anti- and pro-Iraq camps, involved the military commitment of a U.S.-led coalition of twenty-eight countries, and brought tremendous devastation to both Iraq and Kuwait. In addition to the loss of human life and billions of dollars, the toll of the crisis includes deep political divisions between Kuwait and Saudi Arabia on one side, and Iraq, Jordan, and the Palestine Liberation Organization (PLO) on the other.

Factors Leading to the Invasion Iraq's need for money and desire for power motivated the invasion of Kuwait. Iraq emerged from the Iran-Iraq War of the 1980s financially exhausted, carrying a debt of roughly $80 billion. Saddam Hussein (1937–2006), Iraq's president, planned to service the debt—and fund the country's high-tech defense industry, food imports, and reconstruction—with oil revenue. Unfortunately, his plan collapsed when oil prices fell from $20 to $14 a barrel in the first half of 1990. Hussein charged that Kuwait and the United Arab Emirates had exceeded their Organization of Petroleum Exporting Countries (OPEC) quotas, which drove down the price of oil. Hussein accused the United States of keeping Iraq weak by encouraging the overproduction. Finally, he characterized the Kuwaiti drilling as an act of war. He demanded that the price of oil be raised to $25 a barrel, that Kuwait forgive $10 billion of debt incurred during the Iran-Iraq War, and that the Gulf states give Iraq financial aid in the amount of $30 billion. Because Iraq historically considered Kuwait a part of its territory, Hussein also demanded Kuwait pay $2.4 billion for Iraqi oil that he felt Kuwait illegally pumped from the Rumaila oil field, which straddles the Iraq-Kuwait border.

Hussein also wanted to lease the two uninhabited Kuwaiti islands of Warbah and Bubiyan, which would provide Iraq secure access to the Persian Gulf. Because of Bubiyan's close proximity to Kuwait City and previous border disputes between Iraq and itself, Kuwait was hesitant to negotiate with Iraq. Despite its debt, Iraq—a country of seventeen million people—had emerged militarily strong from the Iran-Iraq War. Iraq claimed one million experienced soldiers, 500 planes, and 5,500 tanks, and the capability to develop chemical, biological, and nuclear weapons. As tensions between Iraq and Kuwait increased, officials in the West and Israel grew alarmed. Hussein grew suspicious of Western media's condemnation of Iraqi human rights violations, especially against the country's Kurdish population. On April 2, 1990, Hussein threatened to "burn half of Israel" with binary chemical weapons if it attacked Iraq, as it had in 1981. The threat resulted in an outpouring of Arab sympathy. Because Israel had annexed Jerusalem and the Golan, invaded Lebanon, bombed PLO headquarters in Tunis, and suppressed a civilian uprising in the West Bank and Gaza since 1987—all without Arab response—Hussein was viewed as something of a hero. By calling on a potent mixture of themes, including Western imperialism, Arab impotence, the Palestinian cause, and Islam, Hussein successfully incited Arab anger, alienation, and support.

Iraq Invades Kuwait Although relations between the two countries had been deteriorating for some time, it came as a surprise when Iraq suddenly invaded Kuwait on the morning of August 2, 1990. Within a few hours, Hussein's army had occupied the entire country. Meeting little resistance, the forces killed hundreds of Kuwaitis and jailed and tortured hundreds more. The Iraqis looted the entire country, making off with furniture, automobiles, gold reserves, industrial equipment, and treasures from the Kuwaiti museum. Banks were robbed of their deposits, and schools and hospitals were stripped of their equipment. The occupation was complete.

These U.S. Marines disembarked at a base in Saudi Arabia in August 1990, mobilizing in response to Iraq's invasion of Kuwait. *Gerard Fouet/AFP/Getty Images*

Arab reaction to the invasion was split. The anti-Iraq group was made up of Saudi Arabia, Bahrain, Qatar, the United Arab Emirates, Oman, Egypt, Syria, Morocco, Lebanon, Djibouti, and Somalia; Jordan, the PLO, Yemen, Sudan, Libya, Tunisia, Algeria, and Mauritania were either neutral or pro-Iraq. The split was revealed in an August 3 meeting of the Arab League, who quickly lost hold of the crisis when a U.S.-led coalition of twenty-eight countries made the confrontation a worldwide concern. U.S. President George H. W. Bush (1924–) was quick to galvanize opposition to Iraq. On the day of the invasion, the United Nations (U.N.) Security Council condemned Iraq's actions and demanded its immediate and unconditional withdrawal.

Over the next few days, the Soviet Union and the Organization of Islamic Conference joined in the condemnation. The U.N. imposed economic sanctions on Iraq, but the most significant reaction was Saudi Arabia's August 6 agreement to allow U.S. troops and aircraft on its soil after being shown U.S. satellite photographs of Iraqi troops near Saudi borders. The deployment of U.S. troops to Saudi Arabia was known as Operation Desert Shield. Despite several diplomatic missions by various world leaders, Saddam Hussein refused to withdraw

from Kuwait. Bush gave the Iraqi leader until January 15, 1991, to leave Kuwait or face Western military forces. Hussein stood firm. On January 16, U.S. and allied forces launched Operation Desert Storm with air attacks on Iraq and on Iraqi positions in Kuwait.

The Gulf War Ends Iraq responded by firing Scud missiles at Tel Aviv, Israel. The attack damaged hundreds of buildings and killed many people. Iraq also fired missiles at Saudi Arabia and invaded its borders in late January. After a number of unsuccessful diplomatic attempts and another ultimatum by President Bush, coalition ground forces were launched into Iraq on February 24. Four days later, Kuwait was liberated. Before accepting U.N. Security Council resolutions and agreeing to a cease-fire on February 28, Iraq set fire to almost seven hundred Kuwaiti oil wells.

The Gulf Crisis destroyed Iraq's infrastructure and resulted in the loss of tens of thousands of Iraqi people. Kuwait, though, suffered the ravages of invasion, occupation, and war. The looting and destruction cost $65 billion and reconstruction was estimated at another $25 billion. Because some of the 350,000 Palestinians living in Kuwait supported the Iraq army, hundreds of Palestinians were tortured and killed after the war. Their

A portrait of Saddam Hussein looms large over these U.S. soldiers as they sit near Iraq's border with Kuwait in February 1991. *© Peter Turnley/Corbis*

community lost roughly $8 billion dollars and was reduced in size to about 30,000 after the majority resettled in Jordan. One estimate puts the cost of the Gulf War at $640 billion, but the financial cost pales in comparison to the political divisions the crisis caused.

✪ Major Figures

Saddam Hussein

Saddam Hussein (1937–2006) was the president of Iraq from 1979 until 2003, when the United States overthrew his government after he refused to cooperate with United Nations' weapons inspectors seeking alleged weapons of mass destruction. He was born on April 28, 1937, to a poor, landless peasant family in the village of Ouja, near Tikrit in northern Iraq. His mother, Subha Tulfah al-Mussallat, was supposedly related to the family of the prophet Muhammad. His father died just before he was born. At the age of ten, Hussein decided to attend school in a major act of rebellion. When his mother and stepfather tried to dissuade him, Hussein went to live with his uncle, Khayrallah Tulfah, who went on to become a tremendous influence on Hussein's life.

Hussein's Rise In 1955, Hussein began secondary studies in Baghdad where he became an antigovernment activist. In 1957, at the age of twenty, Hussein became a low-ranking member of the underground Ba'ath (Renaissance) Party, an organization based on a pan-Arab, secular socialist ideology in which the party assumes dominance in all aspects of public life. Two years later, in the fall of 1959, the Ba'ath Party chose Hussein to join a small group of party loyalists given the task of assassinating Iraqi General Abd al-Karim Qasim (1914–1963). Although Hussein claimed to have led the tank assault on the presidential palace dressed in military garb, evidence shows that he did not. Hussein was wounded by a bullet and fled to Syria when the assassination attempt failed. In Damascus, the Ba'ath leadership greeted him with a hero's welcome. Michel Aflaq (1910–1989), the Syrian Christian founder and chief ideologue of the Ba'ath Party, met personally with Hussein and later promoted him to full party membership. In 1959, Hussein moved to Cairo, Egypt, finished high school, and started studying law.

In the mid-1960s, Aflaq bestowed upon Hussein the appointment of Regional Command, the highest decision-making body of the Iraqi branch of the Ba'ath. Until his death in 1989, Aflaq was incredibly influential in the Ba'ath's Iraqi faction. Because of his standing within the party, his relationship with Hussein served to legitimize his protégé's leadership.

On February 9, 1963, General Qasim was overthrown with the help of Ba'ath loyalists. After the overthrow, Hussein left Cairo for Baghdad and became involved in internal security. That same year, Hussein married Sajida, his maternal cousin and the daughter of the uncle who raised him. Hussein and his wife eventually had five children: Uday, Qusay, Raghda, Rana, and Hala.

After the overthrow, the Ba'ath Party came to power and almost immediately split into rightist, leftist, and centrist factions. The centrist faction was led by then-prime minister Brigadier General Ahmad Hassan al-Bakr (1914–1982), a relative of Hussein's from Tikrit. Hussein aligned himself with this faction. In late 1963, just months after the overthrow of General Qasim, the Ba'ath Party was removed from power by President Abdul Salam Arif (1921–1966), a Nasserist Party figurehead. In the autumn of 1964, the Ba'ath planned a coup against Arif, but the plan was exposed. Hussein was arrested and jailed in Baghdad that October, but escaped prison in July 1966. Two years later, the Ba'aths ousted new President Abdul Rahman Arif (c. 1916–1966), who had succeeded his younger brother after the latter was killed in a helicopter crash. In 1968, the new Ba'athist president, General al-Bakr, made Hussein the assistant secretary general of the party and deputy chairman of the Revolutionary Command Council (RCC), the highest decision-making institution in the land. Between 1969 and 1979, Hussein used his power to oust and outmaneuver enemies and opponents. On July 16, 1979, he pushed al-Bakr from office, executed party rivals, and took over the positions of president and RCC chair. Within a few weeks, roughly five hundred high-ranking Ba'athists had been executed for suspected disloyalty to Hussein.

Hussein in Charge

On September 22, 1980, Iraqi aircraft invaded Iran over a longtime dispute for sovereignty rights to the Shatt al Arab waterway and related border disagreements. The invasion evolved into a full-scale war that lasted eight years and cost Iraq roughly one percent of its total population. During the ensuing Iran-Iraq war, Iraq incurred an estimated debt of $80 billion. After the war ended in stalemate in 1988, the Iraqi people faced rapidly rising prices, continued political repression, and increased unemployment. Two years later, in August 1990, Iraq invaded Kuwait, the Delaware-sized country that borders Iraq's southern tip. This invasion inspired a U.S.-led coalition to launch a massive air war followed by a short ground war against Iraq. Iraq was ousted from Kuwait and forced to destroy its nuclear, chemical, and biological weapons programs. Although large quantities of chemical weapons were destroyed over the next eight years, the international

community continued to suspect that Hussein was hiding others. By late 1998, U.N. weapons inspectors had not found any, but Hussein refused to let them inspect the presidential palaces and later refused to permit any further inspections. In October of that year, U.S. President Bill Clinton (1946–) signed into law the Iraq Liberation Act, which committed the United States to overthrowing Hussein.

War in Iraq

Following the September 11, 2001, attacks on the Pentagon and World Trade Center in the United States, President George W. Bush (1946–) feared that terrorists equipped with Iraqi weapons of mass destruction might target the United States. He demanded that Saddam Hussein cooperate with new weapons inspectors sent to Iraq in 2002. When no weapons were found, Bush issued the ultimatum that Hussein either completely disarm or voluntarily leave Iraq. When Hussein refused to leave, tensions mounted until, on March 19, 2003, the United States began a war against Iraq with a "decapitation" strike intended to assassinate Hussein. The Iraqi president survived and went into hiding for nine months, after which time coalition forces found Hussein hiding on a sheep farm near his ancestral home of Tikrit.

Hussein's Last Days

Hussein spent seven months as a U.S. prisoner of war before his legal custody was transferred to the interim Iraqi government in July 2004. Preliminary charges against Hussein, mainly pertaining to genocide, war crimes, and crimes against humanity committed during his presidency, were outlined while he was arraigned in an Iraqi court days after his transfer. Specific atrocities Hussein was accused of include the slaying of religious figures in 1974, the gassing of Kurds in 1988, the killing of the Kurdish Barzani clan in 1983, the invasion of Kuwait in 1990, and thirty years of executions of various political opposition leaders. He and members of his regime were tried before a special Iraqi war-crimes tribunal that Hussein interrupted with walkouts and hunger strikes. Finally, by late December 2006, the former Iraqi president was found guilty of crimes against humanity. He was executed by hanging on December 30, 2006.

George H. W. Bush

George Herbert Walker Bush (1924–) was the forty-first president of the United States and the leader who oversaw the Gulf War. The Republican president served from 1989 to 1993, years marked by international conflict and dramatic change. In the late 1980s and early 1990s, after forty years of tension, the Cold War came to an end. As a result, the Communist empire broke up and the Berlin Wall fell in 1989. With the long-familiar danger from Eastern Europe removed, Bush responded swiftly and decisively when Iraqi President Saddam Hussein invaded Kuwait in 1991, personifying the emerging threat from the Middle East. After American and Allied

During a November 1991 speech from the Oval Office, President George H.W. Bush announced the launching of Operation "Desert Storm." © *Jean Louis Atlan/Sygma/Corbis*

troops defeated Saddam and freed Kuwait, Bush experienced a period of unprecedented popularity. Because of a faltering economy, rising violence in America's inner cities, and continued high-deficit spending, Bush lost his bid for reelection in 1992. In retirement, Bush has kept a relatively low profile.

Bush's Early Years   The second of five children, George H. W. Bush was born in Milton, Massachusetts, on June 12, 1924, and was raised in Greenwich, Connecticut. His father, Prescott Sheldon Bush, was an investment banker before serving as a Republican senator from Connecticut from 1952 to 1963. After Bush graduated from the prestigious Phillips Academy in Andover, Massachusetts, in 1942, he was accepted at Yale University. Instead of attending Yale, though, Bush enlisted in the U.S. Naval Reserve. By 1943, Ensign Bush was the youngest fighter pilot in the Navy. After a mission over the South Pacific in which he was shot down on September 2, 1944, Bush received the Distinguished Flying Cross. On January 6, 1945, Bush married Barbara Pierce, daughter of the publisher of *McCall's* and *Redbook* magazines. Their family eventually grew to include six children, one of whom died of leukemia in 1953.

Bush entered Yale University in the fall of 1945 and graduated three and a half years later with a degree in economics. After graduation, Bush moved his family to Texas where he took a job in the oil business. By 1954, he was president of the Zapata Offshore Company, an outfit that drilled for oil in the Gulf of Mexico.

Bush Enters Politics   Bush was elected chairman of the Harris County Republican Party in 1962. In 1964, he ran for the Senate and lost, but was elected to the House of Representatives in 1966. His two terms in Congress were marked by a largely conservative voting record, though he did support several liberal social measures, including an open-housing bill, abolition of the military draft, and the lowering of the voting age to eighteen.

With the encouragement of then-president Richard M. Nixon (1913–1994), Bush ran for the Senate in 1970 but was defeated by Democrat Lloyd Bentsen (1921–2006). That December, Nixon named Bush the U.S. ambassador to the United Nations. Three years later, during the height of the Watergate scandal, Bush became chairman of the Republican National Committee. When Nixon's personal involvement in the scandal became known, Bush urged the president to resign.

Nixon's successor, Gerald R. Ford (1913–2006), made Bush head of the U.S. Liaison Office in the People's Republic of China in 1974. In 1975, Ford called Bush home and appointed him head of the Central Intelligence Agency (CIA). At the time, the agency was under fire from Congress for engaging in covert activities that overstepped the bounds of its legal mandate. Bush won high marks for improving agency morale and for helping draft an executive order designed to prevent future abuses. When Democrat Jimmy Carter (1924–) was elected in November 1976, Bush resigned his position with the CIA.

The Vice Presidency When Bush sought the Republican presidential nomination in 1980, he was seen as an attractive moderate alternative to ultraconservative Republican candidate Ronald Reagan (1911–2004). When Bush fell behind in the primary, he dropped out of the race. Despite their differences, Bush accepted Reagan's offer of the vice presidential slot. He went on to serve two terms as Reagan's vice president, loyally supporting the Reagan agenda in public, but softening the president's stand on certain issues behind the scenes.

The Presidency In 1988, despite allegations that he had known more than he admitted about the 1987 Iran-Contra political scandal, George Bush was elected president. Widely viewed as a foreign-policy president with little interest in domestic issues, Bush had the good fortune of being in office when the Cold War ended. On the domestic front, Bush worked with Congress to decrease the federal budget deficit while dealing with an inherited scandal from the Reagan administration. The scandal involved the Department of Housing and Urban Development (HUD) and the agency's former secretary, Samuel R. Pierce Jr. It was revealed that Pierce had engaged in favoritism toward prominent Republicans and had influenced peddling. Pierce allegedly wasted millions, perhaps billions, of dollars by mismanaging agency funds.

On the international front, Bush's greatest challenge came when Iraqi President Saddam Hussein invaded Kuwait. Bush rallied the global community to condemn Hussein's actions, which transformed the Arab conflict into an international one. When Operation Desert Storm ground forces defeated the Iraqis and freed Kuwait, Bush's approval rating soared. The Gulf War had the effect of boosting patriotic fervor, thanks to George Bush. His seemingly unstoppable popularity was short-lived, however. Economic and domestic issues persuaded voters to elect Democrat Bill Clinton in 1992.

Life After Politics Once retired, Bush kept a low profile. He preferred to travel and spend time with his family, though he did make the news when he became the first American president to jump out of an airplane at the age of seventy-two. In April 1997, Bush received an honorary doctorate from Hofstra University in Hempstead, Long Island. A year later, he coauthored *A World Transformed*, a memoir of his foreign-policy experiences as president. In 1999, Bush's autobiography, *All the Best, George Bush*, was published. In 2000, Bush's eldest son, former Texas governor George W. Bush (1946–), became the forty-third president of the United States. After the natural and humanitarian disasters of the Indian Ocean Tsunami in 2004 and Hurricane Katrina in 2005, Bush teamed with fellow former-President Bill Clinton to raise money for relief.

Dick Cheney

Richard Bruce Cheney(1941–) is widely known for serving both Bush presidencies, as secretary of defense in the first and vice president in the second. Between administrations, Cheney acted as chief executive at the Halliburton Company, a company he helped to build into one of the world's largest oil-drilling, engineering, and construction service providers. Cheney was also elected to the U.S. House of Representatives to represent Wyoming and served on the House Intelligence Committee.

Cheney's Early Years Richard Bruce "Dick" Cheney was born in Lincoln, Nebraska, on January 30, 1941, and was raised in Casper, Wyoming. He attended the University of Wyoming, where he finished his bachelor's degree in 1965 and his master's in 1966, and went on to study political science at the University of Wisconsin at Madison. Cheney left graduate school in 1968 without finishing his Ph.D. He moved to Washington, D.C., that year and became a staff assistant to Representative William Steiger (1938–1978), a respected Republican from Wisconsin. The job led to a series of appointments in the Nixon administration, including special assistant to Donald Rumsfeld (1932–), director of the Office of Economic Opportunity. Rumsfeld promoted Cheney to deputy when the former became White House counsel. When Rumsfeld became director of the Cost of Living Council, he appointed Cheney his assistant director of operations. These positions, held from May 1969 to March 1973, gave Cheney an enviable opportunity to learn government from the inside. Then, Watergate changed his path. Because Cheney had limited private employment experience, and because Watergate Washington was no place for a young man without a law degree, he decided to seek work in the private sector. In 1973, he became vice president of the investment advisory group, Bradley, Woods, and Company.

The Ford Administration In 1974, Donald Rumsfeld invited Cheney to join him on President Gerald Ford's transition staff. As deputy assistant to the president, Cheney became Rumsfeld's assistant again, albeit on a much higher level. It did not take long for Cheney's passion for anonymity and pragmatic conservatism to earn him positions as assistant to the president and chief of staff when Rumsfeld became head of the Department

Secretary of Defense Dick Cheney addresses U.S. troops in Saudi Arabia at the beginning of the Gulf War. © *Corbis/Sygma*

of Defense. Cheney served Ford from November 1975 until the end of his administration in January 1977.

Congressman Cheney When Democrat Jimmy Carter defeated Gerald Ford and became president in 1977, Cheney briefly returned to private life in Wyoming. Then, in 1978, despite being stricken by a heart attack during his campaign, Cheney was elected to the U.S. House of Representatives. From January 1979 until March 1989, Congressman Cheney defined himself as a compassionate conservative and a natural leader. Well liked by his constituents as well as his party, Cheney captured Wyoming's seat five times. In his second term, Cheney was elected chairman of the Republican House Policy Committee, an unprecedented feat for a sophomore representative. Cheney benefited from the return of the Republicans to the White House under Ronald Reagan. He supported Reagan's plan for defense buildup and the president's foreign policy on Afghanistan and Nicaragua. As a respected Congressman, Cheney was the obvious choice for service on the House Select Committee to Investigate Covert Arms Deals with Iran. As ranking Republican and co-chairman of the committee, he vehemently disagreed with the majority report and defended the Reagan administration on the Iran-Contra episode of 1987.

Cheney as Secretary of Defense Ten years of dedicated service in the House made Cheney a respected national figure. Although he never served in the military and had little experience dealing with the Pentagon, he was appointed secretary of defense. The uncommon perspective he gained from his executive and legislative experience was seen as compensation for those shortcomings. Cheney quickly established control over the massive military-civilian bureaucracy. But his most important test came in 1990 when Saddam Hussein invaded Kuwait.

After President George H. W. Bush committed troops to defend Saudi Arabia, Cheney was responsible for the massive organization of personnel and supplies to the Persian Gulf. American troops joined coalition forces in pursuit of the restoration of the Kuwaiti monarchy as well as the protection of U.S. interests. On January 17, 1991, the forces began a violent air strike against Iraq followed by a ground attack on February 24. This second attack destroyed the bulk of Iraq's military forces in less than 100 hours. Cheney and U.S. Chief of Staff Colin Powell (1937–) became popular heroes when Iraq

General Colin Powell, seen here visiting U.S. troops in Saudi Arabia during the Gulf War, was the first African American to serve as chairman of the Joint Chiefs of Staff. © *Durand-Hudson-Langevin-Orban/Sygma/Corbis*

surrendered and withdrew from Kuwait. After the conflict, Cheney began reducing the U.S. military by closing military bases, among other things. The decision was unpopular, but his solid reputation and stellar professionalism allowed him to proceed with this and other controversial measures. He remained secretary of defense until Democrat Bill Clinton became president in 1994. Cheney left Washington again, this time to become chief executive of Halliburton Company. In 1999, after Cheney transformed the organization into one of the world's largest oil-drilling, engineering, and construction service providers, Halliburton acquired Dresser Industries Incorporated, which increased the former company's $20 million revenue.

Cheney as Vice President In 2000, Texas Governor George W. Bush invited Cheney to be his running partner in the presidential campaign. The two were sworn in as president and vice president, respectively, on January 20, 2001. During their first term in office, the Bush administration was accused of being involved in the Enron scandal and other scandals related to the country's rapid economic decline. It denied any and all accusations. In March 2003, the United States invaded Iraq against a firestorm of criticism. In the following months,

the vice president lashed out at critics, calling their arguments against the war dangerous and naïve. Bush and Cheney defeated Democratic presidential candidate John Kerry in 2004 after a vitriolic campaign. The first several years of the second administration were marked by war in Iraq, an investigation into the September 11 attacks, and scandals involving Cheney's chief of staff, I. Lewis "Scooter" Libby, and former Central Intelligence Agency officer Valerie Plame.

Colin Powell

Four-star General Colin Luther Powell (1937–) was chairman of the Joint Chiefs of Staff during the Gulf War and secretary of state in George W. Bush's first term—he was the first African American to hold either position. He achieved national and international prominence during the Persian Gulf War in 1990 and 1991. After the war, he was considered a good candidate for vice president by Democrats and Republicans alike. Powell resisted being pushed into electoral politics.

Powell's Early Years Powell was born in Harlem, New York, on April 5, 1937, to Luther and Maud Ariel McKoy Powell. His parents had immigrated from Jamaica to Manhattan's garment district. The younger of two children, Powell was raised in the South Bronx in a loving and close-knit family. After graduating from high school, Powell went on to New York's City College where he earned a degree in geology in 1958. He was a standout in the school's Reserve Officers' Training Corps (ROTC) unit, serving as commander of the precision drill team and graduating as a cadet colonel, the highest possible rank. After graduation, Powell joined the Army and was sent to West Germany. In 1962, he began the first of two one-year tours of duty in Vietnam, serving as an advisor to a Vietnamese infantry battalion. During this tour, Powell earned a Purple Heart after being injured by a Viet Cong trap that sent a stake through his foot. In his second tour, Powell served as an infantry officer at the battalion level from 1968 to 1969. On this tour, Powell was awarded a Soldier's Medal after rescuing fellow soldiers from the fiery wreck of a downed helicopter. When he returned to the United States, Powell entered George Washington University and completed an MBA in 1971.

Powell Begins His Political Career

In 1972, Powell received a prestigious White House fellowship in the Office of Management and Budget (OMB). During his tenure there, Powell met two men—Caspar Weinberger (1917–2006), the OMB's director; and Frank Carlucci (1930–), the OMB's deputy director and later President Reagan's national security advisor—who would figure prominently in his future. Powell served as Carlucci's assistant and impressed his boss with his competence and efficiency. Over the next fifteen years, Powell went back and forth from military duty to political appointments. In 1976, he graduated with distinction from the National War College. In 1979, he served as executive assistant to the secretary of energy, after working as senior military assistant to the deputy secretary of defense.

In mid-1983, Secretary of Defense Weinberger invited Powell to become his senior military assistant. Powell agreed and excelled as an organizer and a peacemaker who fostered cooperation between competing agencies and individuals. Powell was one of only five people in the Pentagon who knew about the National Security Council's secret efforts to secure the release of American hostages in the Middle East by selling arms to Iran, then channeling the profits to Nicaraguan *contra* forces fighting the Sandinistas. Unlike other players in the so-called Iran-Contra affair, Powell was honest about what he knew, which enhanced rather than compromised his reputation for integrity and candor when his role in the scandal came to light.

In 1986, Powell left Washington to assume a prestigious and much-coveted position as commander of the V Corps in Frankfurt, West Germany, which put him in charge of roughly 72,000 troops. Six months later, in January 1987, Frank Carlucci asked Powell to return to the capital as his assistant. Powell reluctantly took the job,

but only after President Reagan personally asked him to do so. The first order of business was to repair the National Security Council's damaged credibility. Carlucci and Powell reorganized the staff and changed procedures to reduce the risk of future scandals. When Carlucci replaced Weinberger as secretary of defense, Powell was promoted to succeed Carlucci as head of the National Security Council. His selection was met with universal acclaim, unlike many Washington appointments. Powell served as national security advisor throughout the remainder of Reagan's administration, which allowed him to play a key role in several significant events. In the first, Powell helped persuade Reagan not to use military force to oust Panamanian dictator Manuel Noriega (1938–) and not to pressure Congress for continued support of the Nicaraguan contras in their struggle with the Sandinistas. Powell was also the chief organizer of Reagan's last two meetings with Soviet leader Mikhail Gorbachev (1931–), which led to a major nuclear arms treaty. He became chairman of the Joint Chiefs of Staff under President Bush in 1989—the youngest man to ever hold that position.

The Persian Gulf War

When Saddam Hussein invaded Kuwait in August 1990, Powell's duties shifted to include developing actual military strategies. When the order was given to engage Iraq militarily, Powell directed General H. Norman Schwarzkopf (1934–) to integrate communications, operations, and authority of the multinational force. But Powell planned all of the land, sea, and air campaigns and advised President Bush on the many political decisions that had to be made. The success of Operation Desert Shield and Operation Desert Storm, which led to Hussein's withdrawal and the liberation of Kuwait, made heroes of many. Powell stood tallest among them. His ability to balance U.S. political objectives against military realities and to handle both with exceptional skill and diplomacy restored public confidence in the armed forces. Powell's rise from humble beginnings and his unapologetic patriotism appealed to Americans of all races and ethnicities. As a result, he was urged to run for political office. But Powell, an independent who had served both Republican and Democratic administrations with distinction, harbored no political desires.

Powell was reappointed to a second two-year term as chairman of the Joint Chiefs in October 1991, after which time he retired from the military. He spent the next several years chairing organizations that sought to build and strengthen youth competence and character, namely America's Promise—The Alliance for Youth. To make a difference in the lives of American children, Powell enlisted the time and financial support of companies, nonprofit organizations, and individuals. He returned to political life in 2000, when president-elect George W. Bush nominated Powell to be the sixty-fifth secretary of state. His four-year tenure was made

President Bush meets with General Norman Schwarzkopf, dubbed "Stormin' Norman" after his Gulf War ground offensive, in April 1991. *J. David Ake/AFP/Getty Images*

contentious by the war in Iraq. Powell opposed invading Iraq to eliminate the banned weapons the country was thought to possess, but was outnumbered by more hawkish members of the Bush administration. Despite his private reservations, Powell advanced Bush's policy, which earned the secretary of state criticism from both sides. Republicans accused him of not working hard enough to build international support for the war, while Democrats blasted him for supporting a policy he privately opposed. Powell stepped down as secretary of state a few days after Bush was reelected in November 2004.

Since retiring from public life, Powell has maintained a busy speaking schedule, continued working with America's Promise, became a strategic limited partner in a Silicon Valley venture capital firm, and won the 2005 Alexis de Tocqueville Prize for his 1995 memoir, *My American Journey.*

H. Norman Schwarzkopf

General H. Norman Schwarzkopf (1934–) is best remembered for planning the strategic military strike that crippled Iraqi forces in the Persian Gulf War. The four-star Army general earned the moniker "Stormin' Norman" during the conflict.

Schwarzkopf's Early Years H. Norman Schwarzkopf Jr. was born on August 22, 1934, in Trenton, New Jersey. His father, General Herbert Norman Schwarzkopf (1895–1958), was between Army assignments overseas in World War I and World War II when his only son was born. During World War II, the elder Schwarzkopf was sent to Iran to establish a police force for the Shah. Young Norman joined his father in Tehran months before his mother and sisters could join them. Schwarzkopf was impressed to see that his father's subordinates admired the man as much as he did. But his father was not his only role model. Schwarzkopf also admired Alexander the Great, Ulysses S. Grant, and Creighton Abrams, the man who later served as Schwarzkopf's commander in Vietnam. The young man followed his father on military assignments in Italy, Germany, and Switzerland for five years. Schwarzkopf credits his experience of interacting with Iranians, displaced Jews, Germans, Italians, Yugoslavians, and people of other nationalities and ethnic backgrounds for broadening his mind and attitude about people.

Schwarzkopf Begins His Military Career Schwarzkopf eventually returned to the United States and entered West Point, just as his father had done. After graduating as an infantry second lieutenant in 1956, he attended the Infantry Officer Basic course and Airborne School at the Infantry School at Fort Benning, Georgia. In 1957, Schwarzkopf was sent to Fort Campbell, Kentucky, were he became platoon leader. Later, he became an executive officer in the 187th, the Second Airborne Battle Group. He served in that capacity for two years. In 1959, he was sent to Germany to serve as platoon leader in the Sixth Infantry for a year, followed by a stint as aide-de-camp to the commanding general of the Berlin Command. He returned to Fort Benning in September 1961, to continue advanced infantry officer training, then entered the University of Southern California where he pursued a master's degree in guided missile engineering, which he completed in 1964. After graduation, Schwarzkopf returned to West Point where he became an instructor in the department of mechanics.

In June 1965, he was sent to Vietnam with an airborne brigade as an advisor. He served his three hundred days of duty, then returned to West Point where he resumed his teaching post. The following year, Schwarzkopf became a student again, this time at General Staff College at Fort Leavenworth, Kansas. In December 1969, he was sent on a second tour of duty to Vietnam where he served as commander of the First Battalion, Sixth Infantry, 198th Infantry Brigade of the Twenty-third Infantry Division. He was awarded two Purple Hearts and three Silver Stars, but he returned home from Vietnam incensed over Washington's handling of its part of the war effort. He believed the outcome of the war was not a military defeat, but rather a defeat by politicians on the media's battlefields. Schwarzkopf alternated between administrative work and advanced military and technical training in Washington over the next several years. In October 1974, he was promoted from lieutenant colonel to deputy commander of the 172nd Infantry Brigade in Fort Richardson, Alaska. In 1975, he was promoted to full colonel and was later moved up to commander of the First Brigade, Ninth Infantry Division, in Fort Lewis, Washington. He held the post for almost two years

Becoming General Schwarzkopf served for two years at the Pacific Command post at Camp H. M. Smith in Hawaii from 1978 to 1980. After this appointment, he returned to Washington and was made brigadier general and sent to work as assistant division commander of the Eighth Infantry Division in Europe. He held this post for two years, after which time he returned to Washington and worked an administrative job for a year before being promoted to major general and sent to Fort Stewart, Georgia, to serve as deputy commanding general of the Twenty-fourth Infantry Division. There, he had the high-visibility post as deputy commander of the U.S.

Invasion of Grenada in 1983. Schwarzkopf's contribution to the conflict gained the attention of Pentagon officials who appointed him commanding general of the I Corps at Fort Lewis in 1986, a post he assumed with a third star on his shoulder. In August 1987, Schwarzkopf returned to Washington as senior Army member of the Military Staff Committee of the United Nations. Thirteen months later, he was made a four-star general, moving to the top of the U.S. Central Command (CENTCOM).

Directing the Persian Gulf War One of Schwarzkopf's first projects as four-star general and commander in chief at CENTCOM was to figure out the most likely war scenario involving U.S. troops in the Persian Gulf. Because the Soviet threat was in decline, Schwarzkopf concluded that the Middle East posed the greatest threat. After consulting with his superiors at the Pentagon, he conceived a plan to deal with the possibility of an Iraqi invasion into Kuwait and tested it in July 1990. The possibility quickly became a reality—Iraq invaded Kuwait on August 2. By August 17, the first U.S. troops were sent to Saudi Arabia to defend that country from a threatened invasion by Saddam Hussein's Iraqi army. Over the next several months, more than 500,000 U.S. soldiers were deployed to the region, followed by another 25,000 troops representing coalition countries. More than one hundred ships and twelve hundred aircraft were used to intimidate and finally defeat Hussein. Schwarzkopf oversaw the entire operation, dubbed Operation Desert Shield. His impressive diplomatic and language expertise were put to the test in the multinational and multicultural climate of the coalition army.

Because Hussein chose to ignore a U.N.-endorsed withdrawal deadline, Operation Desert Shield became Operation Desert Storm in January 1991. The goal of the stepped-up operation was to eject Iraqis by force through a well-coordinated plan of air strikes meant to sever Iraqi supply lines, disrupt the Iraqi command and control network, damage weapons facilities, and generally weaken Hussein's fighting unit. Despite the success of the air mission, Schwarzkopf and Chairman of the Joint Chiefs of Staff Colin Powell knew that a ground attack was necessary to complete the mission. The two conceived of a plan that involved a faked amphibious assault on the Kuwaiti coast. It successfully distracted Hussein's troops from their western flank, which allowed 200,000 allied troops and hundreds of tanks to overwhelm the enemy. By February 28, just five days after the ground war started, the conflict was over.

Schwarzkopf was greeted with a hero's welcome when he arrived back in the United States on April 21, 1991. Victory parades were organized in his honor and he received a flood of awards and honors, including the Presidential Medal of Freedom, the French Legion of Honor, and honorary knighthood by England's

Queen Elizabeth II. He retired from the military later that summer.

✪ Major Battles

Air War

United States Air Force leaders responded to the invasion of Kuwait by developing a top-secret plan for an air campaign against Iraq. The aim of Instant Thunder, the code name for the plan, was to destroy eighty-four strategic targets in Iraq in one week. Unlike Operation Rolling Thunder, the gradualistic approach used in bombing North Vietnam in the 1960s, Instant Thunder had the objective of moving quickly to paralyze the Iraqi leadership, degrade military capabilities, and neutralize the Iraqi military's will to fight. Instant Thunder eventually served as the basis for Phase I and Phase II of Operation Desert Storm, the Allied coalition's comprehensive war plan.

Instant Thunder was prepared and ready to launch less than two weeks after Iraq invaded Kuwait on August 2, 1990. Its primary target was Baghdad, Iraq's capital city and home to its leader, because it was assumed that if Saddam Hussein were eliminated, the Iraqi Army would withdraw from Kuwait. Although Instant Thunder sought an airpower-only victory, few believed that airplanes alone—despite their advanced technological capabilities—were sufficient to fulfill the military and political objectives set down by U.S. and coalition forces.

Planning the Air Strike U.S. President George H. W. Bush responded swiftly and decisively to the Iraqi invasion of Kuwait. He rallied international condemnation of the invasion and wide support for a speedy military intervention. The initial plan, Instant Thunder, was designed to help achieve the president's four main objectives: to force unconditional Iraqi withdrawal from Kuwait, to reestablish the legitimate Kuwaiti government, to protect American lives, and to ensure regional stability and security. The United States comprised the bulk of air forces, but Great Britain, France, Argentina, Belgium, Egypt, Germany, Italy, Canada, New Zealand, South Korea, Bahrain, Qatar, the United Arab Emirates, Greece, the Netherlands, and Australia sent either aviation or naval assistance. On August 25, U.N. Resolution 665 was passed, which gave the coalition legal status. Partnerships that would have been unheard of just a year before were forged, such as the example of a Royal Air Force maritime patrol plane that assisted a Soviet warship in intercepting an Iraqi blockade-running ship.

While coalition forces were being organized and built up, Iraqi President Saddam Hussein watched commentators on the Cable News Network (CNN) predict disaster for the coalition. Hussein's air force was considered the sixth best in the world. If he could convince the Arab nations to withdraw from the coalition, Hussein felt sure that he could emerge victorious. Aside from his

The territory of the Gulf War extended to Israel, where U.S. soldiers prepared Patriot missiles to counteract Iraqi fire. *David Rubinger/Time & Life Pictures/Getty Images*

military might, the Iraqi president demonstrated his potential for ruthlessness by announcing that all Western nationals trapped in Iraq would be held at planned targets as "human shields."

In August and September, U.S. Navy, Marine Corps, and Army planners began working closely with Air Force planners to draft the initial air campaign. During the fall of 1990, the Instant Thunder concept evolved into the foundation for the Operation Desert Storm Air Campaign Plan, which was based on achieving five military objectives: 1) isolating and incapacitating the Iraqi regime; 2) gaining and maintaining air supremacy to permit unhindered air operations; 3) destroying nuclear, biological, and chemical (NBC) warfare capability; 4) eliminating Iraq's offensive military capability by destroying major parts of key military production, infrastructure, and power projection capabilities; and 5) rendering the Iraqi army and its mechanized equipment in Kuwait ineffective, thereby causing the army to collapse. The twelve types of targets included: 1) forty-five leadership command facilities in Baghdad and others in surrounding areas; 2) electricity production facilities; 3) telecommunications and command, control, and communication nodes; 4) the Iraqi strategic Integrated Air Defense System (IADS); 5) air forces and airfields;6) nuclear, biological, and chemical weapons research, production, and storage facilities; 7) Scud missiles, launchers, and their production and storage facilities; 8) naval forces and port facilities; 9) oil refining and distribution facilities; 10) railroads and bridges; 11) Iraqi army units, including Republican Guard forces in the Kuwaiti Theater of Operations (KTO); and 12) military storage and production sites. Planners estimated the phased execution of the air attack would last approximately eighteen days.

Operation Desert Storm Begins On November 29, 1990, the United Nations passed Resolution 678 at President Bush's urging. The resolution ordered Iraq to withdraw from Kuwait by January 15, 1991. On January 12, 1991, the U.S. Congress authorized President Bush to use force against Iraq if it did not comply with the U.N. resolution. When January 15 arrived and Hussein's forces were still in Kuwait, coalition forces not already stationed in Saudi Arabia and Turkey headed for the Middle East. The result of years of American research and development, and billions of dollars spent on technology that would win wars quickly and with as few casualties as possible, were about to be put into use for the first time.

On January 17, soon after midnight, a force of Lockheed F-117A Nighthawks flew into Baghdad. These stealth airplanes slipped silently through the mighty Iraqi defenses, dropping Paveway laser-guided bombs on various sites around the city. Aircraft carriers stationed nearby simultaneously launched Tomahawk missiles that also hit their planned targets. Silent aircraft that could not be tracked from the ground, bombs that could be steered to hit targets the size of a chair, and satellites that could inform military intelligence of their location in a trackless desert were unleashed in a massive demonstration of American power.

On the first day, 655 coalition aircraft flew 1,322 sorties against communication centers and airfields. Iraqi fighter pilots, overwhelmed by the technologically advanced enemy, began fleeing for airfields in neutral Iran on the second day. Within twenty-four hours, the coalition was free to destroy Iraq's command and control centers. They cut communications between Baghdad and Kuwait and began aiming at Iraqi troops on the ground, destroying bunkers, tanks, and highways. When Iraq began launching Scud missiles into Israel and Saudi Arabia—into Israel in order to draw that country into war knowing the Arab nations would not fight alongside it, and into Saudi Arabia to try and convince it that hosting the coalition was too risky—the United States protected the two countries with Scud-intercepting Raytheon MIM-104 Patriot missile batteries. Although the

Patriot did not always intercept the Scud, the missile was a wonderful political weapon in that it kept Israel and Saudi Arabia among the U.S. allies.

The Air Strike Ends For a month, coalition helicopters and airplanes assaulted any targets that might contribute to the ground war. They destroyed communications buildings and bridges by dropping "Daisy Cutter" (DC) bombs, bombs that were designed to detonate on contact, over the possible frontline to destroy land mines. There was little left of the Iraqi military. Remaining soldiers had no communications, no reinforcements, and little food and water. On February 24, 1991, the air war ended and the ground war began.

Ground Offensive

The Gulf War, widely recognized by its codename Operation Desert Storm, was predominantly an air campaign of the United States and coalition forces against Iraq from January 17, 1991 to February 28, 1991. The war is largely remembered as a land war because the ground war employed the largest invasion force gathered since World War II. U.S. and allied planes, in 42,000 strikes, dropped 88,500 tons of bombs on Iraq and Iraqi targets in Kuwait. Only the final one hundred hours of the conflict were actually fought on the ground. Of the bombs used, roughly 9,500 were laser- and television-guided "smart" weapons, and roughly 162,000 were conventional bombs. The accuracy of the bombing was astounding. The new American airpower assured a relatively bloodless victory, with only 382 U.S. troops lost in both the air and ground wars—of that number 147 died in battle and 235 died in non-battle-related incidents.

Because thirty-nine of the forty-three days of the war were fought in the air, the last four days were spent fighting virtually defeated Iraqi military. The remaining soldiers had lost all communications with military command. There were no reinforcements and little food or water. Iraqi tanks and vehicles had been destroyed in the bombing, and the once-feared Iraqi troops suffered extremely low morale. For these reasons, U.S. and coalition ground troops met little resistance in the last one hundred hours of the war.

The Ground War Begins On February 24, 1991, forces from the United States, Saudi Arabia, Britain, France, the United Arab Emirates, Bahrain, Qatar, Oman, Syria, and Kuwait began a major ground, naval, and air offensive. Assault elements of the First and Second Marine Divisions launched the attack, easily breaching Iraq's defense lines of minefields, barbed wire, and bunkers. Within nine hours, the Marines destroyed several Iraqi tanks and bunkers, captured the Burgan oil field, Al Jabbir Airfield, and thousands of Iraqi troops. After ten hours, American casualties were reported as being "remarkably light" during the dramatically successful offensive in which over 5,500 enemy prisoners of war had been captured. Except for one engagement between

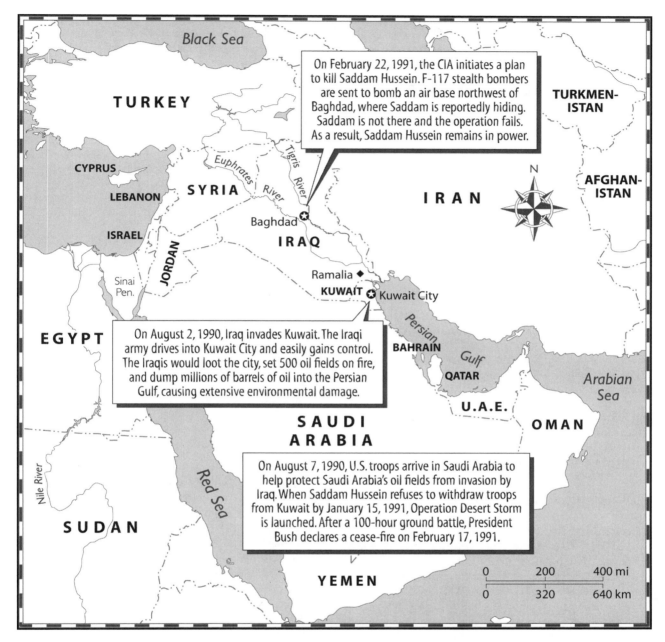

On February 22, 1991, the CIA initiates a plan to kill Saddam Hussein. F-117 stealth bombers are sent to bomb an air base northwest of Baghdad, where Saddam is reportedly hiding. Saddam is not there and the operation fails. As a result, Saddam Hussein remains in power.

On August 2, 1990, Iraq invades Kuwait. The Iraqi army drives into Kuwait City and easily gains control. The Iraqis would loot the city, set 500 oil fields on fire, and dump millions of barrels of oil into the Persian Gulf, causing extensive environmental damage.

On August 7, 1990, U.S. troops arrive in Saudi Arabia to help protect Saudi Arabia's oil fields from invasion by Iraq. When Saddam Hussein refuses to withdraw troops from Kuwait by January 15, 1991, Operation Desert Storm is launched. After a 100-hour ground battle, President Bush declares a cease-fire on February 17, 1991.

U.S. Marines moved north from Saudi Arabia to Kuwait in February 1991 in an effort to oust Iraqi forces. *Reproduced by permission of Gale, a part of Cengage Learning*

a Marine task force and an Iraqi armored unit, which resulted in the retreat of Iraqi tanks and troops, only minor contact with Iraqi forces was reported. For the most part, Iraqi troops opted to retreat rather than engage with and surrender to U.S. and allied forces. On the first day of the ground war, two Iraqi aircraft flew to neutral Iran. Flanked by a joint contingent of Arab troops, U.S. forces swept through the burning oil fields of Kuwait toward Kuwait City. The advance of the troops was aided by artillery barrages and repeated strikes by coalition fighter bombers.

On the second day of the ground conflict, February 25, troops reported the operation was running ahead of schedule. U.S. and coalition forces encountered only light to moderate resistance from Iraqi forces. When U.S. forces engaged the Republican Guards, Iraq's elite military force, they emerged victorious. By this point in the conflict, U.S. and coalition forces had captured over 18,000 prisoners of war and destroyed over 270 Iraqi tanks. The Department of Defense (DoD) reported that 600 fires were burning in the Kuwaiti Theater of Operations (KTO), including 517 oil wellheads. At 5:35 P.M.

(EST), Baghdad Radio announced that Iraqi President Saddam Hussein had ordered his troops to make a fighting withdrawal from occupied Kuwait and return to the positions they occupied before the invasion. The White House responded by stating that they had no evidence to suggest that the Iraqi army was withdrawing and that it was, in fact, continuing to fight.

On the third day of the ground attack, Hussein announced on Baghdad Radio that Iraqi troops had begun withdrawing from Kuwait and that the withdrawal would be completed that day. In his twenty-five-minute speech, the Iraqi president maintained that Kuwait was a part of Iraq, but due to armed forces, his troops were being forced to withdraw. He reminded listeners that Constantinople was not conquered in the first battle, implying that he would attempt to occupy Kuwait again. President Bush called the speech an outrage. He then said, "Saddam is not interested in peace, but only to regroup and fight another day, and he does not renounce Iraq's claim to Kuwait."

The DoD announced that same day that U.S. and coalition forces were engaging, outflanking, outmaneuvering, and destroying armed and fully retreating Iraqi troops throughout the KTO as the ground offensive continued. In the continued effort, twenty-one Iraqi divisions were destroyed or rendered combat-ineffective; a Marine unit, the first U.S. force to enter Kuwait City, recaptured the U.S. Embassy; and Marines engaged Iraqi tanks at Kuwait International Airport. By this point in the ground war, U.S. and coalition forces captured thirty thousand prisoners of war and destroyed over four hundred tanks.

The Gulf War Ends On February 27, 1991, the fourth day of the ground offensive, U.S. and coalition forces engaged in a climactic "classic tank battle," supported by attack aircraft, against approximately three divisions of Republican Guard forces in Iraq near the Euphrates Valley. The remnants of Iraq's forces were surrounded by a mighty wall of U.S. forces along their eastern flank and U.S. and coalition forces along their southern flank. The massive encirclement of Kuwait and southern Iraq around the exhausted and depleted Iraqi forces led to the destruction of two hundred Iraqi tanks, fifty armored vehicles, and twenty artillery pieces. Twenty-nine Iraqi divisions were destroyed or rendered combat-ineffective in the battle. At this point, with Iraqi forces outnumbered two to one, facing a heavily dug-in force, General Norman Schwarzkopf devised a plan that would deliver the final blow of the war. Simultaneous sea and ground operations calling for special forces to conduct mine countermeasures in the Arabian Gulf were put into effect. Aircraft carrier and ground-based air strikes prevented the rebuilding of bridges; U.S. and coalition forces blocked a Republican Guard retreat out of Kuwait and set up a flanking position intended to prevent attacks; U.S. and coalition forces, with the support of

naval gunfire, began engaging remnants of Republican Guard tank units to the east; the First Marine Division seized the Kuwaiti International Airport; and the Second Marine Division encircled and cut off any exits out of Kuwait City. The efforts were a success. General Schwarzkopf declared the near-total destruction of the Iraqi army and stated that Iraq was no longer a regional military threat. At 9:00 P.M. (EST), President Bush addressed the nation and announced the defeat of the Iraqi army. Terms of a cease-fire were outlined and the United Nations formally requested Iraqi compliance. On February 28, the Iraqi government delivered a letter to the United Nations stating its intention to comply with the terms of the cease-fire, thereby ending the brief but devastating war.

✪ The Home Front

Black Monday (1987) and the Ensuing Economic Recession

The stock market crash of Monday, October 19, 1987, was the largest single-day crash in history. The Dow Jones Industrial Average, one of several stock market indices used to gauge the industrial component of America's stock markets, lost more than 22 percent of its value, or $500 billion, that day. The crash led to an economic recession that resulted in several years of high unemployment, massive government budgetary deficits, and slow gross domestic product (GDP) growth.

Causes An extremely powerful bull market—a prolonged period of rising investment prices—characterized the stock market from 1982 to 1987. Companies scrambling to raise funds to buy each other out bolstered the market's strength. The philosophy at the time was that companies could grow exponentially by buying other companies. During such a prolonged bull market, an element of irrationality sets in, as more and more buyers jump into a market that seems to be rising and rising with no end in sight. This influx of money into the market often boosts stock prices much higher than a corporation's actual market value. The end result of such overconfidence in a "never-ending" bull market is a market with overinflated prices and too many buyers. In other words, a market ripe for a downturn.

When the downturn inevitably occurred, it was not one single factor that provoked it, but several. One of these factors was the rise of insider trading investigations. In early 1987, the U.S. Securities and Exchange Commission (SEC) conducted a number of investigations into the illegal practice of insider trading—using nonpublic information to profit on stock transactions. Investors, unsettled by the prospect of further investigations, became wary. Furthermore, because the bull market was so vigorous, economists began to fear inflation. The Federal Reserve quickly raised short-term interest

In 1990, this man's shirt proposed one way of responding to the recession that hit the U.S. economy.　© J. L. Atlan/Sygma/Corbis

rates to curb inflation, but this had the unfortunate effect of damaging stock prices. To protect against stock dips, many institutional trading firms began using portfolio insurance; this created one more factor that helped create Black Monday. Portfolio insurance used futures contracts—agreements to buy or sell specified commodities at a predetermined quantity and price at a predetermined future date—as insurance policies. Individuals holding futures contracts would be able to make money in the event of a market crash, offsetting the losses in the stock holdings.

When the interest rates rose, many of these large institutional firms started using their portfolio insurance all at the same time. This flooded the futures market with billions of dollars within minutes, which caused the crash of both the futures market and the stock market. Common stock holders, frightened by the activity, started selling their holdings simultaneously. The market could not handle so many orders at once. Beyond that, most people could not sell because there were no buyers left.

The Crash Five hundred billion dollars evaporated from the Dow Jones index on October 19, 1987. Markets around the world followed, crashing in the same way, with individual investors losing fortunes instantly. The majority of investors who were selling were only

doing so because they saw everyone else selling. They did not even know why they were doing it. This kind of irrationality led to the extreme market crash and the closing of futures and stock exchanges for the day.

Largely unnoticed during the crash was the sharp rise in the bond market, which received a significant amount of the money that went out of the stocks. Because the government bond market was ten times larger than the stock market, this was good news since gains in bonds more than outweighed losses in stocks. That evening, analysts announced that the Federal Reserve banks would aggressively purchase government bonds to provide financial markets with needed liquidity.

Around the world, markets plunged. The evening after the crash in New York, Tokyo's Nikkei index fell 15 percent, London markets continued to decline, and Australia's market fell 25 percent. The stock markets in Hong Kong and New Zealand simply shut down. Although the New York Stock Exchange (NYSE) opened up 211 points the following day, giving the hopeful nation reason to believe that a "bounceback" had happened, the Dow fell almost 100 points in the first half hour. It rallied and then fell again several times throughout the course of the day, closing up 103 points. Scare headlines and dour predictions ruled the media until the end of October, but the market's recovery and continued strength quickly allayed those fears.

The Aftermath By mid-November, it seemed the crash had not caused the kind of damage that had been expected. October payrolls swelled, performing better than they had since September 1983, department store sales increased on a yearly basis by 1.4 percent, consumer spending rose by 0.5 percent, Christmas sales reached a new record, and the Commerce Department revealed a third-quarter surge of 4.1 percent in the U.S. gross national product.

By the end of the year, several fact-finding commissions were busy investigating the causes of the crash. The most impartial study, conducted by a commission chaired by future U.S. Secretary of the Treasury Nicholas Brady (1930–), placed most of the blame for the crash's severity on portfolio insurance and traders who placed huge orders based on computer programs, or program traders. The Brady Commission made several recommendations, including greater regulatory oversight of index options markets and higher option margins—percentages of the value of an option that a buyer is required to pay up front. The commission also recommended increased cooperation between the stock exchanges and a greater amount of disclosure of information. Each of the Brady recommendations was adopted and the Federal Reserve Board was given the task of oversight.

The Recession The stock market crash of 1987 definitely contributed to the recession of the late 1980s and early 1990s, but the savings and loan crisis, which occurred at the same time and put the savings of millions of Americans in jeopardy, was another significant contributor. The first burst of recession following the stock market crash was short-lived because of an unexpected rise in consumer confidence and increased consumer spending. That combination lifted the United States and Canada out of the economic recession that had plagued North America. But the recovery was largely illusory. By 1990, the economic climate was marked by high unemployment, massive government budgetary deficits, and slow GDP growth. The continued recession affected the United States until 1992.

Savings and Loan Bailout

In 1989, newly elected President George H. W. Bush unveiled a plan to bail out over one thousand failed savings and loans institutions. The massive failures constituted a crisis that has been interpreted in many ways. Some believe it was the greatest scandal in American history. Others describe it as the most profound case of fraud in the history of crime. Others still regard it as the natural result of the so-called climate of greed nurtured by the Reagan administration. Still others saw it as a premeditated conspiracy to move covert funds out of

the country for use by U.S. intelligence agencies. The cost of the crisis has been estimated at $150 billion, of which roughly $125 billion was directly subsidized by the U.S. government. The savings and loan (S&L) crisis contributed to the large budget deficits in the early 1990s and may have contributed to the 1990–1991 economic recession. Estimates predict it will cost over $500 billion over thirty years to completely bail out the failed S&Ls.

Background Savings and loan associations, also known as thrifts, have been around since the 1800s. They are financial institutions originally created to accept savings from private investors and offer home mortgage services to the public. Beginning in 1932 with the creation of the Federal Home Loan Bank System, thrifts were strictly regulated and deposits were insured by the Federal Savings and Loan Insurance Corporation (FSLIC). Although the S&L crisis happened in the 1980s, its origins were in the 1960s and 1970s when market interest rates began to fluctuate with increasing intensity. The fluctuations made it difficult for the S&Ls to survive because interest rate ceilings prevented the institutions from paying competitive rates on deposits. This meant that every time market interest rates rose, consumers withdrew substantial amounts of funds and placed them where they would earn higher rates of return. The effect of consumers withdrawing deposits (disintermediation) and subsequently redepositing funds when the rates rose (reintermediation) left the S&Ls extremely vulnerable. To compound matters, money market funds became sources of competition for the S&Ls, which are not allowed to enter into business other than accepting deposits or granting home loans.

Between 1980 and 1982, statutory and regulatory changes gave the savings and loan industry new powers intended to return them to profitability. The S&Ls, for the first time, were given the authority to make acquisition, development, and construction loans. In 1980, Congress also raised the limits on deposit insurance from $40,000 to $100,000, which was significant because a failed S&L had a negative net worth. By increasing Federal Deposit Insurance Company (FDIC) coverage, those institutions that previously would not have been able to pay off their debt could now take more risk to try to work their way out of insolvency so that the government would not have to take them over. In September 1981, The Federal Home Loan Bank Board allowed troubled S&Ls to issue "income capital certificates," which allowed an insolvent institution to appear solvent. In December 1982, the Garn-St. Germain Depository Institutions Act went into effect. It extended federally chartered S&L powers further, putting S&Ls on a more equal footing with commercial banks. This caused a massive defection of state-chartered S&Ls to the federal system. In response, California, Texas, and Florida allowed state-chartered S&Ls to invest 100 percent of their deposits in any ventures they desired. Deregulation caused the industry to grow just when the Federal Home Loan Bank Board decided to reduce its regulatory and supervisory staff. The savings and loans took advantage of the real estate boom and high interest rates of the early 1980s and lent far more money than was prudent, especially to risky ventures that many S&Ls were not qualified to assess correctly.

The Fallout The relaxation of accounting rules led to fraud and other crimes within the government and the savings and loan industry. This criminal behavior, combined with customer defaults and bankruptcies, led to a massive failure in the industry. In 1980, there were 4,002 active S&Ls. By 1983, 962 of them had collapsed. Some, like Empire Savings of Mesquite, Texas, failed because of "land flips" and other illegal activities. Empire's failure would go on to cost taxpayers roughly $300 million. By 1987, losses at Texas S&Ls made up more than half of all S&L losses nationwide. Of the twenty largest losses in the country, fourteen were located in Texas. The losses sent the state's economy into a major recession. Crude-oil prices dropped by half, office vacancies rose to 30 percent, and real estate prices completely collapsed.

Charles Keating (1923–), the former head of Lincoln Savings of Irvine, California, is probably the most notorious figure associated with the S&L crisis. Keating admitted to committing bankruptcy fraud by taking $1 million from the parent corporation of Lincoln Savings when he knew the corporation was due to collapse in a matter of weeks. He was convicted of fraud, racketeering, and conspiracy in 1993 and went on to serve four and a half years in prison. The Lincoln failure was estimated to have cost taxpayers over $2 billion. Before Keating was convicted, Edwin J. Gray, chairman of the Federal Home Loan Bank Board, was summoned to the office of Senator Dennis DeConcini (1937–). DeConcini and Senators John McCain (1936–), Alan Cranston (1914–2000), John Glenn (1921–), and Donald Riegle (1935–) questioned Gray about the appropriateness of Bank Board investigations into Keating's Lincoln Savings. Because Keating contributed campaign funds to all five senators, they became known as the "Keating Five." DeConcini, Cranston, and Riegle were forced out of politics as a result of the scandal, but McCain and Glenn were exonerated of all charges of influence-peddling.

The Bailout In 1988, the Federal Home Loan Bank Board reported that fraud and insider abuse were the most aggravating factors in the massive wave of S&L failures. A year later, President George H. W. Bush presented his plan to bail out the thousands of failed S&Ls. The Financial Institutions Reform, Recovery and Enforcement Act (FIRREA) abolished the Federal Home Loan Bank Board and FSLIC. It shifted S&L regulation to the newly created Office of Thrift Super-

vision and moved the deposit insurance function to the FDIC. The Act also created the Resolution Trust Corporation to resolve the insolvent S&Ls. Other major provisions of FIRREA included the allocation of funds to the Justice Department to help finance the prosecution of thrift crimes. In 1990, the Crime Control Act mandated a study by the National Commission on Financial Institution Reform, Recovery and Enforcement to research the causes of the S&L crisis and come up with suggestions to prevent future scandals.

✪ International Context

The Fall of the Soviet Union

In the late 1980s, economic and political conflict led to increased tension within the Soviet Union (USSR). Political pressure to either win or end the war in Afghanistan led to military frustration with the Communist political regime. Economic stagnation fostered frustration with the centrally managed financial system. Lastly, Soviet member countries, including the Balkans, the Soviet bloc, and Chechnya and Georgia were experiencing a nationalist resurgence. Soviet leader Mikhail Gorbachev's attempt to engineer a gradual liberalization of the country was initially successful, but different republics' pro-nationalist and Soviet anti-liberal factions weakened Gorbachev's power, ultimately leading to the dissolution of the Soviet Union in late 1991.

Historical Background Problems with the Soviet political and administrative system began to arise in the late 1970s. Not severe enough to cause alarm, these problems did threaten to undermine the superpower status of the Soviet Union and its political stability. The highly centralized system, created under Joseph Stalin (1878–1953) in the 1920s and 1930s, allowed the government to control its people's public and private lives and was generally very successful. It was designed to bring uniformity and equality to all citizens and appealed to a sense of equity. In practice, though, the system was too separated from the public to be truly responsive to its needs.

The Soviet economic system was encumbered by defense expenditures, especially when the arms race with the United States escalated in the 1950s and 1960s. Because Soviet leaders felt it critical to keep abreast of technological advances, many resources were being spent on the military instead of areas that would improve the lives of Soviet citizens. The gap between the people and their leaders was very wide, which resulted in a political system that did not reflect the wishes of the populace. This led to the erosion of Soviet leaders' political legitimacy in the eyes of the disenfranchised and a desire among those individuals to reform the system. After Leonid Brezhnev (1906–1982), the longtime party leader and head of state, died in 1982, the responsibility of rejuvenating the Soviet system fell to his successors.

In the wake of Glasnost, Soviet soldiers prepare to return to Russia from East Germany in 1989.   © *Leif Skoogfors/Corbis*

After two of them died between 1982 and 1985, Mikhail Gorbachev took up the challenge. At the age of fifty-four, Gorbachev was the youngest man to hold the most powerful post in the Soviet Union. Gorbachev's reforms, designed to revive the stagnating Soviet economy and renew public trust in the country's leadership, actually accelerated the Soviet decline and led to its collapse.

Perestroika   Gorbachev identified economic stagnation as his most pressing challenge. As a result, he launched successive campaigns opposing wasted material and human resources. He called on industrial managers and the workforce at large to combat corruption, apathy, and drunkenness at work, but he believed that without a major restructuring of the economy, known as *perestroika*, his plans for rejuvenating the Soviet Union would fail. He also restricted resources earmarked for defense and injected funds into the dilapidated industrial sector. Because it was impossible to withhold defense funds while the Soviet Union was involved in the war against Afghanistan and the arms race with the United States, Gorbachev took unprecedented steps to alleviate tensions with both nations. In May 1989, Gorbachev ordered the withdrawal of Soviet forces from Afghanistan, which quieted tensions between the United States and the Soviet Union. In 1990, Gorbachev's reformist

foreign policy, dubbed "New Thinking," resulted in the political upheavals of Eastern Europe that swept Communist governments aside and brought anti-Russian, pro-Western leaders to power. The new approach led to the celebrated re-unification of East and West Germany in 1990.

Gorbachev's policy of *glasnost*, or openness, was put into effect as a way of addressing the Communist party's legitimacy crisis. *Glasnost* was responsible for the opening of the previously closed Soviet media, among other things, which began running stories about previously taboo subjects like crime, corruption, and prostitution, and the Soviet system began to take on a more responsive, democratic image. Gorbachev's attempt to win the public trust also led to the formation of public organizations, including social and political clubs and associations. Eventually, the clubs pressed for political legitimacy, which brought about the removal of the Communist Party of the Soviet Union's (CPSU) constitutional monopoly in 1990.

The Beginning of the End   Non-Russians who were forced to repress their cultural heritage and traditions during almost seventy years of Soviet rule saw Gorbachev's reforms as permission to reclaim their history. Popular fronts demanding cultural revivals and reassessments of their long-sublimated histories grew in strength, especially in the Baltic states and the Caucasus. In 1990–1991, the threshold between these so-called reassessments and calls for independence was crossed. Gorbachev was willing to appease nationalist demands, but conservative members of the CPSU balked. Reforms had undermined the authority of the Party internally and externally. The CPSU no longer controlled public life, and Gorbachev's gestures toward the West cost the CPSU Eastern European allies. Conservatives expressed fears that negotiating a new Union Treaty would bring about the end of the Soviet Union. Gorbachev tried to calm their fears, explaining that his reform program was necessary for the preservation of a strong and viable Soviet Union. He supported his words by taking a strict approach against calls for independence in the Baltic and Transcaucasia. On August 19, 1991, two days before the new Union Treaty was to be signed, Soviet hardliners attempted a coup that unraveled by August 21, 1991. The failed coup humiliated Gorbachev, who was on vacation when trusted members of his government sought to overthrow him. Because he could not stop the nationalist tide that was sweeping over the country, and because he had lost credibility, Gorbachev resigned from the presidency on December 25, 1991.

The Soviet Union Collapses In June 1991, Boris Yeltsin (1931–2007) won a popular mandate in the presidential elections and became the first Russian leader to stand in direct elections. His courageous behavior during the August coup—Yeltsin inspired mass demonstrations against the 1991 attempt to overthrow Gorbachev's government—brought him and his team of reformers unprecedented popularity and international recognition. He capitalized on his popularity by pressing ahead with radical reform policies. Immediately after the attempted coup, Yeltsin's government banned the CPSU and went so far as to confiscate its assets. It also initiated the process of price liberalization and privatization so that state assets could be distributed to the populace. It did not take long for Yeltsin and his government to completely dismantle the pillars of the Soviet economy.

The disintegration of the Soviet system resulted in triple-digit inflation and price hikes. The crisis was exacerbated by a fall in industrial production. The government found it increasingly difficult to pay its workers, wage earners who were deprived of subsidized government social services due to the privatization of housing, childcare, and retail shops. Economic reforms following the Soviet collapse led to an unprecedented imbalance in the distribution of wealth. While the majority of the population experienced radically lowered living standards, industrial managers and Soviet administrators became wealthy capitalists overnight. While all this was happening, the Soviet republics took advantage of the central government's loosening grip and asserted their own rights to power. Nationalist supporters recognized

the disintegration of the Soviet Union into fifteen separate entities as a natural inevitability and argued that every nation had the right to govern itself. *Glasnost* and *perestroika* made nationalist aspirations possible while the Soviet collapse made independence for those nations a reality.

✪ Aftermath

The Clinton Presidency

William Jefferson Clinton became the forty-second president of the United States in 1993. The young Democrat defeated Republican President Bush in 1992 after vowing to focus on economic issues, especially overcoming the sluggish growth of the American economy. He sought to reshape the Democratic Party by focusing on issues supported by the middle class, including tougher crime laws, jobs for welfare recipients, and tax reform that would shift more of the tax burden to the rich. But Clinton maintained certain traditional liberal goals, including gun control, legalized abortion, environmental protection, national health insurance, and gay rights.

Despite battles with the Republican Congress, Clinton, who was elected to a second term in 1996, successfully met his goals to lower unemployment, control the runaway deficit, and tackle welfare reform. Clinton experienced two major setbacks during his administration. The first was his inability to reform health care. The second was his impeachment by the House of Representatives on charges of having lied under oath and obstructing justice in the attempted cover-up of his affair with White House intern Monica Lewinsky (1973–). Clinton's successes in foreign affairs were mixed. On the one hand, he helped broker peace negotiations in Northern Ireland, was instrumental in ousting the military dictatorship in Haiti, and forced the government of Serbia to end its violence against Muslims in Bosnia and Albanians in the Kosovo region. On the other hand, Clinton failed to mobilize support to end the genocide in Rwanda, and the peace talks he facilitated between Israel and the Palestine Liberation Organization soon devolved into renewed strife that continues today.

The Clinton Administration at Home By the end of his first year as president, Clinton secured the adoption of an economic package that combined tax increases, which fell mainly on the upper class, and spending cuts, which hurt mainly impoverished Americans. Despite the Republicans' dire predictions that the package would result in economic chaos, it had the opposite effect. Clinton's economic policy had the $290 billion deficit shrinking by 1994, and by 1999, generated a surplus of $124 billion. The combination of economic growth, low inflation, and low interest and unemployment rates positioned the American economy as the world's strongest and most robust.

In the last year of his presidency, Bill Clinton met with Palestinian leader Yassar Arafat at a Middle East Peace Summit at Camp David.
AP Images

On some issues, like the passage of the North American Free Trade Agreement (NAFTA), Clinton benefited from Republican support. On others, like welfare reform, Congress accepted Clinton's lead in publicizing the issue, but dominated the actual writing of legislation. By working together this way, Congress passed a sweeping reform bill that fulfilled Clinton's 1992 campaign promise to "end welfare as we know it."

Clinton was besieged by conservative Republicans, especially those on the far right, who made him and the First Lady the subjects of numerous special investigations during his administration. The Whitewater investigation, which looked at the president's and Hillary Clinton's possible participation in financial impropriety in 1978 in Arkansas, was the earliest sustained attack. Another setback occurred in 1997 when the Supreme Court ruled that a sexual harassment suit brought against the president by Paula Jones could go forward while he was in office. Then, in January 1998, news broke that President Clinton had engaged in sexual acts in the Oval Office with White House intern Monica Lewinsky. For the next seven months, the American public was inundated with news of the affair and the related investigation. The scandal led to the eventual impeachment of the president for lying to the grand jury. Because the Senate did not produce the two-thirds majority vote it needed to convict Clinton and remove him from office, the president was acquitted of perjury and obstruction of justice on February 12, 1999. He served the next two years of his second term without incident. Clinton's ratings in public opinion polls hovered around 70 percent in the months following the impeachment. Some of those polls showed that most Americans gave the president low marks for character and honesty and high marks for performance, and viewed the Republican attackers as mean-spirited extremists. Some polls also showed that many voters were happy with Clinton's handling of the White House, the economy, and most matters of public life. However, the president's law license was suspended by the Arkansas bar for five years and he paid a $25,000 fine. Upon leaving office, Clinton did publicly admit his testimony was misleading, and the special prosecutor ended the Whitewater investigation when Clinton left office on January 21, 2001, and stated that Clinton would not be criminally prosecuted for perjury after he left office.

BIBLIOGRAPHY

Web Sites

"The Air Campaign." *Conduct of the Persian Gulf War.* Intelligence Resource Program. <www.fas.org/irp/imint/docs/cpgw6/>(accessed June 6, 2007).

"American War and Military Operations Casualties: Lists and Statistics." *Navy Department Library.* <www.history.navy.mil/library/online/american%20war%20casualty.htm>(accessed June 20, 2007).

"Bill Clinton: A Life in Brief." *AmericanPresident.org.* Miller Center of Public Affairs, University of Virginia. <www.millercenter.virginia.edu/index.php/Ampres/essays/clinton/biography/1> (accessed June 8, 2007).

Doser, Mark. "Black Monday—The Stock Market Crash of 1987." *4A Economics.* Holy Trinity School. <www.newlearner.com/courses/hts/bec4a/ecoho16.htm> (accessed June 8, 2007).

Estes, Kenneth W. "Iraq Between Two Occupations: The Second Gulf War (1990–1991)." *International Relations and Security Networks.* <http://se1.isn.ch/serviceengine/FileContent?serviceID=PublishingHouse&fileid=FB678761-6586-38F1-EFA6-21799C0D073E&lng=en> (accessed June 6, 2007).

Feltus, Pamela. "The Gulf War." *U.S. Centennial of Flight Commission.* <www.centennialofflight.gov/essay/Air_Power/gulf_war/AP44.htm> (accessed June 6, 2007).

"The S&L Crisis: A Chrono-Bibliography." *FDIC.* <www.fdic.gov/bank/historical/s&l/> (accessed June 8, 2007).

"War Chronology: February 1991." *U.S. Navy in Desert Storm/Desert Sheild.* <www.history.navy.mil/wars/dstorm/dsfeb.htm> (accessed June 6, 2007).

Introduction to War on Terrorism

On the morning of September 11, 2001, the United States was the target of organized terrorist attacks. Hijackers seized control of four passenger jets and deliberately crashed them into high-profile targets: the two towers of the World Trade Center in New York city and the Pentagon building outside of Washington, D.C. The fourth airplane crashed into a field in Pennsylvania after passengers aboard overwhelmed the hijackers. These were the most deadly enemy attacks on American home soil in U.S. history.

The War on Terrorism, launched in direct retaliation for these attacks, is a blanket term for American military and security efforts aimed at neutralizing ongoing or potential terrorist plots against the United States and its allies. The war has grown to encompass actions both large and small across the globe.

The nature of the War on Terrorism constitutes a radical departure from previous American conflicts. In stark contrast to America's previous wars, there is no readily identifiable enemy army or national government to strike against; the enemy soldiers wear no uniforms, and it remains unclear as to whether they even constitute enemy combatants in the legal sense.

The stated war goals of the United States, as outlined in President George W. Bush's address to Congress of September 20, 2001, are to build an international coalition of allies to fight terrorists, to destroy the global terrorist infrastructure, and to wage war against any nation that harbors or supports terrorists.

The latter goal led to the invasion of Afghanistan on October 7, 2001. The Taliban, the militant Islamist government of that country, had formed close ties with the al-Qaeda terrorist network and its leader, Osama bin Laden, scion of a wealthy Saudi family and purported mastermind of the 9/11 attacks.

The invasion of Afghanistan met with great success. By employing a combination of conventional, large-scale military operations with the efforts of elite Special Forces units, often working closely with local allies, the Americans were able to decisively rout the Taliban and al-Qaeda forces, chasing the shattered remnants into the rugged hills along the Pakistani border.

Although al-Qaeda's power base had been broken, the organization itself lived on, as did bin Laden himself. The flexible nature of the outfit, which operated in independent cells of four or five operatives each, scattered across the globe, allowed attacks to continue, as subsequent bombings in Bali, London, and Madrid proved.

The second major phase of the War on Terrorism opened in March 2003 with the invasion of Iraq. In contrast to the Afghan war, this action was met with significant international resistance. The United States asserted that Iraqi dictator Saddam Hussein had weapons of mass destruction at his disposal, which he would likely use against his neighbors and abroad. U.S. officials also implied Saddam was linked to al-Qaeda. Evidence of these links was shaky, however.

Four years after the initial invasion of Iraq, no conclusive link between the Iraqi government and al-Qaeda had been produced, nor have any weapons of mass destruction been found. The American public, initially supportive of the war, has grown increasingly weary of what many perceive to be a counter-productive quagmire that only serves to radicalize a new generation of terrorists.

War on Terrorism

✪ *Afghanistan*
✪ Causes

September 11, 2001, Terrorist Attack

The events of September 11, 2001, were directly responsible for propelling the United States into the War on Terrorism. Over the course of a single morning the largest attack on American soil in U.S. history unfolded as three hijacked commercial airplanes were flown into each of the two towers of the World Trade Center in New York City and the Pentagon Building in Arlington, Virginia. These attacks were carried out not by a government or an army but by nineteen men affiliated with an international terrorist network known as al-Qaeda. Referred to as the "Pearl Harbor of the twenty-first century," the events of 9/11 (as the attack came to be called) were a defining moment in post–Cold War America, earning the United States an outpouring of international sympathy and inaugurating major shifts in American domestic and international policy.

Al-Qaeda The September 11 attacks were the product of years of planning. Al-Qaeda terrorist Khalid Shaikh Mohammed first proposed the idea of hijacking planes and flying them into buildings in 1996. Over the next five years, the plan was refined and further developed. A cadre of trusted al-Qaeda operatives entered the United States and began training in the piloting of civilian jumbo jets. Meanwhile, Khalid Mohammed worked with al-Qaeda leader Osama bin Laden to select the targets for the attacks.

The World Trade Center had already been the target of an al-Qaeda terrorist attack in 1993—a truck packed with explosives was detonated in the basement of Tower One with the aim of collapsing the building onto Tower Two, bringing both towers down. The attack caused extensive damage and killed six people, but the towers did not collapse. The failure prompted al-Qaeda to increase its efforts to bring down the Twin Towers. Two other targets—the Pentagon and, allegedly, the U.S. Capitol, both in the Washington, D.C., area—were also selected as targets.

The Attacks on the World Trade Center September 11, 2001 fell on a Tuesday. At Logan International Airport in Boston, Washington Dulles International Airport in Washington, D.C., and Newark Liberty International Airport in Newark, NJ, nineteen men boarded, respectively, United Airlines Flight 175 and American Airlines Flight 11, American Flight 77, and United Flight 93. On their persons they carried small knives (most likely box cutters), which had passed through airport security unnoticed, as well as pepper spray.

The planes were all destined for cities on the west coast and were fully loaded with jet fuel for their cross-country flights. Over approximately the next ninety minutes, starting with Flight 11 at 8:14 A.M. Eastern Daylight Time, the four planes were hijacked by the terrorists onboard. Although exact details varied by plane, the general pattern of events saw the terrorists subduing or killing the flight crew, then herding the passengers and flight attendants to the back of the plane, claiming there was a bomb on the plane and warning against any attempts at heroics. Under the guise of flying the hijacked planes toward a nearby airport, the hijackers instead turned the aircraft toward their assigned targets.

Flight 11 was the first plane to hit, striking Tower One of the World Trade Center at 8:46 A.M. The fuel-laden plane exploded between floors 94 and 98 killing all 92 people aboard the plane and hundreds inside the tower itself, which immediately began burning.

Initially thought to be a horrible accident, the deliberate nature of the crash became increasingly clear when, eighteen minutes later, Flight 175 crashed into Tower Two. Like Flight 11, Flight 175 hit its target traveling at hundreds of miles per hour, laden with more than ten thousand gallons of jet fuel. Unlike the first crash, this second crash was captured by dozens of amateur and

Planes hit the twin towers of the World Trade Center on September 11, 2001, as part of a coordinated terrorist attack. *AP Images*

professional videographers, who had had their cameras trained on Tower One. The haunting image of a silhouetted plane exploding into the side of Tower Two went out live nationwide as the story morphed from one of a tragic accident to that of a deliberate attack.

As massive evacuations of the two World Trade Center towers began, President George W. Bush, who had just sat down in a Florida classroom to read to a room full of elementary school students, was informed by his Chief of Staff that "America [was] under attack." In a move later praised by his supporters and condemned by his critics, President Bush remained in the classroom for another ten minutes before meeting with advisors, issuing a brief public statement, and departing the school for a nearby airport to board Air Force One.

The Attack on the Pentagon and Flight 93 As F-15 fighter jets scrambled to protect New York City airspace, two more planes were hijacked. Flights 77 and 93 were soon turning around and heading toward their Washington, D.C., targets. At 9:37 A.M., Flight 77 slammed into the side of the Pentagon, killing all aboard, along with 125 personnel inside the building—a relatively small death toll owing to the fact that the stricken wing of the building was largely unoccupied at the time thanks to recent renovation work.

After the Pentagon strike all U.S. airspace was shut down—incoming flights from overseas were diverted to Canadian airports. As the 10:00 hour neared along the Eastern seaboard, the only planes in the air were military aircraft, scrambled to protect New York and Washington, D.C., airspace; Air Force One, carrying the president and his staff; and Flight 93, which was approximately twenty minutes from its intended target when a passenger revolt forced the hijackers to roll the plane and deliberately crash it into a Pennsylvania field.

Collapse of the Two Towers Meanwhile, the situation at the World Trade Center had grown increasingly desperate. Thousands of workers were trapped in both towers above the respective crash zones. Many attempted to reach the roofs of the towers in the hope of a helicopter rescue while around two hundred others, driven to desperation by the flames that were quickly spreading through the floors of the two towers, leapt to their deaths, much to the horror of onlookers. Meanwhile, city emergency personnel (the first responders, such as firefighters and police officers) were coordinating evacuation and fire-fighting efforts around and inside the entire World Trade Center complex.

Suddenly, at 9:59 A.M., not quite an hour after it was struck, Tower Two collapsed, "pancaking" more-or-less straight down and unleashing a massive debris cloud of powdered glass and concrete across lower Manhattan. Half an hour later, Tower One followed suit.

Death Toll and Impact The majority of the deaths sustained on 9/11 occurred when the towers collapsed. In all, counting both the airplane passengers and those victims on the ground, the attacks claimed at least 2,973 lives in addition to the 19 hijackers.

As the full impact of the attacks began to sink into the nation's stunned consciousness, messages of sympathy poured in from the international community. Although no claims of responsibility were immediately forthcoming, connections were quickly drawn both in the media and among government agencies between the attacks and al-Qaeda.

When reports of missile attacks around the Afghan city of Kabul were reported on the afternoon of September 11, many assumed it was in retaliation for the terrorist attacks. Al-Qaeda's connections to the Taliban, Afghanistan's ruling party, were well known. Although the attacks were soon attributed to internecine warfare, the implications of the day's events were clear. Indeed, within a month of the attacks the United States and its allies were engaged in open warfare with the Taliban and al-Qaeda. The War on Terrorism had begun.

✪ Major Figures

George W. Bush

In the first year of his first term as American president, George W. Bush (1946–) dealt with terrorist attacks on the United States. The attacks of September 11, 2001, on New York City and Washington, D.C., compelled

After the attacks of September 11, 2001, President Bush addressed the crowd and the nation from the rubble of the Twin Towers on September 14. *AP Images*

him to launch the War on Terrorism with American military in Afghanistan and Iraq. Over time, public support for these initiatives eroded.

Born July 6, 1946, in New Haven, Connecticut, Bush was the eldest child of George H.W. Bush and his wife, Barbara. His father went on to make a fortune in the oil business in Texas. The family moved to Texas when the younger Bush was two years old. George H.W. Bush later served as vice president in the Ronald Regan administration and became a one-term president in 1988.

Education at Phillips Academy and Yale
Bush attended elementary and part of middle school in Texas, where he was a talented athlete but a mediocre student. He had early political experience as a seventh grader by running for class president and winning. For the rest of his education, Bush was sent to an East Coast preparatory school, Phillips Academy. Again shining by playing three sports—baseball, basketball, and football—Bush continued to struggle academically.

Like his father, the younger Bush attended Yale University, where he became president of his fraternity, Delta Kappa Epsilon. Bush graduated in 1968 with an undergraduate degree in history. Returning to Texas, Bush settled in Houston, where his family lived. His first job was working for an agribusiness company. During the Vietnam War, Bush served in the Texas National Air Guard. He was never on combat duty.

Oil Business
Bush applied to and was rejected by the University of Texas Law School. Later, he entered Harvard Business School. Upon completing his M.B.A., Bush returned to Texas in 1975 and went into the oil business. Changing course for a time, Bush ran for a seat in the U.S. House of Representatives in 1978; he lost the election by a small margin and returned to his oil business, Bush Exploration. Bush spent the next few years in the oil industry before selling out his shares in the company that had bought his business, Harken Energy, in 1990.

The Texas Rangers
Politics remained important to Bush, who worked on his father's presidential campaign in 1988. He primarily helped the senior Bush with fundraising. After his father's victory, Bush went back to Texas. He put together a group of seventy investors to buy the Texas Rangers, a Major League Baseball team. Though the Rangers were struggling when the group bought the team in 1988, their fortunes soon began turning around. In 1998, the group sold the Rangers for a tidy profit. Bush himself gained $14 million by the sale.

Texas Governor
In 1994, Bush again sought political office. He ran as a Republican for the governorship in Texas, promising to cut down on crime, institute welfare reform, and achieve autonomy for public school districts. Bush won, defeating incumbent Democrat Ann Richards.

As Texas governor, Bush appealed to both moderates and conservatives. Though still politically untutored—he stated he did not like briefings and meetings—Bush was a popular two-term governor. He gained national attention for his accomplishments in Texas, especially in his second term.

Two Terms as President
In the late 1990s, Bush decided to make a run for the presidency. In 2000, he secured the Republican nomination. With running mate Dick Cheney, who had been Secretary of Defense during Bush's father's administration, Bush eked out a hotly contested victory over Democrat Albert Gore, who had been vice president during Bill Clinton's two terms as president. The race between the two candidates was so close there was no definite winner on election day, and problems with ballots in parts of Florida led to recounts. The controversy dragged on for a month. The recounts were ended by the U.S. Supreme Court, and Bush was declared the winner in early December 2000. Though it was determined that Gore had won the popular vote, Bush had enough electoral votes to win the presidency. Bush won re-election in 2004.

As president, Bush dealt with domestic issues like education reform, pushing his No Child Life Behind legislation through Congress in 2001. What essentially defined his presidency, however, was the War on Terrorism. Less than nine months after Bush took office, terrorists hijacked four jet liners. Two were crashed into the World Trade Center, one into the Pentagon, and the fourth crashed in rural Pennsylvania after passengers fought the hijackers. Among Bush's responses to this attack were creating the Office of Homeland Security and improving security in American airports.

Response to Terrorist Attacks After the Islamic extremist group al-Qaeda took responsibility for the September 11, 2001, terrorist attacks against U.S. targets, Bush authorized the launching of an offensive against the ruling Taliban in Afghanistan later in 2001. The Taliban had harbored al-Qaeda's leader, Osama bin Laden, and many members of his organization. Though the Taliban were soon removed from power, efforts to locate bin Laden ended in failure. Bush remained committed to rebuilding Afghanistan and supporting their efforts to become a more democratic nation.

By 2002, Bush was calling for similar action in Iraq. In a September 2002 address to the United Nations, he demanded military intervention in Iraq because he believed Iraq and its leader, Saddam Hussein, possessed weapons of mass destruction. Though the United Nations declined to get involved or support the American position, Bush gained the support of the Republican-controlled Congress for military intervention in Iraq in October 2002.

Iraq Invasion In mid-March 2003, the United States and a few of its allies, including Great Britain, invaded Iraq. Within a few months, Bush declared victory as Saddam and his political party had been removed from power and Iraq was thought secured. Though Bush said that this victory marked the end of military action in Iraq, the conflict dragged on for years as the American forces struggled to impose order in a country beset by warring religious and political factions.

As his second term in office progressed, Bush faced increasing domestic, even international pressure, about continued American involvement in Iraq. Though he promised Iraqis that he would not pull out troops before their new government was secure, more and more Americans expressed discontent over the situation. By June 2007, Bush's approval rating had reached an all-time low at 26 percent, according to a *Newsweek* poll. The war was a primary reason for the low rating as 73 percent of those polled stated they did not approve of how Bush was managing the war in Iraq.

Despite low ratings, Bush believed in his course. Speaking to the nation in a televised address in January 2007, he proclaimed, "America is engaged in a new struggle that will set the course for a new century. We can and will prevail."

Osama bin Laden

Osama bin Laden is the mastermind behind the Islamic terrorist organization, al-Qaeda, and the group's terrorist attacks on the United States on September 11, 2001. His actions began the War on Terrorism in the 1990s. Despite ongoing efforts to locate him, bin Laden has remained elusive.

Bin Laden was born on March 10, 1957, in Riyadh, Saudi Arabia, the son of Mohammad bin Laden and one of his several wives. His father was a wealthy business owner of a construction company, the Bin Laden Group, which built roads, infrastruce, and mosques in Saudi Arabia. Bin Laden and his fifty siblings split their father's multi-billion dollar estate after his death in 1968 in a helicopter accident.

Educated in Mecca and Jedda and raised in privilege, bin Laden was a dedicated Muslim from earliest childhood. After marrying his first wife at the age of seventeen, he entered King Abd al-Aziz University and studied public management. While a student, he became influenced by a professor, Sheik Abdullah Azzam, who was also a well-known radical Muslim. Bin Laden completed his degree in 1978.

Osama Enters the Fray Bin Laden went to Afghanistan in late 1979 to join the jihad to defend the country

Osama bin Laden's career as a terrorist likely began during his involvement in 1980s efforts to oust the Soviets from Afghanistan. *AP Images*

against the Soviet Union, which had invaded it. He used his considerable wealth to fund the activities of the *mujahideen* (Muslim fighters) in Afghanistan. Bin Laden ensured they were trained, equipped, and fed, as well as had their medical needs met. Bin Laden himself even participated in several battles and demonstrated bravery.

While the Soviet invasion of Afghanistan lasted for a decade, bin Laden continued his activities in support of the jihad fighters. One situation eventually led to the founding of al-Qaeda. In 1984, bin Laden was the co-founder of the *Maktab al-Khidmat* ("Services Office") with Azzam, a member of the Muslim Brotherhood. Despite its innocuous name, Maktab al-Khidmat recruited and trained jihad fighters from around the world.

Founded al-Qaeda About six months after the Soviets retreated from Afghanistan in 1989, Azzam was killed in a car bombing. Though dejected by Azzam's death, bin Laden was also inspired to carry on with what they started. To that end, he launched al-Qaeda, a militant network of jihad fighters, with members of the Egyptian Islamic Jihad. al-Qaeda consisted of thousands of radical Muslims who had been trained and financed through the Maktab al-Khidmat. Still committed to the cause, they were organized into secret cells around the world in their home countries. Led by bin Laden, al-Qaeda launched guerilla attacks against selected targets deemed heretical.

Bin Laden's activities put him in opposition to his home country. He returned to Saudi Arabia in 1990 and began speaking out against the Saudi royal family as well as Saudi foreign policies. Bin Laden's criticisms increased during the Gulf War, when Saudi Arabia invited American troops into the country as part of the war effort in 1990. He was placed under house arrest and later had his passport revoked.

Exile As bin Laden came to be seen as a threat in Saudi Arabia, he was asked to leave the country. He left with his family, which included more wives and a number of children. They moved to Sudan, which had a militant Islamic government. While there, bin Laden founded a few businesses, including a construction company. Bin Laden also established terrorist training camps in the country, which trained a number of established militant Muslim groups and sent them to participate in conflicts involving Muslims.

While living in Sudan, bin Laden remained critical of the Saudi government and actively worked to bring it down. His actions included organizing assassination attempts on Saudis. In response, the Saudi government froze his assests—at least $200 million—in 1993. The following year, bin Laden renounced his citizenship and soon began using the Internet to organize his attacks as well as launder funds to fund them.

As bin Laden was working against Saudi Arabia, he was also targeting the United States and Americans abroad through al-Qaeda. The network was directly or indirectly responsible for killing Americans at a hotel in Yemen, shooting down American soldiers in Somalia, and the World Trade Center bombing, all in 1993. Bin Laden and al-Qaeda also aimed at others in this time period, including the attempted destruction of an airliner on its way to Japan in 1994 and an assassination attempt on the Egyptian president, Hosni Mubarak, in 1995.

Back to Afghanistan Pressured by the United States, Sudan ended its protection of bin Laden in 1996. In response, he moved his family and followers to Afghanistan that May, though his camps continued to operate in Sudan. At the time, Afghanistan was controlled by the Taliban, a strict, fundamentalist Islamic group led by Mullah Mohammed Omar. As in Sudan, bin Laden gave the Taliban financial support and helped rebuild Afghanistan's infrastructure, which had been severely damaged during the Soviet occupation. In return, the Taliban supported the terrorist work of bin Laden and al-Qaeda, and allowed him to found more training camps for al-Qaeda terrorists.

In August 1996, bin Laden declared jihad against both Americans and Jews and called for Muslims to expel them from Saudi Arabia and Israel. Later that year, nineteen Americans died in a suspected al-Qaeda attack on a military complex in Saudi Arabia. Bin Laden took his attack on Americans a step further in 1998 when he issued a *fatwa* (a religious proclamation) that demanded the death of all Americans. al-Qaeda's jihad fighters responded by bombing two U.S. embassies located in East Africa resulting in death or injury to thousands.

An Enemy of the United States Recognizing that bin Laden was a significant threat, the U.S. government moved from labeling him an extremist to watch to indicting him on charges, including for the embassy bombings in November 1998. A $5 million reward was offered for information leading to his arrest at the same time. The following year, he was placed on the Federal Bureau of Investigation's "most wanted terrorist" list.

The Taliban grew tired of bin Laden by the late 1990s because of the international attention and anger he drew to Afghanistan, and they asked him to stop his military and political activities. Despite being kept under watch by Taliban soldiers, bin Laden played a role in the failed campaign to bomb major New Year's Eve celebrations in 1999. More successful was his alleged role in the suicide bomber attack on the *U.S.S. Cole* in Yemen in 2000 in which at least twelve soldiers lost their lives.

Orchestrated 9/11 Attacks On September 11, 2001, al-Qaeda operatives hijacked four major airliners in the United States. Two were crashed into the World Trade Center in New York City, and another hit the Pentagon. A fourth hijacked plane was taken over by the passengers who thwarted the attack by crashing it in Pennsylvania. About 3,000 people died as a direct result of these attacks.

Condoleeza Rice, Tony Blair, and George W. Bush walk to a pickup truck during a September 2002 meeting at the president's Crawford, Texas, ranch. *Stephen Jaffe/AFP/Getty Images*

After September 11, President George W. Bush presented requested proof of bin Laden's involvement in the attacks and demanded the Taliban turn him over. Because of the Taliban's continued refusal, the U.S. government attacked Afghanistan in what was known as Operation Enduring Freedom. Beginning with air strikes and later including ground troops, Americans and non-Taliban Afghanis fought against the Taliban as well as al-Qaeda. Despite efforts to secure bin Laden, it is believed he escaped from Afghanistan during a battle at the Tora Bora cave complex.

After 2001, bin Laden's whereabouts were unclear as he remained in hiding in remote areas. He irregularly issued videotapes and missives in support of al-Qaeda activities in the years after the attack. While it is believed bin Laden could be in Pakistan or even dead, the truth is unknown, though the United States upped the bounty on his head to $25 million.

Tony Blair

The prime minister of Great Britain until June 27, 2007, Tony Blair (1953–) oversaw British involvement in the War on Terrorism. He supported American president George W. Bush's military actions in Afghanistan and Iraq with British troops and funding, sparking much controversy in his own country.

Anthony Charles Lynton Blair was born on May 6, 1953, in Edinburgh, Scotland. He was the son of Leo and Hazel Blair. The family lived in Australia for a time during Blair's childhood before eventually settling in Durham, England. There, Leo Blair worked as a lawyer and as a law lecturer at Durham University.

Leo Blair was running for a seat in Parliament as a member of the Conservative Party in 1963 when he suffered a stroke shortly before the election. Because Blair's father took an extended amount of time to recover, including three years to learn to speak again,

Blair and his two siblings were forced to learn how to take care of themselves. Leo Blair also encouraged his children to become involved in politics.

Law Career While a scholarship student at Edinburgh's Fettes College, Blair questioned authority, showed a talent for acting, and booked engagements for rock bands. He went on to study law at St. John's College, Oxford University. After completing his degree in 1975, Blair served as an intern for Queen's Counsel Alexander Irvine and focused on employment law cases. He then worked as a lawyer until the early 1980s.

Early Political Career After joining the Labour Party, Blair soon became involved in politics. In 1983, he won his first seat in Parliament. Blair was, however, a member of the official opposition (the party with the second most number of seats in the House of Commons) as the Conservative Party held a vast majority in Parliament. Neil Kinnock became the leader of the Labour Party at the same time, and he soon got Blair involved in the national party.

From 1984 to 1987, Blair served as the spokesperson of treasury and economic affairs. He then became the trade and industry spokesperson, and investigated the stock market crash of October 1987. Blair was then a member of the shadow cabinet in 1988, first as shadow energy secretary then as a shadow employment secretary to 1991. (A shadow cabinet is made up of members of the official opposition party in Parliament, who "shadow" or criticize and respond to, the actions of the cabinet.)

When John Smith became leader of the Labour Party in 1992, he named Blair his home secretary. Smith died in 1994, and Blair himself was elected the leader of the Labour Party. When Blair took over, he shifted the message and focus of the Labour Party.

While Labour had traditionally supported unions, nationalized industry, and the welfare state, Blair emphasized greater empowerment of regional and local governments. He also compelled the party to make changes in its charter to move it away from its leftist and socialist-leaning economic and social philosophies. This "New Labour." Party supported free enterprise while emphasizing the importance of controlling inflation and lowering budget deficits.

Prime Minister When national elections were held in May 1997, the Labour Party won a majority of seats in Parliament and Blair became Great Britain's prime minister. He was initially extremely popular with an 82 percent approval rating. Soon after taking office, he instituted reforms to social programs, the National Health Service, and welfare spending. One program gave young welfare recipients access to education to expand their employment opportunities. Blair also encouraged legislation that reduced government restrictions on business and inhibited crime.

By 1998, Blair also helped end the three-decade conflict in Northern Ireland between the Protestant majority and Catholic minority by supporting peaceful Northern Ireland. With solid support from the middle class, Blair was re-elected in June 2001, though with a reduced Labour majority in Parliament. He became the first Labour Party leader to win and complete a second full term. Within a few months after this victory, he became involved in the War on Terrorism after the September 11, 2001, terrorist attacks on New York City and Washington, D.C., were launched by the terrorist organization al-Qaeda. Actively supporting President George W. Bush's efforts in this area, Blair talked to numerous world leaders to gain more backing for fighting the terrorists.

The Cost of Supporting America Blair did much more than talk. He sent British troops to join American forces in removing the Taliban from power in Afghanistan in the fall of 2001. That government had harbored al-Qaeda members and its leader, Osama bin Laden, and allowed the group to train in Afghanistan. While Blair's military actions in Afghanistan were generally supported by the British, his backing of the United States' invasion of Iraq provoked controversy.

By 2002, Blair and other British officials joined the chorus of Americans, led by President Bush, who claimed that Iraq's leader, Saddam Hussein, had weapons of mass destruction as well as an active weapons program. Labeling Saddam a threat to world peace, Bush argued that the Iraqi government supported terrorists. Like Bush, Blair called for a military intervention in Iraq, but found few international supporters. The United Nations did not back military action against Iraq, and many people in Great Britain wanted no part of what they viewed as unwarranted American aggression.

Despite this situation, Blair stuck with Bush and committed a number of British troops to the war when the United States led an invasion of Iraq in March 2003. While Saddam's government was quickly removed from power, the conflict dragged on for years as Iraq was reduced to chaos amidst insurrections and internal power struggles. Because the ostensible cause for the invasion—Saddam' weapons of mass destruction—were never found, public support for both Blair and Bush withered in their respective countries. Blair was accused of exaggerating intelligence to justify British actions in the war. The number of deaths of British soldiers also resulted in less popularity for Blair among his people.

Leaving Office Though the Labour Party's majority eroded further in the September 2005 elections, Blair retained his post as prime minister, becoming his party's longest-serving Labour prime minister. His domestic programs were generally still popular, but his foreign policy, particularly in Iraq, drew wide criticism.

After the national elections in 2005, Blair announced he would step down before the next election cycle. Blair continued to back Bush's actions in Iraq before resigning as Labour Party leader and prime minister on June 27, 2007. He was replaced by Gordon Brown, who had been Blair's chancellor of the exchequer. Blair then became the Middle East peace envoy for the United States, Russia, the European Union, and the United Nations (collectively known as the Quartet).

Mullah Mohammad Omar

The leader of the Taliban regime in Afghanistan, Mullah Mohammad Omar (c. 1959–) was forced out of power in 2001. His oppressive Islamic regime sheltered Osama bin Laden, the founder and leader of al-Qaeda, the group behind the terrorist attacks against the United States on September 11, 2001. After being forced out by the United States and its allies, including anti-Taliban Afghanis, Omar remained a wanted fugitive for many years.

Fought Soviets Omar was born in 1958 or 1959 in the village of Singesar, near Kandahar, a member of the Pashtun tribe. He was educated at a religious school. When he was a young adult, Afghanistan was invaded by the Soviet Union in 1979. Omar joined the mujahedeen, Afghan rebels who fought against the Soviet invaders. During one battle, Omar lost one eye. He eventually became commander of a guerrilla unit.

After seeing fellow members of the mujahedeen terrorizing Afghan villagers, Omar resigned and resumed his studies to be a mullah (a Muslim cleric) at a radical Islamic school that was funded by Saudis. These schools resented the mujahedeen and trained their students to work against them. Omar then became a religious teacher and village cleric.

Founding the Taliban The Soviets left Afghanistan in 1989, and the mujahedeen gained control of the government by the mid-1990s. By this time, Omar was working as a religious teacher in Singesar, an Afghan village. There, he took action against the mujahedeen when he was told two teenaged girls had been kidnapped by certain mujahedeen soldiers, had their heads shaved, and were being raped at a military checkpoint. Gathering other former soldiers and using Soviet rifles, they stormed the checkpoint and freed the girls. The mujahedeen commander was hanged.

Over time, the Taliban emerged as a group organized to resist mujahedeen rule. Omar emerged as the Taliban's leader, proposing that the group follow Islam in its purest form. Their developing ideology was also influenced by the Egyptian Muslim Brotherhood and the Jamaati Isami, which both fought against Western influences in favor of an Islamic state. Omar and the Taliban received support from Pakistan as well as from other Pashtuns.

While in Pakistan to research possible links between "shoe bomber" Richard Reid and Al Qaeda, *Wall Street Journal* reporter Daniel Pearl was kidnapped and murdered by Al Qaeda operative Khalid Sheikh Mohammed. *CNN/Getty Images*

The Taliban Take Afghanistan Originally locating their power base in Kandahar, the Taliban gained other territories in the mid-1990s as the people looked to them for freedom from the oppressive mujahedeen rulers. By 1996, the Taliban had captured Kabul, the capital of Afghanistan and declared themselves in control of the government.

Led by Omar, the Taliban was initially embraced by the people of Afghanistan as a force of stability after years of warfare. However, Omar and the other mullahs who led the regime soon put oppressive laws and practices into place which were based on their interpretation of Islam. For example, women were no longer allowed to work outside of the home and girls were not allowed to attend school after the age of eight. Non-religious music was banned and television stations were shut down. There were public executions and actions against those deemed criminal or deviant. Thieves underwent public amputations of limbs, while accused homosexuals were killed. Such human rights violations led to international condemnation. Only three countries recognized the Taliban as the legitimate government of Afghanistan: Pakistan, Saudi Arabia, and the United Arab Emirates.

In September 2006, five years after the attacks that launched the War on Terror, President Bush hosted a White House Meeting between Afghanistan president Hamid Karzai (r) and Pakistan president Pervez Musharraf (l). *Mark Wilson/Getty Images*

Omar and the Taliban harbored bin Laden and his al-Qaeda followers as the group gave the Taliban much needed financial support. The two men are also connected by family ties: Omar's sister is one of bin Laden's four wives. Bin Laden was believed to be behind a number of terrorist attacks on Americans beginning in 1993, including the bombings of American embassies in east Africa in 1998 and the *U.S.S. Cole* in Yemen in 2000. Though the United States demanded that Omar turn over bin Laden, he refused.

Removal from Power Omar's support of bin Laden eventually led to his own downfall. After bin Laden proved to be the mastermind behind al-Qaeda's terrorist attacks on the United States on September 11, 2001, the United States invaded Afghanistan a month later. As the Taliban was forced to cede power to newly elected Afghan president Hamid Karzai in December 2001, Omar and the other leaders went into hiding. Despite a massive hunt for him, he was not found and American forces were even unsure if he was alive for a time.

Eventually, it became clear that Omar had escaped. Since 2004, he has tried to launch a Taliban insurgency and regain control of Afghanistan.

Pervez Musharraf

The self-appointed president of Pakistan beginning in 2001, Pervez Musharraf (1943–) allied his country with the United States after the September 11, 2001, terrorist attacks. He supported the American invasion of Afghanistan and took strong action against Muslim terrorists living in his country.

Pervez Musharraf was born August 11, 1943, in Delhi, India. His father was a career diplomat while his mother was employed by the International Labour Organization. When the Muslim country of Pakistan was founded as India gained its independence in 1947, the family moved to Karachi, the country's largest city. Because of his father's career, Musharraf spent 1949 to 1956 living in Turkey. Musharraf received his education at Christian schools in Turkey and Pakistan, including Karachi's St. Patrick's High School and Lahore's Forman Christian College. Moving on to the Pakistani Military Academy in 1961, he graduated in 1964.

Early Military Career After completing his education, Musharraf joined the Pakistani Army. He spent the next few decades in the service, beginning with a stint in an artillery regiment. In 1965, Musharraf saw combat in an armed conflict with India and was awarded the Imtiazi Sanad (a medal) for gallantry. He then volunteered for a commando outfit. Later a company commander, he fought in the Pakistani civil war in 1971, which saw the western part of the country split off to form Bangladesh. Throughout his career, Musharraf also held staff and instructional positions.

By 1991, Musharraf was named a major general. He continued his education in the early 1990s as well, studying at the Command and Staff College and the National Defense College, both in Pakistan, as well as the British-based Royal College of Defense Studies. Musharraf went on to teach at both Pakistan-based schools. He later was named the director of general military operations at the Pakistani Army's general headquarters.

Promoted to General Reaching the rank of full general in 1998, Musharraf was appointed the army's chief of staff by Pakistani Prime Minister Nawaz Sharif. Musharraf's predecessor, General Jehangir Karmat, was removed because he advocated the military sharing governmental power through a joint national security council. Though Musharraf promised the prime minister he would not concern himself with politics, he soon broke this vow.

Musharraf gained more power in 1999 when he was appointed chairman of the Joint Chiefs of Staff Committee. Later that year, Musharraf came into conflict with Pakistani Prime Minister Nawaz Sharif over his policies. Musharraf was on official business in Sri Lanka in October 1999 when he learned that Sharif had fired him. Musharraf quickly returned to Pakistan to address the situation.

Sharif Deposed On October 12, 1999, Musharraf was able to depose Sharif in a bloodless coup and take over as Pakistan's chief executive. Musharraf had the support and backing of a number of senior military officers as well as the armed forces. After dismissing parliament and imposing martial law in violation of his country's constitution, he soon promised the Pakistani people that he would stabilize the country by improving the weak economy and dealing with the widespread corruption in the government. Then, civil rule would be allowed to return.

After the coup, Musharraf also kept his positions as the army chief of staff and chairman of the Joint Chiefs of Staff. He added a fourth title on June 20, 2001, when he appointed himself president and head of state as well. Musharraf initially proved a popular leader with widespread appeal, though Islamic fundamentalists and the Indian government were leery of him and his intentions.

As leader, Musharraf tried to deal with the long-standing dispute with India over control of the disputed Kashmir region. He also promised to strengthen protections of human rights. For example, he condemned the practice of honor killings of Pakistani women. (An honor killing is the murder of a family member, usually a

woman, who is believed to have dishonored the family.) Musharraf appeased fundamentalists by allowing the Islamic provisions of Pakistan's constitution to be revived and by supporting the rule of the Taliban in Afghanistan.

American Ally While Musharraf's actions often stymied Pakistan's continued movement toward democracy, he assured the Pakistani people that civilian rule would resume in 2002 when national elections were to be held. Before this could happen, world events affected his country and how he was perceived. The United States depended on him and Pakistan after the September 11, 2001, terrorist attacks on American targets by the al-Qaeda—a terrorist organization supported by the Taliban regime.

Backing the anti-terrorism cause, Musharraf provided support for Americans as they launched Operation Enduring Freedom and invaded Afghanistan to dislodge the Taliban. At the same time, Pakistan was

THE RED MOSQUE

Lal Masjid (Red Mosque) in Islamabad, Pakistan's capital city, had a reputation for radicalism for many years and openly supported the Taliban's extremist regime in Afghanistan. The Red Mosque was attached to seminaries for both men and women, and students there received a fundamentalist Islamic education. The students and clerics associated with the mosque often called for the overthrow—or even assassination—of Pakistan's president Pervez Musharraf, unpopular with Islamic extremists since lending his support to America's War on Terror. The protestors called for the establishment of a religious government.

After Musharraf began destroying many mosques in Islamabad in an effort to quash Islamic extremism, armed female students set up a vigil at the Red Mosque, vowing to fight to the death to protect it. After negotiations with the mosque's occupiers failed, Musharraf order an elite force of army commandos to lay siege to the building in early July 2007. On July 10, 2007, the soldiers stormed the mosque in a blaze of gunfire, but not before approximately 1,300 of those within had fled. About eighty people, ten of them soldiers, were killed in the raid, as fighters within the mosque attacked the soldiers with rocket launchers and machine guns. It took more than a day, but the soldiers were finally able to secure the Red Mosque. Musharraf declared the operation successful, claiming that there were few civilian casualties and that those killed had been violent extremists, many of them foreigners. Though Musharraf's decision to storm the mosque was praised by some, who said it showed he was prepared to be tough with radical Islamic groups within his country, many were outraged by the violence. Some fundamentalist clerics in the region have called for a jihad, or holy war, against Musharraf's regime.

Defense Donald Rumsfeld stands before one of the Stealth Bomber planes that launched an attack on Afghanistan in 2001. *Dave Kaup/AFP/ Getty Images*

known for harboring Muslim terrorists, a situation Musharraf worked to change. He even attempted to get the Taliban to hand over al-Qaeda leader Osama bin Laden so that Afghanistan might avoid American military reprisals and closed the border with Afghanistan. Musharraf was widely criticized in his own country for supporting the United States, and there was a call to overthrow him.

Challenges Continue While Musharraf remained in office even after national elections were held in October 2002, he faced significant challenges. In addition to dealing with ongoing disapproval from fundamentalists inside the country, Musharraf had to deal with domestic crises as well. On October 8, 2005, a magnitude 7.6 earthquake struck Pakistan. Musharraf was criticized for the delay in getting aid to devastated areas.

Musharraf also continued to address corruption within his government. In March 2007, he suspended the chief justice of the supreme court of Pakistan, Ifikhar Chaudhry, accusing him of transgressions and the misuse of authority. Musharraf's actions compelled two hundred lawyers in Pakistan to burn him in effigy. Chaudhry was later reinstated. It was not the only problem faced by Musharraf, as there were widespread violent protests in the country. In the summer of 2007, Musharraf faced several challenges from political rivals determined to wrest power from the unpopular president.

Elections have been called for to determine the future leadership of Pakistan.

Donald Rumsfeld

The U.S. Secretary of Defense under both President Gerald R. Ford and President George W. Bush, Donald Rumsfeld (1932–) played a significant, often controversial, role in shaping policy related to the War on Terrorism.

Born Donald Harold Rumsfeld, on July 9, 1932, in Chicago, Illinois, he was the son of George Donald Rumsfeld and his wife, Jeannette. His father worked in real estate sales and served in the U.S. Navy during World War II.

Raised in Winnetka, Illinois, Rumsfeld attended New Tier High School where he was both an exceptional student and champion wrestler. He also worked hard in his spare time, holding down at least twenty part-time jobs over the course of his teen years. With both an academic and a Naval Reserve Officer Training Corps scholarship, Rumsfeld studied political science at Princeton University. He also played football, serving as captain of Princeton's team, and continued to wrestle. Rumsfeld earned his bachelor's degree in 1954.

Naval Career After completing his degree, Rumsfeld began serving in the U.S. Navy. He spent his three-year tour of duty as an aviator and flight instructor. In 1957,

Rumsfeld was transferred to the Navy's Ready Reserve. He continued to participate in flying drills and administrative assignments for nearly two more decades. When he left active duty, Rumsfeld spent several years working in politics in Washington. He became employed by a Congressman as an administrative assistant. In 1959, he began working as a Congressional staff assistant.

Political Office Rumsfeld took a two-year break from politics and returned to Chicago. There, he was employed at A.G. Becker and Company as an investment broker. Politics, however, still had an allure for Rumsfeld. He ran for a seat representing Illinois's thirteenth district in the House of Representatives in 1962. Rumsfeld won, and the popular representative was re-elected three more times.

In 1969, Rumsfeld resigned from Congress to join the administration of the newly elected Republican President Richard M. Nixon. Rumsfeld served as the Office of Economic Opportunity's director. He was also a member of the president's cabinet and served as an assistant to the president.

Two years later, Rumsfeld took on new positions in the Nixon administration. He became the Economic Stabilization Program's director as well as a counselor to the president. In 1973, Rumsfeld went abroad for Nixon when he was appointed the American ambassador to the North Atlantic Treaty Organization (NATO).

Service in the Ford Administration Rumsfeld went back to Washington, D.C., in 1974. After Nixon resigned (due to political pressure resulting from the Watergate scandal) and Gerald R. Ford took office, Rumsfeld was named the head of the new president's transition team. When the transition was completed, Rumsfeld continued to serve the new president. Ford initially named him the chief of staff in the White House as well as a member of his cabinet.

Late in 1975, Rumsfeld was appointed to a position of considerable power: Secretary of Defense. When Rumsfeld took office on November 20, 1975, he became the youngest defense secretary in the history of the United States. Rumsfeld retained the defense secretary post until early 1977, when the new Democratic administration of Jimmy Carter took office.

Work in the Private Sector Leaving politics behind for a time, Rumsfeld worked in the private sector as a business executive. He became the president and chief executive officer (CEO) of G.D. Searle & Company, an international pharmaceutical corporation, in 1977. Remaining with Searle until 1985, Rumsfeld introduced two new popular flavors of Metamucil® as well as the artificial sweetener Nutrasweet® to the market during his tenure. In 1985, he became Searle's chairman of the board for a time, then served as advisor to William Blair & Company from 1985 to 1990.

While Rumsfeld was working in business, he became politically active again after Republican Ronald Reagan took office as president in 1981. From 1982 to 1986, Rumsfeld served as a member of the president's General Advisory Committee on Arms Control.

Rumsfeld also harbored presidential aspirations of his own. In the spring of 1986, he stated that he planned to run for the Republican nomination for president in 1988, but changed his mind in early 1987. Instead, Rumsfeld continued to serve in the administrations of Reagan and his Republican successor, George H.W. Bush. Rumsfeld was a member of the National Commission on the Public Service, the National Economic Commission, and the National Defense University Board of Visitors.

As the 1990s dawned, Rumsfeld's professional focus was again as an executive. He became the chairman and CEO of General Instrument Corporation, which was involved with broadband technology, in 1990. Three years later, Rumsfeld joined Gilead Sciences as the chairman of its board of directors. He also began serving as an advisor for many companies, such as Sweden's Investor AB.

Rumsfeld continued his public sector work as well. During the first term of President Bill Clinton, he was a member of the High Definition Television Advisory Committee for the U.S. Federal Communication Commission. Rumsfeld later served as the chairman on the Commission to Assess National Security Space Management and Organization as well as the Commission to Assess the Ballistic Missile Threat to the United States. Still a loyal Republican, he campaigned for Republican presidential candidate Bob Dole in 1996.

Return to Defense Department When Republican George W. Bush was elected president in 2000, he selected Rumsfeld to be his Secretary of Defense. Soon after taking office, Rumsfeld was charged with reducing the Pentagon's $300 million budget by trimming down the amount of wasted and excess spending as well as modernizing the military. The military establishment criticized Rumsfeld's efforts, and he had little support outside of the administration.

After the terrorist attacks on the United States on September 11, 2001, however, Rumsfeld became important to Bush's War on Terrorism. When the United States launched an attack on the Taliban in Afghanistan, Rumsfeld sometimes tried to interfere with military decisions—telling Central Command to use more ground troops, for example—but soon backed off.

Forced out of Office While criticism of Rumsfeld was minimal during the first two years of the War on Terrorism, the situation changed after the war in Iraq was launched in 2003. His perceived arrogance and abrasive directness in public statements and press conferences about the war was regularly derided. Rumsfeld also was accused of concealing the whole truth about military

Condoleeza Rice speaks after being named national security adviser during President George W. Bush's first term in office.   *AP Images*

matters and defending American actions in Iraq despite many obvious failures and poor planning. In addition, military leaders did not generally support Rumsfeld because he dismissed their advice and ignored the insurgency which later grew in Iraq.

Despite widespread disapproval at home and abroad, Rumsfeld continued to enjoy the support of President Bush. He retained his position for two more years. But when Republicans lost their majority in Congress in midterm elections in 2006, Bush took it as a sign that the people wanted change: he ousted Rumsfeld in November 2006. Rumsfeld was replaced as Secretary of Defense by Robert Gates.

Condoleeza Rice

During the presidency of George W. Bush, Condoleezza Rice (1954–) served first as national security advisor then as Secretary of State. She helped shape American foreign policy after the September 11, 2001, terrorist attacks on the United States, including the launch of the War on Terrorism in Afghanistan and Iraq.

Born November 15, 1954, in Birmingham, Alabama, Rice was the daughter and only child of John Wesley Rice, Jr., and his wife, Angelena. Her father was a guidance counselor and football coach at a black public high school in Birmingham as well as an ordained Presbyterian minister. Her mother was a teacher and church organist. Rice's parents wanted her to have wide horizons and emphasized achievement. She studied piano, languages, and became a competitive figure skater.

A Gifted Student   An excellent student from an early age, Rice skipped both first and seventh grades while attending segregated public schools in Birmingham. When she was eleven years old, the family moved to Tuscaloosa, Alabama, where her father had a new position as a college administrator. Rice moved to Denver, Colorado, when she was entering tenth grade and attended integrated public schools for the first time.

She completed her last year of high school while beginning her first year of college at the University of Denver.

Having studied piano since the age of three, Rice majored in music and planned on a career as a concert pianist. However, she changed her focus and began studying Russian history and language as well as political science.

Rice earned her undergraduate degree in political science in 1974, then entered Notre Dame University. She earned a master's degree in government and international studies, then planned on joining the private sector. A prospective position as an executive assistant at Honeywell fell through, so Rice became a piano teacher for a time. A former professor and mentor suggested she go back to school, so she returned to the University of Denver's Graduate School of International Studies. She completed her doctorate in 1981 with a dissertation on the Czechoslovak Communist Party and its army.

Academic Career After earning her Ph.D, Rice was offered a fellowship to the Stanford University's Center for International Security and Arms Control. She was the first woman to be offered a fellowship to the center. By 1983, Rice was working at Stanford as a professor of political science, gaining tenure in 1987.

As her professional career was taking off, Rice became politically active and soon went to Washington. When Gary Hart ran for the Democratic nomination in 1984, she served as his advisor. Five years later, Rice joined the staff of the National Security Council, on the recommendation of new national security advisor Brent Scowcroft in the administration of George H.W. Bush. Rice eventually became Bush's advisor on the Soviet Union and Eastern Europe. She helped shape American foreign policy as Communism fell in Eastern Europe.

Resigning from her position in the Bush administration in 1991, Rice returned to California and her teaching career at Stanford. In 1993, she became the provost of Stanford, the first woman to hold the position. Rice faced challenges in the position, including a budget deficit and conflicts with faculty. She remained in the position at Stanford until 1999.

Became Bush Advisor In 1999, Rice joined the staff of George W. Bush, the governor of Texas who was seeking the Republican nomination for president in 2000. Rice served as the leader of his group of foreign policy advisors. After Bush won the nomination and general election, he selected Rice to be his national security advisor and shape the direction of American foreign policy. It marked the first time a woman held the post.

Within a few months, Rice faced significant challenges. The terrorist attacks on New York City and Washington, D.C., on September 11, 2001, put Rice in a key position in Bush's government. She helped advise the president as he launched his first offensive on Afghanistan, where the Taliban regime had harbored the mastermind

behind the attacks, Osama bin Laden, in 2001. Rice also helped create the policies for dealing with Iraqi President Saddam Hussein. The United States invaded Iraq based on the belief that Saddam had weapons of mass destruction at his disposal. The invasion was launched in early 2003 without the support of the United Nations. Rice vocally supported Bush's actions, despite a lack of convincing evidence that such weapons existed. (No weapons of mass destruction were found by the U.S. invasion forces.) She also put together documents explaining the new direction in American foreign policy.

Named Secretary of State After President Bush was elected to a second term in 2004, Rice took on new responsibilities in his administration. Bush named her his Secretary of State, replacing Colin Powell (who resigned on November 15, 2004). In this position, she was the leading diplomat representing the United States. Rice served as the primary advocate of American foreign policy both in the United States and abroad, spending much time traveling to achieve more realistic diplomatic goals. She dealt with nuclear issues in North Korea and Iran as well as tensions in the Middle East, among other concerns.

Rice continued to have to answer questions related to American involvement in Afghanistan and Iraq. Though the United States had quickly toppled both the Taliban and the regime of Iraqi dictator Saddam Hussein, both conflicts had dragged on as reconstruction was taking place and Iraq, especially, had to deal with a long-running insurgency. Rice defended American involvement as necessary to Congress and the American people.

After leaving office when Bush's term ends in early 2009, Rice's plans are unclear. She has been mentioned as a potential presidential or vice presidential candidate.

Richard Myers

During the early twenty-first century War on Terrorism, Air Force General Richard B. Myers (1942–) served as the chairman of the U.S. Joint Chiefs of Staff and as a senior military advisor to President George W. Bush. Myers was born on March 1, 1942, in Kansas City, Missouri, and raised in Merriam, Kansas. There, his family owned and operated a hardware store.

As a child, Myers was afraid of airplanes for many years because he saw one crash in his neighborhood. His parents tried to help him overcome his fear by taking him to watch airplanes take off and land at a local airport. After graduating from Shawnee Mission North High School, he entered Kansas State University (KSU). By college, Myers had conquered his fear of planes enough to join the Air Force Reserve Officer Training Corps at KSU. In 1965, Myers earned his B.S. in mechanical engineering.

Early Air Force Career After completing his degree, he joined the Air Force. He was trained as a command pilot at Vance Air Force Base in Oklahoma and was promoted to first lieutenant by 1966. Myers was stationed at Ramstein Air Force Base in West Germany for several years before being transferred to Indochina to participate in the Vietnam War. By 1969, Myers was stationed at the Udorn Royal Thai Air Force Base in Thailand. From there, he flew combat missions in F-4 Phantoms. Myers logged about six hundred combat hours during his time in Vietnam.

Returning in the United States in the 1970s, Myers took on more support roles in the Air Force, which took him away from flying. Before ending his flying days, he logged more than 4100 flying hours. He also continued his education by earning an M.B.A. from Auburn University in 1977. That same year, he attended Maxwell Air Force Base's Air Command and Staff College in Montgomery, Alabama. Myers continued his education in the early 1980s by earning a diploma from the U.S. Army War College in 1981.

Military Leadership Positions   Myers did post-graduate work at Harvard University in 1991, then was the director of tactical weapons and command and control acquisition programs for the Air Force for two years. In 1993, Myers was sent to Japan, where he commanded U.S. Forces Japan and the 5th Air Force at Yokota Air Force Base for nearly three years. Returning to the United States in 1996, Myers was sent to Washington where he served as the assistant to the chairman of the Joint Chiefs of Staff for a year.

In 1997, Myers began serving as commander of Pacific Air Forces at Hickman Air Force Base in Hawaii and was promoted to general that same year. Returning to the mainland of the United States in 1998, Myers was named the head of the U.S. Space Command and the North American Aerospace Defense Command at Peterson Air Force Base in Colorado. There, he offered vocal support for the development of space-based weapons. Satellites were especially appealing to Myers because they could provide constant surveillance.

Joint Chiefs of Staff   Myers left Colorado for Washington, D.C., in 2000 when he was named vice chairman of the Joint Chiefs of Staff. When chairman Army General Hugh Shelton retired in the fall of 2001, Myers took his place and became the head of the Joint Chiefs of Staff. Myers officially became the fifteenth chairman of the Joint Chiefs on October 1, 2001, shortly after the terrorist attacks on New York City and the Pentagon on September 11, 2001. Myers had been in the Pentagon that day, but survived the attacks.

As President Bush launched the War on Terrorism in Afghanistan and Iraq, Myers advised him, the Secretary of Defense, and the National Security Council on military-related matters. He also pressed Congress for sufficient military budget to fight the costly war on several fronts. Summarizing Myers' accomplishments as the head of Joint Chiefs, UPI NewsTrack quoted the president as saying "He helped design a broad and innovative military strategy to win the war on terror. His leadership and flexibility were essential to the liberation of Iraq, and to adapting our tactics to defeat the terrorists and help Iraqis build a peaceful democracy."

Activities in Retirement   Myers retired from the Air Force and as Joint Chiefs head on September 30, 2005. Before leaving office, he emphasized the importance of winning the war in Iraq and neutralizing al-Qaeda and other terrorists operating there (al-Qaeda is the terrorist organization behind the September 11, 2001, attacks on U.S. targets). Myers was awarded a Presidential Medal of Freedom by President Bush several months after leaving office for his accomplishments.

After retiring, Myers took a job as a professor of military history at Kansas State University beginning in 2006. He also joined the board of directors of several companies that same year, including Northrop Grumman Corporation, Deere & Company, and United Technologies Corporation.

Tommy Franks

Four-star General Tommy Franks (1945–) served as the commander of the United States Central Command during the United States' military action in Afghanistan in 2001 and invasion of Iraq in 2003. Franks is known for his common touch and affinity for the everyday soldier.

Tommy Ray Franks was born on June 17, 1945, in Wynnewood, Oklahoma, the adopted son of Ray, an auto mechanic, and Lorene Franks. The family moved to Midland, Texas, when Franks, their only child, was quite young. While attending Midland's Robert E. Lee High School, he distinguished himself as an outstanding athlete. He entered the University of Texas at Austin in 1963 but dropped out after two years.

Early Military Career   Hoping to improve his prospects, Franks joined the U.S. Army and found his calling. Already a skilled shooter (Franks enjoyed hunting as a youngster), Franks' talent led the army to send him to Artillery Officer Candidate School at Fort Sill in Oklahoma. Upon graduation in 1967, he was commissioned as a second lieutenant and briefly stationed at Fort Sill as a battery assistant executive officer.

Franks was deployed to Vietnam in 1967. He served with honor in the Ninth Infantry Division, the 60th Infantry Division, the Second Battalion, and Fourth Field Artillery as a forward observer, aerial observer, an S-3 assistant, and fire support officer. During his tour in Vietnam, he was wounded three times and earned three Purple Hearts.

In 1968, Franks was sent back to Fort Sill and intended to leave the military when his commitment ended. The service chose him to participate in their degree completion program. Franks changed his mind about the military and re-enlisted. A year later, he was a student at the University of Texas at Arlington. A better student this time around, Franks earned an undergraduate degree in

As commander of the U.S. Central Command from 2000 to 2003, General Tommy Franks led American and Coalition troops in two campaigns: Enduring Freedom in Afghanistan and Operation Iraqi Freedom in Iraq. *AP Images*

business administration in 1971, then completed the Artillery Advance Course offered by the army.

Served as Commander

In 1973, Franks was sent to West Germany and named commander and operations manager of the First Squadron Howitzer Battery. While still stationed in Germany, he later was named head of the 84th Armored Engineer Company as well as regimental assistant of operations. The U.S. Army then sent him back to the United States to continue his education. Franks attended the Armed Forces Staff College, graduating in 1976.

Franks was assigned to the Pentagon later that year. He was named the Investigative Division's inspector general. In 1977, Franks was moved to the office of the Army Chief of Staff. He first served on the Congressional Activities Committee, and later served as an executive assistant. Returning to West Germany in 1981, Franks served as the commander of the Second Battalion, 78th Field Artillery for several years.

Brought back to the United States in 1984, Franks continued his education at the Army War College. He then completed his master's degree in public administration at Shippensburg University in Pennsylvania. Franks graduated with the degree in 1985, and was stationed at Fort Hood in Texas. He became the deputy assistant operations officer of III Corps there. In 1987, Franks was promoted to commander of the Division Artillery, First Cavalry Division. Franks was later named the First Cavalry Division's chief of staff.

Combat General

By now a general, Franks took part in Operation Desert Shield and Operation Desert Storm as the assistant commander (maneuver) for the First Cavalry Division in the early 1990s. He then held a series of high-power positions in the United States and Asia. After serving as the assistant commandant of Fort Sill's Field Artillery School in 1991, he was named the first director of the Louisiana Maneuvers Task Force for the Office of the Chief of Staff of the Army at Fort Monroe in 1992.

In 1994, Franks went to Korea, where he was the operations officer for the Combined Forces Command and United States Forces Korea. A year later, he was put in charge of the Second Infantry (Warrior) Division in Korea. Franks spent two years in the post before returning to the United States in 1997. He then was named commander of the Third U.S. Army at Army Forces Central Command.

Leading Troops in the War on Terrorism

Promoted to four-star general, Franks became commander in chief of the United States Central Command in June 2000. In this position, he was in charge of military operations in twenty-five countries across Asia, Africa, and the Middle East. Thus, Franks was in a key position when the al-Qaeda terrorist attacks on New York City occurred on September 11, 2001.

The day after the attacks, Franks was asked to prepare the United States' military options for presentation to President George W. Bush. Within a week, Franks offered his plan to attack both the terrorists and the Taliban that supported them in Afghanistan in Operation Enduring Freedom. In October 2001, the air strikes suggested by Franks began, and within a month, the Taliban had been defeated. As commander of American forces in Afghanistan, Franks used special operations forces, air support, local militia, and CIA (Central Intelligence Agency) operations to complete his mission.

Though Franks' strategy in Afghanistan was successful, he was criticized by some, including U.S. Defense Secretary Donald Rumsfeld, during the operation. But his triumph gave Franks the support of the Bush administration. Franks was allowed to employ a unique strategy when the United States invaded Iraq in Operation Iraqi Freedom in the spring of 2003.

In Iraq, Franks used small forces to move quickly throughout the country instead of mass ground forces,

Afghans go to the polls for the 2005 election of Afghanistan's first parliament after the overthrow of the Taliban. *Desmond © Boylan/Reuters/Corbis*

which gave the U.S. invasion force an element of surprise. The agile special operations forces proved important to his strategy, as did technologically advanced weapons such as precision bombs. Franks also integrated the four branches of the military, making them more effective.

Retirement As in Afghanistan, Franks' strategy paid off in the short term. The United States took Iraq's capital, Baghdad, in three weeks and soon successfully ousted Iraqi leader Saddam Hussein. Franks remained in charge of the operation for several months and turned down a chance to be the Army Chief of Staff. He retired from the U.S. Army on August 1, 2003.

Franks then penned his memoir, *American Soldier*, which was published the following year. The war in Iraq dragged on, and some critics believed Franks' initial success in Iraq was not as great as initially believed because he did not make adequate provisions for post-invasion Iraq. Franks defended his initial attack strategy and remained convinced that removing Saddam from power was the right thing to do.

Hamid Karzai

Hamid Karzai (1957–) was elected president of Afghanistan after the United States toppled the Taliban regime in 2001.

He was born on December 24, 1957, in Karz, a village near Kandahar, Afghanistan, the son of a Populzai tribal clan chief and the descendent of many rulers of his country. Karzai received his education first in Kandahar, then in Kabul, Afghanistan. Remaining in Kabul, Karzai attended the Habibia School from which he earned his bachelor's degree in political science.

After the Soviet Union invaded Afghanistan in 1979, the Karzai family fled from their home country and settled in Quetta, Pakistan. He continued his education in India, where he earned another degree in political science from Himachal Pradesh University. Karzai then studied journalism at the École Supérieure de Journalisme in Paris, France, in 1985, among other educational experiences.

Efforts Against the Soviets Though living in exile, Karzai actively supported efforts to overthrow the Soviets.

Working with anti-Soviet guerillas called the mujahedeen, he helped funnel weapons and supplies from the United States to Afghanistan. Karzai also served as a political adviser to key resistance leaders he supported.

After the government of Burhanuddin Rabbani was established in the post-Soviet period, Karzai served as his deputy foreign minister. However, chaos, corruption, and infighting were hallmarks of the Rabbani regime, prompting Karzai to resign in 1994. He went back to Pakistan and began supporting the Taliban with funds and weapons. Though the Taliban were conservative Muslims, many people already believed they were extremists. Karzai backed them at this time because many were members of his Pashtun tribe (of which the Populzai clan was a part), and he hoped they would address the problematic issues of the Rabbani administration.

Opposition to the Taliban When the Taliban gained control of the Afghan government in 1996, Karzai realized his error. Their regime was restrictive and oppressive and soon began allowing non-Afghani members of the Taliban to establish terrorist training camps throughout the country. Though the Taliban soon wanted him to be their United Nations envoy, Karzai refused.

Leaving Afghanistan to join his family in Quetta in 1997, Karzai worked against the Taliban government. He initially supported efforts to restore Afghanistan's former king, Mohammad Zahir, into power. A year later, he began working with Pashtun chiefs to launch a movement against the Taliban in Afghanistan.

Elected Tribal Chief Karzai suffered a personal loss when the Taliban killed his father in 1999 in retribution for his actions. Karzai was elected the Populzai tribal chief in his father's place. Despite continued threats from the Taliban, Karzai arranged for a massive funeral procession to take his father's body for burial in Kandahar. His actions garnered him admiration, especially from anti-Taliban supporters, and he vowed to create a government in which all its clans, tribes, and ethnicities were represented. Karzai then began traveling to the United States to request support against the Taliban.

Karzai continued to fight the Taliban, especially after the terrorist attacks on the United States on September 11, 2001. He immediately organized a tribal militia to fight the Taliban, but only the British backed his actions at first.

After the United States linked the September 11 attacks to the Taliban, the Americans began bombing the Afghan targets in October 2001. At the same time, Karzai took his militia forces into Kandahar. He was nearly captured by the Taliban and had to be rescued by American forces. Over the next few months, the United States came to respect Karzai as a Pashtun leader in Afghanistan.

Provisional Leader Later in 2001, as the Americans and their Afghan allies in the Northern Alliance were meeting to form a new government in Afghanistan, attendees chose Karzai as the leader of the provisional administration. He took the post in late December 2001, and began working on organizing a national assembly, or Loya-Jirga. This body would elect another temporary head of state, and this leader would coordinate the formation of the new government.

Karzai was elected president of the Afghan Transitional Authority in the summer of 2002. He was by no means secure in his position as several attempts were made on his life. His vice president, Haji Abdul Qadar, was killed by an assassin's bullet. The threat of violence remained a part of his everyday life.

Karzai worked to ensure a smooth transition to a representative government. He was charged with drafting a new constitution, putting together a new army and unified police force, and ensuring national elections occurred by 2004. Karzai completed these tasks and also secured funding and support from other countries to start the reconstruction process. He ultimately gained $5 billion in aid.

President of Afghanistan Despite continued violence in Afghanistan, elections were held on October 9, 2004. Karzai ran for the office of president and was officially elected to the position with over 55 percent of the vote. He was the first democratically elected leader of Afghanistan. He formally took office on December 7, 2004.

As Afghanistan's president, Karzai still had to deal with rebuilding a ravaged country and its economy. Violence among ethnic groups also remained a problem, and corruption crept back into the government. The Taliban continued to be active in Afghanistan, regaining more and more power. The group led an insurgency, which included terrorist activities throughout the country beginning in 2005. Though international forces supported Karzai's government, the Taliban held control of certain parts of the country at times.

Corruption among Afghan government officials and workers also became more of an issue by late 2006. While some questioned whether Karzai was up for the tough job ahead of him, he remained certain he could be the leader Afghanistan needed during this period of reconstruction.

See also **Gulf War: Major Figures: Dick Cheney**
See also **Gulf War: Major Figures: Saddam Hussein**
See also **Gulf War: Major Figures: Colin Powell**

✪ Major Battles

Aerial Bombardment of Afghanistan

Shortly after the devastating terrorist attacks against the United States on September 11, 2001, President George Bush announced that the operation had been planned and executed by members of Osama bin

Within three weeks of the beginning of the 2003 invasion of Iraq, American troops assumed control of Baghdad.   *Ramzi Haidar/AFP/Getty Images*

Laden's terrorist network al-Qaeda, who were being sheltered by the Taliban—the rigid Islamic government of Afghanistan. A few weeks later, the U.S. military launched Operation Enduring Freedom to topple the Taliban and to root out al-Qaeda strongholds in Afghanistan. The campaign opened with an extensive aerial bombardment, followed by an allied ground assault.

The Taliban   The Taliban, a group of fundamentalist Muslim scholars and clerics, had taken control of most of Afghanistan by 1998. Throughout the 1980s, they had fought (with generous American support) to oust the military forces of the Soviet Union, which had invaded Afghanistan in 1979. After the Soviets withdrew, the Taliban subdued the various warlord factions and brought a measure of stability to the country.

However, the Taliban's strict interpretation of religion, enforced by harsh autocratic rule, incurred general international censure. Furthermore, it was well known that the Taliban sheltered and aided groups that engaged in international acts of terror. Before September 11, 2001, only three countries—Pakistan, Saudi Arabia, and the United Arab Emirates—recognized the Taliban as the legitimate government of Afghanistan.

The economy of Afghanistan suffered, especially after the Taliban destroyed the poppy crop for religious reasons. Afghanistan had supplied a large portion of the world's opium, an illegal drug made from poppies, and the trade had produced the majority of the country's cash income. In addition, a harsh drought brought famine—by 2001, at least five million Afghans depended on foreign aid for survival.

The Ultimatum On September 20, 2001, President Bush demanded that the Taliban hand over bin Laden and other al-Qaeda leaders. He also insisted that they shut down the many militant Islamist training camps in Afghanistan. The country, he asserted, had become "safe harbor" for terrorists. He also insisted that the Taliban should release foreign nationals who had been imprisoned for preaching Christianity.

The Taliban reacted with defiance. They denied having any knowledge of bin Laden's whereabouts and made it clear that they would not hand him over even if they did. America had no right, they argued, to accuse bin Laden without proof of his complicity. They warned that Muslims everywhere would rise up against the West, should Bush carry out his threats. Spokesman Mullah Muhmajin told the press that "if the U.S. attacks us, we will declare jihad [holy war] against America."

It was undeniable that, while Middle Eastern governments publicly condemned the Taliban and al-Qaeda, bin Laden had wide public sympathy in the Arab world. Understanding this, Bush took pains to isolate the Afghan leadership, essentially threatening any government who might sympathize with the Taliban. "Every nation," he said, "in every region, now has a decision to make. Either you are with us, or you are with the terrorists."

Nevertheless, President George W. Bush did not enjoy the broad international support that his father had cultivated during the Gulf War. Aware that France, China, and Russia would oppose an armed invasion of Afghanistan, the Bush administration did not bother to seek United Nations (UN) approval before attacking. Instead the United States turned to Great Britain, who proved a staunch ally. Together the United States and Britain invoked Article 51 of the UN charter, which guarantees the rights of nations to act in self-defense.

They launched a series of air strikes against Afghanistan, beginning on October 7, 2001. Canada and Australia joined the effort after the commencement of hostilities. The military operation was initially codenamed "Infinite Justice." However, that name was deemed to be blasphemous to Muslims. The name was accordingly changed to "Operation Enduring Freedom."

The Attack The air strikes targeted training camps, airfields, anti-aircraft radars, and launchers. The United States also gave air support to the Northern Alliance, the anti-Taliban resistance movement that controlled parts of northern Afghanistan.

The assault was unprecedented in its range of attack—cruise missiles were launched from submarines in the Arabian Sea; B-52 bombers took off from Diego Garcia Island in the Indian Ocean; and B-2 Stealth Fighters began their forty-plus-hour bombing runs from the United States. Even command centers were widely distributed—the U.S. Central Command (CENTCOM) in Florida coordinated with the Combined Air Operations Center (CAOC) in Saudi Arabia. This was made possible by advancements in communication technology. Space satellites provided immediate and constant information flow on enemy locations and activity.

The United States and its allies flew about twenty-five thousand sorties before the end of 2001. Despite America's state-of-the-art targeting and guidance systems, and despite Bush's repeated claims that America had no quarrel with the Afghan people, hundreds of civilians, including some U.N. aid workers, were killed and injured in the bombing. As Donald Rumsfeld said in one interview: "If there were an easy, safe way to root terrorist networks out of countries that are harboring them, it would be a blessing, but there is not. Coalition forces will continue to make every reasonable effort to select targets with the least possible unintended damage, but as in any conflict, there will be unintended damage."

The civilian population faced even greater dangers than the falling ordnance. Foreign aid organizations had largely abandoned the country. After months of famine, with the severe winter approaching, Afghanistan faced a humanitarian crisis of epic proportions. Millions of refugees poured into makeshift camps at the border.

The U.S. military command was haunted by the specter of the Vietnam War, where American tactics had often created more enemies than they had killed. In order to win "the hearts and minds" of the Afghan people, American airplanes dropped thirty-seven thousand food kits over the civilian population, as well as medical supplies and propaganda. The U.N. and other aid organizations also stepped up efforts to meet the growing needs of the people.

The Taliban were quick to condemn the air attacks. They announced that their fighters had shot down an American plane, a claim that the Pentagon denied. Bin Laden himself also responded, releasing a taped message over the Arabic news station Al-Jazeera. The bombings, he said, were part of a global struggle between the "side of faith, and the side of infidelity."

Mazari Sharif

On November 9, 2001, with the help of American air cover and U.S. Special Forces, the UIF (the Northern Alliance) captured the key Afghan city of Mazari Sharif. This victory led to the rapid collapse of the Taliban throughout northern Afghanistan.

The Northern Alliance Afghanistan has never been a homogenous society. The country is made up of various tribes, factions, and ethnic groups that speak different languages and profess different religious creeds. Traditional warlords exert a great deal of local control, and their rivalries and alliances are often complex and changeable. Because of this, over the last few centuries, the many governments of Afghanistan have seldom managed to exert total control over the region.

The Taliban, dominated by the southern Pashtun tribe, came close to controlling all of Afghanistan. By

1998, they had conquered more than 90 percent of the country. They were opposed by the United Islamic Front for the Salvation of Afghanistan (UIF), which held a small region to the north of the country. Called the Northern Alliance by the Western press, the resistance comprised several different factions of different ethnicities, mostly Tajik, Uzbek, and Hazara.

Burhanuddin Rabbani (1940–) served as the titular head of the Northern Alliance. However, he was often upstaged by the charismatic and brilliant Ahmed Shah Massoud (1953–2001). Massoud was assassinated by al-Qaeda agents just two days before the September 11 attacks.

A Bloody History The ancient stronghold of Mazari Sharif has seen its share of conquering armies. The city has both strategic and cultural importance. Standing on the only supply route through the Hindu Kush Mountains, thirty-five miles from the northern border, it serves as a kind of gateway into northern Afghanistan and Uzbekistan. Afghans believe that the city's famous Blue Mosque houses the tomb of Mohammed's son-in-law, Caliph Ali.

The Soviets used the city as a staging base for their Afghanistan operations in the 1980s. After the Soviets withdrew in 1992, Mazari Sharif was left in the hands of Uzbek leader General Abdul Rashid Dostum (1954–). Reportedly, he ruled the city like his own personal kingdom. He and his men had a reputation for extreme brutality, and they were greatly feared by other Afghans.

In May 1997, one of Dostum's men turned against him. The Taliban took the city, and Dostum fled to Turkey. Back in Mazari Sharif, the Uzbek and Hazaras minorities revolted against the Taliban occupation. Some two thousand Taliban soldiers were massacred and buried in shallow graves.

The Taliban retook Mazari Sharif fifteen months later. In retaliation, they went on a six-day killing spree, dragging people from their houses to be summarily executed. They slaughtered about eight thousand of the local people, particularly the Shi'ite Hazaras (Shi'ites belong to a Muslim sect; the majority of Muslims are Sunni, or orthodox).

The Approach After September 11, 2001, the United States declared their support of the Northern Alliance, providing funding and supplies. Around one hundred U.S. Army Special Force operatives also joined the ragged Afghan army. They gave strategic advice and coordinated the U.S. air strikes with the ground assault against the Taliban.

Alliance troops battled for weeks, seizing the territory around Mazari Sharif. The battle proved to be a bizarre combination of the old and the new. Misunderstanding an American order, 250 Alliance fighters bore down on Taliban tanks at full gallop, just after American Green Berets had called in an air strike at that position. One of the U.S. servicemen recalled:"Three or four

bombs hit right in the middle of the enemy position. Almost immediately after the bombs exploded, the horses swept across the objective—the enemy was so shell-shocked. I could see the horses blasting out the other side. It was the finest sight I ever saw."

After General Mohammed Atta finally took Aq Kupruk, the Special Forces and Alliance fighters met at Shulgarah Pass, where they were joined by an anti-Taliban Hazara group, led by Haji Mohammed Mohaqiq. The combined army marched north to Mazari Sharif. They reported that the Taliban had burned out villages in their retreat.

The Taliban Routed By November 9, Alliance forces were poised to take the city. All the previous night, U.S. planes had carpet-bombed defender's positions, particularly the enemy concentrations at the southern gates of the city.

Not all of the Taliban forces made a desperate last stand in Mazari Sharif. Over the previous weeks, many of the Afghan Taliban had given up or defected. However, a great many of the city's defenders were foreigners—mostly Saudis and Pakistanis—who believed themselves engaged in a holy war. Even so, weakened by the air strikes, they could put up only light resistance as the Northern Alliance swept into the city.

Atta's men cleared out pockets of Taliban fighters around the main citadel, while Dostum seized the airport and entered the city from the south. An estimated 600 Taliban fighters died in the overall battle, while the UIF lost anywhere from 40 to 150.

American officials, painfully aware of international scrutiny, begged their allies to show restraint. However, reports of looting, rape, and murder were common after the city fell. Humanitarian groups have claimed that Alliance troops severely mistreated Taliban prisoners.

Mazari Sharif represented a major turning point in Operation Enduring Freedom. The United States had gained a gateway into northern Afghanistan, through which military supplies and humanitarian relief could flow more easily. The Northern Alliance had won an important strategic and psychological victory.

After the city was lost, Taliban defenses began crumbling throughout the country. Afghan warlords, previously loyal to the Taliban, began to switch sides. Soon the Alliance held firm control over all of the northern provinces. Just a week later, the capital city of Kabul fell to the Alliance. By November 26, they were able to surround and defeat the last holdout of Taliban forces in Kunduz.

Fall of Kabul

On November 12, 2001, Taliban fighters abandoned the Afghanistan capital, Kabul, and fell back to their base at Khandahar to the south. The next day the Northern Alliance took possession of the city.

Kabul The ancient city of Kabul, mentioned in the Rig Veda (Sanskrit hymns dating to before 1500 BCE), is

Citizens of Kabul, Afghanistan, wave at the Northern Alliance forces that retook the city after American bombing drove out the Taliban. *Scott Peterson/Getty Images*

the capital of Afghanistan. The majority of the city's citizens are ethnically Tajiks, who speak Farsi (Persian, the language of Iran) even though most people in the region speak Pashto (the language of the Pashtun tribe.)

In the years after the Soviet Union's retreat from Afghanistan in 1992, warlord militias fought over control of Kabul. The civilians of Kabul suffered intensely during this period of chaos and civil war, as the various mujahedeen groups (mujahedeen was the term used to refer to those who fought against the Soviet invasion)—many of which joined the Northern Alliance—indulged in murder, torture, looting, abduction, and rape.

Nevertheless, before the Taliban's rise to power in 1996, Kabul had been relatively modern and cosmopolitan. Under the repressive fundamentalist regime of the Taliban, the religious police had cracked down particularly harshly on the city. Young men could be arrested for shaving, and women would be publicly beaten if they accidentally showed a bare ankle. All secular music was banned. The Taliban forbade anyone to play chess, fly kites, or own any picture of any living thing.

The Bombardment As the seat of the Taliban government, Kabul endured heavy aerial bombardment once the United States launched Operation Enduring Free-

dom in October 2001. Almost all civilians who could afford to leave Kabul did so. U.S. military commanders insisted that they had only selected military targets in the city. They hotly denied targeting non-combatants. Nevertheless, they admitted that mistakes had been made and that bombs had gone astray. Though exact numbers were impossible to calculate, several hundred civilians were probably killed in the bombardment.

Afghans fleeing the city reported that Taliban fighters deliberately moved tanks and anti-aircraft equipment into residential areas. The fighters, they asserted, slept in mosques and hospitals to avoid American fire.

Reports of civilian casualties deeply upset Afghans and outraged much of the international community. Indignation ran especially high in the Arab world. Muslims were also angered by America's stated intent to continue hostilities into the Muslim holy month of Ramadan, which began in mid-November.

The Quick March The fall of Mazari Sharif to the Northern Alliance on November 9, 2001, caused a ripple effect throughout Afghanistan, drastically accelerating the war. Two days after the fall of Mazari Sharif, the Alliance easily retook their former headquarters at Taloqan, which had been lost to the Taliban the year before.

Around the country, local war leaders followed long-established Afghan tradition and switched their allegiance to the winning side.

On November 12, the citizens of Herat, on the western border, rose up against the Taliban. Orchestrated by the United States and Iranian military leaders, the insurrection was timed to coincide with the arrival of Northern Alliance troops under Ismail Khan, former governor of Herat. The Taliban fled, and the city was taken with little bloodshed.

The rapidity of the Taliban's disintegration surprised and concerned Western observers. If the ruling government should dissolve before an interim government could be formed, they argued, a "power vacuum" would form, and Afghanistan could easily dissolve into chaos.

Furthermore, the opposition forces were composed primarily of northern ethnic minorities. Should they seize power on their own, many feared that the Alliance would not be inclined to share that power. Policy analysts agreed that if the Pashtun majority did not form a central part of the new government, it would have disastrous effects on post-Taliban Afghanistan.

The rebel factions were also feared by the people, who remembered their brutality from the pre-Taliban days. Pakistani President General Pervez Musharraf expressed his concerns frankly: "We know the atrocities that were committed between the period when the Soviets left and before the Taliban came, when there were warlords butchering each other. I have heard stories that are hair-raising. The Northern Alliance must be kept in check so we don't return to anarchy."

America wanted to slow things down. President George Bush repeated his earlier appeals to Alliance leaders, urging them not to enter the capital city of Kabul before an interim government could be formed.

On November 12, heavy American bombing all but crippled the defenses around Kabul. The Northern Alliance troops, under General Gul Haidar advanced on the city limits, fighting a few skirmishes with scattered enemy forces. At dusk the army camped for the night in the suburban village of Qarabagh, which had been all but demolished by air strikes.

After 9:00 P.M. that night, Taliban forces fled the city under cover of darkness. It is not clear if their retreat was a planned withdrawal or a panicked rout. Opposition forces entered the city the next morning, arguing that someone needed to restore order to the city. Only a handful of Arab al-Qaeda fighters held out in the Shar-i-Nau park, and these were decimated after a fifteen-minute firefight.

The Liberation The citizens of Kabul greeted the Alliance with cautious joy. While many feared the newly arrived rebel forces, hatred for the Taliban had run deep. People did not throw flowers at the feet of the UIF, but they celebrated, chanting "Death to the Taliban!" Some

pulled out radios to play music on the street; children flew kites; and men rushed to buy razors to shave off their beards. Some women even appeared on the street with their faces unveiled.

Bodies of Taliban fighters lay in the streets to be abused by the crowds. The people of Kabul particularly despised foreigners working with the Taliban—mostly Pakastanis and Saudis. A few such Arab fighters were captured alive and then lynched in front of Western news crews.

Konduz

In November of 2001, Northern Allied forces (Afghan forces supported by the United States against the Taliban regime in Afghanistan) closed in on the city of Konduz, the last Taliban stronghold in northern Afghanistan. The city was defended by at least six thousand al-Qaeda and Taliban troops, while upwards of thirty thousand civilians were trapped inside.

Approach from the East On November 11, Northern Alliance troops under Commander Mohammed Daoud Khan took the village of Taloqan, forty miles east of Konduz. As two senior Taliban leaders defected to the opposition forces on the eve of battle, the victory promised to be easy.

As a result, Daoud's men were overconfident as they chased the retreating enemy toward Kundoz. On November 13, thirty miles east of Konduz, Taliban forces ambushed their pursuers in the village of Bangi. The Alliance retreated in a rout—some trucks even ran over their own soldiers in their rush to escape. Taliban and al-Qaeda fighters only retreated after a withering display of American air power.

The Taliban then entrenched at Selbur, a ridge three miles west of Bangi. They placed mines around the entrance to the village.

Daoud, surprised by the ferocity of the counterattack, decided not to press on immediately. His army held a line for more than a week at Taloqan, while U.S. Special Forces called down a rain of air strikes to soften Konduz' defensive positions.

Approach from the West In the meantime, General Rashid Dostum's forces approached Kunduz from Mazari Sharif. The Uzbek general constantly spoke over the radio to Taliban leaders, some of who surrendered on the spot.

Although only a handful of American Special Forces operatives worked with each unit of the Northern Alliance, the Afghans had been impressed by the effectiveness of U.S. air strikes. Dostum had become particularly enamored with their laser targeting system. Tribal fighters, who had seen decades of warfare, watched while Green Berets would aim a marker gun at a target of Dostum's choosing. A few minutes later Navy F-18 Fighters would fly overhead, almost invisible at an altitude of twenty thousand feet, and drop a thousand-pound laser-guided bomb precisely at that location.

"Put your guns down, take your jackets off, and march in here," Dostum told Taliban troops outside Konduz, "or we'll turn the Americans on to you with their Death Ray."

Negotiation and Surrender   Generally speaking, Afghan Taliban leaders were ready to give up. The city was surrounded, and the Northern Alliance controlled all of northern Afghanistan. The Taliban commander responsible for the north, Mullah Dadullah, and the governor of Konduz, Haji Omar Khan, both announced their willingness to surrender.

However, a large number of fighters inside and around Konduz had come to Afghanistan from abroad in order to fight in a jihad, or holy war. These foreigners—mostly Saudis, Pakastanis, and Chechens—were allied to al-Qaeda, and violently opposed to any talk of surrender.

Many Afghans loathed the foreigners, who had been invited into the country by the Taliban. Opposition groups considered them to be outsiders who had hijacked the government of Afghanistan. Even those sympathetic to the Taliban often blamed al-Qaeda for bringing on the catastrophic American invasion. As cities fell to the Northern Alliance, townspeople turned against the foreigners, brutally murdering them in the streets.

As a result, the al-Qaeda trapped in Konduz found themselves in a tight corner. International human rights groups warned of an impending massacre. Dostum stated that any amnesty offered to the Taliban did not extend to their "guests."

In addition, the Northern Alliance's attitude hardened because the so-called "Arab Afghans" would participate in false surrenders. On one occasion, three Arab Taliban gave themselves up, only to detonate bombs they had hidden on their bodies when they were close enough to their captors. General Pir Mohammed Khaksar, like other Afghan leaders, decided not to risk any more such incidents. He ordered his troops "to kill all the foreigners."

The United States was not much more sympathetic. At a press conference, Donald Rumsfeld stated: "Any idea that those people should be let loose on any basis to bring terror to other countries and destabilize other countries is unacceptable."

On November 21, Taliban leader Mullah Faizal went to Mazari Sharif to discuss terms with Dostum. They announced a general surrender of Konduz. However, the next day violence erupted around the city as Afghan Taliban troops attempted to leave the city. It is not clear who began the fighting.

By November 23, however, up to six thousand Afghan Taliban fighters had walked out of the city. Many of them were greeted with hugs by their tribesmen in the Alliance. Opposition forces swept through the city, brutally eliminating pockets of resistance.

PRISONER CONTROVERSIES

After the fall of Konduz, thousands of foreign prisoners were loaded into stifling metal trucks and taken to prison. A number of them suffocated or died of their wounds along the way and were buried in mass graves. The U.S. military denies that any American soldier participated in, or was aware of, any inhumane treatment of these prisoners of war.

Ironically, America has also come under criticism for leniency toward the enemy. Eyewitnesses—including American soldiers—reported that unauthorized airplanes made several landings inside Kunduz at night, while the airstrips were still under enemy control. The government of India believed that these planes came from Pakistan and that thousands of al-Qaeda fighters, including many high-level Pakistani military officers, were airlifted to freedom. India protested that the American government was buckling under Pakistani pressure and had deliberately allowed terrorists to escape from the city.

The U.S. State Department has not officially confirmed cutting any deal, though it seems unlikely that planes would have been able to pass the American Air Force otherwise.

Kandahar

On December 7, 2001, the Taliban yielded the city of Kandahar to forces of the Northern Alliance (Afghan forces that fought, with the support of the United States against the Taliban regime of Afghanistan). Future President Harmid Karzai negotiated the terms of surrender, which granted amnesty to any Taliban fighter who laid down his arms.

The Bonn Conference   As the Northern Alliance marched virtually unopposed into the capital city of Kabul, many policy experts worried that Afghanistan would collapse once more into anarchy. To prevent this, the international community convened a conference at Bonn, Germany, to decide the future of the country. Four Afghan groups were represented: the followers of Zahir Shah (1914–), the former king of Afghanistan, two other exile factions, and the Northern Alliance.

On December 5, 2001, after days of closed-door meetings, the delegates agreed to create an interim government led by Harmid Karzai, who was, at the time, leading a march on Kandahar. The council further decreed that after six months, a *loya jirga*—a council of tribal elders—would decide on a transitional government. Free elections were to be held by 2004.

This decision was not universally accepted. In Mazari Sharif, warlord Abdul Rashid Dostum refused to acknowledge the interim government, claiming that it did not represent the Uzbek people. Spiritual leader Sayad Ahmad Gailani also complained that the Bonn agreement was unfair to many mujahedeen who had fought against the Soviets.

Defiant Resistance In the meantime, the Alliance had seized control of all of northern Afghanistan. American attention turned toward the southern, Pashtun-dominated provinces, particularly to Kandahar. Mullah Omar had lived in the city, and it was considered the spiritual home of the Taliban.

American intelligence believed that both Osama bin Laden and Mullah Omar were holed up somewhere in or around Kandahar. In late November, one thousand U.S. Marines landed at an airstrip about eighty miles southwest of the city. They immediately set about securing the roads, trying to cut off possible escape routes.

The defensive forces in Kandahar were led by Mullah Akhtar Usmani, the loyal, but practical, Taliban Corp Commander. U.S. officials hoped that he could be rea-

Two of the approximately 2,500 Canadians who have served in Afghanistan as part of the NATO-led International Security Assistance Force stand guard in the southern Afghan city of Kandahar, January 2007. *Shah Marai/AFP/Getty Images*

soned with. Twenty-five-year-old police chief, Hafez Majid was less moderate. He was known as a fanatic devoté of Mullah Omar.

Throughout November, U.S. air strikes pounded down on defensive military posts in and around Kandahar. But even as their strongholds crumbled and the number of defectors skyrocketed, the Taliban leadership remained defiant. In radio announcements on November 28 and 29, Omar urged the fighters in Kandahar to fight to the death. "The fight has now begun," he said. "It is the best opportunity to achieve martyrdom."

Closing In Though more American soldiers had entered the battlefield, the U.S. government still preferred to work through local opposition leaders. In the case of Kandahar, they backed ex-governor Ghul Agha Sherzai. The choice was unpopular with many Taliban and non-Taliban Afghanis. Sherzai had ruled Kandahar from 1992 to 1994, and his reign had been brutal.

After meeting the U.S. ambassador in Pakistan in early November, Sherzai started hiring mercenaries and bandits. When he had gathered a force of around eight hundred Pashtuns, he advanced on Kandahar from the south.

On November 23, with U.S. air support, Sherzai ploughed over heavy Taliban resistance at the village of Tahk-te-pol. Two days later the warlord had reached the Kandahar airport, which he took after seven days of heavy American bombing.

Harmid Karzai had worked all of his life for the liberation of Afghanistan. After fighting against the Soviet, he had initially backed the Taliban in their attempt to unify and stabilize the country. Later, as the regime became more repressive, he turned against it. While his siblings fled to the United States, Karzai remained in Pakistan so that he could continue to work for the opposition.

On October 8, 2001, Karzai sneaked across the border by motorcycle, with only two of his aides. Caught by a Taliban ambush, he was rescued by an American helicopter and taken back to Pakistan. He returned on November 14, the day after the Northern Alliance marched into Kabul, this time accompanied by U.S. Delta Force operatives and officers of the CIA.

Karzai led approximately 100 to 150 Afghan guerillas. Accompanied by U.S. Special Forces units, they approached Kandahar from the north, driving in a ragged caravan of Toyota pickups, Subaru taxis, and Nissan vans. While on the road, Karzai addressed the Bonn Convention by satellite phone, accepting his nomination as chairman of the interim government. According to Lieutenant Colonel David Fox, who acted as his military advisor, "He was the personnel officer, the intelligence officer, the operations officer, the logistics officer, the future plans officer, and the communications officer for his element."

Karzai's force seized the village of Showali Kowt (and the only bridge across the Arghandab River) after two days of heavy fighting. Toward the end of the battle, Karzai's unit was hit by friendly fire—a B-52 bomb that had been given the wrong GPS coordinates. Over thirty Afghans and Americans were killed or wounded. Karzai himself was nicked on the face.

The Deal As the cordon tightened around Kandahar, Karzai spent days speaking by satellite phone to Taliban leaders. By December 7, he had brokered a deal. Taliban fighters would hand over their weapons to Mullah Naqibullah, a well-respected Pashtun tribal elder. They would be allowed safe passage to their home villages. The Taliban surrendered Kandahar province, Helmand Province, and Zabul Province. Ghul Agha Sherzai was made governor of Kandahar, to be assisted by Naqibullah.

When the deal was made public, Mullah Abdul Salam Zaeef, the former Taliban ambassador to Pakistan, asserted that the Taliban had surrendered in order to spare civilian lives.

Washington rejected some of the conditions brokered by Karzai. United States Secretary of Defense Donald Rumsfeld particularly objected to one clause, which would have allowed Mullah Mohammed Omar to "live in dignity" in Kandahar. As it turned out, the point was moot, as it appeared Omar had slipped out of the city during the negotiations.

With the Taliban essentially dissolved, the U.S. military focused its attention on hunting Osama bin Laden, the author of the September 11, 2001, terrorist attacks on U.S. targets. Helicopters were sent over the southern Afghanistan plains. With the Taliban returning to their homes, often still holding their weapons, it became increasingly difficult to tell friend from foe.

Tora Bora

In December of 2001, U.S. Special Forces and allied local tribes assaulted the cave complex of Tora Bora, where al-Qaeda leaders were believed to shelter. Although heavy damage was inflicted on enemy forces, most American military leaders considered the operation to be a failure. Its main target, terrorist leader Osama bin Laden, very likely escaped during the battle.

Cave Hideouts As the United Islamic Front (UIF, also known as the Northern Alliance) wrested control of northern Afghanistan from the Taliban, the United

In preparation for the offensive on the Tora Bora region, in November 2001, a U.S. Navy flight deck crew push a F/A-18C Hornet attack fighter into position on the deck of the USS *Theodore Roosevelt* in the Arabian Sea.   *AP Images*

States turned its attention to the hunt for al-Qaeda. Intelligence suggested that both bin Laden and Mullah Omar hid in the mountains of southern Afghanistan.

Tora Bora was a mountain fortress in the White Mountains in eastern Afghanistan, right on the border of Pakistan. The outpost backed up on the famous Khyber Pass, through which invading armies had marched since the time of Alexander the Great. In the 1980s, the mujahedeen had reinforced and extended the natural caves of Tora Bora, using them as a stronghold in the bitter war against the Soviets.

The Target The American government knew how difficult it was to track down a single man and tried to downplay the manhunt for bin Laden. The greater goal, they insisted, was to disrupt the global terrorist network. However, many American soldiers felt differently. Stunned and outraged by al-Qaeda attacks on U.S. targets on September 11, 2001, most of the C.I.A. operatives and the Special Forces Green Berets had volunteered—even begged—to be sent into Afghanistan. They were looking for revenge. One C.I.A. director summed up the prevailing attitude when he said: "I want bin Laden's head shipped back in a box filled with dry ice."

In late November, intelligence reports indicated a build-up of al-Qaeda forces in the White Mountains. Witnesses reported seeing a tall man (bin Laden is over six feet tall) who seemed to be in charge. Signal intelligence seemed to confirm that the terrorist mastermind was, in fact, in Tora Bora.

Closing In By December of 2001, the Taliban had surrendered all of its strongholds in northern Afghanistan. The United States had proved the effectiveness of "unconventional warfare"—the combination of local armies, a small contingent of Special Force ground units, and high-tech aerial bombardment. U.S. Central Command (CENTCOM) hoped to replicate the success of such strategies in the hunt for bin Laden.

However, the situation had changed. Hidden in caves, al-Qaeda was less susceptible to air attack. Furthermore, the people of the region were mostly ethnic Pashtun tribesmen, who tended to embrace the fundamentalist Islam of the Taliban. They also followed a strict code of ethics that included *melmastia*—absolute hospitality. It was unheard of that a Pashtun chieftan should hand a guest (such as bin Laden) over to his enemies.

The United States attempted to overcome this reluctance by placing a $25 billion bounty on bin Laden's head. C.I.A. operatives also liberally bribed warlords in the region. However, Pashtun tribal militias lacked the Northern Alliance's fierce hatred for al-Qaeda, and their performance was relatively lackluster. At least a few Afghans took the Americans' money, but continued to help bin Laden's forces in any way they could.

Nevertheless, three local militias signed on to hunt al-Qaeda in the region. Tribal forces led by Commander Mohammed Zaman Ghun Shareef, Commander Haji Zahir, and Commander Hazrat Ali fought their way through the snowy mountains. A handful of American Delta Force operators and C.I.A agents joined them at the beginning of December. Together the allies managed to push the remnants of al-Qaeda back into the Milawa Valley, the northern entrance to Tora Bora.

The Truce As Commander Zaman's forces closed in on December 12, an Arab al-Qaeda leader appealed for a cease-fire. He agreed that his men—numbering around eight hundred—would surrender, but only to United Nations officials. Zaman accepted the truce and stopped his men's advance. He gave the Arab fighters until 8:00 A.M. the following morning to give themselves up.

The two other Afghan chieftains were surprised, not to mention angry, to hear of this arrangement. The Americans promptly declared that they would not accept any conditional surrender whatsoever, and they continued to bombard the caves. No fighters surrendered the next day. Many believed that the negotiations had been a ruse, designed to give the al-Qaeda leadership time to escape.

Their confidence in their Afghan allies shaken, American commanders put more Delta Force commandos on the ground. They were joined by the members of the British Special Air Service (SAS), a small but highly respected combat unit. Together with the Afghan fighters, they began a thorough assault of the mountain, taking cave after cave over fierce resistance.

The Escape Evidence quickly surfaced that bin Laden and many others had already made good their escape. The American and British forces only besieged the compound from three directions. They left the fourth side—the long, porous Pakistani border—to the Pakistani army.

General Pervez Musharraf, president of Pakistan, had pledged his support for the United States invasion, not least because of America's thinly veiled threat to attack his own country if he did not. He did so at great political and personal risk, as many of his people supported al-Qaeda and the Taliban. In short, the Pakistani military was, at best, a reluctant ally of the United States. Bin Laden had a great deal of money—both from his own personal fortune and from the looted coffers of the former Afghan government. As a result, hundreds of those supposedly trapped at Tora Bora slipped over the border into friendly territory.

Controversy still surrounds the event. General Tommy Franks and others have expressed doubts that bin Laden was at Tora Bora at all. Others have speculated that the terrorist leader could have died in the battle, either from a missile hit or from poor health. Heavy American bombardment caused many cave-ins, which made it impossible to find all of the al-Qaeda bodies.

U.S. soldiers inspect the body of a man killed in Operation Anaconda. © *Reuters/Corbis*

The battle for Tora Bora yielded some successes—for example, the capture of some high-ranking al-Qaeda operatives. However, many military officers consider Tora Bora to be a significant American military defeat. Some have blamed CENTCOM's fear of incurring American casualties, which led to their unwillingness to commit a large number of conventional troops at a critical moment.

Operation Anaconda

In March of 2002, coalition troops fought al-Qaeda die-hards for eleven days in the Shah-i-Kot Valley. Code-named Operation Anaconda, the battle was, for the Americans, the most costly of the Afghan war.

The Valley On December 22, Harmid Karzai was sworn in as leader of the new Afghanistan interim government. However, it was clear that the country's troubles were not yet over. Karzai did not have universal support. A large number of Taliban prisoners had been released and allowed to keep their weapons. Foreign jihadists (those pledged to fight a holy war, or jihad, against the West) still came into the country, determined to fight the infidels.

By March of 2002, intelligence sources reported that Taliban and al-Qaeda (the terrorist organization

behind the September 11, 2001, attacks on U.S. targets) fighters had begun to regroup in the Shah-i-Kot valley, southeast of Kabul. They were also waging a campaign for the "hearts and minds" of the Afghan people. They circulated pamphlets urging the faithful to join the jihad against the American invaders and even offered bounties on any westerner killed.

Major General Franklin Hagenbeck, in command of the operation, and Colonel John Mulholland, who headed the Special Force Units in northern Afghanistan, had learned from their disappointment at Tora Bora, where they let enemy leaders escape their grasp. This time American troops would entirely encircle the enemy before closing in, hence the name Operation Anaconda. The number of hostiles could not be accurately determined—U.S. military brass estimated around 150. They agreed to commit significant conventional ground forces to the effort.

U.S. Central Command (CENTCOM) had been determined not to repeat the Soviet Union's mistakes—in the 1980s, the Soviets had floundered in the mountains of Afghanistan, losing as many as 250 men a day. As a result, until this point in the Afghan war, the United States had been reluctant to insert conventional (that is, non-Special Forces) troops into the country.

However, the U.S. policy of using native Afghan fighters as proxies backfired at Tora Bora. Furthermore, conventional military officers were complaining vigorously about being left out of the war. After analyzing the situation, the generals came to the conclusion that the Shah-i-kot Valley would have to be stormed by conventional ground troops, with Special Forces support.

The assembled force included over nine hundred American professional infantry troops and Special Forces. Afghan General Zia Lodin led around the same number of troops, who were recruited by the United States and paid $200 a month. Several hundred British, Canadian, German, French, Danish, and Norwegian soldiers also took part in the battle, making a total force of around two thousand coalition soldiers.

The Hammer and the Anvil
On March 1, coalition forces moved into their positions around the valley. Delta commando units set up in the north and south, attempting to cut off possible escape routes. A Navy SEAL unit (SEALS are the Special Forces of the U.S. Navy) approached and seized an enemy observation post to the southeast.

The Taliban and al-Qaeda troops had entrenched themselves up the sides of the valley. They took cover in caves and behind ridges, all the time targeting oncoming allied troops with mortars and heavy machine guns. Once hostilities were underway, it became clear that there were far more than 150 al-Qaeda fighters in the region—the army now estimated anywhere from six hundred to one thousand.

Task Force Hammer, consisting of both American and Afghan troops, attacked the valley from the west. Their approach was botched. Foiled by unexpectedly difficult road conditions, Task Force Hammer arrived late and disordered. An American AC-130 aircraft, due to various instrument failures, took them for an enemy column and attacked. The resulting friendly firefight killed one American commander and wounded several soldiers. Because of miscommunication, Task Force Hammer received minimal air support when they finally reached their position. The Afghan contingent took heavy losses from al-Qaeda mortar fire.

In the meantime, Task Force Anvil, consisting of the 101st Airborne Division (called the Rakkasans) and the Tenth Mountain Division, were airlifted in from the east. They found the enemy more numerous, better prepared, and more determined than they had expected. Some units in the southern part of the valley—the battle's "hot spot"—were pinned down by mortar fire. They held their position all day before being airlifted out, suffering almost thirty wounded but none killed.

Having underestimated the opposition's numbers and firepower, Task Force Anvil did not bring adequate ground artillery. Cover fire was provided by Apache helicopters, who exchanged machine-gun fire nose to nose with enemy positions high in the valley. Air strikes

called in by Special Forces also inflicted heavy damage on al-Qaeda positions.

Battle of Takur Ghar
Heavy fighting raged throughout March 2 and 3, as more units were airlifted into combat or blocking positions. Early on the morning of March 4, two Navy SEAL teams were helicoptered onto the mountain peak of Takur Ghar. Their plan was to set up an observation point looking down over the valley.

As it turned out, al-Qaeda fighters had already dug in at high altitudes. One of the Chinook helicopters, Razor 3, touched down in an area swarming with enemy fighters. It was hit from close range by a rocket-propelled grenade (RPG). Taking heavy fire, the damaged ship immediately took off again. However, in the confusion Petty Officer Neil Roberts fell out of the ship. When the Razor 3 turned back to retrieve him, their instruments seized up, and they were forced to crash land several miles away.

The other chopper, Razor 4, came back to the hot spot to rescue Roberts. The SEAL team landed and found themselves in a heavy firefight, and they were forced off the peak.

Two more helicopters, Razor 1 and Razor 2, were sent in with reinforcements. Razor 1 was misdirected to the hot spot and also took an RPG hit the moment it landed. The Army Rangers on board scrambled for cover. They were soon engaged in a fierce and deadly firefight. Thanks to close air strikes, and to the arrival of backups from Razor 2, the Americans held on for hours. By evening, they had managed to take control of the Takur Ghar peak. Seven American servicemen had been killed.

Finishing Up
Hostilities continued for the next two days, though the fiercest of the fighting had ended. On March 6, American bombs took out a truck leaving the valley, only to discover that it was full of women and children. By March 12, the coalition forces swept the region for enemies and encountered very few.

On March 18 General Tommy Franks declared that Operation Anaconda had ended with "unqualified and complete success." Eight Americans and an unknown number of Afghans had died. Enemy casualties were estimated anywhere from three hundred to eight hundred, but it is widely believed that many more al-Qaeda fighters managed to slip away.

Panjwaii

In 2006 and 2007, Afghanistan witnessed a dramatic resurgence of the Taliban, especially in the Pashtun-dominated Panjwaii region about sixteen miles west of Kandahar. Taliban insurgents began to launch attacks against the government of Afghanistan President Hamid Karzai. In an attempt to put down the uprising and to extend the control of the central government, international peacekeeping forces fought several major battles in the region.

The Karzai Government When Harmid Karzai was peacefully and democratically elected president of Afghanistan in 2004, the international community breathed a sigh of relief. The Taliban had been routed, al-Qaeda was on the run, and a coalition of thirty-seven countries agreed to send peacekeeping and reconstruction forces into the country. It seemed as if Afghanistan was on the road to recovery.

The road was not, however, an easy one. Despite the slow but steady advances of Karzai's government, several of his ministers have been accused of corruption and incompetence. Afghan tribal warlords still held almost complete sway over their districts, and they pay little attention to Kabul. Lawlessness and poverty were rampant in many outlying parts of the country. Poppy farming has resumed and flourished, bringing with it a booming heroin trade. Millions of Afghan refugees still huddle in Pakistani camps, unable to return to a country that could not support them.

International aid flowed into the country, but not enough to address all the ravages caused by decades of war. When the United States invaded Iraq in 2003, many Afghans felt embittered and abandoned because American attention and resources had been diverted away.

Shocked at modern "irreligious" behavior in urban areas (behavior such as shaving for men or appearing unveiled in public for women), disturbed by lawlessness and the continued lack of public infrastructure, and encouraged by foreign jihadists, many Afghans (especially ethnic Pashtuns) began turning back to the Taliban.

Mountain Thrust Beginning in 2006, international coalition forces came under increasing attacks by Taliban insurgents. Suicide bomb attacks targeted international troops, and fighters carried out nighttime raids of small-town government offices. On May 17, clashes between Taliban and Canadian peacekeepers resulted in the death of Captain Nichola Goddard, the first Canadian female to die in combat.

Compared to the ragged Taliban army of 2001, the 2006 insurgents seems better equipped and more prepared for combat. They also rely more heavily on suicide attacks. For these reasons, some military experts suspect that former members of the Iraqi army have been training the new Taliban.

In June 2006, alarmed by insurgent activity throughout the south, the U.S.-led peacekeeping force initiated Operation Mountain Thrust. Eleven thousand coalition soldiers from thirty-seven nations joined forces with three thousand Afghan National Army troops to target insurgency strongholds throughout southern Afghanistan. Canadian units led the Mountain Thrust effort into the town of Pashmul, in Panjwaii, where they encountered particularly fierce resistance. Several Canadian fighters were killed, and the local school was completely destroyed.

In July, Mountain Thrust wound down. Coalition leaders claimed that more than six hundred militants were killed. However, quite a few civilians had also died, and a great deal of property had been destroyed.

By October, it was announced that NATO's International Security Assistance Force would take control of peacekeeping in the region. (NATO, the North Atlantic Treaty Organization, is an alliance between western nations.)

Operation Medusa By September 2, 2006, it became clear the Taliban had regrouped and was once more taking control of the Panjwaii region. In response, NATO launched Operation Medusa, a two-week offensive that involved more than twenty thousand NATO troops. Canadian forces bore the brunt of the fighting, supported by American, British, and Dutch air support.

The Taliban militants in Panjwaii put up a surprising amount of resistance, standing their ground and fighting instead of melting back into the mountains. NATO forces fought with air strikes and with direct artillery fire, taking casualties. Nine Canadian soldiers died throughout the operation, bringing the country's death toll in Afghanistan since 2002 to thirty-six. One died in a friendly fire incident, when an American plane accidentally strafed an allied position. Fourteen British soldiers died when a surveillance plane crashed, apparently from a mechanical failure, at the beginning of the campaign.

It was estimated that more than five hundred insurgents were killed. Taliban spokespeople denied the number.

NATO declared Operation Medusa finished, and successful, on September 17. Nevertheless, an unknown number of Taliban escaped, presumably to fight another day. Insurgent attacks continued sporadically throughout the country, as did anti-Taliban operations.

In October, misdirected NATO air strikes killed thirty-one Afghan civilians. Harmid Karzai insisted with vehemence that NATO should avoid such incidents, though he also called the Taliban "cowardly" for sheltering behind innocents.

Ongoing Operations With the consent of the Afghanistan government, NATO forces continued to cooperate with the Afghan Army in an ongoing attempt to squelch the Taliban resurgence. Coalition forces mounted Operation Mountain Fury and Operation Falcon Summit in 2007.

✪ Homefront

Guantanamo Bay Detainment Camp

The detention center at Guantanamo Bay Naval Base in Cuba stands as perhaps the most controversial landmark in the ongoing War on Terrorism. Set up in the wake of the invasion of Afghanistan as a holding area for the hundreds of al-Qaeda and Taliban prisoners captured

Inmates at Guantanamo Air Force Base on Cuba, are, in the words of the Bush Administration, "unlawful combatants" and thus unqualified for the rights granted by the Geneva Conventions.   *Roberto Schmidt/AFP/Getty Images*

during the last months of 2001, the "Gitmo" prison has earned vocal condemnation from both within and outside the United States for its approach to handling its detainees, which many call illegal, as well as for widespread allegations of the use of torture.

Development of the Detention Center   Guantanamo Bay was acquired in the wake of the Spanish-American War (1898) as a perpetual lease from Cuba to the United States. A naval base constructed there served many purposes over the years; prior to terrorist attacks on U.S. targets on September 11, 2001, it was the primary holding center for Cuban and Haitian refugees picked up at sea by the U.S. Navy.

As the War on Terrorism got under way in late 2001 with the invasion of Afghanistan, the United States soon found itself with hundreds of prisoners and little room overseas in which to keep them. The prisoners taken during the opening weeks Operation Enduring Freedom (the initial attack on Afghanistan) presented a rich intelligence opportunity—the need for a centralized deten-

tion facility in which to conduct interrogations and process terrorism suspects quickly became evident.

Guantanamo Bay was selected ostensibly to provide just such a holding area without bringing suspected terrorists into the United States itself. Critics have charged that the location provided the additional benefit of shielding the goings-on at the facility from media and judicial attention.

Controversial Procedures   From the very beginning, the Guantanamo Bay detainment camp was run according to its own set of rules. Detainees were classified as "enemy combatants," emphatically not prisoners of war. This new, hazily defined term allowed the Department of Defense to bypass international law, called the Geneva Conventions, regarding the treatment of prisoners taken during warfare. This approach was later deemed illegal by a U.S. Supreme Court ruling in 2006, which ruled the detainees should be subject to the Geneva Conventions as if they were prisoners of war.

The detainees at the Guantanamo Bay detainment camp also experienced a unique form of justice, unprecedented in American civil or military law: the military tribunal. This new process put the prisoner at the complete mercy of his captors and ignored several long-standing traditions in American law, including the right to petition for a writ of *habeas corpus*. *Habeas corpus* (Latin for "you have the body") protects people from wrongful imprisonment—for example, it protects them from being held indefinitely without a charge being filed. With such a right suspended, as it is at Guantanamo, a prisoner can be held indefinitely without trial.

During the first five years of its operation, the majority of Guantanamo detainees were released without charges, albeit often after several years in custody. As of late 2006, more than 250 inmates remained in legal limbo with no charges filed against them and no sign of an upcoming trial or release.

Conditions Inside the Prison   The environment of the prison at Guantanamo has also been a source of furious debate. Prisoners' living conditions at the prison are subject to their level of compliance. A compliant detainee gains increased access to the exercise yard and the right to contact with fellow prisoners, whereas uncooperative inmates are put in solitary confinement.

The stories of released prisoners, along with evidence from leaked documents and the testimony of federal agents who visited the detention center, paint a grim picture. Tales of chambers that alternated between blistering heat and teeth-chattering cold, of sleep-deprivation and water torture, of prisoners being hung from walls or of being left hog-tied for days at a time, and of guards and interrogators defacing the Koran (the Muslim holy book), have been told and retold. Repeated hunger strikes by prisoners failed to affect a change in policy—several strikers were reportedly force fed, a direct violation of international policy.

Sean Baker, a guard at the detention center, seemed to corroborate reports of brutality when, posing as an uncooperative inmate during a secret training drill, he was beaten so severely that he sustained permanent brain injuries and suffered from recurring seizures.

Calls for Closure   *New York Times* columnist Thomas Friedman wrote a well-publicized article in 2005 calling for the closure of the base: "It has become worse than an embarrassment. I am convinced that more Americans are dying and will die if we keep the Gitmo prison open than if we shut it down. So, please, Mr. President, just shut it down."

A particularly vocal source of criticism from abroad has come from the United Kingdom, normally a staunch U.S. ally. Several British legal experts and members of Parliament have condemned the prison in the harshest terms. While he was the British prime minister, Tony Blair also went on record expressing his distaste for the center, along with his wish that it would be shut down.

In the wake of the 2006 Congressional elections, in which a Democratic majority was elected in both the House of Representatives and Senate largely on an anti-war policy, the first efforts to shut down the Guantanamo Bay detainment camp were inaugurated in the spring of 2007. The alternative—to house the detainees in federal prisons inside the United States—has been strongly opposed by Republican Congressmen.

Five years after it began operations, the fate of the detention center at Guantanamo Bay remains unclear. As for the prisoners within, the Supreme Court has begun handing down rulings that may go some way toward creating a codified approach more in keeping with American legal traditions.

✪ International Context

NATO Participation

Afghanistan, invaded by the United States in the wake of the terrorist attacks of September 11, 2001, has been under the control of an international coalition of members of the North Atlantic Treaty Organization (NATO) since 2002. Elements of this international force, initially concerned mainly with the area around the capital of Kabul, have increasingly shouldered responsibility for bringing security to the more volatile regions of the country and, since 2006, have also engaged in battles against a resurgent Taliban. Canadian forces in particular have led this fight, sustaining the second highest allied casualty rate in the ongoing occupation.

ISAF   Although the United States military dominated the initial invasion of Afghanistan in October 2001, the need for an international peacekeeping force quickly became evident as the year came to a close. This new NATO-led coalition, dubbed the International Security Assistance Force (ISAF), comprised more than thirty thousand troops from more than thirty countries. Led by a rotating staff of generals, the ISAF has seen its role in Afghanistan steadily expand as the conflict in Iraq has put increasing demands on U.S. manpower in the region.

Although the ISAF has been in Afghanistan since 2002, it is only since 2005 that its troops have been deployed outside the immediate region of Kabul. During that three-year interim, a massive manhunt for Osama bin Laden (leader of al-Qaeda, the terrorist organization behind the September 11 attacks) saw the situation in much of Afghanistan deteriorate as U.S. troops were committed to combat operations at the expense of providing security for a country still unstable in the wake of the collapse of the Taliban. After the Taliban fell, local warlords muscled their way back into power across the country, so for many Afghans, life is little better now than it was under the Taliban. In fact, in many regions opium poppy production (forbidden by the Taliban regime) has skyrocketed, as have corruption and graft.

Canadian Offensives in Kandahar In an effort to curb these disturbing trends, ISAF units were deployed to the dangerous southern provinces, particularly Kandahar. The reemergence of the Taliban in 2006 added a new note of urgency to the increased role of ISAF. Canadian units, which had played a small, if important, supporting role in 2002's Operation Anaconda (during which Canadian sniper teams broke the Vietnam-era record for the longest-distance confirmed kill), would take the lead in ISAF's new role in Kandahar.

In 2006, a squadron of Canadian Leopard tanks was deployed to the region, the first foreign deployment of tanks to Afghanistan since the start of Operation Enduring Freedom. The tanks arrived in time to assist with the mop-up of the months-long Battle of Panjwaii between a revitalized Taliban force and a Canadian-led coalition.

Operation Falcon Summit, kicked off in December 2006, saw a continuation of the Canadian-led ISAF effort against the Taliban. Now enjoying the support of their Leopard tanks, the operation took its objectives without a single allied death.

With ISAF providing badly needed support in the south, and the Canadian-led victories of 2006, the Taliban began using suicide bomb attacks targeting military personnel and reconstruction projects. These new attacks, combined with the country's burgeoning illegal drug trade and evidence of a reemerging al-Qaeda presence, has led many to question the future of Afghanistan and the ability of the NATO coalition forces to guarantee peace and stability in the region.

✪ *Iraq*
✪ Causes

Weapons of Mass Destruction

In 2003, President George W. Bush became convinced that Iraq supported anti-U.S. terrorist activities and possessed significant numbers of so-called "weapons of mass destruction"—chemical, biological, or nuclear weapons. Bush and members of his staff told the American people and the international community that they had reliable

This satellite image comes from Secretary of State Colin Powell's presentation to the U.N. Security Council on February 5, 2003. *U.S. Department of State/Getty Images*

intelligence that indicated these weapons of mass destruction were a direct threat to the United States and that America must, as a matter of self defense, invade Iraq and topple the government.

The Iraqi Threat President Saddam Hussein of Iraq had a long history of military aggression. In 1980, he launched a long and costly war against neighboring Iran. During the eight-year conflict, he received supplies and technology from the United States and other western countries, including chemical and biological weapons (at the time the United States believed Iran was a more potent enemy). Saddam used chemical weapons against Iranian soldiers and civilians. Though the Iran-Iraq war ended in stalemate with both countries crippled economically, Saddam had gained valuable military technology—and he had shown the world he was perfectly willing to unleash the horrors of chemical and biological warfare on his enemies.

In August 1991, Saddam again invaded a neighbor—this time the tiny, but oil-rich, nation of Kuwait, which had loaned Iraq billions of dollars during its war with Iran. Kuwait refused to forgive the debt, straining relations between the countries. Saddam saw a simple solution to his country's financial problem: take Kuwait and take its oil. The international community condemned the invasion, and the United States, with full United Nations support, led a coalition force into Kuwait to push Iraq out. President George H.W. Bush, who had been vice president of the United States during the Iran-Iraq War, was fully aware of the Iraqi military's capabilities and Saddam's ruthlessness. The Gulf War, as the conflict came to be called, ended when Iraq was pushed out of Kuwait in February 1991. Because the stated aim of the conflict was to liberate Kuwait, coalition forces did not seek to capture Saddam or overthrow his government. Saddam remained a thorn in the side of the U.S. government.

Suspicious Intelligence After the Gulf War, United Nations weapons inspectors visited Iraq regularly to verify that Saddam was not developing biological, chemical, or nuclear weapons. The inspectors found and destroyed significant chemical weapons stockpiles. In 1998, however, Saddam kicked the weapons inspectors out of the country. This made it difficult, if not impossible, to verify intelligence about Iraqi weapons programs.

During 2002 and 2003, various U.S. intelligence agencies gathered information about Iraqi weapons that troubled the Bush administration. There were intercepted messages about nerve gas, for example. Compounding the worry was the fact that the chief UN weapons inspector in Iraq, Hans Blix, announced that he believed that Iraq had not declared all the chemical weapons that it possessed. At issue was the accounting system the Iraqis used for its weapons. Documents that showed the numbers of chemical weapons did not match what Saddam declared to the UN. There was no way of knowing what happened to all the weapons. The Bush administration chose to believe that this lack of accounting proved the weapons still existed.

Secretary of State Colin Powell was assigned the task of making the case for military action against Iraq to the United Nations and to the world. He addressed the United Nations on February 5, 2003. The best evidence he had were satellite images of what appeared to be mobile missile launchers with chemical and biological warheads being moved in an attempt to conceal them from UN inspectors. He also explained that the CIA had human eyewitness accounts of mobile biological and chemical labs that were producing weapons of mass destruction. Powell showed sketches of these mobile labs. He also said Iraq had links to the terrorist organization al-Qaeda (which was behind the September 11, 2001, attacks on U.S. targets).

Powell had much popularity and credibility with other leaders of the world, the American people, and the media. Many skeptics were turned into believers after the Powell presentation. World leaders such as Jacques Chirac from France, Vladimir Putin from Russia, and Gerhard Schroeder from Germany still did not believe it was necessary to go to war, however. They believed the evidence was sketchy and could not be verified. Critics of the plan even speculate that the evidence was just a ruse to give the United States an excuse to oust Saddam, who had proved so troublesome over the years.

The United States chose to invade Iraq without international support. No stockpiles of weapons of mass destruction were discovered after the invasion. In 2005, Colin Powell (who had resigned as secretary of state) described his presentation to the UN before the invasion as a "blot" on his record and bluntly stated that "the [U.S.] intelligence system did not work well."

Oil

The 1990s saw a huge expansion of economic growth in western countries, especially in the United States. Oil prices were stable for much of the decade. However, a bustling economy meant that the Americans had a greater demand for and dependence on oil from the Middle East. Demand was exceeding supply even though OPEC (the Organization of the Petroleum Exporting Countries) tried to bump up oil production two separate times in August 2000. At the time, Iraq was churning out 3.6 million barrels per day, its highest output ever. If there was any type of disturbance in the supply of Iraqi oil, it would greatly affect the economy of the United States.

An American Addiction The United States had a clear problem: "it was addicted to oil," as President George W. Bush would later say in a State of the Union speech. Before Bush entered office in 2001, the United States was using nineteen million barrels of oil per day—two times the amount the country used in 1983. It had

Donald Rumsfield shaking hands with Saddam Hussein in 1983 in Baghdad.   *Getty Images*

to import 60 percent of this total. More problematic was the reduced capacity of American oil production—oil output had fallen by 15 percent while domestic demand had grown by 11 percent. The United States had only 5 percent of the world's population, but consumed 25 percent of the world's oil.

Iraq had been crippled by United Nations sanctions since its invasion of Kuwait in 1990. Saddam Hussein, the president of Iraq, began to realize that America's unquenchable thirst for oil might work in his favor. In 2000, Saddam signaled to the West that he would not keep producing at the current level unless the UN voted to relax the sanctions against Iraq. President Bill Clinton, who was in the final months of his second term in office, realized the United States was in a precarious position. The economy had already started to look shaky. Oil traders knew supplies of home heating oil and crude oil inventory in the United States were at low levels and they began bidding up prices. West Texas Intermediate crude futures rose to $37 a barrel. Clinton decided to release one million barrels per day for thirty

days from the U.S. Strategic Petroleum Reserve. This helped stabilize and reduce world oil prices.

To further shake up the world oil market, Saddam seized the initiative and accused Kuwait of illegal drilling and held Saudi Arabia liable for oil revenue losses when the Kingdom closed a pipeline from southern Iraq. Saddam's belligerence made oil traders nervous and the oil prices were in danger of spiking up again. Saddam was able to use oil as a weapon against Western nations and their allies: he cut off the supply of oil to Israel for thirty days in 2002 when Israel re-occupied disputed territory, and he invited other Arab countries to follow suit.

Protecting Oil Sources   President Bush realized that American dependence on oil from the Middle East was a weakness that could easily be exploited by al-Qaeda, the terrorist organization responsible for the September 11, 2001, attacks on U.S. targets. Many Islamic fundamentalists throughout the Middle East supported al-Qaeda leader Osama bin Laden. This popular support for bin Laden made it difficult for Middle East heads of state to align themselves openly with the United States.

Nevertheless, the United States redoubled its efforts to develop strong ties with Saudi Arabia, one of the world's leading oil producers and a leading influence in the Middle East. The Unites States has made the case that stability in the Middle East is in everyone's best interest, and that aggressors like Saddam and terrorists like bin Laden are threats to stability.

Blood for Oil? Critics of the U.S. invasion of Iraq have argued that the real reason for American action against the country was oil. The United States, it was argued, worried that Saddam would cut off supplies of Iraqi oil or that control of Iraqi oil would fall into al-Qaeda hands, with or without Saddam's approval. Indeed, since the invasion, the management and protection of Iraqi oil has been a major U.S. concern. While the Iraqi oil infrastructure was secured during the initial invasion of Iraq in 2003, it endured many attempts at sabotage and terrorism. The Iraqi oil fields currently produce about 1.9 million barrels per day as opposed to 2.5 million barrels a day under Saddam. The northern oil fields in Kirkuk are operating at much less than full capacity thanks to constant vandalism and theft of the oil pipeline. To this date, the Iraqi parliament has yet to pass an oil revenue bill that is palatable to all the different factions in the Iraqi government.

✪ Major Figures

Tariq Aziz

Under Iraqi president Saddam Hussein, Tariq Aziz (1936–) served as the deputy prime minister and foreign minister of Iraq. He was the public face of Iraq for the West from the early 1980s until he was captured during the invasion of Iraq in 2003.

Aziz was born Mikhail Yuhanna in 1936 in Tell Kaif, Iraq, a city near Mosul. Born into a family of Chaldean Christians who practiced a form of Catholicism, he was the son of a waiter, who died when his son was seven years old. (Some sources say his father was a doctor and native of Turkey.) Aziz received nearly all of his education in Baghdad. He earned a degree in English literature from the University of Baghdad in 1958, and later earned a master's degree from the institution as well.

Active in the Baath Party After earning his undergraduate degree, Aziz worked as an educator. By this time, he had become active in the Baath Arab Socialist Party, which at the time was an underground movement working in opposition to Iraq's monarch King Faisal II. He was among the group's leading intellectuals.

In 1958, Aziz began working as a journalist at *Al-jumhuriyah* (*The Republic*). He also was the editor of the Baath Party magazines, *al-Ishtiraki* and *al-Jamahir*. He continued to support the Baath Party when General Abdul Karim Qassem staged a coup to remove the monarch, also in 1958.

By 1963, Aziz was the editor-in-chief of *Al-jumhuriyah*. That year, Qassem was ousted and the now-legitimate Baath Party took over during the so-called Ramadan Revolution. Because of internal conflicts, the Baath Party split up and lost power later that year. Aziz supported a centrist faction led by General Ahmad Hasan al-Bakr.

Allegiance to Saddam During the mid-1960s, Aziz aligned himself with Saddam. Aziz joined a rebellious faction helmed by Saddam and based in Tikrit. Within five years, the Baath Party had reorganized and was again in charge of Iraq. In 1968, Aziz returned to journalism. Though he was denied a position as a national correspondent for a Lebanon-based newspaper because he was believed to be a spy, Aziz was hired as the editor of *Al-thawra* (*The Revolution*), a journal of the Baath Party, with the help of Saddam.

Four years later, Aziz moved from journalism to politics, becoming the first Christian to serve in the Baath government. In 1972, he joined the ruling Revolutionary Command Council's bureau of general affairs. Aziz then became the minister of information in 1974, serving President Ahmad Hasan al-Bakr. That year, he also became a candidate member of the Regional Command of the Baath government. Aziz achieved full membership in 1977.

Deputy Prime Minister In 1979, Saddam became Iraq's president, succeeding al-Bakr. Saddam named Aziz his deputy prime minister and then named him foreign minister as well in 1982. As foreign minister, Aziz became the face of Iraq for the Western World. He soon began working to re-establish full diplomatic relations with Egypt in 1983, and eventually achieved his goal. During the Iran-Iraq War of the 1980s, Aziz asked President Ronald Reagan for American aid in fighting Iran. Improving Iraq's relations with other countries as well, he also secured support from the French and the Soviet Union.

Aziz's job became more difficult in the 1990s, when he had to defend Iraq's invasion of Kuwait on August 2, 1990, as well as Iraq's use of chemical weapons. As the Gulf War began when the United States intervened on Kuwait's behalf, Aziz began negotiating an alliance with Iran to ensure Iraq retained an ally in the conflict. After the end of the Gulf War, Aziz stepped down as foreign minister, but remained deputy prime minister.

In the late 1990s, Aziz continued to be a public, though guarded, spokesperson for Iraq. He accused Western governments of exploiting Iraq over oil in 1998, incurring their irritation. He also had to deal with the United Nations weapons inspectors who regularly visited the country from 1991 to 1998, and he tried to thwart their efforts.

After September 11 After the September 11, 2001, terrorist attacks on New York City and Washington, D.C., Aziz's job became increasingly difficult. The United States invaded Afghanistan to topple the Taliban, an extremist Islamic government that harbored the mastermind behind the attacks, Osama bin Laden. By 2002, the United States was threatening to use similar military force against Iraq because of Saddam's alleged possession of weapons of mass destruction. Aziz attempted to use diplomacy with the Americans, but Iraq was invaded in 2003 and Saddam's government soon fell.

Wanted by the United States, Aziz surrendered to American forces in April 2003, though his wife and two sons had managed to flee to Jordan. Though he initially refused to testify against Saddam or any other fellow members of the erstwhile regime, Aziz was compelled to testify at Saddam's trial in May 2006 and spoke in praise of the former leader.

Allegedly in ill health, Aziz remains in U.S. custody awaiting trial for crimes against humanity.

George W. Casey, Jr.

General George W. Casey, Jr., (1948–) served as the top allied military commander in the war in Iraq from July 2004 to early 2007. His tenure was considered controversial by its end, though Casey himself was regarded as intelligent, self-disciplined, and even-keeled.

Born on July 22, 1948, in Sendai, Japan, Casey was the son of George William Casey, Sr., and his wife, Elaine Casey, Sr., was a career military officer in the U.S. Army, and was stationed in Japan at the time of his son's birth. Casey was raised in various places in the United States and Europe because of his father's occupation.

Casey attended Boston College High School. He ran track and played basketball there and also worked as a golf caddy at a local country club. Casey then entered Georgetown University and studied international relations in the School of Foreign Service while serving in the Reserve Officer Training Corps. He also worked as an equipment manager on a part-time basis for the Washington Redskins, a professional football team.

Early Army Career Casey graduated with his B.S. in 1970, entered the U.S. Army as a second lieutenant, and was stationed in West Germany. Before leaving, he learned his father, by then a major general, had lost his life in a helicopter accident while serving during the Vietnam War. Casey, Sr., died in a crash in Cambodia and was the most senior American officer who lost his life in that conflict.

Casey spent the next two years serving in the U.S. Army. Though he had planned on leaving the service and going to law school when his tour was complete, his father's death, combined with his growing satisfaction in military life, compelled him to change his mind. Casey re-enlisted in 1972 and spent the whole of his professional career in the army. In the 1970s, he held a succession of field command and staff positions.

Casey also continued his education, attending the University of Denver. He earned his master's degree in international relations in 1980. In 1981, Casey was assigned to Cairo, Egypt, where he was a military observer for the United Nations. In 1982, he left the post to return to Colorado. There, he served as an executive officer for the First Battalion, Tenth Infantry, Fourth Division, U.S. Army, stationed at Fort Carson. In 1984, Casey began serving on the staff of the 4th Infantry Division, also at Fort Carson. He then was named commander of the First Battalion, Tenth Infantry, Fourth Division, again at Fort Carson. Casey held this post from 1985 to 1987.

Service in Washington and Europe Moving to Washington, D.C., Casey became a program coordinator for the Office of the Chief of Legislative Liaison in 1988. Then, from 1989 to 1991, he served as a special assistant to the army chief of staff, also in Washington. Casey spent the next four years at Fort Hood in Texas, first as the chief of staff for the First Calvary Division for two years, then as the commander of the Third Brigade for the First Calvary.

Stationed in Europe beginning in 1995, Casey served as an assistant chief of staff for the V Corps. in the U.S. Army in Europe. Remaining in Europe, Casey became the assistant division commander of the First Armored Division, United States Army Europe and Seventh Army in 1996. In this position, he took part in a peacekeeping mission in Bosnia-Herzegovina. Casey left the post in 1997 to go back to Washington, D.C. He then served as the assistant deputy director of politico-military affairs for the Joint Staff from 1997 to 1999. Here, Casey helped coordinate policy for the Kosovo air war.

In 1999, Casey was named the commander of the First Armored Division in Germany. He remained in the position until 2001, when he returned to Washington. Working again at the Pentagon, he was the director for strategic plans, policy, for the Joint Staff from 2001 to 2003. Here, he expressed concerns about the Iraq War and the lack of any post-war planning for the conflict.

After briefly serving as director of the Joint Staff for several months, Casey was named vice chief of staff of the U.S. Army in October 2003. Casey was promoted to four-star general around the same time. In this position, he dealt with War on Terror–related issues, such as organizing the training and ensuring the equipping of American forces serving in Iraq and Afghanistan.

Iraq Military Commander President George W. Bush selected Casey to become the commander of multinational military forces in Iraq in June 2004. Casey replaced Lieutenant General Ricardo Sanchez, who had lost support after the Abu Ghraib prison scandal in which American soldiers were suspected of torturing Iraqi prisoners.

Confirmed by the Senate for the position with bipartisan support, he took over in July 2004 and hoped to ensure terrorism could not be used to achieve political objectives in Iraq.

Stationed in the country, Casey oversaw 140,000 American troops as well as 25,000 allied soldiers. Overall, he was in charge of the role the military played in political and reconstruction issues in Iraq. Among his first goals were to train and equip Iraq's own security forces and aid the Iraq people in their fight against the growing insurgency. He also helped prepare Iraq for national elections, held in late 2005. Despite many problems in Iraq, including an insurgency that seemed to gain strength over time, Casey's tenure was generally considered a success by the administration and he believed that the process for rebuilding Iraq was on track.

Though Casey was supposed to rotate out of the position in July 2006, Bush asked him to extend his tenure for at least six months because of his ability to work well with many senior officers in the Middle East as well as the U.S. ambassador to Iraq, Zalmay Khalilzad. Casey was also admired for his knowledge of the delicate political situation in Iraq. Casey remained in Iraq until early 2007, when General David Petraeus replaced him.

Army's Chief of Staff
Returning to the United States, Casey defended himself during an appearance in front of the Senate Armed Services Committee as part of his nomination to become the U.S. Army's Chief of Staff. There, some Republicans joined the Democratic voices of dissent over the war and how it was handled, accusing Casey of making some poor decisions. Casey defended his actions and was confirmed for the position by the Senate in February 2007. Early in his tenure, Casey announced his desire to increase the number of active duty forces in the U.S. Army by 65,000 by the year 2010.

David Petraeus

After the United States invaded Iraq in 2003, General David Petraeus (1952–) played several key roles in that war. He first commanded the 101st Airborne Division, which occupied northern Iraq, then oversaw the training of the reconstituted Iraqi army. In 2007 he became the head of all American forces there, replacing General George Casey.

David Petraeus was born November 7, 1952, in Cornwall, New York. He was the son of Sixtus and Miriam (Sweet) Petraeus. His father was a Dutch sea captain who served on a "Liberty" ship during World War II. Growing up near the United States Military Academy, Petraeus himself entered West Point after completing high school. After graduating with his B.S. in 1974, he joined the U.S. Army as a second lieutenant.

Early Military Career
Petraeus was first stationed overseas in Italy for four years with the 1/509th Infantry. Coming back to the United States in 1979, he was affiliated with the 24th Infantry Division at Fort Stewart, serving as co-commander, operations officer, and aide-de-camp over the next years. At the same time, Petraeus continued his education, first at the U.S. Army Command and General Staff College. He graduated from the Ft. Leavenworth, Kansas-based school in 1983.

While remaining with the 24th Infantry, Petraeus also became an assistant professor of international relations at West Point for two years, 1985 to 1987. By this time, Petraeus was attending Princeton University. He earned both a master's and doctorate from the Woodrow Wilson School of Public and International Affairs in 1985 and 1987 respectively. He later credited his graduate education in international relations with giving him effective leadership skills.

In 1987, Petraeus returned to Europe as the military assistant to the Supreme Allied Commander in Europe for the North Atlantic Treaty Organization (NATO). In this post, he was stationed in Brussels, Belgium. Going back to the United States a year later, Petraeus held a succession of leadership positions for various divisions through the 1990s and early 2000s.

Wounded in Training Exercise
By the Gulf War in 1991, Petraeus was an assistant to the chair of the Joint Chiefs of Staff. He was wounded in 1991 during a training exercise at Fort Campbell. He was shot in the chest near his heart. This serious injury later required surgery to remove part of his lung. It was not the only non-combat injury Petraeus would suffer. He later broke his pelvis while doing a parachute jump.

Service in Iraq
In 2002, Petraeus became the commander of the 101st Airborne. He led the eighteen thousand soldiers in his division during the invasion of Iraq in 2003, his first combat experience. As the war began, the 101st launched some of the major air strikes that started the war, then provided support for the 3rd Infantry as it moved over land to take Baghdad.

After the 101st secured Mosul, in northern Iraq, Petraeus and his soldiers made it their headquarters for a time. As occupying commander, Petraeus showed himself to be a skilled leader and was widely praised for his handling of the situation as he had his soldiers reach out to the local population. His division did five thousand rebuilding projects in Mosul, including founding a television network and a soccer league for kids.

Petraeus took on a new task in June 2004, becoming the commander of the multinational security transition command. In this position, he was put in charge of helping the Iraqis form their own security forces and training them, as the previous military and many police forces had been dispersed after the invasion. This duty was especially important as an insurgency was gaining strength, and having Iraqi military and police forces were important to the stability of that country. Petraeus continued to aid in the development of the Iraqi military for

Bombs, like the one that targeted a U.S. convoy in Baghdad in November 2005, proved to be a devastating insurgency weapon against both coalition forces and Iraqi civilians. *Karim Sahib/AFP/Getty Images*

fifteen months until late in 2005. Nearly 200,000 Iraqis were trained under Petraeus's command.

Returning to the United States, Petraeus became the commander of the U.S. Army's Combined Arms Center at Fort Leavenworth. He spent two years in the post before being asked to return to Iraq. In February 2007, Petraeus became the Multi-National Force commander in Iraq. He replaced General George Casey, who went back to the United States to become the army chief of staff. Around the same time, Petraeus was promoted to four-star general.

Head of U.S. Forces in Iraq Going back to Baghdad, Petraeus faced significant challenges as support for the war was evaporating in the United States and many areas of Iraq seemed increasingly chaotic. His immediate goal was to secure Baghdad and other parts of Iraq with more American troops. Petraeus believed this effort would help Iraq's government gain better control of the country as well as credibility among the Iraqi people. Petraeus has stated, however, that it might take as long as a decade to stabilize Iraq enough for American forces to leave.

Jalal Talabani

Elected president of Iraq in 2005, Jalal Talabani (1933–) had to deal with controversy and intense instability in his country as the United States continued to occupy Iraq after the 2003 invasion. He had been active in Kurdish politics for decades, seeking autonomy and independence for the Kurdish people, a minority population in Iraq. Talabani also had served on the Iraq Governing Council.

Early Political Activities Born in 1933 in Kelkan, a city in South Kurdistan that was part of Iraq, Talabani was the son of a Qadiri murshid (a sufi teacher; sufism is a kind of Islamic mysticism) and part of a prominent Kurdish family. (The Kurds are a distinct ethnic group and minority people in Iraq and have suffered persecution for centuries.) He became politically active at a young age, founding the Kurdish Student Union at thirteen. Talabani joined the Kurdish Democratic Party (KDP) in 1947, which incorporated the underground union into its organization. In 1951, Talabani became a central council member in the KDP.

Head of the KDP Though his political activities sometimes forced him into hiding, Talabani eventually moved to Baghdad and graduated from Baghdad University with a law degree in 1959. Continuing his political activities, he became the head of the KDP in 1960. He held this position until 1966. At the same time,

Talabani worked as a journalist and editor. He also served in the Iraqi Army as the leader of a tank unit.

By 1961, Talabani was spending much of his time on the issues of the Kurdish people and politics. Talabani assisted in the Kurdish resistance to the Iraqi government. He even went abroad on diplomatic missions on the behalf of the KDP and the Kurdish independence movement.

Though Talabani was the head of the KDP in the early and mid-1960s, there was dissension within the group. He joined a splinter group of mercenaries fighting the KDP in 1966, but it disbanded in 1970. At that time, the KDP reached a peace and autonomy agreement with the Iraqi government, represented by vice president Saddam Hussein. The peace only lasted until the mid-1970s.

Founded PUK   Still unsatisfied with the KDP and the position of Kurds in Iraq, Talabani was the co-founder of and secretary general of the Patriotic Union of Kurdistan (PUK) in 1975. PUK was a separatist political party also acting on behalf of Kurdish interests. There were tensions between Talabani and the leader of the KDP, Massoud Barzani, and each party fought for control of Kurdish political factions.

Within a year, PUK started using armed resistance to fight the ruling Baath Party. This practice continued through the 1980s, when Iraq was fighting Iran in the Iran-Iraq War. The conflict reached new heights in 1988, when Saddam, by then the leader of the Baath Party and the ruler of Iraq, began using chemical weapons against the Kurdish people. Thousands died as a result. Talabani went to Iran temporarily, but never ceased his criticism of Saddam.

Infighting to Autonomy   Despite this situation, infighting between Kurdish factions only grew stronger. The relationship between PUK and KDP continued to weaken during the Gulf War (1990–1991). In 1992, there was a brief respite as the two parties reached a truce and jointly ruled the Kurdish Autonomous Zone created after the war's end. Tensions still existed, however, and Talabani and Barzani ended their joint rule with more armed conflict in 1994. By 1996, Talabani had founded his own Kurdish Regional Government, headquartered in Sulaymaniyya.

Though there was still much hostility between PUK and KDP as well as their leaders, Talabani and Barzani reached a new peace agreement in 1998. Again, they jointly ruled Kurdistan and their alliance only grew stronger over the next few years. Talabani and Barzani worked together for the continued autonomy for the Kurd's living in Iraq and hoped to one day achieve Kurdish independence. More autonomy was gained in late 2002 with the first full session of the Kurdish Parliament. By 2003, Talabani was serving as the vice president of the Kurdish

Though women serving in the armed forces in Iraq are still not assigned combat roles, the story of Jessica Lynch, seen here talking to reporters after her 2003 ordeal, attests to the constant dangers they face. *Getty Images*

Regional Government, which united Iraqi Kurds together within Iraq.

President of Iraq   After the United States invaded Iraq in March 2003 as part of the War on Terrorism, Talabani rose to new political heights. Within a few months, he was appointed to membership in the Iraqi Governing Council, the interim government put in place after the removal of Saddam's regime. Talabani spent two years working on both Kurdish and Iraqi issues, while trying to put a democratic government in place in Iraq.

In 2005, the national assembly of Iraq held elections. Talabani was elected president of Iraq, the first Kurd to become the leader of the predominantly Arab country. As president, he promised to continue pursuing democracy for his country while attempting to unify Iraq's various ethnic and religious groups. Talabani's election was controversial in Iraq. Soon after his election, it was unclear how much support he could maintain among non-Kurds.

Talabani continued to face significant challenges, especially a rising insurgency that contributed to more instability in Iraq. Though Talabani had the support of the Americans, he was sometimes critical of the way they dealt with the situation in Iraq, including the training of Iraq's security forces. This training was important in the face of the continued insurgency and bringing back the peace needed to stabilize Iraq in the long term. Talabani was elected to a second term as Iraq's president in April 2006.

✪ Major Battles and Events

Invasion of Iraq

The invasion of Iraq began on March 20, 2003, with the bombing and cruise missile attack on an area outside of Baghdad where Saddam Hussein was thought to be hiding. The mission of the U.S. military in Iraq was to attack Baghdad and remove Saddam from power and ensure that the Iraqi military would not use weapons of mass destruction to threaten its neighbors in the region. Some have criticized the operation for not having broader strategic goals and for not sufficiently planning for the post-invasion activities that resulted in looting and a counterinsurgency that has continued since 2003.

Initial Attack There were roughly 145,000 soldiers and marines who took part in the initial attack. There were three U.S. Army divisions, one beefed-up marine division, and one British division. The Army had 247 Abrams tanks and around the same number of Bradley infantry fighting vehicles. These forces were represented by the U.S. Third Infantry Division, the light air-assault 101st Airborne Division, and two light brigades from the 82nd Airborne and the 173rd Airborne Brigade plus Special Operations Forces totaling around 65,000 soldiers. The marines were numbered at around 65,000, and the British First Armored Division added 20,000 soldiers. The war plan was weakened by Turkey's decision to not allow American troops to stage an attack from that country. An American division coming down to secure Baghdad from the north and to cut off Iraqi escape routes would have simplified the operation. The Iraqis were weaker than they were in the Gulf War (1990–1991), but they still had around 400,000 troops and 4,000 tanks.

The Third Infantry Division was really more of an armored division, and under the "speed" philosophy behind General Tommy Franks war plan, quickly drove ninety miles from the Kuwaiti border to An Nasiriyah. The tanks and infantry fighting vehicles took a key airfield in the south, and the marines came up to hold it along with the southern oil fields. The Third Infantry Division then turned north and skirted the Euphrates River and bypassed An Nasiriyah. The British took Basra, the second largest city. Special Operations Forces pre-

On May 1, 2003, President George W. Bush landed a jet on the USS *Abraham Lincoln*, then gave a speech declaring the end of major combat operations in Iraq. *Stephen Jaffe/AFP/Getty Images*

vented the enemy from attacking Israel with short-range ballistic missiles; they linked up with Kurdish fighters who were allied with coalition forces. The fighting was heavier than expected. Civilians were firing back at coalition armored columns with assault rifles, machine guns, and rocket-propelled grenades. The fighting became fierce in certain city blocks.

Difficulties One aspect of the attack plan was its long communication and supply lines. The commanders knew that these supply lines would be difficult to protect since the attack began in Kuwait, and Baghdad was roughly three hundred miles to the north. A U.S. Army Reserve transportation unit got lost by taking a wrong turn in An Nasiriyah and was subsequently ambushed several times. The unit suffered eleven killed, nine wounded, and seven captured. One of the soldiers, Private Jessica Lynch, was rescued later in captivity at an Iraqi hospital. Another difficulty was deep attacks to the enemy rear conducted by Apache helicopters. The 11th Air Attack Helicopter Regiment took some determined rifle fire and had to return to base without engaging the enemy. They failed to accomplish their mission of destroying armored vehicles and artillery pieces of the Medina Division north of Kuwait. One Apache was shot down and its crew taken prisoner. Thirty-one of the thirty-two helicopters had been hit by enemy rifle fire.

The weather also played a role in slowing things down. A huge sandstorm hit the area of operations on March 24 and lasted for three days, grounding aircraft and causing the desert to turn into mud. However, the coalition forces were able to use superior technology with radar, infrared, and thermal imaging for target acquisition. They still destroyed Iraqi armored vehicles and artillery—even those that were thought to be well hidden by the Iraqis. These attacks served to lower morale and break the Iraqi's will to fight.

By April 3, the Third Infantry Division held Saddam International Airport. It then used this area as a jumping off point for huge armored attacks into Baghdad. Many of the pundits and retired military officers predicted that the attacking force would get bogged down outside the city. The surprise attacks worked rapidly, although the attacks were not without heavy fighting. Many American armored vehicles took numerous hits from assault rifles and rifle-propelled grenades.

Fall of Baghdad The U.S. Army Third Infantry Division set up a command post outside the Saddam Airport while its tanks and vehicles probed into the city. The marines were approaching from the south and were holding ground and protecting lines of communication and supply. By early April, coalition forces were in control of Baghdad, and Saddam's government had fallen. Saddam himself, however, remained at large.

Experienced military personnel knew better than to celebrate early; they began warning of the Iraqi counter-attack that would be sure to come in the next months. The officers predicted demonstrations against U.S. occupation, terrorist attacks against U.S. personnel, and sabotage against the new government that was sure to come in the coming months.

These warnings proved correct, but the coalition forces still congratulated themselves on achieving their primary mission objectives. The oil fields were intact. Weapons of mass destruction were not used on coalition personnel (indeed, weapons of mass destructions were never found in Iraq), and ballistics missiles were not fired into Israel or at coalition troops.

Unfortunately, the Americans and their allies inherited a country in shambles. Iraqis had to fight for the basics of survival—food, shelter, and water. Electricity and waste treatment services were spotty before the war. It would be a herculean task to restore basic public administration facilities. The Iraqi people would have to wait in long lines for gas. Day-to-day life would be an ongoing misery for many Iraqis.

Capture of Saddam Hussein

The search for deposed Iraqi president Saddam Hussein was conducted by several different military and intelli-

---

"MISSION ACCOMPLISHED" SPEECH

On May 1, 2003, President George Bush decided to address the public concerning progress in the invasion of Iraq. The setting of the speech—and the president's arrival—were both staged for maximum public relations appeal. Bush chose to address sailors aboard the aircraft carrier *USS Abraham Lincoln* in the Pacific off the coast of California. The president arrived in the co-pilot seat of a navy jet that landed on the deck of the ship. The president emerged in a full flight suit. He took stage on the flight deck with a banner that said "Mission Accomplished" behind him in the background. Although he never said the words "mission accomplished," the television cameras were able to convey the banners' message. At the time, the speech was considered a public relations triumph for the administration. However, once the struggle against the Iraqi insurgency became protracted and a civil war looked likely, the publicity stunt proved to be difficult for the administration to explain. Critics of the Iraq invasion have used the "Mission Accomplished" speech as evidence that Bush had not fully considered the ramifications of his actions.

---

gence units. On December 14, 2003, the Coalition Provisional Authority announced it had captured Saddam Hussein alive. It was considered a triumph for the administration of President George Bush, who had made bringing Saddam to justice a major goal.

An Important Visitor Army intelligence had heard from an informant that an important visitor was hiding out near the village of ad-Dawr. Groups of soldiers began to search the village. They came upon a farm building that had a suspicious-looking rug inside. One soldier lifted the rug to find a plastic cover. In this case, standard operating procedure would be to fire down into the hole or drop a hand grenade in case it had been booby-trapped. Before the soldiers could decide what to do, a person came out with his hands in the air. The figure who emerged looked similar to Saddam Hussein—although somewhat difficult to recognize with a thick, disheveled beard and long hair. The person, who turned out to be Saddam himself, was then taken into custody by special operations forces and Fourth Infantry Division soldiers of Operation Red Dawn.

The Coalition Provisional Authority (CPA) put out a call of triumph. CPA leader Paul Bremer told the media that it was time for the insurgents to put down their weapons. Many U.S. commanders said that the insurgency would be defeated with the capture of Saddam. They thought since the head of Iraq was captured it was doubtful that the Baathists or Sunnis loyal to Saddam would be able to retake command of the country.

Baghdad residents read about the December 13, 2005, capture of ousted dictator Saddam Hussein by American troops. *Joe Raedle/Getty Images*

The U.S. intelligence community working in Iraq basked in the glory of the capture and looked forward to the continued success of utilizing more intelligence that would be gleaned from Saddam. Baathists did indeed begin surrendering in substantial numbers after the capture.

After the Capture Not all agreed that the new arrests would bring stability to Iraq. Some intelligence officers regretted that the CPA did not reach out to former Baath Party members (the party of Saddam) and include them in the new government. This would have allowed the new government to gain legitimacy, stability, and expertise. There was some blowback from the Saddam arrest. Video released by the Americans showed Saddam being examined by military doctors. They checked his teeth and looked for lice in his hair. Some Arabs considered this an undignified way to treat Saddam and felt that it led many to resent the Americans. Arab commentators thought that the video images of Saddam's capture and medical examination would never be forgotten by Muslims and that more people would be drawn to the insurgency.

At first, attacks looked to be decreasing against the coalition forces. U.S. military commanders thought that the insurgency was beginning to weaken—even ending in some areas. But America's difficulties in Iraq were just beginning. There were reports of detainee abuses at the prisons American forces were using to house the prisoners taken in Iraq. The numbers of detainees were skyrocketing. U.S. conventional forces were using large sweep and cordon missions to capture suspected insurgents. Military-age males were detained in villages. These prisoners were reportedly dropped off at overcrowded prisons. These new prisoners were often questioned aggressively, then released if they had little knowledge useful to military intelligence officials. Naturally, many of those released joined the insurgency.

U.S. military commanders were reportedly at odds over how to handle the insurgency. Very few were thought to be knowledgeable of urban insurgency tactics. Others thought that the best way to protect their troops was to go on the offensive and kill as many suspected insurgents as possible. This tactic backfired, and the ranks of the various insurgent groups swelled.

Iraqi Insurgency

After the fall of Baghdad to U.S.-led forces and the capture of President Saddam Hussein in 2003, a power vacuum existed in Iraq. Many groups struggled for dominance both at the national and local levels, and most were hostile toward the Americans. Despite the establishment of a new Iraqi government under President Jalal Talabani, Iraq remains unstable. Quashing this insurgency has proven difficult for the United States.

IEDs and Other Challenges The goal of counterinsurgency efforts in Iraq is to win the political support of the Iraqi people—to have them accept the ideals of a representative democracy, adhere to the centralized authority of a federal republic, and conduct free elections for a popularly elected government. For this transformation to happen, the American personnel would need to be seen as facilitators of peace, stability, and rebuilding efforts. Instead the U.S. tactics have sometimes led the Iraqi people to believe that the Americans were not interested in helping them build a better life.

Part of the problem originally was that many American units were not trained for an urban counterinsurgency campaign. U.S. commanders did not agree on how many or what type of troops should be used to fight the insurgency. Large bodies of troops offered more security and force protection, yet offered more targets for the enemy, resulting in higher potential casualties. Smaller numbers of troops reduced the threatening presence of foreigners in Iraq, but fewer soldiers made it harder to stabilize sectors.

Dismounted patrols are necessary to fight an insurgency effectively. Soldiers must physically interact with villagers and collect information to find weapons caches and work with rebuilding efforts. However, this has proven difficult in Iraq. U.S. soldiers and marines must wear elaborate and heavy body armor in temperatures that reach 120 degrees Fahrenheit. It is extremely difficult to patrol carrying the extra pounds. However, if they do not wear the extra protection, they are vulnerable to injury from improvised explosive devices (IEDs), or homemade bombs deployed in unconventional ways.

Another problem facing the U.S. military was the lack of appropriate personnel to stabilize and rebuild the country. There were not enough military police soldiers to handle much of the interrogation and jailing of detainees. Civil affairs personnel, part of the U.S. Army Special Forces, were also in short supply. These specialists serve as political and economic liaisons with local populations. They help Special Forces units set up vital counterinsurgency and counterintelligence links with the local populace.

Limited Progress There were bright spots. The 101st Airborne fought a successful counterinsurgency campaign under Major General David Petraeus in the city of Mosul in northern Iraq. He established unity of command, a unified intelligence effort, and unified actions with the Special Forces. Petraeus was even able to get some Iraqi government employees paid for their services, which went a long way in improving the spirits of the Iraqis.

Petraeus eventually got promoted to Lieutenant General and was given overall command of the Multinational Forces in Iraq in 2007. He came up with a plan to "surge," or reinforce, the American forces with five additional brigades. Petraeus and other observers have said this new strategy will take time to work. However, the American public is becoming more skeptical and hostile to the war in Iraq.

✪ Homefront

Anti-War Movement

Opposition to the war in Iraq, widespread in foreign countries from the very beginning, has grown steadily in the United States as the war has dragged on and American casualties have mounted. The fortunes of the war, and the public attitude toward it, have mirrored the fortunes of President George W. Bush and the Republican-driven policy of the War on Terrorism.

Cindy Sheehan, whose son Casey was killed serving in the war in Iraq, became the face of the anti-war movement when she led a vigil outside the Texas ranch of President Bush in 2005. *AP Images*

ABU GHRAIB

After the fall of Saddam Hussein's government, U.S. forces took control of the Abu Ghraib prison. The prison had been stripped of most of its furnishings and was in terrible disrepair. U.S. forces repaired the facility and added a medical ward, with the intention of using the facility as a detention center. By the fall of 2003, there were thousands of Iraqi men and women incarcerated at Abu Ghraib. Most were civilians who had been picked up in security sweeps. Some were detained because officials thought they might have useful information. Others were common criminals picked up for looting or violence. Others were picked up for loosely defined "crimes against the coalition."

The prison was put under the supervision of Army Reserve Brigadier General Janis Karpinski. Unfortunately, she proved far from capable of overseeing the facility. She was suspended in early 2004 amidst an army investigation into conditions at Abu Ghraib. In a report leaked to the press, investigators described abhorrent practices and conditions at the prison. Detainees were being terrorized, tortured, and abused by army personnel. Ample photographic evidence showed American soldiers almost gleefully brutalizing prisoners.

Revelations of the abuses at Abu Ghraib were a public relations disaster for the United States. Many soldiers were charged and tried for their actions, but critics scoffed that the officers in charge escaped punishment.

Early Anti-War Movements In the wake of September 11, 2001, terrorist attacks on the United States, America enjoyed widespread support of its invasion of Afghanistan, a nation with unmistakable ties to terrorist mastermind Osama bin Laden. A small faction of anti-war protesters led demonstrations and peace rallies across the country.

Attitudes were not nearly so united as it became increasingly apparent in late 2002 that the Bush administration was making a case for war against Iraq. In November of that year, more than 200,000 antiwar protesters marched in Washington, D.C., and San Francisco. As the specter of war loomed ever larger, the size of anti-war demonstrations grew commensurately. The most remarkable of these demonstrations, a coordinated global show of opposition that brought millions out in protest worldwide, saw several hundred thousand Americans marching in protest in New York City, Chicago, Seattle, and San Francisco.

Dormancy After an initial burst of furious opposition, the antiwar movement sustained a dispiriting blow when the invasion of Iraq went ahead unimpeded. Although polls indicated that Americans had favored a diplomatic solution with Iraq, when the war got under way, the majority of Americans supported it. With the apparent success of the invasion, many in the pro-war camp

decried the anti-war protests and it did indeed seem as if the movement had ended for good. But, as the 2004 election race would soon prove, it was not extinct, merely dormant.

The sudden rise of Howard Dean to front-runner status in the run-up to the 2004 Democratic primaries came as a complete shock to political analysts. The secret behind Dean's meteoric rise lay almost entirely in his opposition to the war in Iraq. As the only candidate to take such a stance, Dean reinvigorated the slumbering anti-war sentiment to such a degree that even his fall from grace could not quell it.

Growing Opposition The anti-war movement gained significant traction in the wake of the "official" end of combat in Iraq—President Bush's infamous "Mission Accomplished" speech. The subsequent rise of an armed insurgency in Iraq was an unexpected and unwelcome development and, as the insurgency dragged on and American soldiers died by the hundreds, many began to question the effectiveness of the U.S.-led occupation.

Compounding the problem was the lack of a clear reason for being in Iraq in the first place. President Bush led America into war by insisting that Iraq was an immediate danger to the United States because it was in possession of weapons of mass destruction. Bush also implied that Iraq supported al-Qaeda. However, after the invasion, the feared stockpiles of weapons of mass destruction (WMD) failed to materialize and, government claims aside, no link between Iraqi president Saddam Hussein and al-Qaeda (the terrorist organization behind the September 11 attacks) was ever established.

The anti-war movement was not contained to grass roots organizations and protestors, either. Many retired military personnel and former highly-placed government officials expressed grave doubts about the invasion of Iraq, most notably former National Security Advisor Brent Scowcroft, who published an editorial in the *Wall Street Journal* entitled "Don't Attack Saddam," and former counter-terrorism advisor Richard Clarke. Several diplomats and other experienced government employees resigned in protest over the impending war. The anti-war stance of these men was not born of pacifism or isolationism, but rather of a concern that Iraq was at best a needless distraction from more pressing matters in the Middle East.

For many who lived through America's war in Vietnam in the 1960s and 1970s, the situation with Iraq seemed dishearteningly familiar: the blurring of lines between civilian and soldier, the emphasis on winning the "hearts and minds" of the Iraqis, even the swaggering Secretary of Defense, Donald Rumsfeld, whose brash manner was reminiscent of Vietnam-era Defense Secretary Robert McNamara.

The Anti-War Movement and the Military The fear that Iraq would turn into a situation resembling the Vietnam War, in which American soldiers were caught up in an unwinnable military quagmire, proved a strong motivation for anti-war protestors associated with the military. Many military families quickly grew weary of the extended tours of duty their loved ones in the armed forces were obliged to serve, particularly in the cases of National Guard units deployed in Iraq.

As U.S. casualties steadily mounted, the anti-war movement found a voice in the form of Cindy Sheehan, whose son Casey was killed in Iraq. Rising to prominence with her quest to gain a meeting with President Bush by camping outside his vacation home in Crawford, Texas, Sheehan went on to campaign vigorously for peace, embodying the resurgent anti-war movement.

Political Impact of the Anti-War Movement Despite the reawakened protests, despite the mounting death toll in Iraq, and the scandal at Abu Ghraib prison (where Iraqi detainees were tortured and abused by U.S. soldiers), President Bush won reelection in 2004. Nevertheless, his approval ratings would continue to fall, as would American opinion on the course of the war in Iraq. By 2006, anti-war sentiment in the country had grown to the point that, in the mid-term elections, the Democrats were swept into power in both Houses of Congress, largely on an anti-war agenda.

Ironically, the failure of the newly elected Democrats to immediately act upon their promises to end the war in Iraq led to another round of disillusionment. Cindy Sheehan once again gave a voice to widespread feelings: "Now, with Democrats in control of Congress, I have lost my optimistic naiveté and have become cynically pessimistic as I see you all caving [in].... We do not condone our government's violent meddling in sovereign countries and we condemn the continued murderous occupation of Iraq. We gave you [Democrats] a chance, you betrayed us." Two days later Cindy Sheehan announced her retirement from public anti-war activism.

Despite such setbacks and cynicism, the anti-war sentiment in the United States had never been stronger. Four years after the invasion, the case against U.S. involvement in Iraq had simply grown too long for many to ignore, whether it was the controversial nature of the invasion and the reasons given for it, or the continuing threat to American servicemen in the region, or allegations of government corruption and backroom dealings, or simply the human toll, both American and Iraqi, that the war had so far exacted. A war that had once enjoyed widespread support and was seen by many as a natural extension of the War on Terrorism had, within four years of its inception, led to the largest anti-war movement in America in a generation.

Republican Loss of Congressional Control

The Republican loss of both Houses of Congress in the 2006 midterm elections represented a significant shift in American public opinion, carrying with it major implications for both the War on Terrorism and the conflict in Iraq.

Although the Iraq invasion initially enjoyed popular support, by 2006 ceaseless insurgent attacks, mounting American casualties, and little evidence of any real progress in stabilizing the country had led a majority of voters to name opposition to the war as their top issue going into the elections. A series of scandals involving Republican congressmen, including Tom DeLay, House Majority Leader when he was forced to resign from office amid accusations of corruption, further eroded voter confidence in the Republican-led Congress.

The 1994 midterm elections had swept Republicans into control of Congress, and since the election of George W. Bush in 2000, Republican politicians had dominated the government. This dominance proved double-edged, however, as the increasingly disillusioned and war-weary public placed the blame for foreign and domestic shortcomings squarely on the shoulders of the G.O.P.

A Mandate Against Government Policy In many ways the 2006 elections were a public mandate on the course of American policy, a message sent directly at the Bush administration. From approval ratings hovering in the low seventies at the outset of the invasion of Iraq, President Bush's popularity had steadily plummeted. Managing to secure a second term, Bush's fortunes continued to fall. By the time of the 2006 elections, Bush's ratings rarely rose above 40 percent.

The war in Iraq was not the only issue that led voters to enact such sweeping changes. As with the Iraq war, many of these issues were linked more closely to President Bush than to the Congress; the midterm elections thus functioned as a channel for voter frustration over the direction of American policy both at home and abroad, which had been strongly influenced by the president and what many saw as a compliant Congress willing to offer any number of "blank checks."

The slow government response to the disaster of Hurricane Katrina, which struck the U.S. Gulf Coast in August 2005, had also seriously damaged Bush's public image, as had his unpopular attempts to reform Social Security. Democratic opposition had painted the 109th Congress as the "Do Nothing Congress," thanks to a low volume of legislation and extensive breaks between sessions. Although the Democratic Party had mostly gone along with the Republican agenda after the terrorist attacks on American targets of September 11, 2001—especially when it came to war funding—they constituted the only real opposition party in the minds of most Americans. Their widespread success in the 2006 elections was owed directly to the "message" voters wished to send to President Bush and the Republican leadership in Congress.

Massive Political Changes In the House, the Democrats picked up enough seats to give them a 233-202 advantage. The Senate race was closer—seemingly evenly split at forty-eight seats apiece—but two Independent candidates were lumped in with the Democratic side owing to their own statements of support for the party,

In November 2006, Representative Nancy Pelosi (D-CA) became the first woman speaker of the House as the Democratic Party retook control of both houses of Congress. *AP Images*

giving the Democrats the de facto majority. Meanwhile, Democratic governors were elected in Arkansas, Colorado, Maryland, Massachusetts, New York, and Ohio, bringing the total number of Democratic governors to twenty-eight, compared to the Republican's twenty-two.

California's Nancy Pelosi became the first Representative from that state, and the first woman ever, to be named Speaker of the House. Nevada's Harry Reid took over as Senate Majority Leader.

With such a strong mandate from the voters, the new Democratic agenda quickly shaped up with a series of bold initiatives. Broadly speaking, the goals included withdrawal from Iraq; implementing the recommendations of the 9/11 Commission, which emphasized focusing policy on Afghanistan, Pakistan, and Saudi Arabia; raising the minimum wage, a goal they accomplished with relative ease; and taking steps toward health care reform, including funding stem cell research and lowering Medicare drug costs. The Democrat agenda was spelled out explicitly in July 2006 in the form of the "Six Point Plan," which emphasized domestic security and prosperity, as well as development of energy sources free of foreign entanglements.

Despite these plans, it remains to be seen how much of this ambitious agenda will be enacted. Although the Democrats captured majorities in both Houses of Congress, they were slim majorities and were not large enough to override a presidential veto. Initial Democratic attempts to set a timetable for withdrawal from Iraq were essentially political statements, as President Bush vowed to veto any bill that set such a restriction.

Foreign reaction to the elections was largely positive. Many politicians in Europe and the Middle East praised the voters of America for holding Bush and the Republican Congress responsible for the situation in Iraq and expressed hope that the new Congressional leadership would signal a positive change in what many around the world perceived as a disastrous direction in U.S. national policy.

✪ International Context

Worldwide Reaction Against American Unilateralism

The attacks of September 11, 2001, brought a massive outpouring of sympathy for the United States from nearly all corners of the globe. The September 12 headline of a French newspaper summed up the attitude best: "We Are All Americans." Yet within two years France would lead the opposition to the United States' latest efforts in the War on Terrorism: the invasion of Iraq. This shift in policy and attitude is directly attributable to the rise of American unilateralism and the international backlash it created.

Unilateralism and Neo-Conservatism To act in a unilateral fashion is to literally act in a "one-sided" manner, without the consent of other parties. Comparing the two wars against Iraq, the Gulf War of 1991 and the invasion of Iraq in 2003, gives a good idea of the difference between the two approaches. The Gulf War was a

In March 2003, on the first day of U.S. missile attacks on Iraq, these Berlin students carry a banner proclaiming "Stop Bush." © *Tim Brakemeier/dpa/Corbis*

United Nations–led effort that brought together more than thirty nations for the purpose of liberating Kuwait. By contrast, the 2003 invasion of Iraq was carried out in the face of international condemnation and expressly without the blessing of the United Nations.

The shift in approach between the two wars, and between the two Presidents Bush (George H.W. Bush and George W. Bush), is owed largely to the rise of neo-conservatism, a doctrine of post–Cold War right-wing thought that espoused the moral imperative of America, as the world's sole superpower, to assume a leadership role on a global scale. This would be accomplished by projecting U.S. military strength across the world.

The election of George W. Bush in 2000 placed a strongly neo-conservative administration in charge of directing American policy, and the terrorist attacks of September 11, 2001, gave that administration the political capital to begin pursuing its goals. Strong majorities in Britain, France, Germany, Japan, India, and Russia supported the War on Terrorism. In fact, the new war was supported nearly across the board, the notable exceptions being the Middle East and China.

Loss of International Support

Although a small minority of world leaders criticized the invasion of Afghanistan as a "war of aggression," the widespread global support for the U.S.-led action did not falter; a thirty-country coalition force took over security details in the country after the Taliban was defeated in late 2001.

It was only during the run-up to the invasion of Iraq that international attitudes began to shift. The change came from the ground up, as it were, as popular attitudes in many European countries began to turn against the Bush administration and its emerging policies. Even in countries that officially supported U.S. action, such as Britain, Italy, and Spain, the majority of the populace was soon registering its opposition to the war. Even Russia, which had its own history of Islamic terrorism, saw its popular support for the U.S. War on Terrorism drop by 20 percentage points in the run-up to the Iraq war. In Japan, a mere one in five citizens supported the war and Japan's participation in it, limited as it was.

The motivation behind this shift in opinion was owed largely to what many saw as a transparent power grab on the part of the United States. For many, the case for war with Iraq was tenuous at best. There was a widespread feeling that the United States was rushing to war and was not willing to allow the United Nations time to locate the supposed weapons of mass destruction that constituted the main American reason for war against Iraq. Instead, it was widely believed that the United States was more interested in securing access to Iraq's oil fields and establishing a permanent base in the Middle East from which to project its influence.

France and Germany led the international opposition to the impending military action. France, in particular, was particularly critical of American intentions—

Dominique de Villepin, the Foreign Minister of France, delivered a speech at the United Nations on February 14, 2003, arguing against aggression in Iraq. In return, France became a frequent target of American invective. Charges have also been leveled against France and Germany that their opposition to the Iraq war is in itself financial, driven by concerns of losing out on investments in Iraq's oil industry.

Whatever the high-level motivations, the opposition of what many characterized as American imperialism was in full evidence on February 15, 2003, when simultaneous demonstrations against the impending war drew crowds across the world in excess of five million protesters. The demonstration in Rome surpassed three million participants, while London drew around one million. In all, there were protests in over six hundred cities.

Long-term Implications

The American invasion of Iraq, which went ahead in the face of such massive opposition, seemed only to confirm worldwide fears of America as a superpower out of control. By flouting international law, critics argue, the United States has set a dangerous precedent. The influence of the United Nations as an international regulator has been damaged, which may lead to an increase in aggressive action by nations around the world. And America's reputation as a defender of freedom and human rights has been badly bruised.

BIBLIOGRAPHY

Books

Hiro, Dilip. *Iraq: In the Eye of the Storm*. New York, N.Y.: Thunder's Mouth Press/Nation Books, 2002.

Kaplan, Robert D. *Imperial Grunts: The American Military on the Ground*. New York, N.Y.: Random House, 2005.

Moore, Robin. *The Hunt For Bin Laden: Task Force Dagger*. New York: Random House, 2003.

Ricks, Thomas E. *Fiasco: The American Military Adventure in Iraq*. New York, N.Y.: Penguin Press, 2006.

Suskind, Ron. *The One Percent Doctrine: Deep Inside America's Pursuit of its Enemies Since 9/11*. New York, N.Y.: Simon & Schuster, 2006.

Woodward, Bob. *Plan of Attack*. New York, N.Y.: Simon & Schuster, 2004.

Woodward, Bob. *State of Denial: Bush at War, Part III*. New York, N.Y.: Simon & Schuster, 2006.

Periodicals

Martin, Susan Taylor. "Writer reassess Franks' days as Iraq commander; Authors claim errors during and after the invasion." *Houston Chronicle*. (October 15, 2006): 10.

Mazzetti, Mark. "General Starwars." *U.S. News & World Report*. (September 3, 2001): 20.

McCarthy, Rory. "Taliban Under Siege" *The Guardian*. (Friday November 30, 2001).

McCarthy, Terry "A Volatile State Of Siege After a Taliban Ambush." *Time Magazine.* (Sunday, Nov. 18, 2001).

Moniz, Dave. "Stakes in Iraq Rival Those in WWII, Gen. Myers Says." *USA Today.* (September 27, 2005): 6A.

Web Sites

BBC News. "7 October: US launches air strikes against Taleban". <http://news.bbc.co.uk/onthisday/hi/dates/stories/october/7/newsid_2519000/2519353.stm> (Accessed June 5, 2007).

Boot, Max. "Special Forces and Horses" *Armed Forces Journal.* <http://www.armedforcesjournal.com/2006/11/2146103> (Accessed June 9, 2007).

Gordon, Michael R. "Shifting Fronts, Rising Danger: The Afghanistan War Evolves" *New York Times* (December 9, 2001). <http://www.pulitzer.org/year/2002/public-service/works/story3b.html> (Accessed September 1, 2007.)

Guardian Unlimited "Fears grow over true intentions of Northern Alliance". <http://www.guardian.co.uk/afghanistan/story/0,,566005,00.html> (Accessed September 1, 2007.)

PBS.org. "Frontline: Campaign Against Terror: Interviews: Lt. Colonel David Fox" <http://www.pbs.org/wgbh/pages/frontline/shows/campaign/interviews/fox.html> (Accessed September 1, 2007.)

Other Military Operations and Peacekeeping Missions

✪ U.S. Relations and Operations in Africa

America's involvement in Africa, historically limited by a number of factors, has been steadily increasing since the African nations began to gain their autonomy in the last half of the twentieth century. Recently, a variety of humanitarian crises across the continent caused considerable debate on how best to put America's vast resources to use for aid and support. Additionally, Africa is also considered a secondary front in the War on Terrorism. Military interventions have occurred in both the name of humanitarian relief and antiterrorism.

The Barbary Wars

With one significant exception, American intervention in Africa has been restricted to the postcolonial era. The exception occurred during the formative years of the United States, when the Barbary pirates of the North African coast clashed with the nascent American Navy and Marine Corps.

The coast of North Africa had long been a haven to the semiautonomous states of Tripoli, Tunis, Algiers, and Morocco, known collectively as the Barbary States. The coast was long held in check by the Knights of St. John, based on the island of Malta. However, the destruction of the Knights during the Napoleonic Wars (c. 1799–1815) opened up a power vacuum in the Mediterranean, which the pirates were quick to exploit.

Meanwhile, the United States, newly independent and no longer able to benefit from British naval protection, found its merchant fleet at the mercy of the resurgent Barbary pirates. The United States adopted a policy of paying "protection money" to the Barbary pirates. Thomas Jefferson, ambassador to France under John Adams, vigorously opposed this policy. Upon becoming president in 1801 he immediately cut off the payments, which were amounting to 20 percent of the government's annual revenue by that point.

The result of this new hard-line policy was the First Barbary War, which lasted until 1805. Although an undeclared war, Congress did appropriate funds for its execution, enabling the fledgling U.S. Navy to operate against its North African foes.

The course of the war took a dramatic turn in 1804 with the capture of the *USS Philadelphia* and its crew. On February 16, Captain Stephen Decatur led a raid on the Tripoli harbor, where the *Philadelphia* was moored, to destroy the ship, thus denying its use to the pirates. It was a daring raid and a complete success. Decatur returned home as one of the country's first national heroes.

Two months later, a unit of marines under General William Eaton landed on the "shores of Tripoli." With an assortment of five hundred Arab, Greek, and Berber mercenaries, the Marines executed a fifty-day, five hundred-mile march over vast tracts of Libyan desert to find victory at the Battle of Derne, the decisive conflict of the war. A negotiated settlement was soon reached: in exchange for $60,000, the Barbary states pledged to hand over three hundred prisoners and cease attacks on American ships. Although money had once again been paid, a distinction was drawn: this was no longer tribute, but rather a ransom.

The power of the Barbary pirates was not broken, however. As the United States became embroiled in war with Great Britain in 1812, the Dey of Algiers began renewed raids on U.S. shipping. With the British defeat in 1815, Congress once again sent Stephen Decatur to North Africa to deal with the pirate threat. Within a month of departure, Decatur had captured two Algerian ships and forced the Dey to turn over all American and most European prisoners and to pay America a $10,000 indemnity.

The Second Barbary War marked the effective end of the North African pirates as a significant threat. By the 1830s, the region had been divvied up between France and the Ottoman Empire, even as the rest of Africa began to rapidly fall under European colonial domination.

This domination necessarily prevented the United States from exerting influence in African affairs for over a century.

Postcolonial U.S. Influence in Africa

Many African nations have found the postcolonial transition to self-governing democracy difficult. The United States military has a long history of providing logistical assistance to the young governments, as well as protection to U.S. embassy staff and private citizens.

In 1964, the U.S. Air Force assisted Belgian forces in rescuing two thousand American and European hostages held by Congolese rebels. The United States provided logistical aid and military support to Zaire in 1978 and 1991, and again in 1996, when Zaire was flooded with refugees fleeing the genocide in neighboring Rwanda.

Elsewhere on the continent, the U.S. military has provided increased security for embassies and facilitated evacuation of American citizens in times of unrest, particularly in such unstable countries as Sierra Leone (where American troops intervened in 1992, 1997, and 2000) and Liberia (where American troops intervened in 1990, 1996, 1998, and 2003). The crisis in Liberia in 2003 also required over four thousand military personnel to be dispatched to that country's territorial waters, where they stood by to assist United Nations relief efforts.

The United States has occasionally offered direct military assistance to African nations. In 1983, President Ronald Reagan dispatched two airborne warning and control system (AWACS) surveillance aircraft and eight F-15 fighters to Chad, which was embroiled in conflicts with Libya and internal rebel factions.

Military Operations in Africa

Outright U.S. military intervention in Africa has been rare. The one time it was attempted on a relatively major scale—in Somalia in 1993—has generally been seen as a mistake. Somalia had been wracked by internal strife and the civilian population was suffering. Chaotic conditions on the ground made it difficult for United Nations peacekeeping forces to provide relief and restore order.

A food relief program instituted under President George H. W. Bush was escalated under President Clinton into military intervention that eventually resulted in the Battle of Mogadishu (1993), a short but savage firefight that saw eighteen American servicemen killed and seventy-three wounded.

The disaster in Somalia convinced U.S. leaders of the wisdom of limiting U.S. military action in Africa to air and missile strikes. Libya was the target of such strikes in 1986. Libya was a frequent target of the Reagan administration's fight against terrorism. Operation El Dorado Canyon, a series of air strikes on the night of April 15, 1986, destroyed multiple targets in the Libyan capital of Tripoli. The operation came in response to an escalating series of aggressive confrontations between the two countries, as well as allegations that Libya was funding terrorists and was behind a bombing in a Berlin nightclub that killed two servicemen. The raid was meant to harm Libya's military infrastructure and demonstrate that the United States would take action against nations that supported terrorists.

Aside from the strikes on Libya, the other notable U.S. attack on Africa came as part of Operation Infinite Reach in August 1998, in the form of missile attacks on a suspected nerve gas plant in Khartoum, Sudan. The plant later turned out to be a pharmaceutical factory. The missile attacks, which also targeted al-Qaeda bases in Afghanistan, were in direct response to terrorist bombings of the American embassies in Kenya and Tanzania earlier in the month. In retrospect, the attacks did little to discourage terrorist attacks. A bombing of a Planet Hollywood restaurant in South Africa shortly after the strikes was reportedly carried out in retaliation, and al-Qaeda leader Osama bin Laden pledged renewed attacks on the United States.

Supposed terrorist links between Iraq and Sudan were used as a justification for the U.S. invasion of Iraq in 2003. Meanwhile, Sudan is in the midst of a massive humanitarian crisis in the region of Darfur, where hundreds of thousands of civilians have been murdered and brutalized and millions have been left starving and homeless during several years of armed conflict between the Sudanese military and various rebel factions. The United States has not, as yet, intervened militarily.

Other Military Operations and Peacekeeping Missions

✪ U.S. Relations and Operations in the Caribbean and Central and South America

For a period of time spanning about two decades—beginning with the Spanish-American War (1898) and ending with the Woodrow Wilson presidency (1913–1921)—the United States came closer to building a colonial empire in Latin America than at any other time in its history. After World War II, the Cold War and the subsequent "War on Drugs" kept the destiny of Latin America and the Caribbean closely bound up with the United States. Even as the memory of the past U.S. interventions in Latin America fade away, new issues such as immigration and oil rights continue to cause tension between the United States and its southern neighbors.

The Nineteenth Century and the Monroe Doctrine

As early as 1798, the young American Navy was fighting the so-called Quasi-War against France (1798–1800) and participated in several naval engagements throughout the Caribbean and even a Marine landing in the modern-day Dominican Republic to capture a French ship at port. Antipiracy raids continued throughout the next two decades, with troops landing on Cuba and Puerto Rico to eliminate pirate bases.

Throughout the opening decades of the nineteenth century, the former Spanish colonies of Latin and South America declared their independence. U.S. troops repeatedly landed in Argentina, Nicaragua, Uruguay, and Panama to protect American interests throughout this turbulent time. These landings were the practical expression of the Monroe Doctrine, first developed in 1823 by President James Monroe and John Quincy Adams. In its original form, the doctrine was a moral statement against European colonialism in the Americas, but it did not take long for other interpretations to become attached to it. Protection of U.S. investments in Latin and South America was one of the earliest of such unofficial addendums.

Some businessmen, such as railroad tycoon Cornelius Vanderbilt, even provided covert support to American adventurers who dreamed of carving out personal kingdoms from Latin American countries. The most well known of these men, William Walker, was initially backed by Vanderbilt, but then turned against his sponsor upon achieving the presidency of Nicaragua after a brief coup. Angered, Vanderbilt used his considerable influence to stir up Nicaragua's neighbors and to foment war. An invading Honduran army was able to depose Walker, who was captured three years later and executed.

The "filibusters," as adventurers like Walker were called, were an expression of a rapidly developing American philosophy in the mid-nineteenth century: manifest destiny, the concept that it was the duty of the United States to expand westward and spread its culture throughout the Western Hemisphere. The Monroe Doctrine was invoked in the name of manifest destiny and such conflicts as the Mexican-American War (1846–1848) and the Spanish-American War (1898), which saw the United States acquiring, respectively, fifty-two percent of Mexican territory and the islands of Cuba and Puerto Rico.

The Roosevelt-Taft-Wilson Years

The Spanish-American War marked a shift in U.S. policy in the Americas. A vocal movement within the United States began agitating for colonial expansion. Although an overt colonialist policy was never formally adopted, the two decades following the Spanish-American conflict saw extensive intervention in Latin America and the Caribbean.

One of the most obvious physical American interventions in Latin America was the construction of the Panama Canal, a shipping channel across the Isthmus of Panama. This marvel of engineering was of huge military and economic importance to the United States, as it allowed easier and safe passage of American ships between the east and west coasts (before the canal was built, ships had to round the dangerous southern tip of South America). The United States began construction on the canal in 1904; it was opened in 1914. Of course, the United States could not simply go in and start digging. Acquiring the necessary land required some military wrangling, as what is now Panama was at the time part of Colombia. Colombia was reluctant to let the United States have its way, so President Theodore Roosevelt covertly stirred up and backed a Panamanian revolt. The Republic of Panama was soon declared, and Roosevelt got the necessary treaty allowing construction of the canal.

In the late nineteenth and early twentieth centuries, many Latin American nations were unstable, and the United States feared European colonial expansion along its borders (with justification—various European powers were flexing their muscles off the Atlantic coast of South America at the turn of the twentieth century). The threat of European interferences prompted the development of the Roosevelt "Corollary" to the Monroe Doctrine and "Dollar Diplomacy," so-called for the idea that economic investment in other countries could be used to influence their governments. Together, these new policies constituted the most radical interpretation of the Monroe Doctrine to date. In essence, the Roosevelt Corollary stated that the United States had the right to intervene militarily in any country in the Western Hemisphere that appeared too weak to fend off European intervention.

The Roosevelt Corollary was put into action as the United States intervened extensively in Nicaragua. Nicaragua had long been considered by other powers as a potential site for a second (non-U.S. controlled) canal. Under President William Howard Taft, troops were sent into Nicaragua to back an insurgency funded by U.S. mining corporations. The revolution was successful and American investors flooded into the country, creating a significant U.S.-backed national debt. A U.S.-backed regime was installed in Nicaragua, but it proved unpopular, and soon more troops were sent in to protect it. The U.S. Marines remained in Nicaragua until 1925.

Although President Woodrow Wilson repudiated "Dollar Democracy" upon taking office, his administration saw some of the most extensive U.S. military involvement in the region, particularly in the Caribbean, as U.S. troops occupied Cuba, the Dominican Republic and, most notably, Haiti. In 1915, amid growing concerns of German influence in Haiti and of threats to U.S. business interests there, President Wilson sent marines into Haiti. They remained until 1934, during which time Haiti was essentially under the control of the American military.

The American military also made repeated incursions into Mexico during Wilson's presidency in response to threats and attacks by Mexican revolutionaries (the Mex-

ican Revolution lasted from 1910 to 1921). General John "Black Jack" Pershing's pursuit of revolutionary hero Pancho Villa is perhaps the most well known, but American troops were sent into Mexico several times after that. Furthermore, in the wake of the "Tampico Affair," in which two American soldiers were arrested in Veracruz, President Wilson sent U.S. troops into the city. The troops took the city after pitched street battles and occupied it for six months, from April to November 1914, nearly touching off war between the two countries.

The Cold War and "Hemispheric Defense"

The Great Depression and World War II put a temporary damper on U.S. military activity in Latin America, and the Cold War brought about a new strategy: "hemispheric defense," the dispatching of operatives and troops to various hot spots that threatened U.S. political and economic interests.

The U.S. Central Intelligence Agency (CIA) was involved in the overthrow of the democratically elected Guatemalan government in 1954, the assassination of the Dominican president in 1961, the 1961 invasion of Cuba by exiled dissidents (the so-called "Bay of Pigs" invasion), and innumerable plots aimed at assassinating Cuba's Communist dictator Fidel Castro. The CIA was also behind Operation Condor, a multinational effort in South America aimed at suppressing leftist political movements, most notoriously in Chile, where a CIA-backed coup put the notorious dictator Augusto Pinochet into power. Pinochet's repressive reign was marked by economic recovery at the expense of extensive human rights violations, a price for stability that the CIA seemed willing to accept.

The 1980s and the Ronald Reagan presidency marked the final decade of the Cold War and the last of the CIA-backed operations in Latin America, as well as a new groundswell of controversy over such activities. American backing of the right-wing "contra" rebels fighting against the leftist Sandinista government in El Salvador brought vocal condemnation at home.

The War on Drugs

The final decade of the Cold War saw a new facet of American involvement in Latin American affairs: the "War on Drugs." In an effort to stop the export of illegal drugs (mostly marijuana and cocaine) into the United States, American agents were dispatched to drug-producing countries such as Panama, Colombia, and Bolivia. In addition, the largest U.S. military intervention in sixty years, Operation Just Cause (1989), was motivated in part by the war on drugs.

Operation Just Cause was aimed at deposing Panamanian president Manuel Noriega, whose increasingly totalitarian regime was seen as presenting a threat to the American-controlled Panama Canal Zone. Noriega was also suspected of involvement in drug-related money laundering and trafficking. In total, more than 27,000 U.S. troops took part in the operation, which achieved its goals in less than a month, toppling the Noriega government and bringing him back to the United States for trial.

The years since Operation Just Cause have seen little American military action in Latin America. However, some tensions between North and South remain, from continuing debates over illegal Mexican immigration—which has led some in the United States to propose building a wall along the border—to continuing conflicts with Venezuela's Hugo Chávez, an outspoken critic of American foreign policy, whose country controls vast oil reserves.

Other Military Operations and Peacekeeping Missions

✪ U.S. Relations and Operations in Asia

The United States has a long history of involvement in Asian affairs, stretching back to antipiracy raids in Sumatra and the Pacific Islands in the 1830s and 1840s. With the arrival of Commodore Matthew Perry's infamous "Black Fleet" in Tokyo Bay in 1853, America began playing an active and direct role in Asian affairs. This was an involvement that ultimately resulted in extensive operations across the whole of the vast continent of Asia, first in opposition to Communist expansion and later in fighting against Islamic terrorists.

The Philippine Insurgency

After the Perry expedition forced Japan to participate in trade with the United States in 1853, American trade began steadily expanding into East Asia. In the wake of the Spanish-American War in 1898, in which the United States won the Philippines and the island of Guam, America gained territorial possessions to match its economic expansion.

Although a vocal faction in U.S. politics at the time was in favor of seeing America become a colonial power, the acquisition of the Philippines would bring with it unforeseen trouble. An insurrection began in 1899 that ultimately lasted for fourteen years and required, at its peak, 126,000 American soldiers to contain.

The United States lost four thousand soldiers over the course of the insurgency. The toll on the native civilian population was even steeper—estimates range from anywhere between 250,000 and 1,000,000 deaths due to the conflict and the famines and diseases that accompanied it.

At the core of the conflict was the issue of Philippine independence. The insurrection had actually begun under Spanish rule but continued when it became clear that America had no plans to deal with the rebel government.

After a series of hard-fought victories, the Americans had effectively broken the Philippine army by 1900. This only drove the insurgents to adopt a tactic of guerilla warfare, which in turn drove the American troops to adopt increasingly harsh countermeasures, including burning whole villages and shooting prisoners.

By such harsh measures, coupled with the enormous troop presence on the islands, the American military was gradually able to gain the upper hand. By 1902, the last of the Philippine generals had been either captured or killed, and widespread resistance came to an end. Nevertheless, scattered bands of rebel fighters kept up sporadic attacks against both the U.S. occupiers and their Philippine allies for over a decade.

Nationalist China

Around the time the Philippine insurgency was beginning to die down, America found itself increasingly drawn into affairs in China. Beginning with the Boxer Rebellion and followed soon after by the 1911 Revolution, U.S. troops were sent in ever-increasing numbers to protect American interests in China. American marines were first stationed in Tientsin during the First Sino-Japanese War of 1894–1895. By 1927, over five thousand U.S. troops were on the ground in China, guarding railways and American businesses and embassies. Troop levels declined as the Great Depression turned America isolationist in the 1930s, but the last American soldiers did not leave Peking and the surrounding regions until the outbreak of World War II.

Although ground troops were withdrawn from China, the area proved essential as a base for American planes during World War II. Under General Claire Chennault and his famous "Flying Tigers" squadron, missions were flown throughout the war to support British, American, and Chinese efforts in the China-Burma-India Theater. After the war, Chennault proved instrumental in founding what would eventually become Air America, the covert Central Intelligence Agency (CIA)-operated transportation service that flew missions throughout Southeast Asia before and during the Vietnam War (1959–1975).

Cold War Power Politics

After World War II came to a close, America found itself inextricably bound up in Asian affairs. The Japanese home islands were under occupation. The Korean Peninsula had been split between North and South and the "DMZ," or demilitarized zone, which marked the border, was garrisoned by thousands of U.S. troops. French Indochina, whose first stirrings for independence had been felt after World War I, soon erupted into open rebellion. And China, to the great surprise of many, turned Communist in 1949.

Tibet was soon to become a theater in the "shadow war" waged by the CIA against America's Communist enemies. Invaded by China in 1950, Tibet fought a fierce resistance effort for four years before America quietly intervened, providing weapons and training in guerilla tactics in Saipan and at a base in Colorado. This American backing lasted until 1974, when attempts to normalize relations with China led to a sudden withdrawal of support for Tibetan insurgents operating out of Nepal.

The Cold War largely drove American policy all across Asia, as in the rest of the world. With China and North Korea firmly under Communist rule, and clear signs developing in other nations of strengthening Communist influence, the United States focused on preventing further expansion of the enemy's ideology. The Korean and Vietnam Wars were direct results of America's belief in the "domino theory," which suggested that the next country to fall to communism might touch off a whole sequence of similar revolutions in neighboring states, much like a toppling line of dominoes.

Although the conflicts in Korea and Vietnam are the most well known of America's Cold War efforts in Asia, they were also somewhat anomalous. Much more common were operations in which the CIA and American Special Forces provided arms, equipment, and training to groups fighting against Communist insurgencies or invasions. In one of the last such efforts, during the Soviet war in Afghanistan (1979–1989), Americans trained and equipped the *mujahedeen* freedom fighters who successfully resisted the ten-year invasion. Ironically, many of these same Muslim guerillas, including Osama bin Laden (leader of the al-Qaeda terrorist network), later used their training to help plan and carry out terrorist attacks on the United States and its allies.

Asia and the War on Terror

The War on Terrorism has shifted America's focus in Asia toward the Indian subcontinent, Afghanistan, and the former Soviet Republics of Central Asia. Countries such as Pakistan and Kazakhstan, despite sometimes questionable human rights records, have proven instrumental in assisting American war efforts and in hunting down suspected terrorists.

The current wrangling for influence in Central Asia between America, Russia, and China (among others) has been termed the "New Great Game," a reference to a similar diplomatic and military struggle carried out between Britain and the Russian Empire in the nineteenth century. Because of the presence of weapons-grade plutonium in the Central Asian republics, not to mention their prime placement over extensive oil and natural gas fields, it is doubtful that the "new game," or American intervention in the region, will end any time soon.

Other Military Operations and Peacekeeping Missions

✪ U.S. Relations and Operations in Europe

The American military played decisive roles in the allied victories in World War I and World War II. The second half of the twentieth century saw the deployment of American military and economic assistance to Europe on an unprecedented scale.

The Marshall Plan Postwar Europe lay in ruins in 1945. Many major cities were little more than rubble heaps; strategic bombing and the ravages of war had devastated the continent's infrastructure. Although Germany was overrun by American, British, French, and Soviet troops, all of the European powers, victors included, were on the verge of economic collapse. Famine and disease were a constant menace.

The United States stood alone as the one power to emerge from the conflict stronger than before it entered. The American wartime economy, which had not only sustained the U.S. military effort but also substantially contributed to Allied economies, was quickly converting to a peacetime footing, ushering in a period of unprecedented wealth and prosperity for the country.

This economic vitality would soon be used to assist Europe in its rebuilding process. Although initial plans for postwar Germany had revolved around completely dismantling that country's industrial economy, an American faction led by Secretary of State George Marshall began advocating for economic aid to all European countries in the interest of humanitarian relief and stability on the continent.

The Marshall Plan quickly gained traction in Western Europe; although the Soviets were invited to join in, there were several provisos to the plan that conflicted with their Communist doctrine or violated Soviet leader Joseph Stalin's isolationist policies. Worse, Stalin blocked Czechoslovakia and Poland, both within the postwar sphere of Soviet influence, from accepting benefits under the plan. The "Iron Curtain," a phrase used

by former British prime minister Winston Churchill in a 1946 speech to describe the divide between the democracies of Western Europe and the Soviet-dominated regimes of Eastern Europe, guaranteed that only the Western European countries would benefit from U.S. economic aid.

Over a period of four years, from 1947 to 1951, nearly $13 billion in aid was delivered to Europe in the form of money and material. Austria, Belgium, Denmark, France, Greece, Iceland, Ireland, Italy, Luxemburg, the Netherlands, Norway, Portugal, Sweden, Switzerland, Turkey, the United Kingdom, and West Germany all received aid, and all benefited tremendously. Although a general recovery was already underway, the Marshall Plan sped this process up considerably. By the time the plan ended, Western Europe was on the cusp of a two-decade period of rapid growth and prosperity.

The Cold War The four years of the Marshall Plan also mark the emergence of the Cold War. When the plan was initiated, the Soviet Union was still seen by many as an ally of the West. However, as the Iron Curtain descended, the plan took on an unforeseen aspect as it benefited the countries outside the Soviet Bloc, creating a sharp divide between the two halves of Europe. Even as money poured into Western Europe, so too did American military personnel. By the close of the 1940s, Europeans worried that their continent would once again become a battleground, this time between America and the Soviet Union and their respective European allies.

There were many on both sides, Joseph Stalin included, who viewed war between the two power blocs as inevitable. American antipathy toward the Communist regime of the USSR stretched back to the Bolshevik revolution. In one of America's earliest and most remarkable European military interventions, U.S. troops were sent to aid the White (non-Communist) Russian faction during the Russian Civil War. Landing in the east at Vladivostok and in the north at Archangelsk and Murmansk, American troops, in concert with Japanese and Czech forces, advanced as far as the Volga, shooting it out with Red Russian troops over a two-year period from 1918–1920. This action did not go unforgotten in the Soviet Union—which until its collapse continued to claim damages from the United States—and Stalin later regarded it as a sign of things to come.

The "inevitable" war was very nearly sparked in 1948 with the isolation of West Berlin, which was occupied by the Western Allied powers but situated deep within the Soviet-held zone (soon to become East Germany). The Berlin Air Lift, organized by commanders of the American Air Force, managed to keep the city supplied for nearly a year before Stalin lifted the blockade, motivated in large part by the formation of the North Atlantic Treaty Organization, or NATO, which declared that an attack on a single member state would be considered a declaration of war on all member states.

With that crisis averted, both sides began preparing for war, leading to a semi-permanent American military presence in Europe, particularly in the United Kingdom and West Germany. The latter country became the front line in the ceaseless battle of espionage and brinkmanship that characterized the Cold War and America's containment strategy.

Even after the collapse of the Soviet Union, American military bases in Germany and elsewhere were maintained, providing a staging area for intervention in the Middle East, an especially vital function in the wake of the events of terrorist attacks on American targets on September 11, 2001, and the subsequent War on Terrorism.

Peacekeeping Missions The U.S. has intervened in Europe for reasons beside Cold War power politics. These interventions have taken the form of peacemaking missions, either diplomatic or military. For example, President Bill Clinton played a highly personal role in the Northern Ireland peace process of the 1990s, making several speeches calling for peace and even telephoning Irish and British leaders during the negotiations that led to the Belfast Agreement of 1998, encouraging them to keep talking and not to leave until an agreement had been reached.

The Clinton administration also intervened in the former Yugoslavia, which was wracked by a series of wars and factional conflicts starting in 1991 with the breakup of the country into its constituent states. A savage three-way war in the state of Bosnia, drawn along ethnic and religious lines, drew widespread international condemnation, but little action until the U.S.-led NATO attacks, codenamed Operation Deliberate Force, of August and September 1995.

The sustained bombing campaign, launched primarily from U.S. carriers in the Adriatic Sea, was instrumental in finally bringing the various factions together for peace talks in Dayton, Ohio. The Dayton Accords marked an end to a war that was infamous for its episodes of "ethnic cleansing" and prison camps that many found uncomfortably reminiscent of the atrocities of World War II.

When conflict flared up once again in the region, this time in the Serbian state of Kosovo in 1999, U.S.-led NATO forces were quick to intervene with another bombing campaign. The Kosovo War visited widespread death, displacement, and destruction on the region, but also brought a relatively quick peace. Today Bill Clinton is still honored as a hero among the ethnic Albanians of the region.

American intervention in Europe has played a large role in that continent's movement toward an open economy and the formation of the European Union. Although the U.S. presence in Europe continues to cause diplomatic friction occasionally, on the whole U.S. intervention has proven a positive factor in Europe's postwar history.

Other Military Operations and Peacekeeping Missions

✪ U.S. Relations and Operations in the Middle East

American involvement in the Middle East did not begin in earnest until after World War II, when the end of European colonialism led to a rapidly shifting political situation complicated by the establishment of the Israeli state in 1948. Initially one of the front lines in a series of proxy wars between the United States and the Soviet Union, the Middle East has found itself increasingly at the center of international attention, as terrorist attacks on Western targets, anti-American sentiment, and Islamic extremism have all increased dramatically in the past generation.

The Rise of the Modern Middle East The collapse of the Ottoman Empire in the wake of World War I brought three decades of European dominance to the Middle East, which was quickly growing prosperous from its rapidly developing oil industry. Independence movements, already growing in strength prior to World War II, created the states that comprise the modern Middle East. The complicating factor of the creation of the state of Israel was resolved in 1948, when that country successfully defended itself against attacks from Egypt, Syria, Jordan, Lebanon, Iraq, and Saudi Arabia.

Israel's success was achieved largely through grim determination coupled with arms and equipment smuggled in from Europe. However, as the Cold War began to dictate American foreign policy, Israel would find in America a staunch ally, willing and able to provide economic and military aid to the fledgling country. The roots of Arab anti-Americanism stem partially from this support of a country that is widely regarded in the region as illegitimate, invasive, and anti-Arab.

Cold War Operations The other half of the anti-American equation comes out of Cold War power politics. As the newly formed nations of the Middle East began to carve out their own destinies, several anti-American governments were brought to power throughout the region, namely in Egypt, Syria, Iraq, and Libya. The Soviet Union, eager to capitalize on this and hamper the American petroleum industry's influence in the process, began backing these regimes.

The United States responded in kind, strengthening its alliances with Saudi Arabia and the Arabian emirates, as well as Jordan and Iran, which was ruled by a monarch installed by the Central Intelligence Agency (CIA). The rise and fall of the Shah of Iran, Mohammed Reza Palavi, is illustrative of the lengths to which Western covert forces went to manipulate politics in the Middle East for political and economic gain.

In 1953, in concert with British MI6 (intelligence) agents, members of the CIA, responding to Iranian efforts to nationalize its oil production, initiated Operation Ajax, a manufactured coup against the democratically appointed Prime Minister Mohammed Mosadegh. Through a campaign of mass propaganda and character assassination, CIA and MI6 agents were able to force Mosadegh from office and bring in their own handpicked military strongman. The shah, effectively a figurehead, negotiated a deal that diverted at least half of all Iranian oil profits to American and European companies.

While the KGB (Soviet secret police) and CIA played politics behind the scenes, the two great powers armed and equipped their respective allies, leading to wars in the Middle East in 1956, 1967, and 1973. This complex interplay of foreign interference and ideological clashes would become further complicated by unforeseen developments during the Jimmy Carter administration (1977–1981).

The Carter Years Perhaps President Carter's greatest achievement while in office, the Camp David Accords finally brought some measure of stability and peace to the Middle East by bringing Egypt's Anwar Sadat and Israel's Menachem Begin to the negotiating table. Building on earlier, less successful U.S. efforts to initiate an Arab-Israeli peace process, Carter was able to host the two leaders, who had been making secret peace over-tures of their own, at the presidential retreat at Camp David.

Over the course of thirteen days, issues were slowly hammered out between the two men who could hardly stand to be in the same room with each other. On multiple occasions the talks threatened to dissolve completely, and it was President Carter himself who personally convinced both Begin and Sadat to persevere and not scrap the talks altogether. Carter's personal approach paid off—the landmark Israel-Egypt Peace Treaty was later signed in March 1979.

That same year brought another unexpected development in the Middle East—the Iranian Revolution. The seeds of anti-American resentment and radicalized Islam planted by Operation Ajax bore a bitter fruit for the West when a faction of religious radicals led by the Ayatollah Khomeini toppled the shah's regime. The United States had not only lost one of its key allies in the region, but also gained a vehement enemy.

The degree to which the situation had changed was amply demonstrated when, on November 4, 1979, militant university students overran the U.S. Embassy in Teheran, the Iranian capital. In what came to be known as the Iran Hostage Crisis, sixty-six American citizens were taken prisoner, fifty-two of them were held hostage for a total of 444 days.

A rescue attempt launched in the last days of the Carter presidency was scrapped before it got started due to logistical problems and the loss of eight servicemen after a midair collision. The hostage crisis was eventually resolved diplomatically, and the hostages were released.

America and Iraq   The Iran-Iraq War (1980—1988) provides further insight into American intervention in the Middle East, as Saddam Hussein and his Iraqi Army became proxy fighters against America's newest enemy, Iran.

Throughout the course of the eight-year war, Iraq received extensive aid and equipment from the United States, in spite of evidence of Saddam's use of poison gas on his own citizens. Two years after the end of the war, Saddam invaded the tiny, oil-rich country of Kuwait. The United States and United Nations forces swiftly expelled the invading Iraqi Army during the Gulf War (1990–1991).

Since the Gulf War, American military forces have been a permanent presence in the Middle East, a situation that rankles many in the region. The terrorist bombing of a U.S. Marine barracks in Beirut, Lebanon, in 1983, in which 241 Americans lost their lives, showed just how angry some factions had grown about the American presence—in fact, terrorist leader Osama bin Laden credits the 1982 Israeli invasion of Lebanon and the presence of U.S. forces in Saudi Arabia during and after the Gulf War as the primary motives for driving him to declare a personal war on America.

In the wake of the September 11, 2001, terrorist attacks on U.S. targets and the subsequent invasion of Afghanistan, the George W. Bush administration began making an increasingly vocal case for linking Iraq (as well as Iran) to terrorism, eventually resulting in an American-led invasion of Iraq and the arrest and execution of former ally Saddam Hussein.

How the American presence in Iraq will ultimately affect the stability and future of the Middle East remains to be seen. One thing is certain: after decades of covert operations, the American and allied forces in Iraq, and the support network that stretches into Qatar and Saudi Arabia, constitute the largest-ever foreign intervention in the region, an unprecedented move that will have repercussions for decades to come.

Further Reading

BOOKS

Adams, Henry. *History of the United States of America During the Administrations of James Madison.* New York: Library of America, 1986.

Ambrose, Stephen E. *Nothing Like It In The World: The Men Who Built the Transcontinental Railroad 1863–1869.* New York: Simon & Schuster, 2000.

Arnold, James R. *Grant Wins the War: Decision at Vicksburg.* New York: John Wiley & Sons, 1997.

Ballard, Michael B. *Vicksburg: The Campaign That Opened the Mississippi.* Chapel Hill, N.C.: The University of North Carolina Press, 2004.

Barson, Michael and Steven Heller. *Red Scared! The Commie Menace in Propaganda and Popular Culture.* San Francisco: Chronicle Books, 2001.

Basler, Roy P., ed. *Collected Works. The Abraham Lincoln Association, Springfield, Illinois.* New Brunswick, N.J.: Rutgers University Press, 1953–1955.

Boettcher, Thomas D. *Vietnam: The Valor and the Sorrow.* Boston: Little, Brown and Company, 1985.

Borneman, Walter R. *1812: The War That Forged A Nation.* New York: Harper Collins, 2004.

Brown, Dee. *Bury My Heart at Wounded Knee: An Indian History of the American West.* New York: Viking, 1970.

———. *Hear That Lonesome Whistle Blow: Railroads in the West.* New York: Holt, Rinehart and Winston, 1977.

Brown, William Wells. *The Negro in the American Rebellion: His Heroism and His Fidelity.* Boston: Lee & Shepard, 1867. New York: Johnson Reprint Corp., 1968.

Buell, Hal, ed. *World War II: A Complete Photographic History.* New York: Black Dog & Leventhal, 2002.

Cadbury, Deborah. *Dreams of Iron and Steel.* New York: HarperCollins, 2003.

Caffrey, Kate. *The Twilight's Last Gleaming: Britain vs. America 1812–1815.* Briarcliff Manor, N.Y.: Stein and Day, 1977.

Calloway, Colin G. *New Worlds for All: Indians, Europeans, and the Remaking of Early America.* Baltimore: Johns Hopkins University Press, 1997.

Canney, Donald L. *Lincoln's Navy: The Ships, Men and Organization, 1861–1865.* Annapolis, Md.: Naval Institute Press, 1998.

———. *Sailing Warships of the U.S. Navy.* Annapolis, Md.: Naval Institute Press, 2001.

Carlisle, Rodney, ed. "Israel." *Encyclopedia of Politics*, vol. 1: The Left. Thousand Oaks, Calif.: Sage Reference, 2005.

Catton, Bruce. *The Army of the Potomac: Glory Road.* Garden City, N.Y.: Doubleday, 1952.

Chandler, David G. *The Campaigns of Napoleon.* New York: Macmillan, 1966.

Chapelle, Howard I. *The History of the American Sailing Navy.* New York: W. W. Norton, 1949.

Chidsey, Donald Barr. *The War With Mexico.* New York: Crown Publishers: Harper Perennial, 1968.

Clowes, Wm. Laird. *The Royal Navy: A History From the Earliest Times to the Present*, Vol. 6. London: Sampson Low, Marston and Company, 1901.

Collins, Donald E. *The Death and Resurrection of Jefferson Davis.* Lanham, Md.: Rowman & Littlefield, 2005.

Cowley, Robert, ed. *The Great War: Perspectives on the First World War.* New York: Random House, 2003.

Dalton, Kathleen. *Theodore Roosevelt: A Strenuous Life.* New York: Alfred A. Knopf, 2002.

Daniel, Larry J. *Shiloh: The Battle That Changed the Civil War*. New York: Simon & Schuster, 1997.

Davis, Burke. *Sherman's March*. New York: Random House, 1980.

Davis, William C. *Battle At Bull Run: A History of the First Major Campaign of the Civil War*. Garden City, N.Y.: Doubleday, 1977.

———. *Duel Between the First Ironclads*. Garden City, N.Y.: Doubleday, 1975.

———. *The Pirates Laffite: The Treacherous World of the Corsairs of the Gulf*. Orlando, Fla.: Harcourt, 2005.

———. *Three Roads to the Alamo: The Lives and Fortunes of David Crockett, James Bowie, and William Barret Travis*. New York: Harper Perennial, 1999.

Dillon, Richard H. *North American Indian Wars*. New York: Facts on File, 1983.

Dolan, Edward. *The Spanish-American War*. Brookfield, Conn.: The Milbrook Press, 2001.

Dorland, Gil. *Legacy of Discord: Voices of the Vietnam War Era*. Washington: Brassey's, 2001.

Dowdey, Clifford. *The Seven Days: The Emergence of Lee*. Boston: Little, Brown and Company, 1964.

Dudley, William S., ed. *The Naval War of 1812, A Documentary History, Vols. 1–3*. Washington, D.C.: Naval Historical Center, Department of the Navy, 1985.

Dupuy, Ernest. *World War II: A Compact History*. New York: Hawthorn Books, 1969.

Durand, James R. *The Life and Adventures of James R. Durand*. Sandwich, Mass.: Chapman Billies, 1995.

Dwight, Theodore. *History of the Hartford Convention: with a review of the policy of the United States Government, which led to the War of 1812.*. Freeport, N.Y.: Books for Libraries Press, 1970.

Dyer, Frederick H. *A Compendium of the War of the Rebellion, Compiled and Arranged from Official Records of the Federal and Confederate Armies, Reports of the Adjutant Generals of the Several States, the Army Registers and Other Reliable Documents and Sources*. Des Moines, Iowa: Dyer Publishing, 1908.

Early, Jubal A. *Memoir of the Last Year of the War For Independence in the Confederate States of America Containing an Account of the Operations of His Commands in the Years 1864 and 1865*. New Orleans: Blelock, 1867.

Eisenhower, S. D. *So Far From God: The U.S. War with Mexico 1846–1848*. New York: Random House, 1989.

Evans, Martin Marix. *Passchendale and the Battles of Ypres 1914–18*. London: Osprey Publishing, 1997.

Fair, Charles. *From The Jaws of Victory*. New York: Simon & Schuster, 1971.

Farwell, Byron. *Stonewall: A Biography of General Thomas J. Jackson*. New York: W. W. Norton & Company, 1992.

Fleming, Thomas. *Liberty! The American Revolution*. New York: Viking, 1997.

Flood, Charles Bracelen. *Grant and Sherman: The Friendship That Won the Civil War*. New York: Farrar, Straus and Giroux, 2005.

Foote, Shelby. *The Civil War, A Narrative*. New York: Random House, 1958.

Gallager, Gary W. ed. *The Third Day at Gettysburg & Beyond*. Chapel Hill, N.C.: The University of North Carolina Press, 1994.

Gardiner, Robert. *The Naval War of 1812*. London: Chatham Publishers, 1998.

Gilbert, Martin. *The Second World War: A Complete History*. New York: Henry Holt, 1989.

Grant, Ulysses S. *Personal Memoirs of U. S. Grant*. New York: C. L. Webster & Co., 1885–1886.

Green, Michael D. "Alexander McGillivray." *American Indian Leaders: Studies in Diversity*. Lincoln, Neb.: University of Nebraska Press, 1980.

Griffith, Benjamin W., Jr. *McIntosh and Weatherford, Creek Indian Leaders*. Tuscaloosa: University of Alabama Press, 1988.

Halbert, H. S., and T. H. Ball. *The Creek War of 1813 and 1814*. Tuscaloosa: University of Alabama Press, 1969.

Harvey, Robert. *Cochrane: The Life and Exploits of a Fighting Captain*. New York: Carroll & Graf, 2000.

Hattaway, Herman, and Archer Jones. *How the North Won*. Urbana, Ill.: University of Illinois Press, 1981.

Hickey, Donald R. *Don't Give Up The Ship!: Myths of the War of 1812*. Champaign, Ill.: University of Illinois Press, 2006.

Hiro, Dilip. *Iraq: In the Eye of the Storm*. New York: Thunder's Mouth Press/Nation Books, 2002.

Hoig, Stan. *Sand Creek Massacre*. Norman, Okla.: University of Oklahoma Press, 1961.

Hoxie, Frederick E. *Encyclopedia of North American Indians*. Boston: Houghton Mifflin, 1996.

Isaacs, Jeremy, and Taylor Downing. *Cold War: An Illustrated History, 1945–1991*. Boston: Little, Brown, 1998.

Isserman, Maurice. *The Vietnam War: America At War*. New York: Facts on File, 1992.

James, William. *The Naval History of Great Britain: From the Declaration of War by France in 1793 to the Accession of George IV,* Vol. 6. London: Richard Bentley, 1859.

Jansen, Marius B. *The Making of Modern Japan*. Cambridge, Mass.: The Belknap Press of Harvard University Press, 2000.

Johnson, Curt. *Battles of the American Revolution*. New York: Bonanza Books, 1984.

Johnson, Robert Underwood, and Clarence Clough Buel, eds. *Battles and Leaders of the Civil War, in four volumes*. New York: Thomas Yoseloff, 1956.

Johnson, Rossiter. *Campfires and Battlefields: The Pictorial History of the Civil War*. New York: The Civil War Press, 1967.

Jones, Virgil Carrington. *Roosevelt's Rough Riders*. Garden City, N.Y.: Doubleday & Company, 1971.

Kaplan, Robert D. *Imperial Grunts: The American Military on the Ground*. New York: Random House, 2005.

Karnow, Stanley. *Vietnam: A History*. New York: Viking Press, 1983.

Karsten, Peter, ed. *Encyclopedia of War and American Society*, Thousand Oaks, Calif.: Sage Reference, 2005.

Katz, Solomon H., ed. "Rationing." *Encyclopedia of Food and Culture*. New York: Charles Scribner's Sons, 2003.

Kauffman, Michael W. *American Brutus: John Wilkes Booth and the Lincoln Conspiracies*. New York: Random House, 2004.

Keegan, John. *An Illustrated History of the First World War*. New York: Alfred A. Knopf, 2001.

———. *The Second World War*. New York: Penguin Books, 1989.

Keenan, Jerry. *Encyclopedia of American Indian Wars*. Santa Barbara: ABC-CLIO, 1997.

Kimball, Warren. *The Juggler: Franklin Roosevelt as Wartime Statesman*. Princeton, N.J.: Princeton University Press, 1991.

Kirchberger, Joe H. *The First World War: An Eyewitness History*. New York: Facts on File Ltd., 1992.

Kutler, Stanley I., ed. *Dictionary of American History*. New York: Charles Scribner's Sons, 2003.

Lankford, Nelson D. *Cry Havoc! The Crooked Road to Civil War, 1861*. New York: Viking, 2007.

Lanning, Michael Lee. *The Civil War 100: The Stories Behind the Most Influential Battles, People and Events in the War Between the States*. Naperville, Ill.: Sourcebooks, 2006.

Leech, Margaret. *Reveille in Washington, 1860–1865*. New York: Harper & Brothers, 1941.

Leonard, Elizabeth D. *Lincoln's Avengers: Justice, Revenge, and Reunion after the Civil War*. New York: W. W. Norton, 2004.

Levinson, David, and Karen Christensen, eds. *Encyclopedia of Modern Asia*. New York: Charles Scribner's Sons, 2002.

Lewis, James. *The Louisiana Purchase: Jefferson's Noble Bargain?* Chapel Hill, N.C.:The University of North Carolina Press, 2003.

Long, E. B., and Barbara Long. *The Civil War Day by Day: An Almanac 1861–1865*. New York: Da Capo Press, 1971.

Lukes, Bonnie. *The Dred Scott Decision*. San Diego: Lucent Books, 1997.

Lyons, Michael. *World War I: A Short History*. Upper Saddle River, N.J.: Prentice Hall, 2000.

Mahan, Alfred Thayer. *Admiral Farragut*. New York: D. Appleton, 1892.

Mahon, John K. *The War of 1812*. Gainesville, Fla.: University of Florida Press, 1972.

Markham, Felix M. *Napoleon*. New York: New American Library, 1964.

Marrin, Albert. *The War for Independence: The Story of the American Revolution*. New York: Atheneum, 1988.

McHenry, Robert, ed. *Webster's American Military Biographies*. Springfield, Mass.: G. & C. Merriam, 1978.

McNeill, William, Jerry Bentley, and David Christian, eds. *Berkshire Encyclopedia of World History*, vol. 4. Great Barrington, Mass.: Berkshire, 2005.

McPherson, James M. *Battle Cry of Freedom: The Civil War Era*. Oxford: Oxford University Press, 1988.

———. *Crossroads of Freedom: Antietam*. Oxford: Oxford University Press, 2002.

Meed, Douglas V. *The Mexican War 1846–1848*. London: Routledge, 2003.

Merriman, John, and Jay Winter, eds. "Eastern Bloc." *Encyclopedia of Modern Europe: Europe Since 1914: Encyclopedia of the Age of War and Reconstruction*. Detroit: Charles Scribner's Sons, 2006.

Miller, Donald. *The Story of World War II*. New York: Simon and Schuster, 1945.

Minks, Louise, and Benton Minks. *The Revolutionary War*. New York: Facts on File, 1992.

Mitchell, Joseph B. *Decisive Battles of the Civil War*. New York: G. P. Putnam's Sons, 1955.

Moore, Robin. *The Hunt For Bin Laden: Task Force Dagger*. New York: Random House, 2003.

Morgan, Edmund S. *The Birth of the Republic, 1763–1789*. Chicago: University of Chicago Press, 1956.

Muir, Rory. *Britain and the Defeat of Napoleon, 1807–1815*. New Haven, Conn.: Yale University Press, 1996.

Navy Department Office of the Chief of Naval Operations Naval History Division. *Dictionary of American Naval Fighting Ships, vol. III*. Washington, D.C.: U.S. Government Printing Office, 1968.

Nies, Judith. *Native American History*. New York: Ballantine Books, 1996.

O'Toole, G. J. A. *The Spanish-American War: An American Epic 1898*. New York: W. W. Norton, 1984.

Overy, Richard. *Why the Allies Won*. New York: W. W. Norton, 1995.

Painter, Sue Ann. *William Henry Harrison: Father of the West*. Cincinnati: Jarndyce and Jarndyce, 2004.

Philbrick, Nathaniel. *Mayflower: A Story of Courage, Community, and War*. New York: Viking, 2006.

Pickett, Albert J. *History of Alabama, and Incidentally of Georgia and Mississippi, from the Earliest Period*. Charleston, S.C.: Walker and James, 1851.

Pickles, Tim. *New Orleans 1815*. Oxford: Osprey Publishing, 1993.

Pope, Dudley. *Life in Nelson's Navy*. London: Chatham Publishing, 1997.

Porter, Roy. *The Enlightenment (Studies in European History)*. Hampshire, UK: Palgrave, 2001.

Powaski, Ronald E. *The Cold War. The United States and Soviet Union 1917–1991*. New York: Oxford University Press, 1998.

Purdue, A.W. *The Second World War*. New York: St. Martin's Press, 1999.

Quinn, John F. *Father Matthew's Crusade: Temperance in Nineteenth-century Ireland and Irish America*. Amherst, Mass.: University of Massachusetts Press, 2002.

Ralfe, James. *The Naval Biography of Great Britain: Consisting of Historical Memoirs of Those Officers of the British Navy Who Distinguished Themselves During the Reign of His Majesty George III*, Vol. 2. Boston: Gregg Press, 1972.

Ramsay, Jack C., Jr. *Jean Laffite: Prince of Pirates*. Austin, Tex.: Eakin Press, 1996.

Rehnquist, William H. *Grand Inquests: The Historic Impeachments of Justice Samuel Chase and President Andrew Johnson*. New York: William Morrow and Company, 1992.

Reilly, Robin. *The British at the Gates: The New Orleans campaign in the War of 1812*. New York: Putnam, 1974.

Remini, Robert V. *Andrew Jackson and His Indian Wars*. New York: Viking, 2001.

———. *The Life of Andrew Jackson*. New York: Harper and Row, 1988.

Reynolds, David S. *John Brown, Abolitionist: The Man Who Killed Slavery, Sparked the Civil War, and Seeded Civil Rights*. New York: Alfred A. Knopf, 2005.

Rhea, Gorden C. *The Battle of the Wilderness: May 5–6, 1864*. Baton Rouge: Louisiana State University Press, 1994.

Rich, Joseph W. *The Battle of Shiloh*. Iowa City: The State Historical Society of Iowa, 1911.

Ricks, Thomas E. *Fiasco: The American Military Adventure in Iraq*. New York: Penguin Press, 2006.

Robinson, Charles M., III. *General Crook and the Western Frontier*. Norman, Okla.: University of Oklahoma Press, 2001.

Rodger, N. A. M. *The Wooden World: An Anatomy of the Georgian Navy*. Annapolis, Md.: Naval Institute Press, 1986.

Rommel, Erwin. *Attacks*. Provo, Utah: Athena Press, 1979. Originally published in 1935.

Sandburg, Carl. *Abraham Lincoln*. New York: Charles Scribner's Sons, 1926.

Schneller, Robert J. *Farragut: America's First Admiral*. Dulles, Va.: Potomac Books, 2003.

Sears, Stephen W. *Chancellorsville*. New York: Houghton Mifflin, 1996.

———. *Gettysburg*. New York: Houghton Mifflin, 2003.

Seligmann, Matthew S., and Roderick R. McLean. *Germany from Reich to Republic, 1871–1918*. New York: St. Martin's Press, 2000.

Sherman, General William T. *Memoirs of General William T. Sherman*. New York: D. Appleton, 1889.

Smith, Page. *A New Age Now Begins: A People's History of the American Revolution*. New York: McGraw Hill, 1976.

Stephen, Sir Leslie, and Sir Sidney Lee, eds. *The Dictionary of National Biography*. Oxford: Oxford University Press, 1917.

Strachan, Hew. *The First World War*. Viking Penguin: New York, 2003.

Summers, Harry G., Jr. *Historical Atlas of the Vietnam War*. Boston: Houghton Mifflin, 1995.

Suskind, Ron. *The One Percent Doctrine: Deep Inside America's Pursuit of its Enemies Since 9/11.* New York: Simon & Schuster, 2006.

Swanberg, W. A. *First Blood: The Story of Fort Sumter.* New York: Charles Scribner's sons, 1957.

Sword, Wiley. *Shiloh: Bloody April.* New York: William Morrow, 1974.

Traxel, David *1898: The Birth of the American Century.* New York: Alfred A. Knopf, 1998.

Trudeau, Noah Andre. *Bloody Roads South: The Wilderness to Cold Harbor, May–June 1864.* Boston: Little, Brown and Company, 1989.

Truth, Sojourner. "Ain't I A Woman?," *Inquiry: Questioning, Reading, Writing,* second edition, edited by Lynn Z. Bloom and Edward M. White. Upper Saddle River, N.J.: Pearson/Prentice Hall, 2004.

U.S. Congress, Joint Committee on the Conduct of the War. *Report of the Joint Committee on the War. 1863–1866: The Battle Of Bull Run.* Millwood, N.Y.: Kraus Reprint Co., 1977.

U.S. Department of the Navy. *Official Records of the Union and Confederate Navies in the War of the Rebellion.* Washington, D.C.: GPO, 1922.

U.S. War Dept. *The War of the Rebellion: A Compilation of the Official Records of the Union and Confederate Armies.* Washington, D.C.: GPO, 1880–1901.

Vietnam: A Television History. Boston: WGBH Video, 1983.

Ware, Chris. *The Bomb Vessel: Shore Bombardment Ships of the Age of Sail.* Annapolis, Md.: Naval Institute Press, 1994.

Wheelan, Joseph. *America's Continental Dream and the Mexican War, 1846–1848.* New York: Carroll & Graf, 2007.

Woodward, Bob. *Plan of Attack.* New York: Simon & Schuster, 2004.

———. *State of Denial: Bush at War, Part III.* New York: Simon & Schuster, 2006.

Yans-McLaughlin, Virginia, and Marjorie Lightman. *Ellis Island and the Peopling of America.* New York: The New Press, 1997.

Zobel, Hillard B. *The Boston Massacre.* New York: W. W. Norton, 1970.

PERIODICALS

Anderson, Bonnie S. "The Lid Comes Off: International Radical Feminism and the Revolutions of 1848." *NWSA Journal* (Summer 1998): vol. 10, p. 1.

Cavendish, Richard. "Japan's Attack on Port Arthur: February 8th and 9th, 1904" *History Today* (February 2004).

"Courageous Leadership Will Be Able to Eradicate Partition." *Irish Examiner* (October 2, 2006).

Etcheson, Nicole. "Mistress of Manifest Destiny: A Biography of Jane McManus Storm Cazneau, 1807–1878." *Journal of Southern History* (November 2002): vol. 68, p. 943.

Farrell, David R. "Slavery and the American West: The Eclipse of Manifest Destiny and the Coming of the Civil War." *Canadian Journal of History* (August 2001) vol. 36, p. 383.

"The Foundation of Sinn Fein: November 28th, 1905." *History Today* (November 2005): vol. 55, p. 61.

Gordon, Walter I. "The Capture and Trial of Nat Turner: An Excerpt from the Book *A Mystic Chord Resonates Today: The Nat Turner Insurrection Trials.*" *Black Renaissance/Renaissance Noire* (Spring–Summer 2006) vol. 6, p.132.

Hergesell, Alexandra. "Echoes of World War I." *Europe* (October 2001).

Hodgson, Godfrey. "Storm over Mexico." *History Today* (March 2005): vol. 55, p. 34.

Holden, William. "The Rise and Fall of 'Captain' John Sutter." *American History* (February 1998): vol. 32, p. 30.

Hull, William. "The Scramble for Africa: White Man's Conquest of the Dark Continent from 1876–1912." *The Historian* (Summer 1993): vol. 55, p. 80.

"In Harm's Way; The Sinking of the Lusitania." *The Economist* (April 20, 2002).

Jeffrey, Julie Roy. "The Transformation of American Abolitionism: Fighting Slavery in the Early Republic. (Book review)" *The Historian* (Fall 2005): vol. 67, p. 532.

Kennedy, Paul. "Birth Of A Superpower." *Time* (July 3, 2006).

Kinealy, Christine. "The Great Irish Potato Famine & Famine, Land and Culture in Ireland (Book Reviews)." *Victorian Studies* (Spring 2002): vol. 44, p. 527.

Low, D.A. "The Scramble for Africa: 1876–1912." *The English Historical Review* (November 1994): vol. 109, p. 1319.

Mandelbaum, Michael. "In Europe, History Repeats Itself." *Time Magazine* (December 25, 1989).

Martin, Susan Taylor. "Writers Reassess Franks's Days as Iraq Commander; Authors Claim Errors During and After the Invasion." *Houston Chronicle,* (October 15, 2006).

Mazzetti, Mark. "General Starwars." *U.S. News & World Report* (September 3, 2001): 20.

McCarthy, Rory. "Taliban Under Siege." *The Guardian* (November 30, 2001).

McCarthy, Terry "A Volatile State Of Siege After a Taliban Ambush." *Time Magazine* (November 18, 2001).

Moniz, Dave. "Stakes in Iraq Rival Those in WWII, Gen. Myers Says." *USA Today* (September 27, 2005): 6A.

Norton, Graham Gendall. "Toussaint Louverture." *History Today* (April 2003).

Otte, T. G. "'The Winston of Germany': The British Foreign Policy Elite and the Last German Emperor." *Canadian Journal of History* (December 2001): vol. 36, p. 471.

Quinn, Peter. "The Tragedy of Bridget Such-A-One." *American Heritage* (December 1997): vol. 48, p. 36.

Rolston, Bill. "Frederick Douglass: A Black Abolitionist in Ireland: Bill Rolston Describes the Impact of an Erstwhile Slave, Who Toured the Emerald Isle Speaking Out Against Slavery in 1845." *History Today* (June 2003): vol. 53, p. 45.

Schultz, Eric B. "Time Line of Major Dates and Events." *Cobblestone* 21.7 (2000).

Silvester-Carr, Denise. "Ireland's Famine Museum." *History Today* (December 1996): vol. 46, p. 30.

Stievermann, Jan. "Writing to 'Conquer All Things': Cotton Mather's *Magnalia Christi Americana* and the Quandary of Copia." *Early American Literature* 39.2 (2004): 263–98.

Stoner, Lynn K. "The Santiago Campaign of 1898: A Soldier's View of the Spanish-American War." *Latin American Research Review* (Summer 1996).

Utley, Robert M. "The Bozeman Trail Before John Bozeman: A Busy Land." *Montana: The Magazine of Western History* (Summer 2003).

WEB SITES

The Afghanistan War Evolves" *New York Times* (December 9, 2001). <http://www.pulitzer.org/year/2002/public-service/works/story3b.html> (Accessed September 1, 2007.)

"The Air Campaign." *Conduct of the Persian Gulf War.* Intelligence Resource Program. <www.fas.org/irp/imint/docs/cpgw6/>(accessed June 6, 2007).

"The American Experience, MacArthur, Korean Maps." *PBS.* <www.pbs.org/wgbh/amex/macar thur/maps/koreatxt.html> (accessed May 16, 2007).

"American War and Military Operations Casualties: Lists and Statistics." *Navy Department Library.* <www.history.navy.mil/library/online/american%20war%20casualty.htm>(accessed June 20, 2007).

"Anti-annexation Protest Documents: Liliuokalani to Albert Willis, U.S. Envoy, June 20, 1894." *University of Hawai'i at Manoa.* <libweb.hawaii.edu/digicoll/annexation/protest/liliu4-trans.html> (accessed April 4, 2007)

"The Austro-Hungarian Ultimatum to Serbia, English Translation (23 July 1914)." *World War I Document Library.* Brigham Young University Library. <http://net.lib.byu.edu/~rdh7/wwi/1914/austro-hungarian-ultimatum.html> (accessed April 22, 2007).

"The Battle of Little Bighorn, 1876." *EyeWitness to History.com.* <www.earlyamerica.com/lives/franklin> (accessed April 8, 2007).

BBC News. "7 October: US launches air strikes against Taleban". <http://news.bbc.co.uk/onthisday/hi/dates/stories/october/7/newsid_25 19000/2519353.stm> (Accessed June 5, 2007).

"Bill Clinton: A Life in Brief." *AmericanPresident.org.* Miller Center of Public Affairs, University of Virginia. <www.millercenter.virginia.edu/index.php/Ampres/essays/clinton/biography/1> (accessed June 8, 2007).

Boot, Max. "Special Forces and Horses." *Armed Forces Journal.* <http://www.armedforcesjournal.com/2006/11/2146103> (Accessed June 9, 2007).

Calvert, J. B. "William Henry Harrison and the West." University of Denver, 2001. <www.du.edu/~jcalvert/hist/harrison.htm> (accessed March 9, 2007).

"Chivington, John M. (1821–1894)." *PBS.* <www.pbs.org/weta/thewest/people/a_c/chivington.htm> (accessed April 10, 2007).

Churchill, Winston S. "Iron Curtain Speech, March 5, 1946." *Internet Modern History Sourcebook.* <www.fordham.edu/halsall/mod/churchill-iron.html> (accessed May 11, 2007).

Doser, Mark. "Black Monday—The Stock Market Crash of 1987." *4A Economics.* Holy Trinity School. <www.newlearner.com/courses/hts/bec4a/ecoho16.htm> (accessed June 8, 2007).

"Durant's Big Scam." *PBS.* <www.pbs.org/wgbh/amex/tcrr/sfeature/sf_scandals.html> (accessed April 21, 2007).

Estes, Kenneth W. "Iraq Between Two Occupations: The Second Gulf War (1990–1991)." *International Relations and Security Networks.* <http://se1.isn.ch/serviceengine/FileContent?serviceID=PublishingHouse&fileid=FB678761-6586-38F1-EFA6-21799C0D073E&lng=en> (accessed June 6, 2007).

Feltus, Pamela. "The Gulf War." *U.S. Centennial of Flight Commission.* <www.centennialofflight.

gov/essay/Air_Power/gulf_war/AP44.htm> (accessed June 6, 2007).

Fowler, Mariam R. "Menawa: A Chief of the Upper Creeks." Shelby County Museum, Columbiana, AL. <www.rootsweb.com/~alshelby/Menawa.html>(accessed March 22, 2007)

Frahm, Jill. "SIGINT and the Pusan Perimeter." *National Security Agency.* <www.nsa.gov/publications/publi 00024.cfm#5> (accessed May 19, 2007).

Franklin, Benjamin. *The Autobiography of Benjamin Franklin.* Reprinted at Archiving Early America. <www.earlyamerica.com/lives/franklin> (accessed March 10, 2007). Originally published in 1793.

Guardian Unlimited. "Fears grow over true intentions of Northern Alliance." <http://www.guardian.co.uk/afghanistan/story/0,,566005,00.html> (Accessed September 1, 2007.)

Hamilton, Alexander. *The Works of Alexander Hamilton, (Federal Edition),* Henry Cabot Lodge, ed. Vol. 7. (18thc). Reprinted at The Online Library of Liberty. <oll.libertyfund.org/Home3/HTML.php?record ID=0249.07> (accessed March 27, 2007).

"Henry R. Luce and the Rise of the American News Media." *PBS.* <www.pbs.org/wnet/american masters/database/luce_h.html> (accessed May 9, 2007).

Hermansen, Max. "Inchon—Operation Chromite" *United States Military Logisticsin the First Part of the Korean War.* University of Oslo. <http://vlib.iue.it/carrie/texts/carrie_books/hermansen/6.html> (accessed May 17, 2007).

HistoryNet.com. "Spanish-American War: Battle of San Juan Hill" <www.historynet.com/wars_conflicts/19_century/3033026.html?page=1&c=y> (accessed March 26, 2007).

"History of Korea, Part II." *Life In Korea.* <www.lifeinkorea.com/information/history2.cfm> (accessed May 15, 2007).

"INDEPENDENCE: The Birth of a New America." *Time* (July 4, 1976). Reprinted at <www.time.com/time/magazine/article/0,9171,712235-1,00.html> (accessed March 10, 2007).

Internet Movie Database <http://www.imdb.com> (accessed May 29, 2007).

"Interview with Lt. Col. Charles Bussy, U.S. Army." *CNN.* <www.cnn.com/interactive/specials/0005/korea.interviews/bussey.html> (accessed May 19, 2007).

Jarmul, David "America's Fear of Communism in 1920 Becomes a Threat to Rights." *VOA News. com* (May 17, 2006) <www.voanews.com/specialenglish/archive/2006-05/2006-05-17-voa2.cfm> (accessed May 2, 2007).

Jefferson, Thomas. "Second Inaugural Address." *The Avalon Project at Yale Law School.* <www.yale.edu/lawweb/avalon/presiden/inaug/jefinau2.htm> (accessed April 9, 2007).

Jevtic, Borijove. "The Assassination of Archduke Franz Ferdinand (28 June 1914)." *World War I Document Library.* Brigham Young University Library. <http://net.lib.byu.edu/~rdh7/wwi/1914/ferddead.html> (accessed April 22, 2007).

Kipling, Rudyard. "Recessional (1897)." *The Oxford Book of English Verse.* Originally published in 1919. <www.bartleby.com/101/867.html> (accessed June 4, 2007).

"The Korean War Armistice." *BBC News.* <http://news.bbc.co.uk/1/hi/world/asia-pacific/2774931.stm> (accessed May 18, 2007).

"The Korean War—The Inchon Invasion." *Naval Historical Center.* <www.history.navy.mil/photos/events/kowar/50-unof/inchon.htm> (accessed May 16, 2007).

Liliuokalani, Queen of Hawaii. "My Cabinet—Princess Kaiulani." *Hawaii's Story by Hawaii's Queen.* Originally published in 1898. <digital.library.upenn.edu/women/liliuokalani/hawaii/hawaii-5.html> (accessed April 4, 2007)

Lincoln, Abraham. "Speech at Worcester, Massachusetts, September 12, 1848." *Collected Works of Abraham Lincoln.* <quod.lib.umich.edu/cgi/t/text/text-idx?c=lincoln;cc=lincoln;type=simple;rgn=div1;q1=fences;singlegenre= All;view=text;subview=detail;sort=occur;idno= lincoln2;node=lincoln2%3A2> (accessed April 9, 2007).

Lowell, James Russell. "War." *The Complete Poetical Works of James Russell Lowell.* <www.gutenberg.org/etext/13310> (accessed April 9, 2007).

"Mexican Colonization Laws." *The Handbook of Texas Online.* The University of Texas at Austin, <www.tsha.utexas.edu/handbook/online/articles/ MM/ugm1.html> (Accessed April 4, 2007).

"Modernism and Experimentation: 1914–1945." *Outline of American Literature.* <http://usinfo.state.gov/products/pubs/oal/lit6.htm> (accessed June 6, 2007).

"The Narodna Odbrana (1911)." *World War I Document Library.* Brigham Young University Library. <http://net.lib.byu.edu/~rdh7/wwi/1914m/odbrana.html> (accessed April 22, 2007).

The Navy and Marine Living History Association. "The Battle of Honolulu." <www.navyandmarine.org/ondeck/1800battleofhonolulu.htm> (accessed May 2, 2007).

The Navy Department Library. "The Cruise of the Great White Fleet." <www.history.navy.mil/library/on line/gwf_cruise.htm> (accessed April 2, 2007).

Navy Historical Center. "Report of the Secretary of the navy, 1898." <www.history.navy.mil/wars/spanam/sn98-5.htm> (accessed April 2, 2007).

Paine, Thomas. "Common Sense." Reprinted at the Constitution Society <www.constitution.org/tp/comsense.htm> (accessed March 10, 2007). Originally published in 1776.

———. "The American Crisis: 1, December 23, 1776." Reprinted at the Constitution Society <www.constitution.org/tp/amercrisis01.htm> (accessed March 10, 2007). Originally published in 1776.

PBS.org. "Frontline: Campaign Against Terror: Interviews: Lt. Colonel David Fox." <http://www. pbs .org/wgbh/pages/frontline/shows/campaign/inter views/fox.html> (Accessed September 1, 2007.)

Peace Corps. <www.peacecorps.gov> (accessed June 1, 2007).

Polk, James K. "Polk's War Message Washington, May 11, 1846." *Berkeley Law School Foreign Relations Law.* <www.law.berkeley.edu/faculty/yooj/courses/forrel/reserve/Polk1.htm> (accessed April 30, 2007).

Roosevelt, Theodore. "General Young's Fight at Las Guasimas." *The Rough Riders.* Originally published in 1890. <www.bartleby.com/51/3.html> (accessed March 26, 2007).

"Rufus King and the Missouri Controversy." *The Gilder Lehrman Institute of American History.* <www.gilder lehrman.org/collection/docs_archive/docs_archive_rufus.html> (accessed April 9, 2007).

"The S&L Crisis: A Chrono-Bibliography." *FDIC.* <www.fdic.gov/bank/historical/s&l/> (accessed June 8, 2007).

Schultz, Stanley K. "The Gilded Age and the Politics of Corruption." *University of Wisconsin.* <us. history.wisc.edu/hist102/lectures/lecture04. html> (accessed April 21, 2007).

Smith, Adam. "An Inquiry into the Nature and Causes of the Wealth of Nations by Adam Smith." Project Gutenberg <www.gutenberg.org/etext/3300> (accessed March 27, 2007). Originally published in 1776.

The Spanish-American War Centennial Website. "The Official Report of Spanish Admiral Montojo on the Battle of Manila Bay" <www.spanamwar. com/mtreport.htm> (accessed March 26, 2007).

State of the Union Addresses of James Monroe. <www. gutenberg.org/dirs/etext04/sumon11.txt> (accessed April 8, 2007).

"The Story of Africa: Between World Wars (1914–1945)." *BBC.* <www.bbc.co.uk/world service/africa/features/storyofafrica/13chapter 11.shtml> (accessed May 4, 2007).

Tallmadge, James, Jr. "Tallmadge's Speech to Congress, 1819." *Wadsworth Learning American Passages.* <www.wadsworth.com/history_d/templates/student_resources/0030724791_ayers/sources/ch09/9.3.tallmadge.html> (accessed April 9, 2007).

"Texas Declaration of Independence." *Texas A&M University.* <www.tamu.edu/ccbn/dewitt/decin depen36.htm> (accessed April 30, 2007).

"Thomas Jefferson's Account of the Declaration." Reprinted at USHistory.org. <www.ushistory.org/declaration/account/index.htm> (accessed March 10, 2007).

Travis, William Barret. "Letter from the Alamo, February 24, 1836." *The History of the Alamo & the Texas Revolution.* Texas A&M University <www.tamu.edu/ccbn/dewitt/adp/history/bios/travis/travtext.html> (accessed April 30, 2007).

Treaty of Ghent. <www.loc.gov/rr/program/bib/our docs/Ghent.html> (accessed April 5, 2007).

Truman, Harry S. "The Truman Doctrine, President Harry S. Truman's Address Before a Joint Session of Congress, March 12, 1947." *The Avalon Project at Yale Law School.* <www.yale.edu/lawweb/avalon/trudoc.html> (accessed May 18, 2007).

Utz, Curtis A. "MacArthur Sells Inchon." *Assault from the Sea, Amphibious Landing at Inchon.* Naval Historical Center. <www.history.navy.mil/down load/i-16-19.pdf> (accessed May 17, 2007).

Voltaire. "The Philosophical Dictionary." H.I. Woolf, ed. New York: Knopf, 1924. Reprinted at Hanover Historical Texts Project <history.hanover.edu/texts/voltaire/volindex.html> (accessed March 27, 2007).

"Walton Harris Walker, General, United States Army." *ArlingtonCemetery.net.* <www.arlingtoncemetery. net/whwalker.htm> (accessed May 19, 2007).

"War Chronology: February 1991." *U.S. Navy in Desert Storm/Desert Sheild.* <www.history.navy. mil/wars/dstorm/dsfeb.htm> (accessed June 6, 2007).

Webster, Daniel. "Speech to the Senate, 1848." *The Great Speeches and Orations of Daniel Webster.* <www.gutenberg.org/etext/12606> (accessed April 14, 2007).

Wormser, Richard. "Harry S. Truman Supports Civil Rights (1947–1948)." *PBS.* <www.pbs.org/wnet/jimcrow/stories_events_truman.html> (accessed May 24, 2007).

"WWI—The Great War Remembered." *United States Department of Defense.* <www.defenselink.mil/home/features/2005/WWI/index.html> (accessed April 22, 2007).

Index

WITHDRAWN